EUROPEAN HISTORICAL DICTIONARIES
Edited by Jon Woronoff

Historical Dictionary of the United Kingdom

Volume 2: Scotland, Wales, and Northern Ireland

Kenneth J. Panton
and
Keith A. Cowlard

European Historical Dictionaries, No. 17

The Scarecrow Press, Inc.
Lanham, Md., & London
1998

SCARECROW PRESS, INC.

Published in the United States of America
by Scarecrow Press, Inc.
4720 Boston Way
Lanham, Maryland 20706

4 Pleydell Gardens, Folkestone
Kent CT20 2DN, England

British Library Cataloguing-in-Publication Information Available

Library of Congress Cataloging-in-Publication Data

Panton, Kenneth J. (Kenneth John), 1945–
    Historical dictionary of the United Kingdom / Kenneth J. Panton
and Keith A. Cowlard.
        p.   cm.— (European historical dictionaries ; no. 17)
    Includes bibliographical references.
    Contents: v. 2. Scotland, Wales, and Northern Ireland.
    ISBN 0-8108-3441-3 (cloth : alk. paper)
    1. Great Britain—History—Dictionaries. I. Cowlard, Keith A.
(Keith Arthur), 1946– . II. Title. III. Series.
DA34.P36   1998
941.003—dc20   96-23996

ISBN 0-8108-3441-3 (cloth : alk. paper)

♾™ The paper used in this publication meets the minimum requirements of
American National Standard for Information Sciences—Permanence of
Paper for Printed Library Materials, ANSI Z39.48–1984.
Manufactured in the United States of America.

CONTENTS

EDITOR'S FOREWORD

The United Kingdom is, as the name indicates, united. But this has not kept the component regions from preserving many of their earlier customs and traditions, their language and a somewhat different lifestyle. Sometimes this particularism results in frictions and strivings for greater independence; on occasion it is consecrated with a degree of formal autonomy. To minimize the differences would be as unfortunate as to exaggerate them. However, since it is most often the former which occurs, it is quite useful to have a greater emphasis on the parts. The first volume of the *Historical Dictionary of the United Kingdom* covered the nation as a whole and its most prominent part, England. This second volume focusses on Scotland, Wales and Northern Ireland. It looks more closely at their history and geography, their economy, society and culture, and significant persons, events and institutions which have shaped them. But it also shows how they fit in with the rest of the country.

Like Volume 1, Volume 2 starts with a chronology, one encompassing roughly the same period but highlighting different aspects. The list of abbreviations should again prove helpful in reading not only this book but other documentation. The introduction describes how Scotland, Wales and Northern Ireland were brought together into the nation as well as how and why they have remained true to their earlier selves. The dictionary entries then present specific persons, places, events and institutions, political, economic, social and cultural features. Because some of these entries tie up with others in the first volume and may be treated there as well, refer to the list of entries in Volume 1 in the appendix. This time the bibliography directs readers toward more specific works dealing largely or wholly with the three regions, and includes many titles that might not be included in standard bibliographies of the United Kingdom but are essential in understanding Scotland, Wales and Northern Ireland.

This second volume of the *Historical Dictionary of the United Kingdom* was written by the same authors as the first, Keith A. Cowlard and Kenneth J. Panton. Dr Cowlard was born and grew up in England, and Dr Panton was born and raised in Scotland; together they provide good balance. More important is that both studied geography, in particular the geography of the United Kingdom, and have a better feel for the country than most. They obviously know well its history, economy, society and culture to judge by the informative entries in both volumes. They also know how to impart this information gently, but firmly, after years of experience with British students during the academic year and visiting Americans during the summer. Dr. Cowlard retired from the post of Head of Geography at London Guildhall University in London, England, in 1997 and Dr. Panton, who taught for many years at the same university, has recently taken up an appointment at the University of Southern Mississippi in the United States.

Jon Woronoff
Series Editor

ACKNOWLEDGEMENTS

Even in these days of fax machines and e-mail, transatlantic cooperation over book production is fraught with problems. With one author, the series editor and the text designer in Europe, and another author, the publisher and the printer in North America, communication was no easy task, so we are grateful to all those who took time and trouble to ensure that delays and misunderstandings were few and far between.

Many of those who helped prepare the first volume of this Dictionary again made indispensable contributions. Jon Woronoff, the series editor, always available for consultation, was a major source of advice and support. Neil Gosney, formerly Senior Librarian at London Guildhall University, once more demonstrated his stubborn insistence that every bibliographical citation should be fully authenticated and Gareth Owen, of City Cartographic, spent many hours ensuring that the maps he prepared were as accurate as possible. Don Shewan and Andrew Ellis (also of City Cartographic) took the unembellished printout and disk from a personal computer and, weaving some kind of magic, turned it into a thoroughly professional book layout.

We also owe a debt to several people who had not been involved with Volume 1 but who allowed us to draw on their skills for Volume 2. Carolyn Robbins and her colleague, Betty Blackledge, at the University of Southern Mississippi's Department of Geography, did much typing in the later stages of preparation for one of the authors, as did Frances Sudduth of the University's College of International and Continuing Education. All three, along with Frances's colleagues, Sylvia McNabb and Melissa Ravencraft, sent faxes, dispatched memos and responded to phone calls with a willingness and efficiency which deserves admiration as well as thanks.

In addition, there is an army of library staff who did much (often unwittingly) to help the collection of facts and figures, particularly at the University of Southern Mississippi, London Guildhall University and at public libraries in Cardiff, Edinburgh and Redhill, where we were frequent, demanding (and, therefore, possibly sometimes unwelcome) visitors.

Finally, our families have acquiesced to our love affair with the Dictionary, showing a stoicism which did nothing to assuage our feelings of guilt at abandoning them on weekends and evenings. To Carol and Morven Panton, and to Margaret, Christopher and Katherine Cowlard, our heartfelt thanks for their unstinting support and encouragement. The preparation of these two volumes has been a jaunt along a lengthy, but fascinating, trail, with new horizons constantly opening up and new acquaintances round many bends. We are enormously grateful to all those who walked with us and who thereby added so much pleasure to our journey.

Kenneth J. Panton
Hattiesburg, 1997

Keith A. Cowlard
London, 1997.

NOTES TO THE READER

This *Historical Dictionary of the United Kingdom* consists of two parts: one dealing with England and the United Kingdom, the other with Scotland, Wales and Northern Ireland. Such a division is necessary because the country took its present form only in 1921 and each of its component nations has preserved specific features from the past. Moreover, the strongly held sense of identity which is characteristic of the Scots, the Welsh and the Irish — and which transcends mere regionalism — means that the modern state can only be truly understood in terms of the evolution of its component parts.

Of course, many events and leaders have influenced all four territories. They are, for the most part, detailed in the first volume, which concentrates on matters which relate specifically to England — always the most powerful and influential of the quartet — and which deals with the politics, the economic and social developments and the international ties which have produced a united country with a considerable role in world affairs. This second volume concentrates more specifically on the issues, people and events which have had their greatest impact in Scotland, Wales and Northern Ireland. Most topics will, therefore, appear in one volume alone, but some will appear in both, with different emphases. To assist the reader, a list of the entries in Volume 1 is included as an appendix to this volume.

Below are fuller details of the book's format and the principles adopted in the allocation of entries to each volume.

Abbreviations

This section includes all abbreviations used in the book.

Chronologies

The Chronologies provide simple checklists (in date order) of Historical Events and of Monarchs and leading Political Posts, using the precise year (or nearest relevant year) for the entry. More detailed dates, including month and day when appropriate, are noted in the *Dictionary* entries. Early dates are approximations from recent research publications. Others are based on the prevailing calendar of Britain for the period, with the change from the Julian to the Gregorian calendar occurring in 1752 (see *Dictionary* entry on **CALENDAR** in Volume 1).

The **HISTORICAL EVENTS** Chronology includes those events described in the *Dictionary* to which an exact or approximate date can be given. Entries correspond to the titles used in the *Dictionary*. Events with no precise date, and references to individuals, are omitted.

The **MONARCHS** Chronology lists all Monarchs of Scotland. Dates are the calendar years over which the Monarchs reigned.

The **SECRETARIES OF STATE** and **NORTHERN IRELAND PRIME MINISTERS** Chronologies deal with political posts important to the government of the respective areas.

The Dictionary Section

The conventions employed in the body of the text are noted below:

Entry Conventions

Entries in this section are arranged in alphabetical order, with the title of the entry in **UPPERCASE BOLD PRINT**. When a series of entries consists of two words or more, entries which start with the same word are listed consecutively. In some cases, entries may be listed by a word other than that used first in spoken English (for instance, all battles appear in the form **KILLIECRANKIE, BATTLE OF**, rather than **BATTLE OF KILLIECRANKIE**). All individuals, with the exception of monarchs, are listed by surname. Kings and Queens appear under their given (or Christian) name and number order.

The two volumes of the *Dictionary* cover the major events in the history of Britain and the people who have helped to shape that history, particularly the monarchs, politicians, and military, commercial and industrial leaders of the nation. Given the country's lengthy history, the entries are necessarily selective and that selection remains the responsibility of the authors. In particular, material related to North America has been kept to a minimum because information about Britain's involvement in that part of the world is readily available to US and Canadian readers from other sources.

In addition, the allocation of material to each of the volumes is, to some extent, subjective. All material relating specifically or principally to England appears in Volume 1. All material relating specifically to Scotland, Wales and Northern Ireland appears in this volume. Entries dealing with Ireland prior to 1920 (when Northern Ireland was created) are deliberately limited because a volume dealing with Ireland in its entirety by Colin Thomas and Avril Thomas appears as number 20 in this series of Historical Dictionaries.

Cross-Referencing

Cross-references to related entries elsewhere in the *Dictionary* are shown within the body of individual entries in **UPPERCASE BOLD PRINT** and should be consulted to obtain additional information.

Multiple Entries

In cases where the same title occurs at different dates (as, for example, when three battles occurred at the same place but in different years), the individual occurrences are given either as separate dictionary entries (for major events) or as <u>underlined date</u> entries within the main entry (for lesser events).

Publications

In cases where entries include reference to a publication and no separate entry for that publication exists in the *Dictionary*, the title of that publication is shown in *lower case italic print*.

Names

The names of ships, trains and planes are given in *italic print*.

The Bibliography

The Bibliography is subdivided into sections for Scotland, Wales and Northern Ireland. Fuller details are given in the introduction to the Bibliography.

ABBREVIATIONS

A-Level	Advanced Level high school examinations
AD	Anno Domini (in the year of our Lord)
Ala	Alabama
am	before noon (ante meridiem)
BA	Bachelor of Arts
BBC	British Broadcasting Corporation
BC	Before Christ
BD	Bachelor of Divinity
BSc	Bachelor of Science
C	Centigrade
c.	circa
CDU	Campaign for Democracy in Ulster
CSJ	Campaign for Social Justice
CCDC	Central Citizens' Defence Committee
CLMC	Combined Loyalist Military Command
CLP	Commonwealth Labour Party
Co	Colorado
d	penny, pennies or pence
DC	District of Columbia
DD	Doctor of Divinity
DUP	Democratic Unionist Party
GCSE	General Certificate of Secondary Education
HIDB	Highlands and Islands Development Board
HIE	Highlands and Islands Enterprise
ILP	Independent Labour Party
INLA	Irish National Liberation Army
IPLO	Irish People's Liberation Organization
IRA	Irish Republican Army
IRB	Irish Republican Brotherhood
IRSP	Irish Republican Socialist Party
KBE	Knight Commander of the Order of the British Empire
KCB	Knight Commander of the Order of the Bath
KCMG	Knight Commander of the Order of St Michael and St George
LLB	Bachelor of Laws
MA	Master of Arts
Mass	Massachusetts
MBA	Master of Business Administration
MP	Member of Parliament

MSc	Master of Science
NJ	New Jersey
NORAID	Irish Northern Aid Committee
Pa	Pennsylvania
PhD	Doctor of Philosophy
RAF	Royal Air Force
RUC	Royal Ulster Constabulary
SCE	Scottish Certificate of Education
SDLP	Social Democratic and Labour Party
SDP	Social Democratic Party
SNP	Scottish National Party
TV	Television
UDA	Ulster Defence Association
UDR	Ulster Defence Regiment
UF Church	United Free Church of Scotland
UFF	Ulster Freedom Fighters
UP Church	United Presbyterian Church
UPUP	Ulster Popular Unionist Party
UPL	Ulster Protestant League
UPNI	Unionist Party of Northern Ireland
UUUP	United Ulster Unionist Party
UNESCO	United Nations Educational, Scientific and Cultural Organization
UK	United Kingdom
US	United States
UUP	Ulster Unionist Party
VUPP	Vanguard Unionist Progressive Party

CHRONOLOGIES

HISTORICAL EVENTS

BC

3000	Callanish
2000	Jarlshof

AD

83	Mons Graupius, Battle of
142	Antonine Wall
637	Mag Rath, Battle of
807	Book of Kells
893	Buttington, Battle of
1067	Palatine Counties
1098	Orkney
1138	Standard, Battle of the
1155	Laudabiliter
1174	Falaise, Treaty of
1176	Eisteddfod
1178	Belfast
1258	Galloglasses
1263	Largs, Battle of
1266	Perth, Treaty of
1267	Montgomery, Treaty of
1276–84	Edwardian Conquest
1292	Great Cause
	Stirling Bridge, Battle of
1295	Auld Alliance
1296	Dunbar, Battle of
	Berwick, Battle of
1298	Falkirk, Battle of
1300	Mabinogion, The
1306	Ruthven, Battle of
1318	Dundalk, Battle of
	Berwick, Battle of
1320	Arbroath, Declaration of
1333	Halidon Hill, Battle of
	(Battle of Berwick)
1356	Berwick, Battle of
1357	Berwick, Treaty of
1388	Otterburn, Battle of
1450	Bonds of Manrent
1482	Berwick, Battle of
1494	Poynings' Law
1513	Flodden, Battle of
1532	Court of Session
1536	Union of Wales and England
1542	Solway Moss, Battle of
1543	Union of Wales and England
1544	Rough Wooing

1545	Ancrum Moor, Battle of
1547	Pinkie, Battle of
1548	Haddington, Treaty of
1556–1659	Plantations of Ulster
1557	Lords of the Congregation
1559–67	Tyrone Rebellion
1560	Berwick, Treaty of
1561	Book of Discipline
1568	Casket Letters
	Langside, Battle of
1578	Book of Discipline
1582	Ruthven Raid
1584	Black Acts
1586	Berwick, Treaty of
1589	Northern Earls
1594–1603	Tyrone Rebellion
1594	Ford of the Biscuits, Battle of the
1598	Yellow Ford, Battle of
1600	Gowrie Conspiracy
1601	Kinsale, Battle of
1610	Presbyterian Church in Ireland
1618	Five Articles of Perth
1625	Act of Revocation
1628	The Graces
1638	Covenanters
	National Covenant
	Glasgow Assembly
1639–40	Bishops' Wars
1639	Berwick, Treaty of
1643	Solemn League and Covenant
1644	Distilleries
1645	Auldearn, Battle of
	Kilsyth, Battle of
	Philiphaugh, Battle of
	Glamorgan Treaty
	Levellers
1647	Engagers
1649	Act of Classes
1650	Dunbar, Battle of
1652	Settlement Act
1653–54	Glencairn Rising
1660	Act of Explanation
1661	Restoration Settlement
1662	Settlement Act
1663	Cattle Act
1665	Act of Settlement and Explanation
	(see Settlement Acts)
1666	Pentland Rising
1667	Cattle Act
1672	Court of Justiciary
1679	Bothwell Bridge, Battle of

CHRONOLOGY OF SCOTTISH MONARCHS 841–1603

c. 841 – c. 859	Kenneth MacAlpin (Kenneth I)		1097 – 1107	Edgar
c. 859 – 863	Donald I		1107 – 1124	Alexander I
863 – c. 877	Constantine I		1124 – 1153	David I
c. 877 – 878	Aed		1153 – 1165	Malcolm IV
878 – 889	Eochaid and Giric		1165 – 1214	William I
889 – 900	Donald II		1214 – 1249	Alexander II
900 – 943	Constantine II		1249 – 1286	Alexander III
943 – 954	Malcolm I		1286 – 1290	Margaret
954 – 962	Indulf		1290 – 1292	Interregnum
962 – c. 967	Dubh (or Duff)		1292 – 1296	John
c. 967 – 971	Culen		1296 – 1306	Interregnum
971 – 995	Kenneth II		1306 – 1329	Robert I (Robert the Bruce)
995 – 997	Constantine III		1329 – 1371	David II
997 – 1005	Kenneth III		1371 – 1390	Robert II
1005 – 1034	Malcolm II		1390 – 1406	Robert III
1034 – 1040	Duncan I		1406 – 1437	James I
1040 – 1057	Macbeth		1437 – 1460	James II
1057 – 1058	Lulach		1460 – 1488	James III
1058 – 1093	Malcolm III		1488 – 1513	James IV
1093 – 1094	Donald III		1513 – 1542	James V
1094	Duncan II		1542 – 1567	Mary
1094 – 1097	Donald III (northern Scotland)		1567 – 1603	James VI (James I of England)
1094 – 1097	Edmund (southern Scotland)			

CHRONOLOGY OF PRIME MINISTERS OF NORTHERN IRELAND

1921 – 1940	James Craig		1963 – 1969	Terence O'Neill
1940 – 1943	John Andrews		1969 – 1971	James Chichester-Clark
1943 – 1963	Basil Brooke		1971 – 1972	Brian Faulkner

CHRONOLOGIES OF SECRETARIES OF STATE

SCOTLAND

1926 – 1929	John Gilmour (Conservative)		1947 – 1950	Arthur Woodburn (Labour)
1929 – 1931	William Adamson (Labour)		1950 – 1951	Hector McNeil (Labour)
1931 – 1932	Archibald Sinclair		1951 – 1957	James Gray Stuart
	(Coalition Government)			(Conservative)
1932 – 1936	Godfrey Collins		1957 – 1962	John Maclay (Conservative)
	(Coalition Government)		1962 – 1964	Michael Noble (Conservative)
1936 – 1938	Walter Elliot		1964 – 1970	William Ross (Labour)
	(National Government)		1970 – 1974	Gordon Campbell
1938 – 1940	David John Colville			(Conservative)
	(National Government)		1974 – 1976	William Ross (Labour)
1940 – 1941	Alfred Ernest Brown		1976 – 1979	Bruce Millan (Labour)
	(National Government)		1979 – 1986	George Younger (Conservative)
1941 – 1945	Tom Johnston		1986 – 1990	Malcolm Rifkind
	(Coalition Government)			(Conservative)
1945	Earl of Rosebery (Caretaker)		1990 – 1995	Ian Lang (Conservative)
1945 – 1947	Joseph Westwood (Labour)		1995 – 1997	Michael Forsyth (Conservative)
			1997 –	Donald Dewar (Labour)

WALES

1964 – 1966	James Griffiths (Labour)	
1966 – 1968	Cledwyn Hughes (Labour)	
1968 – 1970	George Thomas (Labour)	
1970 – 1974	Peter Thomas (Conservative)	
1974 – 1979	John Morris (Labour)	
1979 – 1987	Nicholas Edwards (Conservative)	
1987 – 1990	Peter Walker (Conservative)	
1990 – 1993	David Hunt (Conservative)	
1993 – 1995	John Redwood (Conservative)	
1995 – 1997	William Hague (Conservative)	
1997 –	Ron Davies (Labour)	

NORTHERN IRELAND

1972 – 1973	William Whitelaw
1973	Francis Pym
1973 – 1976	Merlyn Rees
1976 – 1979	Roy Mason
1979 – 1981	Humphrey Atkins
1981 – 1984	James Prior
1984 – 1985	Douglas Hurd
1985 – 1989	Tom King
1989 – 1992	Peter Brooke
1992 – 1997	Patrick Mayhew
1997 –	Marjorie Mowlam

Map 1

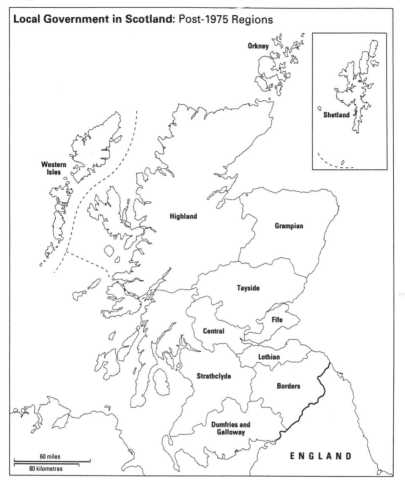

Local Government in Scotland: Post-1975 Regions

Orkney

Shetland

Western Isles

Highland

Grampian

Tayside

Fife

Central

Lothian

Strathclyde

Borders

Dumfries and Galloway

ENGLAND

60 miles

80 kilometres

Map 2

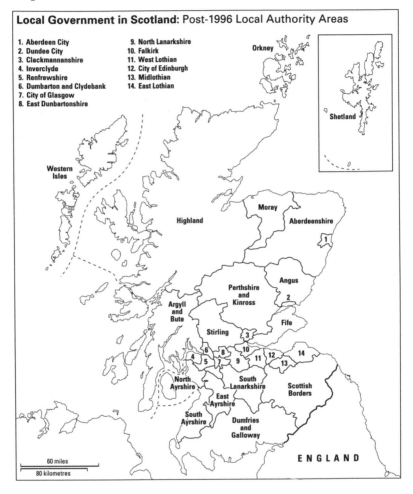

Local Government in Scotland: Post-1996 Local Authority Areas

1. Aberdeen City
2. Dundee City
3. Clackmannanshire
4. Inverclyde
5. Renfrewshire
6. Dumbarton and Clydebank
7. City of Glasgow
8. East Dunbartonshire
9. North Lanarkshire
10. Falkirk
11. West Lothian
12. City of Edinburgh
13. Midlothian
14. East Lothian

Orkney

Shetland

Western Isles

Highland

Moray

Aberdeenshire

Angus

Perthshire and Kinross

Argyll and Bute

Fife

Stirling

North Ayrshire

East Ayrshire

South Ayrshire

South Lanarkshire

Scottish Borders

Dumfries and Galloway

ENGLAND

60 miles

80 kilometres

Map 3

Local Government in Wales: Post-1974 Counties and Major Settlements

Map 4

Local Government in Wales: Post-1996 Local Authority Areas

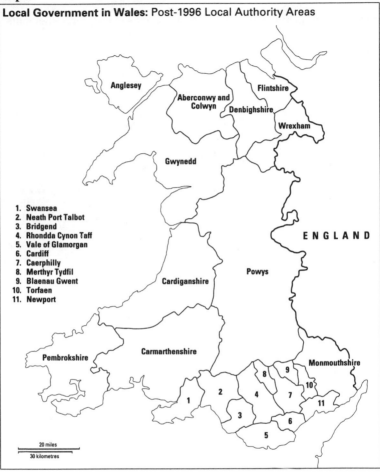

1. Swansea
2. Neath Port Talbot
3. Bridgend
4. Rhondda Cynon Taff
5. Vale of Glamorgan
6. Cardiff
7. Caerphilly
8. Merthyr Tydfil
9. Blaenau Gwent
10. Torfaen
11. Newport

Map 5

Counties and Major Settlements in Northern Ireland

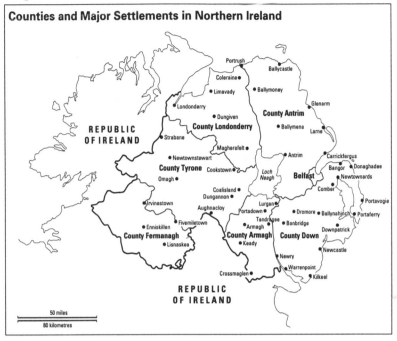

Map 6

Local Government in Northern Ireland: Post-1973 District Councils

Map 7

Local Government in Northern Ireland: Post-1974 Area Board Boundaries

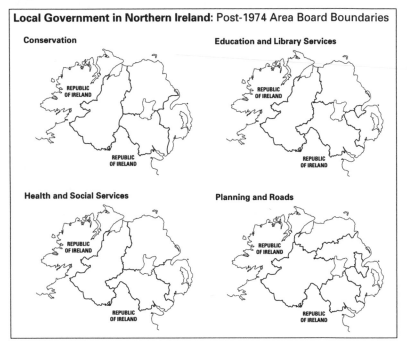

Conservation

Education and Library Services

Health and Social Services

Planning and Roads

INTRODUCTION

Politically, the United Kingdom is a single state. Culturally, it consists of four nations, three of whom — the Scots, the Welsh and the Irish — fought for centuries against English domination and still jealously preserve their individual identities.

When the Romans invaded the British Isles during the first century AD, they advanced westwards, pushing their Celtic predecessors ahead of them. The Anglo-Saxons continued that process from the fifth century and the Normans from the eleventh, but none of these groups was able to establish dominance over the whole area. The uplands of the north and west did not lend themselves to the set piece battles at which the English armies excelled, favouring forms of guerilla warfare which allowed small bands of local people, with an intimate knowledge of the fractured landscape, to harass and demotivate troops based in unfamiliar territory. In the end, technology, economics and heredity led to political unity but, until the comparatively recent introduction of telephones and air travel, Wales, Ulster and Scotland were remote from the United Kingdom's political power base in the southeast of the country. As a result, they were able to preserve facets of their distinctive cultures. Language, religion, education, legal conventions and banking combined to produce worldviews in Belfast, Edinburgh and Cardiff which differed markedly from those in London. In turn, these differing views led to unique traditions of achievement; many writers, for example, have related the Scots' output of philosophers, scientists and engineers to a distinctive education system and the Welsh flair for socialist political oratory to the training grounds of Methodist chapels.

WALES

Wales was the first of the celtic nations to be absorbed into an expanding kingdom dominated by England. Covering an area of about 8,000 square miles, it forms a peninsula, which looks remarkably like a pig's head and extends westward from the British mainland. Most of the territory is hilly, rising to 3,560 feet at Snowdon, in the northwest, and dissected by rivers and streams which complicate travel. The more northerly rocks are volcanic in origin, creating dramatic scenery emphasized by glaciation. Further south, sediments, uplifted and folded, produce gentler, rounded uplands, which are utilized for sheep pasture and, in some areas, are covered by forestry plantations.

The climate is mild, dominated by air masses from the Atlantic Ocean which keep mean January temperatures relatively high at around 50° Fahrenheit (10° C) and mean July temperatures a comfortable 61°

Fahrenheit (16° C). The annual average rainfall is 55 inches, but regional variations can be considerable, depending on altitude and proximity to the sea.

Most of the 2.9 million population concentrate in the south, where settlements such as Cardiff, Swansea and Merthyr Tydfil flourished during the industrial revolution as migrants flooded into the area in search of jobs in the coal mines and the iron works. Clusters of towns along the north coast serve as holiday resorts, but, elsewhere, building is confined largely to valley villages and isolated farmhouses in sheltered locations among the mountains. At 360 people per square mile, the population density is significantly less than the 615 per square mile of the United Kingdom as a whole.

The first significant colonization of the area was effected by celtic peoples, who had established permanent communities by 3500 BC, but limited archaeological remains and a lack of any written culture mean that their numbers, economy and social structure are the subject of much scholarly debate. Roman armies were present from the first to the fourth centuries AD, but Wales was always at the northwestern outpost of their empire and their impact was limited. They built towns in the south, at locations such as Carmarthen, but, elsewhere, their presence was primarily evident in the form of forts linked by a network of roads.

As the Romans left, from about AD 400, they were replaced by Anglo-Saxon peoples, who tilled the clay soils of the lowlands and cut down trees to create fields, establishing farming communities. However, these agriculturalists had little impact on the more mountainous areas, where local groups fought to expand their territorial influence and a series of small kingdoms evolved. Attempts to unite these ministates were frequent but never resulted in more than temporary coalitions of mutually antagonistic fiefdoms; the most successful of the native leaders was Gruffudd ap Llywelyn, who briefly held the whole of Wales before his death in 1063 led to a refragmentation of his estates.

The development of a national identity began as a result of the activities of the Normans. They invaded the British Isles from northwest France in 1066 and, by 1100, had gained control of much of southern Wales. Also, they had stamped their authority along the western limits of Anglo-Saxon settlement, building defensive sites at centres such as Shrewsbury, Hereford and Chester. In these frontier lands, known as the marches, aristocratic barons wielded great authority, presiding over courts of law and exercising a right to build fortifications which was denied to the lords in other areas under Norman jurisdiction. They discovered, however, that their Welsh neighbours were unwilling to submit and frequently found themselves under threat by forces from the west. In particular, Gwynedd and Powys (in the north of Wales) and Deheubarth (in the southwest) retained varying degrees of independence. In essence, the monarchs of England were unwilling to commit the resources clearly necessary to subjugate Wales but were determined to prevent the area from grouping under a single ruler and thus facing them with a united army. That was a strategy which was not easily sustained. In 1095 and 1097, William II sent royal forces to the support of the marcher lords, and, from 1100, Henry I became increasingly involved in Welsh affairs. Also, Henry II took his army into Wales in 1157 and again in 1165, but neither of these incursions had any lasting effect in expanding control. During the 13th century, however, the tide turned against the Welsh. In 1267, under the terms of the Treaty of Montgomery, King Henry III of England accepted Llywelyn ap Gruffudd's right to the title Prince of Wales and to the homage of all lesser rulers in the principality. Edward I, who succeeded Henry in 1272, was less cooperative. Intent on anglicizing the Welsh, rather than simply expanding his empire by demanding homage, he quarrelled continuously with Llywelyn, who found few supporters willing to face the superior military power of the English sovereign. War in 1277 led to confinement of Llywelyn's power to the area of Gwynedd west of the River Conwy, and in 1282 an attempt to reestablish his former authority convinced Henry to put an end to the constant skirmishing. On 11 December, Llywelyn was killed by the English at Builth Wells and, though his brother, Dafydd, took up the cause for several months, the struggle for Welsh independence was over by the summer of the following year.

Edward consolidated his hold by building a series of castles (such as the imposing structures at Conway and Harlech) where he could base his troops. In addition, through the Statute of Rhuddlan in 1284, he introduced English principles of local government and criminal law. A rebellion by Owain Glyndwr threatened to reassert native rule during the early years of the 15th century, but, ultimately, initiated processes which led to the full incorporation of Wales within England. In 1536, the government of Henry VIII extended the county system of local government to the marches, partly in order to make control of the frontier more effective. Wales was given representation in Parliament for the first time, all legal distinctions between Welsh and English people were abolished and the English language was made the principal means of communication in the principality. Further measures in 1543 pushed the Welsh legal system even more closely into line with that of England by creating justices of the peace, who undertook a wide range of administrative duties as well as presiding in courts of law.

The vast majority of the Welsh gentry welcomed the infusion of

English administrative procedures, but, culturally and socially, the people retained their distinctiveness. The agrarian population, numbering only some 250,000, largely illiterate and spread throughout a mountain landscape, continued to converse in their own tongue. Translations of the New Testament and the *Book of Common Prayer* into Welsh by William Salesbury in 1567, and William Morgan's translation of the whole Bible in 1588, served as a focus for religious worship. Also, while Oliver Cromwell ruled between 1653 and 1658 — and the influence of Parliament outweighed royal commands — Nonformists established their own congregations, distinct from the Anglican Church groups, which provided the foundation for a movement that had a lasting effect on the Welsh people.

During the 18th century, the dissenting tradition swelled in a Methodist wave which swept across Wales, particularly in the years from 1735, led by such charismatic preachers as Daniel Rowland and Howel Harris. Griffith Jones' schools, formed so that Christians could learn to read and, therefore, study their Bible more regularly, fostered education, and, by 1850, Wales was one of the few European nations which could claim that most of its members were literate.

The years which followed brought further transformation, wrought by the Industrial Revolution. Between 1801 and 1851, the Welsh population doubled in size from 587,000 to 1,100,000. Over the next 50 years, it nearly doubled again. Immigrants flocked to the coalfields of northeast and, particularly, south Wales and to jobs in the growing manufacturing industries and the docks. Conditions were hard, with wages low, hours long and living conditions squalid. Industrial unrest was increasingly evident from the 1830s, and, coupled with the nonconformist dissenting tradition, manifested itself in a political radicalism which was later to produce such distinguished national leaders as David Lloyd George and Aneurin Bevan.

After the First World War, economic depression hit south Wales. Declining demand for coal and steel caused widespread unemployment and poverty, which fostered emigration and provided fertile ground for the socialist policies of the Labour Party. At the same time, the growing sense of national identity (evident from the mid-19th century, which had brought the growth of a Welsh language press and the establishment of a nationalist eisteddfod) assumed a decidedly political dimension.

Cardiff was recognized as the capital of the principality in 1955, but that failed to satisfy those who demanded clear recognition that Wales was an entity distinct from the rest of the United Kingdom. During the 1960s, membership of Plaid Cymru (the Welsh Nationalist Party) grew rapidly, and the Welsh Language Society campaigned to get Welsh accepted for official purposes, painting out English text on road signs in an attempt to gain recognition for their cause. In response, the Labour Party appointed a Secretary of State for Wales (with a seat in the cabinet) in 1964. The Welsh Language Act, approved by Parliament in 1967, gave Welsh parity with English within Wales, and bodies such as the Welsh Development Agency (created in 1976) and the Welsh Language Board (established in 1988) were appointed to promote specific aspects of social, cultural and economic life.

However, devolution of power to a Welsh parliament — a major aim of many activists — was never approved. A referendum, held in 1979, revealed that only 12 per cent of the electorate was in favour, a figure well below the 40 per cent required for implementation of the plans for a Cardiff-based assembly which the Labour government had published. Since then, although Plaid Cymru has retained regional pockets of support, there has been little agitation for change to the constitutional status quo. In 1997, a second referendum held in the wake of a Labour Party's return to power at a general election earlier in the year, resulted in a tiny margin of 6,721 votes in favour of an elected forum. The 60-strong 'Parliament' which was expected to meet for the first time in 1999, would have a £7 billion budget but (unlike its Scottish counterpart) no powers to raise revenue through taxes. As a result, its critics claimed, it would be a talking shop with no authority to innovate or develop.

SCOTLAND

Scotland occupies approximately one-third of the area of the United Kingdom. In the south, it has a land boundary with England but the rest of its 30,400 square miles is surrounded by sea — the Atlantic Ocean in the west, the North Sea in the east and the Pentland Firth in the north.

Structurally, it can be divided into three parts — the highlands, the central lowland and the southern uplands. The highlands are mountainous, rising to 4,406 feet at Ben Nevis (the highest point in the British Isles) and much eroded by glaciers, which have created a topography of steeply sided valleys and sharp peaks. The central lowland, drained by the Rivers Forth and Clyde, is a rift valley, with outcrops of volcanic hills rising to over 2,000 feet in places. The southern uplands consist of gently rounded hills, composed primarily of sedimentary rocks.

Because of the influence of the sea, the climate is mild, with mean temperatures ranging from January lows of about 37° Fahrenheit (3° Centigrade) to July highs of about 59° Fahrenheit (15° Centigrade). Rainfall is highest in the west, with the mountains around Fort William receiving 140 inches per annum (Dundee, on the east coast, receives about 30 inches). Pine forests formerly clothed much of the land, but most of these have been removed by charcoal burners (who cut down the trees for commercial purposes) and sheep (who nibble young shoots and prevent regeneration). Nowadays, the hills are covered largely by poor grasses (which provide grazing for the sheep) and heather (which provides a habitat for the red grouse, a much-prized game bird).

Since 1919, private landowners as well as the government-supported Forestry Commission have attempted to reintroduce woodland, partly for strategic reasons and partly in an effort to reduce Britain's bill for wood imports. The sitka spruce, a North American species, is now the most common tree in Scotland; planted by foresters, it matures quickly, soon producing a financial return.

The bulk of the 5.1 million people live in the towns and cities of the central lowland, which, because of its reserves of coal and iron ore, became one of Britain's major manufacturing areas during the Industrial Revolution. Elsewhere, despite concentrations in coastal cities (such as Aberdeen) and market towns (such as Hawick), settlement is sparse (Scotland's population density, at 169 people per square mile, is much lower than that of England, which has 960).

There is evidence of a settled population in Scotland from the second millenium BC and of construction of stone circles (such as that at Callanish, in the Western Isles) by Bronze Age people who arrived from about 1800 BC. The Romans, who had a major economic and social impact in southern Britain, had limited influence in the north, where they were at the remotest corners of their empire. Hadrian's Wall, built across the uplands between the Solway Firth and the River Tyne between AD 122 and 128, marked the boundary of their authority. Beyond that, there was a frontier zone contested by the invaders and the native people and never effectively subdued.

From the fifth until the ninth centuries, the land which was to become Scotland was fought over by five distinct groups, who were ultimately to merge in one nation. Much of the land south of the River Forth was controlled by the Britons, a Celtic race, who probably first appeared in the area during the first century BC. The area north of the Forth was occupied by the Picts, a people who have left very limited material remains and whose economy and society have been the subject of much debate. The Scots arrived from the north of Ireland during the late fifth century and initially colonized Argyll (on the west coast of the country) but quickly expanded their authority eastwards and southwards, and the Angles, Germanic invaders, forced the Britons out of the southeast during the early seventh century. In addition, Viking raiders appeared in the later eighth century and, for 150 years, settled on many of the islands and the northernmost parts of the mainland.

The process of uniting these disparate peoples was begun by Kenneth MacAlpin, leader of the Scots. He became King of the Picts in 843 and his successors continued to expand his empire so, by 1250, Scotland was a recognizable political entity.

From the time of Edward I (who reigned from 1272 until 1307), the expansionist English monarchs threatened the country's existence, and frequently occupied much of its territory, but resistance was strong. William Wallace (*c.* 1270–1305) and Robert the Bruce (1274–1329) initially provided charismatic and tactically astute leadership which avoided submission to a significantly more powerful enemy, but, for over 350 years, independence was insecure and warfare drained the nation's coffers.

In 1603, the union of the two countries under a single monarch — James VI of Scotland and I of England — brought peace, despite the challenges to royal authority of James Stuart (the Old Pretender) in 1715 and Charles Edward Stuart (Bonnie Prince Charlie) from 1745 to 46.

Charles's defeat at Culloden (1746) ended attempts to acquire the British throne through military means and represented the last struggles of a dying culture. By the time the Stuarts were leading their rebellions, Scotland had rejected its Gaelic heritage and was developing an anglicized economy centered on the lowland towns. The religious reformation of the 16th century had wrought a social revolution on a scale markedly different from that experienced elsewhere in the British Isles. John Knox and the other leaders of the Protestant movement argued that education was fundamental to their faith and emphasized thrift rather than conspicuous consumption. The Treaty of Union with England in 1707 united both countries under a single parliament and, though much disputed, opened new markets to Scottish merchants. Also, during the middle and later years of the 18th century, Scotland experienced a period of remarkable intellectual vigour, strongly European in character, which produced men of the calibre of philosopher David Hume, economist Adam Smith, architect Robert Adam and poet Robert Burns.

The 19th century brought further change, with the transformation from an agrarian to an urban society as the development of coal and iron resources produced large-scale industrial development in the central lowland. In particular, the population of the west of Scotland grew as Glasgow flourished, becoming a world centre of shipbuilding and engineering. James Watt (who developed the steam engine), John Macadam (who created tarmac road surfaces), Thomas Telford (designer of canals and bridges) and others were responsible for the technological and scientific innovation which allowed enterprizes to develop. Workers migrated to the area from the highlands and southern uplands — some of them former tenants thrown off the land as the lairds replaced human labour with sheep; others attracted by the city's relatively high wages.

From about 1880, the new factory employees increasingly organized themselves into trade unions and, led by such left-wing politicians as James Keir Hardie, contributed to the growth of the Labour Party, which has dominated Scottish politics since the end of the First World War. In part, the radicalism was fuelled by poverty. Poor housing conditions, subsistence level wages and overcrowding, particularly during the economic depression of the 1920s and 1930s, contributed to low living standards and demands for social change.

The Scottish National Party, formed in 1934, also benefited, during the late 1960s and early 1970s especially when it had 11 representatives in the House of Commons and was seen by significant numbers of voters as a credible alternative to Labour. Nevertheless, as in Wales, the proposal to devolve power from Westminster to a regional assembly failed to gain the approval of 40 per cent of the electorate when a referendum was held in 1979, so Scotland continued to be governed from London.

During the 1980s, the economic recession, which blighted the industrialized world, led to the closure of many of the manufacturing plants which had contributed to 19th-century growth. Many Scots held Margaret Thatcher's Conservative government responsible. However, failure to adapt working practices or introduce new technologies had made shipbuilding, chemical, engineering and textile companies uncompetitive in international markets so a narrow, outdated economic infrastructure caused much of the distress.

A change of direction fed growth in computer industries and telecommunications services, notably in Fife, the Edinburgh area and Strathclyde (which focuses on Glasgow). Also, the discovery of oil and gas in the North Sea during the 1970s created many thousands of jobs, particularly at Aberdeen and Lerwick (on the Shetland Islands). Moreover, the growth of tourism, coupled with increasing demands for financial products, has caused a shift in employment from manufacturing to services, confirming Edinburgh's position as the major British banking centre outside London. The resurgent economy fuelled a growing national self-confidence. In 1997, Scots voted decisively for the Labour Party at the general election held in the spring, voting every Conservative Party M.P. in the area out of office, including the Secretary of State for Scotland and the Foreign Secretary. Labour's reward was a referendum asking the people whether they wanted their own Parliament, able to legislate on Scottish affairs and raise money through taxation. This time, the proposals were overwhelmingly approved, with 74 percent of the electorate supporting the assembly and 63 affirming its tax raising powers. *The Scotsman*, in an emotional editorial, claimed that the figures demonstrated the Scots' willingness to believe in themselves.

NORTHERN IRELAND

Northern Ireland occupies about 5,460 square miles of the northeast corner of the island of Ireland and has 1.6 million people. However, its role in the United Kingdom's domestic politics is far greater than its size, either of territory or of population, would suggest.

The fringes of the province are upland, with the Mourne Mountains (in the southeast) rising to 2,789 feet at Slieve Donard. These hills drain to Lough Neagh, passing through landscapes moulded by ice, which formerly scoured the area. The climate is mild and, like that of the rest of the British Isles, greatly influenced by the seas which surround Ireland. Mean January temperatures are about 40° Fahrenheit (4.4° Centigrade) and July temperatures about 58° Fahrenheit (14.4° Centigrade). Annual rainfall totals reach 80 inches in the Sperrin Mountains, to the west of the province, but only about 33 inches in the southeast.

The majority of the people live in the coastal areas, notably in Belfast and Londonderry, the two major cities. Elsewhere, the population congregates in small market towns (such as Newcastle and Omagh) or is spread across the countryside in scattered farmhouses. The 20th-century economy has been dominated by manufacturing industries (particularly shipbuilding, engineering and textile production), but, in recent decades, these have been much affected by world trade recessions and a lack of investment caused by civil disorder in the area. Partly for these reasons, agriculture remains important, with particular concentration on beef, dairying and sheep farming. In additon, the Irish Sea ports (such as Kilkeel and Portavogie) have small fishing fleets.

The nub of Northern Ireland's political problems is an apparently intractable threefold social cleavage between Protestants and Roman Catholics, rich and poor, and republicans (most of whom advocate union of Northern Ireland with the Irish Republic) and loyalists (who are determined to maintain British sovereignty). The three elements of the cleavage are not mutually exclusive, thus compounding the difficulties, and have deep historical roots.

During the 12th century, King Henry II attempted to consolidate

English rule in Ireland by promoting the immigration of settlers from the British mainland, and, in 1366, attempts were made through the Statutes of Kilkenny, which banned marriage between natives and settlers, to keep the two groups apart. In the 16th century, following the Reformation, Henry VIII persecuted those (in Ireland and elsewhere) who persisted in espousing the cause of Catholicism and, in 1607, James VI and I promoted a further infusion of new blood, attracting Protestant farmers from Scotland and England to land in Ulster (the ancient kingdom which forms the core of modern Northern Ireland).

The settlement policies produced two distinct groups — a Roman Catholic, largely landless (and, by implication, poor) peasantry and a relatively affluent Protestant gentry. In 1690, the schism was emphasized following the defeat, at the Battle of the Boyne, of the exiled King James VII and II, who claimed the British throne then occupied by William of Orange. After the victory, Parliament approved measures which prevented Catholics from owning property or exercising any rights of English citizenship. Those provisions were replaced in 1793, when Roman Catholics were given the right to vote, but that change did little to counterbalance the decades of repression.

The bitterness between the religious communities was manifested in violent clashes during the dying years of the 18th century and, in 1800, an Act of Union made Ireland an integral part of Great Britain, placing Protestants under the formal protection of the British Crown.

Under the terms of the legislation, Ireland was given places for 100 representatives in the House of Commons and 32 (4 bishops and 28 peers) in the House of Lords. However, there were many people who found that arrangement less than satisfactory so the disturbances continued (in 1835, for example, there was a major clash between Protestants and Catholics in Belfast).

For the British government, the problems caused by the constant dissent were exacerbated by the great famine of the 1840s, when the potato crop was destroyed by blight and the effects were worsened by a series of severe winters and restrictions on the sale of Irish wheat on the world market. Poverty and starvation were widespread, an estimated 1 million people (about one in eight of Ireland's population) died and 1.25 million emigrated, many to the United States.

As the difficulties mounted, politicians in London, increasingly inclined to the view that Ireland should be allowed to determine its own future, presented home rule bills to Parliament in 1886, 1893 and 1912. The first of these, introduced by William Gladstone, Prime Minister and Leader of the Liberal Party, never got further than debate in the House of Commons and was firmly opposed by the Irish Protestants, who were concentrated in the north and feared that, following independence, their privileges would be removed by the Catholic majority in the rest of the island.

The second bill suffered a similar fate, but the third was approved by the Commons twice before being rejected by the House of Lords. Under the parliamentary procedures of the time, the bill could become law if the Commons accepted it after a third debate, even though the Lords continued to resist. That acceptance was given in 1914, but the outbreak of the First World War prevented implementation of the legislation.

Irishmen of all religions and political persuasions fought together on the European mainland between 1914 and 1918, but domestic troubles continued. In April 1916, a rebellion in Dublin, known as the Easter Rising, was harshly suppressed, and, in 1919, members of Sinn Fein (the Irish nationalist party), who had been elected to Parliament, declared independence for Ireland and formed their own assembly.

The problem for the Liberal government was stark. Most people in Ireland wanted freedom from British colonial rule, but most people in Ulster refused to entertain any suggestion that the link with the Crown should be broken. The preferred solution was the Government of Ireland Act (1920), which proposed partition of the island, with one parliament for the north (based at Belfast) and one for the south (based at Dublin). Both would be subject to the overall authority of the full British Parliament in London. Republicans were unmoved and mounted a violent campaign designed to earn further concessions. Following a truce, called on 11 July 1921, negotiations led to the formulation of an Anglo-Irish Treaty, which was approved on 6 December and created the Irish Free State, with its own parliament. The six northeastern counties — Antrim, Armagh, Derry, Down, Fermanagh and Tyrone — were made a self-governing province of the United Kingdom, with an elected assembly which had power to enact domestic legislation.

The new division left 500,000 Catholics in the new Northern Ireland, a significant minority in an area dominated by 1 million Protestants. With the new parliament at Stormont permanently dominated by a Protestant government, the Catholic groups saw little hope of obtaining positions of political authority at any administrative level and, over the years, effectively became disenfranchised. On the other hand, the availability of jobs in the manufacturing sector of the economy (which was virtually absent in the Free State) encouraged them to remain in Ulster, disaffected but employed.

During the 1950s and, in particular, the 1960s, these Catholic workers increasingly banded together in a civil rights movement which called for social as well as political change. The Irish Republican Army (which had its roots in the Nationalist Volunteer Force, founded in 1913) reemerged from a period of quiescence. In 1969, after months of mounting tension, violence broke out in Belfast and Londonderry. In 1970, troops were sent to Northern Ireland from the mainland in an attempt to keep the peace, but they were viewed by Catholics as agents of colonial rule, thereby provoking trouble simply through their presence. In 1972, as the clashes continued and the Stormont administration seemed unable to assert its authority, the British government, led by Prime Minister Edward Heath, suspended the Northern Ireland parliament and introduced direct rule of the province from London. The move was supposed to be temporary, but a series of senior politicians failed, over the next quarter century, to find any formula which allowed for the return of power to a Belfast-based assembly.

Throughout the 1970s and 1980s, violence was a fact of life in Northern Ireland and, to some extent, in English cities, where Irish Republican Army cells planned attacks such as that upon Mrs Margaret Thatcher and other government leaders at a Conservative Party conference in Brighton in 1984. The Anglo-Irish Agreement, signed in November 1985, raised hopes of peace because it allowed the Republic of Ireland (successor to the Free State) a consultative role in decision making about the province's future. However, although indicative of a cooperative mood both in London and in Dublin, the accord aroused the wrath of Protestant militants, who resented any southern interference in Ulster, and, in the end, brought little change. Nine years later, the IRA's decision to end violence and seek a political solution to the troubles was widely welcomed, but progress towards an understanding between the nationalists and the British government was too slow for the more militant members of the organization and, in 1996, a bombing in London's docklands brought an end to the peace. That resumption of violence proved to be temporary because, the following year, the ceasefire was resumed and negotiations inched towards a political solution to the troubles as Unionist leaders, despite much protest from hardline Protestants, sat at the same table as representatives of Sinn Fein.

CONCLUSION

In the final years of the 20th century, Wales, and Scotland both faced the prospect of constitutional change, with regional assemblies bringing greater local control over national affairs but introducing an element of uncertainty about future trends. Doubts hung over Northern Ireland too, because even the most optimistic negotiators were aware that discussions between parties separated by centuries of bitterness were fraught with problems.

However, despite the political uncertainty, economic and social trends were positive. The period of peace in Northern Ireland from 1994 until 1996 attracted inward investment and encouraged tourists to venture into the province in increasing numbers. Wales and Scotland were proving attractive to foreign investors, with Cardiff experiencing significant development in the service sector and Glasgow claiming to be Britain's first postindustrial city. The old heavy engineering order had changed, and that change brought major social readjustment in its wake, but Scots, Welsh and Irish had retained their national identities and seemed determined both to preserve their individuality and to gain some form of control over their political destinies before the third millenium was far advanced.

THE DICTIONARY

—A—

ABERCROMBY, RALPH (1734–1801). One of the outstanding British generals of the 18th century, Abercromby was largely responsible for restoring the morale and prestige of the army after its setbacks during the campaign in Flanders (1793–99). He also helped to end the French occupation of Egypt, which had been taken by Napoleon in an attempt to cut Britain's routeways to its possessions in India. Born in Menstrie (Clackmannanshire) in October 1734, Abercromby was educated at Rugby School and at the universities of **EDINBURGH** and Leipzig. He began his military career in 1756 as a cornet in the third dragoon guards and served with that regiment during the Seven Years War but changed course in 1774 and was elected member of Parliament for Clackmannanshire. Failing to achieve advancement (primarily because of his opposition to the war in the American colonies), he left politics in 1780 and, in 1793, on the outbreak of hostilities with France, returned to soldiering. He was appointed to the command of a brigade in Flanders, where he served with distinction, particularly when, leading the rear column, he was given the task of protecting the tired and dispirited troops during the retreat from Holland in the winter of 1794–95. Abercromby's rewards were a knighthood and public recognition as his country's most able soldier, but, more fundamentally, he had also become aware of the army's lack of discipline and of the problems caused by officers who owed their positions to wealth and political influence rather than leadership qualities. In 1795, when he was ordered to the West Indies, he put the lessons he had learned to good use, improving the calibre of his men by personal example and by improving their conditions (he adapted uniforms to suit tropical climates, for example). Also, he instituted a series of rewards for courage and self-discipline.

He continued to gain the respect of his troops while he served in Ireland (1797–98), Scotland (1798–99) and Holland (1799), then, in 1800, was given command of Britain's Mediterranean forces. Ordered to evict Napoleon from Egypt, he landed at Aboukir Bay on

1 March 1800 and advanced towards Alexandria. A French attack in the darkness of the early hours of 21 March was repulsed, with the attackers suffering heavy casualties, but Abercromby was seriously wounded in the battle. He died on board his flagship a week later, leaving the army bereft of a leader but much more feared and respected than it had been a decade earlier.

ABERDEEN. Situated on the North Sea coast between the River Dee and the River Don, Aberdeen lies some 120 miles north of **EDINBURGH** and is the major settlement in northeast Scotland. Often called *The Granite City* after the local rock which was used to construct much of its core, it was formed in 1891 by the merger of two previously independent **BURGH**s — Old Aberdeen and New Aberdeen. Old Aberdeen's history dates from 580, when, according to legend, it was founded by St Machar, one of **ST COLUMBA**'s followers. It was made the seat of a bishopric established by King **DAVID I** during the 12th century and, in 1489 and 1498, received charters, which made it a free burgh under the administration of the church. In 1494, it became a centre of learning when Pope Alexander VI authorized the establishment of King's College. The Protestant Marischal College followed in 1593, and, in 1860, the two united as the University of Aberdeen. New Aberdeen developed as a fishing port and commercial centre adjoining the ecclesiastical area and was granted a trading charter by **WILLIAM I**. In 1638, Charles I confirmed the privileges.

Although there were no local mineral resources, Aberdeen grew during the Industrial Revolution, using its natural harbour to export agricultural produce from its immediate hinterland to other parts of Britain and to the European mainland. Local wood provided the raw material for a shipbuilding industry, and the city developed a considerable reputation for the construction of clippers, which specialized in the speedy transport of tea from China. Also, following the development of steam trawlers from the 1880s, Aberdeen evolved into Scotland's major fishing port, and that, in turn, led to the growth of related industries, such as food processing (notably fish curing). Other sources of employment included engineering (particularly ship repair work and the making of agricultural equipment), the production of chemicals and fertilisers, papermaking, quarrying (the granite was much in demand for paving as well as for building), and textile manufacturing (especially linen and woollen goods).

As the settlement expanded, it became the major retail, administrative and educational centre in northern Scotland. Rail, sea and air routes focused on the city, and ferry connections were developed to serve the **ORKNEY** and **SHETLAND ISLANDS**, Iceland and Norway. When oil and gas were discovered under the North Sea during the 1970s, Aberdeen rapidly became the major service and supply centre for the industry, providing a base for over 200 new companies and 6,000 immigrants from the United States, Ireland and other parts of the world. Construction of offices, schools and homes followed hard on their heels, but jobs and income proved vulnerable to fluctuations in world oil prices. Moreover, the fishing industry found conditions increasingly difficult as catches fell and European Economic Community quotas were reflected in reduced returns. Faced with the precarious nature of local employment, planners attempted to diversify the area's economic base, particularly by making efforts to attract a greater number of tourists, and by 1997 employers in certain sections of the economy were complaining that expansion was being restricted by a lack of skilled personnel. In 1991, Aberdeen had a population of 205,000, marginally higher than in 1981.

ABERFAN DISASTER, 21 October 1966. A waste tip, at a coal mine in Glamorgan, collapsed after a period of heavy rain, engulfing the village school. Twenty-eight adults and 116 children died in a tragedy which touched many people around the world and led to new regulations for the construction of large spoil heaps, including provisions for a reduction in the height of tips elsewhere in Britain. An official inquiry blamed the disaster on the National Coal Board's failure to dispose of its industrial waste safely.

ABRAHAM, WILLIAM (1842–1922). The first of a long line of representatives of the South Wales coal industry to become members of English Parliament, William Abraham was elected to represent the **RHONDDA VALLEYS** in 1885, beating a young mine owner at the poll and allying himself with the more progressive elements of the Liberal Party. Born in Cwmafan (Glamorgan) on 14 June 1842, the fourth son of Thomas Abraham and his wife, Mary, he had a very elementary education at the local school, then, at age ten, followed his father into the pits. In 1873, he became a miner's agent, and, in 1877, was appointed full-time organizer of the Cambrian Miners' Association. For the next 30 years, he was one of the main leaders of the Welsh labour movement. A committed Methodist and an able negotiator, he was widely known as Mabon, a pen name he adopted when preparing material for local **EISTEDDFOD**au. He believed that the interests of mine owners and workers were the same and, in 1875, had helped to develop a scheme which related wages to the price of coal. As a result, between 1888 and 1898, the first Monday in the month became known as Mabon's Monday because miners observed it as a holiday in an attempt to limit output and thus keep prices high. In 1898, the South Wales Miners' Federation was formed, and Abraham became its first President. In that role, he attempted to pursue the moderate policies which had become his hallmark in negotiations with the employers but, eventually, his conciliatory approach was brushed aside by more radical, confrontational colleagues impatient for change. In 1912, following a strike over pay in pits where the geological conditions made extraction of coal difficult, he resigned. Although he was never an enthusiastic socialist, he transferred his political allegiance from the Liberal Party to the Labour Party when the Miners' Federation of Great Britain voted to affiliate to that organization in 1908, was made a privy councillor in 1911 and remained in Parliament until 1920. In the House of Commons, he played little part in debates, but on his home territory he was a powerful orator, often wooing his audiences by delivering part of his speeches in **WELSH** and using his fine tenor voice to lead them in popular chapel hymns. He died at Pentre on 14 May 1922.

ACT ANENT PEACE AND WAR, 1703. In 1701, the English Parliament passed the Act of Settlement, which ensured a Protestant succession to the throne through the Hanoverian family line. The Scots were not consulted, even though the monarch ruled both countries, and responded by approving the Act anent (about) Peace and War, which asserted that Scotland's Parliament had the right to choose Scotland's King. The implication was that the choice might be different from that made in England and could be the Roman Catholic **JAMES STUART**, exiled son of James VII and II. (See **ACT OF SECURITY; ALIEN ACT**).

ACT OF CLASSES, 1649. This legislation debarred opponents of the **NATIONAL COVENANT** from holding public or military office in Scotland until they repented. It prevented many experienced soldiers from serving in the army and, therefore, contributed to the Scottish defeat at the **BATTLE OF DUNBAR** on 3 September 1650. The act was repealed in June 1651, following the crowning of Charles II as King of Scotland (on 1 January of the same year) and the need to unite the country in the face of impending English invasions.

ACT OF EXPLANATION, 1660. During the interregnum (the period from 1649 until 1660 when England was ruled as a republic and under Puritan influence), Roman Catholics were displaced from their lands in northern Ireland as the English government attempted to colonize the area with loyal Protestants (see **PLANTATIONS OF ULSTER**). The Act of Explanation, passed by Parliament in November 1660, after the monarchy had been restored, confirmed ownership in the hands of the incomers (mainly demobilized soldiers and Scots farmers), though "innocent papists" could regain their estates if they could prove their loyalty to the Crown.

ACT OF REVOCATION, 1625. This legislation, instigated by King Charles I, cancelled all grants of crown and ecclesiastical land and property made to lay proprietors in Scotland since 1540. It was designed to secure funds for the clergy's stipends, but alienated many landowners, who were little mollified by a concession which allowed them to keep the estates on payment of a fee. Under the feudal system, monarchs frequently made gifts of land to nobles in return for military or other services. Grants made by Regents, who exercised power for sovereigns considered too young to rule, were often revoked when the monarchs assumed control, but the 1625 act was unusual, partly because Charles succeeded to the throne as an adult and partly because it covered the 85 years before his accession.

ACT OF SECURITY, 1703. In 1701, the English Parliament approved the Act of Settlement, which provided that, if William II (of Scotland) and III (of England) and his sister-in-law, Anne (who was expected to succeed him), both died childless, the Crown would pass to Sophia, Electress of Hanover and granddaughter of James VI (of Scotland) and I (of England), or her heirs. The Scots were not consulted about the legislation. Piqued, the **THREE ESTATES** passed the Act of Security, which asserted that, unless Scotland's sovereignty and security were ensured, the successor to Queen Anne would not be the same person as the monarch of England (the implication was that the choice could be **JAMES STUART,** only son of the exiled James VII and II). The Queen declined to give royal assent to the act, so the Scottish Parliament refused to grant her funding until she acquiesced in 1704. England retaliated the following year with the **ALIEN ACT,** which called for the repeal of the Act of Security and the suspension of all trade with Scotland. This political sparring between the two nations occurred at a time of increasing tension in the years prior to the **TREATY OF UNION**. (See **ACT ANENT PEACE AND WAR**).

ACT OF UNION (1800). In 1798, the Society of United Irishmen — a group, formed seven years earlier, which was determined to wrest Ireland from British rule — rose in rebellion against the government of William Pitt the Younger. Support was strongest in Wexford and in **ULSTER,** and aid was promised by France, with whom Britain was at war. The troubles were quickly subdued but were enough to convince Pitt that the only solution to the long-running problems on the island was full political integration with the rest of the British Isles. An act of union was passed by the Westminster Parliament on 1 August 1800. The Irish Parliament approved similar legislation on the same day (though only as a result of widespread corruption and after promises from Pitt that Roman Catholics would be allowed to hold public office), and the United Kingdom was formally established on 1 January the following year. Ireland was represented by 100 Members of Parliament in the House of Commons and by 32 peers in the House of Lords.

ADAM, ROBERT (1728–92). The leading neoclassical architect of his time, Adam was one of a large group of Scots who contributed to science and the arts in 18th-century Europe. (See **SCOTTISH ENLIGHTENMENT**). He was born in Kirkcaldy on 3 July 1728, and learned his trade from his father, William, who was Master Mason to the Ordnance in North Britain and designer of such important country mansions as Hopetoun House and House of Dun. In 1754, after completing his formal education at **EDINBURGH** High School and Edinburgh University, he went to Rome, where, in the company of C. I. Clerisseau (the French antiquary), he studied classical Roman architecture in great detail, making visits to Florence, Naples, Vicenza and Split. In addition, he cultivated the friendship of wealthy English travellers who, he felt, might become patrons in later years.

Adam returned to Britain in 1758 and set up a practice in London, where his friendly personality and connections in affluent, aristocratic circles, coupled with the successful publication of his work on *The Ruins of the Palace of the Emperor Diocletian at Spalatro* (1764), brought him enormous fame and made him the most sought after architect in the country. In 1761 (jointly with Sir William Chambers, his great rival), he was appointed architect to King George III, and, by the 1770s, the Adam style had superseded palladianism in fashionable circles. With his younger brother, James, he designed interiors as well as buildings, and his influence spread well beyond his homeland, with American architects, in particular, modelling their work on his. His best country houses — Kenwood House in Hampstead (London), Osterley House and Syon House in Middlesex and Kedleston House in Derbyshire — were completed in the 1760s and 1770s. In his native Scotland, most of his major works are public buildings, including Register House in Edinburgh. He died on 3 March 1792, and was buried in Westminster Abbey. (See **CULZEAN CASTLE**).

ADAMS, GERARD (1948–). President of **SINN FEIN** and the principal spokesman for the nationalist movement in Northern Ireland, Gerry Adams was born in **BELFAST** on 5 October 1948, the son of Gerald Adams and his wife, Annie. He was educated at St Mary's Christian Brothers' school in the city, then found work as a barman, joining the republican movement in 1964. In 1971, he was interned, suspected of being the leader of the **IRISH REPUBLICAN ARMY** on the militant Ballymurphy housing estate in West Belfast, but was released the following year so that he could take part in secret talks with **WILLIAM WHITELAW,** the Secretary of State for Northern Ireland. By 1973, the security services believed that he was one of a triumvirate shaping the IRA's campaign of violence, and he was arrested again. After attempting to escape from custody he was given an 18-month gaol sentence. In 1978, he was formally charged with membership of the IRA, by that time an illegal organization in the United Kingdom, but, after seven months in custody, was allowed to go free when Lord Lowry, the Lord Chief Justice, ruled that there was insufficient evidence to justify a conviction.

In the years which followed, Adams adopted a less aggressive posture. In 1979, the year after he was elected vice president of Sinn Fein, he told a public meeting in County Kildare that unification of Ireland could not be achieved by military means alone and, in 1983, became part of the formal political process by winning the West Belfast seat at the General Election, ousting the sitting member of Parliament, **GERRY FITT.** An astute tactician and an able speaker, he was appointed president of Sinn Fein in 1984 and, three years later, held on to his House of Commons constituency even though he had never put in an appearance at Westminster, increasing his majority despite a determined attempt by the **SOCIAL DEMOCRATIC AND LABOUR PARTY (SDLP)** to defeat him.

However, despite the electoral successes, Adams faced problems.

Support for Sinn Fein in the **REPUBLIC OF IRELAND** was limited so he found it difficult to claim that he had widespread support for his policies in the South. Public opinion was clearly swinging against sectarian violence, and, in 1989, he was forced to criticise some IRA activities which resulted in the killing of innocent civilians. Moreover, in 1990, his call for talks with the British government prior to a ceasefire was rejected out of hand (the United Kingdom argued that the ceasefire had to come first and that there would be no negotiations with active terrorists) and, in 1992, the SDLP candidate (Joe Hendron) defeated him at the April General Election.

Nevertheless, despite the setbacks, he continued to receive the backing of the republican movement and, in 1993, held a series of meetings with **JOHN HUME,** the moderate SDLP Leader, at the instigation of Roman Catholic clergy. The result was a commitment to explore new avenues which might lead to a settlement in **ULSTER** and, by the autumn, he was spelling out conditions for an end to violence. In January 1994, and despite vociferous British protest, he was granted a visa to enter the United States, where he received national television coverage but failed to deliver the much-expected announcement of an IRA ceasefire. The decision to end the killings came later in the year, allowing Adams and his colleagues to begin talks with British government officials. Inevitably, progress was too slow for some militants, and bombings resumed in London early in 1996, leading to claims that Adams was unable to control IRA activities and that his influence in the organization was waning. Nevertheless, he retained his authority and, in 1997, led a Sinn Fein delegation to the first formal negotiations with **MARJORIE MOWLAM,** the **SECRETARY OF STATE FOR NORTHERN IRELAND,** and **DAVID TRIMBLE,** leader of the **ULSTER UNIONIST PARTY.**

ADVOCATE. These lawyers have the right to appear either for the prosecution or for the defence at cases heard before the higher courts in **SCOTLAND**. Their professional organization is the Faculty of Advocates. (See **LEGAL SYSTEM: SCOTLAND**).

ALEXANDER I (*c.* 1080–1124). King of Scotland for 17 years, Alexander was the fifth son of **MALCOLM III** and **ST MARGARET.** He succeeded to the throne on the death of an older brother, **EDGAR,** and divided the country between himself and younger brother **DAVID I,** taking the area north of Strathclyde and the

RIVER FORTH. He married Sibylla, an illegitimate daughter of Henry I of England, around the time of his accession, and, in 1114, led Scottish troops in support of his father-in-law's campaign against the Welsh. A literate, godly man, he founded an Augustinian Priory at **SCONE** about 1115 and planned to establish other religious settlements but quarrelled with successive bishops of **ST ANDREWS**, and the schemes were never realized. He died in April 1124, probably at **STIRLING.**

ALEXANDER II (1198–1249). The only legitimate son of King **WILLIAM I** of Scotland, Alexander was born on 24 August 1198, and succeeded to the throne on his father's death in 1214. In an attempt to regain former Scottish territories in northern England, he supported the English barons in their struggle against King John, but later paid homage to Henry III, whose sister, Joan, he married in 1221. Joan died childless in 1238, and Alexander, in an attempt to continue the succession, married Mary de Courcy the following year. Their son (later **ALEXANDER III**), born in 1241, was betrothed to Henry's daughter, Margaret, at age one in order to strengthen the relationship between the neighbouring monarchs. However, Henry's claim to overlordship of Scotland and Alexander's desire to regain his English territories were constant sources of friction. In 1249, Alexander died at Kerrara and was succeeded by his son.

ALEXANDER III (1241–86). The only son of **ALEXANDER II** of Scotland, Alexander was born in Roxburgh on 4 September 1241, and succeeded to the throne, at the age of seven, on his father's death in 1249. Despite that inauspicious start to his kingship, he reigned for 37 years, creating a prosperous, united country, which maintained its independence from England. While still an infant, Alexander was betrothed to Margaret, daughter of Henry III of England, but, when they were married in 1251, he managed to evade paying homage to his father-in-law. In 1278, during a visit to the royal court to meet Henry's successor, Edward I, Alexander pledged allegiance for his English estates alone.

In 1263, King Haakon of Norway led a strong attack on Scotland, a response to rumours that Alexander intended to annex the **HEBRIDES.** The Scandinavian force was defeated at the **BATTLE OF LARGS** (1263), and, in 1266, Norway ceded the **WESTERN ISLES** and the Isle of Man to Scotland in return for a fixed payment and an annual rent.

Margaret died in 1275, leaving no living offspring, and, in 1285, Alexander married Yolande, daughter of Robert, Count of Dreux. While riding to join her at Kinghorn on the night of 18–19 March the following year, he was thrown from his horse and killed.

ALIEN ACT (1705). When Queen Anne declined to accept the **ACT OF SECURITY** passed by the **THREE ESTATES** in 1703, the Scots retaliated by refusing to approve the allocation of funds to the monarch until she capitulated the following year. Enraged, the English Parliament introduced the Alien Act, which banned the import of cattle, coal and linen from Scotland and provided that all Scots would be treated as aliens unless they accepted that the throne should pass through the Hanoverian line or sought a full union of the two countries. The potential loss of trade threatened to cripple the Scottish economy, and, after a month of heated debate, the country decided to turn its back on independence. (See **TREATY OF UNION**). The Alien Act was repealed despite protest from some sections of the English public. (See **ACT ANENT PEACE AND WAR**).

ALLIANCE PARTY. A politically moderate, nonsectarian organization, the Alliance Party is committed to the maintenance of Northern Ireland's links with the United Kingdom. It was formed in 1970 and developed support from the predominantly middle class, creating a power base at the **STORMONT** Parliament in 1972, when two Unionist Party MPs and one Independent Nationalist defected to its ranks. Its programme of government reform (involving a formula for the devolution of power from London to a regional assembly in **BELFAST**) has failed to win it any seats at Westminster, but it is recognized as one of the province's four major political parties, taking part in the short-lived **NORTHERN IRELAND POWER SHARING EXECUTIVE** during 1974 and constitutional conferences with representatives of the governments of the United Kingdom and the Irish Republic in 1991 and 1992. In 1993, it captured 7.6 per cent of the poll at the **LOCAL GOVERNMENT (NORTHERN IRELAND)** elections and won 44 seats — its best performance for 16 years.

ANCRUM MOOR, BATTLE OF, 27 February 1545. This battle followed the Scots' change of heart over the Treaty of Greenwich. Signed in July 1543 by representatives of the English Parliament and the **THREE ESTATES,** that document made provision for the marriage of Edward, son of King Henry VIII of England, to **MARY, QUEEN OF SCOTS,** when the Queen reached the end of her tenth year, and included a clause that peace between the two kingdoms would continue for at least a year after one of the parties died. The Estates annulled the agreement in December, but Henry sent troops north to enforce it (a campaign known as the **ROUGH WOOING**). However, his plans to devastate **THE BORDERS** were thwarted by Archibald **DOUGLAS,** Earl of Angus, whose forces heavily defeated the English invaders in a battle fought in a fog at Ancrum Moor, near Jedburgh.

ANDREW, ST. The reasons for Scotland's choice of Andrew (one of Christ's fisherman disciples) as patron saint are lost in legend. According to one account, St Regulus (or Rule) dreamed that he was told by an angel to take some of the apostle's relics from their resting place near the Mediterranean Sea and convey them to a location which would be indicated to him as he travelled. He did as he was told, going northwest until the angel stopped him at the site now called **ST ANDREWS,** where he built a church. Also, there is a tale that relics of St Andrew were taken to Hexham, in northern England, and that some of them strayed into Scotland. The Scottish flag is designed to commemorate Andrew's death: a white saltire cross depicts the X-shaped timbers on which he is supposed to have been crucified (though that story is not known before the 14th century) and the blue background represents the sea on which he spent much of his life. His feast day is 30 November.

ANDREWS, JOHN MILLER (1871–1956). Prime Minister of Northern Ireland from 1940 until 1943, Andrews was born on 18 July 1871, the son of Thomas and Eliza Andrews. He was educated at the Royal Academical Institution in **BELFAST,** then forged a career in the linen industry, ultimately becoming chairman of the family firm. He entered politics in 1917 as a member of Down County Council, and, four years later, was elected to the Northern Ireland Parliament as **ULSTER UNIONIST PARTY** MP for County Down. Almost immediately, he was appointed Minister of Labour, a post which he held until 1937, when he transferred to Finance. On several occasions, he deputised for Prime Minister **JAMES CRAIG,** and there was little dissent when he succeeded to the post following Craig's death in November 1940.

Andrews, however, was ill-fitted for wartime leadership. At the age of 69, and in indifferent health, he lacked the vision necessary for decision making under pressure. Moreover, he inherited a province which had been unprepared for the outbreak of the Second

World War the previous year, and decided to introduce only one new-comer (Lord Glentoran) to a cabinet whose members had failed to win public confidence. Over the next two years, Andrews appeared to his critics to have little grasp of the seriousness of Northern Ireland's situation. He worried greatly about Roman Catholics employed in the civil service, wondering if they were loyal, but showed little resolve in dealing with a wave of labour disputes in 1942 (so much so that Winston Churchill, Prime Minister in London, sent him a telegram saying that he was shocked at what was happening). Increasingly, his own grassroots party colleagues lost confidence in him, and, on 19 March 1943, voted unanimously for changes in cabinet personnel. Andrews refused, but the revolt gathered strength and, on 28 April, he was forced into resignation. **BASIL BROOKE** replaced Andrews who continued to serve in the **ULSTER** Parliament until 1953, but played little further part in politics. He died on 5 August 1956.

ANGLO-IRISH AGREEMENT, 15 November 1985. Sometimes called the Hillsborough Agreement (after the place near **BELFAST** where it was negotiated), this accord superseded the 1973 **SUNNINGDALE AGREEMENT** and was signed by the governments of the United Kingdom and the Irish Republic. It marked a major shift in the British attitude to the problems in Northern Ireland, giving Irish politicians a formal role in the administration of the province's affairs (through an intergovernmental standing conference). Also, it guaranteed that the majority view of **ULSTER**'s population would determine the territory's political status with respect to the United Kingdom. Some commentators interpreted these moves as a major step towards the resolution of **THE TROUBLES,** but they provoked bitter opposition from the **ULSTER LOYALISTS**.

ANGLO-IRISH TREATY, 6 December 1921. Under the terms of this treaty, which ended the **ANGLO-IRISH WAR,** the provisions of the **GOVERNMENT OF IRELAND ACT** (1920) were annulled. The six counties of **ULSTER** were made a self-governing province of the United Kingdom, with an elected assembly (based at **STORMONT,** near **BELFAST**), which had authority to enact legislation governing domestic affairs. The 26 Irish counties outside Ulster became independent of Great Britain as the **IRISH FREE STATE,** with its own parliament in Dublin and with the status of dominion within the British Empire. Provision was made for a boundary commission, which would determine the location of the border between the province and the Free State. The proposals for such a commission led to much unrest in the north, where **ULSTER LOY-ALISTS** feared that large areas of the six counties (Antrim, Armagh, Derry, Down, Fremanagh and Tyrone) would be transferred to Free State control. This led to violent clashes in the north, and, in March 1922, 61 people died in Belfast alone. In the south, hard line nationalists refused to accept division of the island and continued to fight for a united Ireland. (See **FIANNA FAIL; FINE GAEL; PARTITION OF IRELAND**).

ANGLO-IRISH WAR, 1919–21. In Ireland, the period immediately following the end of the First World War was marked by violence and terrorism, events which proved to be the culmination of the campaign for **HOME RULE** and were termed **THE TROUBLES** (a name still applied to current problems on the island). The **IRISH REPUBLICAN ARMY,** led by Michael Collins, began guerilla attacks on the **ROYAL ULSTER CONSTABULARY** (RUC) in 1919. Initially, Britain responded by creating the **BLACK AND TANS,** who reinforced the RUC, and imposing harsh reprisals on nationalist supporters. Then, in 1920, it introduced the **GOVERNMENT OF IRELAND ACT,** which provided for a **PARTITION OF IRELAND.** Formally, the war ended with the **ANGLO-IRISH TREATY,** signed on 6 December that year, but the peace which followed was an uneasy one.

ANTI-PARTITION LEAGUE (APL). The APL was the principal nationalist political party in Northern Ireland in the years immediately after the Second World War. It was formed in 1945 and, through publicity campaigns and speeches in the **ULSTER** Parliament, attempted to achieve the reunification of the province with the Republic of Ireland. Through a network of local branches and the introduction of annual conferences, it restructured the nationalist movement, but it failed to achieve any significant political change, and, from the mid-1950s, its support drifted away to other, more aggressive organizations, such as **SINN FEIN.**

ANTONINE WALL. This fortification was built *c.* AD 142 by Emperor Antoninus Pius to mark the northern boundary of the Roman empire, aid the conquest of the Scottish lowlands and protect against incursions from the north. Thirty-nine miles long, it ran from the **RIVER CLYDE** to the **RIVER FORTH,** and consisted largely of turf on a stone base, with a ditch (or vallum) providing additional security. For a time, some 7,000 troops manned the wall, but by about AD 163 they had abandoned it. Very little of the fabric remains.

APOLOGETICAL DECLARATION. In 1684, opponents of the **TEST ACT,** led by James Renwick (a militant **PRESBYTERIAN** who had joined the **CAMERONIANS** some three years earlier), posted, on church doors and market crosses, statements which rejected the legislation's assertion of the Crown's supremacy over Parliament in Scotland. The movement, strongest in the southwest, threatened that any man who attempted to kill one of its members would forfeit his life. Government response was unequivocal: those suspected of supporting the cause were shot, or sabred, without trial if they refused to reject the declaration. Renwick himself was eventually captured, found guilty of disowning royal authority and executed in **EDINBURGH** on 17 February 1688. (See **COVENANTERS; JOHN GRAHAM; WIGTOWN MARTYRS**).

APPRENTICE BOYS. A movement which advocates Northern Ireland's continued inclusion in the United Kingdom, the organization (a group of clubs founded from 1814 onwards) commemorates 13 Protestant apprentices who closed the gates of **LONDONDERRY** against the army of the Roman Catholic King James VII and II during his campaign to regain the throne in 1689 (see **SIEGE OF LONDONDERRY**). Many of the members are also associated with the **ORANGE ORDER.** The Boys hold a major parade in the city on 12 August every year to celebrate the end of the siege, and a smaller demonstration on 18 December to mark the shutting of the gates. These events frequently lead to conflict between members of the two religious communities, notably in 1969, when the summer parade was accompanied by serious riots. (See **THE TROUBLES**).

ARBROATH, DECLARATION OF, 1320. In 1320, the flower of Scottish nobility gathered at Arbroath Abbey and prepared a letter to Pope John XXII, asking him to urge Edward II of England to recognise Scotland as an independent country with **ROBERT I** as its King. That message became one of the most important documents in the nation's history, and is still invoked by those who advocate a breakup of the United Kingdom. Probably composed by Bernard de Linton, Abbot of Arbroath, and sealed by eight earls and 45 barons, it begins with a brief history of the Scots, who, it claims, had lived in peace until the English stole their freedom. Since then, all citizens, whatever their age or sex, their religion or their rank, had lived in constant danger of such cruelty, massacre, violence, pillage, arson and outrage as "no one could describe nor fully imagine unless he had seen them with his own eyes". King Robert had restored the peace but "if he should give up what he has begun, and agree to make us or our Kingdom subject to the King of England or the English, we should exert ourselves at once to drive him out as our enemy and a subverter of his own rights and ours, and make some other man who was well able to defend us our King; for, as long as but a hundred of us remain alive, never will we on any conditions be brought under English rule. It is in truth not for glory, nor riches, nor honours that we are fighting, but for freedom — for that alone, which no honest man gives up but with life itself". The Pope was asked to counsel Edward to "leave us Scots in peace, who live in this poor little Scotland". If he refused, he would have to assume responsibility for the "slaughter of bodies, the perdition of souls, and all the other misfortunes that will follow".

Much of the preamble to the declaration was mere fiction, relating how the Scots had travelled from Greater Scythia across the Tyrrhenian Sea and reached their northern land after many years among the tribes of Spain. Even so it reflected a unity and sense of common purpose in a nation which had been split by internal dissent only a quarter of a century earlier and, on two counts, set the scene for the rest of the country's history until the **TREATY OF UNION** in 1707. Firstly (and 450 years before the French Revolution was to make the same point), it stated clearly that the will of the people took precedence over the will of the monarch. Subjects were bound to the sovereign "both by law and by his merits" but only in order that they could maintain their freedom. If the King betrayed that freedom, they could replace him. The attitudes and values inherent in that statement were very different from those prevailing in England. Secondly, it was an emotional affirmation that the Scots were one nation and that they had the right to govern themselves as they wanted rather than as some colonial overlord desired.

Pope John was persuaded and advised Edward to make peace. In 1328, Scotland's independence was enshrined in the **TREATY OF EDINBURGH,** by which England renounced all claims to sovereignty.

ARGYLL, DUKES AND EARLS OF. The holder of the dukedom of Argyll is head of the Campbells, one of the most prominent of the Scottish **CLAN**s. The family obtained the barony of Lochow (now

Lochawe) in 1315, and the clan chief (Duncan) was styled Lord Campbell in 1445. In 1457, an earldom was conferred on Colin Campbell (Duncan's younger son), and, in 1641, Archibald (the eighth earl) was created marquis by Charles I. Sixty years later, Archibald's son (also Archibald) became the first Duke of Argyll.

The family has a long record of involvement in Scottish and British affairs. The second earl (Archibald) was killed with **JAMES IV** at the **BATTLE OF FLODDEN** in 1513; the fifth earl (also Archibald) was involved in the murder of **HENRY DARNLEY** (husband of **MARY, QUEEN OF SCOTS**) in 1567; and the eighth Earl (again, Archibald) joined the **COVENANTERS,** establishing a Scottish government with the support of Oliver Cromwell in 1648. He later broke the alliance with the English Parliamentarians over the execution of Charles I and crowned Charles II King of Scotland on 1 January 1651. Archibald, the ninth earl, opposed the **TEST ACT,** fled to Holland and conspired with James, Duke of Monmouth, in his attempts to overthrow James VII and II. (See **ARGYLL'S REBELLION**; **ROB ROY MACGREGOR**).

The first Duke of Argyll supported the Glorious Revolution of 1688-89, accompanying William of Orange on his journey from Holland to London. Also, along with John, Earl of Breadalbane, and Sir John Dalrymple, he was responsible for the **GLENCOE MASSACRE** (1692). His son, John, the second duke, was a supporter of the 1707 **TREATY OF UNION** with England and a distinguished military leader, fighting under the Duke of Marlborough in the War of the Spanish Succession at Oudenarde (1708) and Malplaquet (1709). Archibald, the third duke, was one of the 16 peers chosen to represent Scotland in the House of Lords when the first Parliament of Great Britain met after the Treaty of Union had been ratified. He played a significant role in raising Scottish regiments in support of the Hanoverian monarchy.

The eighth duke, George Douglas Campbell, was a cabinet minister before he reached his thirtieth birthday, serving as Lord Privy Seal, Postmaster General and Secretary of State for India, but ultimately splitting with the Liberal Party during the 1880s as a result of its policies on Ireland. John, his eldest son, became the ninth duke and was Governor General of Canada from 1878 until 1883.

ARGYLL'S REBELLION, May–June 1685. This abortive, badly organized rebellion was led by Archibald Campbell, ninth earl of Argyll, in support of the Duke of Monmouth's attempt to overthrow King James VII and II. Its purpose was to raise an army of **COVENANT-**

ERS who would take control of **GLASGOW**. Loyal Scottish forces, led by the Marquis of Atholl and aided by English troops and warships, pursued the earl (deserted by his small following), who was captured on 18 June and immediately executed without trial. (See **ARGYLL, DUKES AND EARLS OF**).

ARROL, WILLIAM (1839–1913). Responsible for building the railway bridge over the **RIVER FORTH** and founder of a construction company which was to become one of the largest in Britain, William Arrol was born in Houston (Renfrewshire) on 13 February 1839, the son of Thomas Arrol (a cotton spinner who became manager of Coats, the thread manufacturer in Paisley). At the age of ten, he lied about his age in order to get a job in a local textile mill and, four years later, became apprenticed to a blacksmith. Over the next few years, he moved from place to place in order to find work but also studied mechanics and hydraulics at evening classes, eventually opening his own boilerworks in 1868. In 1872, he founded the Dalmarnock Ironworks and concentrated much of his effort on bridge building, primarily for the railway companies. He was responsible, in particular, for the steel bridge over the River Tay (1882–87), whose 85 spans replaced the structure which had collapsed in 1879 (see **TAY BRIDGE DISASTER**), and for the cantilever design of the **FORTH BRIDGE** at Queensferry (1883–90). Also, he was responsible for the steelwork on Tower Bridge in London (1886–94), the bridge over the River Nile at Cairo (1904–8) and the Wear Bridge at Sunderland (1905–9). In 1890, he was awarded a knighthood, and from 1892 until 1906 represented South Ayrshire in the House of Commons as a Unionist MP. He died in Ayr on 20 February 1913, but his firm — Sir William Arrol and Company, Ltd — continued to expand, becoming particularly renowned for its steel-framed factory buildings and the road bridge over the Forth, which was built upstream from the railway bridge and opened in 1964.

ARTS COUNCIL OF WALES (CYNGOR CELFYDDYDAU CYMRU). The Council is the government's principal vehicle for the funding of the arts in Wales and is accountable to the Welsh Office. Based in **CARDIFF**, but with regional offices at Bangor, Carmarthen, Cwmbran and Mold, it consists of a chairman and 15 other members drawn from **LOCAL GOVERNMENT** and the universities, as well as branches of the performing and other arts. With a budget of some £14 million annually in the mid-1990s, it provides financial support for major events, companies (such as Welsh National Opera) and for aspiring individual talents.

ATKINS, HUMPHREY EDWARD GREGORY (1922–96). When Prime Minister Margaret Thatcher announced the composition of her Cabinet after the Conservative Party's General Election victory in 1979, Humphrey Atkins' appointment as Secretary of State for Northern Ireland was one of the few surprises. "Humphrey Who?" asked a headline in the *Sunday News*. Born in Kenya on 12 August 1922, Atkins was the son of farmer and army officer Edward Atkins and his wife, Mary. He returned to Britain in 1925, following his father's gruesome death (he was gored by a rhinoceros), was educated at Wellington College, then served as a lieutenant in the Royal Navy during the Second World War and entered the House of Commons as MP for the London suburb of Merton and Morden in 1955. From 1959 until 1962, he was Parliamentary Private Secretary to the Lord of the Admiralty and, from 1967 until 1979, served as a party whip (in 1973-74, under Prime Minister Edward Heath, he was Government Chief Whip). His appointment to the Northern Ireland post owed something to his position as a close adviser to Mrs Thatcher during the months leading up to the General Election but occurred because Airey Neave, who had been the Conservatives' chief spokesman on **ULSTER** during the latter stages of their time in opposition and the most likely candidate for the office, had been murdered by the **IRISH REPUBLICAN ARMY** in March 1979. One of Atkins' first actions was to increase the strength of the **ROYAL ULSTER CONSTABULARY** in response to an increase in violence in the province during the summer of 1979. In early 1980, he held a constitutional conference at **STORMONT** in an attempt to thrash out a formula which would allow some devolution of power to the Province but although the **ALLIANCE PARTY**, the **DEMOCRATIC UNIONIST PARTY** and the **SOCIAL DEMOCRATIC AND LABOUR PARTY** all agreed to participate, the **ULSTER UNIONIST PARTY** refused to take part so the initiative was unsuccessful. The following year, he proposed a 50-member advisory council but that, too, failed to bring the parties together. Atkins was replaced as Secretary of State by **JAMES PRIOR** in September 1981 and knighted (KCMG) in 1983. In 1985, he voiced his approval of the **ANGLO-IRISH AGREEMENT** and, in 1987, was created a life peer (as Lord Colnbrook of Waltham St Lawrence). He died on 4 October 1996.

AUGHRIM, BATTLE OF, 12 July 1691. This, rather than the more famous **BATTLE OF THE BOYNE,** was the most decisive encounter between the forces of James VII and II and William III in **IRELAND.** James' Roman Catholic **JACOBITE** army, led by the Marquis de St Ruth, was heavily defeated and many leading Irish nobles were killed, thus effectively ending resistance to the Protestant monarchy on the island.

AULD ALLIANCE. Essentially, the auld (or old) alliance, was a series of mutual defence treaties forged between Scotland and France as a result of war with England. The first was signed when, in 1295, **JOHN BALLIOL** was forced by Scottish nobles and churchmen to defy Edward I and enter an alliance with King Philip IV. For nearly 300 years after that, the two countries intermittently called on each other's military support and the bond was cemented through unions involving scions of noble families. The association ended in 1560 with the **TREATY OF EDINBURGH,** which specified that French and English troops should leave Scottish soil. A marriage of convenience on both sides, the alliance always meant more to the Scots though France did continue to provide a safe haven for political refugees from Scotland until the late 18th century.

AULDEARN, BATTLE OF, 9 May 1645. This battle, fought at a site near Nairn (in the **SCOTTISH HIGHLANDS**) after Scotland had become embroiled in England's civil war, ended in a resounding victory for royalist troops led by **JAMES GRAHAM**, Marquis of Montrose. His army, numbering fewer than 2,500 Scottish and Irish troops, defeated a **COVENANTER** force of 4,000 foot soldiers and 400 cavalrymen commanded by Sir John Urry and supporting the Parliamentary cause. Outnumbered, and with an ill-equipped infantry which was forced to live off the land, Montrose, a brilliant military strategist, adopted tactics which confused and unnerved the opposition, sending it into retreat with 2,000 dead.

—**B**—

BAGPIPES. Forms of bagpipe are known throughout Europe and parts of western Asia, but, in the United Kingdom, are most closely associated with Scotland and Ireland. The traditional Scottish pipes took two forms — the cauld-wind (or cold-wind) bagpipes, which used bellows, and the much better known highland bagpipes, in which air from a bag pressed by the player's elbow was fed to a chanter (which contained a reed) and two drones (each of which produced a single note). In its modern form, the highland bagpipe has two tenor drones and a bass drone an octave below. The melody is formed as the piper fingers the holes in the chanter. A unique syllabic notation known as *canntaireachd*, which represents melody notes by vowels and grace-notes by consonants, has been developed for the music.

The highland pipes became widespread during the 15th and 16th centuries, used particularly by the armies of the **CLAN**s as they entered battle. They were proscribed by the government (along with the wearing of **HIGHLAND DRESS**) after the second **JACOBITE REBELLION** but returned as regiments were raised in northern Scotland to supplement the British Army. The combination of pipes and drums, which is the basis of marching bands today, developed after 1881, when a reorganization of the army led to the establishment of pipe bands with all Scottish regiments, lowland as well as highland. After the First World War ended in 1918, musicians returned to their homes, still keen to play, and civilian bands were established in towns and villages up and down the country. In 1930, the Scottish Pipe Band Association was formed to coordinate their activities and established a college in **GLASGOW,** providing a system of examination for aspiring pipers. Bagpipe playing has experienced an upsurge in popularity during the 1980s and 1990s, with the pipe-making industry estimated to have an annual turnover of some £15 million. There are five major producers in Great Britain: the largest is in Somerset but the other four are based in Scotland.

The traditional Irish pipes are bellows-blown, with a chanter and three drones; these drones are accompanied by pipes containing keys which are struck by the player's hand and produce simple chords. The more modern pipes were introduced early in the 20th century as a modified version of the Scottish highland bagpipe, originally in a two-drone version and later with three drones and keys on the chanter to increase the flexibility of the instrument. (See **PIBROCH**).

BAIN, ALEXANDER (1818–1903). Bain, one of the eight children born to weaver George Bain and his wife, Margaret, was intimately involved in developing the theory of associationism, which contends that knowledge is the result of the connections which the mind makes between individual sensations. Born in **ABERDEEN** on 11 June 1818, he worked at his father's trade by day and studied in the evening, eventually winning a scholarship to Marischal College, and graduating in 1840. Through contributions to the *Westminster Review*, he made contact with political philosopher John Stuart Mill, and, in 1848, moved to London, where he wrote two books — *The Senses and the Intellect* (1855) and *The Emotions and the Will* (1859) — which helped him win appointment to the new post of Professor of Logic and English at Aberdeen University in 1860. Texts on grammar and rhetoric, published between 1863 and 1874, and a two-volume work on *Logic* (1870) earned him an honorary doctorate of laws from **EDINBURGH** University in 1869. At the same time, he was pursuing his interest in psychology, publishing a number of studies, including *On the Study of Character* (1861) and *Mind and Body: The Theory of Their Relation* (1873). In these, he adopted a scientific approach to issues which previous authors had dealt with metaphysically, and argued that the mind is a psychophysical unity. In 1876, he founded *Mind*, the first journal of philosophy and psychology. Bain, who was convinced that modern languages should have a greater role in the educational process, resigned his chair in 1880 but continued to publish; his later works included *John Stuart Mill: A Criticism, with Personal Recollections* (1882) and *Dissertations on Leading Philosophical Topics* (1903). He was elected to the post of Rector of his university on two occasions (1881 and 1884) and died in Aberdeen on 18 September 1903.

BAIRD, JOHN LOGIE (1888–1946). The first man to transmit television pictures, Baird was born in Helensburgh on 13 August 1888 and educated at Larchfield Academy, the Royal Technical College and **GLASGOW** University. He reproduced objects in outline in 1924, transmitted recognizable human faces the following year and gave a practical demonstration of the principles of television at a lecture in the Royal Institution in 1926. In 1928, he broadcast pictures from the United Kingdom to the ship *Berengaria* in mid-Atlantic. When the British Broadcasting Corporation began its television service in 1936, it used Baird's system as well as that of Marconi Electrical and Musical Instruments. The following year, his technique was dropped, but he continued his research and, by 1939, had succeeded in developing the technology of colour television. He died at Bexhill-on-Sea on 14 June 1946.

BALLINAMUCK, BATTLE OF, 8 September 1798. This conflict occurred during the **IRISH REBELLION** of 1798, when 850 French troops, under General Joseph Humbert, landed at Killala Bay (County Mayo) on 22 August to join forces with 1,500 Irish nationalists. The British army of 9,000 trained soldiers, led by Lord Charles Cornwallis and far superior both in numbers and in fighting ability, easily trapped invaders and insurgents between two columns and defeated them within 30 minutes. The regular French soldiers were treated as prisoners of war, but the rebels were either killed in flight or summarily hanged. Militant nationalists had hoped that the French invasion would lead to an uprising by Irishmen of all religious persuasions but, in the event, support was limited.

BALLIOL, EDWARD (?–1364). Son of **JOHN BALLIOL,** Edward claimed the Scottish throne, and was supported by Edward III of England. In 1332, he defeated the Earl of Mar (Regent for the young King **DAVID II**) at the **BATTLE OF DUPPLIN MOOR** and, in September, was crowned at **SCONE**. In November, he acknowledged Edward as overlord but, the following month, was driven from the country by forces loyal to David. Edward, infuriated, came to his vassal's aid and roundly defeated the Scots' army on 19 July 1333 at the **BATTLE OF HALIDON HILL:** six earls of Scotland died in the fighting, along with 70 barons and 500 knights, whereas the English lost only 14 men, most of them archers. David was taken to France for safety, and Balliol was installed as King once again, ceding Berwick, Dumfries, Lothian, Peebles and Selkirk to the English King, who was styled Lord Paramount of Scotland. Balliol, however, was always considered a mere puppet by his subjects and never gained the support of the nobility. When David returned in 1341, he fled to England, and, in 1356, formally resigned his title and lands to Edward. He remained in England until his death in January 1364.

BALLIOL, JOHN (*c.* 1250–1314). King of Scotland from 1292 until 1296, Balliol was the youngest son of John de Balliol of Barnard Castle (Durham) and his wife, Devorguilla. In 1290, on the death of **MARGARET, MAID OF NORWAY,** he declared himself heir to the Scottish throne, a claim based on his mother's lineage as daughter of the eldest daughter of David, Earl of Huntingdon and brother of **MALCOLM IV** and **WILLIAM I.** Twelve rivals also claimed the title, and Edward I of England was asked to adjudicate. He accepted, on condition that the claimants first accepted him as overlord; Balliol and eight others agreed. After well over a year of deliberation, Edward's court of 104 auditors eventually accepted Balliol's case, and, on 30 November 1292, he was crowned at **SCONE**. On 26 December, he paid homage to Edward at Newcastle. The overlordship, however, was not popular in Scotland, and Balliol was a feckless, weak-willed leader, so, in 1295, after Edward had demanded military aid for a war in Gascony, Balliol was persuaded to renounce his oath of fealty and conclude a treaty of mutual help with King Philip IV of France (see **AULD ALLIANCE**). Edward was furious and laid to waste eastern Scotland. On 2 July 1296, Balliol was forced to seek both peace and forgiveness, blaming evil counsellors for his actions. He was imprisoned in England until 1299, when papal intervention secured his release. He never returned to Scotland and died in Normandy in 1314. (See **BATTLE OF DUNBAR; GREAT CAUSE**).

BALMORAL CASTLE. Situated on the banks of the River Dee some eight miles west of Ballater in Scotland, Balmoral is the British monarch's summer home. It was originally owned by the Farquharson family, who forfeited the property as a penalty for supporting **CHARLES EDWARD STUART**'s abortive rebellion in 1745, and, ultimately, was acquired by Prince Albert (consort of Queen Victoria) in 1847. The royal family visited the property for the first time in September 1848, and the Queen, in particular, was charmed by the place. However, the building was too small for the needs of an imperial retinue and a new castle was constructed on the site between 1853 and 1856. Built of local granite in a 19th-century interpretation of the 16th-and 17th-century Scottish baronial style, it was designed by William Smith of **ABERDEEN** but much influenced by Albert's concepts of architectural attractiveness. It remains a private (rather than a state-owned) residence to which Queen Elizabeth II, Prince Philip, their children and guests return every August (sometimes to the consternation of hillwalkers, who meet the royal holidaymakers exercising their dogs on paths through the estate). Tourist agencies market the area around the castle as 'Royal Deeside', but critics argue that 'Balmorality' — the sentimental view of kilt-bedecked royalty standing on heather-clad hillsides — contributes to an unrealistic picture of Scotland abroad.

BANK OF SCOTLAND. The oldest of the major Scottish banks and Scotland's largest company in terms of market value, the Bank of Scotland was founded in 1695 and pioneered major commercial developments during the 18th century, notably in joint-stock banking (which was illegal in England and Wales) and the establishment of a network of local branches. Legislation in 1845 allowed it (and the other Scottish banks) to issue its own notes, a right denied to institutions south of the border. In recent years, it has earned a reputation as a cautious lender, and its activities have helped to establish **EDINBURGH** as the United Kingdom's principal financial centre outside London. It has also been at the forefront of electronic banking and, through its mortgages, made major inroads into the English market without incurring the expense of opening a chain of branches. In 1995, the Bank acquired Australia's BankWest, broadening its international commitments. (See **CURRENCY**).

BANNOCKBURN, BATTLE OF, 23–24 June 1314. This critical battle between the Scots (with **ROBERT THE BRUCE** at their head) and the English (led by the weak and ineffectual Edward II) was fought a few miles south of **STIRLING** on the boggy ground alongside the Bannock Burn (or stream). The Scottish force of 8,000–10,000 men, largely armed with pikes and shields, was greatly outnumbered by the 17,000–22,000 archers and knights in the invading army, but Bruce used calthrops (four-pointed metal pyramids) to maim the enemy horses and reduce the impact of the cavalry. Then, the English, in the heat of the struggle, allegedly mistook a crowd of 'sma' folk' (townsmen and freemen) for Scottish reinforcements and fled the field. Edward was forced into retreat, and Bruce was able to raid far south of the border. More enduringly, the victory provided a foundation for independence and helped forge a sense of nationhood.

BEATON, DAVID (*c.*1494–1546). An implacable opponent of the Reformation, Beaton was a leading figure in Scotland's ecclesiastical and political life during the early 16th century. The son of John Beaton (a Fife landowner), he was educated at universities in **GLASGOW, ST ANDREWS,** Paris and Rouen, becoming chancellor of Glasgow Cathedral before he reached the age of 25 and Abbot of Arbroath by the time he was 30. A staunch francophile and advocate of the **AULD ALLIANCE,** he was appointed Bishop of Mirepoix at the insistence of Francis I of France in 1537 and, in 1538, became the first Scotsman to be made a cardinal of the Roman Catholic Church. In 1539, following the death of his uncle (James Beaton) he succeeded to the Archbishopric of St Andrews then, in 1544, was appointed Papal Legate in Scotland by Pope Paul III. From 1522, he was much involved in diplomatic negotiations on behalf of the Scottish court, most importantly in 1537 (when he was responsible for the arrangements leading to the marriage of **JAMES V** to Madeleine, Francis' daughter) and the following year (when he organized James' wedding to **MARY OF GUISE**). Beaton's successes earned him the trust of the King but also the jealousies of competitors for royal confidences, so, when James died in 1542, leaving the infant

MARY, QUEEN OF SCOTS, as the new monarch, he was involved in a contest for the regency with the Earl of Arran, who was sympathetic to the new Protestant faith rather than to the Catholic Church and to England rather than to France. Arran received the support of most of the nobles and was proclaimed Protector and Governor of the Realm on 3 January 1543. Within weeks, the cardinal was gaoled, ostensibly for treason, but he was released after only three months and, later in the year, Arran changed his allegiance, submitting again to the Church of Rome and receiving absolution from Beaton. In December of 1543, Beaton was made Chancellor and used his post to persecute advocates of the Protestant religion, sanctioning the arrest and execution of George Wishart, one of the leaders of the reform movement, in 1546. That was the straw which broke the camel's back. On 29 May, eight weeks after the execution, a group of Wishart's supporters broke into St Andrews Castle and murdered the cardinal. As they attacked him, he is reported to have cried out "I am a priest," a phrase more likely to provoke the reformists than to stay their hands.

BELFAST. The centre of retailing and administration in Northern Ireland, Belfast is located at the mouth of the River Lagan, on **ULSTER**'s eastern seaboard. Archaeological remains indicate that the site was occupied during prehistoric times and documents show that fortifications were constructed by John de Courci, who took part in the Norman invasion of Ireland, but the development of the modern city really began in 1611, when Baron Arthur Chichester built a castle and promoted the growth of a settlement. By 1685, there was a population of some 2,000 people, most of them employed in making fishing nets, sailcloth, rope or bricks. Towards the end of the century, a flourishing linen industry was established, brought by Huguenot refugees from France, and, by the 1740s, Belfast had become the most important town in northeast Ireland. Shipbuilding added to the sources of employment during the 1790s, when William Ritchie opened a yard and a graving dock, and (despite the lack of local coal reserves) engineering became increasingly important following the technological innovations of the Industrial Revolution. Harland and Wolff developed into an internationally renowned company, building such major vessels as the *Titanic*, and mechanization made Belfast one of the world centres of the linen industry. Tobacco products, ropemaking, the manufacture of textile machinery and food processing all added to the industrial mix. In 1888, the settlement formally became a city when Queen Victoria granted it a royal charter and in 1920, following the passage of the Government of Ireland Act, it was chosen as the location of the new Northern Ireland Parliament. (See **STORMONT**). However, the 20th century brought economic decline even though an aircraft factory (destined to become one of the biggest in Europe) was established in 1937. The great depression of the period between the First and Second World Wars hit export industries hard and recovery proved difficult in the face of competition from foreign producers. Harland and Wolff collapsed when orders for tankers dried up during the oil price crisis of the early 1970s and was taken into public ownership in 1975. A similar fate befell the Shorts aircraft company, and now, although back in private hands, both have significantly reduced labour forces. In addition, most of the textile mills, which were heavily dependent on female labour, have closed.

Belfast's economy was also laid waste by the civil disturbances which marked **THE TROUBLES** of the years between 1969 and 1994. The animosity between religious groups has simmered for decades. The Protestant majority consists mainly of descendants of British settlers who migrated to Ulster during the 17th century, but the Roman Catholics trace their roots to native Irish country people who moved into the city to seek work during the 19th-century industrial expansion. The Catholics, believing themselves discriminated against and seeing a better future in a reunited Ireland, took to the streets in a campaign of violence led by the **IRISH REPUBLICAN ARMY.** Pro-unionist groups retaliated, with resultant loss of life and property. The strife led many people to leave the city for safer homes (Belfast's population declined from 417,000 in 1971 to 295,000 in 1981 and 279,000 in 1991). Also, it discouraged potential investors from moving in. However, following the declaration of a ceasefire in 1994, there were signs of regeneration. Major retailers (notably Marks and Spencer, Sainsbury and Tesco) bought sites for development, and tourists in 1995 numbered 435,000 (an increase of 56 per cent over the previous year). Belfast also now has significant employment in transport (it is an important route centre, with air and sea links to the British mainland) and in education (it houses the campuses of two universities). (See **EDUCATION: NORTHERN IRELAND; TYRONE REBELLION**).

BELL, ALEXANDER GRAHAM (1847–1922). The inventor of the telephone, Bell was born in **EDINBURGH** on 3 March 1847, the son of Alexander Melville Bell (who invented visible speech — a system of pictorial symbols which showed deaf students how to use the tongue, lips and throat to produce sounds) and his wife, Eliza. He was educated at McLauren's Academy (Edinburgh), Edinburgh High School, Edinburgh University and London University, then, in 1868, began work as an assistant to his father, teaching elocution at University College, London. The family moved to North America in 1870, and, in 1872, Alexander junior opened a school for the training of teachers of the deaf in Boston. The following year, he was appointed Professor of Vocal Physiology at Boston University and began a series of experiments designed to find a way of using electromagnetic currents to send sounds along wires. On 5 June 1875, working with Thomas A. Watson, he managed to transmit the noise made by the plucking of a steel spring and, on 10 March 1876, conveyed the first clear telephone message ("Mr Watson, come here. I want you."). The Bell Telephone Company was founded in 1877.

Bell also invented the photophone (an instrument which, he demonstrated in 1880, could transmit sound by using the vibrations in a beam of light) and developed a form of phonograph in 1887. In his later years, he turned his attentions to the study of aeronautics. He was the founder of the American Association to Promote the Teaching of Speech to the Deaf (1890) and of the journal *Science* (1883), as well as acting as President of the National Geographic Society (1896–1904). He died on 2 August 1922 in his summer home near Baddeck (Nova Scotia).

BERWICK, BATTLES OF, There have been a number of important battles near the town of Berwick-on-Tweed, a result of its strategic position on the border between Scotland and England. These conflicts made the settlement one of the most fought over in the British Isles.

28 March 1296. The town was taken from the Scots by King Edward I of England, many of the citizens were summarily executed and their fortifications were destroyed. It was briefly recaptured by **WILLIAM WALLACE** in September 1297, but reverted to English control soon afterwards. Edward had the town defences rebuilt, and Berwick remained an important English stronghold until 1318.

1 April 1318. **ROBERT THE BRUCE** wrested the town from English control in 1318 and withstood a long siege by King Edward II the following year.

19 July 1333. This battle, though fought near Berwick, and for control of the town, is more usually referred to as the **BATTLE OF HALIDON HILL**. It resulted in victory for the English, commanded by King Edward III, and the surrender of Berwick to the

victorious forces.

20 January 1356. Within months of a brief recapture of Berwick by the Scots (with the aid of French forces), Edward III again brought the town under English control. It remained in their hands, except for short periods in 1378 and 1384, until, in 1561, it was ceded by Lancastrian King Henry VI to Scotland in order to buy that country's support during the Wars of the Roses.

August 1482. The English had unsuccessfully laid siege to Berwick in November 1481, and tried again in August of the following year. This second attack, led by Richard, Duke of Gloucester, was more successful, but the town was not formally ceded to England until the **TREATY OF EDINBURGH** was approved in 1560. Berwick's status remained anomalous because it was never formally incorporated into England and, in official documents, was referred to, until 1747, as being part of 'England and Berwick'. This much disputed town became a county in 1836, and later part of Northumberland, but remains a curious entity in the body politic (its football team — Berwick Rangers — plays in the Scottish League, for example).

BERWICK, TREATY OF. Four important treaties were signed at Berwick, a vital strategic town on the border between Scotland and England.

3 October 1357. In return for a payment of 100,000 marks, King Edward III of England released King **DAVID II** of Scotland from 11 years of imprisonment. The Scottish government raised taxes on wool in order to pay for the ransom over the next decade, but the debt was never redeemed in full.

27 February 1560. Under the terms of this treaty, Queen Elizabeth I of England agreed to send troops to Scotland to assist the **LORDS OF THE CONGREGATION** in their struggle to expel the French Roman Catholic forces of **MARY OF GUISE** from their country. At the time, Scotland was enduring a civil war, with Mary ousted as Regent to the throne by the Calvinist Lords (followers of the preaching of **JOHN KNOX**), who were attempting to secure Protestant rule. For military reasons, Elizabeth had to prevent the establishment of a French powerbase in Scotland at all costs, even if her actions alienated English Catholics. The treaty is sometimes considered a turning point in Anglo-Scottish relations, leading eventually to the **UNION OF THE CROWNS,** although it was intended only as a mutually convenient pact against a common enemy.

7 July 1586. This mutual defence treaty between Queen Elizabeth

I of England and King James VI of Scotland was designed to counter Roman Catholic conspiracies and forestall invasion of either country by the French. James was granted a pension of £4,000 per annum by the English, and the religious freedoms in both realms were respected. Elizabeth hoped, by that device, to diminish the dangers associated with the activities of the Roman Catholic **MARY, QUEEN OF SCOTS,** who claimed her throne.

18 June 1639. Sometimes known as The Pacification of Berwick, this accord between King Charles I and the **COVENANTERS** ended the first of the **BISHOPS' WARS.** The terms included the disbanding of armies by both sides and a provision that ecclesiastical disagreements would be settled by a free general church assembly. Disputes over civil matters would be adjudicated by a Parliament to be called at **EDINBURGH.** The peace was forced on the King by the inadequacy of funds available to sustain a military campaign, lack of English support for hostilities against Protestant Scotland and the poor condition of the royal armies. However, the treaty settled nothing; both sides later claimed that it had not been properly honoured.

BEVAN, ANEURIN (1897–1960). The architect of the National Health Service, Bevan was born in Tredegar on 15 November 1897, the son of David and Phoebe Bevan. He was educated at Sirhowy Elementary School but left at the age of 13 and followed his father into the coal mines. Over the next six years, he became increasingly involved in trade union activities and, by 1906, was chairman of his local miners' lodge (the regional branch of the labour union), which had over 4,000 members. He had an eye disease which exempted him from military service during the First World War (a conflict which he decried as "a capitalist war"), so he continued his work with the lodge until 1919, when the South Wales Miners' Federation sent him to the Central Labour College in London for two years.

Bevan returned in 1921, only to find that the colliery owners had branded him a troublemaker and were refusing to employ him. He was elected to Tredegar Urban District Council the following year, and became disputes agent for his lodge in 1926, working to further the miners' cause in the general strike that year. In 1929, he contested the Ebbw Vale Parliamentary constituency for the Independent Labour Party and became an MP, transferring his allegiance to the more moderate Labour Party two years later. In 1934, he married Scots-born Jenny Lee, MP for North Lanark, establishing a formidable left-wing alliance in the House of Commons. During the

1930s, he became associated with Stafford Cripps as an opponent of Prime Minister Neville Chamberlain's policy of appeasing Nazi Germany and an advocate of cooperation with communists in opposition to Adolf Hitler. His activities resulted in expulsion from the Labour Party in March 1939, but he was readmitted in December and became a vociferous opponent of Winston Churchill's coalition government for the duration of the Second World War.

After Labour won the first postwar General Election in 1945, Bevan was appointed Minister of Health by Clement Attlee, the new Prime Minister. He introduced socialized medicine in the form of the National Health Service, which nationalized the hospitals and provided free medical care for every British citizen. The principle that medical treatment should be available to all, regardless of their ability to pay, was dear to his heart — so much so that, in April 1951, he resigned from his post as Minister of Labour and National Insurance (after only three months in the job) because the government introduced charges for some aspects of provision.

A dynamic speaker, he acted as a focus for dissident left-wing MPs for the next five years but never found enough support to enforce change. In 1954 and 1955, he was a candidate for the post of party treasurer but was beaten on both occasions by Hugh Gaitskell, who also defeated him in the contest for the leadership which followed Attlee's resignation (also in 1955). At that point, Bevan changed tack and decided to toe the party line. It was a decision which lost him the allegiance of many of the radicals but got him the posts of party treasurer and opposition spokesman on colonial affairs in 1956. Later, he became shadow foreign secretary and, in 1959, deputy leader of the party. Now more mellow, he was in a position to exert considerable influence on the direction of policy, but his health failed and he died at Chesham (near London) on 6 July 1960. Churchill had termed him "a merchant of discourtesy", with some justification — he had described Conservative MPs as "lower than vermin" and called Gaitskell "a desiccated calculating machine" — but he was a man of principle with an agile mind which made him a formidable opponent in parliamentary debate. His autobiography — *In Place of Fear* — was published in 1952.

BISHOPS' WARS, 1639–40. These two short wars were named after the English bishops, who, it was said, were behind attempts by King Charles I to impose, in **SCOTLAND,** the Book of Common Prayer used in the Church of England. Also, they intended to reestablish, by a show of force, the episcopal system that had been abolished by the **COVENANTERS.** The first war started in the spring of 1639 and ended, without bloodshed, almost as soon as it had begun. (See **TREATY OF BERWICK,** 18 June 1639). The second opened in August of the following year and concluded with the treaty of Ripon (26 October 1640), by which Charles, unable to get supplies from England's Short Parliament after his defeat at the Battle of Newburn Ford, agreed to the Scots retaining possession of Newcastle and Durham. That decision led to the recall of the English Parliament, ending a period (known as the Eleven Years' Tyranny) when the King alone ruled.

BLACK, JOSEPH (1728–99). One of the outstanding experimental scientists of the 18th century, Black discovered carbon dioxide, latent heat and specific heat, contributing greatly to the development of a quantitative approach to the study of chemistry. The son of an **ULSTER** wine merchant, he was born in Bordeaux (France) on 16 April 1728 and educated in **BELFAST** and at **GLASGOW** and **EDINBURGH** Universities. In his doctoral thesis, submitted in 1754, he outlined the results of a series of tests on magnesium carbonate, identifying a gas which he termed "fixed air" and which is now known to be carbon dioxide. Two years later, he demonstrated that carbonates become more alkaline when they lose carbon dioxide, and, by 1757, he was aware that the gas was produced when charcoal was burned as well as through fermentation and respiration. Further studies showed that, when ice melts, it absorbs heat without exhibiting any increase in temperature: Black argued in 1761 that this heat must be absorbed by the ice particles and thus become latent in the substance. Pursuing these experiments, he noted that different amounts of heat were required to raise equal masses of different chemicals through the same range of temperature, thus formulating the doctrine of specific heat. Black was appointed lecturer in chemistry at Glasgow University in 1756. In the same year, he was made professor of anatomy but exchanged posts with the professor of medicine and, for some time, practised as a doctor. In 1766, he became professor of medicine and chemistry at Edinburgh. Despite his illustrious career, he published little, and, as a result, others claimed much of the credit for his research. However, he was a close friend of **JAMES WATT** and undoubtedly influenced his work on the development of the steam engine. Black died in Edinburgh on 10 November 1799.

BLACK ACT, 1584. King James VI imposed these retaliatory actions on Scotland after his incarceration following the **RUTHVEN RAID.** They reinforced the powers of the bishops and King in Scottish religious affairs, giving the episcopacy greater authority than it had wielded for nearly 25 years, and were designed to limit the influence of **PRESBYTERIANS.**

BLACK AND TANS. In June 1920, an armed force was hastily recruited in England (mainly from veterans of the First World War) to support the Royal Irish Constabulary during the **ANGLO-IRISH WAR.** Their nickname — the Black and Tans — derives from the mixture of army (khaki or tan) and police (black) uniforms, with which they were issued. Feared and hated in equal measure, members of the unit operated a shoot-to-kill policy against nationalists, inflaming the activities of the **IRISH REPUBLICAN ARMY.**

BLAIR, ANTHONY CHARLES LYNTON (1953–). Widely regarded as the most right wing leader in the history of the Labour Party, Tony Blair became Prime Minister following the Conservative party's general election defeat in May, 1997. He was born in **EDINBURGH** on 6 May 1953, the son of Leo and Hazel Blair and was educated at Durham Choristers' School, Fettes College (Edinburgh) and Oxford University (while an undergraduate, he was the lead singer in a rock band but is adamant that there were no drugs — not even a Clintonesque puff). He joined the Labour Party in 1975, continued his political interests after qualifying as a barrister specializing in trade union and industrial law (see **ALEXANDER ANDREW MACKAY IRVINE**), and eventually entered the House of Commons as the Member of Parliament for the Sedgefield constituency (1983). **NEIL KINNOCK** appointed him spokesman on treasury and economic affairs (1984–87), trade and industry (1987–89), energy (1988–89) and employment (1989–92) — posts which allowed him to build on his interests and use his influence to further the modernization of the party. Under **JOHN SMITH,** he became shadow home secretary and impressed colleagues with his toughness on law and order, traditionally an area of Conservative Party strength.

It was evident after Smith's sudden death in 1994 that Blair would have strong support if he stood for the leadership and, after the withdrawal of his friend, **JAMES GORDON BROWN,** from the contest, victory was inevitable (he won 57 per cent of the vote and became the youngest-ever Labour leader). Almost immediately, he began to move the Labour Party away from its traditional association with organized labour and the socialist cause, making deliberate attempts to woo the business community and the middle-income middle classes. His youthfulness, articulacy and pleasant personality undoubtedly contributed to his appeal, particularly to the grass roots of the Party. A staunch family man, his politics (like those of Smith and Brown) stemmed from mainstream Christian socialism and stressed the need for low rates of unemployment, sound educational provision and decent housing. These values struck a chord with the electorate, who gave the Labour Party a massive vote of confidence in the 1997 general election, returning it to the House of Commons with a formidable 179 seat majority over all other parties. As Prime Minister, he appointed a youthful administration (the oldest member was 51) and used his early days in office to advance policies which clearly enhanced his popular appeal, berating western countries for failing to tackle environmental problems adequately, supporting referenda designed to demonstrate support for the **DEVOLUTION** of powers from Westminster to assemblies in Scotland and Wales, and advocating a more powerful role for the United Kingdom in the European Union. A tall, photogenic figure, he was well received by voters in southern England who had been wary of his more overtly celtic predecessors at the head of the Labour Party. However, some critics have complained of his attempts to manipulate the media and cultivate the rich and influential. An editorial in *The Scotsman* comments on his "loyal, affectionate and effortlessly obsequious remarks" celebrating Queen Elizabeth II's golden wedding anniversary in November 1997, pointed out that "if there is a person of power and privilage to whom he has not yet sucked up that's only because he hasn't found the time" . Also, **ULSTER LOYALISTS** critisised his decision to meet **GERARD ADAMS** and other leaders of **SINN FEIN,** claiming that it amounted to a softening government stance on terrorism.

BLAIR CASTLE. Dating from 1269 but greatly enlarged during the 1740s, Blair Castle is the seat of the Duke of Atholl (chief of **CLAN** Murray) and located close to the small town of Blair Atholl in Perthshire. For centuries, it played a significant role in Scottish history. In 1644, **JAMES GRAHAM,** Marquis of Montrose, rallied the clans at the Castle in support of Charles I's campaign against the **COVENANTERS.** At the time of the **BATTLE OF KIRRIEMUIR,** in 1689, it was in the hands of supporters of **JAMES II,** and, in 1745 and 1746, Prince **CHARLES EDWARD STUART** used it as a campaign headquarters during the second **JACOBITE REBELLION.** Now, the distinctive white-painted building houses the only private army allowed in the United Kingdom. In 1845, Queen Victoria presented colours to the Duke's bodyguard, and these have never been withdrawn although the guard (now known as the Atholl Highlanders) is maintained only for ceremonial purposes.

BLOODY FRIDAY (21 July 1972). The **IRISH REPUBLICAN ARMY,** in an attempt to force the British government to withdraw from Northern Ireland, set off 26 bombs in **BELFAST,** killing 11 people (seven at a bus station and four in a shopping centre). A further 139 were injured. At the time, the incident was the most serious in the city since the resumption of violence in the late 1960s, and, according to many historians, was the point at which London politicians decided that the IRA was a terrorist organization rather than a political movement with which they could negotiate. (See **THE TROUBLES**).

BLOODY SUNDAY (30 January 1972). A march planned for **LONDONDERRY** by the Northern Ireland Civil Rights Association was banned by the British government, but the organizers decided that the event would go ahead. A riot ensued, and the 1st Parachute Regiment opened fire, killing 13 demonstrators. Later, the army claimed that it had responded to shots fired at the soldiers, but none of the victims was armed. In the aftermath of the event, thousands of Roman Catholics in the province went on strike, a crowd estimated to be 30,000-strong burned down the British embassy in Dublin and, in the House of Commons, **BERNADETTE DEVLIN** (MP for Mid-Ulster) punched Home Secretary Reginald Maudling, accusing him of lying about the shootings. Prime Minister Edward Heath instructed Lord Widgery, Lord Chief Justice of England, to hold an enquiry into the events, but the findings — that, though the illegal march had created a highly dangerous situation, the day would have passed without serious incident if the army had adopted a low profile — failed to satisfy the critics. By the time the Widgery Report appeared, the Northern Ireland Parliament had been suspended, and it is widely accepted that the public reaction to the shootings was the reason for the UK government's decision to impose **DIRECT RULE** from Westminster. (See **BOGSIDE**).

BOGSIDE. A dominantly Roman Catholic district of **LONDONDERRY,** Bogside experienced the start of the modern phase of **THE TROUBLES** on 13 August 1969, when it was surrounded by **UL-**

STER LOYALIST paramilitaries and **B-SPECIALS** in a display of sectarian hostility. It also took the brunt of other confrontations on a massive scale, particularly on **BLOODY SUNDAY** (30 January 1972), when 13 people died during rioting.

BONNIE DUNDEE. (See **JOHN GRAHAM**).

BONNIE PRINCE CHARLIE. (See **CHARLES EDWARD STUART**).

BOOK OF DISCIPLINE. Two Books of Discipline were issued in Scotland, each attempting to reform the church.

<u>1561</u>. The first book, prepared by **JOHN KNOX,** was adopted by the reformers as a blueprint for the future organization of the **CHURCH OF SCOTLAND** following the break with Rome. It established kirk sessions (governing councils for each congregation) and general assemblies (national meetings of ministers and lay representatives of individual churches), regulated the collection and disbursement of revenues required to pay ministers, made provision for education in schools and universities (see **EDUCATION: SCOTLAND**) and proposed that funds should be used to relieve poverty.

<u>1578</u>. The second book — the work of Andrew Melville, Principal of **GLASGOW** University — went much further than its predecessor, proposing radical changes to the government of the church through the removal of bishops and the introduction of **PRESBYTERIAN** forms of organization. It also argued that the Church should be free of state control because King James VI was a member of Christ's congregation and not its head on earth. Inevitably, the text created much dissension within the Church and infuriated monarchists.

BOOK OF KELLS. One of the finest examples of the art of manuscript illumination, the Book of Kells is a Latin transcription of the four Gospels from the Holy Bible. Initial letters are lavishly decorated in the tradition of Celtic art, and representations of plants and animals draw heavily on Celtic symbolism. The work was probably begun at the religious settlement on the Scottish island of **IONA** and completed at the Monastery of St Columba at Kells (Ireland), where the monks took refuge from the Vikings in 807. It is now preserved in Trinity College, Dublin. (See **CELTIC CHURCH**).

BOOTHBY, BARON. (See **ROBERT JOHN GRAHAM BOOTHBY**).

BOOTHBY, ROBERT JOHN GRAHAM (1900–86). One of the most colourful of 20th-century Conservative Party politicians and an influential figure at the time of the Second World War, Bob Boothby was born in **EDINBURGH** on 12 February 1900, the son of Sir Robert Tuite Boothby (a prominent financier) and his wife, Mabel. He was educated at Eton College, then took a BA degree at Oxford University, where his irascible charm made him a focus of social and literary circles. His first attempt to become a Member of Parliament — at Orkney and Shetland in 1923 — ended in failure, but he was more successful the following year, winning the seat at East Aberdeenshire and representing it until, in 1958, he was given a peerage (as Baron Boothby of Buchan and Rattray Head) with a place in the House of Lords. Boothby — an urbanite through and through — knew next to nothing about the agricultural concerns of his constituency but had a convincing speaking style, which wooed voters, and displayed great loyalty to the area throughout his time in office. In 1926, he was made Parliamentary Private Secretary to Winston Churchill and, never a man to stand by convention, raised Conservative eyebrows by visiting Moscow at a time when the United Kingdom was gripped by labour problems. Also, he developed an intimate friendship with Dorothy Macmillan, wife of Harold (who later became Prime Minister), beginning a relationship which was to last a lifetime and scandalized many.

Throughout the 1930s, he consistently opposed his own party's attempts to appease Nazi Germany and argued that state investment was needed if unemployment was to be reduced and the economy stimulated. In 1940, following the outbreak of the Second World War, he became Parliamentary Secretary at the Ministry of Food — an important post at a time when maritime supply lines to the UK were being cut by enemy action — but he was forced to resign the following year following allegations of financial improprieties. Boothby never held office again, but he became an outspoken radio and television commentator on political and economic affairs, attacking the financial agreements made by the world powers at the Bretton Woods conference in 1944, criticizing the agreements for dealing with postwar Germany forged by Churchill, Franklin D. Roosevelt and Josef Stalin at Yalta in January 1945, condemning postwar US loans to Britain, advocating European unity (he became a member of the Council of United Europe in 1948) and opposing the invasion of Suez by France and the United Kingdom in 1956. He also lent his considerable weight to campaigns to reform the homosexuality laws. His robust views annoyed many people, and he was always too outspoken — and too unwilling to toe the party line — to achieve high government office, but he brought a refreshingly independent spirit to the mass media at a time when many commentators treated politicians with great deference, and developed a talent for exposing the hypocrisies of public figures. He died in London on 16 July 1986.

BORDERS, THE. The boundary between Scotland and England stretches for some 70 miles as the crow flies, from the mouth of the **RIVER TWEED** in the east to the Solway Firth in the west. The land to the north of that boundary, consisting of the former counties of Berwick, Dumfries, Peebles, Roxburgh and Selkirk, forms an area of rounded sandstone hills known as The Borders. During the 12th century, the area was characterized by religious settlement, with abbeys founded by the Tironensians (1126), Cistercians (1136), Augustinians (1138) and Praemonstratensians (1140) under the patronage of King **DAVID I.** In succeeding centuries, it was contested by the Scots and English armies: battles at **HALIDON HILL** (1333), Otterburn (1388), Flodden (1513), **SOLWAY MOSS** (1542) and **ANCRUM MOOR** (1545) reflected the English desire for overlordship of the whole of Britain and the Scots desire to maintain their independence. In addition, there was much conflict between the major Border families, often over real and alleged cattle thieving.

Following the **UNION OF THE CROWNS** in 1603, more peaceful conditions allowed agriculture to develop. The 19th-century brought the establishment of textile mills at Galashiels, Jedburgh and other centres, using hill streams for power and wool from local sheep as raw material. The industry has suffered in recent decades as a result of competition from artificial fibres, but high-quality goods from firms such as Pringle of Hawick still maintain an international market. In addition, light industries (such as electronics and plastics) have diversified sources of employment, and the tourist industry (originally kindled by Sir **WALTER SCOTT**'s ballads) has generated additional income. (See **SOUTHERN UPLANDS**).

BOSWELL, JAMES (1740–95). The friend and biographer of Samuel Johnson, Boswell is famed for the diaries in which he chronicled life in Georgian Britain. Born in **EDINBURGH** on 29 October 1740, he was the son of Euphonice Boswell and her husband, Alexander (later Lord Auchinleck), an **ADVOCATE** and Ayrshire landowner. At the age of five, he was sent to Mundell's Day School but from eight until 13 was taught at home. From 1753 until 1758, he attended Edinburgh University. But, when Auchinleck learned that young James had fallen in love with a Roman Catholic actress, he transferred his son to **GLASGOW** University. In 1760, James rebelled and ran off to London with the intention of becoming a monk, but the pleasures of the city diverted him and, by the time his father found him, he was suffering from venereal disease.

In 1762, he passed his civil law examinations and, in the autumn, began to keep the diary which was to earn him fame as a recorder of conversation. He returned to London later that year and, on 16 May 1763, had an unexpected meeting with Samuel Johnson in the parlour of Thomas Davies, an actor and bookseller. The two met again the next week, and the friendship grew. During the following winter, Boswell studied law at Utrecht University and, influenced by Johnson, at first made a considerable effort to keep to the straight and narrow. He found, however, that hedonism was more enjoyable and returned to his former promiscuous habits. Leaving Utrecht, he embarked on a European tour, visiting Berlin, Switzerland (where he met Rousseau and Voltaire), Italy, Corsica and Paris. On 26 July 1766, having returned to Britain, he was admitted to the Faculty of Advocates in Edinburgh and for the next 17 years practised as a lawyer in the city, visiting London periodically when the courts were not in session.

In 1768, he published *An Account of Corsica, the Journal of a Tour to That Island, and Memoirs of Pascal Paoli*. In 1769, Boswell married Margaret Montgomerie, his first cousin (thereby deeply disappointing his father, who had hoped for a match which would bring a significant dowry). In 1773, he made a journey to the **HEBRIDES** with Johnson and, over the next few years, began to advance in his profession and in Edinburgh society — he became an Examiner with the Faculty of Advocates, one of the curators of the Advocates' Library and Master of the Canongate Kilwinning Lodge of Masons. However, his practice was not improving, and he turned to alcohol then began to frequent the haunts of city prostitutes.

Between 1777 and 1783, he wrote a series of essays for *The London Magazine* and in 1785 (despite female diversions) published *The Journal of a Tour to the Hebrides*, which met with great success. In 1786, he was called to the Bar in London but spent most of his time preparing a biography of Johnson, who had died in 1784. *The Life of Samuel Johnson* was published in 1791 to much critical acclaim, which praised the reporting of conversations between Johnson and such distinguished companions as David Garrick, Edmund Burke and Joshua Reynolds. But Boswell found himself increasingly friendless: a habitual drunkard, he was shunned by many people who feared that he would feature them in future literary works. He died suddenly in London on 19 May 1795, and for over a century his private papers were believed to have been lost. In 1927, however, a number were sold by Lord Talbot de Malahide (his great-great-grandson). Others turned up in 1930, 1937 and 1940. All of these materials were purchased for Yale University in 1949 and have added much to literary scholars' understanding of Boswell's life and his relationships with his peers.

BOTHWELL, EARL OF. (See **JAMES HEPBURN BOTHWELL**).

BOTHWELL, JAMES HEPBURN (*c.*1536–78). The third husband of **MARY, QUEEN OF SCOTS,** James was the son of Agnes and Patrick, third Earl of Bothwell (whom he succeeded in 1556). In 1560, he met Mary in Paris and clearly made an impression because, when the young Queen set up court in Scotland following her marriage to **HENRY DARNLEY** the following year, Bothwell was appointed to her privy council. An allegation, by the Earl of Arran, that he had plotted to kidnap the sovereign led to his imprisonment in **EDINBURGH** Castle in 1562, but he escaped after five months and fled to France. He was recalled in 1565 to help suppress a rebellion by the Earl of Moray and, shortly afterwards, married Jean, sister of Lord Gordon. During the rebellion and the crisis which followed the murder of Mary's secretary, David Rizzio, on 9 March 1566, Bothwell proved wholly loyal to the Queen and gradually became her chief adviser. Under her patronage, he acquired titles and property which made him one of the most powerful nobles in the land. Also, there was a growing affection between the two and Bothwell clearly wanted to find a way of marrying her. On the night of 9/10 February 1567, Darnley was killed by an explosion in his Edinburgh house. Public opinion held Bothwell responsible, but he was cleared at a rigged trial held on 12 April. Eleven days later, as the Queen was travelling to **STIRLING,** he intercepted her entourage and carried her off to his castle at Dunbar (ostensibly for her safety). Divorce from Jean followed within days and, on 15 May, he married Mary at **HOLYROOD HOUSE.**

At the time, the Queen was pregnant (almost certainly by

Bothwell), but the union lasted only a month. On 15 May, the royal troops, led by Bothwell, were forced to surrender to a rebel army at Carberry Hill, outside Edinburgh. The Earl fled to Scandinavia, and the marriage was annulled in 1570. Bothwell was placed in solitary confinement at Dragsholm (Denmark) in 1573 and died on 14 April 1578, apparently having lost his mind. A man of courage and great loyalty, he had a lust for power which ultimately proved disastrous both to himself and to the Queen he served. (See **CASKET LETTERS**).

BOTHWELL BRIDGE, BATTLE OF, 22 June 1679. The final conflict of the **COVENANTERS'** rebellion in Scotland was fought at Bothwell Bridge, on the **RIVER CLYDE.** James, Duke of Monmouth, with an army of some 10,000 dragoons and foot soldiers, defeated an ill-prepared and ill-equipped force of 4,000 farmers and peasants, killing 200–400 and capturing 1,200.

BOYNE, BATTLE OF THE, 11 July 1690. By defeating the forces of the deposed King James VII and II, King William III put an end to the **JACOBITE** challenge to his authority in Ireland and established control over the whole island, although the war continued for another year. The royal army of 35,000 considerably outnumbered James's 21,000 supporters but the victory was, by no means, overwhelming. James, fearing encirclement, fled the battlefield, and his troops, although forced southwards, escaped with few casualties. The confrontation is celebrated annually by **ULSTER LOYALISTS** as a success for the Protestant cause.

BROCH. Built during the Iron Age, between *c.* 100 BC and *c.* AD 100, brochs were the fortified dwellings of local chiefs and landowners. Found only in Scotland, they were windowless, circular, stone towers with thick walls and only one entrance. The upper part was hollow, allowing for the provision of stairways, rooms and galleries. Most also had an outer wall, which served as a first line of defence and enclosed smaller buildings. About 500 brochs survive, but most of them are now ruins.

BROOKE, BASIL STANLAKE (1888–1973). From 1943 until 1963, Basil Brooke was Prime Minister of Northern Ireland, shaping the economic and social destiny of the province in the years of reconstruction following the Second World War. The eldest son of Gertrude and Arthur Douglas Brooke (the fourth Baronet

Colebrooke) and his wife, Gertude, he was born in Colebrooke, on 9 June 1888, into a family which had a long history of service as administrators, politicians and soldiers. Educated at Winchester and at the Royal Military College Sandhurst, he received a commission with the Royal Fusiliers, then transferred to the Royal Hussars and fought with them during the First World War, winning the military cross and the croix de guerre but losing his religious faith. In 1921, he became a senator in the first Northern Ireland Parliament, following the partition of the island, but he resigned after a few months to take up the post of commandant of the **B-SPECIALS** in Fermanagh, his home county. He returned to politics as the **ULSTER UNIONIST PARTY** representative for Lisnaskea in 1929 and, four years later, was given his first government post, as Minister of Agriculture. It was a job he relished, transforming **ULSTER** farming through the introduction of new marketing arrangements and schemes to improve the efficiency of crop and animal husbandry. In 1941, his energies were diverted to the organization of Northern Ireland's contribution towards victory in the Second World War (a conflict in which he lost two of his three sons).

In May 1943, there was no dissent when Brooke succeeded the ineffective **JOHN MILLER ANDREWS** as Prime Minister. For the next 20 years, he was the dominant figure in Ulster political life. In the years following the end of the war, he promoted the regeneration and development of industry. Also, despite his party's fear of creeping socialism, he adopted most of the welfare state legislation which the Labour Party government was pushing through Parliament at Westminster. As a result, the 1950s was a golden age for the Unionists: standards of living improved and employment opportunities increased, while, south of the border, the Irish Republic's economy stagnated and emigration rates rose. Brooke, created Viscount Brookeborough of Colebrooke in 1952, led his party to five successive General Election victories — in 1945, 1949, 1953, 1958 and 1962 — and there was little criticism of his leadership. However, scholars blessed with hindsight now argue that many of his policies laid a foundation for the civil rights movement and the years of violence which were to mark the last quarter of the 20th century. (See **THE TROUBLES**). He rigorously excluded Roman Catholics from participation in government and (supporting the **ORANGE ORDER**) refused to countenance their selection as Unionist Party candidates, believing that their loyalty to the principle of Northern Ireland's membership of the United Kingdom was questionable. Moreover, concessions to the religious minority were, he felt, politically unnecessary and, in the long term, unwise. During his last years in office, he involved himself in schemes to stem the flow of working class support from the Unionist Party to the Labour Party, but it was clear that his political judgement was declining as unemployment was rising. In March 1963, he was forced into resignation, and, although he remained an MP until 1968, Brooke played little further part in politics. He died in Fermanagh on 18 August 1973.

BROOKE, PETER LEONARD (1934–). Secretary of State for Northern Ireland between 1989 and 1992, Brooke is the son of Baroness Brooke of Ystradfellte and Lord Brooke of Cumnor (who, as Henry Brooke, was Home Secretary under Prime Minister Edward Heath from 1971 until 1973). The family is descended from a long line of landowners in County Cavan (now in the Irish Republic).

Peter Brooke was educated at Marlborough College, Oxford University and Harvard Business School, and contested the Welsh Parliamentary constituency of Bedwellty in October 1974 before winning the City of London and Westminster South for the Conservative Party in 1977. He served as a government whip under Prime Minister Margaret Thatcher from 1979 until 1983, then as Parliamentary Under-Secretary of State at the Department of Education and Science (1983–85) and Minister of State at the Treasury (1985–87). In 1987, he became both Paymaster General and Chairman of the Conservative Party and, in July 1989, succeeded **THOMAS KING** as Secretary of State for Northern Ireland. His first months in that post were marked by public differences with Republic of Ireland government ministers over the role of the **ULSTER DEFENCE REGIMENT** (which had been accused of passing confidential information to loyalist paramilitary groups) and with unionist politicians (who resented his repeated claim that the United Kingdom had no selfish interest in staying in Northern Ireland). Behind the scenes, however, he negotiated with both sides for over two years in an attempt to move towards the devolution envisaged by the 1985 **ANGLO-IRISH AGREEMENT,** and eventually, in 1991, ministers from the Republic met unionist leaders at **STORMONT.** Later in the year, **JAMES MOLYNEAUX** led an **ULSTER UNIONIST PARTY** delegation to discussions in Dublin. The talks were hailed as a milestone on the road to peace, but they broke down and Brooke's reputation stumbled with them. Although he was considered an honourable politician, he had a tendency to make errors of judgement; the most publicly damning was an appearance on a late-night television show in January 1992, when he accepted an invitation to sing a few lines of *My Darling Clementine* only hours after seven minibus passengers had been killed by a bomb planted by the **IRISH REPUBLICAN ARMY**. Also, many nationalists expressed doubts that he really wanted them involved in any administration installed at Stormont. Following the General Election in April 1992, Brooke was replaced as Secretary of State by **PATRICK MAYHEW**. Throughout his period in the Northern Ireland post, the British government refused to negotiate with representatives of **SINN FEIN** because they would not condemn the IRA's campaign of violence in the Province. However, he admitted later that he would have liked to have met **GERRY ADAMS** because of the significant role the organization's president had played in Ulster politics.

BROOKEBOROUGH, VISCOUNT. (See **BASIL STANLAKE BROOKE**).

BROWN, JAMES GORDON (1951–). One of the most politically astute of modern Labour Party statesmen, Brown was made Chancellor of the Exchequer by Prime Minister Anthony Blair in 1997. The son of the Rev Dr John and Mrs Elizabeth Brown, he was educated at Kirkcaldy High School (where he lost the sight of one eye as a result of a **RUGBY** accident) and **EDINBURGH** University, graduating with an MA in 1972 and a PhD in 1982. He was rector of the university between 1972 and 1975 then spent a year as a temporary lecturer before joining the department of politics at **GLASGOW** College of Technology in 1976. He changed career in 1980, joining Scottish Television's current affairs team as a journalist, but by that time was also involved in active politics and, in 1983, became member of Parliament for Dunfermline East. Brown was appointed opposition spokesman on trade and industry in 1985 and shadow chief secretary to the Treasury in 1987. The following year, he deputized for **JOHN SMITH** as the leader of Labour's economics team and greatly impressed his colleagues by the quickness of his wit, frequently winning exchanges with Nigel Lawson (the Chancellor of the Exchequer) in the House of Commons. His popularity with fellow opposition MPs was evident when he topped the poll for shadow cabinet membership in 1988 and again in 1989, but, in 1992, when **NEIL KINNOCK** resigned the party leadership after the General Election defeat, Brown was considered too young to replace him. Smith took the post, with his junior colleague taking over as shadow chancellor and heir apparent. In 1994, however, it was clear that, when Smith's sudden death precipitated another leadership contest, Party members were split between Brown and his close friend Tony Blair. After much heart-searching, Brown withdrew, but he remained a powerful influence on policy making and was rewarded with the post of Chancellor of the Exchequer following Labour's general election victory in May 1997. His first offical action was to transfer responsibility for changing interest rates from the government to the Bank of England, a move widely welcomed by the business community because of the Bank's political independence. Shortly afterwards he announced radical changes in the system of supervising financial institutions and announced a series of reforms designed to protect the interests of investors and shareholders.

BRUCE, JAMES (1730–94). The first British explorer to venture into the upper reaches of the River Nile, Bruce was born in Larbert (Scotland) on 14 December 1730, the son of David and Marion Bruce. He was educated at Harrow School (near London), then privately, and finally at **EDINBURGH** University, where he studied law. In 1754, he married Adriana Allan and joined her family's wine business, but her death after only nine months destroyed his interest in the firm and, in an attempt to detach himself, he set out on a series of travels to Spain and Portugal. He was appointed British consul at Algiers in 1763 and, from 1765 until 1768, journeyed widely in the Mediterranean countries, making drawings of Roman remains. During that period, Bruce determined to find the source of the Nile and set off from Alexandria (Egypt) in July 1768. He sailed up the Nile to Assouan, visited the ruins at Karnak and Luxor, then crossed the Red Sea. From the straits of Babelmandeb, he retraced his steps to Jiddah before travelling to Masuah (the port of Abyssinia), where he arrived on 19 September 1769. On 15 November, he left for Gondar, the capital of the country, and eventually reached the settlement on 14 February 1770, after a journey bedevilled by lack of provisions, quarrels with local chiefs and troubles over the transport of heavy equipment. However, he became a welcome guest at the royal court as a result of his medical skills and was rewarded with governorships which included authority over the territory where the headwaters of the Blue Nile were located. On 28 October, he set off for Geesh, the major village in the area, and, on 14 November, found the source of the River Abbai (the main tributary of the Blue Nile, then considered to be the principal branch of the Nile). In fact, he had been preceded by another European — Pedro Paez, a Jesuit missionary, who reached the area in 1615 — but Paez had not considered his discovery important whereas the Scot had sought it out. Bruce returned to London in 1774, but his account of the journey was disbelieved by many people (only four Europeans had visited Abyssinia in the previous 150 years so knowledge about the country was limited). Eventually, he published a five-volume description of his experiences — *Travels to Discover the Source of the Nile in the Years 1768–73* — in 1790, just four years before he died at his home near Larbert on 27 April 1794.

BRUCE, ROBERT THE. (See **ROBERT I**).

B-SPECIALS. The B-Specials were created in 1920 as part of the **UL-STER** Special Constabulary and, although part-time and unpaid, gained a reputation for no-nonsense policing in Northern Ireland. Its members, the vast majority of them Protestant, were identified as assailants when civil rights marchers were beaten up during protest rallies in the 1960s, and, on 14 August 1969, they fired on a crowd in Armagh, killing one man (the first death in the later 20th-century outbreak of **THE TROUBLES**). The unit was dissolved later in the year. (See **BOGSIDE**).

BUCHAN, JOHN (1875–1940). A novelist and statesman, Buchan was born in Perth on 26 August 1875, the eldest child in the family of four sons and a daughter born to John Buchan (a minister in the **FREE CHURCH OF SCOTLAND**) and his wife, Helen. The family moved to Kirkcaldy the following year, and young John attended the local school, walking three miles there and three miles back every day. Later, they went to live in **GLASGOW,** where John studied at Hutcheson's Grammar School before becoming a law student at the Universities of Glasgow and Oxford. He was called to the bar in 1901 and, for the next two years, served as secretary at the South African High Commission in London. In 1906, he joined the publishing firm of Thomas Nelson and Son as chief literary adviser then, during the First World War, saw service as a staff intelligence officer, rising to the position of director of information in 1917. When the conflict ended, he moved to Reuters News Agency as assistant director and, from 1927 until 1935, served as member of Parliament for the Scottish universities.

In 1935, Buchan was created Baron Tweedsmuir and appointed Governor-General of Canada. He enjoyed the wide open spaces of the Dominion and travelled widely in an effort to publisise the country's enormous potential. During the 1930s, he worked with Canadian Prime Minister Mackenzie King and US President Franklin D. Roosevelt in futile attempts to prevent the Second World War. His first published work appeared while he was at Glasgow University but it was *Prester John* (1910), a tale of an African uprising, which established his wide popularity. A series of romantic adventure stories followed, including *The Thirty-Nine Steps* (published in 1915 and filmed by Alfred Hitchcock in 1935), *Greenmantle* (1916), *Mr Standfast* (1918) and *John Macnab* (1925). The settings include the Scottish Highlands, the Cotswold Hills and South Africa, but in his last work — *Sick Heart River* (published in 1941 and known in the United States as *Mountain Meadow*) — the action takes place in the icy wastes of Canada. Buchan also wrote several biographies including *Sir Walter Raleigh* (1911), *Montrose* (1913), *Sir Walter Scott* (1932) and *Oliver Cromwell* (1934). He died in Montreal on 11 February 1940.

BURGH. In Scotland, the burghs provided a structure for urban **LOCAL GOVERNMENT** which survived for over 800 years. All were communities which had some form of law enforcement, allowing merchants and craftsmen to pursue their trades peacefully and facilitating the collection of taxes, but, even so, they took distinctly different forms. The royal burghs, the first of which were established during the reign of King **DAVID I** in the 12th century, received charters from the sovereign. These documents granted property to citizens, under a system of feudal tenure, in return for agreed rents and acceptance of a responsibility to assist in keeping the peace. Also, they implied an element of royal patronage and protection and gave travelling burgesses exemption from payment of tolls. In 1364, the royal burghs were awarded additional privileges, including monopoly trading rights within specified areas (known as liberties) and control over foreign commerce. Such measures helped prevent conflict (it was in citizens' interests to preserve the peace because that encouraged trade) and facilitated the Crown's task of collecting import and export duties. In addition, the royal burghs, unlike others, had the right to send representatives to Parliament. By the time of the **TREATY OF UNION** in 1707, there were 83 burghs with royal charters, including **ABERDEEN** (created between 1124 and 1153), **EDINBURGH** and **STIRLING** (both 1124–1127), **DUNDEE** (1191–1195) and **GLASGOW** (1611).

In addition, there were 15 ecclesiastical burghs, established by the Roman Catholic church and focusing on religious buildings, such as the abbeys at Arbroath (awarded burgh status between 1178 and

1182) and Dunfermline (created in 1303). Initially, they did not have the trading and other rights of burghs which had received charters from the King, but these were gradually acquired, particularly during the late 15th and early 16th centuries. Two other forms of burgh had more circumscribed privileges. Barons could petition the monarch to create burghs of barony. Most of these were established between 1451 and 1484 and had rights to provide premises for craftsmen and purveyors of goods, to buy and sell goods, to hold a weekly market and an annual fair and to have officers who could carry out official business on behalf of the townspeople. There was, however, no permission to conduct foreign trade. Also, there were burghs of regality, where the controlling lord could administer justice and build a mint. Altogether, 339 burghs of barony and regality were created: some as early as the 12th century (Inverary, for instance, was established between 1165 and 1174), and some nearly 700 years later (Oban in 1811, for example).

The burgh institutions coped adequately with conditions during the medieval and early modern periods but proved increasingly ineffective as industrialization changed the face of Scotland. Water supply and sewage disposal, provision of housing, care for the poor and demands for more democratic control of local affairs all strained administrative structures to breaking point. As a result, during the 19th century, there was a series of attempts to adapt the old system to the new age. Parliamentary legislation in 1833, 1834, 1847, 1850 and 1862 gave householders the right to elect burgh councils and choose commissioners of police, who could levy property taxes (known as rates) to cover the cost of street lighting and paving, improving water and gas supplies, preventing the spread of infectious disease, regulating slaughterhouses and imprisoning vagrants. The new industrial settlements which gained the right to elect councillors under the terms of that legislation were known as police burghs.

Further change came with the Local Government Reform Act of 1929, which replaced the traditional structure of burghs. The four major cities — Aberdeen, Dundee, Edinburgh and Glasgow — became counties of cities, with their councils responsible for all local government functions. The other settlements were reorganized as large burghs (broadly, those with a population of over 20,000) and small burghs. In the 20 large burghs, town councils controlled all administrative activities except educational provision and property taxation (which were the prerogative of the county councils). The elected representatives of residents in the 176 small burghs organized local services (particularly housing and water supply) but left education, policing and other major tasks to the county authorities. Communities of more than 700 people could ask the **SHERIFF** of the county in which they were located to grant them small burgh status. In practice, few did so, although the new towns of Cumbernauld and East Kilbride, created after the Second World War, both took advantage of the provision. The cost of providing services was, in all cases, met partly by central government grants, partly by property taxes, partly by loans and partly by income from miscellaneous sources such as the letting of buildings. However, as had happened during the 19th century, boundaries quickly became obsolete in the face of urban expansion and the need for large-scale planning of water supply, roads and urban renewal. In 1975, following the **WHEATLEY REPORT,** a wholly new system of local government was introduced, sweeping the burghs into the history books. (See **CONVENTION OF ROYAL BURGHS; COURT OF THE FOUR BURGHS.**)

BURKE, WILLIAM (1792-1829) **AND WILLIAM HARE** (?- *c.* 1860) Burke and Hare became notorious in early 19th-century **EDINBURGH** for providing corpses to the University's School of Anatomy. Both were **ULSTER**men who had gone to Scotland in search of work. Hare kept a lodging house in Tanner's Close and provided accommodation for Burke, a labourer. In 1827, when an elderly man who occupied one of the rooms died, Burke and Hare sold the body to lecturer Robert Knox for £7 10 shillings. Knox, needing cadavers for his students to dissect, asked no questions about the source of the corpse so Burke and Hare, thinking they had found a source of easy money, decided to go into business. They attracted at least 15 people to the lodging house over the next year, plied them with alcohol until they were drunk and then smothered them, receiving returns of £8 to £14 for each one. However, the disappearance of the last victim was noticed and the body found in Knox's cellar on 31st October, 1828. Burke and his mistress (Helen Macdougal) were arrested, along with Hare and his wife, but the authorities lacked sufficient evidence to convict all of them. In return for his freedom, Hare turned King's evidence and was freed. Burke was found guilty and went to the gallows on 28 January, 1829. The charge against Helen Macdougal was found not proven (a distinctly Scottish verdict which implies that the prosecution has not done enough to secure a conviction but the jury is not sure of the accused's innocence). Hare is thought to have died in London, a beggar, about 1860. A formal committee of inquiry cleared Knox of complicity in the murders but claimed that he should have taken steps to find out where the bodies had come from. As a result of the case, the Anatomy Act regulating the supply of bodies for research, was passed by parliament in 1832 and remained in force until it was revised in 1984, Knox is the subject of J. M. Barrie's play, *The Anatomist*, which was published in 1931.

BURNS, ROBERT (1759–96). Sometimes regarded as a dialect poet at the periphery of the mainstream of English literature, Burns is venerated in Scotland, where his writing is an integral part of national identity. He was born in Alloway on 25 January 1759, the son of farmer William Burns and his wife, Agnes.

William Burns, although extremely poor, was determined that his children would be educated so Robert attended school whenever possible, initially at Alloway Mill and later at Dalrymple. He read widely in his spare time and (while still a child) began to compose verse, possibly as a result of listening to Betty Davidson, an elderly lady who lived with the family and had a vast store of songs and ballads. In 1784, he rented a farm at Mossgiel (near Mauchline) with his brother Gilbert, and, over the next four years, wrote some of his best poems, including *The Cotter's Saturday Night, Holy Willie's Prayer, To a Louse, To a Mountain Daisy* and *The Holy Fair*. He also found delight in the company of ladies, a character trait which was to lead to a stream of tender love songs, notably *Ae Fond Kiss, O My Luve's Like a Red, Red Rose* and *Ye Banks and Braes o' Bonnie Doune*.

In 1785, he had an affair with Elizabeth Paton, a servant girl who bore his first illegitimate child. The following year, he fell in love with Jean Armour and made her pregnant as well, but her father refused to agree to a wedding, even though, under Scots law, mutual consent followed by consummation constituted a legal marriage. Depressed by a love apparently lost and a farm which would not yield a living, Burns decided to emigrate to Jamaica but delayed long enough to see the publication of his first edition of *Poems, Chiefly in the Scottish Dialect* (1786). The volume was an outstanding success and persuaded him to remain in Scotland. He went to **EDINBURGH,** where he arranged for a second edition to be published in 1787, but also found himself the centre of literary and social attention. The following year, he married Jean Armour, who helped him work a new farm at Ellisland. He knew, however, that he could never make the land profitable and, in 1789, took an appointment as an excise officer at Dumfries.

His artistic energies were devoted to the collection and writing of songs for *The Scots Musical Museum*, edited by James Johnson. In many cases (as, for example, with *Scots Wha Hae* and *Auld Lang Syne*) the words were new, but the tunes were traditional. He also contributed about 100 songs to George Thomson's *Select Scottish Airs*, published in four volumes between 1793 and 1805. But, after his Edinburgh visit, the only major poetical work which he produced was *Tam o'Shanter* (1791), a tale of the supernatural written in octosyllabic couplets and based on a folk story about an incident at the churchyard in Alloway. Increasingly, his health was causing problems. The long years of hard labour on unproductive soil, a poor diet and recurrent heart trouble were wearing him down and, on 21 July 1796, he died in Dumfries, aged only 37. Since then, he has become Scotland's national bard, his birthday celebrated annually with a devotion accorded to no other writer anywhere in the world.

BUTE, MARQUESS OF. (See **JOHN CRICHTON STUART**).

BUTTINGTON, BATTLE OF, 893. This encounter at Buttington (Powys) resulted in victory for an army drawn from Mercia, Wessex and Wales over a Scandinavian force, which had travelled across the breadth of England in an attempt to throw off pursuers. The success encouraged native British groups to cooperate more fully in attempts to repel invasions from the European mainland.

BWRDD YR IAITH GYMRAEG. (See **WELSH LANGUAGE BOARD**).

—C—

CAERPHILLY CASTLE. The largest fortification in Wales (and rivalled, for size, only by Windsor and Dover in the remainder of the United Kingdom), Caerphilly Castle was built during the second half of the 13th century (and principally between 1268 and 1271). It was constructed by Gilbert de Clare, Anglo-Norman Lord of Glamorgan, as a defence against the attacks of the Welsh princes. Initially, a valley was flooded to create a 30-acre lake, then the fortress was erected on three artificial islands. The most easterly of these formed a great dam and the most westerly a walled redoubt. Both protected the centre, which became the core of the stronghold. The fortress was often threatened, but its two concentric walls proved an insuperable obstacle so it was never taken. Caerphilly Castle is now in public ownership.

CALEDONIA. The Romans gave this name to the area of Scotland north of the **RIVER CLYDE** and the **RIVER FORTH.** Attempts to incorporate the territory within their empire were unsuccessful, although they did establish frontier posts within the southern perimeter of the **SCOTTISH HIGHLANDS.** (See **ANTONINE WALL; BATTLE OF MONS GRAUPIUS).**

CALLANISH. Dating from about 3000 BC, the standing stones and tomb at Callanish, on the west coast of the island of Lewis (in the **HEBRIDES**), were one of the major ceremonial sites in prehistoric Scotland. The formation of the stones is unique, with rows leading north, south, east and west from a central circle, which surrounds the burial chamber and a single monolith some 16 feet high. The nature of the ceremonies performed is not known, but the presence of such a major structure indicates that the area was populated by a relatively large and organized society. Moreover, the design of the tomb and fragments of decorated pottery found on the site suggest strong links with communities on the **ORKNEY ISLANDS**, indicating the importance of sea transport even at a very early stage of the settlement process in Scotland.

CALVINISTIC METHODIST CHURCH OF WALES. (See **PRESBYTERIAN CHURCH OF WALES**).

CAMERON COMMISSION. In January 1969, Captain **TERENCE O'NEILL,** Prime Minister of Northern Ireland, announced a commission of inquiry into the claims of the civil rights movement and the causes of the violence which had plagued the province since October of the previous year. The commission was headed by Lord Cameron (a Scottish judge) and included representatives of the Protestant and Roman Catholic communities. Its report, published in September and widely interpreted as vindicating the activists, criticised the Northern Ireland Parliament for being "complacent" and "hidebound", but added, there had been failures of leadership on all sides. Unfair local authority housing policies, religious discrimination over appointments to posts in the public service, manipulation of electoral boundaries to keep the **ULSTER UNIONIST PARTY** in control and the failure of government to investigate complaints by Catholics were all cited as reasons for the unrest and ammunition for subversive elements. (See **EDUCATION: NORTHERN IRELAND**).

CAMERONIANS. An extremist wing of the **COVENANTERS,** the Cameronians were known as the Society Folk when they were founded in 1680 but soon assumed the name of their leader, Richard Cameron. Advocating strict adherence to the terms of the **NATIONAL COVENANT** (1638) and the **SOLEMN LEAGUE AND COVENANT** (1643), they refused to accept the sovereignty of Charles II. On 22 June 1680, they declared war against him but, on 22 July, Cameron was captured by royal troops at Airds Moss (Ayrshire) and killed. Despite that setback, the movement expanded, particularly in the south of Scotland, and, despite ruthless persecution, numbered several thousand adherents by the tenth anniversary of his death. In 1706, John Macmillan became head of the group and, gradually, supporters became known as Macmillanites rather than Cameronians. They founded the Reformed Presbyterian Church in 1743, continuing to grow in strength and also increasing their influence in Scottish communities overseas. In 1876, the majority of members merged with the **FREE CHURCH OF SCOTLAND.** (See **APOLOGETICAL DECLARATION; JOHN GRAHAM; WIGTOWN MARTYRS**).

CAMPAIGN FOR DEMOCRACY IN ULSTER (CDU). In 1965, a group of left-wing Labour MPs established the CDU as a pressure group dedicated to ending the gerrymandering of electoral boundaries and discrimination against Roman Catholics in Northern Ireland. It was active until 1969. (See **CAMPAIGN FOR SOCIAL JUSTICE**).

CAMPAIGN FOR SOCIAL JUSTICE (CSJ). Established in 1964 and based in Northern Ireland, the CSJ was a middle-class organization consisting largely of Roman Catholics. Its aim was the collection of data about social injustice in the province and particularly on discrimination involving employment, housing and the drawing of electoral boundaries. The CSJ cooperated with the **CAMPAIGN FOR DEMOCRACY IN ULSTER** and with the United Kingdom's National Council for Civil Liberties, gaining particularly strong support within the Labour Party.

CAMPBELLS. (See **ARGYLL, DUKES AND EARLS OF**).

CANMORE, MALCOLM. (See **MALCOLM III**).

CARDIFF. Wales's capital city is located on the north bank of the River

Severn some 150 miles west of London. Although the Romans built
a fort on the banks of the River Taf about AD 75, the Norman Earl
of Gloucester constructed a castle on the same site around 1090–93
and King Edward II gave the settlement a royal charter in 1324, Cardiff is essentially a product of the Industrial Revolution. In 1801, it
was a trading and shipping centre with a population of only 1870.
By 1911, it was a major port with 182,000 residents. The expansion
was based on the export of coal, which was mined in the valleys to
the north of the coastal plain (see **RHONDDA VALLEYS**) and in
great demand as a source of power during the early 19th century.
Routeways from these valleys focused on Cardiff but export facilities were limited until **JOHN STUART,** the second Marquess of
Bute, risked the bulk of his fortune on the development of the harbour. The Bute West Dock opened in 1839 and greatly reduced con-
gestion but, even so, it could not cope with the growth of traffic and
further quays were added in 1855, 1874, 1887 and 1907. By 1887,
Cardiff was Britain's chief port in terms of gross registered tonnage
and, second only to New York in the world. In 1841, the Taf Vale
Railway opened, facilitating the carriage of iron ore to Cardiff, and,
in 1850, the South Wales Railway followed, enhancing the transport focus. Employment opportunities expanded as manufacturers of
iron, steel, copper and chemicals made their base in the town and as
shipbuilding and engineering became increasingly important. In particular, the Dowlais Iron Company transferred its operations from
the northern fringe of the coalfield to a new site in the docks during
the 1880s.

The city weathered the economic depression of the years between
the two world wars relatively well. The East Moors iron and steel
works was modernized, an associated company making rods and wire
was established and new flour-milling facilities were built. In addition, after the United States entered the Second World War in 1941,
it made much use of the harbour, bringing a large proportion of its
service personnel, stores and supplies to Britain through the docks.
However, the export trade experienced a significant decline as the
tonnage of coal despatched fell from 10.5 million in 1913 to only
0.25 million in 1963. Also, the 1966 Industrial Development Act denied development area status to Cardiff because of its relative prosperity, and, as a result, over 40 firms relocated to sites, just outside
the city boundary, where they could make use of government grants
and other incentives. Then, in 1978, at a time when the import of
iron ore was about three-quarters of the docks' total trade, East Moors
steelworks was closed, throwing 4,000 employees (mostly men) out

of work.

On the other hand, while traditional sources of jobs fell on hard times, the city's designation (in 1955) as the capital of Wales proved a spur to the growth of administration. Cardiff is the base for the United Kingdom government's activities in the principality (see, for example, **WELSH DEVELOPMENT AGENCY**) and for the County Council of Glamorgan (see **LOCAL GOVERNMENT: WALES**). It is also a centre for the administration of justice (see **LEGAL SYSTEM: WALES**) and for education (see **EDUCATION SYSTEM: WALES**). In addition, several national companies have established regional headquarters, attracted by the good road and rail connections, the proximity to government offices, a plentiful labour force and relatively cheap accommodation. As a result, by the early 1980s, less than one-fifth of the employed population was in manufacturing industry and about three-quarters were in the service sector. One of the consequences of the changed economic structure was 2,700 acres of derelict dockland, with unused, antiquated warehouses and poor quality housing. A Cardiff Bay Development Corporation was created to shape the regeneration of the area and proposes to build a barrage which will enable it to construct a marina around a 500-acre freshwater lake. According to the developers, the plans will create 45,000 jobs and provide 4 million square feet of office space, 6 million square feet of industrial floor space and 6,000 homes. Cardiff is the retail and entertainment centre for South Wales, with an opera house and a pedestrianised shopping area, and has undergone much urban renewal since the 1950s, with most of the working class slums now gone, but it has retained much of its Victorian architecture in the city centre, which has a network of shopping arcades and a covered market. At the time of the 1991 census, it had a resident population of just under 280,000.

CARHAM, BATTLE OF (*c.* 1016). An allied force of Scots (led by King **MALCOLM II**) and Britons from Strathclyde (led by Owain the Bald) met an army of Northumbrians near the River Tweed and defeated it heavily. The victory confirmed the Scot's possession of the lands between the Tweed and the **RIVER FORTH.**

CARNEGIE, ANDREW (1835–1919). An industrialist who amassed a vast fortune in the North American iron and steel industry, then distributed a large proportion of that income through charitable organizations, Carnegie was born in Dunfermline on 25 November 1835. His parents were poor and, like so many 19th-century Scots, decided to seek a better life in the United States. The family settled in Allegheny (Pennsylvania) in 1848, and Andrew started work as a bobbin boy in a local cotton mill at the age of 13. In his free time, he educated himself through books borrowed from a working boys' library, taught himself telegraphy and ultimately obtained a job as a telegraph operator with the Pennsylvania Railroad. Later, he became a superintendent and introduced sleeping cars to the railway system.

Despite his small salary, he began to invest part of his income and acquired a 12.5 per cent interest in what ultimately became the Pullman Company. However, a meeting with Sir Henry Bessemer in 1873 convinced him that iron and steel would become the backbone of American industry, and, from then, the bulk of his investments were channelled in that direction. His empire expanded during the 1870s and 1880s so, by 1892, he had acquired several industrial plant, coal pits and iron mines (all of which supplied raw materials) as well as railway wagons and lake steamships (which transported them). In 1899, he merged his various interests into the Carnegie Steel Company and, at the turn of the century, was producing a quarter of the United States's output of steel.

The following year, Carnegie sold the business to the United States Steel Company and retired in order to devote himself to charitable work, particularly in the form of donations to educational and research institutes and trusts and to bodies promoting world peace. Of total grants amounting to $350 million, nearly one-fifth was used to establish public libraries in the United States of America, the United Kingdom and other English-speaking countries. Bodies which bear his name include the Carnegie Institution of Washington, D.C. (established in 1902 with a grant of $10 million to conduct research in astronomy, biology and the physical sciences), the Carnegie Foundation for the Advancement of Teaching (formed in 1905 by a grant of $15 million to provide pensions for professors in nonsectarian universities in the USA and Canada), the Carnegie Endowment for International Peace (a $10 million trust founded in 1910 with the aim of abolishing international warfare) and the Carnegie Corporation of New York (created, in 1911, through a $135 million donation in 1911 for the advancement of knowledge in the United States and British colonies and dominions). He died in Lenox (Massachusetts) on 11 August 1919.

CARSON, EDWARD HENRY (1854–1935). The principal opponent of schemes to grant independence to the whole of Ireland, Carson was a towering figure in early 20th century British politics. Born in

Dublin on 9 February 1854, the son of civil engineer Edward Carson and his wife, Isabella, he was educated at Portarlington School and then at Trinity College, where he graduated in law. Called to the Irish bar in 1877, he rapidly earned a reputation as an effective speaker and, at the same time, nursed a growing distrust of the nationalist movement. In June 1892, he was appointed solicitor-general for Ireland in the Marquis of Salisbury's Conservative Party administration and, the following month, became a member of Parliament as one of Dublin University's representatives. Three years later, he was widely acclaimed for the way in which he conducted his cross-examination of Oscar Wilde in the author's libel action against the Marquess of Queensbury and, in 1900, was made Solicitor General for England. At the height of his profession, he was recognized as one of the leading lawyers in the land, praised by opponents as well as supporters for his ability to sway doubting jurors and for his talents both to cajole and to browbeat witnesses. Increasingly, however, he involved himself in the struggle to retain **ULSTER** within the United Kingdom. In 1910, he became the Irish Unionists' leader in the House of Commons and, later in the year, turned down the opportunity to head the Conservative Party so that he could devote his energies to their cause. For the next decade, he fulminated against separation, warning that if Ulster was part of an independent Ireland it would have to be governed as a conquered country and that the battalions of volunteer soldiers which he had helped to raise would be willing to fight in defence of the North's distinctive religious and political life. With the help of the pro-unionist faction on the British mainland, led by Andrew Bonar Law, Carson prised increasingly significant concessions from Herbert Asquith's Liberal government before the outbreak of the First World War, in 1914. In May 1915, he accepted the post of Attorney General in Asquith's cabinet but was increasingly disenchanted by the Prime Minister's military policies and resigned in October of the following year. He returned to government as first Lord of the Admiralty in David Lloyd George's coalition administration of December 1916 and, in July 1917, was made Minister without Portfolio. He resigned again in January 1918, believing that Lloyd George, who had earlier appeared to recognize Ulster's case for continued integration with Britain, intended to introduce legislation giving independence to Ireland as a whole. For a further two years, he continued his campaign and, ultimately, gained Parliamentary support. As a result, when the **GOVERNMENT OF IRELAND ACT** became law in 1920, the six counties of Ulster were incorporated within the United Kingdom of Great Britain and Northern Ireland. Carson, feeling that the time had come for a younger man to take over, resigned his position as leader of the Ulster Unionists in February 1921. Three months later, he was appointed lord of appeal and took the title Baron Carson of Duncairn. He died at Minster (Kent) on 22 October 1935 and was given a state funeral in **BELFAST**.

CASKET LETTERS. Eight letters, some sonnets and two marriage contracts said to have been written by **MARY, QUEEN OF SCOTS**, were allegedly discovered in a casket belonging to **JAMES HEPBURN BOTHWELL** in June 1567 and produced the following year by opponents who wanted to prove that the queen and her lover were conspirators in the plot to murder **HENRY DARNLEY** (Mary's husband). Probably, in large part, forgeries (some writers suspect that they were the work of historian George Buchanan, who harboured a deep-seated hatred of the young monarch), they were instrumental in turning opinion against Mary both in Scotland and in England, where she claimed the throne of Elizabeth I. The letters disappeared in 1584 and have never been recovered.

CATTLE ACTS, 1663, 1667. These acts of Parliament were imposed by English legislators in an attempt to restrict the import of beef both from Scotland and from Ireland. They probably had real effect on the trade and production of the two nations. Some authorities argue that the effects of the legislation were considerable, claiming, for example, that the Irish port of Youghal suffered severely as a result of the ban on the export trade. Others maintain that the legislation simply led farmers to diversify and send butter and other dairy products to the European mainland.

CELTIC CHURCH. Christianity was well established in Celtic Britain by the 4th century, aided by the relatively peaceful conditions established during the Roman occupation of much of the islands, and preachers, such as St Dyfrig (in Wales), St Ninian (in Scotland) and **ST PATRICK** (in Ireland), were responsible for converting many of the indigenous people to the faith. However, after the Romans left in AD 410, the pagan Saxon peoples who replaced them drove Christianity out of much of England, leaving believers concentrated in the southwest peninsula, Wales, Ireland and the north of Britain. Isolated from the main centres of Roman Catholicism, the Celtic Church developed its own practices, so by the time St Augustine arrived in Kent in 597, charged by Pope Gregory I with the task of reestablishing Christianity in England, the two religious traditions, although broadly in accord over doctrine, differed in many matters of detail, such as the date of Easter and the correct form of tonsure. Neither was willing to give way — Augustine had a narrow view of the acceptable and the Celts wanted to preserve their individuality — so, although many of the differences were settled at the Synod of Whitby in 664, Celtic influences permeated the organization and worship of the Church in Wales, Scotland and Ireland until after the Norman conquest in 1066.

The Celtic tradition placed heavy emphasis on monasticism, evangelism and scholarship but lacked any form of overall organization. Hermits and missionaries were highly regarded, but the major rites were performed by bishops and abbots (such as **ST DAVID**). Only those ordained by the bishops could celebrate communion. Monks (including **ST COLUMBA**) took their beliefs to isolated islands and to the European mainland, founding monasteries as they went. (See **IONA**). Many also devoted themselves to learning, teaching the Scriptures, collating ecclesiastical rulings and developing the system of confession and penitence. Art flourished, particularly sculpture (many intricately worked stone crosses survive) and the illumination of manuscripts. (See **BOOK OF KELLS**). However, the lack of any form of diocesan structure resulted in increasing fragmentation of the Church, after the Viking invasions of the 9th and 10th centuries. Also, the missionaries' passion for carrying their beliefs far and wide meant that they often failed to consolidate the gains they made. As a result, the special ethos of the Celtic faith increasingly gave way to the reforms wrought by powerful Norman barons from the 11th century onwards.

CELTIC FRINGE. Following the Roman invasion of the British Isles in AD 43, the native Celtic peoples were forced northwards and westwards to the more climatically and topographically inhospitable areas, a process which continued during Anglo-Saxon times (*c.* 450-1066). Nowadays, the term 'Celtic Fringe' is used as a shorthand means of describing, with limited precision, the areas where the Celts found refuge. It encompasses Scotland, Northern Ireland, Wales and southwest England, all of which show political, linguistic and other cultural differences from the rest of the United Kingdom.

CELTIC REVIVAL. During the 18th and 19th centuries, there was a revival of interest in the languages, dress and literature of both Scotland and Wales. The movement, which resulted in the reintroduction of the **EISTEDDFOD,** was also associated with the growth of nationalist sympathies. (See **SCOTTISH ENLIGHTENMENT**).

CENTRAL CITIZENS' DEFENCE COMMITTEE (CCDC). Formed in 1969 through the amalgamation of several Roman Catholic community organizations in **BELFAST,** the CCDC was highly critical of British army tactics in Northern Ireland, claiming that the security forces were discriminating in favour of Protestants. However, it was considerably influenced by the clergy and, on the whole, adopted conservative polices, including advocacy of an end to violence against soldiers and members of the **ROYAL ULSTER CONSTABULARY.** It was involved in talks with the government and army on many occasions during the early 1970s and, in 1973, made an unsuccessful attempt to persuade the **IRISH REPUBLICAN ARMY** to abandon terrorist activities.

CHALMERS, THOMAS (1780–1847). One of the outstanding ecclesiastical leaders of the 19th century, Chalmers was responsible for the rift which split the **CHURCH OF SCOTLAND** in 1843 (see **DISRUPTION OF THE CHURCH OF SCOTLAND**). Born in Anstruther on 17 March 1780, he entered **ST ANDREWS** University at the age of 11 and was ordained as minister at Kilmany (near Cupar) in 1803. He began to teach chemistry and mathematics classes at the university in 1803 and spent much of his time studying the sciences but, following a period of religious crisis about 1810, became increasingly evangelical. In 1815, he moved to the Tron Kirk in **GLASGOW,** where he addressed the practical problems of a fast-growing industrial city, devoting himself to the material as well as the spiritual needs of his congregation. There and at St John's (which became his charge in 1819), his impassioned oratory brought worshippers flocking to hear him preach, and his powerful personality shaped a social welfare system which centred on his church and emphasised self-reliance and independence.

In 1803, he returned to St Andrews as Professor of Moral Philosophy, partly because he wanted to pursue a growing intellectual interest in political economy and partly because he felt he could wield a wider influence over the Church from a seat of learning. By 1828, when he was appointed to the chair of divinity at the university of **EDINBURGH,** he was the accepted leader of a faction, within the Church of Scotland, which wanted to reduce secular involvement in ecclesiastical affairs and give parishioners the right to influence the appointment of their minister. Inevitably, such an attack on the patronage of landowners was resisted fiercely and, in 1843, feeling that the conservatism of the establishment was limiting the church's ability to meet the needs of its members, he led 470 fellow evangelicals to form a breakaway **FREE CHURCH OF SCOTLAND.** He was made moderator (that is, chairman) of the new organization and became principal of its college until his death in Edinburgh on 30 May 1847.

CHARLES, THOMAS (1755–1814). During the late 18th and early 19th centuries, Charles was the principal figure in Welsh Methodism. He was born at Pantdwfn (Carmarthenshire) on 14 October 1755, the second son of Rice and Jael Charles, who earned a living from their small farm. After receiving a schooling at Llanddowror and Carmarthen (where he joined one of the Methodist societies), he went to Oxford University, graduating in 1779 with a BA degree. In 1778, he was appointed curate at Queen's Camel in Somerset, but he was scathing about his parishioners ungodly living and, in 1783 (three years after entering the priesthood), moved to Bala, which became the centre of his preaching. He travelled the length and breadth of north Wales, the first minister to spread the word of Methodism in that part of the country. Convinced that people should be able to read the Bible for themselves, he set up a network of more **CIRCULATING SCHOOLS**; a class was established in one village and, when children were able to read the gospels in **WELSH,** transferred to another. From 1789, he introduced Sunday Schools to Wales, teaching adults as well as young people (the upsurge in religious fervour which occurred in North Wales in 1791 was, in large part, a result of the spread of these schools). In order to supplement the religious education, Charles produced several publications, the most notable of which was *Geiriadur Ysgrythyrol*, a scriptural dictionary which appeared in four volumes between 1805 and 1811 and included much detail about the geography and history of the Holy Land. The main need, however, was for cheap editions of the Bible and, in 1802, he was the prime force behind the foundation of the British and Foreign Bible Society — an organization which has since printed copies of the Bible in nearly 300 languages but which started with a run of 20,000 in Welsh, prepared by Charles himself.

Although Charles was, in effect, the leader of the Calvinistic Methodist movement, he considered himself in full communion with the established Church of England and had no wish to break away. However, increasing numbers of his followers wanted independence, and, by 1811, he was forced to concede that separation was inevitable.

In June of that year, he ordained nine lay preachers to the ministry at a service in Bala and, in August, added a further 13 at Llandeilo, effectively creating the **PRESBYTERIAN CHURCH OF WALES** and giving the nonconformist sects a numerical majority over the congregations of the Anglican **CHURCH IN WALES**. In 1814, he produced a new edition of his Bible but that was to be his final work. He died on 5 October, the exertions of constant travel and the stresses of leadership having taken their toll on his health. (See **METHODIST REVIVAL**).

CHARLIE, BONNIE PRINCE. (See **CHARLES, EDWARD STUART**).

CHICHESTER-CLARK, JAMES (1923–). Prime Minister of Northern Ireland from 1969 until 1971, Chichester-Clark was born on 23 April 1923, the son of Captain J. L. C. Chichester-Clark and Mrs C. E. Brackenbury. He was educated at Eton College then, in 1942, joined the British Army as a second lieutenant in the Irish Guards. At the end of the Second World War in 1945, he remained in the forces, serving as aide-de-camp to the Governor-General of Canada (Field-Marshal Earl Alexander of Tunis) from 1947 until 1949. He ultimately retired, having attained the rank of major, in 1960, when he joined the Northern Ireland Parliament as **ULSTER UNIONIST PARTY** MP for South **LONDONDERRY**. He got his first government job as Assistant Chief Whip in 1963, then rose rapidly through the ranks, over the next four years, as Chief Whip (1963), Leader of the House (1966) and then Minister of Agriculture (1967). On 23 April 1969, he resigned, ostensibly because he disagreed with Prime Minister **TERENCE O'NEILL** over the timing of a 'one man — one vote' reform for local elections. Five days later, however, O'Neill (Chichester-Clark's cousin) stepped down, and, on 1 May, Chichester-Clark was elected to replace him, a compromise choice over two other candidates — William Craig (who was one of the principal architects of O'Neill's downfall) and **BRIAN FAULKNER** (an articulate and able politician who would become **ULSTER**'s last Prime Minister before **DIRECT RULE** from London was imposed by the British government in 1972). In an attempt to defuse the increasingly explosive confrontation between the Protestant and Roman Catholic communities in the province, he immediately extended an amnesty to all those who had been charged with political offences since the previous October (the Rev **IAN PAISLEY** was one of the beneficiaries). However, the gesture did nothing to cool tempers, so the level of sectarian violence increased. In August, following riots in **BELFAST** and Londonderry, troops had to be used to help the **ROYAL ULSTER CONSTABULARY** maintain order and, in the Irish Republic, special camps were organized to house those who sought refuge from the civil disorder. Only weeks later, he was told by British Prime Minister Harold Wilson that the **B-SPECIALS** would be disbanded and faced the problem of coping with **ULSTER LOYALIST** groups angered by the decision. As the months passed, he became increasingly beleaguered, criticized by unionists for failing to adopt more aggressive action against the **IRISH REPUBLICAN ARMY** and by political opponents for failing to introduce reform measures which would halt the violence. Demands for his resignation mounted, and, on 20 March 1971, he gave in, saying that there was "no other way of bringing home, to all concerned, the realities of the constitutional, political and security situation". He was created Baron Moyola of Castledawson the same year but has played little part in politics since.

CHURCH IN WALES. An independent province of the Anglican Communion, the Church in Wales has approximately 97,000 members and 700 clergy in 1,500 parishes. From the 16th century until 1920, the Anglican Church was the established church (that is, the officially recognized state church) in the principality. That status was removed because, by the early years of the 20th century, the great majority of Christians in Wales were Nonconformists, worshipping mainly in Baptist, Congregational and Methodist chapels. Nowadays, the Church is organized within six sees — Bangor, Llandaff, Monmouth, St Asaph's, St David's, and **SWANSEA** and Brecon. Its leader is the Archbishop of Wales, who is chosen by an electoral college composed both of clergy and of laity. The Archbishop presides over the governing body, which has 349 members representing the bishops, priests and church adherents. The governing body meets twice a year, and is the supreme authority on matters of practice and the interpretation of doctrine. In 1996, it approved the ordination of women priests, the last of the four Anglican Communions in the United Kingdom to do so and, in January 1997, the first women were duly ordained into the Church in Wales. (See **CHURCH OF IRELAND; PRESBYTERIAN CHURCH OF WALES; SCOTTISH EPISCOPAL CHURCH; UNION OF WELSH INDEPENDENTS [UNDEB YR ANNIBYNWYR CYMRAEG]**).

CHURCH OF IRELAND. The Irish Supremacy Act of 1537 established the English sovereign (rather than the Pope) as the supreme authority over religious affairs in Ireland. However, the majority of the people maintained their allegiance to Roman Catholicism, and, in 1869, the British Parliament approved legislation disestablishing the Anglican Communion. As a consequence, the bishops, priests and adherents met the following year to consider programmes of administrative reorganization and financial restructuring as a result of the loss of state support. These delegates framed a constitution for the Church of Ireland, which established a general synod as its governing body, with bishops, clerics and laity all represented. That synod now has 660 members and exercises control over Armagh and Dublin, the church's two provinces. In Armagh (which covers Northern Ireland), there are six sees — Clogher; Connor; Derry and Raphoe; Down and Dromore; Kilmore, Elphin and Ardagh; and Tuam, Killala and Achonry. In 1995, they supported some 360 clergy. The senior official is the Archbishop of Armagh and primate of all Ireland, who is elected by fellow bishops. Other episcopal appointments are made by an electoral college. The Church of Ireland has about 161,000 members and 482 places of worship in **ULSTER**. (See **PRESBYTERIAN CHURCH OF IRELAND**).

CHURCH OF SCOTLAND. In 1560, influenced by such radicals as **JOHN KNOX**, the Scottish Parliament turned its back on Roman Catholicism, declaring that the Pope had no authority within its area of jurisdiction and outlawing the celebration of Mass. A new church was established, governed by a general assembly, which consisted partly of clergy, partly of laymen, and was answerable to no higher ecclesiastical authority. For over a century, however, there was debate — and sometimes conflict (see **BISHOPS' WARS**) — about the most desirable form of administration in the reformed institution, and it was not until 1690 that the differences were settled by King William III's rejection of episcopalianism as "contrary to the inclination of the generality of the people". A **PRESBYTERIAN** structure was created, forming the foundations on which the modern Church of Scotland was built. Clauses confirming that Presbyterian organization were included in the **TREATY OF UNION,** which united Scotland with England in 1707, but, in 1712, the United Kingdom Parliament decided to restore the rights of landowners to appoint ministers to congregations on their estates. Inevitably, many church members objected, arguing that they should have the right to select the clergymen they wanted rather than meekly accept the ones their landlord preferred. Also, during the 18th century, an evangelical movement within the Church gained strength, even though some of its more extreme advocates seceded and set up their own sects. By 1834, led by the charismatic **THOMAS CHALMERS,** in control of the general assembly, campaigning for an end to patronage, a return to the traditional tenets of Calvinism and rejection of modernist changes to belief and practice. Nine years later, after a series of bitter exchanges between the factions, it had become clear that moderates and evangelicals could work together no longer and Chalmers led his supporters into a breakaway **FREE CHURCH OF SCOTLAND.** (See **DISRUPTION OF THE CHURCH OF SCOTLAND**).

The schism reduced the prestige and the morale of the established church, as well as its size, but the later 19th century brought recovery as new forms of worship and an emphasis on young people rebuilt confidence. Patronage was abolished by Parliament in 1874, and, in 1929, most of the congregations which had joined the secessionists returned to the fold. A period of amalgamation followed, hastened partly by declines in attendance at Sunday services.

Changes in post-Second World War society also wrought changes in the church. In 1966, the general assembly decided that women could become elders (elected leaders of the congregations who helped the parish minister with pastoral duties), and, three years later, they were admitted to the ministry. Serious attempts were made, through the appointment of industrial chaplains and school chaplains, to exert an influence on people who were finding attractive alternatives to weekly religious devotions. By the last decade of the 20th-century, the institution was in a paradoxical position. Membership was low, and only about one in every 20 Scots darkened its doors each year. But the meetings of the general assembly received much press coverage, the moderator (the assembly chairman, appointed annually) was a figure of national importance and nonchurchgoers accorded the institution considerable significance in social and political life. It was still, to most Scots, the national church and, to many, the nearest thing Scotland had to a Parliament.

Each congregation is led by a minister and a group of elders, all of whom are elected by church members. The congregations are grouped into 47 presbyteries, organized territorially. Each consists of all the ministers within its area, one elder from each church and members of the diaconate. These presbyteries are responsible for the administration of church business at regional level and for conveying local opinions to the general assembly, which meets annually in **EDINBURGH.** The British sovereign sometimes attends in person, and, when absent, is represented by a high commissioner. In 1995, the Church of Scotland had about 700,000 members (a decrease of 130,000 over the preceding decade) and 1,610 congregations (eight of them outside Scotland). (See **BOOK OF DISCIPLINE**; **CAMERONIANS; CELTIC CHURCH; ST COLUMBA; COVENANTERS; FREE PRESBYTERIAN CHURCH OF SCOTLAND; GLASGOW ASSEMBLY; IONA; NATIONAL COVENANT; SCOTTISH EPISCOPAL CHURCH; UNITED FREE CHURCH OF SCOTLAND; UNITED PRESBYTERIAN CHURCH**).

CIRCULATING SCHOOLS. Education for the working classes and the poor, particularly in rural areas of England, was largely absent until the development of the Dame Schools, Sunday Schools and a number of charity schools during the Industrial Revolution. However, in 1699, a Welsh Trust had been established, with **CHURCH IN WALES** and nonconformist support, to organize education in the principality. The circulating schools drew on that Trust for support. Created about 1737 by **GRIFFITH JONES**, vicar of the parish of Llanddowr, they got their name because they used itinerant teachers, who communicated basic reading skills to members of a community, then moved on to another village. (See **THOMAS CHARLES**).

CLAIM OF RIGHT (1689). In March 1689, three months after James VII of Scotland had fled to France, hounded out by the forces of Protestantism, a Convention of the **THREE ESTATES** was called to discuss the constitutional position. (A Convention was less formal than a full Parliament and was usually summoned to deal with specific issues). The delegates concluded that James had deserted his kingdom and that the throne should be offered to William of Orange and his wife, Mary (James's daughter). That offer, however, was conditional on the new monarchs' acceptance of a Claim of Right, which listed the previous King's shortcomings and stated that his successors should accept certain conditions, notably that no Roman Catholics should hold office in government and that the law of the land should take primacy over the royal perogative. In essence, therefore, it insisted that the sovereignty resided in the people rather than the ruler. The extent to which William and Mary accepted the Claim of Right prior to taking the coronation oath became a vexed issue, causing much trouble between them and the Scottish political leaders.

CLAN. An anglicization of the **GAELIC** word for *offspring,* the word *clan* refers to a group of people claiming descent from a common ancestor. In Scotland, the clans — which included adherents to a particular chief as well as blood relatives — were fiercely independent, wearing their own **TARTAN**s and establishing their own codes of conduct. These social and military units were formed during the 14th century, when the monarchy was weak, but derive, in part, from earlier groups, which were linked by loyalty and kinship to a chief and usually underpinned by a feudal form of landholding. After the **JACOBITE REBELLION**s, Parliament systematically tried to curb their power by removing the chiefs' legal rights and prohibiting clansmen from wearing the **KILT** and carrying arms.

CLARSACH. A large triangular harp common in Celtic areas of the British Isles, the clarsach appears to have evolved by the 8th century. Medieval versions had a heavy wooden frame, with about 30 metal strings (usually brass) which were plucked by the musician's fingernails and made a sound akin to that of a bell. The player was known as a clarsair. By the late 18th century, the clarsach was seldom heard because its long resonant notes were out of fashion in an age dominated by harmonic music, and it is still rarely used. The modern harp is descended from the more delicate European harp, which had gut strings plucked by the flesh of the finger.

CLAVERHOUSE, JOHN GRAHAM OF. (See **JOHN GRAHAM**).

CLEGG AFFAIR, PRIVATE LEE. In June 1993, paratrooper Private Lee Clegg was convicted of the murder of Karen Reilly in Northern Ireland three years earlier. Clegg had shot at a stolen car which failed to stop at a checkpoint, believing the occupants to be terrorists. Because there had been four shots, he was judged to have used excessive force and sentenced to life imprisonment. In January 1995, the case was the subject of an appeal, amidst public sympathy in mainland Britain, and Clegg was released on licence. This action caused widespread rioting throughout the province. In February 1998, the Court of Appeal in Northern Ireland adjudged the original conviction to be 'unsafe' and ordered a retrial of the case.

CLYDE, RIVER. Scotland's major waterway, the Clyde rises in the Galloway hills (part of the **SOUTHERN UPLANDS**) and flows, for 106 miles, north and then west before reaching the Atlantic Ocean. Its upper reaches pass through rough, sheep-grazing land, but, along the middle of its course, between Crossford and Hamilton, it is liable to flood; the alluvial soils which it has deposited are intensively farmed (the Clydesdale, one of the United Kingdom's principal draft horses, developed in this area). During the 19th century, the final part of its route became the focus of the shipbuilding industry on which much of Britain's industrial power was based (the luxury liners *Queen Elizabeth*, *Queen Mary* and *Queen Elizabeth II* were Clydeside products). **GLASGOW,** located on both banks of the Clyde, emerged as a major manufacturing centre and port, trading particularly with North America. In 1790, the river was linked by canal to the **RIVER FORTH,** providing a waterway across central Scotland. Towards its mouth, in the Firth of Clyde, holiday resorts such as Rothesay, Girvan and Millport provided escapes for the burgeoning working class populations of the industrial towns. A network of ferry services still links the major settlements downriver from Glasgow, and, with most of the shipyards now closed, the waterway is a major recreational resource for the west of Scotland, with yachting and fishing particularly important.

COLNBROOK, LORD. (See **HUMPHREY ATKINS**).

COLUMBA, ST (*c.* 521–97). An Irish missionary for the Christian faith, Columba was born into one of the ruling families in Donegal about 7 December 521. He was ordained as a priest *c.* 551 and established a number of churches and monasteries, including Daire Calgaich (beside Lough Foyle) and Dair-magh (in Offaly). Some 12 years later, he left Ireland with a dozen followers and built a monastery on **IONA,** an island in the kingdom of **DALRIADA** on the west coast of Scotland, then began to convert the **PICTS,** who had settled there. Columba and his disciples travelled widely, eventually making the monastery at Iona the centre of the Christian faith in Scotland. He returned to Ireland once, in 597, but spent his later years on the island, where he died on the night of 8 June 597. His feast day is 9 June. (See **CELTIC CHURCH**).

COMBINED LOYALIST MILITARY COMMAND (CLMC). The CLMC was created in 1991 to coordinate the policies of three Protestant paramilitary groups in Northern Ireland — the **RED HAND COMMANDO,** the **ULSTER VOLUNTEER FORCE** and the **ULSTER FREEDOM FIGHTERS.** In the summer of that year, it called a halt to terrorism during interparty political negotiations but broke its own ceasefire by killing a **SINN FEIN** representative. The group is alleged, by many observers, to have been responsible for the increase in **ULSTER LOYALIST** violence during late 1991 and 1992.

COMMONWEALTH LABOUR PARTY (CLP). Established in 1942 by Harry Midgley and other members of the Northern Ireland Labour Party who advocated continued British rule in the province, the CLP adopted more conservative social and economic policies than its parent. It was represented by six candidates at the elections for the Northern Ireland Parliament in 1945, but only one — Midgley — was successful and, when he defected to the **ULSTER UNIONIST PARTY** two years later, the organization disintegrated.

COMPANY OF SCOTLAND. (See **DARIEN SETTLEMENT**).

COMUNN GAIDHEALACH, AN. Formed in 1981, this **INVERNESS**-based organization acts as a pressure group for the **GAELIC** language in Scotland (its title is Gaelic for *The Highland Society*). It has branches throughout the country (including the non-Gaelic speaking areas) and is much involved both in educational and in political activities. In the past, it has promoted a variety of activities (such as youth camps) in an attempt to cultivate the study of Gaelic history, literature and music but is now best known for its annual Royal National Mod. The Mod, a festival of Gaelic arts, was modelled on the Welsh **EISTEDDFOD** and first held at Oban in 1892. Since then, it has taken place annually at a different location every year. A competitive event, it attracts several thousand participants, the majority of them children, who take part in choral and individual competitions in *sean nos* (traditional singing), drama, recitation and other skills. The winners of the adult individual events receive gold medals, which carry much prestige in the Gaelic community. In recent years, An Comunn has attempted to broaden its appeal and, in 1997, included a competition for rock bands, reflecting the considerable success of groups such as Runrig and Capercaille in European popular music. The Mod, and the associated non-competitive fringe events which have developed alongside it, generates about £3 million for the community in which it is held but its costs (about £160,000) are covered largely through volunteer fundraising. Local Mods are held throughout Scotland and, in 1987, an annual Mod was inaugurated in the United States.

CONVENTION OF ROYAL BURGHS. By the end of the 13th century, the royal **BURGH**s were holding meetings — known as conventions — to discuss matters of common interest. Although these gatherings had no statutory powers, they exerted a great deal of influence, and were instrumental in enforcing uniformity of practice within member settlements. Also, the convention regulated foreign trade, and, after the **TREATY OF UNION** in 1707, became the principal body representing Scotland's industrial and commercial interests. (See **CONVENTION OF SCOTTISH LOCAL AUTHORITIES; COURT OF THE FOUR BURGHS**).

CONVENTION OF SCOTTISH LOCAL AUTHORITIES. The convention was formed in 1975, following the reorganization of **LOCAL GOVERNMENT** the previous year. Its function is to promote good government, provide a forum for discussion and represent the views of Scottish local authorities at the United Kingdom Parliament in London. It meets formally four times a year, an executive based in **EDINBURGH** and a series of committees carries out the bulk of its work.

COOK, ROBIN FINLAYSON (1946-). Widely regarded as one of the keenest minds in British politics, Cook became Foreign Secretary following the Labour Party's general election victory in May 1997. The only child of school teacher Peter Cook and his wife, Christina, he was born on 28 February, 1946, and educated at Aberdeen Grammar School, the Royal High School of **EDINBURGH** and Edinburgh University (where he graduated with a Master of Arts degree in English Literature). He worked as a tutor-organizer with the Workers' Educational Association from 1970 until 1974, but was clearly intent on finding a place in national and local government in order to promote social change. He contested the Parliamentary constituency of Edinburgh North unsuccessfully in 1970 but was elected to Edinburgh City Council in 1970 and acted as secretary to the Edinburgh branch of the Labour Party from 1970-72. Using these platforms to build support, he was elected to the House of Commons as the MP for Edinburgh Central in 1974 and then for the New Town of Livingston in 1983. His ability to grasp issues quickly, coupled with an abrasive debating style and a passionate belief in social justice, made him a popular figure on the left-wing of his party and led to his appointment as opposition spokesman on economic affairs (1980-83), European issues (1983-84), the City of London (1986-87), health and social security (1887-92), trade and industry (1992-94) and foreign policy (1994-97). He made no secret of his ambition to become

Chancellor of the Exchequer when the Labour Party swept the Conservative Party from office but was denied the post partly because of his radical reputation (which **ANTHONY CHARLES LYNTON BLAIR**, the new Prime Minister, clearly felt would ruffle the feathers of the business community) and the close relationship between Blair and **JAMES GORDON BROWN**, who also wanted the job (and who is known to have a personal dislike of Cook).

Political commentators have frequently claimed that Robin Cook's political career is hampered by his appearance and his knack of making enemies (Simon Hoggart, for example, referred to him as "a red haired gnome" and Edward Pearce scathingly described him as "a pompous little Scot, proud, conceited and rude"). However, Labour's rank and file demonstrated their support by voting him top of their poll for membership of the shadow cabinet in 1994 and, following the 1997 general election success, clearly regarded him as one of the bulwarks of left-wing philosophy in a Cabinet drawn largely from the party's right. As Foreign Secretary, he made it clear that he had no intention of abandoning either his principles or his style when, within days, he announced that human rights would be a central element of the United Kingdom's international relations and, at the United Nations, berated the United States for failing to take effective action on atmospheric pollution.

COUNTRYSIDE COUNCIL FOR WALES. The Council was formed in 1991 through a merger of the Welsh arm of the Countryside Commission and the Nature Conservancy Council. It acts as advisor to the government on wildlife conservation, countryside management and policies affecting the Welsh coastline and inshore waters. Also, it works with the private sector, voluntary organizations and local authorities to promote schemes which will protect the rural environment, encourage recreation outside towns and cities and improve the quality of life for those who live in the countryside. Based in Bangor, it has ten members (drawn primarily from the farming community, the universities and business) who are allocated an annual budget of some £20 million. In 1995, John Redwood (then **SECRETARY OF STATE FOR WALES**) announced plans for a root and branch review of the Council's work, proposing the transfer of responsibilities for monitoring and management to wildlife groups and local authorities. The scheme caused an outcry from conservationists but drew some support from businesses, which felt that, in areas of rural poverty and long-term unemployment, the council was giving scenery and natural environment priority over development.

(See **SCOTTISH NATURAL HERITAGE**).

COURT OF SESSION. (See **LEGAL SYSTEM: SCOTLAND**).

COURT OF THE FOUR BURGHS. The first **BURGH**s to be established in Scotland were Berwick and Roxburgh, both of which received royal charters between 1119 and 1124. **EDINBURGH** and **STIRLING**, with important defensive sites, were awarded charters between 1124 and 1127. The privileges and laws of these four settlements formed the basis of regulations governing the administration of all burghs established later. Meetings of their representatives to agree on common practices were known as the Court of the Four Burghs. (See **CONVENTION OF ROYAL BURGHS**; **LOCAL GOVERNMENT: SCOTLAND**).

COVENANTERS. Scottish discontent with the rule of King Charles I, and particularly with his attempts to impose an episcopacy and a new liturgy on the **CHURCH OF SCOTLAND**, led, in 1638, to a **NATIONAL COVENANT**, by which Scots pledged resistance to the monarch in a **PRESBYTERIAN**, anti-Catholic alliance. Their defiance led to the **BISHOPS' WARS** (1639–40), when Charles attempted to enforce his edicts, but the Covenanters prevailed, invading England, taking Newcastle and forcing his negotiators, through the Treaty of Ripon (1640), to admit defeat. In 1643, they signed the **SOLEMN LEAGUE AND COVENANT**, which committed them to support for Oliver Cromwell's campaign against the royalists in the English civil war. When Cromwell reneged on the agreement, they transferred their allegiance to the **STUART** cause. With widespread support from all social classes, the covenanting movement did much to confirm Scotland's distinct cultural identity and hastened the move away from government by an absolute monarch towards more democratic forms of administration.

The term *Covenanter* has also been used to refer to individuals who resisted the imposition of an episcopacy in Scotland, and suffered persecution as a result, even though they were not fully committed to the principles spelled out in the two covenants. More generally, it has sometimes been employed as a collective name for all Scottish Presbyterians of the time. (See **APOLOGETICAL DECLARATION**; **BATTLE OF BOTHWELL BRIDGE**; **CAMERONIANS**; **GLASGOW ASSEMBLY**; **JOHN GRAHAM**; **BATTLE OF KILSYTH**; **WIGTOWN MARTYRS**).

CRAIG, JAMES (1744–95). The son of **EDINBURGH** merchant William Craig and his wife, Mary, James Craig was responsible for the design and layout of the New Town in Scotland's capital. His exact date of birth is unknown and details of his education scanty, but he is reputed to have been a pupil of Sir Robert Taylor, architect to the Bank of England. In 1767, the city authorities decided to expand Edinburgh to the north, allowing some of the people cooped up in the medieval town to escape to more commodious accommodation. Craig submitted proposals which showed little originality but gained widespread approval, probably because they accorded closely with the fashions of the Georgian age. Poet James Thomson, his maternal uncle, had written in a work on *Liberty*:

> *August, around, what public works I see!*
> *Lo! stately streets! Lo! squares that court the breeze!*

Craig clearly had the same vision because his plans incorporated straight, wide roadways and squares which contrasted with the tortuous alleyways and gloomy courts of the existing city. George Street was the centrepiece, crowning a ridge and terminating in St Andrews Square at the eastern end and Charlotte Square in the west. Princes Street, which ran parallel to the south, and Queen Street, to the north, had houses on one side only, thereby providing imposing views for residents. The Nor' Loch, on the site now occupied by Princes Street Gardens, was preserved as a linear water feature separating the New Town from the Old.

Craig, who was given a gold medal and awarded the freedom of the city, was not responsible for the buildings which lined his thoroughfares: the only important structure which he designed for Edinburgh was Physicians' Hall, built in George Street in 1776–77 and considered to be one of his best works but later demolished to make way for a bank. His success brought fame but not fortune. Although he was involved in some building work both in **GLASGOW** and in Edinburgh, his plans for remodelling the medieval core of the capital, published in 1786, were turned down by the magistrates as the vogue for improvement waned. From 1781, he was constantly borrowing money and, on his death in Edinburgh on 23 June 1795, left many debts.

CRAIG, JAMES (1871–1940). The first Prime Minister of Northern Ireland, Craig was born in Sydenham (a **BELFAST** suburb) on 8 January 1871, the sixth son of whiskey millionaire James Craig and his wife, Eleanor. James Junior was educated privately and then at Merchiston Castle School (**EDINBURGH**) before becoming a stockbroker. During the Boer War (1900–2), he served as a lieutenant colonel with the Imperial Yeomanry but, increasingly, became interested in politics and, in 1903, made an unsuccessful attempt to enter Parliament by contesting the North Fermanagh constituency. At the 1906 General Election, he took North Down for the Unionists, and almost immediately became embroiled in the controversy over plans to give Ireland its independence. A stalwart supporter of **EDWARD HENRY CARSON**, he opposed moves to grant the island home rule and, when it was clear that the government was determined to press the legislation through Parliament, fought to retain the six counties of **ULSTER** as an integral part of Great Britain.

The campaign won, he became Prime Minister of Northern Ireland in June 1921 and held the office for the next 19 years. The tenure was not an easy one. His own experience of government amounted to a few months in two junior posts — one as Parliamentary Secretary at the Ministry of Pensions in 1919–20 and the other as Parliamentary Secretary and Financial Secretary to The Admiralty in 1920–21 — and, initially, he had to construct an administration consisting of people who had even less background in political office. Also, a new police force had to be created and order established, particularly in areas which had supported the separatist cause. Faced with the task of building up an infrastructure for the new province, his focus narrowed and he became engrossed in the affairs of Northern Ireland at the expense of consideration of the territory's wider links with the rest of the United Kingdom and the British empire. Also, although he assumed office amidst promises to recognize the rights of the Roman Catholic minority, as time passed he was more and more influenced by Protestant pressure groups. On the other hand, although Craig's economic policies were sometimes viewed at Westminster as ill-conceived, he introduced much legislation which brought benefits to Northern Ireland's society and economy, including measures dealing with agricultural reform, educational provision, housing standards and road transport. His service was rewarded with a baronetcy in 1918 and, in 1927, a viscountcy. He died suddenly in Glencraig (County Down) on 24 November 1940, and was buried at **STORMONT**, the seat of the Northern Ireland Parliament.

CRAIGAVON, VISCOUNT. (See **JAMES CRAIG**).

CRANNOG. A wooden construction built in a **LOCH,** with the water providing a natural moat, the crannog probably first appeared in Scotland about 1000 BC, providing a defensive base for farming groups. From there, the concept may have spread to Ireland (where there are many similar structures) and Wales (where one has been identified) but there is no evidence of crannogs anywhere in England. Once numbering many thousands, they could shelter anything from a single family to a large community. Some were royal residences, involving much skilled labour in their construction. They were occupied until the 17th-century, when many were destroyed because they had become the haunt of criminals. During the 1990s, archaeological excavation of one of the 18 crannogs on Loch Tay provided evidence of a wealthy settlement with up to 15 inhabitants, who grew wheat and barley and raised cattle, sheep and pigs during the early Iron Age. Wooden dishes, spoons, cups and a butter dish (with a smear of butter) were recovered from the building, which was supported by huge timber piles.

CROFTER'S WAR (1883-88). Also known as the Highland Land War, the Crofters' War was primarily a campaign of civil disobedience fuelled by the frustrations of poverty in the **CROFTING** communities of **THE HEBRIDES** and **THE SCOTTISH HIGHLANDS.** Angered by the actions of landowners and by a lack of Government help, the crofters refused to pay their rent, killed sheep feeding on land which had formerly been common grazing but had been taken over by the landlords for their own use, and poached deer to prevent their families from starving. On occasion, troops were used to keep the peace, but on the whole, the crofter leadership concentrated on gaining publicity for its cause rather than provoking confrontation with the authorities. Its actions were sufficient to force Prime Minister William Gladstone's Liberal Party Government to set up a Commission of Enquiry, chaired by Lord Napier, in 1884. The evidence presented to the Commission, providing incontrovertible proof of the hardships endured by the crofters and the inequities of the tennancy agreements, led to the introduction, in 1886, of the Crofters' Holding Act. That legislation conferred security of tenure, compensation when land was given up and the right to bequeath tenancies. In addition, a Crofters' Commission was established, with power to arbitrate in rent disputes. Initially, most crofters were sceptical but, by 1888, a series of decisions favouring tenants rather than owners had won most of them over.

CROFTING. A form of mixed agriculture on smallholdings, crofting (as legally defined by a series of acts of Parliament dating from 1886) is confined to the former Scottish counties of Argyllshire, Caithness, Inverness-shire, Orkney, Ross and Cromarty, Sutherland and Zetland. To take advantage of the financial and other benefits made available by the UK government, individual crofts must be no larger than 30 hectares or have an annual rental of less than £100. Most of the 17,700 farms which qualify are on rocky or marshy land, with thin acid soils and high rainfall combining to offer limited potential either for arable or for root crops. About two-thirds are on islands, thereby adding remoteness to the problems created by limited size. The average holding has four acres of crops and grassland, four breeding cows, 20 sheep and rights to graze on some 30 hectares of common land.

The system evolved during the agricultural improvements of the late 18th and early 19th centuries as estate owners strove to achieve more economic forms of production. Often, the arrangement was designed to augment the kelp (or seaweed) industry (the plant was used as a fertiliser) and the fisheries. Multi-tenanted farms were reorganized so that individual lots were laid out, with each crofter allocated a rectangular holding running inland from shore to moor and occupying a cottage on his land rather than in a farm village. Grazing rights on the uplands were held in common and oats and potatoes were the major crops. However, most holdings were too small to allow families to eke out a living, and the collapse of the kelp industry in the 1820s, the failure of the potato crops in the 1830s and 1840s, low prices for cattle and the introduction of sheep grazing (which required fewer people than other forms of husbandry) led to increasing poverty. At the same time, populations in the crofting areas were rising, adding to the insecurity. During the 1870s and 1880s frustration spilled over into civil disturbance and, in 1884, forced reluctantly into action, William Gladstone's Liberal Party government appointed a royal commission of inquiry, headed by Lord Francis Napier, to investigate the grievances. The following year, four representatives of the crofters won seats in Parliament at the General Election and, in 1886, Gladstone introduced the Crofters' Holdings Act, which awarded all crofters security of tenure, the right to bequeath tenancies to their families and compensation if they decided to give up their land. The Crofters' Commission, established the same year, was given the power to fix fair rents and draw up regulations governing grazing rights. Further legislation in 1892, 1897, 1911 and 1919 meant, in effect, that anybody who wanted a croft could have one, so, between 1897 and 1939, some 2,600 new crofts were created and a further 5,000 were enlarged, adding more than 250,000 hectares of pasture and 19,000 hectares of arable land.

In 1955, the Crofters' Commission was reorganized and the Crofters Act introduced grants, along with other measures, designed to develop the system and improve the conditions of the crofters. The years which followed brought amalgamation of tenancies, enhancements to stock and pasture and higher standards of housing. In addition, the 1976 Crofting Reform Act gave tenants the right to purchase their croft, and many have done so, notably at Assynt in 1992 and Borve the following year. Even so, by the mid-1990s, the great majority of the farms were being worked part time by families which derived the bulk of their income from other employment and the crofting community was biassed towards the older age groups, with most tenants over the age of 45. Nevertheless, official efforts are still geared towards maintaining the system, partly because it represents a traditional way of life, partly because it underpins the tourist infrastructure by providing accommodation for visitors and partly because it maintains populations in areas long characterized by migration.

CROWN OFFICE. Based in **EDINBURGH,** the Crown Office is responsible for the conduct of criminal prosecutions in Scottish courts of law. Its head is the **LORD ADVOCATE,** who is assisted by the solicitor general. The crown agent, a legally qualified civil servant, is responsible for the administration of the office and of the procurator fiscal service, which initiates proceedings in the sheriff courts. (See **LEGAL SYSTEM: SCOTLAND**).

CULLODEN, BATTLE OF, 16 April 1746. The last battle of the second **JACOBITE REBELLION** was fought at Culloden Moor, near Inverness. Five thousand exhausted, hungry supporters of Prince **CHARLES EDWARD STUART** faced a 9,000-strong Hanoverian army led by William Augustus, Duke of Cumberland, on ground which none of the young pretender's military advisors believed could be defended. With sleet driving into their faces, they were routed within 40 minutes, losing 1,000 dead. Cumberland lost only 50 of his soldiers but took vicious reprisals, bayoneting the wounded, hanging fugitives and burning the homes of those believed to be harbouring those who had fought for the **STUART** cause. The battle — the last to be fought on the British mainland — crushed the rebellion and effectively brought an end to the **CLAN** system. The victorious

Cumberland had the flower 'Sweet William' named after him. The Scots still call it 'Stinking Billy'.

CULZEAN CASTLE. One of **ROBERT ADAM**'s finest works, Culzean Castle stands on sea cliffs four miles west of Maybole (Ayrshire). It was built between 1772 and 1790 but incorporates a medieval keep constructed for the Kennedy family, which has a long association with the site. The oval staircase, the painted ceilings of the staterooms and the collection of armoury form the major features of interest, but there is also a room with exhibits which describe US president Dwight Eisenhower's links with Scotland (the top flat in the castle was given to General Eisenhower as a Scottish home for use during his lifetime, a gesture of gratitude for his contribution to the allied victory in the Second World War). Caves beneath the building are reputed to have served as rallying points for **ROBERT THE BRUCE**'s forces during their struggle against the English invaders. In 1945, the castle was donated to the **NATIONAL TRUST FOR SCOTLAND** by the Marquess of Ailsa and a successful £2.5 million appeal for funds, launched by the organization in 1991, has led to a major programme of structural repairs. The bulding is now the Trust's most visited property and acts as the focal point for a Scotland's first country park, a 563-acre estate created in 1969 and managed by local authorities.

CURLING. Usually considered to be of Scottish origin, although the Dutch have a strong counter-claim, curling is a sport played by two rinks (or teams) of four people. Each competitor pushes two heavy, polished stones along a 138-foot sheet of ice towards a 12-foot diameter target known as 'the house'. The rink's intention is to get its own stones closer to the centre of the house than those of its opponents. Originally an open-air winter recreation for all social classes and with considerable regional variation in rules, it is now largely confined to indoor arenas (for climatic reasons) and regulated by the Royal Caledonian Curling Club, originally formed in 1838. From Scotland, where there are 630 clubs and nearly 20,000 competitive curlers, the game has spread to Canada and the colder regions of the United States, northern and central Europe and Australasia. Its name derives from the players' ability to rotate (or 'curl') the stones and thus make them travel in a curve.

CURRAGH INCIDENT, 20 March 1914. In 1912, Prime Minister Herbert Asquith proposed legislation giving **HOME RULE** to Ireland, which, at the time, was part of Britain. Pro-unionists responded by forming the **ULSTER VOLUNTEER FORCE** (UVF) and pledged to oppose the bill, which, if it became law, would place the dominantly Protestant north of the island in the same country as the dominantly Roman Catholic south. When British army officers, stationed at the Curragh (near Dublin), were informed that those who lived in **ULSTER** could unofficially disappear but that all who remained would be required to keep the peace (opposing the unionists and the UVF if necessary), General Hubert Gough and 56 of his colleagues declared their readiness to be dismissed if ordered into the north. J. E. B. Seely (the Secretary for War) and Sir John French (Chief of the Imperial General Staff) advised Asquith to withdraw the notice but were overruled by the cabinet and resigned, undermining public confidence in the government. The incident convinced **ULSTER LOYALISTS** that the army was on their side, reinforced the widespread public view that the north could not be coerced into an independence it did not want and demonstrated that soldiers might well refuse to quell a Protestant uprising.

CURRENCY. Northern Ireland, Scotland and Wales have the same currency as the rest of the United Kingdom, with 100 pence equalling £1. However, three Scottish banks (the **BANK OF SCOTLAND,** the Clydesdale Bank and the Royal Bank of Scotland) issue their own notes. These are not legal tender (that is, no one is required by law to accept them in exchange for goods or services), but they circulate widely and have the same status as Bank of England notes. Similarly, notes issued by the Bank of Ireland, First Trust Bank, the Northern Bank and Ulster Bank are used in Northern Ireland. All of the notes can be exchanged at banks throughout the UK but frequently traders in England and Wales, particularly those outside the major urban areas, are suspicious of the unusual designs.

CYFRAITH HYWEL DDA. The native Welsh laws were, according to legend, codified at an assembly convened by **HYWEL DDA** in 950. There is no contemporary evidence of such a meeting but scholars agree that Hywel was certainly responsible for consolidating legal practices and applying the the same regulations throughout his realm. The earliest documents outlining these laws date from the 13th century and, with later manuscripts, show how interpretations and principles evolved with changing social, ecclesiastical and political influences. Essentially folk, rather than statute, law, the legal code emphasized reconciliation between opposing parties rather than coercion through threat of punishment. Also, it demonstrated a respect for the rights of women and children absent from the English legal system, which was increasingly imposed in Wales from the early 14th century. (See **LEGAL SYSTEM: WALES**).

CYMDEITHAS YR IAITH GYMRAEG. (See **WELSH LANGUAGE SOCIETY**).

CYMMRODORION, SOCIETY OF. Three societies with this name have been founded with the aim of celebrating Wales and Welsh culture (the word *cymmrodorion* is derived from *Cymru*, the **WELSH** for Wales).

1751. The first society was founded by Richard Lewis, a clerk at The Admiralty, and other Welsh gentry living in London. Their intentions were to sustain the purity of the Welsh language, increase interest in Welsh literature and Welsh history and encourage economic and other activities which would benefit Wales. The organization achieved little, largely because it confined membership to a wealthy elite who had been much influenced by English cultural forces, and disbanded in 1787.

1820. The society was resurrected, again by Welshmen based in London, with the intention of preserving the native culture by encouraging publications in the Welsh language and reestablishing the **EISTEDDFOD**, an ancient bardic meeting of song and poetry. As in its previous incarnation, however, the reliance on anglicized gentry brought only limited success, and it survived for only 17 years. (See **CELTIC REVIVAL**).

1873. In 1873 a further, and more successful, attempt was made to revive the organization, which still exists as a London-based centre of Welsh art and literature, sponsoring national exhibitions, museums and libraries and publishing journals and books on Wales and Welsh culture. (See **WELSH LANGUAGE SOCIETY; YOUNG WALES**).

—D—

DAFYDD AP GRUFFUDD (?–1283). The last of the Welsh princes, Dafydd was the child of **LLYWELYN AB IORWERTH**'s illegitimate son, Gruffudd. In 1246, his older brothers, Owain and Llywelyn, became rulers of part of the northern kingdom of Gwynedd (see **DAFYDD AP LLYWELYN, LLYWELYN AP**

GRUFFUD), and, in 1252, he received a grant of land. Three years later, he allied with Owain against Llywelyn but was defeated in battle at Bryn Derwyn and forfeited his estates. After a second unsuccessful uprising in 1263, he escaped to England and, the following year, took part in the royalist campaign against the rebel Simon de Montfort. He returned to Wales in 1267 but, eight years later, was involved in another intrigue against his brother. Llywelyn responded by seizing his lands again, and he was forced to flee, once more, to the safety of the English court. In 1277, he was with Edward I on the campaign which led to Llywelyn's submission to England and was rewarded with properties of considerable strategic importance on the northern marches. (See **MARCHER LORDS**). For five years, there was relative quiet in the area, but Dafydd found himself at odds in the courts with Edward's representatives over title to land and the actions of his supporters. The brothers agreed to a covert alliance, and, in March 1282, Dafydd attacked Hawarden Castle, overpowered the defenders and captured Roger de Clifford, the King's justiciar. Llywelyn came to his aid, and war broke out again. His brother's death in December left Dafydd in sole control of the campaign's destiny, but he was never widely accepted as a leader and, in June 1283, was betrayed to the English armies. Edward was incensed at what he considered to be an unforgivable lack of loyalty by a man for whom he had so often provided a safe haven. In October, Dafydd was condemned to death. Because he was a traitor, he was dragged through Shrewsbury streets to the gallows. Because he was a murderer, he was hanged. Because he was a blasphemer, his entrails were removed. And, because he had tried to kill the King, he was beheaded and quartered. Dafydd's two sons spent the rest of their lives as prisoners in Bristol Castle, his daughter was sent to a nunnery and his estates in **SNOWDONIA** and Anglesey were forfeited to the English Crown.

DAFYDD AP GWILYM (c. 1320–c. 1380). One of the greatest of the Celtic poets, Dafydd was born in Llanbadarn Fawr, the son of Welsh nobleman Gwilym Gam and his wife, Ardudful. Although comparatively little is known about his upbringing, it is clear that he spent much time in the company of his maternal uncle, Llywelyn ap Gwilym, who was constable of Emlyn Castle and himself a distinguished bard. This immersion in the distinctive Norman-Welsh culture of mid- and south Wales undoubtedly influenced Dafydd's literary style, which differed markedly from that adopted by the northern poets in Gwynedd. In particular, his cywyddau (short odes written in couplets of seven syllables, one rhyme accented, the other not) used vocabulary easily understood by educated listeners and thus helped to establish the structure of the modern **WELSH** language. Also, he introduced new themes, drawing on the traditions of the wandering troubadours to compose poems dealing with love and, especially, with nature. However, his works have not been widely disseminated amongst English-speakers because they lose much in translation; they are intended, in the bardic tradition, to be heard rather than read, so rely for their effect on the music of the words as much as on their sensitivity and wit. The main love of Dafydd's life appears to have been Morfudd, daughter of Madog Lawgain of Anglesey. She returned his affections but was forced by her family to marry an elderly man, whose sole attraction was his considerable wealth. The young couple eloped but was caught and Dafydd was heavily fined, the penalty being paid on his behalf by kinsmen in Glamorgan. It is believed that he died in Llanbadarn Fawr about 1380. (See **IOLO MORGANWG**).

DAFYDD AP LLYWELYN (*c*. 1208–46). Son of **LLYWELYN AB IORWERTH** and his wife, Joan (sister of King Henry III of England), Dafydd was prince of the northern Welsh Kingdom of Gwynedd between 1240 and 1246. In 1238, Llywelyn summoned the Welsh princes to a council at Strata Florida Abbey, where they agreed that Dafydd should be his successor in preference to his elder, but illegitimate, son, Gruffudd. However, following Llywelyn's death on 11 April 1240, Henry used the animosity between Dafydd and Gruffudd, and the aspirations of the other princes, to emphasize his own control over Wales, confining Dafydd's power to Gwynedd alone and insisting that the lesser rulers owed direct allegiance to the English crown. Furthermore, in 1241, he decreed that authority over Gwynedd would pass to the crown of England if Dafydd died without leaving an heir. Dafydd appealed to Pope Innocent IV, offering to make Gwynedd a papal vassal in return for acknowledgment of his rights but Innocent, wary of depriving himself of the large annual payments made to the Vatican by England, declined the offer. In March 1246, Dafydd died suddenly and childless. Gwynedd was divided, Henry taking the east (extending English control) and Owain and Llywelyn (sons of Gruffudd) the west. (See **LLYWELYN AP GRUFFUDD**).

DALRIADA. In the middle years of the fifth century, Dalriada was the kingdom of the Scottii people, who lived in the northern part of the area of Northern Ireland now known as Antrim. Towards the end of the century, these warriors expanded their influence by crossing the North Channel and colonizing Argyll and the Inner **HEBRIDES,** ultimately giving their name to the country of Scotland. For a time, the maritime kingdom was governed as a single unit but, during the sixth-century, Irish Dalriada declined and, by the ninth-century, had lost its political identity. By contrast, Scottish Dalriada prospered and, in 843, united with the kingdom of the **PICTS.** The territory became known as Alba or **SCOTIA** and the old name fell into disuse. (See **KENNETH MACALPIN; BATTLE OF MAG RATH**).

DARIEN SETTLEMENT, 1698–1700. Often described as Scotland's greatest disaster — greater even than the military defeat at the **BATTLE OF FLODDEN** — the Darien scheme was an attempt to establish a Scottish colony at the eastern end of the Isthmus of Panama. The venture, proposed by **WILLIAM PATERSON,** was eagerly supported by Scots merchants and others who had seen previous attempts at colonization fail in Carolina and Nova Scotia. In 1695, the **THREE ESTATES** passed an act authorizing the establishment of a Company of Scotland trading with Africa, America and the Indies. Attempts to mount a joint venture with England and the Hanseatic towns were unsuccessful, but, in Scotland, there was unbridled enthusiasm — £400,000 Scots (about half of the nation's entire wealth) was subscribed by individuals and institutions, beguiled by national pride and Paterson's salesmanship.

In July 1698, five ships set sail from Leith, bound for Darien. They arrived in November and claimed the land as the Colony of Caledonia. Unfortunately, they had chosen one of the most climatically inhospitable areas of central America. Many of the eager settlers had died even before they reached the promised land. Moreover, the leaders of the group were poor organizers, differing frequently among themselves, and the harbour they had selected was unsuitable for sailing vessels. In addition, Spain claimed the area and the Scots had to beat off attacks from their fellow Europeans. Famine, illness and a lack of supplies complicated matters even further. As a result, the settlement proudly named New **EDINBURGH** was never more than a handful of shacks and, when the English colonies in the Americas were told to offer no assistance, the settlers decided to return home, leaving 400 of their fellows (including Paterson's wife and only child) buried on foreign soil. However, by the time that decision was made, four relief ships had set out from Scotland. They reached the colony in November 1699 and reestablished the settlement. This time, the Spaniards mounted a blockade of the harbour, and after a month the Scots surrendered. Caledonia was abandoned for the second and last time on 12 April 1700. Of nearly 2,500 settlers, only 300 survived. Three-quarters of the subscribed capital was lost.

The Scots' reaction was to blame the English for their treachery rather than to attribute the failure to their own lack of forethought, poor management and flawed judgement. The national poverty which resulted was one factor in the Scots' decision to sign the **TREATY OF UNION** with England in 1707. Article Fifteen of that treaty provided that England would give Scotland some £400,000 sterling: a portion of the money was to be used to repay those who had invested in the Darien venture, with the addition of five per cent interest on their capital. One **JACOBITE** ballad of the period laments, with some accuracy, that Scotland's independence was "bought and sold with English gold". The English retort was that the Scots had only themselves to blame. The failure of the settlement provoked the **WORCESTER AFFAIR** in 1704.

DARNLEY, HENRY STEWART (1545–67). The second husband of **MARY, QUEEN OF SCOTS,** Darnley was born at Temple Newsam (Yorkshire) on 7 December 1545, the son of Matthew, Earl of Lennox, and his wife, Margaret. Lennox (a descendant of King **JAMES II**) had claims to the throne of Scotland and Margaret (granddaughter of King Henry VII) to the throne of England, so both were anxious that their son should make a match with Mary, who would become Queen of Scotland on the death of her father (**JAMES V**) and who was considered by the majority of Roman Catholics to be the rightful Queen of England (the Protestant community favoured Elizabeth I, daughter of Henry VIII).

Darnley first met Mary during a visit to the continent in 1559 and renewed the acquaintance early in 1565, following her return to Scotland after the death of Francis II of France, her first husband. While staying at **STIRLING,** he fell ill with measles and was nursed by the young Queen, who fell passionately in love with him. He was created Earl of Ross on 15 May the same year and Duke of Albany on 20 July. On 29 July, they were married in **EDINBURGH,** a match that seems to have been popular only with the young couple and the groom's family. To most of the nobles, Darnley was a vain, immature and ignorant young man, and to most of the Protestant church leaders, the wedding was a victory for papism.

Mary's ardour cooled quickly. Her husband had been declared King of Scots the day before the marriage but wanted to secure the right to rule after his wife's death rather than have the succession pass to any children. She resisted, partly because he was unwilling to devote time and effort to the chores of government, and he quickly grew jealous of her reliance on her secretary, David Rizzio. He was deeply involved in the plot to murder Rizzio on 9 March 1566, and Mary, aware that he was implicated, became increasingly estranged from him despite the birth of their son (later King James VI and I) on 19 June 1566.

Despised by everyone, Darnley fled to his father's house in **GLASGOW,** where he took ill with what is now believed to be smallpox. Mary visited him and, apparently reconciled, persuaded him to return to Edinburgh with her on 31 January 1567 although he was still unwell. They stayed in a house at Kirk o' Field, just outside the city wall, rather than at the royal palace of **HOLYROOD,** ostensibly because Darnley's sickness might infect their child. On the night of 9 February, while the Queen was attending a wedding celebration, the building was blown up. Darnley's body was found in the garden; he had been strangled and was unmarked by the explosion. The identity of the killers has been a source of debate ever since. Some scholars claim that **JAMES HEPBURN BOTHWELL** — Mary's next husband — was responsible. Some argue that Mary herself was involved. Others have suggested that the intention was to kill both Mary and Darnley and put the blame on Bothwell. The mystery is one of the most compelling in Scottish history, largely because of its importance in the romance and intrigue surrounding the Queen's life. In one sense, however, the hopes of the Lennoxes were realised because every British monarch since James VI and I is descended from Darnley. (See **DOUGLAS, EARLS AND MARQUESSES OF**).

DAVID I (1084–1153). The youngest son of **MALCOLM III** and **ST MARGARET,** David was King of Scotland from 1124 until his death and used his comparatively lengthy reign to modernize his country by establishing law and order, supporting the Roman Catholic Church and improving administrative efficiency. From 1113, Scotland was divided between David and his brother, **ALEXANDER I,** the former being responsible for the southern half of the country and the latter for the north. However, when Alexander died in 1124, David was universally accepted as King and set about the reorganization of his estates. The feudal system of land tenure, which he introduced, undoubtedly enhanced his power — as well as that of later monarchs — and brought considerable cohesion to a previously divided kingdom. His wealth (one of the keys to power in the feudal system) was augmented by the establishment of a series of royal **BURGH**s (such as **STIRLING** and Dunfermline), which were given rights to foreign trade in return for cash payments to the monarch. A standard coinage was developed and a uniform system of weights and measures imposed. The Church, with its strong influence on David's subjects through its literacy and learning as well as its theology, was supported with large grants — **HOLYROOD,** Melrose and Jedburgh abbeys were all established during his reign. The progress was periodically interrupted by rebellion at home and by war with England, but, when he died peacefully at Carlisle in May 1153, he left a kingdom more united than at any time in its history and extending further south than it had ever done before. (See **BATTLE OF THE STANDARD).**

DAVID II (1324–71). The son of **ROBERT I** and Elizabeth de Burgh, David was born on 5 March 1324 and ruled Scotland from 1329 until 1371. At the age of four, he was married under the terms of the **TREATY OF EDINBURGH** (1328) to Joanna, the sister of Edward III of England. He succeeded to the throne on his father's death and was crowned at **SCONE** in November 1331. The following year, however, the Scots were defeated at the **BATTLE OF DUPPLIN MOOR** by **EDWARD BALLIOL,** who claimed the crown. Balliol had been supported by the English so, when he was forced south again after only three months, Edward intervened and defeated the Scots once more, this time at the **BATTLE OF HALIDON HILL.** Fearing for his safety, David's supporters sent him to France, where he remained for more than seven years. By 1341, it was considered safe for him to return, but, at the Battle of Neville's Cross, in 1346, he was taken prisoner and spent the next 11 years in captivity in London, Newcastle and Odiham. The condition of his release was that Scotland would pay a ransom of 100,000 **MERKS** over ten years. Such a sum was beyond the country's means but Edward was mollified by intermittent instalments and the suggestion that one of his sons would be made king if David died without leaving a successor. Throughout his reign, David avoided paying homage to Edward and, although prone to extravagant expenditure at times, built Scotland's finances into a position of some strength. Justice was firm, Parliament developed its use of judicial and legislative committees and the civil service worked effectively. When he died at **EDINBURGH** Castle on 22 February 1371, he did not command the popular affection which his father had earned, but he had kept his country independent and relatively prosperous.

DAVID, ST (*c.* 520–*c.* 600). Little is known of the life of David, the patron saint of Wales. According to legend, he was the son of Sant, who was a member of the princely line of Cunedda in Ceredigion, and his mother was St Non, granddaughter of Brychan of Brecknock. He is reputed to have been a pupil of St Paulinus and to have restored his master's sight before settling on the Mynyw peninsula, in southwest Wales. He founded the most important of his many churches there and lived a life of great austerity, never speaking without necessity and never ceasing to pray mentally even when at work. His food was bread, vegetables and salt and his only drink was water. At the synod held at Llandewbrefi (Cardigan) around AD 570 with the aim of suppressing the Pelagian heresy, which appeared to minimize the role of divine grace in man's salvation, David spoke with such authority that he was unanimously elected primate of the Cambrian Church. It appears, however, that he never travelled to north Wales (although it is likely that he visited Cornwall). He died at Mynyw and his body was taken to St David's Cathedral, but, in 1538, his remains disappeared (some stories suggest they were moved to Glastonbury). David's formal canonization by Pope Calixtus II about 1120 has never been proved, but his feast day is recognized as 1 March. More than 50 churches in south Wales are dedicated to him, and his tomb is still a place of pilgrimage. (See **CELTIC CHURCH**).

DAVIES, CLEMENT (1994–62). Leader of the Liberal Party from 1945 until 1956, Davies was born at Llanfyllin on 19 February 1884, the youngest of the seven children of auctioneer Moses Davies and his wife, Elizabeth. He was educated locally and then at Cambridge University, where he studied law before being called to the bar by Lincoln's Inn in 1909. In 1908–9, he lectured at the University College of Wales, Aberystwyth, and then, in 1909–10, practised on the North Wales and Northern Circuits (see **LEGAL SYSTEM: WALES**). A move to London in 1910 led to the growth of a prosperous chambers but the outbreak of the First World War four years later brought new challenges while he served in the procurator-general's office as a government adviser on enemy activities in neutral countries and the high seas then, at the Board of Trade, on commerce with Germany. At the end of the conflict, he resumed his legal career, acting as junior counsel to the Treasury between 1919 and 1925 and becoming a king's counsel in 1926. However, despite his success as a lawyer, Davies, fascinated by politics, wanted a career in the House of Commons and, at the 1929 General Election, successfully contested his home constituency of Montgomeryshire for the Liberal Party. In 1931, he threw his weight behind the National Liberals, who supported Prime Minister Ramsay MacDonald's coalition government, and used his legal mind to particular effect on a series of Parliamentary committees and royal commissions. In particular, between 1937 and 1939, he chaired an investigation into health levels which condemned the poor provision of housing and other public services in Wales, blaming the high incidence of tuberculosis on the lack of decent living conditions. In 1939, he led a group of members of Parliament charged with making recommendations on the most effective administrative strategies to pursue during the Second World War and, according to Lord Boothby (see **ROBERT BOOTHBY**) was one of the principal architects of Winston Churchill's coalition government.

Davies rejoined the mainstream Liberal group in 1942 and, following the defeat of Sir Archibald Sinclair at the 1945 General Election, was appointed leader. It was a difficult time for the party, which had been reduced to only nine MPs and was rent by internal divisions. He was never wholly trusted by many in the organization because of his lengthy association with the National Liberals (who ultimately merged with the Conservative Party) and expended much effort simply on holding the different factions together. It was largely for these reasons that he turned down an invitation from Prime Minister Winston Churchill to serve as Minister for Education in 1951. In addition, Davies was battling with an addiction to alcohol so his success in maintaining the party intact until his retirement in 1956 (when he was succeeded by **JOSEPH GRIMOND**) was an achievement of some note. A passionate internationalist, he convinced Liberals to support the campaign promoting United Kingdom's inclusion in the European Community and advocated moves towards world government. At the same time, he remained a Welshman, fighting for the retention of Welsh culture and acting as president of the royal national **EISTEDDFOD** in 1938 and 1939. Davies was nominated, unsuccessfully, for the Nobel Peace Prize in 1955 and died in London on 23 March 1962.

DAVIES, RONALD (1946-). Appointed **SECRETARY OF STATE FOR WALES** in the first Cabinet appointed by Prime Minister **ANTHONY CHARLES LYNTON BLAIR** following the Labour Party's general election victory in May 1997, Davies was born into a working class Welsh family on 6 August, 1946. His father (also Ron Davies) was a fitter without the means (or the inclination) to provide his son with a privileged education, so young Ron attended Bassaleg Grammar School, Portsmouth Polytechnic and University College Cardiff before becoming a teacher. From 1970-74, he worked as a tutor and administrator with the Workers Education Association then, from 1974 until 1983, was employed as a further education advisor with Mid-Glamorgan Local Education Authority. In 1969, he won election as a local councillor with Bedwas and Machen Urban District Council and Rhymney Valley District Council, where he honed his political skills before capturing the Parliamentary constituency of Caerphilly in 1983. For a period in 1992, he acted as opposition spokesman on agriculture, fisheries and food, supporting consumer interests and environmental conservation rather than schemes which would boost farm profits. A left winger by political incination, he voted for **JOHN SMITH** and Tony Blair, respectively, in the 1992 and 1994 party leadership contests but was critical of Labour's policy of reserving a quota of seats in the shadow cabinet for women.

DEMOCRATIC UNIONIST PARTY (DUP). Founded in 1971 by the Rev **IAN PAISLEY,** the DUP is a Protestant political party committed to the retention of Northern Ireland within the United Kingdom. It superseded the **PROTESTANT UNIONIST PARTY,** which Paisley had formed seven years earlier, and attracted many members from the mainstream **ULSTER UNIONIST PARTY** (UUP). Under its first chairman (Desmond Boal, a leading **ULSTER** barrister), the DUP developed a relatively radical approach to social policy but opposed suggestions for any form of legislative assembly which involved the sharing of power with the **SOCIAL DEMOCRATIC AND LABOUR PARTY** or other groups with a significant Roman Catholic membership. It has consistently condemned all proposals which it considers might threaten Northern Ireland's constitutional position (the 1993 **ULSTER DECLARATION,** for example, was branded "a sellout"). The DUC has had an uneasy relationship with its Ulster Unionist Party allies, sometimes forming electoral pacts (as in 1983) but sometimes differing over tactics (for example, there was friction over the UUP's willingness to enter discussions with government ministers from the Irish Republic in 1991–92). Since 1997, it has been represented at Westminster by two MPs. (See **NORTHERN IRELAND POWER SHARING EXECUTIVE, UNITED ULSTER UNIONIST COUNCIL**).

DEVELOPMENT BOARD FOR RURAL WALES (BWRDD DATBLYGU CYMRU WLEDIG). Established by the Labour government in 1977, the board has an annual budget of £27 million with which to undertake schemes aimed at improving the economic and social health of the dominantly rural mid-Wales counties. Its 13 members are drawn from local authorities and the business community.

DEVLIN, BERNADETTE JOSEPHINE (1947–). One of the principal leaders of the civil rights movement in Northern Ireland during the late 1960s and the 1970s, Bernadette Devlin was born in Cookstown (County Tyrone) on 23 April 1947, the daughter of Elizabeth and John Devlin. She was educated at St Patrick's Girls' Academy in Dungannon, then studied psychology at Queen's University, **BELFAST,** where she became increasingly involved in the republican movement. Fired by the idealism of youth, eloquent and articulate, she became the youngest member of Parliament for over 200 years when, in April 1969, she was elected (with a 4,000-vote majority) to represent Mid-Ulster in the House of Commons while still in her final year as an undergraduate. Her maiden speech (which lasted for an hour and consisted of a stinging criticism of the **ULSTER UNIONIST PARTY** government of Northern Ireland and its leader, Prime Minister **TERENCE O'NEILL**) contained a suggestion that administration from **STORMONT** should be ended and that the province should be ruled directly from Westminster — an idea considered outrageous by many at the time but one which was to be fulfilled in 1972. (See **DIRECT RULE**). In December of the same year, she was sentenced to six months' imprisonment on a charge of incitement to riot, following her part in disturbances in **LONDONDERRY.** At her appeal, heard in August 1970, her lawyer claimed that she had acted from the highest of motives, comparable to "the roles of Joan of Arc and Florence Nightingale" in her concern for the safety of women and children; pictures taken at the time showed her breaking rocks to throw at police. Her sentence completed, she gained further notoriety in 1972, when she stormed across the House of Commons and punched Reginald Maudling, the Home Secretary, accusing him of telling lies about the events of **BLOODY SUNDAY.**

In 1973, she married teacher Michael McAliskey then, the following February, lost her seat at the General Election and faded from the political scene until 1979, when she stood as a candidate for the Northern Ireland seat in the European Parliament, representing **IRISH REPUBLICAN ARMY** prisoners. She failed to win, but was eliminated only on the third count, and her performance undoubtedly encouraged **SINN FEIN** to seek to pursue its aim of a united Ireland through political means. In January 1981, she was the target of an unsuccessful murder attempt by loyalist gunmen at her home at Derrylaughan, in County Tyrone. Since then, she has continued to speak and write about the Northern Ireland situation but is no longer a major figure in the nationalist movement. In 1996, her daughter (Roisin) was sought by the German police, who believed that she had been involved in the bombing of a British army base at Osnabruck the previous year.

DEVOLUTION. The partial transfer of constitutional, legislative or administrative powers from a central authority to a regional or other lower-level authority, devolution falls short of full independence and therefore fails to satisfy the aspirations of those who advocate **HOME RULE.** There has been a number of occasions when it has been discussed, voted upon, or implemented, in the United Kingdom.

Northern Ireland. After the **PARTITION OF IRELAND** in 1921, Northern Ireland became a self-governing province within the United Kingdom. An assembly, based at **STORMONT,** was given powers over domestic legislation, but not over foreign policy or other matters affecting the United Kingdom as a whole. The arrangement ended in 1972, when **DIRECT RULE** was imposed from London at the height of **THE TROUBLES.**

In 1973-74, an attempt to reinstate a form of devolution through a **NORTHERN IRELAND POWER SHARING EXECUTIVE** failed as a result of massive Protestant opposition organized by trade unions.

Scotland The **KILBRANDON COMMISSION,** which reported in 1973, recommended that the Scots should elect their own Parliament, which would have the right to legislate on specifically Scottish issues but be subservient to the UK Parliament on matters relating to the country as a whole. The Labour Government held a referendum in 1979, committing itself to setting up an assembly if 40 percent of the electorate (rather than 40 percent of those who voted in the referendum) approved, but only 33 percent supported the proposal. In 1997, the Labour Party made a commitment to hold a second referendum if it was elected at the general election and, shortly after gaining power, published proposals for a 129-member Parliament which would have wide ranging powers such as health, education and the legal system. In addition, it would have authority to raise or lower the basic rate of income tax by three percent. This time, 62 percent of the electorate turned up to the polling stations and 74 percent of them voted in favour. **DONALD CAMPBELL DEWER,** the **SECRETARY OF STATE FOR SCOTLAND** and architect of the plans, announced that the first elections to the assembly would be held in 1999.

Wales. The **KILBRANDON COMMISSION** Report in 1973 proposed that Wales, like Scotland, should have its own Parliament but a referendum in 1979 showed that only 12 percent of the electorate agreed. In 1997, the Labour Party resurrected the proposals during its general election campaign and, after taking power, published plans for an assembly which would have 60 members and a £7 billion budget but, unlike its Scottish counterpart, no tax raising powers. A referendum (held a week after that in Scotland) produced a tiny majority in favour; 559,419 (50.3 percent) of the voters accepted the plans and 552,698 (49.7 percent) rejected them. The government declared itself delighted with the result and announced that the first elections would be held in 1999 but critics forecast a difficult passage for the legislation setting up the body, particularly as it made its way through the House of Lords. If approved, the legislation would legitimise the first Welsh government since **OWAIN GLYNDWR** called a Parliament at Machynlleth in 1404.

DEWAR, DONALD CAMPBELL (1937-). Appointed **SECRETARY OF STATE FOR SCOTLAND** in the first government headed by Prime Minister **ANTHONY CHARLES LYNTON BLAIR** following the Labour Part's general election victory in 1997, Dewar is the son of medical consultant Dr Alistair Dewar. He was educated at **GLASGOW** Academy and Glasgow University (where he became President of the Union in 1961-62, led debates with **JOHN SMITH** and **ALEXANDER ANDREW MACKAY IRVINE** and graduated MA, LLB). In 1966, by defeating Lady Tweedsmuir, he became the first Labour Member of Parliament for **ABERDEEN SOUTH** but was ousted in 1970. In 1978, he returned to the House of Commons, representing Glasgow Garscadden and, three years later, became opposition front bench spokesman on Scottish Affairs. He moved to Social Security in 1992 and was appointed the party's Chief Whip in 1995. His appointment as Secretary of State in May, 1997, followed a bitter behind-the-scence battle with **GEORGE ISLAY McNEIL ROBERTSON,** who had been shadow Secretary for four years, but was widely welcomed in Scotland, where he was viewed as a pro-**DEVOLUTION**ist. That perception was confirmed over the next four months, during which he introduced a White Paper outlining plans for a Scottish Parliament, campaigned successfully for support for the proposals in a referendum and won a Cabinet commitment to have the new assembly in operation by the end of the decade.

DIPLOCK COMMISSION. In 1972, a government commission, headed by Lord Diplock, proposed that people accused of certain terrorist activities in Northern Ireland should be tried in the absence of a jury because of the risk that jurors or their families might be threatend by supporters of the defendant. The proposal was adopted and hearings by a judge sitting alone became known as Diplock Courts, but the procedure was much criticized by civil liberties groups, which maintained that it rode roughshod over the rights of defendants.

DIRECT RULE. This term is used to describe the system of government adopted by the United Kingdom, from 1972, in an attempt to establish an effective, centralized administration for Northern Ireland. In March of that year, unable to contain escalating violence and increasing bitterness between the Protestant and Roman Catholic communities, **ULSTER**'s Prime Minister, **BRIAN FAULKNER,** resigned, along with his cabinet. The British government (which was led by Prime Minister Edward Heath and was ultimately responsible for the security of the area) reacted by suspending the **STORMONT** Parliament and imposing direct rule from London, with **WILLIAM WHITELAW** designated as the minister answerable to the House of Commons. Over the next two years, attempts were made to restore normality. The Northern Ireland Constitution Act of 1973 provided for a system of devolved authority to an executive based in **BELFAST** and consisting of the main political parties in the province, with the exception of **SINN FEIN** (see **NORTHERN IRELAND POWER SHARING EXECUTIVE**). However, constant disagreement between members led to the group's disintegration in May 1974, and, under the terms of the Northern Ireland Act (approved the same year) responsibility for the running of the province's internal affairs was transferred to London. A Northern Ireland Office was established, headed by a secretary of state with cabinet rank. (See **SECRETARY OF STATE FOR NORTHERN IRELAND**). By 1997, it also had two ministers of state and two Parliamentary Under-Secretaries of State. Its principal subdivisions were the Departments of Finance and Personnel, Economic Development, Education and Environment. During the office's lifetime, successive governments have attempted, unsuccessfully, to find a political formula which would return powers to an authority operating from Ulster. (See **BLOODY SUNDAY**).

DISRUPTION OF THE CHURCH OF SCOTLAND. In 1843, two of every five clergymen in the established (that is, state-recognized) Church of Scotland left to form their own **FREE CHURCH OF SCOTLAND.** The seeds of the dissension had been sown over a century earlier, in 1712, when the UK Parliament in London approved the Patronage Act, which confirmed the right of landlords to appoint ministers to congregations worshipping on their estates. Evangelicals objected to this external control, arguing that church members should have the freedom to choose the men who best met their own needs. Moreover, they rejected the Church of Scotland's willingness to accommodate its beliefs to a changing society and advocated a return to the fundamental Calvinist principles on which the institution had been founded at the time of the Reformation. By 1834, these evangelicals were clearly in the majority, dominating the religious life of Scotland at a time when one-third of the population was attending services every Sunday. In that year, the Church's general assembly (the annual national meeting of clergy and laity) passed a Veto Act giving congregations the right to reject their patron's nominee, but the **COURT OF SESSION** declared it unlawful because it flew in the face of Parliamentary legislation, a ruling which was upheld by the House of Lords (the highest appeal court in the United Kingdom). Moreover, Lord Melbourne's Whig government refused to approve funds for the building of further churches while the dissent simmered. The radicals refused to budge, and, increasingly, a rift appeared inevitable. It came at the general assembly in St Andrew's Church, **EDINBURGH,** in 1843. Dr David Welsh, the retiring moderator (the assembly chairman) announced that he could no longer acknowledge the Church of Scotland as a body independent of secular interference and, accompanied by **THOMAS CHALMERS,** led nearly 200 supporters to the nearby Tanfield Hall, where they formed the Church of Scotland Free. It was an act of considerable courage because, without state support, the breakaway organization faced the task of building new churches and paying the stipends of its clergymen. However, one-third of the members of the Church of Scotland swapped allegiance, as did two-fifths of the ministers, and the Free Church flourished on enthusiasm and the donations of wealthy supporters. For the remainder of the century, the Church of Scotland found itself virtually unrepresented in many areas — and therefore no longer able to claim that it was the church of the Scottish people. It was only in 1929, following the repeal of the Patronage Act in 1874 and Parliamentary recognition, in 1921, of the Church of Scotland's claims to unfettered spiritual jurisdiction, that the divisions were healed when most of the dissident congregations rejoined the established Church.

DISTILLERIES. (See **WHISKY**).

DONALD III. (See **DONALD BANE**).

DONALD BANE (*c.* 1031–1100). The last of the Celtic kings to rule **SCOTIA**, Donald (also known as Donald III) seized the throne on the death of his brother, **MALCOLM III,** in 1093 and attempted to drive out English influences. He was overthrown in 1094 by Duncan (see **DUNCAN II**), Malcolm's son by his first wife, Ingibjorg (daughter of the Earl of **ORKNEY**), but regained control when his nephew was murdered later in the year. Donald, rashly for a man in his sixties, then joined a Northumbrian rebellion against William II of England but was defeated and overthrown by **EDGAR,** second son of Malcolm and **ST MARGARET,** his second wife. Edgar blinded him and kept him in prison until his death.

DOUGLAS, EARLS AND MARQUESSES OF. One of the noble families who exerted considerable influence on the course of Scottish history, the Douglasses take their name from Douglasdale, the ancestral home in Lanarkshire. The two chief branches of the line — the Black Douglas (represented by the Marquessate of Douglas) and the Red Douglas (represented by the Earldom of Angus) — are now merged in the Dukedom of Hamilton and unentailed estates have passed to the Earldom of Home. The first family head mentioned in records is William de Douglas (or Dufglas) whose name appears in documents dating from 1175. His great-great-grandson, James (*c.* 1286–1330), was **ROBERT I**'s most distinguished commander and earned the nickname Black Douglas (some scholars claim that the soubriquet stemmed from his swarthy complexion; others that it was a name given by the English, who feared his frequent raids into their lands in **THE BORDERS**). Before his death, Bruce asked Douglas to carry his heart to the Holy Land, thereby fulfilling the King's vow to take part in a crusade against the Moslems. Sir James left Scotland in 1330 but was killed in a battle with the Saracens in Andalucia (Spain) on August 25. Allegedly, he threw the silver casket containing the heart deep into the enemy ranks, telling it to lead as it had always led, and then spurred his horse after it. Since then, the Douglasses have incorporated a heart on their coat of arms. William Douglas (*c.* 1327–1384) was created first Earl of Douglas in 1358. As a result of an affair with his wife's sister-in-law, Margaret Stewart, Countess of Mar and Angus, he had a son (George, *c.* 1378– *c.* 1402), who became the first Earl of Angus in 1389, starting the Red line of the family. The sixth Earl of Angus (Archibald, *c.* 1489– 1557), married Margaret Tudor (widow of **JAMES IV**) in 1514. Their daughter, Margaret, was the mother of **HENRY DARNLEY**, second husband of **MARY, QUEEN OF SCOTS**, and father of **JAMES VI AND I.**

William (*c.* 1425–52), eighth Earl of Douglas, was Lieutenant-General of Scotland under **JAMES II,** but differences between the two grew. On 22 February 1452, he was stabbed to death in Stirling Castle by the King himself. The title was inherited by his brother, James (1426–91), who fled to England and forfeited the Lordship, which passed to the Earl of Angus. William (1589–1660), the 11th Earl of Angus, was created Marquess of Douglas by Charles I in 1633. His son, William (1634–94), married Anne, Duchess of Hamilton, and, through her, acquired the Hamilton estates, becoming the third Duke of Hamilton in 1660. Archibald, the third Marquess (1694–1761), was made Duke of Douglas in 1703, supporting the government forces against the armies of **JAMES STUART** (the Old Pretender) at the **BATTLE OF SHERIFFMUIR** in 1715. When he died leaving no son to inherit his title, the Dukedom became extinct and the Hamiltons became heirs male of the house of Douglas. Archibald's nephew, also Archibald (1748–1827), was created first Baron Douglas of Douglas in 1790. He had three sons but none left any male issue. The estates passed by marriage to the Earls of Home in 1857.

DOWDING, HUGH CASWELL TREMENHEERE (1882–1970). The strategist behind the Royal Air Force (RAF)'s defence of the United Kingdom against the German Luftwaffe during the Battle of Britain in 1940, Dowding was born in Moffat (Dumfriesshire) on 24 April 1882 to school teacher Arthur Dowding and his wife, Maud. He was educated locally at St Ninian's School and then at Winchester College before going to the Royal Military Academy, Woolwich. In 1900, he joined the Royal Artillery and spent six years in India, but his interest turned to aviation and, in 1913, he gained his pilot's certificate. When the First World War began the following year, he joined the Royal Flying Corps and served with distinction in France, rising to the rank of Brigadier-General in 1917. After the RAF was formed in 1919, Dowding received a permanent commission and commanded bases at home and in Iraq before becoming Director of Training at the Air Ministry (1926) and Commander of Fighting Area, Air Defence of Great Britain (1929). In 1930, he joined the Air Council as the Air Member for Supply and Research and, for six years, was heavily involved with the rapidly changing technology of aircraft design.

When Fighter Command was formed in 1936, Dowding was appointed Commander-in-Chief and, for the next four years, made plans to defend the United Kingdom against an attack from the European mainland. In 1940, he persuaded the War Cabinet to keep his fighter squadrons at home rather than deploy them in support of the army in France and, in the weeks of July and August during which the Germans sent wave after wave of planes across the English Channel, masterminded the use of limited resources in order to prevent the Luftwaffe from achieving supremacy in the air. Under his supervision, administrators designed rotas which gave plane crews as much rest as possible, deployed personnel throughout the south of England, stockpiled materials at strategic sites and constantly monitored radar screens so that London and other major cities could prepare for night-time raids. To a considerable extent, victory in the Battle of Britain was won because of Dowding's tactical skills.

In November 1940, when it was clear that the RAF was in charge of the skies and required a more offensive plan of action, Dowding was replaced by Air Vice-Marshal Sholto Douglas and persuaded by Prime Minister Winston Churchill to visit the USA as a representative of the Ministry of Aircraft Production, but his lack of political acumen, particularly an unwillingness to compromise, limited the success of the expedition. He returned in 1941 and retired the following year, devoting himself to the study of spiritualism and becoming something of a guru to aspiring airmen. In 1943, his contribution to the war effort was rewarded with the title Baron Dowding of Bentley Priory (the name was taken from the location of his operational headquarters) and, following his death at his home in Tunbridge Wells (Kent) on 15 February 1970, his ashes were placed in Westminster Abbey.

DOWNING STREET DECLARATION. (See **ULSTER DECLARATION**).

DUNBAR, BATTLES OF. There were two major battles at Dunbar

(SCOTLAND).

27 April 1296. This struggle brought defeat for **JOHN BALLIOL,** King of Scots, who had French assistance. It resulted in the collapse of Scottish defiance of King Edward I of England, the stripping of crown and lands from Balliol and the taking of Edinburgh by the English.

3–4 September 1650. The Scottish Parliament had declared Charles II the country's lawful King, and Oliver Cromwell began a march on Edinburgh. Six weeks of fruitless pursuit of the Scots followed, during which time Cromwell's forces suffered losses from sickness, until the diminished Parliamentarian army of 11,000 was surrounded at Dunbar by a Scots force of 23,000. The English were victorious, killing some 4,000 Scots and taking 10,000 prisoners, thereby subduing **COVENANTER** resistance north of the border. The Roundhead cavalry was decisive against the Scots, whose muskets failed in the heavy rain that day. Many of the 5,000 captives died of maltreatment and starvation on the long march they endured to Durham, and only 200 survived to be transported to Virginia. (See **ACT OF CLASSES.**)

DUNBLANE MASSACRE (13 March, 1996). Thomas Watt Hamilton (a 43-year-old man with a grudge against authorities which had prevented him from continuing with youth work and who was alleged to have had an unhealthy interest in young boys) walked into a primary school in Dunblane (near **STIRLING**) with four semi-automatic pistols and killed 15 of the pupils, all aged five or six, along with their teacher. He then turned the gun on himself. The incident shocked Britain and led to the introduction of stringent laws limiting access to handguns.

DUNCAN I (c. 1010–40). The son of Bethoc, daughter of King **MALCOLM II** of **SCOTIA,** and her husband, Crinan (the lay abbot of Dunkeld), Duncan was made King of Strathclyde by his maternal grandfather, probably about 1034. He succeeded Malcolm as King of Scotia in the same year, uniting the two kingdoms. Duncan then ruled for six uneasy years, besieging Durham Castle unsuccessfully and twice being beaten in battle by Thorfinn, Earl of **ORKNEY,** before **MACBETH** killed him during (or soon after) a conflict which took place near Elgin.

DUNCAN II (c. 1060–94). The eldest son of **MALCOLM III** and his first wife, Ingiborg of Norway, Duncan was given as hostage to

William the Conqueror in 1072 in order to ensure the Scottish King's good behaviour. He was brought up at the royal court in London, but, in 1094, returned to Scotland and (with English support) overthrew **DONALD BANE,** taking the crown for himself. However, once Donald had fled, Duncan sent his army back south and, later in the year, was murdered, allegedly on the orders of **EDMUND,** his half-brother.

DUNDALK, BATTLES OF. There were two battles at Dundalk, now in the **REPUBLIC OF IRELAND.**

14 October 1318. This was a conflict fought between a Scottish force of 3,000 men led by Edward Bruce, brother of **ROBERT THE BRUCE,** and an Anglo-Irish army led by John de Bermingham, Lord of Louth. Edward had been proclaimed King of Ireland by the people of **ULSTER** in 1316, one year after he had invaded the island. (Following the success at the **BATTLE OF BANNOCKBURN,** the Scots invaded both England and Ireland.) He was killed during the battle and his forces dispersed, his head being sent to King Edward II in London. Ireland suffered economically from the devastation of the Scottish occupation and its scorched-earth policy, and, though the English control on the island was reestablished by this success in battle, it never regained its strength, perhaps marking the beginnings of the slide into Anglo-Irish conflict so marked in later centuries.

November 1689. This engagement, following the **BATTLE OF DUNKELD** and the **BATTLE OF KILLIECRANKIE,** resulted in defeat for a small force of troops loyal to William III of England and led by Duke Friedrich Hermann of Schomberg. The brief success for the forces of James VII and II was later expunged by the **BATTLE OF THE BOYNE.**

DUNDEE. Situated on the north bank of the River Tay, 50 miles north of **EDINBURGH,** Dundee is one of the major commercial centres on the east coast of Scotland and second only to **GLASGOW** in industrial importance. Its name is derived from the **GAELIC** *Dun Taw* or *Dun Daig(h),* which means *the fort on the River Tay.* It is first mentioned in records in 1045 and, by the end of the 12th century, was owned by the Earl of Lennox, brother of King **WILLIAM I.** During the reign of **ROBERT I,** it was confirmed as a royal **BURGH** and, by the end of the medieval period, had become one of the richest settlements in the country, trading with the Netherlands, the Baltic countries, France and Spain. These international contacts brought it into contact with the Protestant ideas carried through Europe at the time of the Reformation, ideas whose ready acceptance among the mercantile classes earned it a reputation as The Scottish Geneva.

Dundee suffered during the civil wars of the 17th century, particularly when General George Monck's Parliamentary army captured the garrison in 1651, killed one-sixth of the inhabitants and carried away much of the town's wealth. It took over a century for prosperity to return, brought by the growth of the linen industry, the expansion of the whaling fleet and the development of banking and other services for the Tayside region. The Industrial Revolution introduced additional sources of employment, particularly jam, jute and journalism. The jam-making was based on the production of soft fruits, such as raspberries and blackcurrants, on the fertile soils north of the Tay (the Keiller family, who owned one of the largest processing plant, deserve enduring fame for introducing marmalade to the civilized world). The jute trade was based on local whale oil and fibres from the Indian subcontinent, with Dundee dominating British production, manufacturing fabrics ranging from sackcloth to high-quality carpets. And, towards the end of the 19th century, D. C. Thomson and Co became a major publishing firm. Its output included newspapers (notably the locally marketed *Dundee Courier* and the national *Sunday Post*, both of which still thrive), magazines (many of them, such as *The People's Friend*, aimed at female readers) and an enormously popular range of children's comics such as *The Beano* and *The Dandy*.

The growth associated with these industries led to Dundee's designation as a city by Queen Victoria in 1889, but commercial success was built on a low-wage economy, with the labour force heavily dominated by women (particularly in the jute and food-processing trades), so the recession of the 1920s brought high unemployment and great poverty. Since the Second World War, however, incomes have risen as the industrial base has diversified and light industry (particularly electronics and activities related to the exploitation of North Sea oil) has increased in importance. Also, there have been considerable improvements in living standards as the local authority has swept away many of the tenement slums. During the 1960s and 1970s, in particular, new building virtually doubled the size of the built-up area of the city without any significant increase in population. At the reorganization of Scottish **LOCAL GOVERNMENT** in 1975, Dundee lost the right to govern its own affairs, becoming simply a district within Tayside region, but its privileges were restored in 1996, when it was made one of the 29 new single-tier authorities. At the time of the 1991 census, it had a population of 165,873 (down 6.7 per cent from 1981).

DUNDEE, VISCOUNT. (See **JOHN GRAHAM**).

DUNKELD, BATTLE OF, 21 August 1689. The town of Dunkeld in the **SCOTTISH HIGHLANDS** was occupied by a force of 1,200 men led by the Earl of Angus, a supporter of William III. It was attacked by an army of 5,000 **JACOBITE** Highlanders, loyal to James II, commanded by Alexander Cannon and fired by the recent success at the **BATTLE OF KILLIECRANKIE.** At first, the invaders were successful in fierce hand-to-hand street fighting, but eventually the occupiers, with their leaders killed and almost out of ammunition, set fire to the buildings which sheltered the Highlanders, causing a rout. The battle marked the turning point for the Jacobite advance and the end of major Highland support for the Jacobite cause.

DUNLOP, JOHN BOYD (1840–1921). The inventor of the pneumatic tyre, Dunlop was born in Dreghorn (Scotland) on 5 February 1840. His father was a farmer but young John's health was too delicate for the rigours of agricultural work so, after attending the local school, he was allowed to continue his education at Irvine's Academy in **EDINBURGH.** He qualified as a veterinary surgeon in 1859 and, eight years later, opened a practice in **BELFAST** and began to raise a family. In 1887, his nine-year-old son, John, complained of being jolted and jarred as he rode his tricycle, with its solid rubber tyres, on the streets around his home. Dunlop attempted to solve the problem by fastening air tubes to wooden rims and fitting them over the rear wheels, much to his son's satisfaction. The improvement also impressed local businessmen and, in December 1888, Dunlop patented his invention. The following year, with tubes made to his specification in Edinburgh, and the cooperation of Edlin and Company of Belfast (manufacturers of the tricycle), he founded the business which was to become the Dunlop Rubber Company Ltd, producing tyres for bicycles and, later, for cars and other forms of transport. A patent for a vulcanized pneumatic rubber tyre had, in fact, been taken out by another Scot, Robert William Thomson, in 1845, but it was believed that production costs would be too high to generate mass sales and the idea had apparently been forgotten by the time Dunlop tried to improve his child's toy. Thomson's patent invalidated

Dunlop's but, even so, the firm prospered through developments to valves, rims and other elements of vehicle wheels. Most of the financial investment came from William Harvey du Cros (in 1889) and Ernest Terah Hooley (in 1896) so Dunlop himself derived little financial benefit from the expansion. In 1892, he moved to Dublin, where he died on 23 October 1921.

DUNS SCOTUS, JOHN (*c*. 1265–1308). One of the greatest of medieval scholars, Duns Scotus was probably born in Duns (Scotland) and became a Franciscan monk about 1280. He was ordained as a priest at St Andrew's Church, Northampton (England), on 17 April 1291 and, over the next five years, lived and taught in the universities at Oxford, Paris and (probably) Cambridge. He was awarded a doctorate at Paris in 1305 and, two years later, was appointed Professor at Cologne. His major works are considered to be *Opus Oxoniense* (his Oxford lectures, also known as the *Ordinatio*), *Opus Pariense* (his Paris lectures, as recorded by a student but probably revised by Duns Scotus himself), *Tractatus de Primo Principio* and *Quaestiones Quodlibetales*. These works were in various stages of completion at the time of his death and were collected and edited by his colleagues and disciples (the *Ordinatio*, for example, is derived from over 100 codices and appeared in over 30 editions, the first in 1472).

Devout, and with an acute intellect, Duns Scotus thrived on disputation, adopting a rigorously rational form of debate which found many admirers. He argued that there is a world, external to the mind, which human beings can perceive without recourse to the five senses (a philosophical position now known as Scholastic Realism). Moreover, he believed that the will of every individual was essentially free, the summit of human perfection. And God, he argued, was logical, creating a logical universe and revealed in the beings he created.

Such views attracted adherents throughout Europe and Duns Scotus became the accepted leader of Franciscan scholarship. Long after his death in Cologne (Germany), on 8 November 1308, his reasoning continued to be a source of disputation in university classrooms and learned treatises, his philosophy contrasted, in particular, with Thomism (the arguments of Thomas Aquinas, who was followed by the Dominicans). The Scotists were sometimes labelled *Dunses* because of their conservatism (hence, adding *dunce* to the English language) but, ultimately, many of Scotus's tenets (such as that of the immaculate conception) were to become accepted Roman Catholic orthodoxy.

DUPPLIN MOOR, BATTLE OF. 11 August 1332. In the summer of 1332, **EDWARD BALLIOL,** encouraged by Edward III of England (who provided spearmen and archers) and supported by nobles whose estates had been forfeited by **ROBERT I** because they had assisted English efforts to subjugate Scotland, mounted a campaign to win the Scottish throne. At Dupplin Moor, near Perth, he met, and defeated, a Scots army led by the Donald, Earl of Mar and guardian of the realm during the minority of **DAVID II.** Mar was among the dead, and, six weeks later, Balliol was crowned King at Scone.

—E—

EASTER RISING, 24–29 April 1916. One of the most serious events in the history of the Irish **HOME RULE** movement, the rising involved an armed force of 2,000 nationalists drawn from James Connolly's Citizen Army and Patrick Pearse's **IRISH REPUBLICAN BROTHERHOOD.** By 1916, the older Brotherhood was beginning to be overshadowed by the growing **SINN FEIN** movement, and these events could be seen as the last of the old-style Irish rebellions. The insurrection began on Easter Monday, when many British troops were on leave. Dublin's General Post Office on O'Connell Street was quickly taken, and Pearse proclaimed the establishment of an Irish Republic, with himself as head of the provisional government. Bitter fighting took place in the streets as British reinforcements arrived, but, within a week, the rising was put down, the rebels surrendering without provoking the countrywide revolt they had intended. Fifteen leaders were executed, 450 people were killed, 3,500 were arrested and 2,000 deported. Because the rebellion occurred during the First World War, those involved were treated as traitors. Nevertheless, the harsh treatment meted out to those who organized the attempted coup turned the people who died into martyrs and thus did much to rally support for the nationalist movement during **THE TROUBLES.**

EDGAR (*c.* 1074–1107). The second son of **MALCOLM III** and **ST MARGARET,** Edgar, with the support of King William II of England, gained the Scottish throne by overthrowing **DONALD BANE** in 1097. He established a base on the castle rock in **EDINBURGH,** probably because of the site's defensive qualities and its strategic location between the **SCOTTISH HIGHLANDS** (where he had limited power) and areas under English control. Edgar ceded the **HEB-**

RIDES and the Kinytre peninsula to the Norwegians in order to prevent invasion, and ruled as William's vassal, welcoming the Norman lifestyle and patterns of organization into his Celtic kingdom. He never married and was succeeded by his brother, **ALEXANDER I.**

EDINBURGH. Scotland's capital was founded by the Celtic Gododdin tribe, who built a fortress on the extinct volcano which was later to become the site of a medieval castle. Located between the southern shores of the **RIVER FORTH** and the scarp slope of the Pentland Hills, the city lies 380 miles north of London and 45 miles east of **GLASGOW.** Development began during the reign of **MALCOLM III,** who built a hunting lodge on Castle Rock. After 1128, when **DAVID I** (Malcolm's son) founded an Augustinian abbey at **HOLYROOD,** a mile to the east, houses spread down the sloping ridge between the two foci (the road connecting the two sites is now known as the Royal Mile). The protection afforded by the castle, virtually impregnable on three sides, and the periodic presence of royalty, attracted merchants and craftsmen to the town, even though control changed hands several times as English monarchs fought to assert overlordship and the Scots fought to establish the country's independence. In those days, the capital of Scotland was wherever the sovereign happened to be, but, during the reign of **JAMES II,** who had been born and crowned at Holyrood, Edinburgh emerged as the most important town in the kingdom and the usual location for meetings of Parliament. That growth in status was accompanied by a growth in population, but the limitations of the topography and the need for protection meant that the settlement had to expand upwards rather than outwards. Stone tenements as high as 11 stories crowded together, separated by narrow alleyways (known as wynds). In such conditions, infection spread readily and the Old Town became a foul, foetid slum. The problems worsened after the **UNION OF THE CROWNS** in 1603 because many of the wealthy followed James VI and I to London, but, even so, the city was the focus of the **SCOTTISH ENLIGHTENMENT,** the flowering of the arts during the 18th century which was to earn Edinburgh a reputation as the 'Athens of the North'.

In 1767, the **BURGH** authorities held a competition to design a new suburb to the north of the medieval settlement. The winning designs, submitted by **JAMES CRAIG,** were hardly imaginative, but they appealed to the fashions of Georgian Britain and resulted in the construction of wide streets, creating a New Town with gracious squares and low-density living which contrasted with the overcrowding and tortuous lanes of the medieval city. Victorian growth added suburbs to the west, south and east and the appointment of Dr Henry Littlejohn as the city's first medical officer of health in 1862 brought improvements to housing, sanitary conditions and health standards in the Old Town.

During the 20th century, Edinburgh has strengthened its role as a service centre (in the mid-1990s, the services provided jobs for more than three-quarters of the employed population). It is the major British financial centre outside London and has three universities (the University of Edinburgh, Heriot-Watt University and Napier University) as well as technical colleges and other educational institutions. Scotland's principal courts of law are located in the city, as is central government's **SCOTTISH OFFICE** and it will be the site of the new Scottish parliament (see **DEVOLUTION**). Tourism is a major source of income and is an important employer. (See **LOCAL GOVERNMENT: SCOTLAND**). There is little heavy industry so manufacturing is confined to brewing, printing, electronics and related products. At the reorganization of local government in 1975, Edinburgh lost its status as a county and became a district within Lothian Region. However, in 1996 it was reconstituted as one of 29 new unitary authorities. At the time of the 1991 census, it had a population of 418,914 (down by 1.5 per cent since 1981).

EDINBURGH, TREATY OF. Two important treaties were signed in Edinburgh.

_1328._ During the autumn and early winter of 1327, emissaries from the court of King Edward III of England visited **ROBERT THE BRUCE** in **EDINBURGH**, hoping to persuade him to abandon his military campaigns in their northern territories. On 17 March 1328, Bruce agreed to a peace, provided that the English withdrew all claims to sovereignty over Scotland and recognized Robert as its King. The treaty (ratified by the English Parliament at Northampton on 4 May and sometimes known as the Treaty of Northampton) was ostensibly an agreement between equals, but the English were well aware that they were surrendering and termed the arrangement the 'Shameful Peace'.

_1560._ Under the terms of this treaty, England and France agreed to withdraw their troops from Scotland. Also, **MARY, QUEEN OF SCOTS,** and her husband, Francis II of France, were required to remove the arms of the English Crown from their heraldry as a consequence of the Scots negotiators' acceptance that Elizabeth I was the legitimate Queen of England. Mary refused to ratify the document, but, even so, it formally brought the **AULD ALLIANCE** between Scotland and France to an end though, after the **JACOBITE REBELLIONS,** Paris continued to provide a refuge for supporters of the **STUART** cause.

EDINBURGH INTERNATIONAL FESTIVAL. One of the major events on the world cultural calendar, the **EDINBURGH** Festival is a celebration of the arts held for three weeks in late August and early September each year. It was the brainchild of Rudolph Bing, general manager of Glyndebourne Opera, who became increasingly convinced, as the Second World War dragged on, that the European arts scene would take many years to recover from the conflict. Edinburgh, he believed, had an opportunity to mount an event which would aid the process of reconciliation. He managed to persuade the **LORD PROVOST** of the city that his plan was viable, and, in 1945, the local authority allocated £20,000 to support the venture. Contributions from businesses and individuals swelled the fund, so, in 1947, Bing was able to launch his first programme of music and drama, including foreign companies (such as the Vienna Philharmonic Orchestra) as well as British groups (like the Old Vic Theatre Company from London) and organizations based in Scotland (the Scottish National Orchestra, for example). With over 180,000 tickets sold at a time of postwar austerity, the jamboree was a major success and its immediate future assured. Ian Hunter took over as Artistic Director from 1950 until 1955, adding fine arts to the portfolio, with major exhibitions of the works of Cezanne, Degas, Gaugin and Renoir, and his successors stamped their own personalities on the list of offerings — Robert Ponsonby (1956–60) brought over the first Russian orchestra in 1960, Peter Diamand (1966–79) developed a strong emphasis on opera and Frank Dunlop (1984–91) strengthened the theatrical component as well as attempting to provide more material aimed at a mass audience.

Increasingly, groups which were not part of the official programme turned up in the city and staged productions in churches, school halls, youth centres and any other accommodation they could find. Initially, the organizers of the official events tried to discourage such independent activity, but the Festival Fringe, as it became known, proved unstoppable. By 1997, there were more than 500 companies offering shows at over 100 venues and operating a central booking service. Many of the performers are from university dramatic and music groups, and many of their performances, particularly the satirical ones, get radio and television coverage. There is also an International Film Festival, an International Jazz Festival, a Military Tattoo (every two years) and, a Book Festival, all held alongside the official festival. The events bring much tourist income to the city, but there are regular complaints that local residents are inconvenienced and that the great bulk of the programme is too highbrow (and too expensive) for ordinary citizens. Late in 1995, Brian McMaster, who had taken over as artistic director in 1992, had his appointment confirmed for an additional five-year term after the **SCOTTISH ARTS COUNCIL** praised the Festival productions. Accounts showed that he had attracted increased sponsorship from commercial organizations.

EDMUND (? - ?). The third son of King **MALCOLM III** of Scotland and **ST MARGARET,** his second wife, Edmund swore allegiance to his uncle, **DONALD BANE,** who succeeded his father in 1093. As reward, he was given Lothian to rule. The following year, he was allegedly responsible for the murder of his half-brother, who had ousted Donald and ruled **SCOTIA** as **DUNCAN II.** Donald seized the opportunity to return to power but, in 1097, was dethroned by **EDGAR,** Edmund's older brother. Edmund retired to a monastery, where he died and, in accordance with his wishes, was buried in chains as a symbol of remorse.

EDUCATION: NORTHERN IRELAND. The structure of educational provision in **ULSTER** is similar to that in England and Wales but has been much affected by the religious denominations' control of schools. The contest for the souls as well as the brains of Ireland's youth was evident as early as the beginning of the 19th century, when Roman Catholics were offered cheap — or even free — education in Church of England and nonconformist classrooms provided they attended Protestant religious education sessions. Following the partition of the island in 1922, the **ULSTER UNIONIST PARTY** government at **STORMONT** tried to create an integrated system of schooling but, by that time, sectarian opinion was deeply entrenched and the scheme was dropped. Instead, the Roman Catholic community was allowed to retain ownership and control of its own educational institutions with the understanding that it would raise some of the capital expenditure and accept state-nominated representatives on its boards of governors. All running costs were to be met from the public purse. The Protestant groups, by contrast, agreed to transfer their schools to the state, which would meet all the running and capital costs and also make appointments to the governing bodies. In effect, the deal meant that Catholic children would be educated in institutions controlled by the Roman Catholic church, leaving the other schools essentially Protestant in ethos. Moreover, because Catholic schools were only partly funded by the government, they frequently lacked facilities regularly found in other schools.

The Education Act of 1947, which introduced compulsory secondary schooling and contained the major elements of legislation passed for England and Wales three years earlier, preserved the religious divide. At the age of 11, children would take an examination and the most able 20 per cent would attend grammar schools. The rest would go to intermediate or technical schools. However, parents, whose sons and daughters failed to reach the required standard could pay for their children to attend institutions with an academic bias and a far higher proportion of Protestants was able to find the necessary funds. Catholics, therefore, dominated the vocational secondaries but, even so, the 1969 **CAMERON COMMISSION** was able to claim that the 1947 act had led to the expansion of the Catholic middle class, which, in turn, had provided a foundation for the civil rights movement because it was "less ready to acquiesce in the situation of assumed (or established) inferiority and discrimination than was the case in the past".

Opinion polls have consistently suggested that about half of all parents would prefer their children to be educated in religiously integrated schools, but it was not until 1989, under the terms of the Education Reform (Northern Ireland) Order, that the government made formal provision for state funding of nonsegregated institutions. In practice, such schools are only recognized when local people establish them and demonstrate that they have a long-term future so, by 1995, only 28 of the province's 1,300 schools were integrated. In addition, the conversion to comprehensive (that is, nonselective) education, which took place in the rest of the United Kingdom during the 1950s and 1960s, did not occur in Ulster so Northern Ireland is the only extensive area of Britain where children are segregated for schooling on the dual grounds of religion and intellectual ability.

Funding for Northern Ireland's schools is provided by the Department of Education for Northern Ireland and channelled to institutions through five education and library boards, which have responsibility for specific areas of the province (see Map 7, page xxi). Children begin compulsory education at the age of four (a year earlier than their peers in the rest of the UK) and may leave when they reach their 16th birthday. The first seven years are spent at primary school, the remainder at secondary school. About 60 per cent of the secondary pupils are in grammar schools, where they follow an academic curriculum. The remainder, in the nongrammar secondaries, receive a broader education, which includes an emphasis on technology, business studies and other applied subjects in accordance with the provisions of the 1947 Act. At the age of 16, pupils from all secondary schools take a range of examinations in order to gain General Certificate of Secondary Education (GCSE) qualifications. About 72 per cent remain in some form of education after they reach the minimum leaving age in order to attempt further qualifications, notably the Advanced Level (or A-Level) exams, which are necessary for entry to higher education.

There are two universities in Ulster. Queen's University, established in 1845, is based in **BELFAST.** The University of Ulster, created in 1984 through the merger of the New University of Ulster and Ulster Polytechnic, has campuses at Belfast, Coleraine, Jordanstown and **LONDONDERRY.**

The vast majority of children are educated within the state system. There are only 21 independent schools, with some 950 pupils, in Northern Ireland and no privately-funded universities.

EDUCATION: SCOTLAND. The Scots system of education is different both in history and structure from that in the rest of the United Kingdom. Its roots lie in the forces which fanned the Reformation, causing a social upheaval in Scotland much greater than that in other parts of the British Isles. In 1561, **JOHN KNOX** called for a mass education system which would teach children about Protestantism, and, in 1646, the **THREE ESTATES,** supporting the **CHURCH OF SCOTLAND,** passed legislation which required every landowner, without exception or excuse, to pay for parish schools. Such idealistic schemes could not be realised in 16th and 17th century conditions, but, even so, they helped give learning and scholarship a place of distinction in Scottish cultural life.

The Industrial Revolution led to the growth of towns during the 19th century, especially on the coalfields of central Scotland, and a series of measures was adopted to ensure that children in these settlements received some schooling. The most important item of legislation was the 1872 Education Act, which introduced compulsory education for all youngsters aged five to 13 and established school boards, consisting of elected representatives of the local community. A further act, in 1912, transferred administrative responsibilities from the boards to ad hoc authorities based on the counties and the cities of **ABERDEEN, DUNDEE, EDINBURGH, GLASGOW** and Leith. In 1929, the **LOCAL GOVERNMENT** (Scotland) Act passed control of public education to the county councils.

In 1947, the school-leaving age was raised to 16 and, in 1962, the Education (Scotland) Act consolidated earlier legislation, making the local authorities responsible for meeting educational needs within their areas and the **SECRETARY OF STATE FOR SCOTLAND** (through the Scottish Education Department) responsible for supervizing the work of the schools insisted that adequate provision was made for all pupils.

In 1997, there were 3,924 schools in Scotland, the vast majority (3,798) funded by local authorities. Ten were grant-aided (that is, they received financial support directly from the **SCOTTISH OFFICE**) and 116 were independent, depending for income on fees charged to pupils but subject to inspection by the state in order to ensure that standards were maintained.

Children begin formal education in primary school at the age of five and transfer to the secondary sector at the age of 12. In the 1950s and 1960s, selection for these secondaries on the basis of academic ability was replaced by a comprehensive (that is, nonselective) system of allocation. The switch to comprehensive education occurred in England at the same time but, for political reasons, was much more acceptable to the Scots and is now universal. The content of the curriculum is not prescribed by statute (as it is in England), but, at the age of 16 (in their fourth year of secondary schooling), all pupils take the Standard Grade examinations of the Scottish Certificate of Education (SCE), set by the Scottish Examination Board.

Pupils may leave school when they reach their 16th birthday but about 25 per cent remain in full-time education and follow a rather more broad course of studies than is common in the rest of the United Kingdom. At 17, they take Higher Grade SCE examinations, which form the basis of university entry qualifications. About 44 per cent of Scotland's young people go on to degree level studies, compared with 32 per cent in England.

There are 13 universities in Scotland: **EDINBURGH** and **GLASGOW** each have three, **ABERDEEN** and **DUNDEE,** two. The others are in Paisley, **ST ANDREWS** and **STIRLING**. (See **BOOK OF DISCIPLINE**).

EDUCATION: WALES. Responsibility for provision of public education in Wales is vested in the **SECRETARY OF STATE FOR WALES,** with the bulk of the finance coming from the **WELSH**

OFFICE and the local authorities (see **LOCAL GOVERNMENT: WALES**). The structure of the provision is very similar to that in England, but Welsh education has much stronger roots in nonconformist religious ideals, which stress respect for education and literacy. Some of the first schools in the principality were established by Methodist and Baptist Ministers, others by the Society for the Propagation of Christian Knowledge (which founded 96 establishments in Wales between 1700 and 1740). During the 19th century, in particular, learning was viewed as an escape route from poverty, but many authorities considered the **WELSH** language an obstacle to the acquisition of culture and, partly because of that attitude (which forced children to acquire fluency in English in order to succeed), levels of attainment remained low even though a network of elementary schools was created by the Liberal government in 1870.

In 1881, a report by the Aberdare Committee, established to inquire into secondary and higher education in Wales, revealed that only 1,540 children were getting a grammar school education, with a further 2,946 in various private institutions. Armed with that information, Welsh MPs agitated for an increase in provision at all levels and, in 1883–84, university colleges were founded at Bangor and **CARDIFF.** Then, in 1889, the Intermediate Education Act paved the way for the creation of publicly funded secondary schools.

Attempts by Prime Minister Arthur Balfour's Conservative government to reform the structure of educational funding through the Education Act of 1902 met with enormous resistance from nonconformists because the terms of the legislation provided that the cost of running Church of England schools would be paid by the rates (the local property taxes). At the 1904 local authority elections, opponents of the measure gained majorities on every Welsh county council, and the government passed the Education (Local Authority Default) Act — which quickly became known as the Coercion of Wales Act — in an attempt to force the councils to conform by threatening to deprive them of grants if they continued to resist. However, in 1905, Balfour fell, and, in the aftermath of its General Election victory, the incoming Liberal Party administration announced that it would not implement the Coercion Act.

The period immediately after the First World War brought increased participation in secondary education (the number of children aged over 11 and getting some formal classroom instruction rose from 24,000 in 1918 to 40,000 in 1930) and that, in turn, led to greater demand for further and higher education (for example, the University of Wales's complement of students doubled between 1913 and 1930 and more teachers were produced than the Welsh schools could employ). Also, in the wake of a report by the Welsh department of the board of education, published in 1927, more instruction was conducted in Welsh.

Following the passage of the 1944 Education Act, many of the changes in Welsh education paralleled those occurring in England. However, there was a significant increase in the number of schools using Welsh as the medium of instruction. By 1970, 41 primary schools were using the language for all their teaching and, as the children grew older, secondary schools followed suit. The introduction of a national curriculum, a result of the passage of the 1988 Education Reform Act, served to standardize lesson content, and, in addition, provided for compulsory instruction in Welsh (it is government policy that, by 1999, all pupils will be taught the language throughout the period of compulsory schooling).

The great majority of Welsh schools are state-funded (there are only 64 independent schools in the principality). Children start their education in primary schools at the age of five. At 11, they transfer to secondary schools, 99.6 per cent of which are comprehensive (that is, they do not select pupils on the basis of ability). Pupils may leave when they reach their 16th birthday. Some 3,600 youngsters with special educational needs attend schools designed to help overcome physical, mental and other forms of disability.

There are two universities — the University of Wales (which is a federal institution with colleges at Aberystwyth, Bangor, **CARDIFF,** Lampeter and Swansea) and the University of Glamorgan (which converted from polytechnic status in 1992). (See **THOMAS CHARLES; CIRCULATING SCHOOLS; GRIFFITH JONES; WELSH KNOT**).

EDWARDIAN CONQUEST, 1276–84. The Normans attempted to subjugate Wales soon after they took control of southern England in 1066, but the mountainous landscape and widely spread settlement system made conquest difficult. Their influence in the south was great, but native leaders, such as **LLEWELYN AB IORWERTH** and **LLEWELYN AP GRUFFYD,** held the north and, eventually, united Wales into a single political entity. In 1276, however, Edward I of England began a campaign to conquer his Celtic neighbours. A rebellion by the Welsh in 1282 led to the death of Llewelyn ap Gruffyd and the crushing of resistance, as local rulers transferred allegience to the English. By 1283, Edward was in control, building a series of spectacular castles (such as that at **HARLECH**), both as a means of establishing towns populated by his countrymen and as a means of military domination. The **STATUTE OF RHUDDLAN** (1284) extended English legal and administrative principles to the area, and, in 1301, Edward (the eldest son of Edward I) was given the title Prince of Wales. In effect, Wales and England became one country, though formal union came only in 1543. (See **UNION OF WALES AND ENGLAND**).

EISTEDDFOD. In **WELSH,** *eisteddfod* means *sitting, session* or *assembly.* During the Middle Ages, eisteddfodau — festivals of literature and music — were regular events in Wales, patronised by bards who competed against each other according to rules governing the oral traditions of story-telling and alliterative poetry. By the 18th century, they had degenerated into drunken gatherings in taverns, but, in 1789, were revived as formal events by the **GWYNEDDIGION,** an organization founded in London by expatriot Welshmen in 1770. From 1819, provincial eisteddfodau were introduced by local societies and, in the same year, **IOLO MORGANWG** linked his annual *gorsedd* (an assembly of bards) to the national eisteddfod. The **SOCIETY OF CYMMRODORION** provided patronage and administrative support from 1820, and, in succeeding decades, the events became major foci of Welsh cultural life. In 1947, the national eisteddfod was given a permanent home at Llangollen and is now heavily subsidised by state funds, with significant media coverage, particularly for the announcement of the winner of the annual bardic competition. (See **CELTIC REVIVAL**).

EMERGENCY PROVISIONS ACT, THE NORTHERN IRELAND, 1991. This act of Parliament brought together several earlier legislative measures designed to deal with aspects of **THE TROUBLES,** including sanctions against terrorists and provision for members of the security forces to stop and search people in **ULSTER.** It has been renewed annually since 1991 and remains a bone of contention with nationalists. (See **DIRECT RULE**).

ENCYCLOPAEDIA BRITANNICA. One of the world's major works of reference, *Encyclopaedia Britannica* was first published in **EDINBURGH** in a series of parts between 1768 and 1771. It was financed by "a society of gentlemen in Scotland" (that is, by subscribers), engraved by Andrew Bell and printed by Colin Macfarquhar. William Smellie is generally believed to have been the first editor, but there have been claims that James Tytler, who edited the second edition (published in parts between 1777 and 1784), was also responsible for the first. Also, the preface to the third edition (published in parts between 1788 and 1797) refers to Macfarquhar as the editor of the first two editions and the first half of the third. *Encyclopaedia Britannica* broke new ground by including essays on specific issues in the same alphabetical sequence as short articles explaining technical terms and other matters. In 1901 (after nine editions), ownership transferred to the United States when publishers Horace E. Hooper and Walter M. Jackson bought the rights to the publication from A. and C. Black. In 1920, it was purchased by Sears, Roebuck and Co. and, in 1923, by publisher William J. Cox (in conjunction with Hooper's widow). Sears, Roebuck bought the company again in 1928. In 1932, Cox resigned as publisher, and Elkan Harrison Powell (vice president of Sears, Roebuck) replaced him. In 1941, the rights were transferred to the University of Chicago, and two years later a new board of directors was formed with William Benton, vice president of the university, as chairman. Robert M. Hutchins, president of the university, was appointed chairman of a board of editors. The headquarters of the *Encyclopaedia* based in Chicago. *Britannica* is now in its 15th edition and is published in 32 volumes. Editorial advice is supplied by the faculty of the University of Chicago, supplemented by advice from committees whose members are drawn from 22 other universities worldwide. The entries are prepared by more than 4,000 authors from over 100 countries.

ENGAGERS. On 26 December 1647, representatives of one of the **COVENANTER** factions signed an engagement (or treaty) with King Charles I, who had been deprived of his English throne by the Parliamentarians, led by Oliver Cromwell. Under the terms of the agreement, Charles recognized the **SOLEMN LEAGUE AND COVENANT** and agreed to establish Presbyterianism in England for a trial period of three years. In return, the Scots promised military aid to help him regain his throne. However, although the engagers had widespread support from noble families, they were opposed by the **CHURCH OF SCOTLAND,** which wanted the Presbyterian form of ecclesiastical organization established permanently. The dispute affected the morale of the army sent to help Charles, and it was heavily defeated at the Battle of Preston (17–19 August 1648).

ERSKINE, JOHN (1675–1732). The leader of the rebel forces during the first **JACOBITE REBELLION,** Erskine was born in Alloa in February 1675, the son of Charles, Earl of Mar, and his wife, Mary. He succeeded to the earldom on his father's death in 1689. Nicknamed 'Bobbing John' because of his frequent changes of political allegiance, he was, initially, a strong supporter of the **TREATY OF UNION** between Scotland and England (1707), and was chosen as one of the Scots peers appointed to the new Parliament of Great Britain, but argued for its repeal in 1713. He was appointed Secretary of State for Scotland the same year, and, when Queen Anne died in 1714, Erskine sent her successor (George I) a fawning letter offering his continuing services. George had other ideas and dismissed Erskine, who promptly left for Scotland. On 6 September 1715, he raised the standard of the exiled **STUARTS** at Braemar and called on **JACOBITE**s to relieve their native country from "oppression and a foreign yoke too heavy for us and our posterity to bear". The clan chiefs of the **SCOTTISH HIGHLANDS** rallied to the cause despite rather than because of Mar — motivated as much by hatred of the union as by loyalty to **JAMES STUART,** the Old Pretender. On 9th September, they marched south, with Erskine at their head, and captured Perth a week later. The next logical move would have been to **STIRLING,** where the castle was held for the King by 5,000 troops under the **DUKE OF ARGYLL.** However, Mar, whose force numbered some 10,000, stayed put, hoping that his army would be augmented by supporters from France and England and listening to his aides dispute over strategy. Eventually, on 10 November, he broke camp and, three days later, met Argyll at Sheriffmuir (see **BATTLE OF SHERIFFMUIR**). The Jacobites outnumbered the Hanoverians by nearly three to one, but Mar's inept leadership negated that advantage. After some hesitation, he led a haphazard, ill-disciplined charge over ground determined by the enemy. The result was a shambles, with no clear victor, and Mar retreated to his headquarters at Perth. Morale at a low ebb, the Jacobites drifted back to their homes in the glens, and, by the time James Stuart arrived at Peterhead from France on 22 December, Bobbing John had only a few hundred men left. The Pretender returned to the continent disillusioned and accompanied by Mar, who continued to scheme both with the Jacobites and with representatives of the British government but was trusted by neither. Ultimately, he abandoned the Stuart cause in 1725 and died at Aix-la-Chapelle (France) in May 1732.

EWING, WINIFRED MARGARET (1929–). Mrs Ewing led the **SCOTTISH NATIONAL PARTY** (SNP) to a by-election victory at Hamilton in 1967, spearheading a revival in nationalist fortunes. Born in **GLASGOW**, Winnie Ewing was the daughter of wholesale stationer George Woodburn and his wife, Christina. She was educated in the city at Queen's Park School and Glasgow University, where she studied law. After qualifying as a solicitor in 1952, she lectured at the Scottish College of Commerce for some years but, in 1956, opened her own legal practice. Increasingly, she got involved in the nationalist movement and, when the Hamilton seat became vacant in 1967, was adopted as the SNP candidate. At the General Election the previous year, Tom Fraser had held the seat for Labour with a 16,500-vote majority in a straight fight with the Conservatives. However, Fraser resigned when he was appointed chairman of the North of Scotland Hydro-Electric Board and the nationalists, encouraged by opinion polls showing their rising popularity, decided to contest the vacancy. Winnie Ewing was the ideal representative — articulate, personable and a product of the west of Scotland — and her supporters, who included large numbers of young people, campaigned enthusiastically, but, even so, it was a surprise to many commentators when local voters deserted their traditional Labour Party allegiance and carried her to the House of Commons with a majority of 1,799. As the SNP's first MP for over 20 years, she immediately became the standard-bearer for the party, expected to outline the official view on all issues, appearing regularly on television and radio and writing columns for daily and weekly newspapers. Her popularity undoubtedly enhanced the SNP's image and, even though Labour recaptured Hamilton at the 1970 General Election, she won Moray and Nairn in 1974, by which time the nationalists were polling 30 per cent of the Scottish vote and sending 11 MPs to Westminster. Mrs Ewing became a Member of the European Parliament in 1975, following the United Kingdom's successful application to join the European Community, and gained the highlands and islands for the SNP in the first direct elections to that Parliament in 1979. Since then, she has increased her majorities at successive polls, eventually gaining 58.4 per cent of the total vote in 1994. In 1979, she was elected SNP president.

—**F**—

FALAISE, TREATY OF, 1174. This treaty between King **WILLIAM I** of Scotland, and King Henry II of England followed the former's capture at the Battle of Alnwick on 13 June. William had supported rebel English barons in their campaign against Henry and had claimed Northumberland for himself. Under the terms of the treaty, which was named after the French town where the Scottish King was held in exile, William was forced to swear allegiance to the English Crown.

FALKIRK, BATTLES OF. There were two major battles at Falkirk. 22 July 1298. King Edward I of England, with a force of 15,000 men, overcame a Scottish army, led by **WILLIAM WALLACE,** in a battle in which the English cavalry and longbowmen (archers) proved decisive against the enemy spearmen, avenging their defeat at the **BATTLE OF STIRLING BRIDGE.**
17 January 1746. The **JACOBITE** forces of the Young Pretender, **CHARLES EDWARD STUART,** gained a victory over the royalist army, commanded by Henry Hawley, but that was their final success in the second **JACOBITE REBELLION.** Three months later, they were routed at the **BATTLE OF CULLODEN.**

FALKLAND PALACE. Located in the former royal **BURGH** of Falkland, in central Scotland, the palace was a favourite residence of the **STUART** kings, who used it as a base for hunting in the forests of Fife. It was built between 1501 and 1541 by **JAMES IV** and his son, **JAMES V** (who died there in 1542, shortly after his defeat by the English at the **BATTLE OF SOLWAY MOSS**). James V's daughter, **MARY, QUEEN OF SCOTS,** spent some of the happiest days in a tragic life at Falkland, hawking, hunting deer and walking in the gardens. The east wing of the palace (which houses the King's bedchamber and the Queen's room) was partly destroyed by fire in 1654, while Oliver Cromwell's Parliamentarian troops were in residence. Only the foundations of the north wing remain. However, the south range (incorporating the chapel royal) was rebuilt by the Marquess of Bute, who acquired the property in 1887. The palace, which houses one of the few royal tennis courts in Britain, is now owned by Queen Elizabeth II but managed by the **NATIONAL TRUST FOR SCOTLAND** and open to visitors between April and October. In 1970, the building, along with its gardens and orchard and the adjoining streets of the royal burgh, became the first urban conservation area to be designated in Scotland under the terms of the 1967 Civic Amenities Act.

FAULKNER, ARTHUR BRIAN DEANE (1921–77). The last Prime Minister of Northern Ireland before the British government imposed

DIRECT RULE on the province from London, Faulkner was the son of businessman James Faulkner and his wife, Nora. He was educated at Elm Park School (County Armagh) and the College of St Columba at Rathfarnham (in the Irish Republic), then pursued a management career in the textile industry before gaining election to **STORMONT** as the **ULSTER UNIONIST PARTY** representative for East Down in 1949. In 1956, he was appointed government Chief Whip and Parliamentary Secretary at the Ministry of Finance and, three years later, became Minister for Home Affairs. In 1963, he moved to the Ministry of Commerce and worked hard to attract investment to **ULSTER** but found Prime Minister **TERENCE O'NEILL** a difficult superior and, in 1969, resigned in protest at the creation of the **CAMERON COMMISSION** inquiry into the activities of the civil rights movement. Later that year, O'Neill stepped down, and Faulkner lost his party's leadership election by only one vote to **JAMES CHICHESTER-CLARK.** He returned to the government as Minister of Development, responsible for carrying out a programme of local authority reform, but, on 20 March 1971, Chichester-Clark, disheartened by London's refusal to increase security measures in the face of escalating violence in the province, stepped down.

Three days later, Faulkner became Prime Minister. Despite moderate views and an attempt to placate the civil rights movement by including a Roman Catholic in his cabinet, he failed to find a means of stopping conflict between the religious communities and inflamed his opponents by introducing internment without trial only five months after taking office. In March of the following year, the British government disbanded the Northern Ireland Parliament and introduced direct rule from Westminster. Faulkner, who fully believed that such drastic measures would never be taken, initially refused to play any part in the move, claiming that Ulster could not be treated like a "coconut colony". By 1973, he had mellowed sufficiently to lead the Unionist team in the talks that led to the **SUNNINGDALE AGREEMENT,** which proposed a **NORTHERN IRELAND POWER SHARING EXECUTIVE** to govern the province and the formation of a Council of Ireland, including representatives from the Republic. Most loyalists were unwilling to approve of the Council, and, early in 1974, Faulkner resigned as Unionist leader. He struggled on as head of the executive until the spring but, faced by sustained labour troubles, gave up at the end of May. An attempt to form a breakaway party (the **UNIONIST PARTY OF NORTHERN IRELAND**) failed, and, in 1976, he announced his retirement from politics. Early the following year, he was awarded a life peerage as Baron Faulkner of Downpatrick but died on 3 March as a result of a hunting accident at Saintfield (County Down).

FIANNA FAIL. Formally constituted as a political party in 1926, Fianna Fail initially consisted of republican nationalists who opposed the **ANGLO-IRISH TREATY** (1921). **SINN FEIN** refused to accept that agreement because, as the new Irish Free State was a member of the British Commonwealth, members elected to the Dáil (the Irish Parliament) had to take an oath of allegiance to King George V. Eamon De Valera (who had been imprisoned in 1923 for armed resistance to the treaty) eventually accepted that such a fundamentalist position was untenable because it excluded Sinn Fein from the democratic process and, in 1926, led a breakaway movement, which called itself Fianna Fail (Warriors of Ireland). It drew much support from the working classes and advocated reunification of Ireland, preservation of the Irish language, the breakup of large farms and reallocation of land to smallholders, and a self-sufficiency economy. In 1932, the party was elected to power, with De Valera as Prime Minister, and, since then, has had more experience of government than any other political group in Ireland. (See **FINE GAEL).**

FIFTEEN, THE. (See **JACOBITE REBELLION,** 1715).

FINE GAEL. Those members of **SINN FEIN** who supported the **ANGLO-IRISH TREATY** (1921) formed Cumann na nGaedheal (the Society of Gaels), which won the **IRISH FREE STATE**'s first elections in 1923 and governed the country until 1932, when it was ousted by **FIANNA FAIL.** In the wake of the defeat, the organization merged with two smaller political groups, the Centre Party and the National Guard, to form Fine Gael (the Family of Gaels). The party's policies tend to be more conservative than those of Fianna Fail and its support is drawn principally from the wealthier members of the middle class.

FITT, BARON. (See **GERRY FITT**).

FITT, GERRY (1926–). Born in **BELFAST** on 9 April 1926, the son of Mary and George Fitt, Gerry Fitt has been one of the central political figures during **THE TROUBLES** in **ULSTER.** After completing his education at the Christian Brothers' School in his native city, he joined the merchant navy before (in 1962) becoming a member of the Northern Ireland Parliament, representing the Dock Division of Belfast on behalf of the Eire Labour Party. In 1966, he was returned to the House of Commons as the Republican Labour member for Belfast West and, four years later, founded the **SOCIAL DEMOCRATIC AND LABOUR PARTY (SDLP),** along with other nationalist politicians, serving as its leader for nine years. In that role, he was the accepted figure head of the moderates in the Roman Catholic community, condemning violence by all parties and, as a result, enduring the animosity of extremists from both sides. He resigned from the SDLP in 1979 in order to sit in the Commons as an independent socialist but lost his seat at the 1983 General Election. Shortly afterwards, he was created a Baron.

FIVE ARTICLES OF PERTH, 1 August 1618. These articles were imposed on a general assembly of the **CHURCH OF SCOTLAND** called by King James VI and I in an attempt to reinforce his introduction of the episcopacy into Scotland by reforming liturgy and creating a "decent and comelie" (attractive) church service. The articles covered observance of Christmas, Good Friday and Easter, kneeling at holy communion (the most controversial article of all, with its connotations of Catholic Mass), early baptism of infants, private confirmation and communion at home for the sick and dying. The Scottish Parliament, largely with the help of 11 of the recently created bishops, passed the articles in 1621, bringing the kirk (church) closer, in practical terms, to the Church of England. However, the general assembly again registered its disapproval by rejecting them in 1638. (See **GLASGOW ASSEMBLY**).

FLEMING, ALEXANDER (1881–1955). One of the pioneers of modern medicine, Fleming revolutionized the treatment of infectious disease through his discovery of penicillin. Born on 16 August 1881 at Lochfield, an upland sheep farm near Darvel (in Scotland), he was the son of Grace and Hugh Fleming. After receiving his early education at local schools and at Kilmarnock Academy, he moved to London at the age of 14, then spent six years as a clerk with a shipping company before registering as a student at St Mary's Hospital medical school. On graduating in 1908, he was offered a post in the school's bacteriology laboratory (allegedly as much because of his successes with the hospital rifle club as because of his distinction in medical studies) and pioneered the use of vaccines against syphilis and typhoid. His research was interrupted by the First World War, but, while serving as a captain with the army medical corps in France, he found that lysozyme (an enzyme present in mucus) had antibiotic properties and, therefore, was a potential form of treatment for infectious disease.

Returning to St Mary's as lecturer in bacteriology in 1920, Fleming continued to experiment with means of reducing illness caused by bacteria. In 1928, he was appointed professor of bacteriology at the University of London and, in the same year, discovered that a mould had contaminated a culture of staphylococci bacteria which he was studying. That mould (which Fleming identified as penicillium notatum) had created a bacterium-free zone around itself and investigations showed that it retained its antibiotic effects even when prepared in liquid form and diluted 800 times. He published his findings in the *Journal of Experimental Pathology* the following year, but their implications were largely ignored by his colleagues and he did not have sufficient background in biochemistry to advance the studies significantly. However, in 1939, Howard Florey (professor of pathology at Oxford University) and Ernst Chain (lecturer in chemical pathology at the same institution) developed a method of producing the drug for clinical use, and, six years later, all three men received the Nobel prize for medicine. Fleming was made a fellow of the Royal Society in 1944, was awarded a knighthood in 1945 and, in 1946, became principal of the Wright-Fleming Institute of Microbiology. He died in London on 11 March 1955, following a heart attack, and was buried in St Paul's Cathedral.

FLODDEN, BATTLE OF, 9 September 1513. In the early summer of 1513, King **JAMES IV** of Scotland, responding to a request for help from Louis XII of France, launched a major campaign against the English. This reinforcement of the **AULD ALLIANCE** amounted to no more than poorly organized raids into northern England until, in September, two armies met at Flodden Hill, near Berwick (Northumberland). The Scots contingent of about 25,000 men was defeated by an English force of 20,000, led by the 70-year-old Thomas Howard, Earl of Surrey. James was killed, along with 10,000 of his troops, three bishops, nine earls and 13 barons (the dead are the *Flowers o' the Forest* in the haunting Scottish lament written to commemorate the loss). The English cannon, bowmen and halberds were far superior to the Scottish artillery and long spears and the defeat was far reaching — never again did the Scots support the Auld Alliance with the same enthusiasm. Scotland lost a whole generation of its military and noblemen and, with its King and his son killed, faced the long minority monarchy of **JAMES V,** which weakened the crown still further.

FOOTBALL. Soccer has long been the most popular sport amoung the urban working classes throughout the **CELTIC FRINGE,** with the exception of the coal mining valleys of south Wales, where **RUGBY** dominates. It is cheap, requiring only a ball and four jackets, which serve as goal posts. Also, it is a game in which the small can excel, so it suited the physique of city boys suffering from the inadequate diets so common in the years after the Industrial Revolution. The first recorded international football fixture took place between Scotland and England at Brewcastle (Cumbria) in 1599; the score is not known but several Englishmen were taken prisoner and one was disembowelled. In its modern form, however, the sport took shape during the second half of the 19th century.

In Scotland, the first club — Queen's Park — was formed in 1867, and a Scottish Football Association (with eight members) in 1873. From the start, the strength of the game lay in **GLASGOW** and the manufacturing areas along the **RIVER CLYDE,** with Rangers and Celtic winning more honours than any other club. Rangers was formed in 1873 by three steadfastly Protestant families. Celtic, based in the city's east end, first took the field in 1888 with sides consisting largely of players with Irish Catholic origins. The religious divide was accentuated during the First World War as a result of unrest in Ireland (see, for example, **EASTER RISING)** and has continued ever since (Rangers did not sign a Catholic player until 1989). The Old Firm, as the two clubs are jointly known, dominate domestic competition, which is based on four leagues with a system of relegation and promotion. The season extends from August until May.

The Irish Football Association was founded, with eight clubs, in 1880 and established its headquarters in **BELFAST,** where the shipyards and factories provided much of the game's support. A competitive league was formed in 1890 and withstood partition of the island in 1922 (some **ULSTER** clubs defected to the Football Association of Ireland, based in Dublin, but quickly returned to the fold, which remained intact until Derry City joined the **REPUBLIC OF IRELAND**'s league in the mid-1980's). Linfield has long been the strongest side in Northern Ireland but has been unable to compete financially with the wealthy English clubs so regularly sees its young talent lured away.

The roots of Welsh soccer are in the north east of the country, close to the industrial populations of Cheshire and Lancashire, in northern England. The Football Association of Wales was formed in Wrexham in 1876 by a group of Welshmen trying to raise a team for an international fixture against Scotland. A cup competition was introduced the following year and is open to all clubs, regardless of league affiliation, so regularly involves English sides. In 1902, a league was formed but has consistently faced problems because the principality's major teams prefer to play in the English League, where the competition is stronger. As a result, winning the Welsh League does not carry the automatic qualification for European competition which accompanies success in Scotland, Northern Ireland and England.

For historical reasons, the three Celtic nations still field their own sides in international competitions and have distinct soccer traditions. In recent years, for example, they have not experienced the crowd violence which has often marred games in England. The Scots, in particular, have gained a reputation to travelling to the ends of the earth in support of their team, earning the nickname The **TARTAN** Army (one group actually tried to commandeer a submarine in an attempt to get to the World Cup finals in Argentina in 1978).

FORD OF THE BISCUITS, BATTLE OF THE, 7 August 1594. This battle was an engagement during the unrest, led by Hugh O'Donnell, which immediately preceded the **TYRONE REBELLION** (1594–1603). It was fought at a ford across the River Arney, near Enniskillen (**ULSTER**), between English troops led by Sir Henry Duke and Sir Edward Herbert, and an Irish force commanded by Hugh Maguire and Cormac Tyrone. The English army was marching to lift a siege of Enniskillen Castle and deliver supplies when 1,000 rebels ambushed it at the ford (a tactic used again at the **BATTLE OF THE YELLOW FORD**). The 600 infantry and 46 cavalry troops of the government side were overcome by their attackers, who had few casualties and claimed a tactical success in the encounter (though Enniskillen was relieved soon after by English forces). The spilling of rations, intended for Enniskillen, during the battle led to the ford being renamed the Ford of the Biscuits.

FORSYTH, MICHAEL BRUCE (1954–). **SECRETARY OF STATE FOR SCOTLAND** from 1995 until 1997, Forsyth is the son of garage owner John Forsyth and his wife, Mary. He was born in Montrose on 16 October 1954 and educated at Arbroath High School and **ST ANDREWS** University, where he founded a Conservative Association in 1972 and became the organization's first president. After graduating, he set out on a business career in London, but his interest in politics led him to serve on Westminster City Council from 1978 until 1983 and then to become member of Parliament for the **STIRLING** constituency. His rise up the government hierarchy was steady. In 1986, he was made Parliamentary Private Secretary to the Secretary of State for Foreign Affairs and, the following year, was promoted to Parliamentary Under-Secretary of State. He was successively Minister of State at the Scottish Office (with responsibility for health, education, social work and sport) from 1990 until 1992, at the Department of Employment from 1992 until 1994 and at the Home Office from 1994 until 1995. His appointment as Scottish Secretary in July 1995 was not well received. Conservative Party popularity was at an all-time low in Scotland, traditionally a Labour stronghold, and Forsyth had a reputation as a right-winger in the Margaret Thatcher mould. Some of his early decisions confirmed the worst expectations (for example, he refused to join the leaders of the other major parties as joint patrons of the European Movement in Scotland). However, as he eased his way into office, he lived up to his reputation as a smooth political operator, proving that he was unwilling to be bound by the decisions of his predecessors and increasingly giving the impression that he was ready to accept consensus on controversial issues. In particular, he announced that he was happy to support devolution of power to a Scottish Parliament provided that the sovereignty of Westminster was not undermined, indicated that he was willing to give more responsibility to local authorities, took action to assist residents in some **CROFTING** communities to acquire the freehold of the land they farmed and made proposals on law and order which avoided the more extreme policies being pursued in England. Following the loss of his seat at Labour's landslide General Election victory in 1997, he announced that he had no interest in furthering his political career and accepted a post as director of the merchant bank, Robert Fleming. He was knighted later in the year.

FORTH, RIVER. The Forth rises on the slopes of Ben Lomond, at the southern edge of the **SCOTTISH HIGHLANDS,** and flows eastwards, with much meandering, for 115 miles across the central valley of Scotland before meeting the North Sea. The final 50 miles, where the waterway widens, is known as the Firth of Forth. The river is tidal as far as **STIRLING,** which was the lowest crossing until the railway bridge was opened at Queensferry in 1890 (see **FORTH BRIDGE**) and the road bridges at Kincardine in 1936 and Queensferry in 1964. Upstream of Stirling, the floodplain alongside the river has been cleared of peat and provides fertile land for arable crops and grazing. Downstream, the banks are more industrialized, with large electricity-generating stations at Kincardine and Longannet and a major oil refinery and petrochemical complex at Grangemouth. There is also a naval shipyard at Rosyth (near North Queensferry) and port facilities at Methil, Burntisland and Leith. Formerly, small settlements such as Anstruther, Pittenweem and Granton supported fishing fleets, but, faced with European Union quotas and falling profitability, most skippers have gone out of business. The towns, however, provide the basis of a tourist trade. In 1790, a 35-mile canal was completed between the River Forth and the **RIVER CLYDE,** allowing water-borne traffic to pass between the east and west coasts of Scotland, but it fell into disuse during the 20th century and much is now filled in. The largest riparian communities are at Stirling (in the west) and **EDINBURGH** (in the east).

FORTH BRIDGE. The railway bridge over the **RIVER FORTH** between North and South Queensferry was one of the world's first steel cantilever structures. A considerable engineering marvel even now, it enhanced Britain's technological reputation during the late 19th century and became a national symbol of invention and progress. The bridge was designed by Benjamin Baker and built during the 1880s, causing considerable controversy because many people found it aesthetically displeasing (for example, poet and artist William Morris denounced it as "the supremest specimen of all ugliness"). Although the banks of the Forth are, for the most part, thick clays, there is a rock outcrop which causes the river to narrow at Queensferry and also forms the islet of Inchgarvie midway across the waterway. Baker used that rock as a foundation for three 1,350 feet cantilevers, which he joined by two suspended spans, each of 350 feet. The bridge was, therefore, nearly a mile long, with 3,400 feet crossing the water. The tubes used to construct the cantilevers were 12 feet in diameter and manufactured at **WILLIAM ARROL**'s works near **GLASGOW.** Altogether, the bridge used 58,000 tons of steel and cost £3 million. Maintenance of its large surface area has been a problem, painting alone taking a full year, but the structure is still in use, carrying trains between the north of Scotland and **EDINBURGH.** It remains the lowest crossing of the Forth but a suspension bridge with a main span of 3,300 feet was built a few yards upstream and opened to road traffic in 1964.

FORTIFIED HOUSES. During the 15th and 16th centuries, fortified tower houses became a popular form of residence for the nobility, particularly in Scotland and Ireland. Given the political instability of the times, homes which were relatively cheap to build and provided a fair measure of security against small-scale attacks were attractive alternatives to expensive castles. Built of stone, they consisted of several suites of rooms, one above the other and including kitchens and other facilities needed by a baron's family and servants. Houses constructed during the late 16th and the 17th centuries had walls less thick than their predecessors, creating larger rooms, and more windows were incorporated. As peaceful conditions prevailed, battlements and other military embellishments became increasingly stylized and buildings extended horizontally in order to provide more, and higher standard, accommodation. By the late 18th century, defence was no longer required and the fortified houses were superseded by country houses. Craigievar Castle (near Alford, Scotland) is one of the best examples of the vogue. Built by William Forbes in 1626, its lower walls are unadorned but its roof line displays turrets, cupolas and corbelling typical of an architectural style which became known as Scottish baronial. It is now in the care of the **NATIONAL TRUST FOR SCOTLAND.**

FORTY-FIVE, THE. (See **JACOBITE REBELLION,** 1745).

FREE CHURCH OF SCOTLAND. The Free Church was formed as a result of fundamental differences within the **CHURCH OF SCOTLAND** and maintains strict adherence to the 1647 Westminster confession of faith (the definitive statement of Presbyterianism). During the 18th and early 19th centuries, an evangelical movement gained strength within the established Church, advocating a return to the basic principles of Calvinism on which the Reformation had been built and objecting to the right of landowners to appoint ministers to congregations on their estates. Decisions by the secular courts, which upheld the rights of patronage, caused much bitterness, and, on 18 May 1843, **THOMAS CHALMERS** and others marched out of the general assembly of the Church of Scotland in **EDINBURGH** and formed the Free Church of Scotland. Over 400 ministers went with them, giving up their homes and their incomes for their beliefs.

The new organization faced great financial problems — it had no church buildings, no schools or training colleges, no missionary centres abroad and no means of financing its clergy — but its supporters gave liberally, and, within five years, it was firmly established, with particular strength in the western areas of the **SCOTTISH HIGHLANDS.** In 1851, census returns showed that the numbers attending the Free Church and the established church were very similar. The following year, it absorbed the smaller Original Secession Church, and, in 1876, at a time of strong conservative theological views, united with the Reformed Presbyterian Church. (See **CAMERONIANS**).

The last decade of the 19th century was marked by a modernist approach at the training colleges for ministers in **ABERDEEN, EDINBURGH** and **GLASGOW** and by the secession, in 1893, of a number of congregations (mainly in the Highlands) who opposed the progressive views and formed their own **FREE PRESBYTERIAN CHURCH OF SCOTLAND**. Also, there was an increasingly close association with the **UNITED PRESBYTERIAN CHURCH,** and, on 31 October 1900, the two combined to form the **UNITED FREE CHURCH OF SCOTLAND** (UF Church). A group of 63 conservative congregations, mainly in **GAELIC**-speaking areas of the western highlands and the **HEBRIDES,** remained outside the union and, in 1904, won a ruling by the House of Lords (the supreme court in the United Kingdom) that it had legal title to the properties which had been owned by the Free Church and taken over by the UF Church. Members became known as The Wee Frees and exerted considerable influence in areas of their church's strength, preventing the opening of shops and the operating of ferries on Sundays. In 1996, the Church had approximately 20,000 members, 140 places of worship and 110 ministers. Its governing body, the general assembly, has lay and clerical members and meets annually.

FREE PRESBYTERIAN CHURCH OF SCOTLAND. In 1893, a group of conservative congregations within the **FREE CHURCH OF SCOTLAND** broke away to form the Free Presbyterian Church. Based mainly in the **SCOTTISH HIGHLANDS,** they disagreed with the relaxation of the Free Church's strict adherence to the 1647 Westminster confession of faith, which maintained that the ultimate doctrinal authority was the Scriptures as written in their original languages and that "some men . . . are predestined unto everlasting life, others foreordained to everlasting death." Still staunchly Calvinist, the Free Presbyterian Church emphasizes observance of the Sabbath as a day of worship, free from the demands of work. In 1997, it warned its members that dancing at weddings was a sin and asked them to give up either the practice or the faith. The Church has 20 ministers, 63 congregations and about 4,200 adherents. (See **PRES-**

BYTERIAN CHURCH IN IRELAND; PRESBYTERIAN CHURCH OF WALES).

FRIENDS OF IRELAND. Based in Washington, DC, this organization was established in 1981 by a group of leading Irish-Americans, including Congressmen Edward Kennedy and Tip O'Neill. It supports unification of Ireland but only with the agreement of the citizens of **ULSTER.** In 1985, it was instrumental in ensuring US support for the **ANGLO-IRISH AGREEMENT.**

FRIENDS OF IRELAND GROUP. Established in 1945, the group consisted of left-wing Labour members of Parliament, most of them backbenchers, who were opposed to the **ULSTER UNIONIST PARTY**'s policies in Northern Ireland. It cooperated with the **ANTI-PARTITION LEAGUE** in attempts to influence Clement Attlee's government but became increasingly ineffectual after the Conservative Party's General Election victory in 1951.

FRIENDS OF THE UNION. An organization consisting largely of Conservative Party politicians opposed to the 1985 **ANGLO-IRISH AGREEMENT,** the Friends of the Union was formed in 1986. Its primary aim is to secure the continued place of Northern Ireland within the United Kingdom. Founder members included Ian Gow, MP, who resigned from Margaret Thatcher's government in protest at the agreement and was murdered by the **IRISH REPUBLICAN ARMY** in 1990.

—G—

GAELIC, SCOTS. Gaelic is a member of the Celtic branch of the Indo-European language family and a descendant of old Irish. The date of its introduction to Scotland is unclear, but it seems certain that communities of Gaelic speakers were established in the west of the country by the late fifth century. From then, it spread through most of the **SCOTTISH HIGHLANDS,** the central lowlands and the **SOUTHERN UPLANDS,** reaching its greatest extent about the 11th century. Over the next 900 years, its influence waned in the face of the seemingly inexorable march of English so, by the time of the 1991 census, only 70,000 people (1.5 per cent of the Scottish population) could speak, read or write the language. At that time, the proportion of Gaelic speakers was highest in the northwest, and particularly in the Outer **HEBRIDES,** the Isle of Skye and Lochalsh. In 1993, a report by the **SCOTTISH OFFICE** suggested a renaissance, claiming that the language (and the culture associated with it) had been experiencing a period of growth. Since 1989, the budget for Gaelic television programmes has been over £8 million annually (*Machair*, a soap opera with a dominantly Gaelic dialogue, obtained an average audience of over 500,000 viewers each week), Gaelic rock groups (such as Runrig) have consistently topped record charts and the number of school pupils being educated in Gaelic is increasing. The language has a long oral tradition celebrated at an annual Mod, similar in concept to the Welsh **EISTEDDFOD** and organized by **AN COMUNN GAIDHEALACH**. *Gairm*, a periodical established in 1951, publishes poems, short stories and articles on topical issues in Gaelic, and the Gaelic Books Council, created in 1968, subsidizes the production of original works in the language.

GALLOGLASSES. These well-armed mercenaries, employed from the 13th century by **ULSTER** chiefs in their struggles against the English, take their name from *gall óglaigh*, an Irish Gaelic phrase meaning *foreign warriors*. They were first identified in Tyrconnell in 1258 and came mainly from the west of Scotland and the **HEBRIDES**. Speaking a mixture of Gaelic and Norse, they were formidable, well-disciplined soldiers, fighting with traditional Viking heavy axes, who settled in Ulster and served the Irish well during the English invasion of the island. Their last engagement was the **BATTLE OF KINSALE** (1601), at which England subdued the **TYRONE REBELLION.**

GALLOWAY LEVELLERS. During the early 18th century, the enclosure of land for cattle grazing became popular in the Galloway area of Scotland. Tenants who opposed the movement formed groups which broke down (or levelled) the newly built field walls. They campaigned not only against enclosures, but also the related evictions and high agricultural prices, and were the Scottish equivalent of the English levellers and the Irish **WHITEBOYS.** They were finally routed by troops sent from **EDINBURGH** in June 1724.

GEDDES, PATRICK (1854–1932). A pioneer of modern town planning, Geddes was born in Ballater on 2 October 1854, the son of Janet and Alexander Geddes (an army quarter-master). He was educated at Perth Academy, then spent a year working in a bank before training as a biologist in London (under T. H. Huxley) and Paris (under Henri de Lacaze-Duthiers). After an illness in Mexico during 1879 led to a temporary period of blindness, which affected his ability to work with microscopes, he was forced to reevaluate his career. As a result, Geddes turned increasingly to theoretical matters and developed an interest in social organization which had been stirred during his time in France. He was appointed Professor of Botany at the University of **DUNDEE** in 1883 but, three years later, made his home in **EDINBURGH** and established what writers of the time claimed was the world's first sociological laboratory. Geddes travelled widely in Britain and abroad, visiting Cyprus in 1897 and becoming Professor of Sociology and Civics at Bombay University (India) from 1919 until 1923. In 1924, he settled in Montpellier (France), and, in 1931, was awarded a knighthood. By that time, however, his health had been poor for some years, and he died in his adopted city on 17 April 1932.

Although he never earned a degree, he became internationally renowned for his work on the role of sex in the processes of evolution and for his advocacy of the need to understand the principles of ecology. It was those principles, he believed, which determined the development of human communities: people, work and place interacted to shape social change. In the Scottish tradition, he had a great breadth of academic interest (he counted biologist Charles Darwin, geographer Elisée Reclus and anarchist Peter Kropotkin among his friends) and that was reflected in his sociological studies, which drew particular attention to the relationship between city and region and to means of regenerating urban areas. He also created student-administered halls of residence in Edinburgh and established a Scots college in Montpellier. His major works were *The Evolution of Sex* (written with J. A. Thomson and published in 1900), *City Development* (1904) and *Cities in Evolution* (1913).

GEOFFREY OF MONMOUTH (*c.* 1090–1155). Geoffrey's *Historia Regum Britanniae* (*History of the Kings of Britain*) was one of the most influential medieval texts and brought the exploits of King Arthur and his Knights of the Round Table to public attention for the first time. Little is known about the author's early life, but he was probably born in, or near, Monmouth about 1090 and served as a canon with a group of Augustinian monks in Oxford, where he seems to have spent most of his days. He was ordained as a priest in 1152 and consecrated as Bishop of St Asaph's the same year but never visited the see before his death in 1155.

The *Historia* was published between 1136 and 1139 and claimed to be an account of the history of Britain from the time of the first humans until the Anglo-Saxon invasions. Scholars have failed to identify any of the sources which Geoffrey meticulously documented so the work is fiction rather than fact, but its impact was considerable because, at the time, it was believed to be true. Nearly one-third of the text recounts the exploits of King Arthur in a manner which led to a retelling of the tales throughout Europe in romantic forms which continue to catch the popular imagination. For the Welsh, a more important focus was Brutus, who, according to Geoffrey, was the first Briton. Brutus, he claimed, had fled from Troy when it was taken by the Greeks, and, as a consequence, Britons shared a common — and noble — ancestry with the Romans, because Rome was founded by Aeneas, who was also a Trojan. The belief that Brutus had once ruled the whole island provided a powerful foundation for the argument that the Welsh had a moral right to the throne of Britain and that, in turn, helped to foster support for the 15th century campaign for independence led by **OWAIN GLYNDWR.**

GERALD DE BARRI. (See **GIRALDUS CAMBRIENSIS**).

GERALD OF WALES. (See **GIRALDUS CAMBRIENSIS**).

GIANT'S CAUSEWAY. About 59 million years ago, much of western Britain was characterized by volcanic activity. Along the northern coast of **ULSTER** between Ballycastle and Portrush, lava flows cooled rapidly when they met the sea and created thousands of irregular hexagonal pillars, resembling a vast stone honeycomb. The rocks later weathered into a series of steps, which stretch for 100 yards into the ocean. There is an alternative explanation for the phenomenon. Local legend tells that the Causeway is a road built by a race of giants and leading to the island of Staffa, which lies off the west coast of Scotland and has a similar structure. The area is now owned by the **NATIONAL TRUST.**

GIRALDUS CAMBRIENSIS (*c.* 1146–*c.* 1223). One of Wales's greatest Latin authors and an advocate of the independence of the Welsh church (see **CELTIC CHURCH**), Giraldus was born in Manorbier Castle (near Pembroke), probably in 1146. The youngest son of William de Barri and his wife, Angharad, a descendant of the princes of south Wales, he was very conscious of his mixed Anglo-Norman and Welsh ancestry. In 1175, after receiving an education at the Church School in Gloucester and the University of Paris, he returned to Wales as Archdeacon of Brecon. The following year, he was nominated as Bishop of St David's, in succession to his uncle, but King Henry II of England refused to confirm the post because Giraldus was not of pure Norman blood and he returned to France to study theology and canon law. He became a chaplain to the King in 1184 and, in that capacity, travelled widely, accompanying Prince John (later King John) to Ireland in 1185–86 and Archbishop Baldwin of Canterbury to Wales in 1188. These journeys produced a series of writings which add enormously to scholars' understanding of 12th-century society, in particular *Itinerarium Cambriae* (*A Journey through Wales*, which was completed in 1191) and *Descriptio Cambriae* (*A Description of Wales*, which appeared in 1194). The works are often emotional and uncritical, but they provide rich detail of customs and traditions, many of which are still celebrated, and outline the characteristics of the common people (the Welsh, according to Giraldus, were hospitable and generous but lazy and given to vacillation). Much of Giraldus's later life was devoted to attempts to win the Bishopric of St David's and make the see independent of Canterbury. The efforts were in vain, but the fight helped to deepen a developing sense of Welsh nationhood. He resigned his archdeaconry in 1204 and probably died in 1223.

GLAMIS CASTLE. The early home of the Queen Mother, Glamis Castle is located in Angus, five miles southwest of Forfar, and is the seat of the Earl of Strathmore and Kinghorne. It is built in the Scottish baronial style and dates largely from the 17th century, though some parts are as old as the 11th century, when **MACBETH** was **THANE** of Glamis. In 1930, it was the birthplace of Princess Margaret, the first royal baby to be born in Scotland for 300 years.

GLAMORGAN TREATY, 25 August 1645. During the latter stages of the first civil war in England, King Charles I, desperate for more troops, sent the Earl of Glamorgan to Ireland to negotiate in secret with the Roman Catholic gentry, who were engaged in the **IRISH REBELLION.** Charles was prepared to accede to almost any demand from the Irish in return for 10,000 troops to swell his forces. At Kilkenny, Glamorgan made a public treaty which agreed to rescind **POYNING'S LAW,** grant an amnesty to the rebels and return confiscated lands. At the same time, he agreed to a secret treaty, which gave Irish Catholics freedom of worship in churches in Ireland not then in the possession of the Church of England. The English Parliament became aware of the treaties, and Charles was forced, on 16 January 1646, to deny Glamorgan's mission and disclaim the agreements.

GLASGOW. Scotland's most populous city straddles the **RIVER CLYDE**, lying some 20 miles from its mouth and about 45 miles west of **EDINBURGH.** There is evidence of prehistoric settlement in the area and of attempts by **ST MUNGO** to build a church for his Christian converts during the second half of the sixth century. By the 12th century, the township had become an important ecclesiastical centre and significant enough commercially to be created a **BURGH** of barony. For most of the next 600 years it lay outside the mainstream of Scottish life, which focused on the royal court at Edinburgh and **STIRLING.** In 1707, however, the **TREATY OF UNION** opened up England's North American colonies to Scottish merchants and Glasgow developed a thriving tobacco trade with bases in Virginia. Later, sugar from the West Indies and cotton from the southern United States underpinned the prosperity, attracting men and women from the **SCOTTISH HIGHLANDS** to jobs in the docks and the textile industry. The city became the focus of a major cotton-spinning and linen-producing region, which increased both in importance and in concentration after steam superseded water as the major source of power during the 19th century. Bleaching, dyeing and fabric printing provided ancillary employment, and good harbours on the Clyde enabled the finished articles to be exported by sea to the furthest corners of the British empire. The advent of the steamship added a further boost to the economy because local iron ore and coal provided raw materials for a major shipbuilding industry, and, from about 1850, Glasgow became the most important centre of marine engineering in the United Kingdom. The expanding pool of technical skills was also utilized by firms manufacturing railway engines, and the amalgamation of several of these enterprizes under the banner of the North British Locomotive Company Ltd in 1903 formed the largest company of its kind in Europe, capable of turning out more than 500 engines a year. In addition, shipbuilding and railway engineering spawned a great range of other manufacturing and construction businesses which stretched along the Clyde and, in addition, engulfed inland towns such as Paisley (which gave its name to the fabric pattern), Kilmarnock and Lanark. However, the emphasis on heavy industry made the Glasgow conurbation vulnerable to recession, particularly during the period between the two world wars, and that, in turn, created conditions which favoured left-wing politics. **RED CLYDESIDE** became famed for political activism and provided fertile ground for the growth of the Labour and Communist Parties.

Glasgow also earned a reputation for some of the most squalid slums in Europe. Industrial success attracted migrants in large numbers so the city's population grew from an estimated 12,766 in 1708 to 83,769 at the time of the first census in 1801 and over 500,000 in 1891. The incomers crowded into whatever accommodation they could find, creating conditions in which infectious disease spread readily. In 1842, one official report condemned Glasgow as "the filthiest and unhealthiest of all the British towns". Solutions proved elusive, and the Gorbals, in particular, became a byword for poverty and crime. But, from the late 1960s, the city authorities made a concerted effort to raise living standards, encouraging some people to leave for new towns, such as Cumbernauld and East Kilbride, whilst pioneering innovative housing programmes for those who remained. In addition, a comprehensive programme of slum clearance, coupled with transport improvements and conservation plans for some of the most distinguished Victorian buildings in Britain, laid the foundations for a concerted effort to attract new business to the city during the 1980s and 1990s. Posters claiming that *Glasgow Smiles Better* appeared on the London Underground and in national newspapers, helping to change the stereotype of a violent, bleak and poverty-stricken people. Investment in retail and service facilities greatly improved the city centre environment. A series of major events — such as the Garden Festival of 1988 and the European City of Culture programme in 1990 — attracted thousands of visitors. Others came to hear the productions of the Scottish National Orchestra and Scottish Opera at the Theatre Royal. And, to a large extent, the campaign worked.

Glasgow has been hailed as Britain's first post-industrial city, with studies showing that it is high on the list of places in which European businessmen would be happy to locate. However, the recession of the 1990s and central government efforts to control local authority spending have reduced the pace of change. Urban renewal has slowed, with efforts being concentrated on peripheral housing estates, and, in some areas of the city, unemployment is still high. The population at the time of the 1991 census was 663,000 (down by 11.0 per cent over the previous decade but enough to make Glasgow Scotland's most densely populated city, with 33.5 people per hectare, twice the figure for Edinburgh). The population of the Strathclyde region, of which Glasgow is the focus, was 2,248,000 (down 4.8 per cent from 1981). (See **GLASGOW ASSEMBLY;**

GLASGOW BOYS).

GLASGOW ASSEMBLY, 28 November 1638. In 1637, King Charles I imposed the English Book of Common Prayer on Scotland, an action which led protestors to frame a **NATIONAL COVENANT** in February of the following year. The strength of the opposition convinced the King to make concessions so he agreed to withdraw the prayer book, rescind the **FIVE ARTICLES OF PERTH** and call a meeting of the general assembly of the **CHURCH OF SCOTLAND** (the first gathering for over 20 years of the only ecclesiastical forum where decisions were likely to win widespread national support). The assembly took place without the bishops (who feared to attend) and was dominated by **PRESBYTERIANS** and **COVENANTERS,** who gained approval for a radical programme which annulled the five articles, outlawed the prayer book and abolished the episcopy. Inevitably, the move led to confrontation with the monarchy and, ultimately, to the outbreak of the **BISHOPS' WARS.**

GLASGOW BOYS. From 1882 until about 1895, a group of about 20 artists, based in **GLASGOW**, developed a distinctive school of painting which had considerable influence in Europe (and particularly in Germany, where they exhibited many of their works after 1890). Eschewing the detailed approach which had characterized earlier 19th-century studies, they adopted a simple, robust style which emphasized rich, exuberant colouring. W. Y. MacGregor's *The Vegetable Stall* (1884) and George Henry's *Galloway Landscape* (1889) are the most acclaimed of their canvases, with the latter considered by some critics to be one of the masterpieces of European Postimpressionism. However, the vigour was short-lived. Affected by international trends, the Glasgow boys moved away from their original forthright style to more contrived compositions and, by the end of the century, had disbanded.

GLEN. In Northern Ireland and Scotland, valleys are termed *glens*. The word is derived from the **GAELIC** *gleann*, which refers either to a rocky defile or to a large depression between hill masses. (See **GREAT GLEN**).

GLENCAIRN RISING, 1653–54. In June 1653, William Cunningham, Earl of Glencairn, was appointed by King Charles II as commander of the royalist forces in Scotland. He arrived in August to begin a rebellion against Oliver Cromwell's Commonwealth (which, by ordinance of 12 April 1653, had incorporated the Scots). The rising, mainly in the **SCOTTISH HIGHLANDS,** was beset by dissension between the **CLAN** chiefs, shortage of equipment and inadequate leadership so the authorities quickly suppressed it with a final defeat at Dalnaspidal (Tayside) on 19 July 1654. As a consequence, the participating noble families were fined and had land confiscated, though the experience led to some later conciliation from Cromwell in order to prevent recurrence of rebellion in Scotland.

GLENCOE MASSACRE, 13 February 1692. King William III signed orders that the **LORD ADVOCATE** should make an example of the MacDonald **CLAN** for the failure of their chief, MacIain of Glencoe, to swear allegiance to the Crown. MacIain, delayed by a blizzard, eventually took the oath, but because he was a few days late, the command to exterminate his people was not withdrawn. Soldiers arrived in Glencoe early in February and asked for food and shelter. Unsuspecting, the MacDonalds welcomed them because, in the **SCOTTISH HIGHLANDS,** the obligation to provide hospitality was absolute, whatever the enmity between host and visitor. After 12 days of eating, drinking and gossiping, the troops arose at dawn on Saturday 13 February, and turned on the people who had looked after them. Robert **CAMPBELL** had been ordered to put under the age of 70 to the sword but bungled the operation. MacIain, along with 36 of his men, was killed, as were three or four women and children. Many others, however, died later in the bitter winter of the mountains after fleeing from the scene. There had been more brutal deaths in the highlands but this 'murder under trust' was condemned throughout Scotland. Sir John Dalrymple, Master of Stair, the King's principal Secretary of State in Scotland and the man who had signed the original order, was forced to resign. The Campbell name was reviled throughout the land.

GLENDOWER, OWEN. (See **OWAIN GLYNDWR**).

GLENSHIEL, BATTLE OF, 10 June 1719. This curious encounter followed Britain's inclusion in the Quadruple Alliance of European powers which was opposed to King Philip of Spain's designs on France and Italy. **JACOBITE** sympathisers in the **SCOTTISH HIGHLANDS,** led by the Duke of Ormonde, agreed to mount a rising, which would be coordinated with a Spanish invasion of England. Spain was to send a main force of 29 ships and 5,000 men to southwest England and a smaller contingent of 307 men to Scotland.

The former was hit by a storm and failed to arrive, but the latter, led by George Keith, landed in western Scotland in April. However, the rebels argued about leadership, and, after the government troops had destroyed their base at Eilean Donan Castle, they took up poor positions at the end of Loch Duich, where they were mercilessly attacked. The Scots fled, leaving the Spaniards to surrender.

GLYNDWR, OWAIN (*c.* 1354–*c.* 1416). The last prince of an independent Wales, Glyndwr was educated at the Inns of Court in London and may have served in the armies of Richard II and Henry IV of England. In 1400, he led a rebellion against English rule in north Wales. That revolt ended in defeat by Henry's forces at Welshpool on 24 September, but the unrest remained and, in 1401, erupted into violence in the south of the principality. Over the next few years, Glyndwr had a series of victories and captured both Lord Grey of Ruthyn and Sir Edmund Mortimer. Grey brought financial assistance through his ransom and Mortimer allied himself with the Welshman, marrying his daughter, Catherine. The high points for the rebels came in 1404, when Aberystwyth and **HARLECH CASTLE**s were taken, making Glendower the de facto ruler of much of Wales. In July of that year, he made an alliance with King Charles VI of France, but, by 1405, his hold on the country was weakening. In March, he was defeated by English armies at Grosmont and, in May, at Pwll Melyn (where his eldest son, Gruffydd, was taken captive). In June, Henry had quelled rebellion in the north of England, and, with his country at peace, was able to turn his full attention to the troubles in Wales. French support enabled Glyndwr to threaten Worcester during the late summer, but these allies returned home early in 1406, leaving him with very meagre military resources. Aberystwyth and Harlech were retaken in 1408, removing Glendower's territorial power base. He continued sporadic guerilla attacks, but the campaign was effectively over and Henry V was able to regain English control. Glendower probably died in 1416, having failed to achieve the independent Wales he sought, but in recent times he has become something of a folk hero, particularly for those who wish to achieve **HOME RULE.**

GOLF. Although games which involved hitting a ball with a stick were popular as early as Roman times, it is generally accepted that the modern game of golf evolved in Scotland. The earliest written reference to the sport was a decree, issued by the **THREE ESTATES** in 1457, which banned it because it was interfering with archery practice. Further legislation in 1471 and 1491 bolstered the ruling, but, even so, it remained a popular pastime for the aristocracy; there are records that **JAMES IV, JAMES V, MARY, QUEEN OF SCOTS** and James VI and I were all devotees. During the 18th and 19th centuries, the first clubs were formed, based on east coast links courses (that is, on open land along the shores of the North Sea). The Honourable Company of **EDINBURGH** Golfers was founded in 1744 and drew up a set of 13 rules, which were adopted ten years later by the Society of **ST ANDREWS,** now the Royal and Ancient Golf Club. (The Old Course at St Andrews originally had 22 holes but, by 1764, had been redesigned to provide only 18, a number copied by all of the world's full-length courses). The Musselburgh Golf Club introduced a competition for ladies in 1810, and, in 1860, the first British Open Championship was held at Prestwick. In 1919, the Royal and Ancient took over the management of the Open and of the British Amateur Championship, effectively becoming the governing body of men's golf throughout the British Empire. Since then, and particularly over the past two decades, the sport has spread widely around the world and is now played in over 60 countries. Scotland has over 700 courses and reaps a considerable income from tourists who want to play such major championship venues as Carnoustie, Gleneagles and Muirfield as well as St Andrews. In addition, Scots have had a considerable influence on the development of equipment for the sport and on administrative procedures.

GOVERNMENT OF IRELAND ACT, 23 December 1920. This Act of the British Parliament partitioned the island of Ireland into two parts — Northern Ireland (comprising the six counties of **ULSTER**) and Southern Ireland (comprising the remaining 26 counties). Each part was to have its own regional Parliament, but would be subject to the national Parliament in London, where both areas would be represented. A Council of Ireland, comprising 20 members from each of the Irish assemblies, would debate matters of common interest. The act was intended to be temporary, but satisfied neither party (Ulster representatives rejected the concept of a council, while **SINN FEIN** rejected the idea of the southern Parliament because of its subservience to London). As a result, **THE TROUBLES** continued, and the legislation was eventually replaced by the **ANGLO-IRISH TREATY** (1921), which created the **IRISH FREE STATE.**

GOWRIE CONSPIRACY, 5 August 1600. A puzzling event at best, this alleged conspiracy took place at Gowrie Castle (near Perth), home of the Ruthvens, Earls of Gowrie. King James VI of Scotland claimed that he was lured to the castle by John Ruthven on the pretext of meeting an old man with a large pot of gold, then was attacked but saved from death by his retainers. Ruthven and his brother were killed in the mélée. Historians suggest, however, that the King invented the story as a justification for eliminating enemies. In 1582, the earl's father had instituted the **RUTHVEN RAID,** which succeeded in abducting the young James and imprisoning him in Ruthven Castle. Eighteen years later the monarch took his revenge on the family. Also, some scholars suggest that the King made a homosexual advance to Ruthven and that the incident was precipitated by his rejection. Others claim that Ruthven's grandfather held a knife to the abdomen of **MARY, QUEEN OF SCOTS,** when she was pregnant with James so bad blood had existed for many years between the protagonists. James used the incident to test the allegience of the **EDINBURGH** clergy, who were required to give prayers of thanksgiving for the monarch's deliverance.

GRACES, THE, 24 May 1628. A delegation of Old English landowners from Northern Ireland offered King Charles I financial aid in return for concessions to Irish Catholics. On 24 May 1628, he agreed 51 Graces, or concessions, in return for the sum of £40,000 to be paid annually for the following three years. The Graces included institution of an Irish Parliament, a limit of 60 years on Crown confiscations of land and the right of recusants to practise in the Law. A 'Parliament' was held, but later declared null and void as it contravened **POYNING'S LAW,** and by December 1629, suppression of Irish Catholic religious houses was resumed in Northern Ireland. After the Civil War, the English Parliament did not feel bound by any of the provisions of The Graces.

GRAHAM, JAMES (1612–50). One of the outstanding generals of the 17th century, Graham was the son of John (first Earl of Montrose). He was educated at **ST ANDREWS** University and, as a young man, travelled widely in Holland, France and Italy. In 1638, he was one of the four noblemen who prepared the **NATIONAL COVENANT,** which asserted that Scotland's monarchs could rule only through Parliament, but, after meeting King Charles I the following year, spoke out against the growth of antiroyalist feeling in the country. Created Captain General of Scotland in 1643 and Marquis of Montrose the following year, he raised an army of Scottish highlanders, supported by a contingent of Irishmen, to fight for the King's cause and, showing considerable skill, defeated **COVENANTER** troops at Tippermuir (near Perth) on 1 September. Graham's forces then followed up with victories at **ABERDEEN,** Inverlochy, Auldearn and Alford before the success at Kilsyth (see **BATTLE OF KILSYTH**), on 15 August 1645, appeared to place the lowlands at his mercy. However, soldiers filtered back to the glens and many of the **ULSTER**men went home so, on 13 September he was routed at the **BATTLE OF PHILIPHAUGH.** On 3 September 1646, he fled to Norway and, for more than three years, travelled Europe in search of men and equipment. Determined to avenge Charles's execution on 30 January 1649, he attempted an invasion of Scotland the following year, landing on the **ORKNEY ISLANDS** in March but losing many of his small band of followers as a result of shipwreck on the crossing to the mainland at Caithness. He found little support for a rising in the **SCOTTISH HIGHLANDS,** and when, on 27 April, his tiny band of followers was cut to pieces in a fight with the defending army at Carbisdale, Montrose fled into the mountains. Eventually, he sought shelter from one of the Macleods of Assynt, who preferred the £25,000 reward for turning the fugitive over to the government. The marquis was taken to **EDINBURGH** and hanged at the mercat cross on 21 May. In 1661, his remains were buried in the high kirk of St Giles, where a monument was erected to his memory in 1888. (See **BLAIR CASTLE**).

GRAHAM, JOHN (1648–89). Scourge of the **COVENANTERS** and leader of the 1689 **JACOBITE** rising in Scotland, Graham was the son of Magdalene and William Graham of Claverhouse (near Dundee). He was educated at **ST ANDREWS** University, then, from 1672 until 1677, served as a volunteer in the French and Dutch armies and is reputed to have saved the life of William of Orange (later William III) at the Battle of Seneff in 1674. In 1678, he was given command of a troop of horses raised to combat the threat posed by the Covenanters in southwest Scotland, and, the following year, was appointed sheriff-depute for the area. On 1 June 1679, he was lucky to escape with his life from a skirmish with a Covenanter force at Drumclog, but three weeks later, at the **BATTLE OF BOTHWELL BRIDGE,** he commanded the cavalry unit which helped to defeat the rebel army. For the next three years, Graham spent much of his time in London but, from 1682 until 1685, as **SHERIFF** of Wigton, returned to his attempts to suppress Covenanter activities. (See **APOLOGETICAL DECLARATION**). His harsh tactics earned him the nickname Bluidy (Bloody) Clavers although historians now believe that his reputation for atrocity was probably overenhanced and that no more than ten **CAMERONIANS** were murdered on his orders.

When the Protestant William of Orange arrived in Britain in 1688, Graham, promoted to Major-General two years earlier, was second-in-command of a Scottish army which marched into England in support of King James VII and II. He returned without seeing action and, in November of the same year, was created Viscount Dundee, but continued to contest William's right to the Scottish throne. In 1689, he persuaded an army of highlanders to rally to the **STUART** cause. Bonnie Dundee was declared a rebel, and a large reward was offered for his capture but, undaunted, he led his men to meet William's troops in the **BATTLE OF KILLIECRANKIE** on 27 July and forced them to retreat. It was a bittersweet victory because Dundee was shot dead in the struggle and buried nearby at Old Blair. His regiments pushed south to Dunkeld but were repulsed by a force of Covenanters, and the rebellion petered out as they drifted home.

GRATTAN'S PARLIAMENT. The Irish Parliament of 1782–1800 was named after Henry Grattan, an **ULSTER** politician who led the patriotic opposition and became a charismatic figure among the **IRISH VOLUNTEERS** after drawing up a Declaration of Rights in 1780, presenting a series of brilliant speeches in support of Irish freedoms and denouncing proposals for the union of Ireland with Great Britain. In 1782, Ireland's legislature, taking advantage of British military preoccupation elsewhere and a change of government in London, passed his Declaration, which altered the legislative authority of Westminster, repealed **POYNINGS' LAW** and ensured that bills from Ireland could go to London only from the Irish Parliament and not from the governor. This Constitution of 1782 gave apparent legislative freedom to the Irish assembly, but, with Britain retaining an executive in Dublin, the real advantages were superficial and were removed entirely by the **ACT OF UNION** in 1800.

GREAT CAUSE, 1292. This term is applied to the process of adjudication by King Edward I of England between the claims of 13 nobles to the throne of Scotland. He chose **JOHN BALLIOL.** (See **BATTLE OF DUNBAR**).

GREAT GLEN. Following the line of a major geological fault, the Great Glen runs for 66 miles across Scotland from **INVERNESS** to Fort William, continuing northeastward beneath the Moray Firth and southwestward beneath Loch Linnhe. It is marked by a string of **LOCHS** including Loch Ness, Loch Oich and Loch Lochy. Road transport from the northwest of the **SCOTTISH HIGHLANDS** to the south is channelled along the **GLEN** and, in 1822, a canal (designed by **THOMAS TELFORD**) was built to allow fishing vessels to pass from the east to the west coast of Scotland without negotiating the stormy waters of the Pentland Firth, off the north coast. The valley floor is used primarily as grazing land, and forests cover many of the hill slopes.

GRETNA GREEN. A village in southwest Scotland, less than a mile north of the English border, Gretna made an industry out of wedding eloping couples. Under Scots law, a marriage was recognized if the partners declared, in front of witnesses, that they wanted to be united. That practice had been outlawed in England in 1754 but remained valid in Scotland (which retained its own **LEGAL SYSTEM** under the terms of the **TREATY OF UNION),** so, during the late 18th century, Gretna became a goal for young people whose intention to marry had encountered parental disapproval. The declaration ceremony was usually presided over by the local blacksmith, but, in practice, anybody could officiate. In 1856, a change in the law required at least one of the contracting parties to live in Scotland for 21 days before the wedding (thus giving ardour a chance to cool and irate parents an opportunity to retrieve their runaway offspring). Then, in 1939, marriage by declaration was abolished. However, Gretna's reputation survived, and there are now over 4,000 weddings in the village each year, about ten per cent of them involving people from abroad. Some of the participants are attracted by the area's romanticized past, but most are simply avoiding the fuss of a big ceremony at home.

GRIMOND, BARON. (See **JOSEPH GRIMOND**).

GRIMOND, JOSEPH (1913–93). Leader of the Liberal Party from 1956 until 1967, Grimond was born in **ST ANDREWS** on 29 July 1913, the son of Joeseph and Helen Grimond. He was educated at Eton College and Oxford University, where he was a Brackenbury Scholar and graduated with a first class honours degree in politics, philosophy and economics. He was called to the Bar in 1937 and served as a major with the Fife and Forfar Yeomanry during the Second World War. In 1945, he was appointed Director of Personnel with the European Division of the United Nations Relief and Rehabilitation Administration, then, in 1947, became secretary of the **NATIONAL TRUST FOR SCOTLAND.** He entered Parliament in 1950 as the MP for **ORKNEY** and **SHETLAND** (one of the most remote constituencies in Britain) and retained the seat until his voluntary retirement in 1983. For his first six years in the House of Commons, he was Liberal Chief Whip then, in 1956, was elected leader of the party (succeeding **CLEMENT DAVIES**). In that role, he advocated British membership of the Common Market, making the Liberals the first British political party to commit itself to closer integration with the countries of western Europe. He also proposed a policy of co-partnership between management and labour in industry and argued that the United Kingdom should abandon its independent nuclear arsenal.

Grimond's leadership and imaginative policies appealed to many on the political middle ground and led to a doubling of the Liberal vote at the 1959 General Election, but the party's support was widely spread so it failed to improve on its six House of Commons seats. That disparity between votes and seats led to advocacy of a system of proportional representation — a policy which appealed to the minority parties but which threatened the vested interests of the Labour Party and the Conservative Party. The Liberals did well again in 1964 but reverses in 1966 encouraged Grimond to step down from the leadership though he remained an MP and was acting leader for a few weeks in 1976 after Jeremy Thorpe's resignation.

Outside Parliament, he was a trustee of the Manchester Guardian and Evening News Ltd (1967–83), Rector of **EDINBURGH** University (1960–63) and **ABERDEEN** University (1970–73), and Chancellor of the University of Kent (1970–90). He was raised to the peerage as Baron Grimond in 1983 and died on Orkney on 24 October 1993. Very much an ideas man, Grimond was an outstanding public speaker, who appealed to the university community and the educated middle classes but, in the end, was ground down by the emotional roller-coaster effect of by-election victory and General Election defeat. When he resigned in 1967, an editorial in the *New York Times* claimed that under him the Liberals had been a "small, first-rate, irrepressible minority — a leavening in Parliament, a yeast".

GRUFFUDD AP LLYWELYN (*c.* 1007–63). Gruffudd, the son of Llewelyn ap Seisyll (who controlled the northern territory of Gwynedd), was the only native Welsh ruler to exert authority over the whole area covered by modern Wales, an achievement won through ruthless acquisition of territory by force of arms. In 1039, he killed Iago ab Idwal to acquire Gwynedd and Powys and, shortly afterwards, defeated a Mercian force at Crossford, on the River Severn. Over the next 18 years, he became the dominant force in Wales, adding the Kingdom of Deheubarth to his estates by 1055 and driving Cadwgan ap Meurig out of Glamorgan in 1057. Gruffudd was also intent on expanding into the fertile borderlands settled by the Mercians some three centuries earlier. In 1055, for example, he burned Hereford and, in 1062, led a force to pillage lands east of the Severn. In 1063, however, Harold, Earl of Wessex, mounted a retributive campaign and chased him further and further into the hills. On 5 August, he was killed somewhere in **SNOWDONIA.** The circumstances of his death are not clear, but it is likely that he was either murdered by his own followers or betrayed by them to Harold's army.

GWYNEDDIGION. Formed in London in 1770, the Gwyneddigion was a society of Welsh patriots dedicated to supporting the principality's distinctive cultural characteristics. Its membership — more proletarian than that of the **CYMMRODORIAN** — revived the **EISTEDDFOD**au in 1789 and was much influenced by the radical views of the French Revolution, which began the same year. In particular, it proved receptive to the new concepts of religious and political freedom spreading from mainland Europe and focussed debate by publishing many works advocating social reform, support for the **WELSH** language and the widening of educational opportunity. Also, the Gwyneddigion made the contents of several traditional manuscripts (such as the poems of **DAFYDD AP GWILYM**) more widely available, providing a foundation for much 19th-century Welsh scholarship.

—H—

HADDINGTON, TREATY OF, 7 July 1548. The Duke of Somerset, (Lord Protector during the minority of Edward VI and thus ruler of England between 1547 and 1549), continued the policy of **ROUGH WOOING** in his relations with the Scots, defeating them at the **BATTLE OF PINKIE** in 1547. The Scots sought help through the **AULD ALLIANCE** and met at Haddington on 7 July 1548 with French representatives. The resultant treaty promised French military assistance against the English and the acceptance of the Earl of

Arran as regent in Scotland, while, in return, the Scots agreed to send **MARY, QUEEN OF SCOTS,** then only five years old, to France, where she would eventually marry the Dauphin, heir to the throne. The treaty underlined the failure of English policy towards Scotland and the ever present influence of its enemy, France, north of the border.

HAGUE, WILLIAM JEFFERSON (1961–). Appointed **SECRETARY OF STATE FOR WALES** by Prime Minister John Major in 1995, Hague always seemed destined for a career in politics. He was born on 26 March 1961, the son of Stella and Timothy Hague, attended Wath-upon-Dearne Comprehensive School and, in 1977 (at the age of 16), addressed the Conservative Party's annual conference, announcing that it was time to "roll back the frontiers of the state" and reverse the evils of socialism. Margaret Thatcher, the party leader, called him "possibly another young Pitt", and the *Daily Mail* labelled him "Maggie's Bionic Babe". He continued his education at Oxford University, where he was President of the Union and of the Conservative Association in 1981, then took an MBA at the Institut Européen d'Administration des Affaires (near Paris) before embarking on a career as a management consultant. In 1983, he worked as a part-time political adviser to Geoffrey Howe and Leon Brittain at the Treasury and, in 1987, made his first, yet unsuccessful, attempt to become a member of Parliament by contesting Wentworth, his home constituency. In 1989, he won Richmond and, the following year, was made Parliamentary private secretary to Norman Lamont (Chancellor of the Exchequer). In 1993, he became Parliamentary Under-Secretary of State at the Department of Social Security and in 1995 was moved to the post of Minister for Social Security and Disabled People. His appointment as Welsh Secretary was roundly condemned in the principality, where the Labour Party dominates. A native Englishmen who did not even represent a Welsh constituency, he was considered by many to be a symbol of political overlordship (in fact, most Labour, Liberal and **PLAID CYMRU** representatives boycotted his first appearance as Secretary of State in the House of Commons). Almost immediately, he raised hackles by approving a motorway project that would damage several important wildlife habitats but, after that, he kept a relatively low profile, apparently preferring to work with local individuals and organizations rather than promote radical change. Following the Conservatives' defeat at the 1997 general election, John Major resigned the leadership of the party and Hague replaced him even though his critics claimed that he had neither the charisma nor the intellectual abilities of the new Labour Prime Minister, **ANTHONY CHARLES LYNTON BLAIR.**

HAIG, DOUGLAS (1861–1928). Commander-in-Chief of the British forces in France for much of the First World War, Haig was born in **EDINBURGH** on 19 June 1861, the son of John and Rachel Haig. He was educated at Clifton College, Oxford University and the Royal Military Academy Sandhurst then, in 1885, joined the 7th Hussars and served in the Sudan (1898) and the Boer War (1899-1902), rising to the rank of captain in 1891. In 1902, he took command of the 17th Lancers and, the following year, was posted to India as Inspector-General of Cavalry. He returned to Britain in 1906 and spent three years at the War Office as Director of Military Training before going back to the subcontinent as Chief of the General Staff (1909).

In 1912, he took command of the 1st Cavalry Brigade at Aldershot then, at the outbreak of the First World War in 1914, led the 1st Army Corps into Europe. The following year the Corps was expanded into the 1st Army and Haig was made Commander-in-Chief. The administrative problems were considerable. Volunteers had to be trained and integrated both with the regular army and with the Territorial Army at a time when the French were attempting to make Haig commit more troops to the front line. Moreover, the size of the fighting force — at the time, the largest British army ever assembled in war — made efficient supply and coordination difficult to achieve. The Battle of the Somme (1916), fought at the insistence of General Joffre of France and against Haig's advice, resulted in such a high casualty rate that politicians in London (including Prime Minister David Lloyd George) questioned the strategy adopted by the leaders in the field. Events at Passchendaele (Belgium) in 1917 added fuel to the flames even though Haig had been promoted to Field Marshal by King George V the previous year and had received a letter of support from former War Minister Lord Richard Haldane. In March 1918, however, he held the army together in the face of a heavy onslaught by German troops and, working in concert with General Foch of France, forced the enemy to retreat and, ultimately, to surrender.

In 1919, he was created Earl Haig of Bemersyde and, from then, devoted much of his time to the interests of ex-servicemen, helping to unite a number of charitable organizations into the British Legion (1921) and travelling the world in his attempts to further the welfare of officers and men who had suffered as a result of the fighting. He died in London on 29 January 1928 and was buried at Dryburgh Abbey, in the Scottish **BORDERS.**

HALIDON HILL, BATTLE OF, 19 July 1333. Sir Archibald Douglas attempted to relieve Berwick from occupation by the forces of King Edward III of England and **EDWARD BALLIOL,** the puppet king on the throne of Scotland. However, the English bowmen proved superior against a Scottish force bogged down in marshy ground and Douglas was killed, along with five other earls. This conflict is sometimes known as the **BATTLE OF BERWICK.**

HALLOWEEN. Halloween festivities on 31 October are a modern version of the Celtic festival of samhain, which marked the end of summer, and are particularly celebrated in Scotland and Ireland. For the Celts, Halloween signified the end of the old year and the beginning of the new. Cattle were returned to the farms from distant pastures, laws were reenacted and landholding arrangements reviewed. Ghosts and spirits were believed to roam the earth during the night, and the souls of the dead returned to their old homes. It was thought that these supernatural beings played tricks on those who failed to please them and had to be placated by fire, hence the tradition of lighting bonfires (though these are now more common on 5 November, Guy Fawkes Night, an introduction from England during the 20th century). The spirits themselves have their latterday manifestation as guisers — children who dress up, cover their faces with masks, carry a turnip lantern and knock on neighbours' doors, offering songs or a dance in return for sweets or fruit. Halloween was also considered to be a favourable time for predicting prospects for health, marriage and fortune. Many of the activities associated with these predictions involved the use of apples, which were originally of sacred significance because of their connections with harvest thanksgiving ceremonies. Thus, one party game still played involves 'dooking': apples are floated in a tub of water and anybody who can lift one out with his or her mouth will have good luck during the coming year. Halloween festivities were introduced to the United States by Irish and Scots emigrants and increased in popularity during the 19th century. 'Trick or treat' is the North American equivalent of guising, and the native pumpkin, rather than a hollowed-out turnip, is used to make the lantern. The name 'halloween' refers to the Christian feast of Hallowmass, held on 1 November.

HARDIE, JAMES KEIR (1856–1913). The first member of the Independent Labour Party to become a Member of Parliament, Hardie was born in Legbrannock (Lanarkshire) on 15 August 1856, the illegitimate son of Mary Keir, a domestic servant who later married carpenter William Hardie. He had no formal education, beginning work as a message boy at the age of seven and becoming a coal miner at ten. He quickly got involved in trade union politics and was eventually blacklisted by employers, branded as a troublemaker because of his attempts to persuade low-paid underground workers to take industrial action in an effort to improve their income. In 1878, unable to find a job, he opened a stationer's shop and started to write for the *Glasgow Evening Mail* while he acted as an unpaid official of several embryo miners' organizations. Two years later, he was invited to become secretary of the Ayrshire Miners' Union and, in 1887, launched *The Miner* (a monthly periodical which dealt both with events in the coal industry and with current political issues).

Keir Hardie had become an influential figure in the Scottish Labour Party by 1888, but polled only a few hundred votes at the Mid-Lanark Parliamentary election in that year. In 1892, he was more successful, entering the House of Commons as the Independent Labour MP for West Ham (South) and quickly establishing himself as a militant advocate of the rights of the working classes and the unemployed. The following year, he became the first chairman of the Independent Labour Party, which had been formed by the amalgamation of small socialist associations, but much of his influence was dissipated when he lost his Commons seat in 1895. From then until 1900, he edited *The Leader* (a periodical which had developed from *The Miner*) and attempted to persuade the trade unions to support the formation of a new political party which would represent working people and be independent both of the Liberal Party and of the Conservative Party.

The establishment of the Labour Representation Committee in 1900 was the fulfillment of a dream, but, although he won the Merthyr Tydfil seat for the new party at the General Election that year, only one other of its candidates joined him in the Commons. In 1906, however, he was one of 29 Labour victors, a group large enough to have its own organization at Westminster. Keir Hardie was elected chairman of the first Parliamentary Labour Party, an indication of his status in the movement, but ill-health forced him to give up the post the following year. As conflict with Germany appeared increasingly inevitable, he tried to persuade socialists throughout Europe to unite in a general strike if war broke out, but had little success. The Labour Party's decision to support Britain's war effort disillusioned him further and he died of pneumonia in **GLASGOW** on 26 September 1915, believing he was a failure.

HARLECH CASTLE. The small coastal settlement of Harlech, lying some 11 miles north of Barmouth, in north Wales, is the traditional capital of Merioneth. Although there is a local tradition that the site of the castle, which dominates the town and the countryside around, was first occupied during the tenth century, archaeological evidence indicates that the present structure was built between 1280 and 1284, during the reign of Edward I of England, as the Plantagenet barons of the House of Anjou attempted to subdue the Welsh. During the early 15th century, it was held by **OWAIN GLYNDWR**, who, according to tradition, was crowned Prince of Wales at the fortress in the presence of ambassadors from Castile, France and Scotland. In 1460, it provided a safe haven for Margaret of Anjou after her husband, King Henry VI of England, had been taken captive at the battle of Northampton, during the Wars of the Roses, and, in 1468, it was the last Lancastrian castle to fall to the Yorkist armies. Royalist forces held Harlech for King Charles during the first Civil War, which began in 1642, but it was surrendered to Roundhead troops under the command of Major General Thomas Mytton in 1647. It is now owned by the state and open to the public.

HARRIS, HOWEL (1714–73). One of the leaders of the 17th century **METHODIST REVIVAL** in Wales, Harris was born in Trefeca (Breconshire) on 23 January 1714, the second son of carpenter and farmer Howel Harris and his wife, Susanna. He was educated at Llwynllyd Academy before working as a schoolmaster in Llangorse following his father's death in 1730. On Whit Sunday 1735, at a service conducted by the Vicar of Talgarth, he decided to devote his life to spreading the Christian gospel and began to preach. A charismatic orator, he attracted large congregations, sometimes holding as many as five meetings in one day. As he made contact with other missionaries, such as **DAVID ROWLAND** and **WILLIAM WILLIAMS,** he worked with them to create cells of believers, many of whom had learned to read in **GRIFFITH JONES' CIRCULATING SCHOOLS.** These small bands of worshippers met regularly to study the Bible, and it was from them that the organization of the **CALVINISTIC METHODIST CHURCH OF WALES** evolved. In 1750, a clash with Rowland led Harris to retire to Trefeca, where he settled with a group of supporters and attempted to put his ideals into practice. Each member of the Family, as he called his community, had an allotted task, which made a contribution to overall welfare. Extended families lived together, profits went into a common fund, agricultural innovations were welcomed, a college for ministers was established and a militia was formed (five members of that tiny army served with General Wolfe at Quebec in 1759). In 1760, he returned to the mainstream Methodist movement and, once again, began to preach to congregations of thousands. Over the next ten years, he spoke at many gatherings outside Wales and to families at great country houses but the death of his wife in 1770 seemed to sap his energies and he died on 21 July 1773.

HEANEY, SEAMUS JUSTIN (1939–). Winner of the Nobel prize for literature in 1995, Heaney was born in **LONDONDERRY** on 13 April 1939, the son of cattle dealer Patrick Heaney and his wife, Margaret. He was educated at St Columb's College in the city, and then at Queen's University, **BELFAST,** where he graduated with a first class honours degree in 1961. He began his working life in Belfast, spending a year as a teacher at St Thomas's Secondary School (1962–63), then three years at St Joseph's College of Education before being appointed lecturer in English at Queen's University in 1966. From 1972 until 1975, he made his living as a freelance writer, then returned to teaching at Carysfort College in 1975. He was appointed Boylston Professor of Rhetoric and Oratory at Harvard in 1985 and Professor of Poetry at Oxford University in 1989, thereby holding two of the most prestigious teaching posts in the world of English literature. *Eleven Poems* (the first of his collections of poetry) appeared in 1965 and was followed a year later by *Death of a Naturalist*, which won the Somerset Maugham Award and the Cholmondeley Award. A clutch of prizes followed, culminating in the Whitbread Award (for *Haw Lantern*) in 1987 and the Nobel prize eight years later. The Nobel committee praised the "lyrical beauty and ethical quality" of his work and commended him for speaking out about violence in Northern Ireland. (The irony that the wealth of Nobel, an explosives merchant, should bring honour to a man of peace was probably not lost on Heaney.) His early work reflects his rural childhood, conjuring up images of thatching, threshing, cow milking and blackberry picking but later poems consider the roots of **THE TROUBLES** in **ULSTER.** He has renounced his British nationality, and lives in Dublin.

HEBRIDES, THE. Collectively, the islands lying off the west coast of Scotland are known as the Hebrides. They form two groups. The

Outer Hebrides lie farthest from the mainland, include Harris and Lewis, and are sometimes termed the Outer Isles or the Western Isles. The Inner Hebrides (of which Skye, Mull, Jura and Islay are the largest) lie closer to the British coast. The economy of the islands is dependent on agriculture (see **CROFTING**), fishing and (increasingly) tourism, with some industry (such as food processing, textiles and **WHISKY** distilling) locally important. The number of permanent residents has been declining since the late 18th century as young people have sought jobs in the major cities in Britain and abroad but, more recently, there have been indications that the trend is reversing in some places. On Skye, for example, the population in 1980 was just over 7,000 but by 1995 had risen to 12,000. In part, the rise is due to the creation of new employment opportunities as a result of the influx of holidaymakers, but there is also evidence that many people have left urban areas and taken their skills to the islands, establishing small craft businesses and other enterprises.

HENDERSON, ARTHUR (1863–1935). One of the founding fathers of the Labour Party, Foreign Secretary under Prime Minister Ramsay MacDonald and winner of the Nobel Peace Prize, Henderson was born in **GLASGOW** on 13 September 1863, the younger son of cotton spinner David Henderson. When he was nine years old, his father died, and the family moved to Newcastle following his mother's remarriage. Henderson had only an elementary school education before starting work as an apprentice at Robert Stephenson's foundry at the age of 12. As he grew up, he was increasingly involved in trade union activities and then in local and national politics. Also, while in his teens, he became a convinced Christian, adopting the Wesleyan tenets of cooperation and service to others as guiding principles for his public and private conduct. He was elected to Newcastle City Council in 1892 and, in 1903, won a by-election at the Parliamentary constituency of Barnard Castle. Despite his limitations as a speaker, he made a considerable impression in the House of Commons, working with Ramsay MacDonald, **JAMES KEIR HARDIE** and others to further the interests of the working classes. In 1906, he was appointed chairman of the Parliamentary Labour Party and, in 1911, became secretary of the Labour Party, holding that demanding post until 1934. When the First World War broke out in 1914, Henderson emerged as Leader of the Labour majority which supported British involvement. In 1915, Prime Minister Herbert Asquith included him in the wartime coalition government as President of the Board of Education and then, in 1916, as Paymaster General but his most important role was as adviser on the deployment of labour resources. When David Lloyd George succeeded Asquith in December 1916, Henderson became a member of the five-man cabinet which directed the war effort but resigned the following year when the Prime Minister refused to send delegates to a European socialist conference, supported by Russia and held at Stockholm.

Henderson's experience at the conference made him a convinced internationalist, but, in the period following the end of the war, he was forced to devote much of his energy to domestic matters as he lost his House of Commons seat in 1918, won Widnes in 1919, lost it in 1922, won East Newcastle early in 1923, lost it later in the year and finally won Burnley in 1924. MacDonald made Henderson Home Secretary in the first Labour administration (1924) but used him largely in the international arena, where he played a central role in the London conference called in 1924 to discuss the Dawes Plan for German reparations for the First World War and spent much time at Geneva establishing a protocol for the settlement of international disputes through arbitration. That background prepared him for his appointment as Foreign Secretary in 1929 and, despite a relatively short period in office, enabled him to play a significant part in the meetings of the League of Nations, working particularly for disarmament in Europe. In 1931, along with most Labour Party Members of Parliament, he split with MacDonald over economic policy and led the opposition to the national government in the House of Commons but lost his seat in October of that year.

He spent much of the remainder of his life on disarmament negotiations in Geneva, acting as Chairman of the World Disarmament Conference in 1932 and receiving the Nobel Peace Prize in 1934 in recognition of his contribution to minimizing conflict. Although he returned to Parliament as the MP for Clay Cross in 1933, his health was in decline, and he died in London on 20 October 1935. Never a charismatic leader, he was typical of the Scottish lad o' pairts, rising from a humble background to posts of great responsibility, and was held in high regard for his integrity and his loyalty to the Labour movement.

HERETABLE JURISDICTIONS ACT, 1747. Following the collapse of the second **JACOBITE REBELLION** in 1746, this Act of Parliament removed certain legal rights which had been inheritable in Scotland since early times. It brought Scotland more in line with English custom.

HIGH COURT OF JUSTICIARY. (See **LEGAL SYSTEM: SCOT-LAND**).

HIGHLAND CLEARANCES. Eviction of tenants from their farms in the **SCOTTISH HIGHLANDS** followed the suppression of the second **JACOBITE REBELLION** and reached a peak with the introduction of new techniques during the agricultural revolution from about 1790 until 1840. Depopulation was inevitable because the traditional subsistence existence would no longer support the numbers of people living on the land but clearance was promoted with great brutality by landowners determined to turn their estates over to sheep grazing in order to reap sufficient profits to maintain their own lifestyles. Many of the people emigrated to the United States, Canada, Australia and New Zealand, founding Scottish communities in these areas. The changes effectively brought an end to the **CLAN** system.

HIGHLAND DRESS. (See **KILT; PLAID; SGIAN DUBH; TARTAN**).

HIGHLAND GAMES. The original Scottish highland games were trials of strength and agility held at **CLAN** gatherings. The breakup of the clan system after the second **JACOBITE REBELLION** brought these activities to an end, but they were resurrected in a more formalized context during the 19th century, helped by Queen Victoria's affection for Scotland. Events at Aboyne, Ballater, Braemar, Dunoon and Oban had been established by 1871 and were followed by others at locations throughout the country, including places (such as Alva) well outside the **SCOTTISH HIGHLANDS.** Usually, the local clan chief, or some other dignitary, acts as president of the games, and participants compete at highland dancing, playing the **BAGPIPES,** running, field events and wrestling. The most distinctively Scottish of the athletic competitions is tossing the caber — a task which involves throwing a wooden pole, about 17 feet long and some 90 lb in weight, through 180° of vertical trajectory. Traditionally, only men could take part in the dancing, but, during the 20th century, most organizers have allowed women to compete. Some critics have complained about the commercialisation surrounding the modern games, but, for many communities, the influx of visitors provides a welcome source of income. In some towns and villages, it has proved difficult, in recent years, to find people willing to serve on organizing committees and, as a result, games have been abandoned.

HIGHLAND LAND WAR (1883-8), (See **CROFTER'S WAR**).

HIGHLANDS AND ISLANDS DEVELOPMENT BOARD (HIDB).
The board was established by Act of Parliament in 1965 and given
a remit to improve social and economic conditions in the **SCOT-
TISH HIGHLANDS.** It was responsible to the **SECRETARY OF
STATE FOR SCOTLAND** and exercised its powers over an area
of 3.6 million hectares (47 per cent of Scotland), of which only about
5 per cent was woodland and 7 per cent suitable for crops. The bulk
of the remainder was rough grazing for sheep and deer. It attempted
to establish a growth pole policy, with development focussed on three
sites — Caithness (which had an atomic power station at Dounreay),
Fort William (where a pulp and paper mill opened in 1966) and
Invergordon (where bauxite was smelted). However, although the
board could borrow money, acquire land and premises by compulsory purchase and enter into partnership with private businesses, it
had no powers to carry out strategic planning (and therefore no powers to coordinate resource use) so its ability to attract and direct development was limited. Its greatest success was the promotion of
small-scale enterprises which helped to create jobs in village
communities and, as a result, stemmed migration. Grants to knitwear
manufacturers, fishery firms, fish farmers, food processors and to the
GAELIC Books Council for provision of mobile libraries have all
provided employment, much of it for women, who often have difficulty finding work in rural environments. It was reconstituted in 1991
as **HIGHLANDS AND ISLANDS ENTERPRISE.**

HIGHLANDS AND ISLANDS ENTERPRISE (HIE). The successor
to the **HIGHLANDS AND ISLANDS DEVELOPMENT
BOARD,** Highlands and Islands Enterprise was formed in 1991 and
is charged with promoting economic improvements in the **SCOT-
TISH HIGHLANDS** from the estuary of the **RIVER CLYDE** to
the **SHETLAND ISLANDS,** the **HEBRIDES** and Morayshire. It
has developed a business strategy which focuses on four main areas
— food and drink; knowledge, information and telecommunications;
manufacturing and production; and tourism — and operates through
ten regional Local Enterprise Companies, which help local firms to
market products and assist companies to secure funding from the
European Union. An annual budget of some £75 million provides
financial assistance through loans and grants, builds factories and
offices, supports business advisory services and promotes products.
Partly as a result of its activities, unemployment has declined and

population is increasing.

HIGHLANDS, SCOTTISH. Geologically, the highlands lie north of a fault line running from Helensburgh (on the north bank of the **RIVER CLYDE,** some 22 miles west of **GLASGOW**) to Stonehaven (on the northeast coast of Scotland, 16 miles south of **ABERDEEN**). However, popular perceptions usually exclude the flat plains of the north and east coasts. The much-eroded remnants of a mountain chain, once part of the North American Appalachian system and formed over 300 million years ago, the highland hills rise to 4,406 feet at Ben Nevis, near Fort William. They were scoured by ice during several glaciations and are now characterized by thin, acid soils and steep-sided **GLENS**. Rainfall is high (over 100 inches per annum in the west), and much tree cover has been removed, partly for commercial reasons and partly because sheep grazing has prevented regeneration. Land suitable for arable farming is limited so agricultural enterprises concentrate on sheep and cattle rearing. Tourism, however, is the mainstay of the modern economy, with sea fisheries and small industrial activities (such as the manufacture of glassware) at some locations. Deer stalking, grouse shooting and salmon fishing supplement income on many estates but are dependent on an affluent clientele and suffer during recessions. It was in this part of Scotland that the **CLAN**s were based, and, although they were broken up in the aftermath of the second **JACOBITE REBELLION,** echoes of the society they nurtured are still found in the continued use of the **GAELIC** language, in activities such as the playing of the **BAGPIPES** and in the sports at **HIGHLAND GAMES.** Population is scattered, with Fort William, **INVERNESS** and Oban the major settlements. (See **AN COMUNN GAIDHEALACH; GREAT GLEN; HIGHLANDS AND ISLANDS DEVELOPMENT BOARD; HIGHLANDS AND ISLANDS ENTERPRISE; KILT; PLAID; SGIAN DUBH; TARTAN**).

HILLSBOROUGH AGREEMENT. (See **ANGLO-IRISH AGREEMENT**).

HOGMANAY. The derivation of the Scots' name for New Year's Eve is disputed but is probably a corruption of the 16th-century northern French dialect *hoginane*, which meant *a gift at new year*. Within living memory, hogmanay was a more important celebration than Christmas over most of Scotland, and many of the yuletide customs (such as hanging up stockings) were observed on the night of 31 December. The most significant ritual was first-footing. Men would go from house to house, exchanging tots of whisky and leaving short-bread or black bun (a heavy fruit cake) and coal (signifying food and warmth) at each home. It was considered lucky to have a dark-haired man as a first-foot. Also, a drink of the first water drawn from a well after midnight was believed to bring good health and fortune in love. New Year's Day was a time for team games, particularly football and **SHINTY**. Hogmanay is still an important event in the Scottish calendar, but the incidence of first-footing has diminished in the face of seasonal television programmes. (Criticizing the attempts of TV producers to mark the passing of the old year and the start of the new is a much-loved sport in Scotland). Rigorous police attention to those who drink and drive has also reduced mobility, but parties are common, particularly amongst the young, and 1 January is a time for family reunions. (Steak pie is the traditional meal). Many Scots residents in England return home for the new year, leading to enormous traffic jams on the southbound roads as they head back home at the end of the holiday.

HOLYROOD HOUSE. The palace at the eastern end of **EDINBURGH**'s royal mile is one of the sovereign's official residences in Scotland. It is located beside an abbey established by King **DAVID I** in 1128 and given to the monks of St Augustine. That abbey became one of the wealthiest in the country and provided accommodation for members of the royal family until, in 1501, **JAMES IV** began construction of his own residence in the courtyard. Most of that 16th-century building has since been swept away as a result of a series of major extensions and improvements, which began during the reign of Charles II in 1672 and involved the carting of glass from France, white lead from Holland and marble from Italy. Holyrood Park (sometimes called King's Park) lies behind the building, and provides a large area of open, hilly grassland for public recreation. The palace itself can be visited when Queen Elizabeth II is not in residence.

HOME RULE. The United Kingdom is a unitary state, with administrative control centralized at the national Parliament in London. However, in Ireland, Scotland and Wales there is a long history of campaigning both for **DEVOLUTION** of limited powers to regional assemblies and for home rule (that is, complete political independence).
<u>Ireland</u>. In the 1840s, the **YOUNG IRELAND** movement had called for the repeal of the **ACT OF UNION** (1800), and a Home

Rule Party was established in 1870. The first home rule bill was introduced to Westminster by Prime Minister William Gladstone in 1886, but, together with one in 1893, it was rejected by the House of Lords. A third bill, when Ireland was facing civil war, was passed in 1914 but was opposed by the **ULSTER** Unionists and **SINN FEIN** and later suspended because of the First World War. The **GOVERNMENT OF IRELAND ACT** (1920) partitioned Ireland and the **ANGLO-IRISH TREATY** of 1921 finally established the **IRISH FREE STATE** and Northern Ireland as separate entities, with the north getting its own Parliament at **STORMONT** but Westminster retaining authority over matters relating to the United Kingdom as a whole. (See **SOCIETY OF UNITED IRISHMEN**).

Scotland. Nationalism has been a political force in Scotland since the 1880s, when Gladstone responded by appointing an Under-Secretary of State at the Home Office who was given specific responsibility for matters related to Scotland. That action defused some of the movement, though the **SCOTTISH HOME RULE ASSOCIATION** was created in 1886 and 15 bills advocating home rule were presented, unsuccessfully, between 1908 and 1939. The **SCOTTISH NATIONAL PARTY** remains wedded to the full independence ideal for Scotland. (See **NATIONAL PARTY OF SCOTLAND; SOCIETY OF UNITED SCOTSMEN**).

Wales. Because of its longer incorporation into union with England, **WALES** has not experienced widespread support for home rule, though there was a brief period of agitation by the **YOUNG WALES** movement at the end of the 19th century. **PLAID CYMRU,** the nationalist party (formed in 1925), has independence as its ultimate objective.

HOWARD, MICHAEL (1941–). Successively Secretary of State for Employment, Environment, and Home Affairs in Prime Minister John Major's governments, Howard was born on 7 July 1941, the son of Bernard and Hilda Howard. He was educated at Llanelli Grammar School and then at Cambridge University, where he was president of the union in 1962. He qualified as a barrister in 1964 and contested the Liverpool Edge Hill Parliamentary constituencies for the Conservative Party in 1966 and 1970 but did not enter the House of Commons until 1983, when he won the Folkestone and Hythe seat. Howard's progress under Prime Minister Margaret Thatcher was rapid. He served as Parliamentary Private Secretary to the solicitor general (1984–85) and Parliamentary Under-Secretary of State at the Department of Trade and Industry (1985–87), then held ministerial office with responsibility for local government (1987–88), water and planning (1988–89), and housing (1989–90). He was made Secretary of State for Employment in 1990, moved to the Department of the Environment in 1992, and was transferred to the Home Office in 1993. The following year, he resisted demands for his resignation after Semtex explosive was found in Whitemoor Prison following the escape of five **IRISH REPUBLICAN ARMY** prisoners. In 1995 and 1996, he continued to demonstrate his political survival skills, crossing swords with senior judges after the courts had ruled that he had abused his powers over the introduction of a cost-cutting scheme for compensating victims of crime and the imposition of a mandatory 15-year sentence on two schoolboy murderers. In 1997, when John Major resigned after the Conservatives' General Election defeat, Howard was one of six candidates for the leadership of the Party, which was won by **WILLIAM HAGUE.** Howard was appointed spokesman on Foreign Affairs in Hagues' shadow cabinet.

HOWE, BARON. (See **RICHARD HOWE**).

HOWE, RICHARD EDWARD GEOFFREY (1926–). A leading figure in Margaret Thatcher's Conservative Party administrations throughout the 1980s, Howe was born on 20 December 1926, the son of Mr B. E. and Mrs E. F. Howe of Port Talbot. He was educated at Winchester College, then served as a Lieutenant in the Royal Signals between 1945 and 1948. After completion of his national service, he went to Cambridge University, where he studied law and in 1951 became chairman of the Conservative Association. In 1952, he was called to the Bar and between 1957 and 1960 was managing director of the *Crossbow* periodical, acting as editor from 1960 until 1962. He first attempted to enter Parliament at elections in Aberavon in 1955 and 1959, eventually winning the Bebington seat, which he held from 1964 until 1966. He represented Reigate from 1970 until 1974 and East Surrey from 1974 until 1992. In 1965 he became a Queen's Counsel and sat on the opposition front bench as spokesman for labour and social affairs. He was knighted in 1970 and appointed Solicitor General by Prime Minister Edward Heath, moving to the Ministry of Trade and Consumer Affairs in 1972. When Harold Wilson took the Labour Party to power in 1974, Howe reverted to the Opposition benches as Spokesman on Social Services (1974–75) and Economic Affairs (1975–79).

Margaret Thatcher appointed him Chancellor of the Exchequer in

1979, Secretary of State for Foreign and Commonwealth Affairs in 1983 and Leader of the House of Commons in 1989. During his four years as Chancellor, he reduced the rate of inflation, and, by 1989, his status in the party was such that, when the Prime Minister carried out a Cabinet shuffle in which he lost his post as Foreign Secretary, he was able to insist on the title of Deputy Prime Minister and the grant of an official country residence. In 1990, he argued that Britain should take a leading part in talks about the establishment of a single European currency but Mrs Thatcher was unconvinced, declared the plans unacceptable and attacked the notion of a federal Europe dominated by what she believed was the socialist ethos of Brussels. On 1 November, Howe could take no more and resigned, the last minister from her 1979 cabinet to go. In a bitter House of Commons speech 12 days later, he told MPs that the Prime Minister had a "nightmare" vision of a Europe "positively teeming with ill-intentioned people scheming . . . to extinguish democracy". That view, he claimed, presented "increasingly serious risks for the future of our nation". The resignation and its vituperative aftermath exposed deeply entrenched Conservative differences over Europe and highlighted Mrs Thatcher's autocratic approach to government, eventually leading to her final departure from Downing Street on 22 November.

Throughout his period in politics, Howe had maintained links with business and commerce. He was a director of the AGP Research Group and of the Sun Alliance Insurance Group between 1974 and 1979 and of EMI Ltd between 1976 and 1979. Since 1991, he has been a director of BICC plc and of Glaxo Holdings. He was awarded an honorary doctorate by the University of Wales in 1988 and raised to the peerage as Baron Howe of Aberavon in 1992.

HOWELL THE GOOD. (See HYWEL DDA).

HUME, DAVID (1711–76). One of the great advocates of empiricism, Hume was born on 26 April 1711, the younger son of Catherine and Joseph Hume, who farmed land near Berwick-upon-Tweed. David showed an aptitude for learning, entering **EDINBURGH** University in 1723. In 1734, after working in a Bristol merchant's office, he moved to France and spent three years there, preparing *A Treatise of Human Nature*, published in three volumes in 1739–40. The work got little attention, but *Essays, Moral and Political* (1741–42, two volumes) was better received, and on the basis of that success, he applied for the chair of moral philosophy at Edinburgh in 1744.

Turned down because of allegations of heresy and atheism in *Treatise*, he spent seven years travelling through England, France, Austria and Italy, earning money to support his studies and publishing further philosphical works, including *Three Essays Moral and Political* (1748) and *Philosophical Essays Concerning Human Understanding* (also 1748). He returned to Edinburgh in 1751 and was made Keeper of the Advocates' Library the following year. Surrounded by books, he turned to historical studies, publishing *Political Discourses* in 1752 and *History of England* in six volumes between 1754 and 1762. These texts brought him to the notice of scholars throughout Europe, with translations produced in French and German.

In 1763, Hume moved to France as Secretary to the British Embassy, and was lauded by Paris society. Returning to Britain in 1766, he brought Jean Jacques Rousseau with him, providing him with refuge from persecution at Wootton, Staffordshire. Rousseau, however, became convinced of Hume's bad faith and returned to his homeland, provoking a bitter quarrel between the two philosophers. In 1769, Hume went back to Edinburgh, where he took ill and died on 25 August 1776. On his deathbed, he wrote *Dialogues Concerning Natural Religion* (1779) and his autobiography, *The Life of David Hume, Written by Himself* (1776).

Hume's work was greatly influenced by George Berkeley and John Locke. His philosophy was founded on the principle that all knowledge comes from the senses or from logic but that no theory of reality is possible because sense impressions provide no proof of the existence of physical objects and no certain foundation for the establishment of scientific laws. He also maintained that moral actions are based on social custom, not reason, and on an innate feeling of sympathy for one's fellows. The arguments led Auguste Comte to frame his positivist philosophy and strongly influenced the work of Jeremy Bentham, John Stuart Mill and Immanuel Kant. (See **SCOTTISH ENLIGHTENMENT**).

HUME, JOHN (1937–   ). The leader of the **SOCIAL DEMOCRATIC AND LABOUR PARTY (SDLP)**, Hume has gained a reputation as a leading voice of Roman Catholic moderates in Northern Ireland. He was born in **LONDONDERRY** on 18 January 1937, the son of Mr and Mrs Samuel Hume, and attended St Columb's College (Derry) and St Patrick's College (part of the University of Ireland). He became president of the Credit Union League of Ireland (a forerunner of the SDLP) in 1964, was elected to the Northern Ireland

Parliament in 1969, joined the **NORTHERN IRELAND ASSEM-BLY** in 1973 and participated in the **NORTHERN IRELAND CONSTITUTIONAL CONVENTION** of 1975–76. In 1979, he was made leader of the SDLP and also took his place as a member of the European Parliament. Four years later, he was elected member of Parliament for the Foyle constituency and, since then, has earned a considerable reputation from politicians of all parties as an opponent of violence and extremism in **ULSTER**. His attempts to reduce the conflict have also been recognized through honorary degrees awarded to him by the University of Massachusetts, the Catholic University of America, St Joseph's University (Philadelphia) and Tusculum College (Tennessee).

HURD OF WESTWELL, LORD, (See **HURD, DOUGLAS**).

HURD, DOUGLAS (1930–). **SECRETARY OF STATE FOR NORTHERN IRELAND** from September 1984 until September 1985, Hurd is the eldest son of Baron Hurd and his wife, Stephanie. He was educated at Eton College and Cambridge University before working with the Diplomatic Service (1954–66). In 1966, he joined the Conservative Party's research section and, in 1974, was elected as Member of Parliament for Mid-Oxfordshire. Prime Minister Margaret Thatcher attached him to junior posts in her government from 1979, but his appointment as Northern Ireland Minister was something of a surprise and probably precipitated by the resignation of several senior members of the administration. Hurd's tenure at **STORMONT** was brief, but critical because it involved him in the negotiations leading up to the signing of the **ANGLO-IRISH AGREEMENT** in November 1985. In the late summer of 1985, he was moved back to London as Home Secretary and, in that capacity, was active in promoting antiterrorist measures (in 1988, for example, he prohibited radio and television stations from showing interviews with members of proscribed organizations). He was appointed Foreign Secretary in 1989 but resigned in 1995 so that he could spend more time with his young family. He was raised to the peerage as Lord Hurd of Westwell in 1997.

HUTTON, JAMES (1726–97). One of the fathers of the modern earth sciences, Hutton argued that the causes of geological phenomena could be attributed to processes still operating in the landscape and not to cataclysmic forces or (as the neptunist school claimed) to the existence of a primeval ocean which deposited mineral material on the seabed. Born in **EDINBURGH** on 3 June 1726, he studied at the university in his home city and also in Paris, qualifying as a Doctor of Medicine. He then turned to agricultural improvement, a task which gave him an opportunity to observe geological formations and speculate on their causes. From 1768, he devoted himself entirely to scientific matters, aiming to develop a theory which would account for the shape of the land in historical terms. In 1785, he published his views in a paper delivered to the Royal Society of Edinburgh and entitled *Theory of the Earth, or an Investigation of the Laws Observable in the Composition, Dissolution and Restoration of Land upon the Globe.* The essence of his argument was that the forces of nature which shape the earth's surface and interior operate uniformly throughout time and that, by implication, the forces shaping the landscapes of the present operate in the same ways as those which shaped landscapes of the past. Much emphasis was placed on the role of water. Rivers erode hills and deposit material beneath the ocean; these deposits are later uplifted to form mountains, allowing the process of erosion to start again.

Those claims have become accepted tenets of 20th-century geology but, at the time, they were a challenge to the accepted orthodoxy, which maintained that major earth surface features (such as mountain ranges) were shaped over a comparatively short period by catastrophic forces. In particular, the last sentence of his paper, which concluded that "The result . . . of our inquiry is that we find no vestige of a beginning — no prospect of an end", was taken as evidence of his atheism. (In practice, he was a sincere Christian and had merely followed sound principles of scientific investigation). A poor communicator, he never managed to convince the sceptics, but his friend John Playfair, Professor of Natural Philosophy at Edinburgh University, took over his mantle, explained the theories with great clarity and ensured their wider acceptance. Hutton died in Edinburgh on 26 March 1797, unaware of the measure of his contribution to science. (See **SCOTTISH ENLIGHTENMENT**).

HYWEL DDA (?–950). The grandson of **RHODRI MAWR,** Hywel (known in English as Howell the Good) was one of the most successful of the pre-Norman rulers in Wales. The son of Cadell, King of Seisyllwg (an area roughly encompassing Cardiganshire and the valley of the Towy), he gained control of Dyfed when his father-in-law, Llywarch ap Hyfaidd, died in 904. Following his father's death about 910, he ruled Seisyllwg with his brother, Clydog, for ten years and then (following Clydog's death) on his own, the joint Kingdom being known as Deheubarth. Territorial acquisitions continued until, in 942, he added Gwynedd to his estates when his cousin, Idwal Foel ap Anarawd, was killed in battle. That, in effect, made him King of the whole area of modern Wales, with the exception of parts of the south and southeast. Hywel's reign was characterized by a lack of conflict, largely because he was willing to accept a position as vassal to English monarchs. He made a pilgrimage to Rome in 928, but his most enduring achievement was the codification of the Welsh laws (see **CYFRAITH HYWEL DDA**), which were to provide a foundation for social organization in Wales until the 16th century. When he died, probably in 950, his kingdom passed to his son, Owain.

—I—

IBROX PARK DISASTER, 2 January 1972. The home ground of the **GLASGOW** Rangers **FOOTBALL** Club was the venue for a match with local rivals, Glasgow Celtic. When the teams drew level on goals, the pressure of the crowds in the stadium caused barriers to collapse, killing 66 people in the resultant crush. This was one of a number of incidents which led to the Safety of Sports Ground Act of 1975.

INTERNMENT. A policy adopted, in 1971, in Northern Ireland to combat terrorist activity during **THE TROUBLES,** internment involved the imprisonment of suspected members of terrorist organizations without formal trial proceedings. From 1971 until 1975, when the policy was abandoned, nearly 2,000 people were detained, the vast majority from nationalist organizations.

INVERGORDON MUTINY, August 1931. Large cuts in Royal Navy pay led ratings at the Invergordon base in Scotland to refuse to report for duty. The cuts were moderated, so the mutiny ended quickly and peacefully, but the incident created a run on sterling, which forced the government to abandon the gold standard.

INVERNESS. The principal settlement in the **SCOTTISH HIGHLANDS,** Inverness sits astride the River Ness at the northern end of the **GREAT GLEN.** Its location, commanding routes along the coast as well as to the interior, has long been strategically important. The site was occupied by prehistoric peoples as early as 4000

BC and, by AD sixth century, had become one of the **PICTS'** major strongholds. By 1153, the town had been made a Royal **BURGH** by King **DAVID I** and had used the trading privileges accompanying that designation to develop a thriving sea trade with mainland Europe, exporting fish, furs, wool and timber and importing hemp, which was used to make ropes. Its castle, believed to have been built by **MALCOLM III,** was a royal residence throughout the Middle Ages and was fought over as late as the first **JACOBITE REBELLION** in 1715. The railway arrived in 1855 and, between 1866 and 1871, the Cathedral of St Andrew was built, making Inverness an ecclesiastical centre of the Episcopal Church in Scotland. Because the area is distant from supplies of coal and minerals, the city was less directly affected by the Industrial Revolution than were other parts of the country but, after the end of the Second World War, there was considerable expansion of light manufacturing, particularly food processing. Also, since the 1970s, the settlement has developed as a service centre for oil exploration companies in the North Sea. As the administrative focus of the northern and central highlands, Inverness provides employment in local government and ancillary activities, such as printing.

IONA. A tiny island of little more than five square miles, Iona lies in the Inner **HEBRIDES,** off the west coast of Scotland. A centre of Christian worship for over 1,400 years, it still draws many thousands of pilgrims annually. About 563, **ST COLUMBA** arrived from Ireland with 12 disciples, established a monastery and began to convert the **PICT**ish peoples who had settled on the Scottish mainland and the offshore islands. His successors continued the missionary work, but a series of Viking invasions in 794, 801, 806, 840 and 986 resulted in the destruction of the monastery and, on the last occasion, the murder of the abbot and 15 monks. However, the Reilig Oran (the graveyard to the southwest of the church) remained as the last resting place of Scotland's kings until into the 11th century. Forty-eight Scottish, eight Norwegian and four Irish monarchs are reputed to be buried there, including **MACBETH.** In 1938, George MacLeod, minister at Govan in **GLASGOW,** established the Iona Community in an attempt to intermesh spiritual and material aspects of the Christian faith, as Columba had done. His leadership led to restoration of many of the buildings and to the reconsecration of the abbey in 1959. (See **BOOK OF KELLS**).

IRELAND, REPUBLIC OF. In 1937, the **IRISH FREE STATE** was renamed Éire, then, in 1949, left the Commonwealth of Nations and became the Republic of Ireland.

IRELAND ACT, 1949. This Act of the UK Parliament recognized the Republic of Ireland and declared that Northern Ireland would remain a part of the United Kingdom unless the people of the province, through their elected representatives in the Parliament at **STORMONT,** declared otherwise. It remains the basis of the loyalist stance on the political relationship between **ULSTER** and Great Britain.

IRISH FREE STATE. The Free State, consisting of the 26 southern counties of Ireland, was created by the **ANGLO-IRISH TREATY** in 1921 and given dominion status within the Commonwealth of Nations. It renamed itself Éire in 1937, and became the **REPUBLIC OF IRELAND** in 1949.

IRISH INDEPENDENCE PARTY (IIP). Formed in 1977, the IIP advocated British withdrawal from Northern Ireland. That withdrawal was to be followed by negotiations over the province's political future. The party fielded four candidates at the 1979 General Election but failed to win any seats and, from 1982, found its supporters drifting away to **SINN FEIN,** which had decided to enter electoral contests. By 1989, its membership was so small that it decided not to contest the **LOCAL GOVERNMENT** elections in **ULSTER.**

IRISH LAND ACT. Five major Acts of Parliament have affected land rights, always an important issue in Irish affairs, and a main focus of the agitation by the **IRISH LAND LEAGUE.**

1 August 1870. This act provided compensation for tenants who were evicted from their holdings and included recognition for the improvements they had made to the property. It also made provision for disputes over land rights to be settled by courts of arbitration. Although this was a major improvement in the tenants' favour, the legislation still allowed landlords to raise rents as high as they wished and to refuse new leases so it did little to reduce agrarian problems.

22 August 1881. Parliament conceded the three Fs demanded by the **IRISH LAND LEAGUE** — fair rents, freedom to sell and fixity of tenure — but that move, too, was received in Ireland with hostility.

14 August 1885. Known as Ashburne's Act, after its proposer, this

legislation provided for loans to tenants of the whole sum needed to buy the lands that they worked. The loans were to be repaid over 49 years at four per cent interest. The £5 million sum earmarked to support the legislation was exhausted within three years and had to be augmented in 1888 and 1891.

5 August 1891. Balfour's Act, promoted by Arthur Balfour, the Chief Secretary for Ireland and later to become Prime Minister, provided for more tenurial changes but restricted its provisions to purchases by land stock rather than cash. Its primary aim was to ease housing shortages.

21 July 1903. George Wyndham, the government's Chief Secretary for Ireland, produced proposals to wipe out poverty and rehouse one-third of the population which were widely accepted on both sides of the Irish Sea. His legislation provided a fund of £100 million to help tenants buy their land from the larger estates and to give bonuses to owners who agreed to sell. Although further action was required in 1909 to compel all landlords to sell, the measure greatly accelerated the pace of landholding changes.

Together, these Acts led to the purchase of properties totalling 11 million acres for just over £100 million.

IRISH LAND LEAGUE, 1879. In the wake of a severe agricultural depression in Ireland, a rash of evictions from tenancies and popular unrest about agrarian conditions, the League was formed in October 1879 by Michael Davitt, with Charles Parnell as its first president. Land reform and protection for tenants were its major aims. Its most successful tactic was boycotting — ostracism of estate owners and managers who were involved in evictions. The term is derived from the specific case of Captain Charles Boycott, who was eventually forced to leave Ireland by these tactics. The organization was suppressed by the Coercion Act of 1881 but was reincarnated as the Irish National Land League the following year. It contributed to the climate of public opinion which resulted in the **IRISH LAND ACT**s, and which linked these directly to the movement for **HOME RULE.**

IRISH NATIONAL LIBERATION ARMY (INLA). Established in 1975 as the paramilitary wing of the **IRISH REPUBLICAN SOCIALIST PARTY,** INLA draws most of its support from the Roman Catholic areas of **BELFAST** and County **LONDONDERRY.** It was declared illegal by the British government in 1979 after claiming responsibility for placing the car bomb which killed Conservative

Party MP Airey Neave in London. Since then, INLA has gained a reputation as one of the most violent of the Northern Ireland terrorist groups, including among its victims 17 people (11 of them soldiers) killed as a result of a pub bombing at Ballykelly (County Londonderry) in 1982. An internal feud in late 1986 and early 1987 led to 12 killings and was followed by a period of relative inactivity but, by 1990, it had resumed its hardline, high profile position. (See **IRISH PEOPLE'S LIBERATION ORGANISATION**).

IRISH NORTHERN AID COMMITTEE (NORAID). Founded in 1969 and based in the United States, the NORAID organization's stated aim is to raise funds for the families of nationalists killed or imprisoned as a result of attempts to persuade the British government to renounce sovereignty over Northern Ireland. It has been dogged by controversy since its creation, largely because of assertions that much of its income is used to provide arms for the **IRISH REPUBLICAN ARMY.** NORAID has about 100 branches in American centres of sympathy for the republican cause (Boston, Chicago and New York, for example) but has been denounced by senior politicians in Ireland and the United States of America as well as in the United Kingdom. (In 1991, Tom Foley, Speaker of the US House of Representatives, described it as a "disgusting charade").

IRISH PEOPLE'S LIBERATION ORGANIZATION (IPLO). The IPLO was born in 1986–87 as the result of a feud within the **IRISH NATIONAL LIBERATION ARMY.** It was responsible for sending letter bombs to two Members of Parliament in 1988 and, the same year, admitted responsibility for a series of explosions in **BELFAST,** its main area of support. In addition, it is suspected of a lengthy list of murders (five in 1991 alone). Many observers believe that, in 1992, the **IRISH REPUBLICAN ARMY** attempted to break up the organization because of its suspected involvement in drug dealing.

IRISH REBELLION. Three incidents in Anglo-Irish history are termed the Irish Rebellion by historians.
22 October 1641. An insurrection in **ULSTER** was organized by the native Roman Catholic gentry, who owned land but were under severe economic pressure and fearful of the growing power of the settlers who had arrived during the plantation period (see **PLANTATIONS OF ULSTER**). They massacred hundreds of Protestant immigrants and swore loyalty to King Charles I (fearing that, if Parliament were to oust him, their Catholic religion and their landhold-

ing traditions would have no champion in London). The rebellion was eventually put down by troops loyal to Oliver Cromwell. (See **GLAMORGAN TREATY; SETTLEMENT ACTS**).

23 May–21 June 1798. The **SOCIETY OF UNITED IRISH-MEN,** a secret group intent on independence for Ireland, planned an armed rebellion, in concert with a French landing in **ULSTER.** The French force of 15,000 troops initially sailed into Bantry Bay on 22 December 1796, but was turned back by storms. Believing the invasion was imminent, the Society decided not to seek immediate confrontation and the initiative was lost. When the rising did occur in 1797, it was quickly suppressed and the rebels were defeated at the **BATTLE OF VINEGAR HILL** and the **BATTLE OF BALLINAMUCK.** It did, however, emphasise the political problems facing the British government in Ireland and led, eventually, to the **ACT OF UNION** in 1800.

22–29 April 1916. (See **EASTER RISING**).

IRISH REPRESENTATIVE PEERS, 1800. The **ACT OF UNION** between Great Britain and Ireland, in 1800, dissolved the Irish Parliament and gave the Irish a right to representation at Westminster. The delegates included 28 Irish peers, who were elected by their colleagues to represent them in the House of Lords. Those not chosen for the Lords were entitled to seek election to the House of Commons. This arrangement ceased with the establishment of the **IRISH FREE STATE** in 1922.

IRISH REPUBLICAN ARMY (IRA). The IRA is the military wing of **SINN FEIN** and the largest organization advocating the use of violence as a means of forcing the United Kingdom government to renounce political control of Northern Ireland. Formed as a guerilla group fighting to gain Irish independence from Britain between 1919 and 1921, the organization split when the **IRISH FREE STATE** was created in 1921. Part of the force became legitimate, forming the core of the republic's new army, but the rest (those opposed to a continued British presence in Northern Ireland) continued the campaign, carrying out bombings in England in 1939-40 and also in **ULSTER** from 1942 to 44 and from 1956 to 62. However, internal differences led to a further split in 1970. One faction, which became known as the official IRA, argued that there was little public support for the destruction of life and property and that reform would be more speedily achieved by winning representation in the Parliaments of the republic, the United Kingdom and Ulster. The other, now known as the provisional IRA, favoured a continuation of the terrorism. The officials, left wing in their political orientation, were involved in further physical intimidation (bombing a Belfast public house in 1971, for instance), but, in May 1972, they called a ceasefire, which has remained in force.

The provisionals, by contrast, grew in strength and continued to target the army, the **ROYAL ULSTER CONSTABULARY** and members of loyalist groups, claiming responsibility for several hundred deaths each year. In 1981, its victims included the Rev Robert Bradford, **ULSTER UNIONIST PARTY** Member of Parliament for South **BELFAST** and the first MP to be murdered as a result of the conflict in Northern Ireland. Three years later, Prime Minister Margaret Thatcher narrowly escaped death when a bomb exploded in her hotel during the Conservative Party's annual conference in Brighton. In 1994, the IRA called a halt to the killings and indicated that it wanted to explore the possibility of achieving a peaceful solution to the Northern Ireland problem, but negotiations advanced too slowly for many of the provisionals' members and, in February 1996, the campaign resumed with the bombing of an office block in London's docklands. Following the Labour Party's General Election victory in 1997, the truce was reinstated to allow the new government to begin talks about a permanent solution to The Troubles with representatives of Northern Ireland's political parties, including Sinn Fein. (See **GERARD ADAMS**; **ANGLO-IRISH WAR**; **BELFAST**; **BLOODY FRIDAY**; **IRISH VOLUNTEERS**.)

IRISH REPUBLICAN BROTHERHOOD (IRB), 1873. The Fenian Brotherhood, a revolutionary society of Irishmen dedicated to the creation of an independent Ireland, was established in New York in 1858. Following an unsuccessful insurrection of 1867, it reformed itself as the Irish Republican Brotherhood in 1873. It was particularly active in **BELFAST** during the early years of the 20th century but was replaced by the **IRISH REPUBLICAN ARMY** following the failure of the **EASTER RISING** in 1916.

IRISH REPUBLICAN SOCIALIST PARTY (IRSP). Founded in 1974 by Seamus Costello, who had been expelled from the **IRISH REPUBLICAN ARMY** and was eventually shot dead in Dublin in 1977, the IRSP is the political wing of the **IRISH NATIONAL LIBERATION ARMY**. It has maintained links with **SINN FEIN** and has developed contacts with left-wing European organizations, but, apart from gaining two local council seats at **BELFAST** in 1981, has had little impact at elections.

IRISH VOLUNTEERS. Two groups have carried this title. 4 November 1779. A Protestant Irish force was created during the American War of Independence to protect Ireland from invasion by France. (Britain was then also at war with France and Spain.) Its members paraded in Dublin as guardians of freedom and, by 1782, may have numbered up to 80,000 men, becoming such a popular and formidable force for Irish patriotism that it enabled **GRATTAN'S PARLIAMENT** to secure some measure of commercial and legislative independence from London. The volunteers were formally disbanded in 1793.

25 November 1913. A citizens' army, formed in the south of Ireland to fight for independence from Britain, adopted Eamon de Valera as its president in October 1917 and was declared an illegal military organization, along with **SINN FEIN** (its political wing) in 1918. The volunteers undertook some ambushes of British supplies, along with other guerilla actions, but were eclipsed by the breakaway of their more extreme elements as the **IRISH REPUBLICAN ARMY** in 1919.

IRVINE OF LAIRG, LORD. (See **ALEXANDER ANDREW MACKAY IRVINE**).

IRVINE, ALEXANDER ANDREW MACKAY (1940–). Appointed Lord Chancellor (the British government's principal law officer) following the Labour Party's general election victory in 1997, Irvine was born into a working class Argyllshire family on 23 June 1940. His father (Alexander, a slater) and mother (Margaret, a waitress) educated him at **INVERNESS** Academy, Hutcheson's Boys Grammar School **(GLASGOW)** and Glasgow University. A brilliant undergraduate, he read economics, philosophy and law and graduated MA, LLB, but his student days influenced more than his academic future because he met **JOHN SMITH,** with whom he became close friends and, as a result, joined the Labour Party. After reading law at Cambridge University (where he gained First Class BA Honours with Distinction, First Class LLB Honours and the George Long Prize in Jurisprudence), he lectured at the London School of Economics (1965–69) before turning to a full time legal career, initially specializing in employment law, then turning to highly lucrative commercial work. At the age of 37, he was made a Queen's Counsel (the youngest in the country). During the 1980s, Irvine helped **NEIL**

GORDON KINNOCK force militant left wing members out of the Labour Party and, in 1987, was rewarded with a peerage (as Lord Irvine of Lairg). He also had a formative influence on **ANTHONY CHARLES LYNTON BLAIR,** whom he had taken into his chambers during the late 1970s. Irvine introduced Tony Blair to another young pupil (Cherie Booth) and proposed a toast at their wedding in 1980. Over the next 17 years, as Blair's political star shone even more brightly, Irvine became one of the opposition leader's closest advisers, particularly on **DEVOLUTION** policies. He was made shadow Lord Chancellor in 1992, so his 1997 appointment in Blair's first Cabinet was no surprise.

—J—

JACOBITE. The term Jacobite is derived from the Latin *Jacobus*, meaning James. Followers of the **STUART** cause, the Jacobites supported the cause of the exiled Roman Catholic King James VII and II after the Glorious Revolution. (See **BATTLE OF THE BOYNE; BATTLE OF CULLODEN; BATTLE OF KILLIECRANKIE; TREATY OF LIMERICK; BATTLE OF PRESTONPANS; JACOBITE REBELLION, 1715; JACOBITE REBELLION, 1745; JOHN ERSKINE; BATTLE OF FALKIRK; BATTLE OF GLENSHIEL; JOHN GRAHAM; FLORA MACDONALD; BATTLE OF SHERIFFMUIR; CHARLES EDWARD STUART; JAMES STUART**).

JACOBITE REBELLION, 1715. The **JACOBITE** risings were in support of the exiled **STUART** Kings. In 1715, **JOHN ERSKINE,** Earl of Mar, raised the Stuart standard at Braemar and, leading the Scottish highlanders in a rebellion known as The Fifteen, occupied Perth. However, the inconclusive **BATTLE OF SHERIFFMUIR,** near **STIRLING,** was followed by the advance of the royalist army and desertions from the ranks of the rebels. The earl fled with **JAMES STUART,** the Old Pretender, to France on 5 February 1716, and the Crown confiscated the estates of the nobles who had joined the cause. Parliament passed a Disarming Act (which forbade the ownership of swords and guns) and a **CLAN** Act (which allowed the tenants of clan chiefs to withhold rents). Prime Minister Robert Walpole instigated a purge of Jacobite sympathisers, but wide public sympathy for the political motives behind the rebellion persuaded him from pursuing the policy with much vigour.

JACOBITE REBELLION, 1745. The Forty-Five rising was precipitated by the landing of **CHARLES EDWARD STUART,** commonly referred to as Bonnie Prince Charlie, in Scotland in August 1745. Raising his standard at Glenfinnan, he rallied an army drawn largely from the Catholic or Episcopalian **CLAN**s of the **SCOTTISH HIGHLANDS,** captured Perth and **EDINBURGH,** then plundered as far south as Derby in England, taking Carlisle on the way. But, at the **BATTLE OF CULLODEN** (1746), his 5,000 highlanders were defeated by an army of 9,000 under the Duke of Cumberland; all hopes of a **JACOBITE** resurgence were lost and the clans were broken. Charles escaped to France in September 1746. (See **BATTLE OF FALKIRK; BATTLE OF PRESTONPANS**).

JAMES I (1394–1437). James became King of Scotland on the death of his father, **ROBERT III,** in 1406, but, for the first 18 years of his reign, had no contact with his country, having been taken prisoner by pirates whilst on his way to France earlier that year and detained in England by King Henry IV. In his absence, Robert's harsh and acquisitive brother, the Duke of Albany, acted as Regent; on his death (in 1420), his son, Murdoch, succeeded him. During that time, Scotland suffered greatly, but, for James, the period was not entirely unproductive — he was educated well (learning several languages), developed a taste for poetry (he wrote the lengthy poem *The Kingis Quair*), experienced at first hand the strengths and weaknesses of the English administrative system and gained military experience in France with King Henry V. After Henry's death in 1422, terms for James's release were agreed and he returned to Scotland (along with his bride, Lady Joan Beaufort, granddaughter of John of Gaunt). He went back with a vengeance. Determined to restore order and royal authority, he rounded up many of the most powerful nobles (including Murdoch) and executed them, adding their estates to his own. He reorganized financial administration and the judiciary, encouraged learning (particularly at **ST ANDREWS** University), supported the Roman Catholic Church by founding a Carthusian monastery at Perth and introduced a series of social changes (including the banning of after-hours drinking). In practice, many of these measures had little effect, but they promoted the image of a monarch set on reform and the reestablishment of firm rule. Inevitably, however, he made enemies and, on 20 February 1437, he was murdered at Blackfriars Priory in Perth. The act was an attempt by Sir Robert Graham, who bore James several grudges, to place on the throne Walter, Earl of Atholl and son of **ROBERT II** by his second marriage to Euphemia of Ross. Instead, after three days of torture, Walter was crowned with a coronet of red-hot iron engraved 'The King of Traitors'.

JAMES II (1430–60). Born in **EDINBURGH** on 16 October 1430, James became King of Scotland at the age of six, when his father, **JAMES I,** was murdered in Perth. Because of his youth, he had no formal control over the running of his country until after his marriage to Mary of Gueldres, daughter of Duke Philip of Burgundy, in 1449. By that time, Scotland had suffered greatly as the most powerful families — notably the **DOUGLAS**es and the Livingstones — squabbled over the reins of power. But when James did gain control, he pursued many of the policies introduced by his father in an attempt to increase the country's prosperity and reduce the incidence of lawlessness. The estates of nobles whose loyalty was suspect were forfeited, judicial practices were reviewed, a new coinage was issued and offices of state were no longer treated as hereditary entitlements. At home, he imposed his authority on the most powerful of the lords. Abroad, he attempted to establish his position in negotiations with France, a traditional Scottish ally (see **AULD ALLIANCE**), and with Norway, which claimed the **ORKNEY ISLANDS** and **SHETLAND ISLANDS**. Also, he led attacks on the English, who still had a number of footholds in Scotland. As a result, despite the inauspicious start to his reign, by the time he died on 3 August 1460 he had a powerful hold on his country's affairs. His death was a tragedy, both personally and nationally. He was killed by a cannon, which burst whilst firing a salvo during a siege of Roxburgh Castle. James was still only 29, and the Crown passed to his son, **JAMES III**, who was a significantly less effective leader and allowed the kingdom to descend into near anarchy for much of his reign.

JAMES III (1452–88). Born in May 1452, James was only eight when he succeeded to the throne of Scotland on the death of his father, **JAMES II**. During his childhood, the country was governed firstly by his mother, Mary of Gueldres (who died in 1463), then by James Kennedy, Bishop of **ST ANDREWS** (who died in 1465), and finally by a group of nobles led by the Boyd family. From 1469, following his marriage to Margaret, daughter of King Christian I of Denmark, Sweden and Norway, he took charge himself. As part of the marital arrangements, full sovereignty over the **WESTERN ISLES** was formally ceded to Scotland. Three years later, Christian also gave up his claim to the **ORKNEY ISLANDS** and **SHETLAND ISLANDS,** bringing an end to a long running source of dispute.

James was also able to extend his power in the **SCOTTISH HIGHLANDS** by charging John MacDonald, **LORD OF THE ISLES,** with treason and depriving him of the earldom of Ross. However, although intrigued by diplomacy, James did not have the self-discipline to attend to affairs of state in the way his father had done and preferred the company of artists and intellectuals to that of nobles and soldiers. The great families, offended by their loss of patronage and jealous of the King's favourites, allowed their discontent to turn into revolt, often encouraged by English support. Eventually, the barons murdered six of the King's companions and imprisoned James himself in **EDINBURGH** Castle. He was released by a force led by his brother, the Duke of Albany, who had previously been accused of plotting against the sovereign, but the reconciliation did not last and the duke fled to France. Even so, problems remained because the discontent was not confined to the wealthy. A series of bad harvests, coupled with rising prices and increasing lawlessness, had promoted a hostile mood amongst the common people, who attributed the country's woes to James's lack of leadership. Eventually, in 1488, the dissatisfaction turned into a rebellion led by the Homes, the Earls of Angus and Argyll, the Bishop of **GLASGOW** and James's own son (later **JAMES IV**). The King, no soldier, led his loyal troops to battle against the rebels at Sauchieburn, near Stirling, on 11 July, but his force was cut to pieces. James fled, and, it is said, was thrown from his horse. He asked a peasant woman to find him a priest. She did as he requested but, when the King asked for absolution, the man drew a knife and killed him. James had been a sensitive man, patron of the arts and supporter of scientific inquiry. These, however, were not the qualities required of a monarch in 15th-century Scotland.

JAMES IV (1473–1513). Arrogant, extravagant and promiscuous, James was one of the most universally popular of the Scottish monarchs. He succeeded to the throne on the death of his father, **JAMES III,** after the Battle of Sauchieburn in 1488 (having been with the rebel troops who defeated the royal army) and, although only 15, immediately involved himself in government. He built up the navy, expanded the system of peripatetic judges, began the manufacture of cannon in **EDINBURGH,** supported the foundation of a university at **ABERDEEN,** established a College of Surgeons and encouraged the introduction of the country's first printing press. In these domestic policies, he was greatly aided by an extended period of peace with England. Relationships with Scotland's southerly neighbour were difficult at first, with a series of border forays and skirmishes, but a seven-year truce treaty signed in 1497 and marriage to **MARGARET TUDOR,** daughter of King Henry VII, provided security for both countries. The marriage had enormous significance because, in 1603, it led to the **STUARTS'** accession to the English throne and the **UNION OF THE CROWNS** of England and Scotland.

The peace ended when Henry VIII became King of England in 1509. His attitude towards Scotland was more aggressive than that of his predecessor and when, in 1513, he invaded France, James found himself under pressure to support his continental ally. Several advisors counselled caution, but, when Henry declared that he owned Scotland, James gathered his army and marched south. He met the English force, led by the Earl of Surrey, at the **BATTLE OF FLODDEN** on 9 September 1513 and was utterly routed, dying in the battle, along with his illegitimate son, Alexander (the Archbishop of **ST ANDREWS**), nine earls and 13 barons.

A cultured man, he spoke several languages and was an able administrator. Wherever he went — and he travelled widely — he spent money on all social classes, and, at his court, gathered musicians and acrobats as well as political advisers. His love affairs were numerous, his gambling energetic and his affection for pageantry and chivalry widely respected. An immensely personable man, he gave Scotland a place of increased importance in European politics, a lengthy period of relative freedom from internecine strife and improved standards of living. But he was no general, and the defeat at Flodden was a result of lost opportunities.

JAMES V (1512–42). A 17-month-old baby when he inherited the throne of Scotland on his father's death in 1513, James was the only legitimate son of **JAMES IV.** He had an unhappy childhood, separated for much of the time from his mother, Queen Margaret (**MARGARET TUDOR**), with no brothers or sisters as playmates and developing a growing hatred for his stepfather, Archibald **DOUGLAS,** the sixth Earl of Angus. During his youth, the regency was assumed firstly by his mother then, on her remarriage in 1514, by his second cousin, John Stewart, Duke of Albany. It was a period of growing disorder, precipitated by disputes between the pro-English Douglas faction and the pro-French Albany faction. Eventually, Angus gained the upper hand and held the King captive in **EDINBURGH** until he escaped in 1528. From that time until his death, James ruled in his own right.

One of his principal concerns was the reestablishment of law and order, a process which included a punitive tour of the borders, stronghold of the Douglases, in 1529–30. He also made strenuous efforts to increase his income in order to support an extravagant lifestyle which included construction of a Renaissance palace at Falkland (see **FALKLAND PALACE**). In part, that income came from two judicious marriages. The first, in 1537, was to Madeleine, daughter of Francis I of France: that helped cement the **AULD ALLIANCE** between the two countries and brought a considerable dowry. Madeleine, however, was not in good health and died after only six months. In 1538, James married Mary, daughter of Claude, Duc de Guise, and widow of Louis d'Orleans, Duc de Longueville — a match which brought another sizeable dowry but also ranked him firmly with the enemies of England.

In 1542, Henry VIII of England sent an army to invade Scotland. The Scottish nobles refused to support James, partly because the memory of the **BATTLE OF FLODDEN** was still vivid, partly because many of them supported the new Protestant faith and partly because they had no love for a King who relied more on clergy than earls for advice. As a result, the royal forces were routed in the **BATTLE OF SOLWAY MOSS** on 24 November. James was deeply affected by the defeat and returned to Falkland, where he died on 14 December, having just heard of the birth of his daughter, Mary (later **MARY, QUEEN OF SCOTS**). His death was greeted with sadness by the common people, with whom he had mingled in an attempt to find out the reality of circumstances in his kingdom. He developed the habit of travelling around the country representing himself as a humble tenant farmer — the Gudeman (or Goodman) of Ballengeich. The disguise probably fooled nobody, but it endeared him to a peasantry more used to oppression than consideration.

JARLSHOF. An archaeological site preserved by windblown sand on **SHETLAND,** Jarlshof has allowed scholars to reconstruct a sequence of occupation from *c.* 2000 BC to medieval times. Only one hut constructed by the first settlers remains, but it is clear that the people were farmers, keeping sheep and oxen. Six dwellings from the Late Bronze Age have been discovered, along with evidence that the occupants grew grain and reared sheep and cattle. In the Iron Age, circular stone huts were built, along with souterrains (which were probably used for storing food) and a **BROCH** for defence. In second and third centuries, wheelhouses were constructed, circular in form and divided into rooms radiating from the centre. Viking settlers built farmsteads on the site during the ninth century and a farmhouse was erected at the end of the 13th century. That was superseded, in the late 16th century, by a stone house built for a laird. The site was named Jarlshof by **WALTER SCOTT,** who included the laird's house in his novel, *The Pirate* (1822).

JENKINS, BARON. (See **ROY JENKINS**).

JENKINS, ROY HARRIS (1920–). A cofounder of the Social Democratic Party, Jenkins was born on 11 November 1920, the son of Arthur Jenkins (who was Labour Party member of Parliament for Pontypool from 1935 until 1946) and his wife, Hattie. He was educated at Abersychan Grammar School, University College **CARDIFF** and Oxford University, graduating with first class honours in philosophy, politics and economics. He served in the Royal Artillery from 1942 until 1946, rising to the rank of Captain and unsuccessfully contesting the Solihull Parliamentary constituency for the Labour Party in 1945.

After leaving the military, Jenkins was a staff member at the Industrial and Commercial Finance Corporation Ltd until 1948, when he won election as Labour MP for Central Southwark. He held the seat for two years, but moved to Stechford in 1950 and continued to represent voters there until 1976. In 1959, he introduced (as a private member's bill) legislation which became law as the Obscene Publications Act, a controversial measure which strengthened the position of authors, publishers and printers faced with charges of pornography. He was made Minister of Aviation in 1964, promoted to Home Secretary the following year and then became Chancellor of the Exchequer (1967) until the General Election of 1970 brought the Conservative Party to power. For the next two years, he was deputy leader of the Labour Party, resigning in 1972 as a protest against Prime Minister Harold Wilson's decision to hold a referendum on Britain's membership of the European Economic Community. He campaigned strenuously in support of continued links with Europe and returned to the government as Home Secretary for a second time in 1974.

When Wilson resigned in 1976, Jenkins was one of the candidates for leadership of the party but lost to James Callaghan and forsook the House of Commons for the Presidency of the European Commission (1977–80). In 1981, he joined other Labour MPs concerned about plans to give more power to the trade unions and activists in the party, and, along with David Owen, William Rodgers and Shirley Williams, issued a statement warning of a drift towards extremism. As a counterweight, this group, christened the Gang of Four by the tabloid press, founded the Social Democratic Party (SDP), pledged to unite moderates of the political left. Jenkins failed in his attempt to win Warrington for the SDP in 1981 but was appointed leader the following year and captured **GLASGOW** Hillhead. He resigned the leadership in favour of Owen in 1983 but remained an MP until 1987, when he was created Baron Jenkins and took his seat in the House of Lords as leader of the Liberal and Social Democratic Party peers. In the same year, he became Chancellor of Oxford University, a recognition both of his administrative skills and of his contribution to historical studies through his biographies of such leading statesmen as Clement Attlee (1948), Herbert Asquith (1964) and Harry S Truman (1986).

Throughout his career, Jenkins has maintained interests outside politics, acting as governor of the British Film Institute from 1955 until 1958, adviser to the John Lewis Partnership from 1954 until 1962, director of financial operations for the same company from 1962 until 1964, president of the University of Wales Institute of Science and Technology from 1975 until 1981 and director of Morgan Grenfell Holdings in 1981–82. His autobiography — *A Life at the Centre* — was published in 1991.

JOHNSTON, THOMAS (1881–1965). **SECRETARY OF STATE FOR SCOTLAND** from 1941 until 1945, Johnston is credited with initiating much of the legislation which provided the foundation of the Scots' post-Second World War economic recovery. Born in Kirkintilloch on 2 November 1881, the first child of grocer David Johnston and his wife, Mary, he was educated locally and at Lenzie Academy, then worked as a clerical assistant before a relative gifted him a small printing firm and the editorship of two weekly newspapers. Convinced of the need for political reform, he launched the periodical, *Forward*, as a platform for socialist views in 1906 and used it to support an antiwar campaign from 1914. In 1922, he won the Parliamentary constituency of West Stirlingshire for the Labour Party and, from 1929 until 1931, served in Prime Minister Ramsay MacDonald's government, first as Under-Secretary of State for Scotland and then as Lord Privy Seal. Throughout the 1930s, he worked hard to raise public awareness of the threats posed by the rise of Adolf Hitler and, in 1939, was appointed Civil Defence Regional Commissioner for Scotland, responsible for taking over control of government in an emergency. In that role, he was a considerable success, working well with men who would have been political enemies in more stable times, and, in 1941, Winston Churchill rewarded him with the post of Secretary of State for Scotland in the wartime administration. Johnston flourished. He stipulated that he should be advised by a Council of State consisting of all those former Scottish Secretaries who were still alive, whatever their political affiliation, and used that foundation to introduce schemes designed to enhance Scotland's economic infrastructure. Most importantly, he founded the Scottish Council (Development and Industry) to assist the creation of new manufacturing firms and established the North of Scotland Hydro-Electric Board to supply power to the **SCOTTISH HIGHLANDS,** which have no indigenous fossil fuels. The construction work associated with hydro projects caused considerable controversy because of its impact on the environment and on local communities, so, in 1945, when he retired from politics (and declined the peerage offered in recognition of his services), he agreed to take on the chairmanship of the board in order to assume control of its development. In addition, he was chairman of the Scottish National Forestry Commissioners (1945–48) and of the Broadcasting Council for Scotland (1955–56). He also served as Chancellor of the University of **ABERDEEN** (1951–65) and worked with the Scottish Tourist Board, ultimately retiring as chairman from both that and the hydro board in 1959. He died at his home in Milngavie on 5 September 1965.

JONES, GRIFFITH (1683–1761). One of the pioneers of adult education in Britain, Jones made a major contribution to the spread of literacy in Wales during the early 18th century through the development of **CIRCULATING SCHOOLS.** A native of Penboyr (Carmarthenshire), he attended the local grammar school, then (although he had been born into a Nonconformist family) was ordained a deacon in the Anglican Church in 1708 and a priest the following year. In 1711, he was appointed Rector at Llanddowror. An outstanding orator, he drew enormous crowds to his sermons but became convinced that salvation had to be sought through the printed, as well as the spoken, word so that Christians could study the Gospels alone or in small groups. The vast majority of his flock could not read, were too poor to support a parish school and had little time to spare from their farming duties so Jones devized a scheme for part-time learning during the autumn and winter, when the long, dark nights and bad weather limited agricultural activities. Itinerant teachers, most of them working-class men, spent three to six months based at a suitable parish building (often the church itself) and taught WELSH to all those who wanted to learn. Griffiths himself trained the instructors, who used the *Bible* and the *Catechism* as their basic texts, but he was staunchly supported by Bridget Bevan, the wife of Carmarthen's Member of Parliament, and by gentry such as Sir John Phillips (his patron at Llanddowror) and John Vaughan (squire of Cwrt Derllys). By the time of his death on 8 April 1761, his schools had educated more than half the Welsh population and engineered a major social revolution because, in the last decades of the 18th century, Wales was one of very few nations with a literate majority. His success aroused widespread and continuing interest. Catherine the Great of Russia had a report on the circulating schools prepared in 1764, and, as late as 1955, the United Nations Educational, Scientific and Cultural Organization (UNESCO) recommended them as a model for educational practice in Third World countries. (See METHODIST REVIVAL: WALES).

JONES, JOHN PAUL (1747–92). Widely credited with being the father of the US Navy, Jones was born in Kirkbean (Scotland) on 6 July 1747, the fifth child of estate gardener John Paul and Mary his wife. He was given the same name as his father and, at the age of 12, apprenticed to John Younger (a merchant shipper based in Kirkcudbright). He sailed several times between Britain and her American colonies and, in 1768, became master of a brig. Two years later, he had his ship's carpenter flogged for laziness. The man died some weeks afterwards, and Paul, when he reached Scotland in November 1770, was arrested on a charge of murder. Released on bail, he sailed for the West Indies, seeking evidence of his innocence, but, in September 1772, killed the leader of his mutinous crew.

After that, he fled to the American mainland and added Jones to his name (apparently as a token of regard for his friend Willie Jones, a plantation owner and politician in North Carolina). On the outbreak of the War of Independence in 1775, he was commissioned as a Senior Lieutenant in the rebel navy and, the following year, became Captain of the sloop *Providence*. In 1778, in command of the *Ranger*, he was active in British waters and, on 23 April, landed at Whitehaven (Cumbria), where, in an audacious raid, he spiked the cannon at two forts. On the same day, he descended on the Solway Firth and attacked the home of Lord Selkirk, intending to take him captive, but was thwarted by his absence. On 24 April, off Carrickfergus (Northern Ireland) he captured the British vessel, *Drake*, and its 20 four-pound guns. Then, in August 1779, captaining the elderly French East Indiaman *Bon Homme Richard* and accompanied by the 32-gun *Pallas* and two other ships, he threatened the port of Leith (outside **EDINBURGH**) but was forced to retreat because the winds were against him. Turning south along the English coast, he met Britain's Baltic merchant fleet sailing in convoy off Flamborough Head (near Scarborough) and guarded by the *Serapis* (commanded by Richard Pearson), with the *Countess of Scarborough* in support. Jones engaged the *Serapis* on the night of 23 September and captured her after a battle in which an estimated 302 of his crew were killed and his vessel sunk. Transferring the remainder of his men to the enemy ship, he escorted the *Countess of Scarborough* (which had been taken by the *Pallas*) to Holland. When he returned to the United States in 1781, he was greeted as a hero, and, on 14 April, officially thanked by Congress.

In 1788, on the advice of Thomas Jefferson (then US Ambassador to France), Jones accepted Catherine the Great's offer of a post as Rear Admiral in the Russian Navy, but the experience was a personal disaster. Although he served with distinction in the Black Sea campaign against the Turks, he was never given the credit he felt he deserved. Moreover, he complained that his authority was constantly queried by junior officers. In March 1789, he was falsely accused of assault and given leave to return to France, where he died, a broken man, on 18 July 1792. In 1905, his remains were returned to the United States and buried in the chapel at the Naval Academy in Annapolis (Maryland), where his grave is a national shrine.

—K—

KAILYARD SCHOOL. During the late 19th century, a group of novelists achieved great popularity by publishing sentimental, romanticized stories about Scotland. The plots concentrated on everyday incidents in the life of rural communities and clearly appealed to urban populations made insecure by the rapid changes of the industrial age. The most renowned of these authors was J. M. Barrie, who is best known for *Peter Pan* (1904), which is set in London, but who had made his name through *Auld Licht Idylls* (1888) and *A Window in Thrums* (1889). The school got its name from a work by Ian Maclaren Brown, who wrote *Beside the Bonnie Brier Bush* (1894) and took his title from a **JACOBITE** song which includes the line *There grows a bonny brier bush in our kailyard*. A kailyard is a cabbage patch.

KELVIN OF LARGS, BARON. (See **WILLIAM THOMSON**).

KENNETH I. (See **KENNETH MACALPIN**).

KENNETH II (? – *c.* 995). The son of **MALCOLM I**, Kenneth ruled **SCOTIA** from 971 until 995. In 1973, he recognized Edgar, King of England, as his overlord and, in return, was granted the throne of Lothian, taking the Scottish boundary to a location very similar to its present position. With his southern flanks secure, he turned on the Vikings, who were harassing the northeast of his kingdom, but it is not clear whether his campaigns were successful. Kenneth died in 995, probably in a feud, but legend tells that he was killed by a lady who sent him an apple held in the hands of a statue. When the King took the fruit, a tiny brass arrow was released and went straight to his heart.

KENNETH III (?–1005). Son of Duff and grandson of **MALCOLM I**, Kenneth became ruler of **SCOTIA** in 997 by murdering King Constantine. He may have ruled jointly with Giric, his son, until he was murdered by **MALCOLM II**.

KENNETH THE HARDY. (See **KENNETH MACALPIN**).

KENTIGERN, ST. (See **ST MUNGO**).

KILBRANDON COMMISSION, 1973. In 1969, Prime Minister Harold Wilson set up a commission, headed by Lord Kilbrandon, to investigate the constitutional position with respect to **DEVOLUTION**. At the time, violent clashes between sectarian groups were increasing in Northern Ireland (see **THE TROUBLES**), and, in Scotland and Wales, the nationalist parties — the **SCOTTISH NATIONAL PARTY (SNP)** and **PLAID CYMRU** — were experiencing growing political support. The commission report, published in 1973, during the Edward Heath administration, proposed elected assemblies for Scotland and Wales to take over the administrative functions of the **SCOTTISH OFFICE** and the **WELSH OFFICE**. Wilson, returned to power in 1974, introduced the necessary legislation to establish referenda in the two regions to test regional opinion on the plans. These took place in 1979 but neither produced the necessary 40 per cent vote in favour, which was required if the new Parliaments were to be established. The experience was a disaster for the Labour Party, which lost a vote of no confidence (tabled by the SNP) and fell on 28 March 1979, allowing Margaret Thatcher to move into Downing Street.

KILLIECRANKIE, BATTLE OF, 27 July 1689. Scots **JACOBITE**s under **JOHN GRAHAM,** Viscount Dundee, with his loyal **CLAN**s and Irish troops, defeated King William III's force of 3,000 troops at Killiecrankie, but Dundee was killed by an English sharpshooter and the highland opposition to the Glorious Revolution lost its charismatic leader.

KILSYTH, BATTLE OF, 15 August 1645. At this battle, fought near **STIRLING** during the English civil war (in which the Scots had become embroiled), royalist forces led by **JAMES GRAHAM,** Duke of Montrose, defeated the **COVENANTERS** and destroyed their power base. Although this was, perhaps, his greatest victory, it came too late to influence the course of the war.

KILT. The pleated skirt which forms part of the Scotsman's national dress evolved from smocks formerly worn by both sexes in Scotland and Ireland. During the 17th century, these long shirts were replaced by the belted **PLAID** and, by the end of the 18th century, that, in turn, had been superseded by the kilt. The processes involved in this transition are hotly debated but it seems likely that the garment was actually designed by an Englishman. About 1730, Thomas Rawlinson was operating an iron furnace in Lochaber. Wanting to make the plaid more suitable for his labour force, he abbreviated it by cutting round the waist, throwing away the top half, stitching the pleats and converting the front into a flat apron. At the time of the second **JACOBITE REBELLION** in 1745, the kilt was worn only by small numbers of men in the **SCOTTISH HIGHLANDS,** but, even so, it was a sufficiently distinctive badge of nationality for the Hanoverian government to ban its use from 1 August 1747. Until the law was changed in 1782, it was worn only by men attached to regiments raised in the highland counties for service in the British army. In the last decade of the 18th century, however, it was adopted by many civilians and, in 1822, was popularised further when King George IV paid a state visit to **EDINBURGH.**

In the early years of the 19th century, **WALTER SCOTT**'s novels and poems fostered middle-class interest in Scotland, so George's decision to wear highland dress at official engagements during the visit both reflected current fashion and gave the kilt the royal seal of approval. Although now little used as everyday wear (except by hoteliers who rely on the tourist trade), it is common garb on formal and semiformal occasions such as weddings. (The Scot would wear a kilt on occasions at which the American would wear a tuxedo or the Englishman a suit and bow tie). The **TARTAN** which decorates the fabric denotes the wearer's **CLAN,** family or regimental affiliations. Traditionally, a sporran (an ornamental pouch) is worn in front of the kilt but nothing is worn underneath. (Generations of soldiers have had to step on a mirror so that superior officers could check that their buttocks were bare). Technically, the kilt is worn only by men; women wear kilt skirts. (The tailoring of the two garments is different because the disparity between male waist and hip measurements is less than that of the ladies, with resultant effects on the pleating). An orange form of kilt is also worn by men in Northern Ireland but is largely confined to musicians and dancers. (See **SGIAN DUBH.**)

KING, THOMAS JEREMY (1933–). **SECRETARY OF STATE FOR NORTHERN IRELAND** from 1985 until 1989, Tom King was born on 13 June 1933, the son of Molly and J. H. King. He was educated at Rugby School then, from 1951 until 1953, carried out his national service in the army. Three years at Cambridge University followed before he began a business career in Bristol. In 1970, he was elected Member of Parliament for Bridgwater, representing the Conservative Party, and held government posts under Prime Ministers Edward Heath and Margaret Thatcher before getting the Northern Ireland appointment in September 1985. Within weeks, he had to face the wrath of the loyalists over the **ANGLO-IRISH AGREEMENT** and complaints from the government of the Irish Republic, which rejected his claim that, by signing the document, it had implicitly accepted that there would never be a united Ireland. In 1986, he decided to end the deliberations of the **NORTHERN IRELAND ASSEMBLY,** clearly believing that it had become little more than a focus for anti-government rhetoric, and, over the next two years, initiated a dialogue with the leaders of the unionist parties and the **SOCIAL DEMOCRATIC AND LABOUR PARTY.** In July 1989, he was transferred to the post of Defence Secretary and, in 1992, approved the merger of the Royal Irish Rangers and the **ULSTER DEFENCE REGIMENT,** a move which satisfied many critics, who felt that the regiment was too pro-Loyalist. King was dropped from the government following the 1992 General Election.

KINNOCK, NEIL GORDON (1942–). Leader of the Labour Party from 1983 until 1992, Kinnock was born on 28 March 1942, the son of Gordon (a steelworker and former coal miner) and Mary (a nurse). He was educated at Lewis School (Pengam) and University College, **CARDIFF,** becoming president of the students' union in 1965 and graduating with a BA degree in industrial relations and history (1966). He worked as a tutor organiser for the Workers' Educational Association from 1966 until 1970, when he gained election to the House of Commons as member of Parliament for Bedwellty, sponsored by the Transport and General Workers' Union.

Over the next decade, Kinnock gradually enhanced his political experience, serving on the Select Advisory Committee on Public Expenditure (1971–74) and a similar Committee on Nationalized Industries (1975–78). Prime Minister Harold Wilson made him Parliamentary Private Secretary to Michael Foot, Secretary of State for Employment (1974–75). He became a member of the Labour Party's National Executive in 1978, and Foot himself brought him to the Opposition Front Bench as spokesman on education between 1979 and 1983.

A skillful orator with a rousing style reminiscent of a Welsh chapel preacher, Kinnock was the natural choice of the party's left wing when Foot resigned the leadership in 1983 and won the ensuing election by a large majority over Roy Hattersley. He faced the daunting task of rebuilding the morale of party workers depressed by two successive General Election defeats (1979 and 1983), developing policies in tune with the needs of the 1980s and meeting the challenge of the new Social Democratic Party, which aimed to dominate the political middle ground. Kinnock immediately set about isolating the more extremist left-wingers (notably those associated with the Militant Tendency organization) but, even so, lost the 1987 General Election by a considerable margin (229 seats compared with the Conservative Party's 375) after a campaign which resembled that of a US presidential candidate rather than a British political party. Over the next five years, he worked hard to change Labour's image as the champions of state control, and opinion polls just before the 1992 election indicated that he would be the next Prime Minister. At the last moment, however, John Major's Conservatives made up the leeway and gained a Commons majority of 21 seats (helped, according to some commentators, by Kinnock's overconfidence during the final few days of the campaign). In the wake of the defeat, Kinnock resigned and was replaced as leader of the party by **JOHN SMITH.** In 1994, he was appointed to the post of European Commissioner by the Prime Minister and was given the transport portfolio. His wife,

Glenys, had been elected to the European Parliament earlier in the year.

KINSALE, BATTLE OF, 24 December 1601. During the **TYRONE REBELLION** in Ireland, a force of 4,500 Spaniards captured the port of Kinsale, which was then placed under siege by an English army of 11,000 infantry and 850 cavalry, commanded by Lord Charles Mountjoy. A detachment of rebels, led by the Earl of Tyrone, attempted to relieve the Spanish invaders, but was beaten off in an encounter which lasted only three hours. The Spanish surrendered and were allowed to sail home. The defeat proved a turning point for Ireland — the Irish armies never recovered their former strength, their foreign support was gone and the Tyrone Rebellion collapsed. In the end, the English dominated the island. For that reason, some scholars have referred to these events at Kinsale as Gaelic Ireland's **BATTLE OF CULLODEN.** (See **BATTLE OF THE FORD OF THE BISCUITS; GALLOGLASSES; BATTLE OF YELLOW FORD**).

KNOX, JOHN (*c.* 1514–72). One of the principal architects of the Reformation in Scotland, Knox was born in or near Haddington, probably in 1514. Little is known of his early life, but it is believed that he trained for holy orders either at **ST ANDREWS** University or at **GLASGOW** University then, for a short time around 1540, was a Roman Catholic priest. By 1545, however, he was associating with Protestant reformer George Wishart, who was accused of heresy and burnt at the stake the following year. For some months, Knox moved from place to place in order to avoid arrest but, in 1547, spent several weeks in St Andrews and, during that time (and very much against his will) became the spokesman for the reform movement. His own inclination was for the peace of the scholar rather than the danger and hurlyburly of politics, but he was persuaded to deliver a sermon advocating Protestantism and met with such a positive response that he believed God had called him to preach rather than study. In June of the same year, however, he was captured by Catholic forces and despatched to the French navy as a galley slave for 19 months. He was released in 1549 through the intervention of Edward VI, the Protestant King of England, but with his health seriously and permanently impaired. With Scotland still under the sway of Catholicism, it was impossible for Knox to go back to his own country, but the English government was happy to license him to preach and sent him to the rowdy border town of Berwick, where he established a Puritan congregation (and met Marjorie Bowes, who became his wife). Later, he became a royal chaplain and was offered the bishopric of Rochester, an appointment which he refused because he did not trust the government and because he did not want to be bound to it through patronage. In 1553, with the accession of Mary Tudor (Mary I), England became pro-Catholic again. Knox fled to Geneva, where he met John Calvin and adopted his doctrine that salvation is achieved through faith alone and restricted to those predestined by God to be saved. In Switzerland, he ministered to an increasing band of English Protestant exiles and published a treatise entitled *First Blast of the Trumpet against the Monstrous Regiment of Women* (by *regiment* Knox meant rule). He subscribed to the widely held medieval belief that government by women was contrary to natural law and to religion. The work was directed against **MARY OF GUISE** (the Roman Catholic regent in Scotland), Mary Tudor and Diane de Poitiers (mistress of Henry II of France and one of the powers behind the throne). Publication, however, coincided with the accession to the English throne of the Protestant Elizabeth I, who retaliated by banning Knox from her country.

In 1559, he returned to Scotland, where Mary of Guise was attempting to halt the spread of the new faith. The country disintegrated into civil war, but, in April 1560, Mary died and her French supporters withdrew, leaving the Protestants victorious. Knox organized the new church on **PRESBYTERIAN** lines, with authority placed in the hands of a national assembly, regional synods, local presbyteries and individual congregations. Papal authority was abolished and ministers were to be elected by the people, not imposed. Proposals for the education of children and relief of the poor were also developed but eventually abandoned because of lack of finance. When **MARY, QUEEN OF SCOTS,** arrived from France in 1561, Knox vainly attempted to make her abandon her Catholic beliefs and make Protestantism compulsory. Thwarted, he attacked her at every opportunity and advocated her execution when she abdicated in 1567. He preached at the coronation of her son, James VI and I (who eventually confirmed Protestantism as the official religion in Scotland), and played a large part in the political struggle between the faction supporting Mary and that supporting the infant James. His health was deteriorating, however, and on 24 November 1572, shortly after preaching his last sermon, he died in **EDINBURGH.** His *History of the Reformation in Scotland*, telling the story of the struggle for the establishment of the Protestant faith from his own standpoint, was published posthumously in 1584. (See **BOOK OF DISCI-**

PLINE; CHURCH OF SCOTLAND).

—L—

LALLANS. The speech of central and southern Scotland is derived from the dialect of English spoken in the north of England and is commonly known as Scots, Broad Scots or Lallans (a linguistic form of *lowlands*). **WALTER SCOTT** and **ROBERT BURNS** had used Scots but, during the 19th century, it was increasingly affected by the incorporation of standard English words and phrases. In the 1920s, nationalist poet and journalist Christopher Grieve (writing under the pen name **HUGH MACDIARMID**) revived the tongue in his work, resurrecting long-forgotten words and inventing others to suit his needs. Other writers followed his lead, and the movement became known by its supporters as the Lallans Revival. Detractors called it Plastic Scots.

LAND AUTHORITY FOR WALES (AWDURDOD TIR CYMRU). Established by the Conservative Government under the terms of the Local Government's Planning and Land Act (1980), the Authority is empowered to purchase land which can then be sold to developers in either the public or the private sector. It also produces regular Housing Land Availability Studies in consultation with local authorities and builders. The organization is based in **CARDIFF** and is self-funding, drawing its resources from the land sales. Its eight board members are appointed by the **SECRETARY OF STATE FOR WALES** and include representatives of the local authorities and the business community.

LANG, IAN BRUCE (1940–). **SECRETARY OF STATE FOR SCOTLAND** and President of the Board of Trade under Prime Minister John Major, Lang was born on 27 June 1940, the son of James Lang (a wealthy insurance broker) and his wife, Maude. He was educated at Lathallan School (Montrose), Rugby School and Cambridge University (where he graduated with a BA degree in 1962), then embarked on a business career. Lang joined the Conservative Party after leaving university and fought Parliamentary elections at Central Ayrshire (1970) and Glasgow Pollok (1974) before taking the Galloway seat from the **SCOTTISH NATIONAL PARTY** in 1979. Two years later, he was made Assistant Whip by Margaret Thatcher and worked closely with John Major. After that, his rise up the hierarchy was rapid — Lord Commissioner of the Treasury (1983–86), Parliamentary Under-Secretary of State at the Department of Employment (1986) and at the **SCOTTISH OFFICE** (1986–87), Minister of State at the Scottish Office (1987–90) and then Secretary of State for Scotland, with a seat in the cabinet, in 1990. The last of these positions was, in effect, a reward for helping to organize John Major's campaign to win the leadership of the Conservative Party following Margaret Thatcher's resignation. Over the next five years, he concentrated on attracting inward investment (at the expense of promoting indigenous business, according to critics), presided over the closing of the Ravenscraig steel works (Scotland's last large site of heavy industry) and proved lukewarm about proposals to devolve power from London to **EDINBURGH.** He also planned to privatize publicly owned water supplies, forestry land and ferry services to the **HEBRIDES,** but was forced to back down in the face of monumental public protest. After moving to the Board of Trade in 1995, he adopted a liberal approach to company mergers and continued his policy of encouraging foreign investment in areas beyond the immediate hinterland of London. He lost his seat in Labour's landslide General Election victory in 1997 and, indicating that he had had enough of politics, returned to a business career. He received a knighthood shortly afterwards.

LANGSIDE, BATTLE OF, 13 May 1568. **MARY, QUEEN OF SCOTS**, was imprisoned in Loch Leven Castle (Fife) in 1567 and was forced to abdicate by her half-brother, James Stuart, Earl of Moray, the Regent of Scotland after her marriage to the Earl of Bothwell. She escaped on 2 May 1568 and was joined by upwards of 5,000 supporters, including earls, bishops and lairds. On her way to Dumbarton Castle, on the **RIVER CLYDE,** her force was intercepted by a smaller army sent by Moray and soundly beaten. Archibald Campbell, the **EARL OF ARGYLL,** led her army poorly (or perhaps treacherously), and the defeat led Mary to the fateful decision to flee to England and throw herself on the mercy of her cousin, Queen Elizabeth I.

LARGS, BATTLE OF, 2 October 1263. Scandinavians had long held control over large parts of Scotland including the **ORKNEY ISLANDS** and the **WESTERN ISLES.** This encounter was between a force led by King Haakon IV of Norway and King **ALEXANDER III's** Scottish army. During a storm, ten provision ships, sailing with a large Viking fleet, were blown ashore near Largs, on the Ayrshire coast. Their crews were attacked by the Scots and Haakon responded by landing a large supporting force. However, the Norsemen found themselves facing an army led by King Alexander III rather than a band of local peasants, and hastily retreated. There was no large-scale battle, but Haakon retired to Orkney and, within three years, the areas which he had held in northern Britain were firmly under Scottish control.

LAUDABILITER, 1155. This was the title of the papal bull, or letter, given to John of Salisbury, Archbishop Thomas Becket's clerk, by Pope Adrian IV (the only Englishman ever to be appointed Pope) to present to King Henry II of England. It sanctioned Henry to invade Ireland (1171). This was intended by the Pope to reform the Catholic Church in Ireland, which still retained vestiges of Celtic practices, but also helped Henry to remove the threat of a united Ireland under Richard de Clare. (See **CELTIC CHURCH**).

LEGAL SYSTEM: NORTHERN IRELAND. When Northern Ireland was created in 1921, its legal system was devised on lines very similar to those of England and Wales. Major cases are heard in **BELFAST** by the Supreme Court of Judicature, which is headed by the Lord Chief Justice of Northern Ireland and consists of a High Court of Justice, a Crown Court and a Court of Appeal. Important matters of civil law are considered in the High Court, more minor matters in the County Courts, which sit in towns throughout the Province. Decisions to prefer criminal charges are taken either by the Director of Public Prosecutions (in the case of major offences) or by the **ROYAL ULSTER CONSTABULARY** (in the case of less serious charges). Major criminal trials take place in the Crown Court before a judge, accompanied (except for hearings related to certain terrorist activities) by a jury. Most charges relating to lesser offences are presented in the Magistrates Courts but offenders below the age of 17 appear at special Juvenile Courts, which are presided over by a Magistrate with legal qualifications and two other individuals, both of whom must have experience of dealing with young people and one of whom must be a woman.

As a result of the civil unrest which has plagued Ireland since the late 1960S (see **THE TROUBLES**), special laws have been enacted to govern the investigation and trial of those suspected of terrorist offences. In particular, on 9 August 1971, the government used the terms of the Special Powers Act (originally passed in 1922) to introduce internment without trial and, in 1973 (following the

DIPLOCK COMMISSION report), Parliament approved legislation which allowed trials for certain terrorist offences to be held in the absence of a jury on the grounds that intimidation of jurors could lead to miscarriages of justice. The 1974 Prevention of Terrorism Act provided for the exclusion from Northern Ireland (and, if necessary, from the rest of the United Kingdom) of people who were alleged to be involved in terrorism and a further act in 1976 made the soliciting of funds for terrorist groups and activities, and contributing money to such causes, criminal offences. In 1978, the Emergency Provisions Act widened the security authorities' powers of search and arrest. Also, the wearing of paramilitary clothing (including hoods) was banned and membership of several organizations associated with violence — including the **IRISH REPUBLICAN ARMY (IRA), RED HAND COMMANDO,** the **ULSTER FREEDOM FIGHTERS (UFF),** the **ULSTER VOLUNTEER FORCE (UVF)** and the **IRISH NATIONAL LIBERATION ARMY (INLA)** — was confirmed as illegal. In 1991, a further Emergency Provisions Act consolidated antiterrorist legislation relating solely to Northern Ireland and gave the courts power to confiscate the proceeds of terrorist activities (including funds raised to support the proscribed organizations).

LEGAL SYSTEM: SCOTLAND. Following the **TREATY OF UNION** in 1707, Scotland retained its distinctive legal system, which had a considerably greater infusion of Roman law than was the case in England and therefore put more emphasis on principle than on precedent. Although the two nations' systems have grown more alike over the past 300 years (largely because most of the legislation passed at Westminster applies to the United Kingdom as a whole), the administration of justice is still carried out on fundamentally different lines north of the border.

In Scotland, the police have no power to initiate criminal proceedings. That responsibility rests with the **LORD ADVOCATE** when the offence is serious and with the Procurators-Fiscal (public prosecutors, who are qualified lawyers and based in major towns) when the charges are more minor. The supreme criminal court is the High Court of Justiciary, which sits in **EDINBURGH** and in larger towns. Trials are always held before a judge and a jury of 15, and may end with a verdict of guilty, not guilty or not proven.

At a lower level, there are six **SHERIFF**doms, each with a Sheriff Principal at its head. These sheriffdoms are divided into Sheriff Court Districts, which have resident, legally qualified Sheriffs, who act as judges. The Sheriffs may try cases along with a jury, but may also consider lesser offences on their own.

The most minor charges are brought before lay Justices of the Peace (of whom there are about 4,200), who preside over local courts, except in **GLASGOW,** where there are Magistrates Courts. When the offenders are children under the age of 16, hearings usually take place informally before a panel of three lay people.

Since 1926, the High Court has also acted as the ultimate Court of Appeal in criminal cases.

The supreme civil court is the Court of Session, which was founded by King **JAMES V** in 1532. It sits only in Edinburgh, is presided over by the Lord President and is divided into an Inner and an Outer House. The 15 Outer House judges may hear cases on their own or may be accompanied by a 12-person jury. Appeals go to the Inner House, which is divided into two divisions, each of equal status and with four judges. From there, if permission is granted, they pass to the House of Lords. Court of Session judges are known as Lords of Session and also serve as judges in the High Court (where the Lord President is known as the Lord Justice General).

The Sheriff Court also has wide powers in civil actions, with the exception of divorce proceedings, and there are other courts which deal with specific disputes, notably the Sheriff Court of Chancery (which hears cases involving title to heritable property) and the Scottish Land Court (which adjudicates on disagreements relating to **CROFTING** and other agricultural land). There is, however, no equivalent of the English Coroner's Court. In cases of sudden death, investigations are carried out in private by the appropriate Procurator Fiscal and may result in a fatal accident inquiry, held before a Sheriff. (See **ADVOCATE; CROWN OFFICE; LORD JUSTICE CLERK; LORD JUSTICE GENERAL; LORD LYON; KING-AT-ARMS**).

LEGAL SYSTEM: WALES. The administration of justice in Wales has evolved as an integral part of that operating in England, with its roots in the medieval courts established by the monarch and the aristocracy. (See **STATUTE OF RHUDDLAN**). Major cases are heard by the Supreme Court of Judicature, which consists of the Court of Appeal, the High Court of Justice and the Crown Court. The High Court, which takes civil cases, has three divisions — Chancery (which deals with equity, bankruptcy and probate litigation), the Queen's Bench (which concentrates on actions relating to commercial law, personal injury and professional negligence) and the Family Division (which considers all matters relating to domestic disputes). Judges sit alone and hear Welsh cases at Caernarvon, **CARDIFF,** Mold and **SWANSEA**. Disputed judgements go to the Civil Division of the Court of Appeal and, if necessary, to the House of Lords, the ultimate appeal court in the United Kingdom.

Less important civil cases are dealt with locally by the County Courts.

The Crown Prosecution Service (led by the Director of Public Prosecutions) is responsible for conducting criminal proceedings initiated by the Welsh and English police forces, with the exception of some minor offences and certain fraud investigations. The Crown Court tries the most serious charges, and is organized on the basis of six circuits, one of which covers Wales and the area of England around Chester. Cases are heard at Caernarvon, Cardiff, Carmarthen, Dolgellau, Haverfordwest, **MERTHYR TYDFIL,** Mold, Newport, Swansea and Welshpool. Appeals are heard by the Criminal Division of the Court of Appeal and, if necessary, by the House of Lords.

Minor criminal cases are usually heard in local towns at Magistrates' Courts, where unpaid lay judges sit without a jury and are advised by legally qualified officials.

All judicial appointments are made by the Sovereign, who acts on the advice of the Prime Minister and the Lord Chancellor (the government's principal law officer in Wales and England). (See **CYFRAITH HYWEL DDA**).

LIMERICK, TREATY OF, 3 October 1691. After the **BATTLE OF THE BOYNE,** King William III of England was assured of ultimate victory in Ireland against the **JACOBITE** forces loyal to James VII and II. Limerick, however, held out against his army until October 1691, when the 14,000 strong Irish contingent inside the town despaired of receiving aid promised by France and agreed a treaty of surrender. The terms included amnesty for troops swearing allegience to William, toleration for Roman Catholics and guaranteed property rights. Jacobites were allowed to leave the country. (French vessels were permitted to land and, as a result, up to 11,000 Irishmen may have enlisted into the French army). Only the last agreement was properly honoured, and the treaty was effectively annulled by the subsequent **PENAL CODE** (1695) and other legislation which worked against the spirit of the agreement.

LIVINGSTONE, DAVID (1813–73). An explorer and missionary, who added greatly to European knowledge of Africa during the 19th century, Livingstone was born in Blantyre (near **GLASGOW**) on 19 March 1813. His parents — Neil and Agnes Livingstone — were not affluent so, at the age of ten, he was sent to work as a piecer in a cotton mill in order to supplement the family income. However, he was determined to educate himself, spent part of his first earnings on a Latin grammar book and (even though he had to start work at 6 am) studied medicine, Greek and divinity at evening class. In 1840, he was admitted as a licentiate to the Faculty of Physicians and Surgeons at Glasgow University with a degree in medicine, accepted by the London Missionary Society as a suitable person to spread the Christian gospel to the heathen, and despatched to; Kuruman in southern Africa.

Livingstone quickly developed an empathy with the native people, and pushed into relatively unexplored territory in his attempts to establish bases from which he could work. As he travelled, he became increasingly fascinated by the African environment and sought to expand knowledge of the continent as well as knowledge of Christianity. In 1850, he followed the Chobe River to the tribal lands of the Makalolo and, in doing so, learned of the slave trade. "The strangest disease I have seen in this country seems to be brokenheartedness," he wrote, "and it attacks free men who have been captured and made slaves". From that point, his life focused on attempts to break the trade by finding routes, from the interior to the coast, suitable for an interchange of goods which would prove more profitable than buying and selling people. In 1853, he started a journey which took him from Linyanti, the Makololo settlement on the Chobe, along the Zambezi to Loanda on the west coast. He arrived at the port a sick man, having suffered several severe bouts of fever, but was welcomed as a hero by the European sea captains, who offered to take him back to Britain. He refused. Knowing that his 27 African companions had no way of getting home without him, he led them all the way back to Linyanti. It was clear that the route he had pioneered was too difficult for commerce so, in 1855, he set off again, this time hoping to find a way of reaching the east coast by following the Zambezi to the sea. After only 50 miles, he reached a great cataract which he called Victoria Falls in honour of his Queen and, for the rest of the trip, passed through countryside where travel was easy, eventually reaching the Portuguese port of Quilimane and the Indian Ocean. Leaving his African companions to work on plantations until he could return, he set sail for Britain, arriving home in time to spend Christmas 1856 with his wife, Mary, and their three sons.

Livingstone's fame had preceded him, but he clearly preferred the rigours of Africa to the fanfares of London. Moreover, he received a curt letter from the Missionary Society reminding him that he was expected to save souls, not fill the blanks on the map of the Dark Continent, and regretfully he severed his links with the institution. In 1858, the government commissioned him to conduct further explorations of east and central Africa, and, in March, he set off on an expedition which was to last for six years. He led his tribesmen back along the Zambezi, becoming the first European to see Lake Nyasa but losing his wife, who went out to join him, fell ill and died at Shupanga. He was recalled by the Foreign Office in 1864 but, before long, was persuaded to go back and search for the sources of the Congo, Nile and Zambezi. In April 1866, he landed at the mouth of the Rovuma River and made his way past Lake Nyasa to Lake Tanganyika, Lake Mweru and Lake Bangweulu. That journey took him well into uncharted territory and sapped his already fragile health. Unable to communicate with friends in Europe, he appeared to have vanished and was believed dead until, in 1871, Henry Morton Stanley of the New York *Herald* found him at Ujiji on Lake Tanganyika, and, with a most un-American restraint, greeted him with the words "Dr Livingstone, I presume". However, Livingstone declined to accompany Stanley to the coast, preferring to continue his search for the headwaters of the Nile. In August 1872, he made his way along the eastern shores of Lake Tanganyika and then attempted to find a route through the swamps of the Lake Bangweulu region. Suffering from constant bouts of dysentery, he reached Chitambo (in present-day Zambia) but could go no further and died on 30 April 1873. His African companions embalmed his body and carried it, along with his papers, to the coast. From there, it was taken back to Britain and laid to rest in Westminster Abbey. His obiturist in *The Scotsman* wrote that "the memory of David Livingstone will have a monument and in the love and admiration of [Africa's] inhabitants". In practice, however, he is seen by many people on the continent as an agent of colonial oppression. In 1996, a campaign in Zambia attempted to have the word *liberator* erased from his statue there.

LLYWELYN THE GREAT. (See LLYWELYN AB IORWERTH).

LLYWELYN AP GRUFFUDD (*c.* 1222–82). The campaign for Wales's independence from England came to an end with the death of Llywelyn ap Gruffudd, grandson of **LLYWELYN AB**

IORWERTH, who had begun the movement nearly a century earlier. The child of Gruffudd (eldest son of Llywelyn ab Iorwerth) and his wife, Senena, he was the only native Welshman to be recognized as Prince of Wales by the English Crown. When **DAFYDD AP LLYWELYN** died childless in 1246, Llywelyn ap Gruffudd became joint ruler of the western part of the Principality of Gwynnedd with his brother, Owain (King Henry III of England took the east). In 1255, however, Llywelyn defeated Owain and his younger brother, Dafydd (see **DAFYDD AP GRUFFUDD**), in battle at Bryn Derwyn and set himself the task of reestablishing the empire built by his grandfather. Taking advantage of England's preoccupation with domestic affairs, he won control of Merioneth, Ceredigion and southern Powys, gaining such supremacy that, in 1258, he was able to style himself Prince of Wales and persuade lesser rulers to attest loyalty to him rather than to Henry. The rights to the title and to the homage were accepted by the English through the **TREATY OF MONTGOMERY** (1267), by which time Llywelyn had established his authority over most of the area of modern Wales. He was prepared to accept the need to pay allegiance to the King of England, but, in his own land, he was supreme, providing a foundation for the growth of a sense of nationhood.

However, Edward I, who succeeded Henry in 1272, had different aims from his predecessor, seeking to anglicize the Welsh rather than merely incorporate them within his empire. Faced with the might of the English armies, the Welsh rulers deserted Llywelyn during 1276 and 1277 and an attempt to renew his power in 1282, when he asserted that Wales was free and entitled to the same rights as any other free country, persuaded Edward to break him completely. Llywelyn was killed in a skirmish near Builth on 11 December and, although Dafydd took up his mantle, continuing the struggle for some months, the fight for Welsh independence was effectively over. (See **STATUTE OF RHUDDLAN**).

LLYWELYN AP IORWERTH (1173–1240). The most able of the medieval Welsh princes and the initiator of a long struggle for independence from England, Llywelyn was the son of Iorwerth Drwyndwn and his wife, Mared. He was probably born in Dolwyddelan Castle (in the principality of Gwynedd) but was raised by his mother's family in neighbouring Powys and, in 1194, began an attempt to regain what he regarded as his rightful estate, defeating his uncle, Dafydd ab Owain, in battle near the estuary of the River Conwy. By 1202, he had won control of most of north Wales. Three years later, he married Joan, illegitimate daughter of King John of England, but that alliance failed to prevent him from quarrelling with his father-in-law, probably over Llywelyn's continued attempts to expand his suzerainty. In 1211, John invaded Wales and forced his son-in-law to submit, but his aggressive attempts to exert overlordship were resented by local leaders as well as by some of the **MARCHER LORDS.**

Llywelyn took advantage of the political uncertainties to reassert control over much of his former territory, capturing a series of important castles in the process. The strength of his position was such that, through the Treaty of Worcester in 1218, he was able to get confirmation of his right to the lands stretching from Carmarthen (near the southwest coast) to Montgomery (on the English border) from King Henry III, John's successor. In 1223, he lost some of that estate to William Marshall, Earl of Pembroke, but, in 1228, attempts by Hubert de Burgh to reduce his authority further were resisted and ultimately led Llywelyn to invade south Wales, destroying Brecon and Neath as he went. In the peaceful interludes between conflicts, he sought to extend his political influence through strategic marriages for his son, **DAFYDD AP LLYWELYN,** and his daughters, all except one of whom were wed into the Anglo-Norman lordships of south Wales. Also, for the last two decades of his reign, the bulk of his estate enjoyed considerable prosperity, the position of the Welsh church strengthened and the arts were encouraged. Towards the end of his life, by which time he had earned the sourbiquet Llywelyn the Great, he joined the Cistercian monastery at Aberconwy and died there on 11 April 1240.

LOCAL GOVERNMENT: NORTHERN IRELAND. When Ireland was divided under the terms of the **GOVERNMENT OF IRE-LAND** Act (1920), the arrangements made for local government in **ULSTER** closely resembled those which operated in England and remained in place for over 50 years. Authorities exercised powers, granted to them by the national Parliament in London, over territories which were also centrally determined. In 1973, just before the pattern changed, County Councils administered Antrim, Armagh, Down, Fermanagh, Londonderry and Tyrone. **BELFAST** and **LON-DONDERRY** (the major cities) had County Borough status, giving them all the rights and responsibilities of the County Councils (although, technically, Londonderry was run by a Development Commission). The towns of Ballymena, Bangor, Carrickfergus, Coleraine, Lisburn, Larne, Newtownards and Portadown had Borough Councils which concentrated on local issues (such as refuse collection), leaving wider matters (such as strategic planning) to the county authorities. In addition, there were 25 Urban District Councils, with more limited powers, in the smaller settlements and 26 Rural District Councils in agricultural areas.

On 1 October 1973, that structure was replaced by a two-tier system of 26 District Councils organized within six counties (see Map 5, page xxi). (These counties are simply territorial units with no administrative duties). The District Councils (see Map 6, page xxi) are responsible for the provision of entertainment and cultural facilities (including sports grounds and museums) and for the shaping and implementation of measures relating to environmental health, cleansing and sanitation, protective services (such as safety in the home), regulatory services (such as consumer protection and licensing of cinemas) and the administration of cemeteries, crematoria, gas undertakings, markets and slaughterhouses. Members are elected for four years using a system of proportional representation based on the single transferable vote. In 1997, Fermanagh, with 187,684 square miles, was the largest of these authorities and North Down, with 8,159 square miles, the smallest. The most populous was Belfast City (with 281,000 residents) and the least populous Moyle (with 14,600).

When the District Councils were established, many important responsibilities (such as education, housing provision and planning) were transferred from local authority control either to ad hoc bodies or to the government departments at **STORMONT.** However, it soon became clear that this concentration of control in Belfast was creating problems of overcentralization and, in 1974, a series of Area Boards was created in order to provide some element of local accountability and interest (see Map 7, page xxii). These Area Boards operate over groupings of the 26 Districts. In all cases, the majority of the members are appointed by the **SECRETARY OF STATE FOR NORTHERN IRELAND** and the remainder are delegates of the District Councils.

LOCAL GOVERNMENT: SCOTLAND. In Scotland, as in the rest of the United Kingdom, local authorities exercise powers allocated to them by Parliament in London, a system of government which has its roots in institutions established during the medieval period. From the 12th century onwards, many towns gained Royal **BURGH** status, receiving, from the monarch, charters which gave them rights over the regulation of trade and the provision of services within defined territories. Also, a system of shires evolved, each one the area over which a **SHERIFF,** as representative of the king, attempted to ensure that the laws of the country were observed. In addition, churches provided a focus for the parish, which was the territorial basis on which education and relief for the poor were organized. During the 19th century, however, that system failed to cope adequately with the changes wrought by the Industrial Revolution and was increasingly criticized by advocates of democracy in local government. In 1889, reforms introduced elected County Councils for the first time, and, in 1929, the whole system was reshaped to meet 20th century conditions. Scotland was divided into 33 counties, each administered by a County Council, which exercised control over functions such as education and property valuation. The major settlements — **ABERDEEN, DUNDEE, EDINBURGH** and **GLASGOW** — were termed Counties of Cities and given similar responsibilities. Twenty lesser towns (broadly, those with more than 20,000 residents) were labelled Large Burghs and allocated the same duties as the County Councils, with the exception of educational provision and property valuation. In addition, 176 Small Burghs were created and their Councils made responsible for local services such as water supply and refuse collection. County Councils were charged with the smooth running of local government in the landward (or nonurban) areas of the counties but could devolve functions to District Councils. Members of County and District Councils served for three years and were all elected at the same time. Burgh councillors served for the same period but one-third of the members of each Council were elected annually.

The new system undoubtedly improved matters for a time, but, over the next four decades, it increasingly creaked at the hinges as change in the distribution of local authorities failed to match change in Scotland's economy and society. By the 1960s, it was clear that some counties (such as Kinross) had become too small to support a full professional staff. On the other hand, in industrial central Scotland, towns and cities had expanded beyond their official boundaries, posing problems of water supply, sewage disposal, housing and transport, which were being tackled by ad hoc bodies composed of representatives from several local authorities. The multiplication of these bodies was making overall planning difficult and adding to the expense of the administrative process.

In 1975, following the publication of the **WHEATLEY REPORT,** a new structure was imposed under the terms of the Local government (Scotland) Act of 1973 (see Map 1, page xvii). Nine regions — Border, Central, Dumfries and Galloway, Fife, Grampian,

Highlands, Lothian, Strathclyde and Tayside — were given authorities which exercised executive powers and controlled resources for strategic planning (including provision of roads, policing, fire services, education and social work). Within these Regions, District Councils (53 in all) were allocated responsibility for building control, housing, local health services, provision of amenities and local planning. In addition, there were three island areas — ORKNEY ISLANDS, SHETLAND ISLANDS and the WESTERN ISLES — which were granted all purpose councils because of their isolation and distinct cultural identities. For the next 21 years, these authorities shaped the detail of life and work in Scotland, but did not meet with unqualified approval. The major cities, once rulers of their own destinies, had been reduced to District level and resented the loss of status and power; Glasgow, with a population of 681,000 in 1995, had no more legal responsibility than the township of Nairn, in the SCOTTISH HIGHLANDS, which had only 11,000. One region — Strathclyde — housed nearly half of Scotland's citizenry and another (Highland) covered one-third of its area. Moreover, like often partnered unlike within the same authority. Central Region, for example, included large areas dominated by industry as well as extensive areas devoted to farming and forestry; in these circumstances, councillors' views about the best use of limited resources frequently differed.

An attempt to make councils more representative of local needs was introduced in 1996, when the network of regions and districts was replaced by a pattern of 32 unitary authorities based largely on amalgamations of the District authorities (see Map 2, page xviii). The cities (as well as some of the larger towns, such as Falkirk) regained power over their own affairs, and some predominantly rural areas (such as East Lothian) were separated from urban centres. The impact of change, however, was greatest in central Scotland because most of the Highlands remained within a single authority, as did Dumfries and Galloway and the Borders. Grampian and Tayside were divided into only six Councils, including Aberdeen and Dundee.

Representatives on the new authorities hold their seats for four years. When the first elections were held in April 1995, the Scottish National Party won overall control in Angus, Moray, and Perthshire and Kinross. Independents dominated in Argyll and Bute, Borders, Highland, Orkney, Shetland and the Western Isles. No party had a clear majority in Aberdeenshire, Dumfries and Galloway or East Renfrewshire. Labour held the remaining 20 authorities, leaving the Conservatives in the anomalous position of holding a majority of seats in the United Kingdom Parliament but controlling not a single Scottish local authority. (See **CONVENTION OF ROYAL BURGHS; CONVENTION OF SCOTTISH LOCAL AUTHORITIES; COURT OF THE FOUR BURGHS**).

LOCAL GOVERNMENT: WALES. Local government in Wales has evolved on similar lines to that in England, a result of the absence of a distinctive legal system in the principality and of any recent history of self-government. It took shape during the 19th century, largely as a response to the social and economic changes wrought by the Industrial Revolution. The 1888 Local Government Act established 13 County Councils and transferred to them most of the responsibilities previously shouldered by the Justices of the Peace. The first election of councillors, held in January of the following year, inaugurated a social revolution, sweeping away rule by the landowning aristocracy and replacing it with a more democratic system representative of nonconformist views. Of the 590 seats available, 390 were taken by the Liberal Party, which dominated local service provision until the rise of the Labour Party in the period between the two world wars.

During the 20th century, the Councils were allocated an increasingly large portfolio of duties (as were those in the rest of the United Kingdom) but administrative boundaries changed little. By the 1960s, there was much concern that too many authorities had neither a sufficiently large territorial base nor a big enough population to allow them to carry out their duties effectively. The Local Government Act of 1972 brought radical reform. The structure of 13 County Councils, four County Boroughs (which had similar responsibilities to their English counterparts) and 164 District Councils (carrying out duties at a local level within the county framework) was dissolved on 31 March 1974. It was replaced by a two-tier system akin to that introduced in England at the same time, consisting of larger authorities with a more balanced population distribution. (See Map 3, page xix).

There were eight new Counties, most of them with names derived from the ancient tribes of Wales. The largest in terms of area was Dyfed (covering some 2,200 square miles) and the largest in terms of residents was Mid-Glamorgan (with 538,100). Within these counties, there were 37 districts (23 of which were granted Borough status), each of which was responsible for the provision of local services, leaving broader functions (such as strategic planning and provision of education) to the County authorities. The political composition of these new authorities was, for the most part, left of centre.

For example, 273 of the 501 County Councillors represented the Labour Party in 1995 and only 29 represented the Conservatives. At district level, Labour held 646 of the 1,473 seats and the Conservatives, 109.

A further change on 1 April 1996 replaced the two-tier structure with unitary authorities, primarily in an attempt to reduce friction between levels of local government and eliminate the costs inherent in a multilayer system. Eleven County Councils and 11 County Boroughs were created (see Map 4, page xx), many reviving names dropped in the 1974 reorganization. Boundary changes were kept to a minimum by amalgamating the former Districts to form the new authorities, on which representatives hold their seats for three years.

When the first elections were held in May 1995, the Conservatives were almost wiped from the Welsh local government map, winning only 21 of the 392 places available on the County Councils and 20 of the 579 available on the District Councils. Labour took 281 of the County seats and 450 of the District seats, but **PLAID CYMRU** earned the headlines, taking control of the Caernarvonshire and Merionethshire authority in northwest Wales. (See **LOCAL GOVERNMENT BOUNDARY COMMISSION FOR WALES**).

LOCAL GOVERNMENT BOUNDARY COMMISSION FOR WALES. Established in 1974, the commission keeps the territories and electoral arrangements for **LOCAL GOVERNMENT** in Wales under review. It makes proposals for improvements to the **SECRETARY OF STATE FOR WALES** or to the Home Secretary, either of whom can accept the suggestions or implement them after modification. Following the passage, in 1994, of the Local Government (Wales) Bill, the commission was given the task of reviewing boundary anomalies and electoral arrangements in the 22 unitary authorities which replaced the existing structure of counties and districts in 1997.

LOCH. In Scotland, lakes are known as *lochs*. The word is **GAELIC** and can refer either to an inland body of water or to an arm of the sea. A small loch is a *lochan*. (See also **LOUGH**).

LOCH NESS MONSTER. Loch Ness is a freshwater lake formed along a glaciated part of the **GREAT GLEN** fault line in Scotland. It is 24 miles long and, in places, about 1,000 feet deep. Early evidence of the existence of a resident monster, which is now known as Nessie, came from serpent-like images in Neolithic rock carvings and from a biographer of sixth century **ST COLUMBA** who wrote of a savage beast repelled by the Saint with his cross. The first 20th century sighting was by Mr and Mrs Mackay, proprietors of the Drumnadrochit Hotel, in 1933. Indistinct photographs, submarine explorations of the peaty waters, sonar surveys and other investigations have failed to prove or disprove the monster's existence but have caught the public imagination and greatly enhanced the tourist industry. Some people believe that the creature may be a descendent of plesiosaurs trapped as the land rose after the last ice age and cut the loch off from the sea. Others point out that the *Water Kelpie* (or *water horse*) is an abiding element of **GAELIC** folklore and that the Loch Ness example is only the best known of many. Reputedly, the best time to catch a glimpse of Nessie is in the early evening during April or May (just before the start of the tourist season), and after a few glasses of malt **WHISKY.**

LOCKERBIE DISASTER, 21 December 1988. A Pan Am jumbo jet, Flight 102 from Frankfurt (Germany) via Heathrow (London) to New York, was sabotaged by a bomb in midair and fell on Lockerbie, in southern Scotland. All 259 passengers and crew died and 11 people on the ground were killed, as the plane plunged into the small town. Libyan terrorists were suspected of the atrocity, and attempts to extradite two suspects were made in 1993. In 1995, however, a leaked US intelligence document suggested that Iran may have been responsible.

LOMOND, LOCH. One of the largest of the Scottish lochs, Loch Lomond lies at the western edge of the **TROSSACHS,** 25 miles west of **STIRLING** and 20 miles northwest of **GLASGOW.** A long triangle, some 620 feet deep, it stretches for some 24 miles from north to south and, at its base, is about five miles from east to west. Because it straddles the geological fault which separates the **SCOTTISH HIGHLANDS** from the Central Lowlands, its head lies amongst glaciated mountain ranges and its foot amidst gently undulating, wooded hills and farmland. The main road from Glasgow to Oban and Fort William follows the western shore, passing a small hydro-electricity generating station at Inveruglas, five miles from the loch's northernmost point. As a result of its proximity to Glasgow, Loch Lomond has become an important focus of recreation for city-dwellers; Balloch (at its southern tip) has a large marina, a paddle steamer takes tourists for pleasure trips during the summer and there are facilities for camping, hillwalking, hiking and fishing. The loch is featured in **WALTER SCOTT**'s poem *The Lady of the Lake* (1810) and his novel *Rob Roy* (1818), but is, perhaps, best known from *The Bonnie, Bonnie Banks of Loch Lomond*, a plaintive **JACOBITE** song supposedly written by a supporter of the Stuart cause awaiting death in a London prison. *Lomond* may be derived from the Celtic word *llumnan* (meaning *beacon*), which may have referred to Ben Lomond, the hill, 3,192 feet high, which dominates the skyline east of the loch.

LONDONDERRY. Northern Ireland's second largest city sits on a hill beside the mouth of the River Foyle, some 75 miles northwest of **BELFAST.** Originally, it was known as Derry (from the Gaelic word *doire*, which means *oak grove*), and that name is still widely used. **ST COLUMBA** established a monastery on the site during the sixth century, but the settlement's history has been anything but peaceful. It was plundered by the Vikings, attacked by the Normans on several occasions, used as a military base while the English monarchs attempted to exert control over Ireland during the 16th century and besieged for 105 days by the forces of King James VII and II during 1689 (see **SIEGE OF LONDONDERRY**). In 1610, merchants from the City of London were allocated the area as a centre for colonization, the town's name was changed to Londonderry and representatives of the London authorities built defensive walls, which still survive. The main source of employment has been the textile industry but attempts have been made to diversify the city's economic base by building industrial estates. Furniture manufacture, food processing and light engineering now complement the shirt-making, with many jobs in administration and services, including education. Londonderry has a population of 95,300. (See **APPRENTICE BOYS; BOGSIDE**).

LORD ADVOCATE. The holder of this post is the government's principal law officer in Scotland, advising the Prime Minister on constitutional and legal matters relating to Scottish affairs and acting as prosecutor for the Crown in important cases.

LORD JUSTICE CLERK. In Scotland, the Lord Justice Clerk is the judge immediately junior to the **LORD JUSTICE GENERAL.** He hears civil cases in the **COURT OF SESSION** and criminal cases in the **HIGH COURT OF JUSTICIARY.**

LORD JUSTICE GENERAL. The senior judge in Scotland, the Lord

Justice General heads the **HIGH COURT OF JUSTICIARY** and the **COURT OF SESSION.**

LORD LYON, LYON KING-AT-ARMS. The Lord Lyon is the monarch's senior herald in Scotland. He presides over the Lyon Court, which has jurisdiction in cases concerning armorial bearings and matters of precedence (the ranking of titles).

LORD OF THE ISLES. The Lord of the Isles was head of a group of Scottish families, whose members were attached to **CLAN** Donald by ties of blood or through land tenure arrangements. These MacDonalds claimed descent from Somerled, Viking king of the **WESTERN ISLES** during the mid-12th century. After the territory had been ceded to Scotland by Norway in 1266 (see **TREATY OF PERTH**), their leaders ruled the area as they saw fit, remote from the influence of the Scottish monarchs. Educated men, they issued land charters in Latin and governed with the assistance of a council of advisors. During the 15th century, John MacDonald became the first of these powerful clan chiefs to call himself Dominus Insularum (Lord of the Isles). Holding estates on Islay (and in Lochaber and Morvern, on the Scottish mainland), he gained Barra, Harris, Knoydart, Moidart and Uist through his first marriage and, in 1354, won acceptance by the MacDougalls of his rights to Mull and parts of Jura and Tiree. His second marriage — to Margaret, daughter of King **ROBERT II** — brought him Kintyre and Knapdale. John's grandson (Alexander) became Earl of Ross, but his successor (also called John) forfeited the title to **JAMES III** as the penalty for an ill-judged alliance with Edward IV of England. In 1493, the island fiefdom was also taken from the MacDonalds by the Crown following a rebellion led by Alexander of Lochalsh, the second Earl's nephew, against the rule of **JAMES IV.** Attempts by the clan to retrieve its authority during the early years of the 16th century failed, and the Lordship of the Isles remains a royal title, held by the heir to the British throne (currently, Prince Charles).

LORD PROVOST. This official is the Chief Magistrate and leader of the City Council in **ABERDEEN, EDINBURGH, GLASGOW** or Perth.

LORDS OF THE ARTICLES. By the late 1300s, much of Scotland's Parliamentad had been delegated to a committee because of the problems involved in convening regular sessions of the **THREE**

ESTATES. The committee members were required to "determine the articles", a task which involved drafting bills, presenting them to Parliament for approval and, on occasion, actually passing laws. In its early days, the composition of the group reflected the distribution of political opinion in the Estates but, during the early years of the 17th century, James VI and I and Charles I ensured that their supporters were in the majority and thus controlled much of the legislature's business. Those attempts to ensure that the royal view had a permanent majority were considered an abuse of power so the committee was abolished in 1641. It was reconstituted following Charles II's return to the monarchy in 1660, but disbanded again in 1689.

LORDS OF THE CONGREGATION, 3 December 1557. A number of Scottish noblemen, led by the Earl of **ARGYLL,** signed a Covenant with God, by which they rejected Roman Catholicism, "renouncing the Congregation of Satan with all the superstition, abomination and idolatry thereof", demanding the use of the new English Book of Common Prayer in church services and supporting the Reformation cause. They were joined by sympathisers opposed to the anti-Protestant policies of the government of **MARY OF GUISE** after feelings were heightened both by the marriage of **MARY, QUEEN OF SCOTS,** to Francis, Dauphin of France, in 1558 and by the return of the Calvinist firebrand, **JOHN KNOX,** to Scotland the following year. In 1560, the lords entered into the **TREATY OF BERWICK** with Elizabeth I in an attempt to protect their interests.

LOTHIANS. The predominantly agricultural area focussing on **EDINBURGH** is known as the Lothians. The name, which is of Celtic origin, originally referred to the lands which stretched from the **RIVER TWEED** to the **RIVER FORTH** but, nowadays, is usually applied to the more restricted territory incorporating the counties of West Lothian, Midlothian and East Lothian. Industrialization is largely confined to the more westerly regions, whose coal mining and iron making made a significant contribution to Scotland's 19th-century economic development. The east is largely rural, with arable farming along the coast and sheep rearing in the hills, but there is also an important income from recreation and tourism (**GOLF** courses such as Muirfield, near Gullane, provide venues for major tournaments). The major administrative centres outside Edinburgh are Linlithgow and Haddington.

LOUGH. In Northern Ireland, lakes are known as *loughs*. The word is derived from the gaelic *LOCH* and is used in that form in Scotland.

LULACH (? – 1058). King of the Scots in 1057 and 1058, Lulach was the son of Gilcomgan, the mormaer (or king's steward) in Moray. His mother was probably Gruoch, who was later to marry **MACBETH**. When, in 1057, Macbeth was killed in battle by Malcolm (later **MALCOLM III**), son of **DUNCAN I**, Lulach was regarded as the true monarch by those who adhered to the **PICT**ish traditions. However, he was a simple-minded man, unable to exercise authority, and on 17 March 1058, after a reign of only a few months, was killed at Strathbogie (Aberdeenshire) by Malcolm's supporters. His body was taken to **IONA** for burial, and Malcolm became undisputed King of Scotland.

—M—

MABINOGION, THE. A collection of Welsh folktales dating from the 11th to the 13th centuries, *The Mabinogion* is based on two manuscripts — *The White Book of Rhydderch* (written *c.* 1300–1325) and *The Red Book of Hergest* (written *c.* 1375–1425). The first four stories describe heroic, hierarchical societies and focus on events in the lives of Pwyll, Branwen, Manawyddan and Pryderi, all of noble families. Five of the remainder deal indirectly with King Arthur. There is much emphasis on travel between Wales and Ireland, suggesting trading and other links between the Celtic kingdoms.

MABON. (See **WILLIAM ABRAHAM**).

McADAM, JOHN LOUDON (1756–1836). The inventor of a system of road surfacing which provided the basis of Britain's highway network during the Industrial Revolution, McAdam was born at Carsphairn, in southwest Scotland, on 21 September 1756, the son of James and Suzannah McAdam. He was educated at Maybole School, but, in 1770, when his father died, went to live with a merchant uncle in New York and was put to work in his business. Thirteen years later, he returned to Scotland a wealthy man, bought an estate at Sauhrie (Ayrshire) and established himself in the local community, serving as Deputy County Lieutenant and Magistrate. One of his duties involved inspection of local roads, a task which made him aware of the limitations on travel caused by poor surfaces. In an attempt to improve matters, he embarked on a series of experiments which he continued when, in 1798, he moved to Falmouth as agent with responsibility for revictualling the British Navy in western ports. The experiments demonstrated that roads should be built slightly above the level of the surrounding land (so that good drainage could be maintained) and that they should be covered with thin layers of hard stones, all of similar size (so that there would be a firm, durable platform, impervious to water).

In 1815, McAdam was made Surveyor General of Bristol's roads and speedily improved the quality of the highways under his care. His experience was distilled in two works — *A Practical Essay on the Scientific Repair and Preservation of Roads* (1819) and *Present State of Road-making* (1820) — which received much attention from engineers at a time when the development of a good transport infrastructure was seen as an essential component of economic advance. By the mid-1820s, his system was used widely and in 1827 he was appointed General Surveyor of Roads in Great Britain. Parliament offered him a knighthood and a sum of £8,000 as recompense for the expenses he had incurred while carrying out his experiments. He declined the first and accepted the second (which was accompanied by a £2,000 gratuity). Although he spent most of the remainder of his life in England, McAdam made regular visits to Scotland and, on 26 November 1836, during one of these journeys, died at Moffat. By that time, he had become one of a select group of inventors whose names have been incorporated into the English language — *tarmacadam* (often abbreviated as tarmac) refers to a road surface throughout the industrialized world.

McALISKEY, JOSEPHINE BERNADETTE. (See **JOSEPHINE BERNADETTE DEVLIN.**)

MACALPIN, KENNETH (?–*c.* 859). Sometimes known as Kenneth I and sometimes as Kenneth the Hardy, Kenneth MacAlpin made significant steps towards uniting Scotland under one king. Born on **IONA,** he succeeded to the throne of Galloway in 834, when his father died fighting the **PICTS,** and, about 841, added **DALRIADA** to his territories. Two years later, he also became King of the Picts, though it is not clear how that was achieved. Legend tells that he murdered seven other claimants, but it is more likely that he gained the throne through his mother as Pictish inheritance was based on the female line. He was proclaimed King on Moot Hill at **SCONE,** a sacred Pictish site, and later enhanced the settlement's importance by bringing Lia Fail — the **STONE OF DESTINY** — to it. The stone, it was believed, had been a pillow for either the prophet Jacob (Genesis, chapter 28) or **ST COLUMBA,** and Kings of Scotland were crowned on it until Edward III of England took it to Westminster Abbey in 1296. Kenneth's united kingdom was sometimes known as **SCOTIA** but more usually as Alba. Of the King himself, comparatively little is known, though chronicles claim he was astute. He certainly seems to have had the military skill to resist Danish incursions and to have attempted to impose law and order on his kingdom. When he died in 859, he was buried on Iona.

MACBETH (*c.* 1005–57). Despite the reputation created by William Shakespeare's portrayal of his character, there is no reason to suspect that Macbeth was anything other than a competent King of Scotland. He succeeded to the throne after killing **DUNCAN I** in a battle near Elgin in 1040, or by murdering him (there is uncertainty), and appears to have dealt successfully with several threats to his powers. By 1050, he was in Rome on a pilgrimage, indicating that he felt secure enough to leave his country for several months. He died in 1057, killed by Malcolm (Duncan I's son and later **MALCOLM III)** in battle at Lumphanan, (far from Dunsinane Hill, where Shakespeare arranged his death in the play which bears his name). Reputedly, he is buried on **IONA.** (See **LULACH**).

MACDIARMID, HUGH (1892–1978). A founder of the **SCOTTISH NATIONAL PARTY (SNP)** and one of Scotland's greatest poets, MacDiarmid was born Christopher Murray Grieve in Langholm on 11 August 1892, the son of the James Grieve (the local postman) and his wife, Elizabeth. He was educated at Langholm Academy and **EDINBURGH** University, then worked as a journalist on newspapers in Scotland and Wales before joining the army in 1915. Before he returned home suffering from malaria in 1918, he served in Salonica; his first book — *Annals of the Five Senses*, published in 1923 — consists of poems written there. At the end of the First World War, he returned to journalism with the *Montrose Review*. In 1922, apparently influenced by the prose style of James Joyce's *Ulysses*, he rejected English as a valid medium for Scottish poetry and began to write in a synthetic Scots tongue (also known as **LALLANS**), which utilized various dialect forms for its effect. In the same year, he founded the monthly *Scottish Chapbook*, which he used as a forum for advocacy of a Scottish literary revival. His masterpiece — *A Drunk Man Looks at a Thistle* — appeared in 1926 and presents an image of Scotland based on his own personality. During the 1930s,

MacDiarmid's work became increasingly political and metaphysical as he embraced dialectical materialism and expressed his admiration for the Soviet Union. In 1932, he was expelled from the **NATIONAL PARTY OF SCOTLAND,** because of his extremist views (which he had helped to create four years earlier), and, the following year, joined the Communist Party. (He was also expelled from that organization in 1937 but was accepted back into the fold in 1956). In the years before the outbreak of the Second World War, he found that Lallans was unable to convey the moods and feelings he wanted to express so he returned to standard English for poems such as *Second Hymn to Lenin* (1934). The volumes which he published after the war consisted primarily of lengthy, content-laden poetry which explore Celtic consciousness. MacDiarmid took great delight in creating controversy (in *Who's Who*, he listed anglophobia as his principal recreation) and in expressing his political views in an extreme form in order to raise hackles. He died in Edinburgh on 9 September 1978.

MACDONALD, FLORA (1722–90). The daughter of Ranald Macdonald, a farmer on South Uist (in the **WESTERN ISLES**), and Marion, his wife, Flora Macdonald earned her place in **JACOBITE** folklore when she helped Prince **CHARLES EDWARD STUART** escape capture after the **BATTLE OF CULLODEN.** Her father died when she was only two, and her mother was abducted (and married) by Hugh Macdonald of Skye when she was six, but, at the age of 13, she was adopted by Lady Clanranald, wife of her **CLAN** chief, to whom she was related. In June 1746, she was visiting Benbecula when the prince arrived, fleeing the Hanoverian troops. Felix O'Neal (one of his companions) sought her help. At the time, nobody was supposed to leave the island without permission but Flora's stepfather was in charge of the local militia and she asked him to let her go because she had to visit her mother. Macdonald acquiesced and clearly knew about the deception. Disguising Bonnie Prince Charlie as a maid and referring to him as Betty Burke, she sailed with him to Portree, on the Isle of Skye, where they separated (and where the Young Pretender gave her a gift of his portrait in a golden locket). However, their boatmen proved to be less than loyal and suspicions about her role in the escape led to arrest and then imprisonment in the Tower of London. She was freed in 1747, having acquired considerable celebrity status, and, in 1750, married Allan Macdonald of Skye. In 1774, they emigrated to North America, where Macdonald fought on the British side during the War of Independence and was taken prisoner. Flora returned to Scotland in 1779, where her husband rejoined her two years later. She died at Kinsburgh, her husband's family home, having produced nine children, on 5 March 1790. Her heroism is commemorated in **ROBERT LOUIS STEVENSON**'s *Skye Boat Song* (1896).

MACDONALD, JOHN ALEXANDER (1815–91). The first Prime Minister of Canada, Macdonald was born in **GLASGOW** on 11 January 1815, the son of evicted Crofter Hugh Macdonald and his wife, Helen. (See **CROFTING**). In 1820, his family emigrated to Kingston (now in Ontario), where Macdonald was educated at the Royal Grammar School and at 15, was apprenticed to a lawyer. He was called to the Bar in 1836 and had built up a successful business by the time he entered the House of Assembly as the Conservative representative for Kingston in 1844. He was given his first government post as Receiver-General three years later and, during the Conservatives' period in opposition between 1848 and 1854, built up an influential following, which he retained after his party returned to power.

In 1857, Macdonald was appointed Prime Minister of Upper Canada. Over the next decade, his tact and diplomacy earned the respect of Westminster politicians, who were convinced of his loyalty to the Crown, and won him allies among the disparate cultural and regional groups who controlled Britain's North American colonies. From 1864, he led the move to advocate a formal confederation of these territories and, when the Dominion of Canada was formed on 1 July 1867, became Prime Minister. In addition, he was made a Knight Commander of the Order of the Bath in recognition of his services to the empire.

During Macdonald's period in office, he helped to weld potentially conflicting interests together (notably by promoting the construction of a transcontinental railway) and expanded the dominion by incorporating Prince Rupert's Land (1870), North West Territory (1870), Manitoba (1870), British Columbia (1871) and Prince Edward Island (1873). However, in 1873, he was implicated in a financial scandal and, although he denied any wrongdoing, was forced to resign. He returned to office in 1878 and remained in power for 13 years, resisting regional movements which threatened Canadian unity and opponents who wanted to eliminate trade barriers with the United States. (Free trade, Macdonald believed, would ultimately lead to annexation). However, the rigours of leadership took their toll on his health, and, on 6 June 1891, he died at his home near

Ottawa, after suffering a stroke during a General Election campaign.

MACGREGOR, ROB ROY (1671–1734). MacGregor was a cattle thief and outlaw romanticized by **WALTER SCOTT**'s novel *Rob Roy*, published in 1818, and by William Wordsworth's poetry. The younger son of Donald MacGregor (brother of the **CLAN** chief) and his wife, Margaret, he was born early in 1671 and raised at the farm in Balquhidder (in the **SCOTTISH HIGHLANDS,** some 30 miles northwest of **STIRLING**) which the family worked as tenants of the Duke of Atholl. His physique was unusual (according to Scott, he could tie his garters — two inches below his knees — without stooping), but his letters show that he received a sound basic education and had many of the attributes of a highland gentleman of the times. His income was probably earned mainly by providing local farmers with protection against cattle thieves, of which he was undoubtedly one of the most successful. (Both theft and protection had long been considered honourable occupations in upland Scotland). The MacGregors suffered severe penalties for their part in the 1689 **JACOBITE** uprising led by **JOHN GRAHAM** of Claverhouse, and, in 1693, Rob Roy took the surname Campbell (his mother's maiden name). In 1712, he borrowed money from the Duke of Montrose in order to purchase cattle but became entangled in debt as a result of treachery. Montrose destroyed his property and, in midwinter, evicted his wife and children from the farm. In 1716, he began a campaign of harassment directed at the Duke, and his activities became the stuff of legend; stories were told of how he robbed rent collectors, escaped from capture and gave money to the needy. Ultimately, through the good offices of the **DUKE OF ARGYLL,** the two men were reconciled. However, despite their support, he was arrested by English troops, charged with aiding **JAMES STUART** — the Old Pretender — and marched to London, where he was confined to Newgate Prison. In January 1727, he was taken to Gravesend for deportation to Barbados but, at the last minute, was pardoned and spent the rest of his life at Balquhidder, where he died, peacefully, on 28 December 1734.

MACINTYRE, DUNCAN BAN (1724–1812). Macintyre (known in **GAELIC** as Donnchadh Bànn Mac an t-Soir) is the most renowned of highland Scotland's 18th-century poets. Born in Glenorchy (Argyll), he never received a formal education and remained illiterate throughout his life, so his work was written down by others. He never learned to speak English but, in the Gaelic oral tradition, reputedly knew all of his poems — some 7,000 verses — by heart. Although he fought on the Hanoverian side at the **BATTLE OF FALKIRK,** he spent a large part of his life as a forester, employed by the Earl of Breadalbane and the **DUKE OF ARGYLL.** That job brought him into daily contact with the mountain environment, the subject of most of his best poems, including *Moladh Beinn Dòbhrain* (*Praise of Ben Doran*) and *Oran Coire a' Cheathaich* (*Song to Misty Corrie*), compositions which show a detailed understanding of the habits of the deer and other inhabitants of the high hills. A lyrical style and a personal involvement with landscape and events are also evident in Macintyre's songs of praise to the Campbells (who dominated Glenorchy) and his love poems (the best of which were written to Mairi, his wife). From 1793 until 1799, he served with the Duke of Breadalbane's Fencibles (a body of militiamen) and, when that group was disbanded, with the city guard in **EDINBURGH.** However, the three editions of his works which were published in 1768, 1790 and 1804 appear to have given him financial security, and, from 1806, he was able to live on the proceeds of the sales. He died in Edinburgh in October 1812 and was buried in Greyfriars churchyard. Translations by **HUGH MACDIARMID** retain much of the beauty and emotion of the originals.

MACKAY OF CLASHFERN, BARON. (See **JAMES MACKAY**).

MACKAY, JAMES PETER HYMERS (1927–). Lord High Chancellor under Prime Ministers Margaret Thatcher and John Major, Mackay was born on 2 July 1927, the son of railway porter James Mackay and his wife, Janet. He won a scholarship to George Heriot's School (**EDINBURGH**), then studied at Edinburgh University before obtaining a post as Lecturer in Mathematics at the University of **ST ANDREWS** in 1948. In 1950, he moved to Cambridge but stayed for only a short time before returning to Edinburgh, where he graduated with a law degree in 1955. Mackay's acute mind quickly earned him a reputation with legal colleagues, and he was appointed Queen's Counsel in 1965. He was **SHERIFF**-Principal of Renfrew and Argyll from 1972 until 1974, Vice Dean of the Faculty of Advocates from 1973 until 1976 and Dean for a further three years. In 1979, he was created Baron Mackay of Clashfern and appointed **LORD ADVOCATE** of Scotland even though he was not a member of the Conservative Party, which formed the Government. In 1984–85, he served as a Senator of the College of Justice in Scotland and then, for two years, was a Lord of Appeal in Ordinary before being appointed Lord High Chancellor by Mrs Thatcher in 1987. In that post, he introduced radical changes to the legal profession in England, reducing the privileges of barristers and incurring the wrath of fellow-lawyers in the process. He also instigated major amendments to social legislation, notably through the introduction of simplified divorce proceedings, a move which drew much criticism from right-wing Conservatives, who felt that he was threatening the stability of the family. A deeply religious man, he shocked many fellow-members of the **FREE PRESBYTERIAN CHURCH OF SCOTLAND** by attending requiem mass for a Roman Catholic colleague in 1989. Mackay claimed that he had done no wrong, but his Church disagreed and expelled him.

MACKINTOSH, CHARLES RENNIE (1868–1928). One of the leaders of the *art nouveau* movement, Mackintosh was born in **GLASGOW** on 7 January 1868, the son of police superintendent William Mackintosh and his wife, Margaret. He was educated in the city at Allan Glen's School and then, while serving as an apprentice to architect John Hutchison, at Glasgow School of Art. In 1889, he joined the practice of Honeyman and Keppie, becoming a partner five years later. Over the next decade, he gained an international reputation, exerting a considerable influence on European architectural design, and producing posters, craftwork and furniture characterized by a lightness and elegance which contrasted with the popular styles of the period. Many of the patterns incorporated floral features — a reflection of a love of gardening which Mackintosh had inherited from his father.

His outstanding architectural work is considered to be the new building for the Glasgow School of Art (1897–1909), four tearooms (also in Glasgow) built for Miss Cranston between 1896 and 1904 (Mrs Cranston's tearooms became a Glasgow institution, attracting the well-to-do from all over the city), and Hill House in Helensburgh (1903–4). All contrast curved motifs with rectilinear patterns, utilizing traditional Scottish design features but adapting them to modern tastes. Mackintosh's drawings were exhibited throughout Europe, where he was much admired, but, after 1909, he received no major architectural commissions and, in 1914, resigned his partnership and moved to England, spending part of his time in London and part in Suffolk. Between 1923 and 1927, he lived in France and devoted himself to painting in watercolours. He died in London on 10 December 1928.

In 1997, the Heritage Lottery Fund awarded a grant of £3.5 million towards the cost of refurbishing the lighthouse, Mackintosh's first major building. The former newspaper offices in Mitchell Street, Glasgow, had lain empty for twenty years but would be converted into a complex of shops, offices, conference facilities and galleries showing design exhibitions.

MACMILLANITES. (See **CAMERONIANS**).

MADOG AP OWAIN GWYNEDD (1150–c. 1180). The belief that Madog was the first European to set foot in America was a potent force for Welsh migration to the United States during the 18th century. The story appears to have its roots in Richard Hakluyt's *Voyages,* published in 1582, and David Powel's *The Historie of Cambria,* 1584. Drawing on earlier works (including poems by the bards), Powel claims that Madog left Wales to avoid conflicts with his brother after the death of their father, Owain Gwynedd, in 1170. He travelled to Ireland and then north to a strange new land which, according to Powel, must have been Florida. On the basis of that experience, he returned to Wales, gathered resources for a second expedition, set off with ten ships and founded a settlement on the other side of the Atlantic. Madog never returned from that second journey so evidence for his colony was circumstantial, based on details such as supposed linguistic links between **WELSH** and the vocabulary of some Indian languages. John Dee took up the tale in 1577, arguing that King Arthur had carved out a large empire in the lands of the north Atlantic and that Madog had confirmed Welsh title to the territory. Queen Elizabeth I, as the successor to the Welsh princes, exercised sovereignty throughout the area (Dee, in fact, coined the term British Empire, using British as a synonym for Brythonic). The theory had many champions (including **IOLO MORGANWG**) and, during the late 18th century, they found their case supported by mounting rumours of a tribe of Welsh-speaking Indians, known as the Madogwys, who lived in the American interior. During the 1790s, the tale encouraged many Welsh men and women, already predisposed to emigration as a means of escaping from poverty, to set sail for the United States. Among them was John Evans of Waunfawr, who left with the intention of converting the Madogwys to Christianity and prepared the first maps of the Missouri valley as he searched for them. The suggestion that the Welsh might have discovered America provided a potent fuel for national pride, but support for the belief waned during the 19th century in the face both of increased knowledge and more critical scholarship. At the **EI-**

STEDDFOD of 1858, a prize was offered for the best essay on the discovery of North America by Prince Madog ap Owain Gwynedd. The most distinguished submission was presented by Thomas Stephens, but he could not be given the award because his work was a sustained explanation of why the discovery could not have occurred.

MAG RATH, BATTLE OF, 637. The Scottish Kings of DALRIADA had held lands in Ireland since the early sixth century. This short confrontation resulted in their heavy defeat near County Down at the hands of the Uí Néill Irish chieftains, and the effective loss of their interests in the island.

MAID OF NORWAY. (See MARGARET, MAID OF NORWAY).

MALCOLM I (?–954). Malcolm was the eighth King to follow KENNETH MACALPIN as ruler of SCOTIA in less than 100 years, an indication of the turbulent conditions in north Britain during the ninth and tenth centuries. The son of Donald (who ruled from 889 until 900), Malcolm succeeded Constantine when, in 943, that monarch entered a monastery. With the help of King Edmund of England whom he accepted as overlord, he gained control of Strathclyde, but much of his reign was spent attempting to suppress rivals from Moray, in the northeast of his kingdom. In 954, he was poisoned by Indulf (one of these opponents) and buried on IONA.

MALCOLM II (c. 954–1034). The son of KENNETH II, Malcolm gained the throne of SCOTIA in 1005 by killing his predecessor, KENNETH III, and ruled for 29 years, keeping control through a mixture of diplomacy, cunning and threat. He extended his kingdom southwards by wresting Lothian from English hands and kept Strathclyde in subjugation by installing his grandson (later DUNCAN I) as ruler. However, in 1031, he was forced to submit to King Canute following an Anglo-Danish invasion of his lands, and, in the winter of 1034, was poisoned at GLAMIS CASTLE by a group of followers, who drowned when the ice broke beneath their horses' feet as they tried to make their escape across a frozen LOCH.

MALCOLM III (c. 1031–93). Known as Canmore (or Big Head — probably a literal reference to his physiognomy), Malcolm was the son of DUNCAN I and became the King who took Scotland out of the dark ages into the mainstream of European culture. He succeeded to the throne, in 1058, by killing **LULACH** (king for only four months) after several years in exile at the court of Edward the Confessor in England. His friendship with the southern aristocracy was evident in 1068, when, following the Norman invasion, he provided a safe haven for Edward the Aethling (the Saxon pretender to the English throne), his mother and his two sisters, one of whom (**ST MARGARET**) became Malcolm's second wife. In 1072, however, he was forced to pay allegiance to William I of England, handing over Duncan, his eldest son, as a hostage ensuring good behaviour. The relationship between these neighbouring monarchs, was always an uneasy one. A series of incursions into England between 1079 and 1091 severely tried the patience of the Norman kings, and, in 1093, he had to pay homage once more, this time to William II. Later the same year, he invaded England again and was killed at the battle of Alnwick. The available evidence suggests that Malcolm's was a devious, ruthless rule, but he made no attempt to turn Scotland into a feudal kingdom on Norman lines and could communicate in **GAELIC,** English and Latin. His marriage to Margaret undoubtedly fanned the flames of William I's wrath, but the couple established a formidable dynasty: three of their six sons — **EDGAR,** Alexander (later **ALEXANDER I**) and David (later **DAVID II**) — became kings, one daughter (Matilda) married Henry I of England and the other (Mary) married Eustace III, Count of Boulogne. Much of that international matrimonial success was undoubtedly due to Margaret, a devout Christian who had been raised in Hungary and brought to Scotland the civilizing subtleties of European manners and customs. (See **MACBETH**).

MALCOLM IV. (1141–1165) Henry, son of King **DAVID I** of Scotland, died in 1152, while his father was still on the throne. As a result, when David died the following year, the succession passed to Malcolm, his grandson and the product of Henry's marriage to the Anglo-Norman Ada de Warenne. The new monarch (known as *The Maiden,* either because he was celibate or because of his gentle nature) spent most of his 12-year reign suppressing rebellion. In 1157, he surrendered Cumbria and Northumberland to Henry II of England, to whom Malcolm, as Earl of Huntingdon, owed a feudal obligation of military service. Never in good health, he died at Jedburgh in 1165.

MALT TAX, 1713. After the **ACT OF UNION** in 1707, which created the United Kingdom of Great Britain by joining England and Scotland under one Parliament, attempts were made to standardize taxation across the nation, but the Scots were allowed freedom from excise payments under the Malt Tax. (With its importance to the **WHISKY** industry, this was an important concession). However, in 1713, the tax was extended to Scotland (though at a rate of 3d per bushel, half that levied in the rest of the country), and it caused a furore. The **SCOTTISH REPRESENTATIVE PEERS** and Scottish members of Parliament protested, and there were disturbances in the major cities, with troops firing on a mob in **GLASGOW**. In June 1713, the Earl of Findlater even put a motion to dissolve the new union to the House of Lords, citing the tax as one element of the argument. There were further protests when the tax was increased to the full rate in 1725 and extended to beer and ale.

MARCHER LORDS. The Norman barons who administered the Welsh **MARCHES,** the Marcher Lords defended themselves in heavily fortified castles. The border between England and Wales was vital in the fight against Welsh rebels so the Marcher Lords were given special privileges, as at the Mise of Lewes (1264), when those who had supported Simon de Montfort against Henry III were released from prison in order to return to their lands and rebuild their defences. Many of the castles were also associated with markets, and these developed into a string of towns along the border, including Chepstow, Monmouth and Ludlow. Although intended to provide a buffer zone between the two nations, the Marcher Lords frequently proved problematical, and their privileges ceased at the **UNION OF WALES AND ENGLAND** in 1536 and 1543.

MARCHES. After the Norman conquest, the borderlands between England and Wales were taken, usually by force, from the Welsh inhabitants. Most were divided into the Englishry (the lowland area with a castle for military control, a manor for food production and a borough to provide a trading town centre) and the Welshry (the upland area of mostly poorer land, where Welsh customs survived). The Marches were abolished at the **ACT OF UNION** of 1536, but the term is still used today to describe the border areas between England and Wales. The word originally came from the French *marche,* which means a disputed frontier zone. Originally, the leader of a marchland was a **MARCHER LORD,** a term which was the origin of the titles *Marquess* and *Marquis.*

MARGARET, MAID OF NORWAY (*c.* 1283–90). When King **AL-EXANDER III** of Scotland died in March 1286, he was succeeded by his granddaughter, Margaret, the only child of Eric II, King of Norway, and Alexander's own daughter, also named Margaret. The child was proclaimed Queen in July and, three years later, was betrothed to Edward, son of Edward I of England. In September 1290, she set off for Scotland from Scandinavia but took ill during the voyage and died on the **ORKNEY ISLANDS** (then still in Norwegian hands). From there, her body was taken back to Bergen, where she was buried. A court, over which Edward I presided, appointed **JOHN BALLIOL** King of Scotland, condemning the country to two decades of English overlordship and civil war. In 1301, a woman claiming to be Margaret was condemned as an imposter and burned to death in Bergen. However, many people were convinced that her case was just and honoured her as a saint.

MARGARET, ST (*c.* 1046–1093). Queen of **MALCOLM III** of Scotland, Margaret was the daughter of Edward Aethling of England and granddaughter of the Anglo-Saxon King Edmund Ironside. She was born in Hungary, where her parents were living in exile, but spent some time in Northumberland before fleeing to Scotland, in 1068, after the successful Norman invasion of the British Isles. The following year, she married Malcolm in Dunfermline — a match of opposites, because she was a devout, pious Christian and he a rude, violent soldier. Some scholars have argued that Margaret's influence was the beginning of the end for Celtic independence because she began a process of romanizing the indigenous church which was to be continued by her sons (see **ALEXANDER I** and **DAVID I**), helped Benedictine monks establish a settlement and encouraged her husband to develop a Norman lifestyle. A biography written by Turgot, Bishop of **ST ANDREWS** and Margaret's confessor, describes the Queen as a lively woman, who would nevertheless have preferred the nunnery to the royal court and gave much of her wealth to the poor. She died in **EDINBURGH** on 16 November 1093, was canonized by Pope Innocent IV in 1249 and remains the only Scottish royal saint. Her feast day is 10 June.

MARTYRS OF '68. The 1867 Parliamentary Reform Act expanded the franchise by giving votes to every male householder in the Welsh and English boroughs and to all men occupying property rated at a value of £12 or more in rural areas. The result was a 232 per cent increase in the number of people entitled to vote at Parliamentary elections in Wales; in **CARDIFF** and **SWANSEA** the electorate rose threefold and in **MERTHYR TYDFIL** more than tenfold. At the General Election in 1868, the new voters chose to exercise their rights by supporting Liberal Party candidates rather than the landowning, anglicized Conservative Party representatives who had previously held a monopoly of power. However, there was no secret ballot, and many landlords sought vengeance on tenants and employees who had voted against them. In Caernarvonshire, it was claimed that 80 workers at Penrhyn Quarry lost their jobs in the wake of the defeat of George Douglas-Pennant, son of Baron Penrhyn, by Love Jones-Parry (one of the sponsors of the **PATAGONIA** settlement scheme). In Cardiganshire, 43 farm tenants were given notice to quit, as were 26 in Carmarthenshire. A fund to help the homeless 'martyrs' raised £20,000, and several MPs (including **HENRY RICHARD,** who had won one of the two Merthyr seats) raised the matter in the House of Commons. The events served to strengthen the resolve of the Welsh radicals and helped lead to the introduction of secret ballots in 1872.

MARY OF GUISE (1515–60). Mary of Guise (also known as Mary of Lorraine) was the mother of **MARY, QUEEN OF SCOTS,** and acted as Regent for her daughter from 1554 until 1560. She was born at Bar-le-Duc in Lorraine, on 22 November 1515, the eldest child of Claude, Duc de Guise (one of the most powerful men in France) and Antoinette de Bourbon, spending her childhood among the French aristocracy. On 4 August 1534, she married Louis, Duc de Longueville, but he died three years later. Seeking a second husband, she rejected the suit of Henry VIII of England in favour of **JAMES V** of Scotland. Mary arrived in her new realm in June 1538 and married James at **ST ANDREWS** shortly afterwards (legally, the couple had been united by proxy some weeks earlier at a French ceremony). She bore the King two sons (James and Arthur), both of whom died in 1541, and a daughter (Mary), who was born on 7 or 8 December 1542, just a week before her father died following the **BATTLE OF SOLWAY MOSS.** James, Earl of Arran, was appointed Regent, but he failed to keep the country peaceful, and, in August 1548, the five-year-old Queen was sent to France, bargained as the bride of the Dauphin in return for military support against the English invaders. When she reached her twelfth year, Mary, according to French legal opinion, was entitled to govern her kingdom through a ruler of her own choice. On 12 April 1554, Arran unwillingly resigned. Mary of Guise, appointed in his place, initially adopted policies of religious tolerance in face of entrenched anti-

Catholic views, but the appointment of members of the Guise family to positions of power at her court eroded support from the Scottish nobles. In the spring of 1559, apparently under pressure from France, she abandoned conciliation and began a campaign to suppress Protestantism. An attempt to compel ministers to accept Roman Catholicism led to a riot in Perth, and, shortly afterwards, the armies of the Protestant nobles drove her from **EDINBURGH**, declaring, on 21 October, that she was no longer Regent. Mary, helped by French reinforcements, regained the city within weeks but, seriously ill with dropsy, survived only until 11 June 1560. **JOHN KNOX** is reported to have celebrated her death in ways which, according to historian Jenny Wormald, "made it clear why charity has not been thought a notable feature of Scottish Calvinism." Her body was taken to France for burial at Reims, and Scotland was left to the rule of her 18-year-old daughter.

MARY OF LORRAINE. (See **MARY OF GUISE**).

MARY, QUEEN OF SCOTS (1542–87). Mary is one of the most romantic figures in the pageant of Scottish history, her life usually depicted as a series of sorrows and tragedies borne with dignity and courage. Born at Linlithgow Palace on 7 or 8 December 1542, she was just one week old when she became Queen on the death of her father, **JAMES V.** Five years later, her mother (**MARY OF GUISE**) sent her to France in order to ensure her safety whilst the nobles struggled for power and Henry VIII of England attacked villages and religious houses in the southern parts of her realm. She was raised at the French court, becoming a skilled linguist and a noted musician but apparently failing to acquire any political acumen. In 1558, at the age of 15, she married Francis, the sickly Dauphin of France, in an alliance which meant that Mary was destined to become Queen of her adopted country but which was also clearly intended to lead to a situation in which Scotland would unite with her continental ally under one sovereign.

Mary also had a claim to the throne of England. Roman Catholics maintained that Henry VIII's marriage to Anne Boleyn should not be recognized because it followed an invalid divorce from Catherine of Aragon; Elizabeth Tudor (later Elizabeth I), their daughter, was therefore illegitimate and Mary (granddaughter of Henry VII's daughter, Margaret) the rightful heiress.

Francis became King of France in 1559 but died the following year. Seeing no future on the continent, Mary accepted an invitation from the Scottish nobles and returned to her native country in August 1561. She had much popular support, but her interests lay primarily in gaining the Crown of England. Inevitably, that led Elizabeth to regard her as a threat and therefore to attempt to limit her powers. And, at home, she annoyed her counsellors by failing to provide leadership and surrounding herself with a coterie of foreigners. An eminently marriageable young woman, she would have welcomed any husband who would help her gain the English throne and fell for the charms of her cousin **HENRY DARNLEY,** who, according to Catholic supporters, had a claim to the crown of England second only to Mary's own. The match was supported by Philip II of Spain, who wanted the Protestant English monarchy changed because it threatened his provinces in the Netherlands. He promised Mary that, if she married Darnley, he would finance an invasion of England.

The wedding took place on 29 July 1565, but the couple was soon estranged. Mary quickly turned from the jealous, arrogant and cruel Darnley to other admirers. Unwilling to tolerate her philandering, Darnley led a group of conspirators into his wife's apartments at **HOLYROOD PALACE** on 9 February 1566 and murdered David Rizzio, her Italian secretary and favoured companion. Mary, six months pregnant, never forgave him either for the humiliation or for endangering her unborn child. A brief reconciliation, during which her son (later James VI and I) was born, was followed by an affair with **JAMES HEPBURN BOTHWELL,** Earl of Bothwell. Darnley became an embarrassment, threatening to cause a scandal by leaving Scotland, and, towards the end of 1566, Mary discussed with her advisors the possibility of freeing herself from her marital ties. In January of the following year, Darnley fell ill and Mary took him to **EDINBURGH,** ostensibly to nurse him. He was lodged in the upper floor of a house in Kirk o' Fields, with Mary occupying a room below. On the night of 9 February, Mary went to a wedding festival at Holyrood Palace, and, in her absence, the house was blown up. Darnley was found later in the grounds, along with his valet. Both were unmarked by the explosion and strangled. Bothwell was acquitted of complicity in the murder at a trial held in May, divorced his wife and married Mary.

Universally disparaged, the Queen now found herself in conflict with the Protestant nobles, who resented Bothwell's power. She was taken prisoner and held first in Edinburgh, then at Loch Leven Castle, where she was forced to sign a deed of abdication, effectively handing over the throne to her son. She escaped from captivity in May 1568 and rallied loyal supporters but was defeated at the **BAT-**

TLE OF LANGSIDE and fled to England. For Elizabeth, that raised a difficult problem. Mary's death would eliminate the major threat to her Protestant crown but might unite the Catholic forces against her and lead to her downfall. For 19 years, Mary was held prisoner then, in October 1586, was brought to trial at Fotheringhay Castle, charged with colluding with Bothwell in Darnley's murder. The evidence was questionable, and Mary conducted her defence with a dignity which aroused much sympathy and admiration, but she was found guilty and, on 8 February 1587, executed in the great hall of the castle. Elizabeth had taken three months to authorize the death warrant and, in the end, had insisted that the paper should be placed innocently amongst other documents for her signature. Mary had played for high stakes and lost but showed great courage and determination. In many ways, her downfall was due to her inability to control her sexual relationships; despite her charm, she — like so many members of the House of **STUART** — had a personality which contained its own self-destruct mechanism. (See **CASKET LETTERS**; **GOWRIE CONSPIRACY**; **JOHN KNOX**).

MASON OF BARNSLEY, BARON. (See **ROY MASON**).

MASON, ROY (1924–). **SECRETARY OF STATE FOR NORTHERN IRELAND** from 1976 until 1979, Mason is the son of Mary and Joseph Mason. He was born on 18 April 1924 and educated at Royston Senior School, following his father into the coal mines at the age of 14. After serving his political apprenticeship as a Branch Official of the National Union of Mineworkers for six years from 1947, he was elected Member of Parliament for the safe Labour Party seat at Barnsley in 1953. From 1960 until 1964, he was Opposition Spokesman on Defence and Post Office Affairs, then became Minister of State at the Board of Trade (1964–67), Minister of Defence Equipment (1967–68), Postmaster-General (April–June 1968), Minister of Power (1968–69), President of the Board of Trade (1969–70), Opposition Spokesman on Board of Trade Affairs (1970–74) and Secretary of State for Defence (1974–76). Mason's appointment to the Northern Ireland post in 1976 was interpreted as indicative of Prime Minister Harold Wilson's determination to adopt tougher policies dealing with civil disorder in the province. He caused controversy after only a few weeks by sending elite Special Air Service units to trouble spots in South Armagh and by attempting to persuade the mass media not to publish accounts of terrorist incidents when issues of national security were involved. In 1977, he held a series of meetings with representatives of **ULSTER**'s main political parties in an attempt to find a political solution to **THE TROUBLES** but could make no headway and turned his attentions to other issues, notably reform of the courts and the introduction of legislation which brought the rules relating to divorce and homsexuality into line with those in the rest of the United Kingdom. Mason lost office when the Conservative Party returned to power in 1979 and was created Baron Mason of Barnsley in 1987.

MAWHINNEY, BRIAN STANLEY (1940–). One of very few **ULSTER**men to gain high office in the United Kingdom's mainstream political organizations, Mawhinney was appointed Chairman of the Conservative Party and Minister Without Portfolio in Prime Minister John Major's Cabinet in 1995. Born on 26 July 1940, the son of Coralie and Frederick Mawhinney, he was educated at the Royal **BELFAST** Academical Institution before taking degrees at Queen's College Belfast (BSc), the University of Michigan (MSc) and the University of London (PhD). Initially, he embarked on an academic career, holding posts as Assistant Professor of Radiation Research at the University of Iowa (1968–70) and as lecturer (then senior lecturer) at the Royal Free Hospital School of Medicine in London (1970–84).

Mawhinney's first attempt to enter Parliament — at Stockton-on-Tees in 1974 — was unsuccessful, but he won Peterborough for the Conservatives in 1979 and distinguished himself on the back benches of the House of Commons. (In particular, he proposed a plan for a Northern Ireland assembly which was the foundation of the 'rolling devolution' scheme announced by **JAMES PRIOR** in 1982). He earned successive appointments as Parliamentary Private Secretary at The Treasury, the Department of Employment and the **NORTHERN IRELAND OFFICE** between 1982 and 1986, then was promoted to the posts of Under-Secretary of State for Northern Ireland (1986-90) and Minister of State for Northern Ireland (1990-92). In Belfast, response to his period in office were mixed; Unionists criticized his support for the **ANGLO-IRISH AGREEMENT** and the Roman Catholic Church condemned his support for schools which would take pupils from both of the major religious communities. However, he played an important role in the negotiations which led to interparty discussions and talks between the unionist parties and representatives of the Irish Republic's government in 1991.

In the reshuffle of ministerial responsibilities, which followed

John Major's General Election victory in 1992, Mawhinney was moved to the Department of Health as Minister of State. He then spent a period as Secretary of State for Transport (1994–95) before taking over the party chairman's post. In the 1997 General Election, he won the newly created seat at Cambridgeshire North West (a constituency which included much of his former Peterbrough base). He was knighted in John Major's resignation honours list and given the post of shadow Home Secretary by **WILLIAM HAGUE,** who became leader of the opposition. A close friend of Major and a committed Christian (he was a member of the Church of England's general synod from 1985 until 1989), Mawhinney has little time for liberal views on drug addiction and sex education but has advocated greater awareness of environmental matters in policy making. A polished speaker (he can use his Irish brogue to great effect), he has a reputation for bullying his civil servants, but supporters claim that he is simply a hard man who cannot tolerate fools gladly.

MAXTON, JAMES (1885–1946). In the period following the First World War, **GLASGOW** was the most left-wing city in Britain (see **RED CLYDESIDE**), and Maxton was one of the most influential leaders of the socialist movement. He was born in Pollokshaws (now a Glasgow suburb) on 22 June 1885, the son of teacher James Maxton and his wife, Melvina, and educated at Hutcheson's Grammar School and Glasgow University. In 1904, he joined the Independent Labour Party (ILP) and, although he worked as a teacher from 1906 until 1916, became increasingly involved in political activities, developing a reputation as a witty, effective orator. In 1916, Maxton was imprisoned on a charge of sedition after making an antiwar speech and, in 1918, unsuccessfully contested Bridgeton (one of the Glasgow constituencies) for the ILP at the General Election. Four years later, he returned, won the seat and held it until his death. In the House of Commons, he relished the rough and tumble of party politics and proved to be an outstanding debater, although his fiery style often got him into trouble. (In 1923, for instance, he was suspended during a debate on cuts in public health expenditure because he called some MPs murderers). Succeeding Reginald Clifford Allen as Chairman of the ILP in 1926, he mounted a campaign of opposition to the Labour Party's more moderate policies, finally withdrawing his organization's support for Prime Minister Ramsay MacDonald in 1932. After that split, although he continued to intervene in debate and attract crowds to his meetings around the country, Maxton became increasingly isolated from mainstream politics. Failing health curbed his energies, and he died at Largs on 23 July 1946.

MAXWELL, JAMES CLERK (1831–79). A theoretical physician who made major contributions to the study of electricity, Maxwell was born in **EDINBURGH** on 13 November 1831, the son of Frances and John Maxwell. He was educated at Edinburgh Academy, Edinburgh University and Cambridge University then, in 1856, became Professor of Natural Philosophy at Marischal College, **ABERDEEN**. Four years later, he moved to the Chair of Physics and Astronomy at King's College, London, but retired in 1865 so that he could pursue a programme of private research at the family estate in Kirkudbrightshire. In 1871, he was persuaded to move to Cambridge, where he spent the rest of his working life as the University's first Professor of Experimental Physics and founder of the Cavendish Laboratory, now a world-famous research institute. His intellectual abilities were obvious by the time he was 14, when he prepared a paper for the Royal Society of Edinburgh which described how to draw perfect oval curves. In 1857, he established the nature of Saturn's rings and, in 1861, demonstrated the potential of colour photography by producing a picture of a tartan ribbon. In 1866, he made contributions to the kinetic theory of gases but his most significant achievements were in the field of electromagnetic induction. In a series of studies, beginning with *Physical Lines of Force* (published in 1862) and culminating with *Treatise on Electricity and Magnetism* (1873), Maxwell expressed, in mathematical form, the results obtained from Michael Faraday's experiments. His initial formulae outlined the relationship between changes in magnetic fields, induced electromotive forces and electric currents. From that basis, he demonstrated that an oscillating electric charge could produce an electromagnetic field, which would convey energy in the form of transverse waves. The energy in those waves would be divided equally between a magnetic field and an electric field, with the fields being perpendicular to each other and to the direction in which the wave was travelling. That discovery, in turn, led to a consideration of the relationship between the velocity of the waves and the velocity of light and to the suggestion that visible light was a manifestation of the electromagnetic waves he had inferred mathematically. In addition, he argued that his work predicted the existence of lower frequency electromagnetic waves known as radio waves, an assertion which was to be proved accurate some years later. Maxwell died of cancer at Cambridge on 5 November 1879, still in his prime, but his work is considered to have provided a foundation for the advances made by Max Planck and Albert Einstein.

MAYHEW OF TWYSDEN, LORD (see **PATRICK BARNABUS BURKE MAYHEW**).

MAYHEW, PATRICK BARNABUS BURKE (1929–). In 1992, Prime Minister John Major appointed Patrick Mayhew to the post of **SECRETARY OF STATE FOR NORTHERN IRELAND,** widely regarded as the least desirable job in British politics. Mayhew was born on 11 September 1929, the son of Sheila and A. G. H. Mayhew. He was educated at Tonbridge School (Kent) and Oxford University, where he was President of the Union in 1952. He completed his National Service as a Captain in the 4th/7th Royal Dragoon Guards, was called to the Bar in 1955 and became a Queen's Counsel in 1972. In 1970, he lost a contest for the Parliamentary constituency of Camberwell and Dulwich but was successful at Tunbridge Wells in 1974 and held the seat until his retirement from politics in 1997. He was appointed Under-Secretary of State at the Department of Employment in 1979 and Minister of State at the Home Office in 1981. In 1983, he became Solicitor General and, in 1987, Attorney General. John Major transferred him to the Northern Ireland Office in 1992, with the joint task of maintaining security and finding a diplomatic means of ending the conflict. He maintained a high profile in **ULSTER** and has held many meetings with local politicians, Ulster Members of Parliament and representatives of the Government of the Irish Republic, in an attempt to find a peaceful solution to **THE TROUBLES.** After the **IRISH REPUBLICAN ARMY** agreed to end its campaign of violence in 1994, the discussions formally included representatives of **SINN FEIN** and concentrated on achieving multiparty agreement on the government of the province and on its political status. Mayhew retired from politics at the 1997 General Election and was raised to the peerage as Lord Mayhew of Twysden shortly afterwards.

MERK. Formerly a unit of currency in Scotland, the merk was equivalent to 13.33 pence sterling.

MERTHYR RISING, 3 June 1831. The town of **MERTHYR TYDFIL** trebled its population in the first three decades of the 19th century as it developed the largest concentration of ironworks in Britain and became the largest town in Wales, but poverty and falling incomes among the iron workers and coal miners of the district, combined with the controversy surrounding the Parliamentary Reform Bill then before Parliament, led to riots in the town. Troops sent to put down the rising fired on the protesters, killing 20, and enraged the crowds, who forced 450 troops to retreat until order was restored by reinforcement cavalry. Richard Lewis, one of the leaders, was condemned to death for wounding one of the soldiers. The incident did, however, lead to the introduction of the Truck Act, which reduced the dependency of the miners and ironworkers on the employers by insisting on payment of wages in money, not goods or tokens.

MERTHYR TYDFIL. Located on the River Taf some 25 miles northwest of **CARDIFF,** Merthyr is named after Tudful (a fifth-century Christian martyr). Archaeologists have found pottery dating from the first century in the vicinity, but, despite that evidence of early settlement, the town is essentially a product of the Industrial Revolution. Local reserves of iron ore were worked from the 1500s, with charcoal from local forests used for smelting, then, between 1757 and 1783, four new ironworks were established, spawning a series of subsidiary firms and leading to increases in population. Exports of finished products to North America began about 1780, the Glamorganshire Canal was built to provide a means of transporting goods to the docks on the River Severn at Cardiff during the 1790s and, by 1801, Merthyr was the largest town in Wales (albeit with only 7,700 people). The development of steam power led to the exploitation of local coal supplies so, by 1845, Merthyr, with 18 blast furnaces, was the biggest producer of iron in the world. By 1861, the population had climbed to over 50,000, but, as reserves were worked out, more and more ore had to be imported, and businesses began to seek cost-efficient locations near the coast. Also, during the depression years between the First and Second World Wars, the drop in trade forced many companies to shut down (including the enormous Dowlais steel works, which closed in 1930). By 1932, about half of the adult male population was out of work, and employment was concentrated increasingly in the coal mines. Since then, attempts have been made to widen the economic base by attracting new industry, notably light engineering. Enhanced road transport and rehabilitation of derelict land have helped to improve the local infrastructure. The town has a history of radical politics. At the General Election of 1900, it was the only Parliamentary constituency in Britain to elect a socialist MP (**JAMES KEIR HARDIE**) and in 1976, upset by the policies of the long-time Labour Party majority on the local council, it appointed a **PLAID CYMRU** authority in its place. At the time of the 1991 census, it had a population of 57,400. (See **MERTHYR RISING**; **HENRY RICHARD**).

METHODIST REVIVAL (WALES). During the 18th and early 19th centuries, Wales experienced a flowering of Methodism which parallels similar religious movements in mainland Europe and North America. By tradition, it began on 30 March 1735, when **HOWEL HARRIS** was moved by a sermon at Talgarth to devote his life to spreading the Christian gospel. Aided by **DANIEL ROWLAND, WILLIAM WILLIAMS** and others, he set up a series of cells (known as *seiadau* in **WELSH**) where groups of believers (many of whom had learned to read at **GRIFFITH JONES'S CIRCULATING SCHOOLS**) could study their Holy Bible. The Revival was an emotional experience for those involved. All the major preachers had undergone spiritual upheavals and exhorted their congregations to participate in meetings by dancing and singing. At the *seiadau*, individuals were encouraged to confess their sins and articulate their religious feelings. Initially a southern movement, it spread into north Wales during the late 18th century. The reasons for its strength have been much debated. The weakness of the Anglican Church in Wales, the form of organization (based on neighbourhood cells), the emphasis on education, the personal involvement in worship, and the use of Methodism as a form of protest against the squirarchy probably all played a part. Similarly, assessment of the impact of the revival has historians at odds. Some claim that it conditioned the working classes to accept the discipline of the factory system without protest and that the emphasis on sin and evil killed off many of the joyful elements of Welsh folk culture. Others argue that it cultivated values such as honesty, thriftiness and temperance. (See **THOMAS CHARLES**).

MIRRLEES, JAMES ALEXANDER (1936–). Winner of the Nobel prize for economics in 1996, Mirrlees was born on 5 July 1936. He was educated at Douglas-Ewart High School (Newton Stewart), **EDINBURGH** University (where he graduated with an MA in mathematics in 1957) and Cambridge University (where he took a BA in mathematics in 1959 and was awarded a doctorate in economics in 1963). He began his teaching career as an assistant lecturer at Cambridge (1963) but was appointed Edgeworth Professor at Oxford University in 1968 and spent 27 years there before moving back to Cambridge as Professor of Political Economy in 1995. In addition, he has been a visiting professor at several US universities and has served on advisory bodies in Asia and Africa as well as the United Kingdom. Mirrlees received his Nobel prize (jointly with William Vickrey of Columbia University, New York) for studies on economic decision making in circumstances of uncertainty and partial information. Many British scholars regard his work as arid and mathematical, but others argue that his papers on income tax structures have had a major influence on policy making and that he has played a large part in the restructuring of economic institutions in the United Kingdom, from the design of managerial remuneration to the privatization of publicly owned industries and services.

MOD, ROYAL NATIONAL. (See **AN COMUNN GAIDHEALACH**).

MOLYNEAUX OF KILLEAD, LORD. (See **JAMES HENRY MOLYNEAUX**).

MOLYNEAUX, JAMES HENRY (1920–). Leader of the **ULSTER UNIONIST PARTY** since 1979, Molyneaux was born on 27 August 1920, the son of Mr and Mrs William Molyneaux. He was educated at Aldergrove School (Antrim) and served with the Royal Air Force during the Second World War, becoming Member of Parliament for Antrim South in 1970. In 1974, he was appointed leader of the **ULSTER UNIONIST PARTY** in the House of Commons and, in 1979, became leader of the party as a whole. He opposed the **ANGLO-IRISH AGREEMENT** (1985) but proved willing to engage in talks with the government of the Irish Republic and, in 1993, proposed a form of assembly to govern Northern Ireland which would involve formal contacts with the south. Often dominated in the media by **IAN PAISLEY** (who has compared him to Judas Iscariot and Neville Chamberlain), he urged Prime Minister John Major not to accept the **IRISH REPUBLICAN ARMY**'s 1994 promise to renounce violence because it failed to include a commitment that the peace would be permanent. He also maintained that convicted terrorists should serve their full prison sentences whatever the outcome of peace negotiations but stressed his willingness to sit in the same debating chamber as representatives of **SINN FEIN** and other nationalist organizations. Molyneaux gave up the party leadership in 1995, claiming that his departure would give new blood time to prepare the campaign for the next General Election, but he had been undoubtedly stung by Major's decision to exclude him from discussions about Northern Ireland's future and by unionist criticism of his ineffectiveness. He was knighted the following year and promoted to the House of Lords as Lord Molyneaux of Killead in 1997. Apart from his political activities, Molyneaux is a leading Freemason, holding the posts of Deputy Grand Master of the Orange Order and Sovereign Grand Master of the British Commonwealth Royal Black Institution. (See **ORANGEMEN**).

MONS GRAUPIUS, BATTLE OF, AD 83 or AD 84. This was the final defeat for Calgacus, leader of the peoples of **CALEDONIA,** by the Roman governor, Agricola. The battle was fought at a site somewhere in the central lowlands of Scotland, and the Caledonians were said to have lost about 10,000 of their army, believed to number around 30,000 men. (The Romans' short sword and larger shield and their skillful use of cavalry and auxiliary troops proved decisive). As a result, the invaders temporarily subjugated the local population, but the area never became a part of the Roman Empire proper, and the Romans abandoned attempts to colonise the area.

MONTGOMERY, TREATY OF (1267). Under the terms of this agreement between Henry III of England and **LLYWELYN AP GRUFFUDD,** the Welshman accepted English overlordship but was recognized as the principal leader of his people, entitled to the homage of lesser chiefs. He was officially accorded the title **PRINCE OF WALES,** which had first been used by his uncle, **DAFYDD AP LLYWELYN.** By implication, the treaty gave Wales an identity as a single unit; previously, it had been perceived more as a collection of territories exhibiting varying degrees of independence.

MONTROSE, MARQUIS OF. (See **JAMES GRAHAM**).

MORGAN, WILLIAM (*c.* 1545–1604). The first person to translate the Holy Bible into **WELSH,** Morgan was the son of tenants on the Wynn family's estate at Gwydir, near Caernarvon. The Wynns appear to have taken charge of young William's education because, in 1564, he entered Cambridge University — a situation which his parents could not possibly have financed. He proved to be a fine student, learning Hebrew, Latin, Greek, French and English and graduating with four degrees (BA in 1568, MA in 1571, BD in 1578 and DD in 1583). At the time, Cambridge was a centre of Protestantism; Morgan's experiences there probably converted him from the Roman Catholic beliefs which he would have brought from Wales. Ordained in 1568, he was appointed vicar at Llanbadarn Fawr (near

Aberystwyth) in 1572, transfered to Welshpool in 1575 then, in 1578, was promoted to Llanrhaiadr-ym-Mochnant (near Denbigh).

In 1563, Parliament had asked the Welsh bishops to provide a version of the Scriptures in their own language, but the only significant steps towards that end had been the publication of **WILLIAM SALESBURY**'s translations of the New Testament and the *Book of Common Prayer* in 1567. While based at Llanrhaiadr, far from any sources of scholarship, Morgan apparently determined to complete the task, translating the Old Testament himself and changing the wording of Salesbury's New Testament by incorporating a simpler, more contemporary vocabulary. The work was published in 1588, and copies were sent to all the parish churches in Wales. Within 30 years, Richard Parry, Bishop of St Asaph, was claiming that most of these copies had vanished or were worn out, so, in 1620, a revised version was prepared by John Davies. Over the next 180 years, that revision was published 28 times, with further editions appearing during the 19th century. Morgan's poetic, sensitive use of language thus helped establish a standard form of written Welsh which was to be taught to working people for over 200 years (at **GRIFFITH JONES**'s **CIRCULATING SCHOOLS,** for example).

In 1585, Morgan was elected Bishop at Llandaff (where he published a new edition of the *Book of Common Prayer*). Six years later, he moved to the somewhat wealthier see at St Asaph, where he completed a new version of the New Testament and died on 10 September 1604.

MORGANWG, IOLO (1746–1826). One of the leading figures in the 18th-century cultural revival in Wales, Iolo was born Edward Williams at Penmon (Glamorgan) on 10 March 1746. He was educated at home by his mother, then became apprenticed as a stonemason (his father's trade). From 1770, he travelled much of southern Britain as he sought work and became an active member of the **GWYNEDDIGION** Society, founded in London in 1770 to further the study of Welsh literature. After seven years of wandering, he returned to south Wales and, in 1797, because his trade interfered with his health, opened a bookshop in Cowbridge. From there, he made long journeys (always by foot) to seek out documents dealing with Welsh history. Also, he compiled lists of words which had formerly been part of the vocabulary of **WELSH** and coined new ones in an attempt to make his native language suitable for use in all contexts.

Finding the work of a bookseller cramping, he moved to Flemingston and attempted to earn a living as a land surveyor. However, he was easily sidetracked by his studies, learning Latin, Greek and French whilst continuing his search for sources which would add to his knowledge of Wales's past. He had no interest in money, and, as a result, his family lived in considerable poverty; moreover, his principles led him to reject property he had inherited from slave-owning relatives in Jamaica.

Iolo published many poems in English and wrote over 3,000 hymns, many of which were featured in the worship of the South Wales Unitarian Society, which he helped to found in 1802. Also, he made major contributions to studies of the history of Glamorgan. However, it is for his poetry and other writings in Welsh that he is most remembered. In 1789, he published a volume of poems which, he claimed, were the work of the 14th-century writer, **DAFYDD AP GWILYM.** This attempt to prove that Dafydd was a native of Glamorgan was later proved to be a forgery, but the fact that work was accepted as genuine for over a century was testimony to Iolo's literary genius. He also coedited *The Myvyrian Archaiology*, three volumes purporting to consist of Welsh literature dating from the sixth century and published between 1801 and 1806. They also contained many of his own compositions, masquerading as older material.

Iolo's imagination was as fertile as his intellectual curiosity. As a result, he embellished the history of Wales, but did so with such skill that he deceived scholars until well into the 20th century. More positively, he did much to further interest in Welsh culture and shape a sense of national identity. In particular, he was instrumental in linking the *gorsedd* (the meeting of the bards) to the **EISTEDD-FOD** and composed many tunes and songs. After he died, at Flemingston, on 18 December 1826, scholars found his little cottage crammed to the ceiling with manuscripts which are still the focus of academic research.

MORMAER. A Governor appointed by the monarch to rule one of the Scottish provinces north of the **RIVER FORTH,** the mormaer was the equivalent of the English earl.

MOURNE MOUNTAINS. The granitic mass of the Mourne Mountains forms the highest area of upland in Northern Ireland, rising to just under 2,800 feet at Slieve Donard. Located in the southeast of the province, the hills have a maximum extent of nine miles and a breadth of five. Their major economic use is sheep farming, but the hard rocks also provide the foundations of reservoirs which supply water to **BELFAST** and other settlements. The lower elevations (which consist primarily of shale) are largely wooded.

MOWLAM, MARJORIE (1949–). Mo Mowlam was appointed **SEC-RETARY OF STATE FOR NORTHERN IRELAND** by Prime Minister **ANTHONY CHARLES LYNTON BLAIR** following the Labour Party's general election victory in 1997. The daughter of Frank and Bettina Mowlam, she was educated at Coundon Court Comprehensive School in Coventry, Durham University (where she gained a BA degree in social anthropology) and the University of Iowa (where she graduated MA, PhD). She joined the Labour Party in 1969 and was research assistant to Tony Blair in 1971–72 but left politics to build a transatlantic academic career, lecturing at the University of Wisconsin (1976–77), Florida State University (1977–78) and Newcastle University (1979–83). She then spent three years as an administrator at the Northern College in Barnsley (1984–87) before entering the House of Commons as the representative for Redcar, a benificiary of Labour's policy of guaranteeing women a quota of reatively safe seats. She rose through the ranks rapidly, gaining experience as the opposition spokesman on Northern Ireland (1988–89), trade and industry (1989–92), the citizens' charter and women's affairs (1992–93, national heritage (1993–94 and finally Northern Ireland for a second time (1994–97). Her extrovert nature was an asset to Blair's campaign for the leadership of the party following **JOHN SMITH**'s death in 1994 and sometimes shocked establishment figures, as when she suggested (also in 1994) that Queen Elizabeth II should move into a modern house, with a kitchen designed by Terence Conran, so that Buckingham Palace and Windsor Castle could be sold. The bluffness, however, was married to considerable diplomatic skill, which she used to considerable effect within weeks of taking office as Secretary of State by persuading the nationalist **SINN FEIN** leaders and representatives of the unionist political parties to meet for discussions on the future of **ULSTER.**

MOYOLA OF CASTLEDAWSON, BARON. (See **JAMES CHI-CHESTER-CLARK**).

MUIR, JOHN (1838–1914). One of the founding fathers of the modern conservation movement, Muir was born in Dunbar on 21 April 1838. He emigrated with the rest of his family to the United States in 1849 and settled on a farm near Portage, Wisconsin. In 1859, he registered at the University of Wisconsin but, bridling at the restrictions of academic life, left in 1863 without gaining a degree. For some years, he went on lengthy walking tours of the US Midwest and Canada, developing an interest in the natural environments through which he travelled, and writing about his journeys. In 1868, he visited the Yosemite Valley in California and carried out a series of studies which showed that it had been formed by glacial erosion. His researches also took him to Nevada, Oregon, Washington and Utah as well as to Alaska, where he discovered Glacier Bay and the Muir Glacier. During the 1880s, he devoted himself to horticulture and published a series of newspaper articles which focussed on the forests and landscapes of the American west. These helped win widespread public support for the conservation movement and led ultimately to the designation of Yosemite and other areas of the United States as national parks.

In 1891, he resumed his travels, studying forests and woodlands in Africa, Australia and South America. In 1908, President Theodore Roosevelt (who was greatly influenced by Muir's writings) established Muir Woods National Monument in his honour. The monument covers 500 acres of western California and encompasses a virgin stand of redwoods.

Muir died in Los Angeles on 24 December 1914. In 1983, a John Muir Trust was established in his native Scotland as a memorial to the first person to call clearly for conservation of wild places for their own sake. Since then, it has purchased nearly 20,000 acres of mountain, moorland and coastline "for their wildlife, for the spiritual enrichment of present and future generations, and for the benefit of local communities".

MUNGO, ST (?–*c.* 612). Also known as St Kentigern, Mungo is, by tradition, the first Bishop of **GLASGOW**. Little is known of his life but, according to legend, he was of royal descent. He is said to have been a renowned preacher, travelling throughout southwest Scotland, and to have opposed the Pelagian heresy, which was believed to minimize the role of divine grace in man's salvation. He established a see in the kingdom of Strathclyde but was exiled after a pagan uprising and went to Wales, where he met **ST DAVID** and was given land at Llanelwy to found a monastery (the predecessor of St Asaph's Cathedral). About 573, however, he returned to Strathclyde when the pagan rulers were overthrown by King Rydderch. He is reputed to have appointed St Asaph as his successor in Wales and to have co-operated with **ST COLUMBA** in spreading Christianity in Scotland.

MUNROS. Munros are Scottish hills over 3,000 feet in height. They are named after Sir Hugh T. Munro, who first published a list of them in the *Scottish Mountaineering Club Journal* in 1891. Since then, the table has been refined as the calculation of height has become increasingly accurate but it remains essentially subjective, depending on individual editors' judgements about what qualifies as a mountain and what is merely a subsidiary top. The latest revision, in 1997, listed 284 Munros, seven more than the previous list (1981). The validity of the changes was hotly debated in the national press because 'Munro bagging' has become an enormously popular pastime in Britain as a result of the explosion of outdoor activities since the 1960s. Since the Rev. A. E. Robertson first collected all of them in 1901, at least 303 other people have followed in his footsteps. Part of the attraction is that a reasonably fit individual can climb all the Munros within a lifetime and visit scenically attractive parts of the country while doing so. Also, only one hill (the Inaccessible Pinnacle, on the Isle of Skye) requires rock climbing skills and equipment. In addition, other authors have published alternative lists so Corbetts (hills in the **SCOTTISH HIGHLANDS** which are at least 2,500 feet high and have an ascent of 500 feet on all sides), Grahams (hills in the highlands between 2,000 and 2,500 feet in height) and Georges (hills in the Central Lowlands and **SOUTHERN UP-LANDS** at least 2,000 feet high) all have their aficionados.

—N—

NAPIER, JOHN (1550–1617). Through the invention of logarithms, Napier made major contributions to the development of mathematics and to the purgatory experienced by generations of schoolchildren. The eldest son of Sir Archibald Napier and his wife, Janet, he was born at Merchiston Castle (**EDINBURGH**) in 1550 (when Sir Archibald was still only 15) and registered at **ST ANDREWS** University in 1563. There is no record that he ever graduated, and it seems likely that he interrupted his studies in order to travel abroad, a fashionable activity for wealthy young men during the 16th century. By 1571, he was back in Scotland and involved in the religious disputes which rent the country. A convinced Protestant, he was deeply concerned that King James VI was rumoured to have enlisted the support of the Roman Catholic Philip II of Spain in his attempt to gain the throne of England, following the death of Queen Elizabeth I, and urged the Scottish monarch to take action against supporters of the Papacy. He amused himself by trying to invent weapons which could be adopted by the army (for example, he designed a chariot, built of metal, which allowed shot to be discharged through small holes), but much of his leisure time was spent attempting to improve methods of mathematical calculation. In 1614, he published *Mirifici logarithmorum canonis descriptio*, which contained an outline of the nature of logarithms, a table of natural sines and their logarithms for every minute of the quadrant and an explanation of the uses of logarithms in trigonometry and other calculations. *Mirifici logarithmorum canonis constructio*, which appeared in 1619, described the construction of the logarithms, made systematic use of the decimal point to separate the integral and fractional parts of numbers and presented propositions for the solution of spherical triangles. Napier was responsible for other contributions to the sciences — notably through his means of carrying out basic multiplication and division by using small rods — but his devotion to study led him to overwork and the consequent tiredness put strains on his health. He died in Edinburgh, exhausted and suffering from gout, on 4 April 1617.

NASH, BEAU. (See **RICHARD NASH**).

NASH, RICHARD (1674–1762). The first of the dandies who became arbiters of good taste in Georgian England, Nash was born in **SWANSEA** on 18 October 1674, the son of Richard Nash, owner of a bottle factory. He was educated at Carmarthen Grammar School and (for one year) at Oxford University, then, in 1692, bought himself a commission as an ensign in the Guards. The army officer's lifestyle took him into contact with London society, but a lack of private means prevented him from becoming as fully integrated with the social round as he wished so he forsook military barracks for the Inner Temple in 1693, hoping that, in the world of legal affairs, he would learn "the art of living without money". A charismatic figure, he became a common sight at the gaming tables and organized the lawyers' celebrations when William I became king in his own right in 1695. After Queen Anne visited Bath in 1702, the aristocracy followed, and the city quickly became a fashionable place in which to live.

Nash arrived in 1705 and, soon afterwards, was made Master of Ceremonies by the city fathers. Immediately, he introduced a series of social reforms designed to replace raucous behaviour with gentility. Swords and riding boots were banned from the ballroom, and young ladies were given the front row of chairs at dances, while their mothers (who were "past perfection") sat in the row behind. The infrastructure of the city was improved as well — streets were paved, lighting was introduced and the charges levied by hotelkeepers controlled. Nash himself became known as the King of Bath and strutted around wearing a white beaver hat as the badge of his status. With his big nose and bull-like features, he could never be called handsome, but he exerted remarkable influence over the rich and famous and made love to a string of attractive young ladies. Also, he was chivalrous and generous (he founded a hospital for the poor and once handed his night's proceeds from the gaming tables to a man who seemed unhappy).

From 1715, Nash opened the social season at the spa town of Tunbridge Wells in Kent and, in 1735, became Master of Ceremonies there, but antigambling legislation introduced in 1745 destroyed his source of funds and reduced him to a pauper. He died in Bath on 3 February 1762, and, despite his impecunious circumstances, was buried with much pomp and pageantry in the Abbey.

NATIONAL COVENANT, 1638. Protest at attempts by King Charles I to change forms of worship in Scotland led to the breakdown of relations between people and monarch and ultimately to the signing of a covenant, which was both a statement of protest and a public affirmation of alliance by the signatories. The document lists measures taken by the **THREE ESTATES** to condemn popery and commits its supporters to unite in upholding the true Protestant religion. (See **CAMERONIANS; COVENANTERS; SOLEMN LEAGUE AND COVENANT**).

NATIONAL PARTY OF SCOTLAND (NPS). The National Party was formed in 1928 by individuals, such as Christopher Murray Grieve **(HUGH MACDIARMID)** and the Honourable R. S. Erskine of Mar, who believed that Scotland had a distinct national identity and should have a government to run its own affairs. Very quickly, however, it attracted left wingers unhappy with the lack of progress made by the **SCOTTISH HOME RULE ASSOCIATION.** For four years, it was plagued by dissension between radical and conservative elements over policy-making - a dissension which was reflected in poor performances at elections - and by the difficulty of presenting its case to a population more concerned about the implications of the inter-war economic recession. In 1932, some members of the Conservative Party who favoured

HOME RULE formed the Scottish Party and the leadership of the NPS, after expelling extremists such as Grieve from its ranks, negotiated to merge with them, forming the **SCOTTISH NATIONAL PARTY.**

NATIONAL TRUST. Since its foundation in 1895, the aim of the National Trust has been the preservation and conservation of places of historic interest or natural beauty in England, Wales and Northern Ireland. It owns nearly 600,000 acres, making it the largest private landholder in the United Kingdom, and has about 1,700,000 members. Under the terms of the 1907 National Trust Act, its land and buildings are inalienable and cannot, therefore, be sold or mortgaged. Like its sister body, the **NATIONAL TRUST FOR SCOTLAND,** it is independent of central government and funds its activities through membership subscriptions, bequests and donations. In Northern Ireland, the Trust has 32 properties. Many of these (including the **GIANT'S CAUSEWAY**) are on the coast of County Antrim and County Down, and several are important wildlife habitats. (For example, Blockhouse and Green Islands, at the mouth of Strangford **LOUGH,** provide nesting sites for Arctic, Common and Roseate Terns). **ULSTER** buildings in its care range from the Crown Liquor Saloon (a Victorian public house in **BELFAST**) to Florence Court (an 18th-century mansion in County Fermanagh). In Wales, the Trust's 76 properties include 5,000 acres of coastland on the Gower peninsula (an Area of Outstanding Natural Beauty, west of **SWANSEA**) and 8,000 acres of the Brecon Beacons, an upland **NATIONAL PARK** north of the industrial areas of the valleys. In Gwynnedd, its 38,000 acre Carneddau and Ysbyty estates in **SNOWDONIA** incorporate some of the highest mountains in the United Kingdom. Its buildings include the medieval Powys Castle at Welshpool, the Conwy suspension bridge (built by **THOMAS TELFORD**) and Dolaucothi Gold Mines, first exploited by the Romans and last worked in 1938.

NATIONAL TRUST FOR SCOTLAND. The Trust was founded in 1931 and functions independently of the **NATIONAL TRUST,** which had been established 36 years earlier and concentrates its activities on England, Wales and Northern Ireland. Its remit, outlined in various Acts of Parliament, is to care for, and conserve, landscape and historic buildings while ensuring that the public has access to its holdings. By 1997, it owned over 100,000 acres (making it one of the biggest landholders in Scotland) and managed properties at over 100 locations, including the sites of the **BATTLE OF BANNOCKBURN** (1314), the **BATTLE OF KILLIECRANKIE** (1689) and the **BATTLE OF CULLODEN** (1746). It is responsible for preserving some of the most dramatic scenery in the **SCOTTISH HIGHLANDS** (notably at Glencoe, Kintail and Torridon) and for looking after such historic buildings as Brodick Castle (Isle of Arran), **CULZEAN CASTLE** (Ayrshire) and **FALKLAND PALACE** (Fife). In addition, it carries out the restoration of small houses, as at Culross (Fife) and Dunkeld (Perthshire), in an attempt to provide modern living standards while maintaining the architectural characteristics of the exteriors. The Trust depends on donations, legacies and the subscriptions of its 250,000 members for financial support, and is recognized as a charity for tax exemption purposes.

NEW LANARK. One of the 18th-century philanthropic settlements, New Lanark dates from 1783, and was built by Richard Arkwright and David Dale. It was purchased by **ROBERT OWEN** in 1785, rebuilt and extended. The village included a cotton mill, schools, housing and social facilities. One of the precursors of the Garden Cities, it was a commercial venture which endeavoured to give workers better living conditions but also tied them to the company store and derived longer working hours and lives by supporting a healthy existence and a teetotal environment.

NORTHAMPTON, TREATY OF, 1328. (See **TREATY OF EDINBURGH**).

NORTHERN EARLS, 1589. This term was used to describe the three Scottish Catholic Earls, Huntly, Crawford and Errol, who were able to defy the authority of King James VI of Scotland after his minority ended. They conspired, in 1589, with King Philip II of Spain on a projected invasion of Scotland, following the English defeat of the Spanish Armada, and, in 1592, Huntly murdered James Stewart, Earl of Moray (an opponent of the King — there is some evidence that the King or his followers had alerted Huntly, to the whereabouts of Moray). The murder of this prominent nobleman resulted only in a brief period in prison for Huntly and the Northern Earls continued to defy the authorities until forced into exile and renunciation of Catholicism by the King in 1597. King James may have been lenient with them for so long for fear of assassination or of antagonising English Catholics at a time when his ultimate succession to the dual crowns seemed possible.

NORTHERN IRELAND ASSEMBLY. Two bodies have been known as the Northern Ireland Assembly. The first (1973–74) was associated with the **NORTHERN IRELAND POWER SHARING EXECUTIVE.** The second (1982–86) was intended to provide for "rolling devolution" of powers from Westminster to a new body based at **STORMONT,** the extent of the powers depending on the extent of the cooperation between the province's political parties. Elections for the 78-member body were held in October 1982, using a form of proportional representation, but both of the major nationalist organizations — the **SOCIAL DEMOCRATIC AND LABOUR PARTY** and **SINN FEIN** — opposed the arrangement so, when the Assembly met in November, it represented primarily **ULSTER LOYALIST** views representative of only one section of the community. By June 1986, when it was dissolved, having failed to convince republican supporters to participate, it had become little more than a forum for unionist criticism of the **ANGLO-IRISH AGREEMENT** (1985). (See **JAMES MICHAEL LEATHES PRIOR**).

NORTHERN IRELAND CONSTITUTIONAL CONFERENCE. During the first three months of 1980, representatives of the **DEMOCRATIC UNIONIST PARTY** (DUP), the **SOCIAL DEMOCRATIC AND LABOUR PARTY** (SDLP) and the **ALLIANCE PARTY** met Secretary of State **HUMPHREY ATKINS** in **BELFAST** to discuss plans for the government of Northern Ireland. The **ULSTER UNIONIST PARTY** (UUP) rejected an invitation to attend. The negotiations came to naught because, although the representatives all favoured devolution of power to the province, they could not agree on a format. The DUP wanted majority rule (a stance supported by the UUP), but the Alliance and the SDLP wanted a system of power sharing, with all interests represented, and no compromise could be found.

NORTHERN IRELAND CONSTITUTIONAL CONVENTION. Created in 1975, the Convention was mandated to devise a system of government which would command widespread support in **ULSTER**. It was chaired by Sir Robert Lowry (Lord Chief Justice of Northern Ireland) and consisted of 78 members elected by a system of proportional representation. However, the body was dominated by the **UNITED ULSTER UNIONIST COUNCIL** which rejected any form of legislative assembly based on the power-sharing principles favoured by the **ALLIANCE PARTY**, the **SOCIAL DEMO-CRATIC AND LABOUR PARTY** and the **UNIONIST PARTY OF NORTHERN IRELAND.** By March, 1976, it had failed to find any formula acceptable to Parliament in London, and meetings were discontinued.

NORTHERN IRELAND OFFICE. This department was created by the Northern Ireland (Temporary Provisions) Act of 1972 for the **SEC-RETARY OF STATE FOR NORTHERN IRELAND,** who, under the Act, took direct control, on behalf of the British Parliament, of the affairs of the province. (See **DIRECT RULE**).

NORTHERN IRELAND POWER SHARING EXECUTIVE (1973–74). In March 1972, the Northern Ireland Parliament was suspended and replaced by **DIRECT RULE** of the province from London. The following year, in an attempt to find a form of administration which would involve all of the main political parties in **ULSTER,** Prime Minister Edward Heath's government proposed the establishment of an assembly, which would rule through a power sharing Executive. The 78 members of the Assembly would be appointed by proportional representation, thereby ending the monopoly of power which the **ULSTER UNIONIST PARTY** had enjoyed at **STORMONT** ever since Northern Ireland had been created in 1921. Talks involving Heath, Liam Cosgrave (Taoiseach of the Irish Republic), **WILLIAM WHITELAW** and **FRANCIS PYM** (successive **SEC-RETARIES OF STATE FOR NORTHERN IRELAND**) and representatives of the major political organizations led to elections on 28 June, 1973. Twenty-six of the representatives chosen were opposed to the concept of an assembly (eight were members of the **DEMOCRATIC UNIONIST PARTY**, seven represented the **VAN-GUARD UNIONIST PROGRESSIVE PARTY** and 11 were drawn from other **ULSTER LOYALIST** groups). Fifty-two were in favour, 24 of them backing **ARTHUR BRIAN DEANE FAULKNER** of the UUP, 19 supporting the **SOCIAL DEMO-CRATIC AND LABOUR PARTY** (SDLP), eight representing the **ALLIANCE PARTY** and one coming from the Northern Ireland Labour Party.

Talks were held by those who favoured the formation of an executive and, on 22 October, an administration was formed with six representatives of the Unionists, four from the SDLP and one from Alliance. Brian Faulkner was Chief Executive with **GERRY FITT** as his Deputy. However, on 4 January 1974, Faulkner's attempts to get the UUP to accept the power sharing proposals were defeated. Faced with mounting critisism, he resigned the leadership of his party, and his opponents (including Vanguard, the Democratic Unionists and many of his former UUP colleagues) withdrew from the Assembly to form the **UNITED ULSTER UNIONIST COUNCIL** (UUUC). The General Election in February demonstrated support for candidates who opposed the Executive and, on 28 May, a general strike called by the UUUC, the Ulster Workers' Council and the Protestant parliamentary organizations, brought Northern Ireland to a standstill. Faulkner resigned and direct rule from London was resumed. As a result of their success, the loyalist groups were convinced that they could defeat any measures which Westminster attempted to introduce without their consent and thus, in effect, prevented any further political initiative for many years. (See **DEVOLUTION**).

NOVA SCOTIA. In 1621, King James VI and I granted Sir William Alexander a charter which gave permission for the development of a "Nova Scotia in North America". Sir William (who had been tutor to Prince Henry, the King's eldest son) wanted to establish a Scottish colony which would match those founded by the English and other European powers. However, despite the temptation of baronetcies for settlers, few migrants were tempted to leave Scotland and, in 1632, the territory was ceded to King Henri IV of France as part of the settlement which led to the marriage of his daughter, Henrietta Maria, to Charles I, King of England, Scotland and Ireland.

—O—

OFFA'S DYKE. Offa, King of Mercia from 757 until 796, marked the western limit of his sovereignty with a massive earth wall running from the River Dee (in the north) to the River Wye (in the south), a distance of about 150 miles. The wall was not continuous because, along some stretches of the frontier, forests provided an effective indication of the boundary but, despite the erosion of 12 centuries, long stretches (amounting to some 80 miles) remain. The dyke follows an alignment which provides commanding views westwards from Mercian territory and has become the traditional boundary between Wales and England.

OFFICIAL UNIONISTS. Changing political allegiances in Northern Ireland have led several groups, who favour a continued constitutional association between **ULSTER** and the United Kingdom, to break away from the **ULSTER UNIONIST PARTY** (UUP). Members of the UUP are often referred to in the media as official unionists.

OLD PRETENDER. (See **JAMES FRANCIS EDWARD STUART**).

O'NEILL OF THE MAINE, BARON. (See **TERENCE MARNE O'NEILL**).

O'NEILL, TERENCE MARNE (1914–90). Prime Minister of Northern Ireland from 1963 until 1969, O'Neill infuriated many Protestants in the province (because of his willingness to consider closer cooperation with the Republic of Ireland) and alienated Roman Catholics (who anticipated social change and were disillusioned). He was born in London on 10 September 1914, the son of Captain Arthur O'Neill (who was killed in action the same year) and his wife, Annabel. After completing his education at West Downs School (Winchester) and Eton College, he took several jobs (including a spell at the Stock Exchange) before serving with the Irish Guards during World War II. In 1946, he was returned, unopposed, as the **ULSTER UNIONIST PARTY (UUP)** member for the Northern Ireland Parliamentary constituency of Bannside and, two years later, was made Parliamentary Secretary to the Minister of Health. In 1953, he became Deputy Speaker and held the post for two years before moving to a position as Parliamentary Secretary at the Ministry of Home Affairs. For a short period in 1956, he was in charge of that department before Prime Minister **BASIL BROOKE** made him Minister of Finance, a post in which he earned considerable respect for his efforts to persuade firms to set up business in **ULSTER.** On 25 March 1963, he succeeded Brooke as Prime Minister, although opponents claimed that **BRIAN FAULKNER** was the natural successor and that O'Neill got the post more because of his aristocratic connections than his political talents.

The early months of the new premiership were auspicious. O'Neill's UUP attracted recruits as the Northern Ireland Labour Party lost support and a Ministry of Development was established on 1 January 1965 to build on the economic successes of his time as finance minister. However, he courted controversy by inviting Sean Lemass, Taoiseach of the Irish Republic, to visit **BELFAST** on 14 January 1965, without telling his Cabinet colleagues (who, he claimed later, would never have sanctioned the event), and incurred the wrath of right-wing loyalists, including **IAN PAISLEY,** who resented any contact with the Roman Catholic south. Also, he failed to build the bridges between the two religious communities which he had promised during his first days in office, and, as a result, the civil rights movement grew in strength and influence. Violent clashes during a protest march in **LONDONDERRY** on 5 October 1968 convinced him that change was necessary, so he announced a programme which included a new system of allocating public housing and alterations to the conduct of county council elections. However, the plan was criticised by members of his own party, who argued that the civil rights organizations were fundamentally republican and strongly influenced by the **IRISH REPUBLICAN ARMY.** O'Neill challenged his critics by calling a General Election for 24 February 1969 and scored a considerable success: 39 unionists won seats and 27 backed his leadership. However, the loyalist movement remained rent by bitter divisions, and, in March, changes to the executive of the civil rights movement put power squarely in the hands of militants. Street violence and terrorism increased, several MPs seemed to waver in their allegiance to the Prime Minister and, on 28 April, O'Neill resigned, even though he retained much grassroots support. He was promoted to the House of Lords as Lord O'Neill of the Maine in 1970 and frequently took part in Parliamentary debates on Ulster issues but also devoted considerable time to business interests. He died at his home in Lymington (Hampshire) on 12 June 1990. Although he was a decent, humane man, his patrician background meant that he never understood the aspirations and concerns of Ulster's working class citizens.

O'NEILL'S REBELLION. (See **TYRONE REBELLION**).

ORANGEMEN. (See **ORANGE ORDER**).

ORANGE ORDER. The largest Protestant organization in Northern Ireland, the Orange Order is committed to retaining **ULSTER**'s political links with Britain. It is estimated to be 90,000–100,000 strong (no Roman Catholic, and no one with close relatives who are Catholic, can be a member). Formally titled The Loyal Orange Institution, the Order was founded in 1795 in memory of King William III (William of Orange), who defeated the Catholic King James VII and II at the **BATTLE OF THE BOYNE** in 1690. The victory is celebrated in processions held each year on 12 July, the anniversary of the struggle, and has frequently precipitated clashes between religious factions. It is strongly represented in the pro-union political parties. (For example, **JAMES MOLYNEAUX,** former leader of the **ULSTER UNIONIST PARTY,** has held senior posts including that of Imperial Grand Master). The Orange Order has branches in Africa and North America. Members are known as Orangemen.

ORKNEY ISLANDS. The Orkneys — a group of about 70 islands, only about 20 of which are inhabited on a permanent basis — lie off the northern coast of Scotland. Archaeological records show that they were first settled over 5,000 years ago (see **SKARA BRAE)** and that, following Viking raids during the late 8th-century, they became part of the Norse empire. In 1469, King **JAMES III** of Scotland married Margret of Denmark and, three years later, annexed the islands because his father-in-law (King Christian I of Norway, Sweden and Denmark) had failed to pay the full dowry due. On the outbreak of the First World War in 1914, **SCAPA FLOW** became a major base for the British fleet and, in 1919, the captured German navy was scuttled there. There is a long tradition of young men leaving the islands for jobs at sea but the modern economy is based on the off-shore oil industry (a major terminal for the oil has been built at Flotta) and on agriculture (the main products are eggs, beef, pigs and cheese). Kirkwall (a royal **BURGH** since 1486) is located on Mainland, the largest island. In 1991, the Orkney population numbered 19,450.

OWEN, ROBERT (1771–1858). A pioneer of social reform and founder of the settlement at **NEW LANARK,** Owen was born on 14 May 1771 in Newtown (Montgomery), the son of postmaster, saddler and ironmonger Robert Owen and his wife, Anne. He received an elementary education at local schools, then worked as a salesman in several shops in Wales and England before setting up his own business making machinery for the cotton industry in Manchester. In 1790, he was appointed manager of a large cotton mill and adopted innovative approaches to production, improving output and profitability but becoming increasingly concerned that more attention was being paid to the technology of the industry than to its employees. In 1794, he formed the Chorlton Twist Company and, shortly afterwards, offered to buy the mills at New Lanark, on the **RIVER CLYDE,** primarily as an attempt to ingratiate himself with the owner, David Dale, whose daughter he wished to marry. Both proposals were accepted. Owen wedded Anne Dale in 1799 and took over New

Lanark the following year. At that time, the mills employed about 2,000 workers, including some 500 children brought from the poorhouses of **GLASGOW** and **EDINBURGH**. The new proprietor improved their housing conditions, opened a shop where they could buy good quality produce and established a school. Initially, the workforce was suspicious, but he won them over in 1806, when he paid them their full wages even though the mill was closed for four months as a result of an American embargo on cotton exports. Despite the social investment, the company proved to be a commercial success, but some of the partners wanted greater returns for their investment so, in 1813, Owen reorganized the business, involving colleagues who were happy to accept a five per cent return on their capital. His success was widely recognized throughout Europe, and he used his influence to promote factory reform (albeit with limited success) and propound a philosophy that each individual's character is formed by forces over which he or she has no control.

From about 1817, the formulation of plans for social change took up more and more of Owen's time and energy, and his proposals for the alleviation of poverty through the development of agricultural settlements, possibly by the state, has led modern historians to regard him as one of the founding fathers of socialism. Although he rejected all forms of Christianity, he attempted, in 1825, to put his schemes into practice in consort with the followers of George Rapp and build a utopian community in the United States at New Harmony (Indiana). Initially, development went well, but, faced with disagreements over government and organization, Owen left the group to its own devices three years later and £40,000 poorer. He returned to Britain and to considerable support for his view that the ills of society could only be cured by a transformation of the social order. There was much resistance from employers, but his theories proved attractive to the urban working classes and ultimately shaped the growth of labour unions and the development of the Cooperative movement. At the age of 82, he converted to spiritualism, and, on 17 November 1858, died at Newtown.

—P—

PAISLEY, IAN RICHARD KYLE (1926–). One of the major political figures in Northern Ireland, Paisley was born on 6 April 1926, the second son of Isabella and the Rev. J. Kyle Paisley. He was educated at Ballymena Model School, Ballymena Technical High

School, South Wales Bible College and the Reformed Presbyterian Theological College (**BELFAST**). Ordained as a minister by his Baptist father in 1946, he founded his own denomination — the Free Presbyterian Church of **ULSTER** — in 1951 and, by the early 1990s, had attracted over 10,000 members. An outspoken critic of the Church of Rome, he was imprisoned in 1966 and 1969 for militant anti-Catholic activities. As he expanded his religious commitments, he became increasingly involved in politics and contested the Ulster Parliament's Bannside constituency as a Protestant Unionist in 1969, winning the seat at another election the following year. When the Parliament was suspended in 1972, following the imposition of **DIRECT RULE** from London, he campaigned strenuously for its restoration.

In 1970, Paisley became a Member of Parliament at Westminster, representing Antrim North on behalf of his own **PROTESTANT UNIONIST PARTY,** which combined with other Protestant groups in 1971 to become the **DEMOCRATIC UNIONIST PARTY.** His speeches in the House of Commons have been staunchly pro-British and against any form of association with either the Irish Republic or the Church of Rome, but Catholic constituents admit that he shows no religious partiality in his day-to-day work on behalf of the people in the area he represents. A member of the **NORTHERN IRELAND ASSEMBLY** in 1973–74 and of the 1975–76 **NORTHERN IRELAND CONSTITUTIONAL CONVENTION,** he gained Northern Ireland's seat at the European Parliament in 1979 and staged a one-man protest against the decision to invite Pope John Paul II to address it in 1988. In December 1985, he resigned his Antrim seat as a protest against an **ANGLO-IRISH AGREEMENT** which established a joint secretariat staffed by officials from both London and Dublin and gave the Republic the right to raise with the British government matters relating to internal Ulster affairs. He was reelected to the same seat in January 1986, having effectively created conditions for an unofficial referendum in the constituency. A charismatic figure who arouses disgust and affection in equal proportions, Paisley is widely regarded as the leader of the Protestant community in the six counties and as a dominant figure in the fundamentalist church community both in the United Kingdom and in the United States of America.

PANTYCELYN, WILLIAMS. (See **WILLIAM WILLIAMS**).

PARK, MUNGO (1771–1806). One of a long line of Scots who helped fill the blank spaces on European and North American maps of the world (see **JAMES BRUCE** and **DAVID LIVINGSTONE,** for example), Park added much to knowledge of the course of the River Niger, in west Africa. The seventh of a family of 13 children, he was born in Foulshiels (Selkirk) on 10 September 1771 and educated at the local school before becoming a surgeon's apprentice in 1786. In 1789, he entered **EDINBURGH** University, where he studied medicine and developed an interest in botany, then, in 1791, moved to London in search of work. He engineered an introduction to Sir Joseph Banks, president of the Royal Society, and, as a result of that friendship, was appointed assistant surgeon on the sailing ship *Worcester*. During 1792–93, he travelled to the East Indies with the vessel, returning with a collection of plants for his patron and details of eight new species of fish, which he had discovered in the waters around Sumatra.

In 1794, again supported by Banks, Park offered his services to the African Association, which had been founded in 1788 with the object of sponsoring exploration on the continent. He sailed from Portsmouth on 22 May 1795, reached the mouth of the Gambia River on 21 June, then travelled 200 miles upstream to the trading post at Pisania. From there, he set off across the basin of the Senegal River on a journey which was fraught with incident. His belongings were stolen by local people as he travelled, he was imprisoned by an Arab chief at Ludamar for four months and, at Camalia, he was struck by fever and took seven months to regain his strength. On 10 June 1797, he eventually returned to Pisania, having followed the course of the Niger for many miles. Park's account of his journey (*Travels in the Interior of Africa*, published in 1799) brought him fame and made him a welcome guest at society dinner tables. For a time, he settled into the routine of a surgeon's practice at Peebles, but it was clear to his friends (who included novelist **WALTER SCOTT**) that he hankered after further travel, and, on 31 January 1805, he set off for the Gambia once again, heading an expedition originally proposed by Lord Hobart, Secretary of State for the Colonies. On 19 August, his party of 40 Europeans left Pisania for Bamako, on the Niger. By the time the group reached their destination, on 19 August, 29 had died, victims of dysentery and other illnesses. The remnant of the expedition travelled downstream to Segou by canoe. Park based himself for two months at the nearby settlement of Sansanding then, on 19 November, accompanied by the four companions who had survived the rigours of travel in the tropics, set sail down the river, intent on tracing the route to its end, which he believed must be at the sea. Early the following year, rumours of his death began to reach the Gambia but it was not until 1812 that they were confirmed. At Busa, about 1,000 miles below Sasanding, the travellers had been attacked by natives and all of the Europeans were drowned. However, the journey was not entirely unavailing because stories of the courage and determination shown by Park and his colleagues stimulated public interest in Africa and encouraged others to follow in their footsteps. One of those was Park's son, Thomas, who, on 31 October 1827, died 200 miles from the mouth of the Niger while trying to find more details of his father's fate.

PARTITION OF IRELAND, 1921. The **GOVERNMENT OF IRELAND ACT** of 1920 established a **BELFAST**-based assembly to administer the six northern counties of **ULSTER**. However, the **ANGLO-IRISH TREATY** of 1921 superceded that legislation by creating the independent **IRISH FREE STATE** as a Dominion of the British Empire, distinct from, and partitioned from, the six counties of Ulster, which remained within the United Kingdom. A Boundary Commission in 1925 secured the exact line of the border between the two parts of the island.

PATAGONIA. During the 19th century, Welsh emigrants, led by Michael D. Jones, attempted to establish a colony in Patagonia and retain their culture by using their native language and following traditional customs. On 28 July 1865, a party of 163 landed on the coast of South America near the Chubut River and founded Y Wladfa Gymreig (The Welsh Colony). They were joined by a group of Welsh settlers from Brazil in 1868 and augmented by additional shiploads from Wales during the 1880s and early 1900s so, by 1914, the community numbered some 3,000. Initially, they acted as an independent state, with their own constitution, elected assembly, courts of law, schools, chapels and press. **WELSH** was the lingua franca. However, the Government of Argentina was unwilling to allow the incomers to retain their independence (partly because they feared that Britain would use the base as a means of seizing territory, as had occurred in the Falkland Islands in 1833). As a result, disputes flared over obligations to serve in the Argentinian army and over the use of Spanish in schools. In the end, though, it was social rather than political pressure which led to the colony's demise. The Welsh had done much to further the economic development of the Chubut valley and that attracted immigrants from abroad, notably Chile, Spain and Italy. As they flowed in, the Welsh became a cultural minority. To historians, the main significance of the venture is the evidence it provides of a sense of Welsh nationalism during the years of the Industrial Revolution. Even so, descendants of the original emigrants made a considerable contribution to the growth of commerce in South America and several still live in Patagonia, using the Welsh language for conversation.

PATERSON, WILLIAM (1658–1719). Known in Scotland as the Scot who founded the Bank of England and in England as the man behind the ill-fated **DARIEN SETTLEMENT,** Paterson was born at Tinwald, near Dumfries, in April 1658. As a young man, he travelled widely in Europe and the West Indies, then attempted to persuade the English government to support an expedition designed to build a settlement in Darien, the eastern part of the isthmus of Panama. He was unsuccessful but, even so, set himself up as a merchant in London and, in 1694, organized the Bank of England. The following year, after disagreeing with fellow directors over bank policy, he resigned and turned again to the Darien scheme. This time he was more fortunate. The Scottish Parliament agreed to back the plans and financial support came from merchants keen to expand their trading networks. An unexplained loss in the funds of the company set up to direct the venture led to Paterson's exclusion from the planning group (with hindsight, it seems unlikely that he was guilty of embezzlement), but he accompanied the settlers in 1698 as a private citizen. When it was clear that the venture would fail because of poor management, he used his own funds, administrative skills and network of contacts in a vain attempt to keep the settlement alive. His personal losses were great and not confined to his financial resources; his wife and only child died in Darien, and he became gravely ill. He returned to London late in 1699 and devoted his energies to proposals for monetary reform, the union of the Scottish and English Parliaments, Free Trade and expeditions to the West Indies. He died on 22 January 1719, shortly after the British government compensated him for his financial losses in the Darien scheme.

PATRICK, ST (*c.* 390–*c.* 461). The patron saint of Ireland, Patrick was born about AD 390 at a place called Bannauenta, which has still not been identified but which may have been at Dumbarton or in Cumbria or near the mouth of the River Severn. In about AD 406, he was carried off to Ireland as a slave. For six years, he tended his master's sheep but then, while he was asleep, heard a voice telling him to be ready to make great efforts, which would ultimately take him to freedom in the land of his birth. As a result, he ran away from his master and travelled 200 miles to a ship, which was preparing for departure. At first, his request for free passage was turned down, but, in the end, the sailors relented. After three days at sea, they struck land, travelled through a lengthy tract of uninhabited country and ultimately reached home. After a while, fresh visions came and he began to gather disciples and preach the Christian gospel, eventually converting most of Ireland's population. The church which he established was episcopal, not monastic, and had its headquarters at a site in Armagh which had been presented to him by a local King named Daire. It is possible that he died about AD 461 and was buried at Saul, on Strangford Lough, where he had built his first place of worship. His feast day is 17 March, the putative day of his death.

PEACE PEOPLE. In August 1976, Danny Lennon (a member of the **IRISH REPUBLICAN ARMY** and close friend of **GERARD ADAMS**), was shot by a member of the security forces during a car chase in **BELFAST.** The vehicle, out of control, mounted the pavement and killed three young sisters. A wave of revulsion followed the deaths, and two local women — Mairead Corrigan (the girls' aunt) and Betty Williams — called on people of all political and religious persuasions to reject violence. The movement caught the public imagination and attracted tens of thousands of supporters to rallies, the press provided international publicity and Miss Corrigan and Mrs Williams were awarded the Nobel Peace Prize. However, it proved impossible to maintain the momentum and the central figures increasingly bickered over strategy. Betty Williams moved to the United States, there was no change in the policies of the paramilitary groups and, eventually, the group simply faded away.

PEACE WALL. This was the high wall built by British troops in 1969, following riots in **BELFAST,** to physically separate the Protestant Shankill Road area from the Roman Catholic Falls Road and mitigate the recurrence of violence at this interface between the two groups. (See **THE TROUBLES**).

PENAL CODE, 1695–1727. This series of laws (paralleling the Penal Laws in England) sought to suppress Roman Catholicism in **IRELAND** and reduce the rights of Catholics in the administration of the territory and their wealth. All were, strictly speaking, in contravention of the **TREATY OF LIMERICK** (1691).

<u>1695</u>: Catholics were forbidden to keep a school, send their children abroad for education or hold a university degree.

<u>1695</u>: The Disarming Act forced Catholics to surrender all arms, on pain of a heavy fine or life imprisonment.

<u>1697</u>: Priests and bishops in contact with Rome were expelled, and priests were forbidden to enter Ireland.

<u>1697</u>: The Intermarriage Act forbade marriages between Protestants and Catholics.

<u>1698</u>: Catholics were excluded from the Bar.

<u>1704</u>: The Act for the Suppression of Papacy forbade trusteeship to Catholics and ensured that lands of a Catholic descended to all his heirs, not the eldest son, unless that son became a Protestant. No Catholic could buy land, or lease it, for more than 31 years and none could settle in Limerick or Galway.

<u>1709</u>: Any informer who could prove that land had been passed to a Catholic heir could become the owner of that land.

<u>1727</u>: Catholics were deprived of the franchise in municipal and Parliamentary elections.

The draconian nature of the laws, which were not relaxed until 1778, greatly exacerbated the tensions between Catholic and Protestant and between Irish and English, particularly in Northern Ireland where they were a precursor to the present-day resentments.

PENTLAND RISING, 28 November 1666. The terms of the **RESTORATION SETTLEMENT** (1661), and the quartering of English troops on local people, were greatly resented in Scotland, at a time when the **COVENANTERS** were gaining wider support, the **PRESBYTERIANS** feared suppression and the economic conditions of the nation were declining. The capture of Sir James Turner (commander of the occupying English forces) by the Covenanters started a spontaneous uprising, and the rebels came close to **EDINBURGH,** only to be confronted by British Dragoons, led by Sir Thomas Dalyell, at Rullion Green, in the Pentland Hills. The 1,000-strong but poorly equipped and untrained peasant rebel force was quickly defeated. Thirty were executed, and others suffered transportation to Barbados.

PERTH, TREATY OF (1266). Under the terms of this treaty, Norway ceded the **HEBRIDES** and the Isle of Man to Scotland in return for a payment of 4,000 **MERK**s of refined silver and an annuity of 100 merks. There is no record of that annuity ever having been paid.

PHILIPHAUGH, BATTLE OF, 13 September 1645. After the **BAT-TLE OF KILSYTH, JAMES GRAHAM,** Marquis of Montrose and the King's military commander in Scotland during the English Civil War, was in the ascendant and the **COVENANTER** allies of the Parliamentary side in apparent decline. But it was notoriously difficult to keep even victorious troops together when standing armies were not the norm, and Montrose's forces began to dissipate. On 13 September 1645, a Covenanter army of about 6,000 (including 4,000 cavalry), led by Lieutenant-General David Leslie, mounted a surprise attack at dawn on the royalist supporters of Montrose (who now numbered only about 1,500) at Philiphaugh, near Selkirk. The royalists were overwhelmed and given no quarter — all were killed, wounded or captured and the Irish contingent was summarily executed at the behest of the **PRESBYTERIAN** clergy. The battle marked the end of King Charles I's cause in Scotland.

PHOENIX PARK MURDERS, 6 May 1882. Lord Frederick Cavendish, Duke of Devonshire, was appointed Chief Secretary for Ireland in 1882 and charged with promoting Prime Minister William Gladstone's attempts to negotiate with the nationalist groups in Ireland. Soon after arriving in Dublin, he and his Under-Secretary, Thomas Burke, were brutally stabbed to death in Phoenix Park. English reaction to this act of terrorism by a group known as 'The Invincibles' was swift — a new Coercion Act (designed to suppress violence) was passed, the **IRISH LAND LEAGUE** (founded in 1879 to promote land tenure reform) and Charles Parnell discredited by association (though his involvement was later disproven), and the cause of conciliation greatly harmed. The perpetrators were eventually arrested; five were hanged and three were sentenced to life imprisonment.

PIBROCH. An anglicization of the **GAELIC** *piobaireachd*, the term is often used as a synonym for *BAGPIPE playing* or *bagpipe music*. However, it can also refer to *ceol mor* (great music) — a collection of some 250 tunes (including marches, laments and salutes), the majority of which were first written down between 1790 and 1840 but devised by the pipers to the **CLAN** chiefs during the militaristic period from the late 16th century until the aftermath of the **BAT-TLE OF CULLODEN** in 1746. *Ceol beag* (little music) consists of more recently composed reels, slow airs, jigs and strathspeys, and is played much more frequently, even though it is considered distinctly inferior by the purists. The pipes are one of the hardest musical instruments to master (cynics suggest that it is hard to know whether a beginner is trying to to kill them or play them). Traditionally, it took seven years to learn the basics. About 12 major pibroch contests for individuals are held each year, and competition is intense.

PICTS. The Pictish kingdom of the northerly tribes of Scotland presented the main opposition to the Romans in the third century AD. The name is possibly derived from the Latin word *pingere* meaning *to paint* — a reference to the people's habit of painting their faces with the blue dye-filled herb, woad, at times of war. The Picts were defeated by Magnus Maximus in AD 383, during an attempted invasion of England and united with the Scots under **KENNETH MACALPIN** *c.* AD 843. (See **DALRIADA**).

PINKERTON, ALLAN (1819–84). The founder of the first private detective agency in the United States, Pinkerton was born in **GLASGOW** on 25 August 1819 and completed an apprenticeship as a cooper before emigrating to North America in 1842. He settled in Illinois and established a business at Dundee (near Chicago) but soon became involved in the processes of law enforcement. In 1846, having played a part in the capture of a group of counterfeiters, he was made deputy sheriff of Kane County. Shortly afterwards, he transferred to Cook County but, in 1850, set up his own firm — the Pinkerton Detective Agency — which specialized in the apprehension of train robbers. Under his direction, it expanded rapidly, aided by a series of well-publicized coups, including the foiling of an assassination attempt on US President-elect Abraham Lincoln in 1861. During the Civil War (1861–62), Pinkerton (operating under the name of E. J. Allen) was head of the North's secret service in the Confederate states, but he returned to his business as soon as the conflict was over. Although, in Scotland, he had been a supporter of the Chartist movement, which had sought to improve the political and economic situation of the working classes, he was an implacable opponent of labour unions, believing them to be against the best interests of employees in manual jobs. As a result, he was much criticized for the policies he adopted during a series of industrial disputes in 1877. Pinkerton died in Chicago on 1 July 1884, but the firm continued to expand under the direction of his sons, Robert and William, and is now an international concern.

PINKIE, BATTLE OF, 10 September 1547. This battle was fought between an English force of 16,000 men (4,000 cavalry and 12,000 infantry) supported by 80 heavy guns and part of the English fleet, against a Scottish army of 23,000 infantry with some artillery. The English army, led by the Duke of Somerset, Protector of England, was attempting to enforce the Protector's plans to marry ten-year-old Edward VI to five-year-old **MARY, QUEEN OF SCOTS,** and thereby reduce French influence north of the border (see **ROUGH WOOING**). The Scottish forces were led by James, Earl of Arran, Regent of Scotland, and this engagement was the last formal battle to be fought between the national armies of the two countries.

The Scots held a strong position, but the Regent mistook as a retreat English troop movements aimed at securing a better position on a hill known as Pinkie Cleuch, and ordered his troops to cross the River Esk and attack. The Scots were cut to pieces by the English heavy artillery, naval bombardment, archers and handguns and the survivors mercilessly pursued by the cavalry. As a result of the battle, the English occupied **EDINBURGH** and Mary escaped to France, eventually to marry the French Dauphin. Anti-English sentiments gained wider acceptance, and the actions after the battle strengthened support for the **AULD ALLIANCE.**

PIPER ALPHA DISASTER, 6 July 1988. A North Sea oil-drilling rig stationed off **ABERDEEN** exploded, killing 167 men. The incident led to the Cullen Inquiry, which made several recommendations for safety improvements in the North Sea oil extraction industry.

PLAID. The long **TARTAN** woollen cloth draped over the shoulder of the Scottish **BAGPIPE** player originated during the 17th century as a belted plaid. A piece of fabric some 18 feet long and 6 feet wide was laid on the ground over a belt, then folded into pleats along its full length. The wearer then lay with his back on the material and folded the sides over him to form a long apron. He then clasped the belt around his waist and stood up. His lower half was now covered by a pleated skirt, and the rest of the cloth could be wrapped around his shoulders. When he needed to sleep, the owner simply lay down and wrapped the plaid around him. Adaptations to the belted plaid during the first half of the 18th century led to the development of the **KILT,** which is now the distinctive element of Scottish highland dress. The modern piper's plaid is only about ten feet long and is fringed at both ends. It is attached to the tunic by a brooch. A shorter plaid is sometimes worn by men at formal evening functions. In North America, *plaid* is often used as a synonym for *tartan*.

PLAID CYMRU. The Welsh National Party was formed in 1925 during the annual National **EISTEDDFOD** in Pwllheli and contested its first parliamentary election (unsuccessfully) in 1929 but did not emerge as a significant political force until after the Second World War. In 1966, Gwynfor Evans (President of the Party from 1945–1991) won a by-election at Carmarthen and, in the wake of the publicity, membership grew rapidly. During the 1970s, gains were made at **LOCAL GOVERNMENT** level in several places, culminating in overall control of **MERTHYR TYDFIL** Borough Council in 1976. In the 1987 general election, Ynys Mon was wrested from the Conservatives and, two years later, the party won 12.9 per cent of the popular vote (but no seats) in the elections for the European Parliament. The 1990s saw the Plaid Cymru established as second only to the Labour Party in Welsh politics, advocating self-government for the **PRINCIPALITY** within the European Union. In 1995, it won 114 seats (more than the Conservatives or the Liberal Democrats) on the new local government authorities (taking control of the Caernarvon and Meironnydd Council) and, at the 1997 general election, returned four MPs to the House of Commons, all from constituencies in its **WELSH**-speaking rural heartland of northwest and west Wales.

PLANTATIONS OF ULSTER, 1556–1659. Colonization of Ireland, and particularly Northern Ireland, was achieved by the encouragment given to Scottish and English families to establish homes, on lands often confiscated from the Irish people, in settlements known as plantations. By anglicizing the population, giving land and property to the settlers and imposing English government and language on **ULSTER** (and, indeed, the whole of Ireland), it was hoped that the subjugation and allegiance of the region would be secured. At times the process bordered on what in the present day would be called ethnic cleansing, with the intention to replace the Gaelic population with English and Scots through any and all possible means. The plantations really began in 1556, when the areas of Offaly and Leix were renamed King's and Queen's Counties; these were followed by two unsuccessful plantations in Ards and Antrim in 1572, modelled on those attempted in North America. The **TYRONE REBELLION** targeted the plantations, and many were destroyed in the last decade of the 16th century, while renewed efforts were made from 1609, with complete removal of native populations and the taking of Derry as a plantation by the City of London, renaming it as **LONDONDERRY**. The **IRISH REBELLION** of 1641 again attacked plantations and savage reprisals were exacted, with massive confiscations from the 1650s, following the **SETTLEMENT ACTS** in 1652, 1662 and 1665. This policy became one of the main planks of Anglo-Irish hostility and an important element in the historical antecedents of **THE TROUBLES.** To this day the Irish refer to Londonderry as Derry.

PORTEOUS RIOTS, 7–8 September 1736. During a time of protest in Scotland at the anti-smuggling moves which followed the **UNION OF THE CROWNS,** smuggler Andrew Wilson gained much public sympathy for helping an accomplice to escape from prison in **EDINBURGH.** At his hanging on 14 April 1736, a riot broke out, and, fearing an escape attempt, the City Guard fired on the crowd, killing six people. Captain John Porteous was accused of giving the order to fire and condemned to death, but his execution was postponed by Queen Caroline, then acting as Regent in the absence of King George II. On the night of 7 September, a mob broke into Porteous's prison cell, dragged him out and hanged him in the street. The incident provided **WALTER SCOTT** with the plot for *The Heart of Midlothian.*

POTATO FAMINE, IRISH, 1845–50. Potato Blight affected the Irish crops for several years from late 1844. In a population heavily reliant on this staple crop, the disease, coupled with a series of harsh winters, caused widespread famine and starvation throughout the island and a mass exodus to other countries, particularly England and the United States of America. The lack of real help from mainland Britain during the crisis survives in the popular imagination as yet another example of Anglo-Irish disinterest and hostility.

POYNINGS' LAW, 1494. Sir Edward Poynings was sent as Lord Deputy to Ireland by King Henry VII to reestablish English control of the island. Poynings forced the Irish Parliament to pass an act which forever afterward bore his name — all future acts before the Irish Assembly had to be approved by the English Parliament before they became law. A similar act made laws passed in England automatically apply to Ireland. Both were hated by Irish Parliamentarians and republicans (especially the **IRISH VOLUNTEERS**) and became another thorn in the side of Anglo-Irish relations until their repeal in 1782.

PRESBYTERIAN CHURCH IN IRELAND. Although some Puritan

groups had adopted a **PRESBYTERIAN** structure during the 16th century, the movement really became established in Ireland in 1610, when Protestants from Scotland and England were settled on the island in an attempt to anglicize it (see **PLANTATIONS OF ULSTER**). Initially, these immigrants were organized within the Anglican Communion but, faced with increasing persecution from King Charles I and Archbishop William Laud, who attempted to impose a religious orthodoxy and use the episcopacy as a means of achieving absolute power for the monarch (see **BISHOPS' WARS**), most eventually turned elsewhere. For many thousands of these Christians, the solution to the problems caused by the discrimination was flight to North America. Others joined Nonconformist sects which, during the 18th and early 19th centuries, grew in number as breakaway groups flourished and new forms of worship became popular. Eventually, in 1840, the Synod of **ULSTER** (the largest Presbyterian organization) merged with the Secession Church to form the Presbyterian Church in Ireland. Fourteen years later, the Synod of Munster, which had its greatest strength in Dublin and in the southwest, joined the Union. The modern Church is conservative in doctrine and, in 1997, had approximately 195,000 members in Northern Ireland, 455 churches and 400 ministers. It is governed by a General Assembly, which meets annually and is presided over by a Moderator, who is elected for a one-year term. (See **CHURCH IN IRELAND; CHURCH OF SCOTLAND; FREE PRESBYTERIAN CHURCH OF SCOTLAND; PRESBYTERIAN CHURCH OF WALES**).

PRESBYTERIAN CHURCH OF WALES. During the second quarter of the 18th century, **HOWEL HARRIS** (1714–73) and **DANIEL ROWLAND** (1713–90) experienced religious conversions, became itinerant preachers and provided the foci for a Christian revival in Wales. Initially, they cooperated with leaders of the English Methodist movement, such as Charles and John Wesley, and therefore remained within the fold of the Church of England. However, doctrinal differences led to disagreement and the paths increasingly diverged as the Welsh emphasized the tenets of Calvinism. By the end of the century, the Methodists had become a Church within a Church but were unable to appoint their own ministers, and the movement's senior figures were looking enviously at the sects outside the Anglican community which had that right. In 1811, **THOMAS CHARLES,** faced with growing demands for independence and the threat of Parliamentary legislation which would restrain unlicensed preachers, reluctantly ordained nine ministers at Bala and 13 at Llandeilo. That action, which effectively removed all of his supporters from the established (or state) Church, had two effects. Firstly, it altered the balance of ecclesiastical power in Wales because it placed the great majority of Christians in the Nonconformist camp, although the landowning classes retained their allegiance to the Church of England. Secondly, it led the Calvinistic Methodists to reorganize themselves as the Presbyterian Church of Wales (the institution's popular name — the Calvinistic Methodist Church of Wales — reflects that background). Two associations of congregations were created, one for the south of the principality, the other for the north, and, in 1823, a creed based on Calvinist principles was adopted. A General Assembly was formed to unite the two associations in 1864 and, since then, has met annually, presided over by a Moderator who holds office for one year. The doctrine and constitutional structure of the Church were confirmed by Act of Parliament in 1933. In 1997, the Presbyterian Church of Wales had some 53,000 members, 950 congregations and 130 ministers. (See **CHURCH IN WALES; CHURCH OF SCOTLAND; FREE PRESBYTERIAN CHURCH OF SCOTLAND; PRESBYTERIAN CHURCH IN IRELAND; UNION OF WELSH INDEPENDENTS [UNDEB YR ANNIBYNWYR CYMRAEG]**).

PRESBYTERIANS. This Protestant sect followed the Calvinistic rejection of the episcopacy and created a strong local or parish presbytery administration. It is strongest in Scotland (Presbyterianism is the organizational basis of the **CHURCH OF SCOTLAND**). (See **BISHOPS' WARS; BLACK ACTS; COVENANTERS; ENGAGERS; JOHN KNOX; NATIONAL COVENANT; PRESBYTERIAN CHURCH IN IRELAND; PRESBYTERIAN CHURCH OF WALES; SOLEMN LEAGUE AND COVENANT**).

PRESTONPANS, BATTLE OF, 21 September 1745. In this engagement during the **JACOBITE REBELLION, CHARLES EDWARD STUART** led a force of 2,500 Highlanders and routed an English army under Sir John Cope, capturing 1,600 men. The battle was said to have lasted barely four minutes, with the "hideous shout" of the charging Highlanders putting the whole Hanoverian army to flight. The success convinced Charles to mount an invasion of England in an attempt to capture London.

PRINCE OF WALES. This title was first used, during the early 13th century, by **DAFYDD AP LLYWELYN** and was officially accorded to his nephew, **LLYWELYN AP GRUFFUDD,** following the signing of the **TREATY OF MONTGOMERY** in 1267. In 1301, Edward I of England delegated the administration of his Welsh territories to his 17-year-old-son, the future Edward II, who had been born in Caernarvon, and invested him as Prince of Wales at a ceremony in Lincoln. Since then, the title has been almost continually invested in the heir to the throne, presently **PRINCE CHARLES.**

PRINCIPALITY. The term was originally applied to those parts of Wales that were held by the English Crown, excluding the **MARCHES,** and dates from the investiture of Edward, the first **PRINCE OF WALES,** in 1301. It is now applied to the whole of Wales.

PRIOR OF BRAMPTON, BARON. (See **JAMES PRIOR**).

PRIOR, JAMES MICHAEL LEATHES (1927–). **SECRETARY OF STATE FOR NORTHERN IRELAND** from 1981–84, Prior is the son of Mr and Mrs Charles Prior of Norwich. He was born on 11 October 1927 and educated at Charterhouse School and Cambridge University (where he earned a first class honours degree in estate management). He received a commission in the Royal Norfolk Regiment in 1946 and served in India and Germany, then pursued a career as farmer and land agent in East Anglia. In 1959, he was elected Member of Parliament for Lowestoft, representing the Conservative Party. Between 1963 and 1970, he served as Parliamentary Private Secretary to the President of the Board of Trade (1963), the Minister of Power (1963–64) and Edward Heath, Leader of the Opposition (1965–70). When Heath became Prime Minister in 1970, Prior was rewarded with the posts of Minister of Agriculture (1970–72) and Lord President of the Council and Leader of the House of Commons (1972–74). Margaret Thatcher made him Secretary of State for Employment after her General Election victory in 1979 and appointed him to the Northern Ireland post in September 1981. At the time, he was known to differ with the Prime Minister over economic policy and was being widely tipped as a possible, more moderate, successor. The appointment was widely interpreted as Mrs Thatcher's personal form of revenge. Prior made clear that he wanted to find a political settlement to **THE TROUBLES** in **ULSTER,** but the **DEMOCRATIC UNIONIST PARTY** and the **ULSTER UNIONIST PARTY**, wary of suggestions that they might have to share power with nationalist organizations, were unwilling to support any initiatives and called for tougher security measures against terrorists. The **SOCIAL DEMOCRATIC AND LABOUR PARTY,** on the other hand, objected to the lack of overt assurances that they would be involved in any system of devolved government for the province. In 1982, Prior announced a plan for 'rolling devolution' of administration to **STORMONT.** An elected Assembly would be charged with advising the Government in London and would be given increasing powers as it gained support within the community. Elections were held in October, but the refusal of the nationalist groups to participate in debates condemned the body to a role as a forum for a limited range of views. Prior was replaced as Secretary of State by **DOUGLAS HURD** in September 1984. In 1987, he left the House of Commons and was created Baron Prior of Brampton, but his part in Northern Ireland's politics was not forgotten because, in 1992, the **IRISH REPUBLICAN ARMY** placed a bomb at his London home (he was absent at the time). Prior has been Chairman of the General Electric Company since 1984 and holds several other directorships.

PROGRESSIVE UNIONIST PARTY (PUP). The PUP is the political wing of the outlawed **ULSTER VOLUNTEER FORCE,** one of the major protestant terrorist organizations in Northern Ireland. Formed in 1977, it is a dominantly working class group which maintains that **ULSTER** should remain part of the United Kingdom but that nationalists should have an executive role in any form of government created for the province. In 1997, it held three seats on **BELFAST** City Council but failed to win any House of Commons representation at the general election.

PROTESTANT UNIONIST PARTY (PUP). The term Protestant Unionist was first used by four candidates at the 1964 local government elections in **BELFAST.** During the next seven years, the Rev **IAN PAISLEY** and his supporters won seats at the Stormont and Westminster Parliaments under the PUP banner but, in 1971, it was assimilated by the **DEMOCRATIC UNIONIST PARTY.**

PYM OF SANDY, BARON. (See **FRANCIS LESLIE PYM**).

PYM, FRANCIS LESLIE (1922–). **SECRETARY OF STATE FOR NORTHERN IRELAND** for three months in 1973–74, Pym was born on 13 February 1922, the son of Leslie Pym (a former Member of Parliament for Monmouth) and his wife, Iris. He was educated at Eton College and Cambridge University, then served as a Captain with the 9th Lancers in Africa and Italy from 1942 until 1946. At the close of the Second World War, he embarked on a business career but became increasingly involved with local and national politics and, in 1961, entered the House of Commons, representing Cambridgeshire and the Conservative Party. He held posts as Party Whip from 1961 until 1970 then, for the three years following Edward Heath's General Election victory, was Parliamentary Secretary to the Treasury and Government Chief Whip. When he moved to **ULSTER,** he was well briefed on the situation in the province because he had insisted on attending meetings of Cabinet committees dealing with **THE TROUBLES** and immediately became involved in implementing the **SUNNINGDALE AGREEMENT** and establishing the **NORTHERN IRELAND POWER SHARING EXECUTIVE.** However, he had little opportunity to make his mark before Harold Wilson brought the Labour Party back to power at the General Election in February 1974. Pym was later involved in discussions over security matters during his period as Defence Secretary (1979–81) and over relations between the United Kingdom and the Republic of Ireland while he was Foreign Secretary (1982–83). He left the House of Commons in 1987, having found himself at odds with many of the policies introduced by Prime Minister Margaret Thatcher, and was created Baron Pym of Sandy.

—R—

RADICAL WAR, 1820. 'Radicals' were the advocates of fundamental social and, especially, political change who agitated for Parliamentary reform, civil rights and the repeal of laws in order to alleviate the economic distress prevalent towards the end of the 18th century. Radicalism and Chartism grew rapidly in the early years of the 19th century, particularly in the wake of the Napoleonic Wars and the ensuing economic slump. In England, the wave of riots and unrest culminated in the Peterloo Massacre of 1819, while, in Scotland, it resulted in the so-called Radical War of 1820.

In Scotland, unemployment was high and economic distress widespread, especially amongst workers in the textile industries which had been most affected by the mechanization introduced during the Industrial Revolution. Protest meetings were held in **EDINBURGH, GLASGOW** and Paisley during 1819, and 27 Radicals suspected of sedition were arrested in Glasgow in 1920. A strike for seven days by 60,000 workers was followed by an unsuccessful attempt at uprising, which began with the seizure of the Carron Ironworks but was quickly suppressed by a force of Hussars near Falkirk. Three of the leaders were executed and 19 others transported to Australia, passing into Scottish folk history as martyrs to the Scottish cause.

RAEBURN, HENRY (1756-1823). Scotland's most distinquished portrait painter, Raeburn was born in **EDINBURGH** on 4 March, 1756, the younger son of mill owner Robert Raeburn and his wife, Ann. He was educated at Heriot's Hospital then became apprenticed to James Gilliland, a goldsmith and jeweller. His employer was much impressed by the new employee's ability to create miniature portraits in watercolour and encouraged him to such an extent that Raeburn turned to painting full-time. Marriage in 1778 to Ann Elder, daughter of a landowner and a wealthy woman in her own right, brought financial security and allowed him to spend two years in Rome (1785-87), studying the works of the Italian masters. Over the next thirty years, he completed studies of nearly all the leading figures of Scottish society, often working on several pictures at once and entertaining three or four subjects a day at his studio. **JAMES BOSWELL, DAVID HUME, JAMES HUTTON, WALTER SCOTT, ADAM SMITH** and other products of the **SCOTTISH ENLIGHTMENT** all sat for him, but he kept neither a record of their appointments, nor an account of their payments so art historians have had difficulty compiling a full chronology of his work. He was knighted by George IV when the King visited the Scottish capital in 1822 and, the following year, was appointed His Majesty's Painter in Scotland. However, within weeks of receiving the title, he took ill and, on 8 July, died in his native city. He was buried in St John's Church, in the New Town.

Today, Raeburn is best known for *Reverend Robert Walker Skating on Duddingston Loch* — a picture which has appeared on so many shortbread boxes and oatcake tins that it has become known, somewhat sarcastically, as Scotland's *Mona Lisa.* However, despite that association with modern tartan souvenirs, Raeburn is still highly regarded by modern critics. Reviewers of a major exhibition of his work, held at the Royal Scottish Academy in 1997, praised his ability to turn "the standard repertoire of portrait poses into a highly inventive composition" (Tom Lubbock in *The Independent)* and noted how his "freedom of brushwork eventually develops the power to express extraordinary depths of emotion" (Iain Gale in *The Scots-*

man). Later the same year, two miniatures discovered at the offices of a London publisher, were identified as Raeburn's earliest known works. Thought to date from 1772, when the artist was just 16, they show James Gilliland and his wife, Elizabeth.

RAMSAY, ALLAN (1713–84). One of the products of the **SCOTTISH ENLIGHTENMENT,** Ramsay was a portrait painter whose work hangs in many galleries in the United Kingdom and the United States. Born in **EDINBURGH** on 13 October 1713, he was the son of poet Allan Ramsay, whose collections had made the Scottish ballad tradition available to **ROBERT BURNS** and whose own pastoral, *The Gentle Shepherd* (published in 1725), had been immensely popular. The work of the younger Ramsay was shaped during a period in Italy between 1736 and 1738, when he studied with Francesco Imperiali and Francesco Solimena (his *Dr Mead* of 1747, for example, is in the Italian grand manner). Following that training, he settled in London and became extremely popular with wealthy patrons. He spent a second period in Italy between 1755 and 1757, but painted little after that, turning more to classical studies, socializing and writing political pamphlets. He died at Dover on 10 August 1784, but the continued popularity of his work is evidenced by the £551,000 paid for his *Portrait of Sir Edward and Lady Turner* in 1993. Other of his paintings and drawings are held by the National Gallery of Scotland, the Scottish National Portrait Gallery, the Huntington Gallery in San Marino (California) and the Ringling Museum in Sarasota (Florida).

RAMSAY, WILLIAM (1852–1916). The discoverer of the noble (or inert) gases, Ramsay was born in **GLASGOW** on 2 October 1852. He studied at Glasgow University from 1866 until 1870, then moved to Germany, where he worked in Heidelberg in 1870–71 and Tubingen in 1871–72. He was awarded a doctorate at Tubingen in 1873 and, the following year, became a tutorial assistant at the university. In 1880, he was appointed to the Chair of Chemistry at the University of Bristol and, in 1881, became Principal. In 1887, he moved to University College, London, and remained there until he retired in 1913.

As a young researcher, Ramsay had catholic interests, but, in the early 1890s, he became interested in the reasons for the difference between the densities of atmospheric and chemical nitrogen. In 1894, using equipment which would remove oxygen and nitrogen from the air, he identified a previously unknown heavy gas, which he called argon, and argued that it was this gas's great density which accounted for the difference between the densities of the two forms of nitrogen. The following year, while attempting to find additional sources of argon, he discovered that air contains helium, previously unknown on Earth. At the time, both helium and argon were believed to be chemically inactive so they were termed inert gases and were placed in a new group on the periodic table, numbered zero. However, consideration of their position suggested that three other such gases should exist and, in 1898, Ramsay, working with M. W. Travers, discovered neon, krypton and xenon in liquid air residues, from which nitrogen and oxygen had been removed. In later years, studies of helium led Ramsay to focus on the decay of radioactive materials and, as a result of cooperation with Whytlaw Gray, he was able to show that radium emanation (now called radon) is also one of the noble gases. Ramsay's work on the new family of elements was recognized by the award of the Davy Medal of the Royal Society in 1895, a knighthood (KCB) in 1902 and the Nobel prize for chemistry in 1904. He died in High Wycombe on 23 July 1916.

REBECCA RIOTS, 1839 and 1842–44. These were protests in Wales against the Poor Law provisions, high rents, tithes and corrupt local government. Tenant farmers, disguised as women, attacked turnpike tollgates and the Carmarthen Workhouse, but the disturbances were quelled by soldiers and the police. The riots were partially successful, however, because an Act of Parliament in 1844 altered the turnpike trust laws and reduced the adverse economic impact of the tollgate system. The troubles derive their name from a Biblical reference much quoted by the protestors; in chapter 24, verse 60, of the Book of Genesis, Rebecca's mother and brother bless her and express the hope that her descendants will "possess the gate of those which hate them". The Welsh troublemakers divided into groups; the leader of each was known as Rebecca and "her" followers were known as her "daughters".

RED CLYDESIDE. During the years of the First World War and its immediate aftermath, the areas of heavy industry along the banks of the **RIVER CLYDE** from **GLASGOW** to Gourock were, politically, well to the left, earning the area the soubriquet Red Clydeside. The movement was fragmented, with the Communist Party, the Independent Labour Party (ILP) and the Labour Party all gaining adherents. Supporters were opposed to the war (see, for example, **JAMES MAXTON**) and resented the squalor of the living conditions to which the urban working classes were condemned. They gained much public support and, at the 1922 General Election, won ten Parliamentary seats. At Westminster, however, they found themselves an ideological minority, little understood even by fellow socialists; Beatrice Webb wrote in her diaries, covering the years 1924–32 but published in 1956, that "The dour Scot objects to any social intercourse" — a reflection of the Clydesiders attempts to keep to themselves and thus avoid compromising their views. The movement had little impact nationally although Maxton led the ILP into a breach with the mainstream Labour movement, and, in 1924, John Wheatley became housing minister in the first Labour government, led by Ramsay MacDonald, introducing state subsidies which provided the foundation for an effective programme of municipal housing.

RED HAND COMMANDO. Formed in 1972, Red Hand Commando is one the Northern Ireland Protestant paramilitary organizations responsible for the murder of Roman Catholics in the province. Outlawed by the UK government in 1973, it is thought to have strong links with the **ULSTER VOLUNTEER FORCE** and is believed to have been involved in the killings of two news agents, who sold the nationalist *Republican News* in **BELFAST** during 1991.

REES, MERLYN (1920–). **SECRETARY OF STATE FOR NORTHERN IRELAND** from 1974 until 1976, Rees (who changed his surname to Merlyn-Rees by deed poll in 1992) was born in Cilfynydd (near Pontypridd) on 18 December 1920. He was educated at Harrow Weald Grammar School, Goldsmith's College (London), London School of Economics and London University Institute of Education, then served in the Royal Air Force during the Second World War, reaching the rank of squadron leader. Between 1949 and 1960 he taught history and economics, initially at Harrow Weald and then at Luton College of Technology, but he also became increasingly involved in politics and unsuccessfully contested the Parliamentary constituency of Harrow East for the Labour Party in 1955 and (twice) in 1959. In 1963, he won the seat at Leeds South, then served as Parliamentary Private Secretary to the Chancellor of the Exchequer (1966–68) and at the Home Office (1968–70) before becoming Labour's Northern Ireland spokesman in 1972. Prime Minister Harold Wilson appointed him Secretary of State for Northern Ireland following the General Election in 1974, giving him the task of coping with unionist opposition to the **SUNNINGDALE AGREEMENT** and the **NORTHERN IRELAND POWER**

SHARING EXECUTIVE. A campaign of terrorism by the **IRISH REPUBLICAN ARMY (IRA)** added to his problems and a strike by loyalist workers opposed to the Sunningdale accord exacerbated matters further. After 15 days of industrial action, during which road blocks prevented traffic movement and power stations closed down, **BRIAN FAULKNER,** the leader of the Executive, resigned and Rees reintroduced **DIRECT RULE** from London.

In November 1974, the IRA bombing of two public houses in Birmingham forced him to introduce legislation tightening security laws and, in particular, allow for the deportation of nationalists to the Irish Republic. The following February, the IRA called a ceasefire, and, to help sustain it, Rees decided to end the controversial process of internment by speeding up the release of suspected terrorists who had been detained without trial. Also, he established seven incident centres, manned by IRA representatives, in Roman Catholic areas — an attempt to defuse potentially violent situations by allowing people with a grievance to talk to sympathetic members of the republican community, who would pass the complaint on to government officials. Ostensibly, the aim was to politicize the IRA, encouraging the organization to further its aims by democratic means rather than by violence, but the move failed. The nationalists shunned the **NORTHERN IRELAND CONSTITUTIONAL CONVENTION** and, by the summer of 1975, the ceasefire was effectively over. In September 1976, following the demise of the Convention, Rees returned to London and the post of Home Secretary, which he held until Labour's defeat at the 1979 General Election. In opposition, he served as the party's spokesman on home affairs (1979–80) and energy (1980–83) before retiring from the House of Commons in 1992 and receiving a life peerage, as Baron Merlyn-Rees, for his political service.

REPUBLICAN LABOUR PARTY (RLP). The RLP was founded in 1960, when two members of the Northern Ireland Parliament — **GERRY FITT** (Dock Labour Party) and Harry Diamond (Socialist Republican) — agreed to unite under one political banner. Strongly rooted in **BELFAST,** where it had a number of successes at local government elections, it was active in the civil rights movement and advocated a policy of achieving reform in **ULSTER** by nonviolent means. However, it lacked a strong central administration and fell apart soon after Fitt decamped to the new **SOCIAL DEMOCRATIC AND LABOUR PARTY** in 1970.

RESTORATION SETTLEMENT, 1661. This was the political, constitutional, religious and legal framework of Acts of Parliament that were passed by the reconstituted Parliaments of England, Scotland and Ireland in order to effect the Restoration of King Charles II to the thrones of England and Scotland. All acts passed since 1641 in England and 1640 in Scotland were annulled by the Act Rescissory of 1661. The Act of Indemnity and Oblivion limited the scope of vengeance on involved politicians, and through the Declaration of Breda, Charles accepted Parliamentary government. In Scotland, the Settlement was opposed by the **COVENANTERS** and many clergy as it reimposed the episcopy and did not remove all restrictions in worship, but, generally, it was broadly accepted by a population tired of religious and regal controversy and hopeful of better economic conditions. In Ireland, the **SETTLEMENT ACT** of 1662 confirmed Protestant ownership of lands confiscated from Catholics, but allowed Catholics innocent of rebellion to petition for the return of their lands. The Church of Ireland moved further towards Anglicanism, and Presbyterianism continued to be suppressed. The settlement in each part of the United Kingdom was therefore different and selective of the elements most advantageous to Westminster.

REVOLUTION SETTLEMENT, 1689–90. This legal and constitutional framework was agreed by the Convention Parliament to confer the Crown upon William and Mary following the Glorious Revolution of 1688–89. The English Parliament considered that, legally, James II had left the throne vacant, while the **THREE ESTATES** considered that he had forfeited it. William agreed, in January 1689 (when he was already King of England), to administer Scotland until his status could be established by the Scottish Parliament. The Scots took the opportunity to abolish the episcopacy and subsequently to reestablish Presbyterianism (see **PRESBYTERIANS**). By the **CLAIM OF RIGHT,** they restricted the monarch to Protestantism and by the Articles of Grievances they restricted the Royal Prerogative and condemned the **LORDS OF THE ARTICLES.** On 11 May 1689, William was offered the Scottish Crown. Like the earlier **RESTORATION SETTLEMENT**, this Settlement was different in the two nations, which at this time were still constitutionally quite discrete, though legally united.

RHODRI MAWR (*c.* 820–78). One of the most gifted of the Welsh rulers, Rhodri Mawr (or Rhodri the Great, in English) united the area from Anglesey (in the north) to the Gower Peninsula (in the south) under one government and succeeded in keeping the marauding Vikings at bay. The son of Merfyn Frych (whose court in north Wales had been a centre of scholarship) and his wife, Nest, Rhodri became King of Gwynedd on his father's death in 844. He inherited the western kingdom of Powys from Cyngen, a maternal uncle, in 855, and the southern kingdom of Seisyllwg from Gwygon, his wife's brother, in 877. Although these large territories were acquired peacefully, Rhodri gained a considerable reputation as a warrior, notably as a result of a victory over the Viking leader Gorm (also known as Horm and Horn), in a naval battle off Anglesey in 856. He also resisted incursions by Saxons from Mercia, on the eastern borders with his kingdom, and was killed fighting them in 878. On his death, his estates were divided among his six sons so the potential for the continuation of a centralized monarchy and a uniform political structure was lost. (See **HYWEL DDA**).

RHONDDA VALLEYS. The Rhondda valleys in south Wales were the source of much of the coal which fuelled British railroad engines and navies during the second half of the 19th century. Two rivers — Rhondda Fawr and Rhondda Fach (Big Rhondda and Little Rhondda) — cut through sandstones to reveal the coal measures, which were first worked in 1807 to provide raw material for the iron industry of **MERTHYR TYDFIL** and neighbouring towns. Increasing awareness of the coal's steam-raising properties promoted further expansion, notably after the opening of the Treherbert pits in 1855, and brought people flooding to the valleys in search of jobs. The population rose from 542 in 1801 to 24,000 in 1871 and 168,000 in 1924. Hamlets expanded and merged into each other, creating rows of terraced cottages along the hillsides. Coal extraction was exhausting and heavily male dominated, but whole communities benefited from the establishment of libraries, social facilities and chapels, and residents developed a strong sense of local identity. However, in the period between the two world wars, demand for coal slumped. Industrial recession, the greater efficiency of steam engines and competition from other areas combined to produce diminishing output and high unemployment (in 1923, 87 per cent of the employed population in the Rhondda valleys were in mining so recession hit hard). Pits closed and people moved out, as they still do. Coal mining has virtually vanished from the valleys, but alternative sources of work have been hard to find. Despite the best efforts of local and national authorities, large areas of derelict land, problems of subsidence as a result of underground workings, lack of open space for building and a dominantly working class culture have deterred firms from moving in. The population in 1991 was 76,000, less than half its 1924 peak of 168,000, and, although the industrial heritage is now being marketed as a tourist attraction, the decline is likely to continue.

RHUDDLAN, STATUTE OF, 1284. Sometimes known as the Statute of Wales, this document contains the plans devised by Edward I of England for governing the Welsh territories won from **LLYWELYN AP GRUFFUDD.** Three new counties — Anglesey, Caernarvon and Meirionnydd — were created in the northwest; other changes were made to the preexisting counties of Cardigan, Carmarthen and Flint. Each area was placed under the authority of a sheriff (an English office new to Wales), whose main duties were to administer justice and collect monies owed to the Crown. An English system of courts was established, with English law used for criminal cases but Welsh practices retained for some civil matters (notably disputes over land). The statute was not designed solely as a repressive measure, and some scholars have argued that a strong and uniform legal system brought benefits to Wales. However, the spread of English law, at the expense of the native laws of **HYWEL DDA,** removed one element of Welsh identity and, therefore, of nationhood.

RICHARD, HENRY (1812–88). The first Welsh Nonconformist radical to be elected to Parliament, Richard heralded a process of change which was to oust the Conservative Party from control of all but a few constituencies in the **PRINCIPALITY.** The son of the Rev Ebenezer Richard, a Methodist minister, and his wife, Mary, Richard was born in Tregaron (near Lampeter) on 8 April 1812 and educated at Llangeitho Grammar School. In 1830, he entered Highbury Congregational College in London and, five years later, became pastor of a chapel in the city's Old Kent Road. He served as a minister until 1850, by which time he had become an advocate of arbitration as a means of solving international disputes and had earned, as a nickname, The Angel of Peace. In 1848, Richard was elected secretary of the Peace Society and, in that capacity, attended a series of conferences in Brussels (1848), Frankfurt (1850), London (1851), Manchester (1853) and **EDINBURGH** (also 1853). His efforts bore fruit; in 1856, he successfully urged diplomats in Paris to insert an arbitration clause in the treaty ending the Crimean War.

Richard, although he was British first and Welsh second, also published a series of articles in English newspapers such as the *Morning Post*, advocating the end of the anglicized, Conservative gentry's monopoly of power in Wales. It was a campaign which touched the emotions of people in his homeland, and, at the 1868 General Election (held the year after the Parliamentary Reform Act had expanded the franchise), Liberal Party candidates gained 23 of the 33 seats (see **MARTYRS OF '68**). Even so, most of these Liberals were from the landed class; Richard (who topped the poll at **MERTHYR TYDFIL**) was the most lowly born of their number, earning his victory through a series of eloquent speeches, which supported religious Nonconformists and demonstrated his understanding of the economic plight of the working classes. In the House of Commons, he quickly became known as the Member for Wales and was instrumental in taking knowledge of Welsh issues to a wider audience, speaking on topics relating to church affairs, education, land reform and the state of the **WELSH** language. A highly respected Parliamentarian, he died at Treborth (near Bangor) on 20 August 1888.

RIFKIND, MALCOLM LESLIE (1946–). **SECRETARY OF STATE FOR SCOTLAND** under Prime Minister Margaret Thatcher and Secretary of State for Defence, then Foreign Secretary, in John Major's governments, Rifkind the son of Mr and Mrs Elijah Rifkind. Born in **EDINBURGH** on 21 June 1946, he was educated in the city at George Watson's College and Edinburgh University (where he graduated LLB, MSc). After a year's lecturing at the University of Rhodesia (1967–68), he qualified as an **ADVOCATE** in 1970. Also that year, he fought an unsuccessful Parliamentary election for the Conservative Party, but, in 1974, won the Edinburgh Pentlands constituency and, in 1975, became the Opposition Spokesman on Foreign Affairs. From that point, and despite his opposition to his party's policy of refusing to consider **DEVOLUTION** of power to Parliaments in Scotland and Wales, his rise was rapid. Mrs Thatcher gave him his first taste of government as Parliamentary Under-Secretary of State at the **SCOTTISH OFFICE** (1979–82), then moved him to a similar post at the Foreign Office (1982–83). He was promoted to Minister of State in 1983 and entered the Cabinet as Scottish Secretary of State, introducing a series of educational reforms and helping to attract several high-tech industries to **SILICON GLEN**. In 1990, he became Transport Secretary and, two years later, under John Major, transferred to the Ministry of Defence. In 1995, Rifkind was appointed Foreign Secretary, the first Jew to hold the post since the brief, two-month stint of Rufus Issacs, Marquess of Reading, in 1931. During his first months in that office, he attempted to placate those Conservatives who were opposed to close links with Europe by advocating bonds with the United States and the growing economies of Asia. In February of the following year, he clashed with Germany's Chancellor Helmut Kohl, who accused Britain of dragging its feet on European integration, but, in September, argued that the United Kingdom should not disassociate itself from plans to introduce a single currency for members of the European Union. A contemplative, thoughtful politician, Rifkind was a powerful debater and developed a reputation for plain speaking in Cabinet meetings (he was ready to resign over poll tax policies in 1990, for instance). After losing his seat when the Labour Party won a landslide victory in the 1997 General Election, he joined Australian-owned BHP Petroleum to help develop its international oil and gas interests but admitted he wanted to find a way back into full-time politics. He was knighted (KCMG) shortly afterwards.

ROBERT I (1274–1329). Known as The Bruce, Robert was the scion of a Norman family which arrived in Scotland during the 12th century. He was born on 11 July 1274, and became Earl of Carrick in 1292, when his father resigned the title in his favour. After the abdication of King John (see **JOHN BALLIOL**) in 1296, he appears to have shifted his support several times between Edward I of England (his superior under the feudal system) and those, such as **WILLIAM WALLACE,** who supported the cause of Scottish independence. The die was cast on 10 February 1306, when he met John The Red Comyn, Earl of Badenoch, in Greyfriars Church, Dumfries. The details of the meeting are not clear, but there is no doubt that tempers rose, possibly because the two men were rivals for the vacant throne, and Bruce stabbed Comyn to death in front of the altar. In most circumstances, such a sacrilegious crime would inevitably have lead to the murderer's arrest but Bruce turned matters to his advantage. While his brothers seized Dumfries Castle, held by the English, Robert rode to **GLASGOW,** fell on his knees before Bishop Wishart (one of the country's leading churchmen) and sought absolution. Wishart willingly gave it, and, on 25 March 1307, Bruce was crowned King of Scotland at **SCONE.**

Inevitably, Edward viewed Bruce as a traitor and attempted to crush him. Defeated at Methven and at Tyndrum in the spring and summer of 1306, his wife taken prisoner and three of his brothers executed, Robert was forced to seek refuge on Rathlin Island, off the coast of **ULSTER.** In February 1307, he returned to Scotland, landing in Ayrshire and gradually building support amongst the nobles and churchmen, a process which was undoubtedly facilitiated by the death of Edward I in July of the same year and the accession of his less ambitious (and politically more inept) son, Edward II. Gradually, Bruce's supporters gained control of the major fortresses in Scotland, and, by the spring of 1314, **EDINBURGH** had fallen, leaving only Berwick and **STIRLING** in English hands. Spurred into action at last, Edward sent a large force, including the flower of English chivalry, to raise the siege at Stirling. Bruce, heavily outnumbered, met the invading army at the **BATTLE OF BANNOCKBURN** on 24 June and routed it. However, despite the victory, Edward was unwilling to accept either Scotland's independence or Bruce's sovereignty, and it took another 14 years of war, including a series of raids into the north of England by Scottish troops, before the Treaty of Northampton recognized Robert I as King of Scotland and renounced all English claims to overlordship.

The years after Bannockburn gave Bruce an opportunity to return his country to forms of government which had been in abeyance since 1296; royal finances were built up again, trade was revived and institutions of law and order were restored (so much so that Bruce became known as Good King Robert by the common people). He died of leprosy at Cardross on 7 June 1329 and was buried at Dunfermline Abbey, but, according to his instructions, his heart was removed and carried by Sir James Douglas on a pilgrimage to the Holy Land (see **EARLS AND MARQUESSES OF DOUGLAS**). En route, Douglas was killed in battle. Surrounded by Saracens, he threw the heart deep into the enemy ranks, telling it to go first as it had always done, then charged after it to his death. But there is a legend that the casket containing the heart was brought back to Scotland and buried in Melrose Abbey and, in 1996, a lead container was unearthed during excavations. Inside, there was a second container, cone-shaped and accompanied by a brass plaque which explained that the object had been found under the floor of the chapter house in 1921. Archaeologists claimed that it would be impossible to verify that any contents were the heart of King Robert so the casket was reburied. (See **BATTLE OF RUTHVEN**).

ROBERT II (1316–90). Robert was the first of the monarchs who were ultimately to unite England and Scotland under one king. (See **STUARTS**). The son of Walter, hereditary Steward of Scotland, and Marjorie, the daughter of **ROBERT I,** he was born on 2 March 1316, by caesarian section, after Marjorie died in childbirth following a riding accident. He proved to be a popular young man and was, at different times, proclaimed heir both to his grandfather and to

DAVID II. While David was exiled in France, and again while he was captive in England, Robert acted as Regent. He succeeded to the throne by hereditary right, at the age of 54, when David died in 1371 but, by that time, was past both his physical and his mental peak and made little impact on the affairs of his kingdom. The civil service, which his predecessor had established, gradually fell into disuse, royal income waned as the practice of direct taxation lapsed and much customs revenue filled the coffers of officials rather than those of the Exchequer. In 1384, after 13 years of feeble government, he handed over the reins to his eldest son, John (known as **ROBERT III**). Robert died at Dundonald on 19 April 1390 and was buried at **SCONE**.

ROBERT III (1337–1406). The eldest son of **ROBERT II** and Elizabeth Mure, Robert ruled Scotland from 1390 until 1406. Originally named John, he changed his name on his accession to the throne on 19 April 1390 because of its associations with the much despised **JOHN BALLIOL.** Lame, sickly and depressive, he failed to provide either the leadership or the imagination which Scotland needed after his father's limp rule and the country descended into a lawless, strife-torn state. His wife, Annabella, attempted to turn the tide by creating their elder son, David, a Duke (the first in Scottish history) and making him Lieutenant of the Realm. Robert, the King's brother (who had been appointed Governor of Scotland by **ROBERT II**), was unwilling to accept the situation and demanded a dukedom for himself. David, Duke of Rothesay, was a dissolute young man and a poor administrator, easy prey for his uncle (now Duke of Albany), who imprisoned him in **FALKLAND PALACE,** where he died three years later. By that time, the Queen was also dead and only the King's seven-year-old son, James (later **JAMES I**), stood between Albany and the throne. In 1406, the young Prince was sent to France for safekeeping, but his boat was taken by pirates and the boy was imprisoned in the Tower of London by Henry IV of England. The news proved too much for the aging King Robert, who died, grief stricken, in Rothesay on 4 April 1406.

ROBERTSON, GEORGE ISLAY McNEILL. Appointed Minister for Defence in the first government formed by Prime Minister **ANTHONY CHARLES LYNTON BLAIR** following the Labour Party's general election victory in 1997, Robertson is the son of police inspector George P. Blair and his wife, Marion. Born in Dunoon on 12 April 1946, he was educated at the local grammar school and at Dundee University (where he graduated with an MA degree in 1968) before joining the staff of the General and Municipal Workers' Union (1970-78). In May 1978, he won the parliamentary constituency of Hamilton at a by-election, allying himself with Labour's right wing. After the departure of several of his colleagues to the Social Democratic Party in 1981 (see **ROY HARRIS JENKINS**), he spent twelve years as a front bench spokesman on foreign affairs, specialising in European issues, before **JOHN SMITH** put him in charge of the team dealing with Scottish matters. Following the murder of 15 children and their teacher at a school near his home in **DUNBLANE** (March 1996) he delivered an impassioned speech to a packed House of Commons, arguing that guns have no place in a civilised society, but in the months before the general election he often failed to articulate party policies on **DEVOLUTION** clearly. Blair's decision to make **DONALD CAMPBELL DEWAR,** rather than Robertson, the **SECRETARY OF STATE FOR SCOTLAND** was considered by some commentators to be a snub for the man who had been responsible for explaining Labour's views on Scotland over the previous four years but those allegations were roundly denied. Robertson himself expressed satisfaction with his responsibility for the United Kingdom's defence strategies and his place in the new Cabinet.

ROB ROY. (See **ROB ROY MACGREGOR**).

ROCKALL. A 70 foot high lump of granite lying in the Atlantic Ocean some three hundred miles west of the **WESTERN ISLES,** Rockall was claimed for Britain in 1955 when a group of Royal Marines landed on it. Since then, ownership has been contested by Denmark, the Faroe Islands, Iceland and the Republic of Ireland. The island was incorporated into the United Kingdom, as part of Inverness-shire, by the 1972 Rockall Act. In 1997, however, the British Government ratified the United Nations Convention on the Law of the Sea, which states that no country can use uninhabited land with no economy as the basis of territorial claims. In effect, the decision meant that the UK signed away its rights to 60,000 square miles of ocean and seabed around the outcrop. Representatives of the fishing and mining industries objected furiously, pointing out that the right to exploit deep sea fish species and possible oil reserves were being given up, but the politicians refused to budge. Technically, Rockall remains part of the United Kingdom (albeit a contested part) because it lies within 200 miles of the island of **SAINT KILDA** which is now the most westerly point from which the country's territorial limits are defined) but the seas around it are now regarded as international waters.

ROUGH WOOING, 1544 and 1545. A series of punitive expeditions into Scotland was undertaken by Henry VIII of England following the failure of his plans to marry his son, the future Edward II, to **MARY, QUEEN OF SCOTS,** when she became of age (ten). Obsessed with subduing the Scots and ending their **AULD ALLIANCE** with France in order to turn his attention to European ventures, he was spurred on by victory at the **BATTLE OF SOLWAY MOSS** in 1542. The policy continued even after his death in 1547 and hardened the Scots' resolve to continue the links with the French. (See **BATTLE OF ANCRUM MOOR; TREATY OF HADDINGTON**).

ROWLAND, DANIEL (1713–90). One of the leaders of the 18th-century **METHODIST REVIVAL** in Wales, Rowland was born at Pantybeudy (Cardiganshire), the second son of the Rev Daniel Rowland and his wife, Janet. He was educated at Hereford Grammar School then, in 1731, became an Anglican curate at Llangeitho and Nantcwnlle, where John, his older brother, had succeeded as rector after their father's death. He was ordained a priest four years later, but was increasingly attracted by Methodist philosophies and, following a meeting with **HOWEL HARRIS** in 1737, began to preach on unconsecrated sites in an attempt to establish congregations (known as societies) which were prepared to follow the Calvinist tradition rather than the Arminianism of brothers Charles and John Wesley. When the first Methodist association (the central assembly) was formed in 1743, Rowland was appointed deputy moderator. His sermons were eloquent and the message — that those who did not have a personal awareness of Christ's suffering were condemned to eternal hell — was readily understood. He and Harris attracted enormous audiences, sometimes numbering thousands of listeners, but, in 1746, they differed on a theological issue. Harris inclined to the Sabelian doctrine that Father, Son and Holy Ghost are different forms of the same being and that, as a result, God died on the cross as Christ was crucified. In 1750, he was disowned by most adherents and Rowland became the undisputed leader of Welsh Calvinist Methodism for over a quarter of a century. Basing himself at Llangeitho (near Lampeter), he continued to preach and write until his death on 16 October 1790. (See **WILLIAM WILLIAMS**).

ROYAL AND ANCIENT GOLF CLUB. (See **GOLF**).

ROYAL ULSTER CONSTABULARY (RUC). The RUC was formed in 1922 as the official police force for the six counties of Northern Ireland which remained part of Britain when the rest of the island gained independence as the **IRISH FREE STATE.** Because of its role in preserving the political status quo, it has always been strongly Protestant and, during the civil unrest of the last three decades, has been much criticised by the nationalist community, which has frequently alleged that it does not act impartially. In 1969, a government inquiry into the policing of the province, chaired by Lord Hunt, recommended sweeping changes, proposing that the RUC should be disarmed, lose its paramilitary role and remodel itself on the other police forces in the United Kingdom. In the wake of the reforms, the number of serving officers increased (from some 5,000 in 1970 to nearly 8,500 in 1991), and the constabulary was given primary responsibility for peace keeping in **ULSTER,** with support from the **ULSTER DEFENCE REGIMENT** and the Army. Civilian support services also expanded, particularly from 1982. Since the signing of the 1985 **ANGLO-IRISH AGREEMENT,** there has been close co-operation between the RUC and the Garda, its counterpart in the Irish Republic. (See **B-SPECIALS**).

RUGBY. The game of rugby spread from England to Scotland, Wales and Northern Ireland about the middle of the 19th century and became particularly popular in schools. The first international match, between Scotland and England, was played in 1871. Two years later, a Scottish Football Union was formed, consisting of eight clubs. In 1874, an Irish Football Union and a rival North of Ireland Football Union were established; in 1879, they merged as the Irish Rugby Football Union. A Welsh Rugby Union was formed in 1881. Traditionally, club matches have been organized on a friendly basis. League competitions have been introduced only within the last decade, as the Celtic nations have tried to build national sides which can match the success of Australia, New Zealand and South Africa, the modern world powers. Ireland, where the sport is largely confined to the fee paying schools and the universities, has been less successful than the others in international matches. However, the Irish administration survived the partition of the island in 1922 and fields teams, representing Ireland, which draw on players from both **ULSTER** and the **REPUBLIC OF IRELAND.** In Wales, the game is almost a religion in the coal mining valleys (partly because it allows the small and fleet of foot to turn out alongside the large and strong), but has suffered in recent years as young men have found alternative recreations and resisted the discipline of regular training. Scotland made a distinctive contribution to the evolution of rugby by inventing a seven-a-side version of the sport, which originated in Melrose, where, in 1882, a local butcher promoted a competition to raise funds for the local club. Now, there is a World Sevens Tournament (first held in 1973), the British season ends with a series of sevens events, and countries in Asia and the Pacific have taken to the speed and flamboyance of sevens with relish.

RUNRIG. A system of communal farming, runrig (or, alternatively, rundale) was common throughout Scotland during the medieval period. Individual tenant farmers lived in a village (rather than on their own farms) and worked rigs (or ridges) of land which were intermingled with those of other tenants. The rigs nearest the houses were normally devoted to oats or bere (barley) and separated from the rougher moorland (which was used for grazing) by a stone or turf wall. In addition, both the plough and the animals used to pull it were shared. The origins of the system have been the subject of much scholarly dispute, but there is evidence that it has its roots in the socioeconomic conditions of the 12th century. Remnants remain but, for the most part, it was swept away during the 18th and 19th centuries, a casualty of the enclosure movement and the increased mechanization of the agricultural revolution.

RUTHVEN, BATTLE OF, 20 June 1306. **ROBERT THE BRUCE** had been proclaimed King of Scotland on 17 March 1306 and proceeded to rally support to his cause. His forces met with an English army led by Aymer de Valence of Pembroke at Ruthven on 20 June 1306 and were decisively defeated. Bruce escaped, but many of his followers were captured and subsequently executed. Following this defiant act, savage retribution was meted out to supporters and relatives of Bruce in both Scotland and England.

RUTHVEN RAID, 22 August 1582. Sixteen-year-old King James VI of Scotland was captured by a Protestant faction led by William Ruthven, Earl of Gowrie, and John Erskine, Earl of Mar, while on a hunting expedition, and imprisoned in Ruthven Castle. They aimed to overthrow the government and establish a **PRESBYTERIAN** and pro-English administration. Neither Queen Elizabeth I of England, nor the English Parliament, offered any support, and the King managed to escape in June 1583. Gowrie was executed in 1584, and the incident confirmed James's anti-Presbyterian prejudices. (See **BLACK ACTS; GOWRIE CONSPIRACY**).

—S—

SALESBURY, WILLIAM (*c.* 1520–84). The first person to translate the New Testament into **WELSH,** Salesbury was born at Llansannan (Denbighshire), probably in 1520. The second son of Foulke and Elen Salesbury, he was educated at Oxford University then (possibly) at the Inns of Court in London. He was raised as a Roman Catholic but, while studying at Oxford, was swayed by the ideals of the Reformation and, by 1550, had become a Protestant. Between 1547 and 1552, he published a considerable library of works on a variety of themes, including the first Welsh and English dictionary (1547) and a translation of the epistles and gospels (1551). In 1603, Parliament ordered the Welsh bishops to arrange for a translation of the *Book of Common Prayer* and the New Testament to be prepared in their own language. Salesbury cooperated in the task with Richard Davies, bishop of St Davids, and other scholars, working at the bishop's palace at Abergwili but shouldering most of the burden himself. His New Testament, prepared from the Greek and published in 1567, is now regarded as a stylistic masterpiece, but, at the time, was much criticized, primarily because Salesbury (despite his deep love of the Welsh language) had peppered the text with Latinizations and employed unusual spellings and mutations. The criticisms may have stung because he abandoned his plans to translate the Old Testament and, although he continued to work on translations with Davies until they quarrelled over an etymological matter in 1576, produced no further significant work before his death in 1584. Although claims that Salesbury saved the Welsh language, at a time when it was under attack by English institutions, are probably overstated, there is no doubt that he helped ensure that it became a written, as well as an oral, form of communication. (See **WILLIAM MORGAN**).

SALMOND, ALEXANDER ELLIOT ANDERSON (1954–). Leader of the **SCOTTISH NATIONAL PARTY** (SNP) since 1990, Salmond was born on 31 December 1954, the son of Mary and Robert Salmond. He was educated at Linlithgow Academy and **ST ANDREWS** University, graduating with an MA degree in economics and history. He worked as an economist with the Department of Agriculture and Fisheries (Scotland) from 1978 until 1980, then, from 1980 until 1987, with the Royal Bank of Scotland, where he specialized in energy matters. In 1987, he was elected Member of Parliament for Banff and Buchan and, in the House of Commons, acted as joint SNP/**PLAID CYMRU** spokesman on energy and environment issues. Originally appointed to the organization's national executive in 1981, he became vice chairman in 1985, deputy leader of the party in 1987 and leader in 1990. By 1996, Salmond had gained an unprecedented grip on his party's organization and policy making, siphoning power away from the elected executive committee to an inner cabinet whose members he appoints himself. An articulate speaker, he has used his economic training to good effect in policy documents which make a case for the breakup of the United Kingdom and an independent Scotland's membership of the European Union. In 1997, he was widely praised (by opponents as well as supporters) for his passionate but cogent advocacy of the case for **DEVOLUTION** in the campaign which led to an overwhelming referendum vote in favour of the establishment of a Scottish Parliament with tax rasing powers.

SCAPA FLOW. This sheltered harbourage in the far north of the United Kingdom, amoung the **ORKNEY ISLANDS,** was a vital naval depot during both world wars. It was the main operational base for the British Navy during the First World War. In 1918, the entire German High Seas Fleet was interned there while the Allies awaited the outcome of the Paris Peace Conference. However, on 21 June 1919, as the victorious powers argued over the allocation of the vessels, the German crews began to scuttle their ships. Fifty-one vessels, including ten battleships, were sunk. During the Second World War, a defensive causeway (known as the Churchill Barrier), was built to link some of the islands and Scapa Flow once again became a key naval port.

SCONE. The traditional site for the coronation of monarchs in Scotland, Scone lies some two miles northeast of Perth. It became the capital of the kingdom of the **PICTS** during the eighth century and retained that status after **KENNETH MACALPIN** united the Picts with the Scots in 843. In 1296, Edward I of England took the **STONE OF DESTINY,** on which the kings were crowned, to London, but Scone remained the location for coronation ceremonies until 1651, when Charles II was confirmed as monarch. During the early 19th century, a country house with extensive parks was built on the site.

SCOTIA. Although originally applied to Ireland, this term was later used as the name of the kingdom established by **KENNETH I,** who united **DALRIADA** and the **PICT**ish territories north of the **RIVER FORTH** during the ninth century. As control was extended into Strathclyde and Lothian, the name was increasingly used with reference to the whole of Scotland.

SCOTT, WALTER (1771–1832). Often regarded as the founder of the historical novel, Scott was one of the most influential figures in European literature during the early 19th century. He was born in **EDINBURGH** on 15 August 1771, the son of Sir Walter Scott (a Writer to the Signet) and his wife Anne Rutherford (daughter of a professor of medicine). He was educated at Edinburgh High School (1778–83) and Edinburgh University (1783–86), then became apprenticed to his father and was called to the Bar in 1792. In 1799, he was appointed Sheriff-Depute of Selkirkshire and, in 1802–03, published *Minstrelsy of the Scottish Border*, a three-volume collection of ballads. His first original poem — *The Lay of the Last Minstrel* — appeared in 1805 and was followed by a series of narrative poems, including *Marmion* (1808), *The Lady of the Lake* (1810) and *Rokeby* (1813), which brought him fame and fortune. In 1811, he purchased Abbotsford, in his beloved border country (see **THE BORDERS)**, and built himself a mansion designed to look like a Norman castle. However, as George Byron's star waxed, Scott's waned and he turned to a new career as a novelist. *Waverley* was completed in 1814 (and was published anonymously because Scott felt that writing fiction was not an activity expected of a man with his legal status). The book was immensely popular, and Scott responded by producing well over 20 historical narratives between 1815 and 1831. Collectively, these are known as The Waverley novels and include *Rob Roy* (1817), *The Heart of Midlothian* (1818) and *Redgauntlet* (1824). He wrote with great speed and made few revisions (*Guy Mannering*, which appeared in 1815, was, he claimed, the work of six weeks at Christmas), so he was able to sustain the prolific output needed to supply an apparently insatiable public. In 1820, he was rewarded with a baronetcy and, in 1822, was responsible for organizing the visit of George IV to Edinburgh. The King's appearance in a **KILT** created a vogue for **TARTAN** and that, in turn, led to the creation of innumerable plaids which had no connection whatsoever with **CLANS** or the **SCOTTISH HIGHLANDS.** The tartan image which Scotland presents to the world in order to sustain its tourist industry is largely the creation of Sir Walter Scott.

The bubble burst in December 1825 and January 1826, when Archibald Constable (Scott's publisher) and James Ballantyne (his printer) went bankrupt. Scott had financial interests in both and vowed to pay his creditors in full. Over the next six years, his output increased further as he tried to pay off his £114,000 debt: poems, novels, stories, essays and biographies (including the first biography of Napoleon in English) streamed from his pen, but his health broke, and, in March 1831, he suffered a paralytic stroke. The government provided a frigate to take him to the Mediterranean in the hope that a change of climate would help him recover, but other strokes followed, and he died, at Abbotsford, on 21 September. After his death, publisher Robert Cadell took over his copyrights and paid off his debts. Demand for Scott's works continued into the early 20th century but then declined until the 1930s, when European Marxist critics brought renewed attention to the novels. British scholars initiated a reappraisal of his work in the 1950s, rejecting criticism that he was a mere glorifier of the past and arguing that the Waverley novels are his masterpieces. (See **THE TROSSACS**).

SCOTTISH ARTS COUNCIL. Originally formed in 1947 as the Scottish Committee of the Arts Council of Great Britain, the Council was given its present name (and considerably increased authority) in 1967. In 1994, it became completely autonomous, responsible to, and financed by, the **SCOTTISH OFFICE.** Central government's main means of promoting the arts in Scotland, it is expected to devise and execute policies which will encourage the arts and make them more accessible to the public. The 16 members (appointed by the **SECRETARY OF STATE FOR SCOTLAND**) serve for a maximum of five years and administer a budget of around £25 million. About half of the available funds go to the four national companies — the Royal Scottish National Orchestra, Scottish Ballet, the Scottish Chamber Orchestra and Scottish Opera — and a further third provides support for some 60 major organizations (including theatres, art galleries, literary groups and musical companies). The remainder is used to award grants to individuals, commission new works, fund a scheme which takes authors into schools and subsidize initiatives which broaden the appeal of the arts in the Scottish community. Traditionally, council members have given their services free, but, in 1996, Magnus Linklater, demanded a salary of £20,000 in order to act as chairman, working a two-day week. He argued that, as a working journalist, he could not afford to do the job for nothing, but his demand caused controversy because the council's own data showed that about half of all artists earn less than £5,000 a year from their work.

SCOTTISH CIVIC TRUST. Formed in 1967, the trust encourages high standards in the planning and construction of building projects, promotes schemes which will enhance the quality of the environment, makes recommendations regarding plans to alter or demolish structures of historical importance and encourages the growth of local amenity societies. Its most conspicuous successes have been through conservation work in **NEW LANARK** and the New Town of **EDINBURGH,** an urban regeneration programme in **GLASGOW** and the formation of such special interest groups as the Scottish Environmental Education Committee.

SCOTTISH ENLIGHTENMENT. The second half of the 18th century witnessed the development of a significant intellectual movement in Scotland, based largely on **EDINBURGH** and affecting the sciences as well as the arts. It was marked by an emphasis on the philosophical bases of knowledge, the practical implications of science and the social benefits of study. Those involved included philosophers **DAVID HUME** and **ADAM SMITH,** physicist **JOSEPH BLACK,** geologist **JAMES HUTTON** and engineer **JAMES WATT.** The movement was less evident in literature (poet **ROBERT BURNS,** for example, was never part of the mainstream), though novelist **WALTER SCOTT** was associated with its later period. Several learned societies (such as the Royal Society of Edinburgh) were founded during the period, as were many academic journals. The **ENCYCLOPAEDIA BRITANNICA** was also first published at this time (1768–71).

SCOTTISH ENTERPRISE. Formed in 1991 through a merger of the Scottish Development Agency and the Training Agency in Scotland, Scottish Enterprise is a statutory body responsible for improving the skills of the population, promoting economic progress and enhancing the quality of the environment. Covering the whole of Scotland south of the **HIGHLANDS AND ISLANDS ENTERPRISE** territory, it works through 13 area-based local enterprise companies, each of which has a board of management consisting of people from the region and cooperates with private as well as public organizations. The major foci of their activity are technical training, job creation and income generation.

SCOTTISH EPISCOPAL CHURCH. When the **CHURCH OF SCOTLAND** was established in 1690, those Christians who supported an episcopacy formed their own organizations. Initially, there were two groups — those who pledged allegiance to William of Orange as King of Britain and those who supported the claims to the throne made by **JAMES STUART** and his son, **CHARLES EDWARD STUART.** After Charles died in 1788, leaving no legitimate heir, the second faction accepted the validity of the Hanoverian line of succession, and, during the 19th century, congregations gradually merged to form a single Scottish Episcopal Church. At the same time, there was an increasing adoption of the trappings of the Church of England. The Thirty Nine Articles of Religion, the use of the Prayer Book at Matins and Evensong and the obligatory wearing of a surplice by clergy all became part and parcel of worship until eventually, in 1864, the authority of the Scottish bishops was fully recognized by Anglicans south of the border. The Scottish Episcopal Church remains an autonomous member of the Anglican Communion, and is organized territorially on the basis of seven sees (**ABERDEEN** and **ORKNEY;** Argyll and The Isles; Brechin; **EDINBURGH; GLASGOW** and Galloway; Moray, Ross and Caithness; and **ST ANDREWS**, Dunkeld and Dunblane). It is governed by a General Synod, which meets annually and is presided over by a Primus elected by the Bishops. In 1997, the Church had 54,000 members, 230 clergy and 314 congregations, but, like most of the mainstream religious organizations in the United Kingdom, it was facing problems of declining numbers, having experienced a reduction in membership of nearly one-third over the previous 25 years. (See **CHURCH IN IRELAND; CHURCH IN WALES**).

SCOTTISH HIGHLANDS. (See **HIGHLANDS, SCOTTISH**).

SCOTTISH HOME RULE ASSOCIATION (SHRA). During the 1880s, Prime Minister William Gladstone's advocacy of the cause of **HOME RULE** for Ireland encouraged many members of his Liberal Party to make similar claims for Scotland. The SHRA, formed in 1886 and supported by representatives from all walks of Scottish life (including the aristocracy), provided a platform for these arguments. After the First World War ended in 1919, it adopted an increasingly radical stance as its leadership, which included **THOMAS JOHNSTON** (later to become **SECRETARY OF STATE FOR SCOTLAND)**, became more dominated by socialist sympathisers. However, although Johnston won election to the House of Commons in 1922 and the 1920s brought an increase in support for the Labour Party, the organization failed to win any concessions from governments in London and, in 1928, senior members defected to the new **NATIONAL PARTY FOR SCOTLAND.**

SCOTTISH NATIONAL PARTY (SNP). The SNP was formed in 1932 through the union of the **NATIONAL PARTY FOR SCOTLAND** and the more right wing Scottish Party. It represented the views of those who felt that the major political parties were unlikely to grant any form of **HOME RULE** to Scotland and, more broadly, reflected a more growing interest in national identity. However, although it captured its first parliamentary seat at Motherwell in 1945, it enjoyed limited electoral success until, in 1967, **WINIFRED MARGARET EWING** unexpectedly defeated the Labour Party candidate at a by-election in Hamilton and supporters began to win seats at **LOCAL GOVERNMENT** level. The 1974 general election produced 11 MPs and 30 per cent of the popular vote but the party failed to sustain the momentum and, in 1979, only two of the victors held on to their seats. That collapse led to a lengthy period of internecine strife, with one faction favouring a leftward shift move in policy and another arguing that the focus should be on independence from the rest of the United Kingdom, regardless of other considerations. A new sense of direction did not become apparent until 1988, when the SNP committed itself to a compaign for Scottish independence within the European Community. The following year, the election of **ALEXANDER ELLIOT ANDERSON SALMOND** as national Convener (party leader) confirmed the organization's orientation as a left of centre, social democratic grouping. At the 1997 general election, it won six seats and, despite initial doubts, urged supporters to vote for a Scottish assembly in the **DEVOLUTION** referendum held in September of the same year. The subsequent decision by the Labour government to establish a Scottish parliament which could raise taxes and legislate on domestic matters was welcomed by many members as a step towards full independence.

SCOTTISH NATURAL HERITAGE. A government agency created in 1992 through the amalgamation of the Nature Conservancy Council for Scotland and the Countryside Commission for Scotland, Scottish Natural Heritage is charged with securing the conservation and enhancement of Scotland's physical environment. It promotes projects which improve public access to areas of outstanding beauty and advises voluntary bodies on policies and proposals designed to preserve wildlife under threat. However, it has been accused by several writers of being too influenced by the opinions of landowners and insufficiently representative of the general public. Scottish Natural Heritage is based in **EDINBURGH**. (See **COUNTRYSIDE COUNCIL FOR WALES**).

SCOTTISH OFFICE. The Scottish Office, based in **EDINBURGH**, is the British government's headquarters in Scotland. Because the nation retained its own legal, banking and education systems after the 1707 **TREATY OF UNION** (see **BANK OF SCOTLAND; EDUCATION: SCOTLAND; LOCAL GOVERNMENT: SCOTLAND**), successive administrations found it necessary to appoint a series of committees (such as the Board of Agriculture and the Board of Health) to ensure that legislation was appropriately and effectively applied in the Scottish context. During the 19th and early 20th centuries, in particular, as the Industrial Revolution brought radical social and economic change, the number of organizations multiplied and, in 1939, the Scottish Office was created in an attempt to rationalize the situation. It was headed by the **SECRETARY OF STATE FOR SCOTLAND** and had four Departments (Agriculture, Education, Health and Home Affairs), each of which was responsible to a Permanent Under-Secretary of State. Further duties were added over the next 50 years and, by the 1990s, the number of Departments had increased to five — the Department of Agriculture and Fisheries for Scotland, the Scottish Development Department (formed in 1962), the Scottish Economic Planning Department (formed in 1973), the Scottish Education Department and the Scottish Home and Health Department. In addition, a series of government supported organizations (such as the Scottish Development Agency, formed in 1975) are answerable to the Scottish Office or directly to the Secretary of State.

SCOTTISH REPRESENTATIVE PEERS, 1707. The **TREATY OF UNION** between Scotland and England in 1707 made provision for 16 Scottish aristocrats to be elected by all Scottish peers to represent them in the House of Lords. This frequently allowed the London administration to exert great control over Scottish affairs, particularly since Westminster paid the peers' substantial pensions and any Scottish peers not elected held no rights to stand for the other House, the House of Commons. The 1967 Peerage Act extended the right to sit in the House of Lords, for the first time, to all Scottish peers.

SECRETARY OF STATE FOR NORTHERN IRELAND. As the government's principal minister responsible for **ULSTER,** the Secretary of State heads the **NORTHERN IRELAND OFFICE** and has a seat in the cabinet. After its formation in 1921, the province's internal affairs were shaped by its own Parliament, based at **STORMONT.** However, the failure of that Parliament to find a solution to **THE TROUBLES,** and stem increasing civil unrest, led the United Kingdom government to impose **DIRECT RULE** from London in March 1972, with a Secretary of State appointed to take charge of security, economic development and other matters. Two years later, a Northern Ireland Office was created, as a department of government and with the Secretary of State at its head, to facilitate the administration of the province. No politician has found a means of solving the problems posed by the conflict in **ULSTER** so, not surprisingly, the position has become the least desirable of senior government posts. (See **HUMPHREY ATKINS; PETER BROOKE; DOUGLAS HURD; THOMAS KING; ROY MASON; BRIAN MAWHINNEY; PATRICK MAYHEW; MARJORIE MOWLAM; JAMES PRIOR; FRANCIS PYM; MERLYN REES; WILLIAM WHITELAW).**

SECRETARY OF STATE FOR SCOTLAND. Following the **TREATY OF UNION** in 1707, a Secretary of State was created to take responsibility for the new government's business in Scotland, but the post was abolished in 1746. For much of the next 180 years, the nation's affairs were in the hands of the **LORD ADVOCATE** (who was responsible to the Home Secretary) or (from 1881) an Under-Secretary of State at the Home Office who was given specific responsibility for matters relating to Scotland. In 1926, however, Stanley Baldwin's Conservative government resurrected the post and appointed John Gilmour, MP for Pollok and an able administrator, to the position. The Secretary of State for Scotland has a place in the Cabinet and acts as head of the **SCOTTISH OFFICE.** In addition, he is responsible for the appointment of members to committees such as the **SCOTTISH ARTS COUNCIL.** (See **DONALD CAMPBELL DEWAR; MICHAEL FORSYTH; THOMAS JOHNSTON; IAN LANG; MALCOLM RIFKIND).**

SECRETARY OF STATE FOR WALES. The Secretary of State is the government minister responsible for Welsh affairs, acts as head of the **WELSH OFFICE** and has a seat in the Cabinet. The first appointment was made in 1964, at a time when the major political parties were concerned that a growing awareness of Wales's cultural identity was being reflected in increased support for **PLAID CYMRU,** the nationalist organization. (See **WILLIAM JEFFERSON HAGUE; RON DAVIES**).

SELECT COMMITTEES ON SCOTTISH AND WELSH AFFAIRS. During the late 1970s, the Labour government, under Prime Minister James Callaghan, established a series of Parliamentary committees which were intended to scrutinize the activities of the major departments of state. Initially, the **WELSH OFFICE** and the **SCOTTISH OFFICE** were omitted from these arrangements because it was expected that **DEVOLUTION** of power to elected assemblies in **CARDIFF** and **EDINBURGH** would render them unnecessary. However, early in 1979, referenda on the devolution proposals failed to gain the support necessary for implementation and, after the Conservative Party was elected to power in May of that year, select committees for Wales and Scotland were created on lines similar to those committees attached to the other government departments. They normally have 11 members, who represent the balance of political power in Westminster rather than in the **CELTIC FRINGE.** As a result, when Wales returned only six Conservative Party MPs amoung its 38 representatives to the House of Commons, the Conservative government was forced to nominate three members from English seats for the committee and face the inevitable accusations of colonial rule.

SETTLEMENT ACTS (Scotland, Ireland and Wales). There were three main acts affecting areas outside England:

Act of Settlement (Ireland), 1652. This was imposed by the Westminster Parliament on Ireland, and punished the participants in the **IRISH REBELLION** of 1641. One hundred leaders of the rebellion were executed, and their estates confiscated. Those who had killed an Englishman (except in battle) lost their estates and their lives, other military leaders lost two-thirds of their estates, members of the Parliamentary forces lost one-third of their estates and all confiscated lands were given to supporters of Oliver Cromwell. Those whose personal estate was valued less than £10 per annum were granted a free pardon.

Act of Settlement (Ireland), 1662. This attempt to mitigate the harshness of the 1652 Act was part of the **RESTORATION SETTLEMENT.** Protestant Irish adjudged to be innocent of rebellion regained their lands and innocent Catholics likewise, though in the latter case such arrangements rarely became reality, as the Protestant settlers had become too well entrenched, particularly in northern Ireland.

Act of Settlement and Explanation (Ireland), 1665. This legislation redistributed some of the land confiscated from Catholics and given to supporters of Cromwell, in order to compensate loyalists in Ireland. All contested or doubtful cases were to be found in favour of Protestants. (See **ACT OF EXPLANATION; TREATY OF LIMERICK**).

The Settlement Acts were the main legislative elements of the **PLANTATIONS OF ULSTER** policy.

SGIAN DUBH. The sgian dubh (**GAELIC** for *black knife*) is the dirk carried in the stocking of Scotsmen when wearing the **KILT**. It is a utility knife, rather than an armament, adopted between 1747 and 1782, when men in the **SCOTTISH HIGHLANDS** were banned from carrying weapons in an attempt by the Hanoverian government to prevent a repetition of the **JACOBITE REBELLION**s.

SHERIFF. A nonhereditary officer of the Crown, the Sheriff carried out the routine administration of a shire (a division of the royal estate). The main tasks involved collection of taxes and administration of justice. In Scotland, the Sheriff Courts are still an integral part of the **LEGAL SYSTEM**. (See **STATUTE OF RHUDDLAN**).

SHERIFFMUIR, BATTLE OF, 13 November 1715. Both sides claimed victory after this engagement, fought towards the end of the first **JACOBITE REBELLION. JOHN ERSKINE,** the Earl of Mar, led an army of 12,000 in support of **JAMES STUART,** and met the Duke of **ARGYLL**'s 3,300 royalists. It was an indecisive battle in the Ochil Hills, near **STIRLING,** each side losing about 500 men. Despite his numerical superiority, Mar exhibited poor tactical skills and decided to withdraw, abandoning his men to their fate. That action, along with the defeat at the Battle of Preston next day, effectively ended the rebellion.

SHETLAND ISLANDS. A group of some 100 islands lying about 130 miles north of the Scottish mainland, the Shetlands are one of the least accessible areas of Britain. Consisting of a complex of sedimentary, metamorphic and igneous rocks, which rarely rise above 1,000 feet, they were invaded, during the eigth and ninth centuries, by the Vikings, who ruled them until 1472, when they were annexed by the Scottish Crown. Until comparatively recent, the main occupations have been **CROFTING,** fishing, seafaring and the production of woollen goods (Fair Isle, which gave its name to a distinctive knitwear pattern, is one of the Shetland Islands). However, during the 1970s, the discovery of fossil fuels beneath the North Sea transformed the economy. Europe's largest oil and gas export terminal was opened at Sullom Voe in 1978, airport facilities were improved and harbours expanded. In addition, the influx of labour led to enhanced retail and service provision, notably in Lerwick, the islands' main settlement. Local authority income from the activities of the oil companies has been invested in a trust fund, which supports local charities and commercial enterprises. Tourism is also a source of employment, but the Shetlands are distant from major centres of population so the number of visitors is limited. There are air and sea connections to the Scottish mainlands and to Norway. (See **JARLSHOF**).

SHINTY. One of the traditional sports of the **SCOTTISH HIGHLANDS,** shinty bears some resemblance to hockey. Two teams of 12 players each try to score goals by hitting the ball (made of leather and cork) into their opponents' net with a stick (known as a caman). The side scoring most goals over a 90-minute period wins. Players can stop the ball with their feet and carry it on their caman. The earliest written records of the game date from the 14th and 15th centuries, but **GAELIC** legends tell of warriors playing matches long before then and it is likely that the sport was introduced to Scotland by the Irish (along with Christianity and the Gaelic language) some 2,000 years ago. In the late 19th century, the Camanachd Association was founded to standardize the rules and now about 40 teams compete in a variety of league and cup competitions, drawing crowds of up to 5,000 for major events. Until recently, the sport has been a male stronghold, but increasing numbers of women and girls are playing, particularly in school teams.

SIEGE OF LONDONDERRY (1689). On 17 April 1689, beginning a campaign to regain his throne, the exiled Roman Catholic King James VII and II besieged the town of Derry (now **LONDONDERRY**), which was held by supporters of the Protestant cause. Despite a lack of food and water, the ravages of disease and a hail of cannon balls, the settlement held out until it was relieved on 30 July. The 105-day siege was the last of its kind in Britain. (See **APPRENTICE BOYS**).

SILICON GLEN. Because of its popularity as a location for high-tcch industries, Scotland's central valley had become widely known as Silicon Glen. In 1991, **SCOTTISH ENTERPRISE** created a unit specifically to encourage firms involved in software development, with the result that by 1995, employment growth in that sector of the economy was three times the European average. In addition, Scotland had a higher proportion of students studying computer-related disciplines than any other region on the continent and wage costs were significantly lower than in other industrialised countries. **EDINBURGH,** the university campus at **STIRLING,** South Queensferry (on the **RIVER FORTH**) and the new towns of East Kilbride and Livingstone were favoured sites, attracting such multinational companies as IBM, GEC Marconi and Hewlett-Packard, as well as providing a base for small independent firms.

SIMPSON, JAMES YOUNG (1811–70). A pioneer in the use of anaesthetics, Simpson altered the course of medicine by employing chloroform to reduce the pain of childbirth. Born in Bathgate (Scotland) on 7 June 1811, the seventh son of banker David Simpson and his wife, Mary, he went to **EDINBURGH** University at the age of 14, studying arts and then medical sciences, and graduated in 1832. He was elected Senior President of the Royal Medical Society of Edinburgh in 1835 and, in 1840, was appointed Professor of Midwifery at the university. By 1847, he was using ether as an anaesthetic in obstetrics but was aware of its limitations and carried out a series of experiments on himself and his assistants in an effort to develop a more effective substitute. He discovered that chloroform was more efficient and published a full account of its effects, but his advocacy of the drug met with much resistance, both from the medical profession and from religious leaders, some of whom argued that it was a woman's duty to bring forth children in suffering. Only after it was administered to Queen Victoria during the birth of her ninth child, Prince Leopold, in 1853 did it gain widespread acceptance. Simpson continued to make contributions to other areas of gynaecology and, in 1866, was awarded a baronetcy in recognition of his work. He died in London on 6 May 1870.

SINN FEIN. This Irish National Party (the words are Gaelic for "We Ourselves") was formed in 1902 and rose to prominence during the **HOME RULE** crisis of 1913–14. Eamon de Valera, a commander in the **EASTER RISING,** became leader in 1917 but broke away with a group of supporters to form **FIANNA FAIL** in 1926. The rump membership, fundamentalist in attitude, continued to advocate a united, independent Ireland and the party became the political wing of the **IRISH REPUBLICAN ARMY** (IRA). In 1994, however, it announced that the IRA would forsake violence and call a ceasefire. Shortly afterwards, its leader held a much-publicized meeting with the Taoiseach of the Irish Republic (Albert Reynolds), who had refused to hold talks with the group while the killing continued. Three years later, following the Labour Party's General Election victory in May, 1997, it was admitted to formal multi-party talks on the future of Northern Ireland. (See **ANTI-PARTITION LEAGUE**; **FINE GAEL**; **GERARD ADAMS**; **PETER BROOKE**; **THE TROUBLES**; **ULSTER DECLARATION**).

SKARA BRAE. In 1850, a violent winter storm blew the turf and sediments from a sand dune on the **ORKNEY ISLANDS** and revealed a Neolithic settlement of nine dwellings which had been covered by gales some 5,000 years before. Because of their exposure to Atlantic winds, the Orkneys were virtually treeless when the buildings were constructed so domestic furnishings were carved from stone and were in an excellent state of preservation, allowing archaeologists to reconstruct the lifestyles of the inhabitants in considerable detail. For example, rectangular fireplaces could be seen on the floors of some of the huts. Stone structures beside the hearths have been interpreted as beds. Others, upright and fitted with compartments, are believed to have served as dressers. Wall recesses may have been cupboards and small clay-lined depressions in the ground may have been filled with sea water and used to keep shellfish fresh. The function of the settlement is still unclear.

SMITH, ADAM (1723–90). A political economist and philosopher, Smith exerted enormous influence on the development of economic and political theory in North America and Europe through his book *An Inquiry into the Nature and Causes of the Wealth of Nations* (1776). The exact date of his birth is unknown although the records show that he was the son of lawyer Adam Smith and his wife Margaret, and that he was baptized in Kirkcaldy on 5 June 1723. He was educated at the Universities of **GLASGOW** and Oxford then, in 1748, was appointed Lecturer in Rhetoric and Belles-Lettres at **EDINBURGH.** He returned to Glasgow as Professor of Logic in 1751, transferring to the chair of Moral Philosphy the following year and publishing his dissertation on the *Theory of Moral Sentiments* in 1759. In 1763, he resigned his university post to take up a position as tutor to the Duke of Buccleuch and, from 1764 until 1766, travelled with his young charge, primarily in France, where he discussed economics with some of Europe's leading scholars, including François Quesnay and Jacques Turgot.

On his return to Scotland, Smith began work on *The Wealth of Nations*, which was fundamental in creating the academic discipline of political economy. In the text, he stressed the advantages of a division of labour and advocated increased use of machinery as a means of improving levels of production in manufacturing industry. In addition, he made a persuasive case for free trade, arguing that government should facilitate the ability of every individual to compete in a market unrestricted by regulation. The result, he maintained, would be fair prices and maximum benefit to society. In 1778, he was appointed Commissioner of Customs in Scotland and, in 1787, became Rector of Glasgow University. During that time, he seems to have been working on one study of the theory and history of law and another on the arts and sciences, but shortly before he died in Edinburgh on 17 July 1790, he destroyed most of the manuscripts. *Essays on Philosophical Subjects*, published in 1795, contains material which may well have formed part of the second of these treatises. (See **SCOTTISH ENLIGHTENMENT**).

SMITH, JOHN (1938–94). Leader of the Labour Party from 1992 until 1994, Smith was born in Dalmally (Scotland) on 13 September 1938, the son of Archibald Smith a school headmaster and his wife, Sarah. He was educated at Dunoon Grammar School and **GLASGOW** University, where he studied law and, in 1960, was Chairman of the Labour Club. He was called to the Scottish Bar in 1967 and became a Queen's Counsel in 1983, displaying oratorical skills which had become evident as early as 1962, when he won a national debating competition organized by *The Observer* newspaper. He contested the East Fife Parliamentary constituency unsuccessfully in 1961 and 1964 but won at Lanarkshire North in 1970. Four years later, he was given his first government post — Parliamentary Private Secretary to Willie Ross, the **SECRETARY OF STATE FOR SCOTLAND.** He then became Under-Secretary of State at the Department of Energy during 1974–75 and Minister of State at the same department in 1975–76. From 1976 until 1978, he was Minister of State in the Privy Council Office (where he was responsible for piloting the Scotland and Wales **DEVOLUTION** bills through the House of Commons) and, in 1978–79, as Secretary of State for Trade, was the youngest member of Prime Minister James Callaghan's cabinet.

After Labour's General Election defeat in 1979, Smith acted as Party Spokesman on Trade, Prices and Consumer Protection until 1982 and on Energy during 1982–83. At the 1983 General Election, he was returned as Member of Parliament for Monklands East and given the employment brief. For three years from 1984, he had responsibility for issues relating to trade and industry then, in 1987, became Shadow Chancellor of the Exchequer. It appeared that his career might be cut short when he suffered from a heart attack the following year, but he recovered and returned to the House of Commons in 1989. At the 1992 election, he retained his seat with a majority of 15,712 and, when **NEIL KINNOCK** resigned after Labour's fourth consecutive defeat, was elected Leader of the Party.

In that role he frequently faced Prime Minister John Major in Parliamentary debate, with mixed success. His detractors alleged that he lacked the dynamism that would have enhanced his public image but supporters claimed that his quiet Scottish brogue, his calm demeanour and his middle-of-the road policies encouraged confidence. The accuracy of the latter's assessment was evident following his sudden death in London, following a heart attack, on 13 May 1994. There was universal regret at his passing, with even his political opponents praising his integrity. John Major described him as "one of the outstanding Parliamentarians of modern politics".

SNOWDONIA. The Snowdonian mountain mass, an eroded anticline consisting primarily of volcanic rocks, slates and gritstones formed some 445–510 million years ago during the Ordovician period, is located in northwest Wales. Snowdon (known in **WELSH** as Y Wyddfa, or The Viewpoint) is the highest mountain in the United Kingdom south of the **SCOTTISH HIGHLANDS,** reaching 3,560 feet above sea level. The area has been heavily glaciated, presenting a dramatic scenery of sculpted summits and steeply sided valleys, often with long, finger lakes. Although much of the land was once forested, the majority of the trees have been felled and the vegetation now consists largely of rough grassland, which provides feeding for hill sheep. Most of the area forms a national park, which covers some 845 square miles and is a focus for tourists, particularly climbers and hillwalkers. A rack-and-pinion railway climbs from the village of Llanberis to the top of Snowdon, but most of the people who reach the summit do so on foot, causing considerable problems of erosion in the fragile environment.

SOCCER. (See **FOOTBALL**).

SOCIAL DEMOCRATIC AND LABOUR PARTY (SDLP). The SDLP was founded in 1970 by Roman Catholic nationalists in Northern Ireland. It had consistently adopted a moderate stance, rejecting the terrorist campaign waged by the **IRISH REPUBLICAN ARMY (IRA),** supporting power sharing policies (see, for example, **NORTHERN IRELAND POWER SHARING EXECUTIVE)** and advocating closer links with the Irish Republic. Since 1979, it has been led by **JOHN HUME,** who is widely credited with negotiating the IRA ceasefire in 1994. In 1995, Jonathan Stephenson, the party's vice-president, urged his colleagues to broaden the organization's base by encouraging Protestants, young people and minority groups to join the fold. At the 1997 general election, the SDLP won three Parliamentary seats and gained 24.7 per cent of the popular vote. (See **GERRY FITT).**

SOLEMN LEAGUE AND COVENANT, September 1643. The Long Parliament and the **COVENANTERS** formed an alliance during the Civil War, the Scots providing an army on the understanding that, after the defeat of Charles I, **PRESBYTERIANISM** would be established in England. The covenant was crucial to the Parliamentary cause, ensuring Scottish support at the Battle of Marston Moor. (See **ENGAGERS; NATIONAL COVENANT).**

SOLWAY MOSS, BATTLE OF, 24–25 November 1542. This was a decisive defeat for the Scots, near Carlisle, at the hands of the forces of King Henry VIII, brilliantly led by Thomas Howard, Earl of Norfolk. At the time, Henry was determined to subdue **SCOTLAND** because of its continued support for France (see **AULD ALLIANCE)** and the cause of Roman Catholicism, and in order to release his own armies for foreign ventures. **JAMES V** precipitated the battle by invading England, but his army was weakened through the absence of many Scottish nobles who were reluctant to repeat the experience of the **BATTLE OF FLODDEN.** It is said that the defeat finally caused the death of King James on 14 December. (See **ROUGH WOOING).**

SOUTHERN UPLANDS. A succession of rolling hills rising to over 2,000 feet, the southern uplands stretch from west to east along Scotland's boundary with England, forming a natural barrier to transport. Bounded to the north by a fault line which crosses the country for 130 miles between Girvan (on the Atlantic coast) and Dunbar (on the **RIVER FORTH**), the hills consist largely of sedimentary rocks originally laid down during the Ordovician and Silurian periods, some 395 million to 510 million years ago. The folding of the strata, intrusion of volcanic material, further deposition, sculpting by ice and, most recently, the forces of rivers and rain have all helped to shape the scenery. The dominant agricultural activity is sheep farming, which has provided the foundation for a wool textile industry, particularly towards the east in towns such as Galashiels and Hawick. Arable and root crops are confined to the valleys and the coasts. Woodland cover is increasing as a result of reafforestation programmes begun during the 1980s and 1990s, but critics have complained of the loss of open landscape and of planting policies which stress economic gain from fast-growing conifers, which detract from the visual quality of the landscape. Tourism is a major source of income, with outdoor activities such as hillwalking and fishing attracting visitors. The medieval abbeys at Dryburgh (where **WALTER SCOTT** is buried), Jedburgh and Melrose also provide foci for holidaymakers. Apart from the production of knitwear, there is little manufacturing activity, but towns such as Dumfries, Moffat, Peebles and Berwick-upon-Tweed, which serve primarily as market and administrative centres, provide bases for some light industry. (See **THE BORDERS**).

ST ANDREWS. For many years the ecclesiastical heart of Scotland, St Andrews is located on the North Sea coast of Fife, some 13 miles southeast of **DUNDEE**. It dates from the sixth century, when the **CELTIC CHURCH** established a settlement on a rocky, windswept, sandstone headland near the estuary of the River Eden. Two hundred years later, the **PICTS** built a more substantial place of worship and dedicated it to **ST ANDREW,** whom they adopted as their patron saint. The site became a place of pilgrimage after relics of the saint were deposited in the Church and, by the tenth century, had acquired such celebrity that the bishop of the Scots moved his seat there from Dunkeld. Between 1127 and 1144, Augustinian monks began the construction of a cathedral and, about 1160, King **MALCOLM IV** granted the town the status of royal **BURGH.** In 1410, a university (Scotland's first) was founded, and, by the end of the century, the combination of educational, religious and commercial prestige had made St Andrews one of the most important towns in Scotland. The ecclesiastical importance waned following the Reformation, which led to the abandonment of the cathedral (now in ruins), and a lack of local coal reserves meant that the settlement never developed any significant manufacturing activity during the

Industrial Revolution. However, the university remained and provides a significant source of employment. Also, miles of sandy beach have attracted holidaymakers during the 20th century, and the pilgrims who once made their way to the shrine of St Andrew have been replaced by those who go to the Royal and Ancient **GOLF** Club (founded in 1742) and the links courses surrounding it. The town is also the administrative and market centre for eastern Fife.

ST KILDA. Lying in the Atlantic Ocean 110 miles west of the Scottish mainland, the seven cliff girt islands which make up St Kilda are one of the most remote parts of the British Isles. Until 1930, Hirta (the largest of the islands) was inhabited by a small community which lived by gathering seabirds (young gannets for food, young fulmars for oil and young puffins for meat and down). Sheep provided wool, and supplemented the meagre diet. Fishing was also important, but catches were limited by heavy seas, frequent storms and a paucity of landing places. In 1930, the last 36 inhabitants were evacuated at their own request, and the island was bought by the Marquis of Bute. In 1957, it was bequeathed to the **NATIONAL TRUST FOR SCOTLAND,** which is using parties of volunteers to reconstruct the village where most of the community lived. St Kilda, which houses the world's largest gannetry, was designated a world heritage site by UNESCO in 1987, the first Scottish location to be placed on the list.

STANDARD, BATTLE OF THE, 22 August 1138. This engagement was fought between the forces of King **DAVID I** of Scotland and an English army rallied by Thurston, Archbishop of York, from the local countryside near Northallerton in the County of Yorkshire. David had been mounting a series of raids into northern England, exploiting the anarchy and disorganization of King Stephen's reign, which had followed the death of Henry I and the ensuing disputed succession (David was an uncle of Queen Matilda, who was a rival to Stephen's claim to the throne). The Scottish force may have numbered 10,000 men, while the Anglo-Norman force was nearer 8,000, and ably led in the field by William, Count of Aumale. The Scots were defeated, being less well equipped and suffering heavy casualties from the English archers. The battle takes its name from the banners or standards of St Peter of York, St Wilfred of Ripon, and St John of Beverley, carried by the English on a wagon in the thick of the battle to denote the sense of holy war engendered by the Archbishop amidst rumours that the Scots were intent on slave taking.

STEEL OF AIKWOOD, LORD. (See **DAVID MARTIN SCOTT STEEL**).

STEEL, DAVID MARTIN SCOTT (1938–). Leader of the Liberal Party from 1976 until 1988, Steel was born in **EDINBURGH** on 31 March 1938, the son of the Very Rev David Steel (Moderator of the General Assembly of the **CHURCH OF SCOTLAND** in 1974–75) and his wife Sheila. He was educated at the Prince of Wales School in Nairobi, at George Watson's College (Edinburgh) and at Edinburgh University, where he was president of the Liberal Club in 1959 and of the Students' Representative Council in 1960. From 1962 until 1964, he was Assistant Secretary of the Scottish Liberal Party and, in 1964–65, worked as an interviewer with BBC Television. He unsuccessfully contested the constituency of Roxburgh, Selkirk and Peebles in 1964 but won the seat at a by-election the following year, becoming the youngest Member of Parliament at the time. In 1967, he introduced a private member's bill which would allow women to have an abortion if two doctors confirmed the need on medical grounds and steered it to fruition as the Abortion Act. From 1970 until 1975, he was Liberal Chief Whip and, in 1976 (following Jeremy Thorpe's resignation), was elected Leader of the Party, the first to gain the office as the result of a poll of supporters outside Parliament.

In 1977, Steel became the youngest member of the Privy Council, and it was clear that his moderate policies, boyish good looks and approachable personality appealed to many voters. He negotiated a Lib-Lab Pact with James Callaghan's minority Labour Party government and, in 1982, formed an alliance with the new Social Democratic Party, sharing leadership of the group with David Owen until 1988. However, despite his own public prestige and a quarter of the popular vote, the alliance returned to Parliament after the 1983 General Election with only 23 seats — a result of the lack of any geographical concentration of support. Immediately after the 1987 election, he called for a full merger of the Liberals with the SDP and announced that he would not stand for leadership of the new party. Instead, he accepted the role of Foreign Affairs Spokesman for the Liberal Democratic Party, formed the following year. In 1989, he campaigned unsuccessfully for a seat in the European Parliament as representative for Central Italy and, in 1993, announced his intention to retire from politics.

Among his other activities, Steel has introduced religious programmes on television (1966–67, 1969 and 1971–76), acted as President of the Anti-Apartheid Movement in Great Britain (1966–69) and been Chairman of the Scottish Advisory Council of Shelter. He was Rector of Edinburgh University from 1982 until 1985 and Chubb Fellow at Yale in 1987. Since 1991, he has been a Director of Border Television. He published his autobiography — *Against Goliath: David Steel's Story* — in 1989, was knighted (KBE) in 1990 and was promoted to the House of Lords as Lord Steel of Aikwood in 1997.

STEVENSON, ROBERT LOUIS BALFOUR (1850–94). A novelist, poet, story writer and essayist, Stevenson was born in **EDINBURGH** on 13 November 1870, the only son of Thomas Stevenson (Engineer to the Board of Northern Lighthouses) and his wife, Margaret Isabella Balfour. Sickly from birth, his education was much interrupted by illness but he entered Edinburgh University in 1866 with the intention of pursuing a career at the Bar. In 1875, he qualified as an **ADVOCATE** but, by that time, his teenage interest in writing had flourished and a series of essays and reviews, followed by *An Inland Voyage* (1878) and *Travels with a Donkey* (1879), was bringing him to the notice of literary society. In 1876, he met Fanny Vandergrift Osbourne, an American separated from her husband, and fell in love. He followed her to the United States (the story of his travels is told in *Across the Plains* and *The Amateur Emigrant*, published in 1892 and 1895 respectively) and, in 1880, married her. The couple returned to Scotland, where Stevenson discovered he had tuberculosis. Over the next few years, they travelled much of Europe in search of a cure, and, during that time, he completed *Treasure Island* (1883), his first full-length novel and a work which established his reputation as an adventure writer. By the spring of 1885, he was seriously ill and settled for a time in Bournemouth. The period there (from January 1886 until July 1887) was a fruitful one in terms of literary output: he revised *A Child's Garden of Verses* (which had first appeared in 1885) and wrote *Kidnapped* (the first of his Scottish romances) and *The Strange Case of Dr Jekyll and Mr Hyde* (both published in 1886).

In 1887, still seeking a remedy for his tuberculosis, Stevenson returned to the United States, where publishers competed in attempts to persuade him to sign contracts. For a time, he lived in the vicinity of Saranac Lake, where he began *The Master of Ballantrae* (1889), but, in June 1888, set sail from San Francisco, accompanied by his wife, his mother and his stepson. The voyage was intended to be a vacation, but he never returned. For over two years, the little group wandered the South Seas, eventually settling in Samoa, where he became known as Tusitala (The Storyteller). Works written during that time included *Catriona* (published in the United States as *David Balfour* in 1893), *The Ebb-Tide* (1894) and the unfinished *Weir of Hermiston* (1896). He died suddenly of a cerebral haemorrhage at Vailima on 3 December 1894. Since then, his reputation has fluctuated. Although much lauded by his contemporaries, the pendulum swung soon after his death, and he was increasingly regarded as a second-rate writer of children's fiction. More recent scholarship, however, has restored him to his pedestal, emphasizing the originality of his prose and the moral subtlety of his adventure stories.

STEWARTS. (See **STUARTS**).

STIRLING. Throughout the Middle Ages, Stirling was at the centre of Scotland's struggle for independence from English rule. (See **BATTLE OF BANNOCKBURN; BATTLE OF SHERIFFMUIR; BATTLE OF STIRLING BRIDGE**). Its castle, one of the most imposing in the United Kingdom, stands atop the neck of an extinct volcano and commands routeways along the **RIVER FORTH** from **EDINBURGH** (37 miles east) to the **SCOTTISH HIGHLANDS**. The early history of the site is unknown, but there is evidence that King **DAVID I** made the settlement a royal **BURGH** sometime between 1124 and 1127 and that, in 1226, **ALEXANDER II** confirmed the trading privileges associated with that status. (In 1997, five bodies believed to date from the 12th century were found during excavations at the castle). A market developed downhill from the castle, separated from the fortification by the houses of the nobles and dominated by the Church of the Holy Rude, where **MARY, QUEEN OF SCOTS,** and her son, James VI and I were crowned in 1543 and 1567, respectively. However, following the **UNION OF THE CROWNS** in 1603, the royal court moved to London and there was no longer any need for easily defended strongholds. Stirling lost much of its prestige, and many of the large houses, built by the aristocracy, were subdivided for poorer families. Broad Street, the location for the market, became a stinking slum where infectious disease spread readily. Following the arrival of the railway in 1848, commerce moved to the flat lands at the base of the hill, and Stirling developed as an administrative centre, building on its commercial expertise and serving the coal-mining and manufacturing towns of the central valley of Scotland as well as much of the agricultural area of the southern highlands. From 1953, programmes of urban improvement raised the quality of the urban fabric and development is now greatly influenced by conservation legislation. For example, building to the west of the castle is rarely permitted because it might spoil the view. Tourism is a significant source of income and employment (the castle alone gets some 300,0000 visitors each year). The town is also an educational centre (with a university established in 1967), the headquarters of **LOCAL GOVERNMENT** for the surrounding area, a location for sittings of the **HIGH COURT OF JUSTICIARY** and an important retail complex (the shopping hinterland stretches as far as Oban and Fort William, over 90 miles away).

STIRLING BRIDGE, BATTLE OF, 11 September 1297. King Edward I temporarily subdued Scotland until, in 1297, **WILLIAM WALLACE** and Andrew Moray led a rebellion against **JOHN BALLIOL,** the puppet king. The two sides met in battle outside **STIRLING,** at the bridge over the **RIVER FORTH,** where the rebels outmanoeuvred the overconfident 300-strong English cavalry and 10,000 infantry led by John de Warrene, Earl of Surrey. Five thousand of the invaders were slaughtered and the body of Hugh de Cressingham, one of their leaders, was subsequently skinned by the Scottish forces. The victory, for a time, freed Scotland from English rule. The exact location of the bridge eluded historians for centuries because the structure, they thought, was destroyed during the fighting. However, in 1997, divers found masonry believed to come from one of the piers.

STONE OF DESTINY. Known in Scotland as the Stone of **SCONE** and associated by legend with the prophet Jacob, who took a boulder for a pillow (Genesis, Chapter 28), and with **ST COLUMBA,** this was the rock on which Scottish kings were crowned until it was seized by King Edward I of England in 1296. A 450-pound slab of Old Red Sandstone, it was incorporated into a wooden chair in the early 14th century and has been used at the coronation of English and British sovereigns ever since. It was stolen from Westminster by Scottish nationalist students in 1950 but replaced in the Abbey in 1952 (though it was widely believed in Scotland that the stone returned was not the one taken). In 1996, **MICHAEL FORSYTH,** the **SECRETARY OF STATE FOR SCOTLAND,** announced that the Stone of Destiny would be returned to its homeland and, on 31 November (**ST ANDREW**'s day), it was placed in **EDINBURGH** Castle. The media, however, interpreted the event as a political gesture by an unpopular government in the dying months of its administration and public interest was muted.

STONE OF SCONE. (See **STONE OF DESTINY**).

STORMONT. Stormont Castle, near **BELFAST,** was the seat of Northern Ireland's parliament from the establishment of the province in 1922 until the legislative was suspended fifty years later. It is now the base for the UK's **DIRECT RULE** of **ULSTER** from London. Stormont lies in 300 acres of parkland about four miles east of **BELFAST** city centre. The administrative complex comprises the Parliament Buildings (designed by Sir Arnold Thornley in the Greek classical style and completed in 1928), Stormont Castle (the office of the **SECRETARY OF STATE FOR NORTHERN IRELAND)** and Stormont House (formerly the residence of the Speaker of the Northern Ireland House of Commons). It now houses the **NORTHERN IRELAND OFFICE,** through which the British government administers the province. (See **DEVOLUTION**).

STUART, CHARLES EDWARD (1720–88). One of the great romantic heroes of Scottish history, Bonnie Prince Charlie (the Young Pretender) was the elder son of **JAMES STUART** (the Old Pretender) and Maria Clementina Sobieska. Born in Rome on 31 December 1720, he was the last serious **STUART** claimant to the British throne. A handsome man, he spoke four languages and had a tough physique. In 1744, his father named him Prince Regent and sent him to Paris to promote French plans for an invasion of Britain. Bad weather and the threat of a strong navy presence in the English Channel resulted in the abandonment of the scheme, but Charles, in the headstrong Stuart tradition, decided to go it alone. He pawned his mother's rubies to raise funds and set out from Nantes in June 1745 with 700 men in two ships. One of the vessels turned back, damaged after an encounter with an English man-of-war, but Charles persevered and landed at Eriskay, in the Outer **HEBRIDES,** on 23 July. From there, he sailed to Loch nan Uamh, on the west coast of Scotland and, on 19 August, raised his standard in Glenfinnan, beginning the second **JACOBITE REBELLION.**

Although some of the **CLAN** chiefs shunned him, as did the bulk of the **PRESBYTERIANS** (who deplored his Roman Catholic convictions), within a week he had gathered 2,000 followers. On 20 August, the army set off south, taking Perth on 4 September and **EDINBURGH** on 17 September. The first major confrontation with the government forces, led by Sir John Cope, took place at the **BAT-**

TLE OF PRESTONPANS on 21 September: the Hanoverian troops were routed. Early in November, the **JACOBITES** marched into England and, by 4 December, had reached Derby, virtually unchallenged. By that time, however, the Highlanders were far from home and many had deserted. Moreover, their officers were divided by personal jealousies, and the promised support from England and France had not materialized. After much debate, Charles decided to retreat and, on 6 December, turned north, closely pursued by the Duke of Cumberland.

By April, he had reached **INVERNESS** and, despite advice that his depleted, exhausted, hungry army should be allowed to take to the hills and adopt a strategy of guerilla warfare, insisted on facing the Hanoverian forces in full-scale battle. The two sides met at the **BATTLE OF CULLODEN** on 16 April 1646. The Pretender's ill-prepared and ill-equipped men were cut down in droves by the fitter, better-trained, regular soldiers. And the Stuart cause died with them. Charles skulked in caves and glens for five months, accompanied by a handful of supporters, with a £30,000 reward on his head. In September, two French ships reached Loch nan Uamh, where he had arrived with such high hopes the previous year, and took him to safety on the continent. His exploits had earned him a reputation as a folk hero, but he quarrelled with his father over his brother Henry's elevation to the position of Cardinal in the Catholic church and with Louis XV of France over the terms of French support for a new invasion attempt. When Britain and France made peace at Aix-la-Chapelle in 1748, both nations agreed that Charles should be expelled. He refused to go, was arrested and, on 17 December, was taken to the border. He then disappeared, but is known to have been in London in 1750, attempting to raise money for a new tilt at the throne. On his father's death in 1766, he went to live in Rome, but the Catholic powers in Europe saw no cause to support his claims. Moreover, by that time, his vanity, boasting and drunkenness had destroyed the image of the young gallant.

In 1772, he married Princess Louise de Stolberg, but the match was childless and unhappy. Alone and ill, he sent for Charlotte, his daughter by his mistress, Clementina Walkenshaw. Charlotte reconciled him with his brother and looked after him until he died in Rome on 31 January 1788. (See **BLAIR CASTLE; FLORA MAC-DONALD**).

STUART, JAMES FRANCIS EDWARD (1688–1766). James Stuart (the Old Pretender), was accorded the titles of James VIII of Scotland and James III of England by the **JACOBITES.** Born on 10 June 1688 in London, he was the son of James VII and II and Mary of Modena. His unexpected appearance raised the spectre of a Roman Catholic successor to the throne and, in large part, led to the Glorious Revolution later the same year (the circumstances surrounding his birth, and its consequences, are the source of the nursery rhyme *Rock-a-bye-baby*). At the time, there were rumours that the child was an imposter (none of the Queen's previous five children, all born more than six years earlier, had survived) and that it had been smuggled into Mary's bed in a warming pan, but scholars now accept that these tales were unfounded.

James spent most of his youth in France, but he fervently believed that he was the rightful King both of Scotland and of England and was recognized as such by Louis XIV when James VII and II died in 1702. Queen Anne, who succeeded to both thrones on the death of William III in 1702, almost certainly wanted James Stuart to succeed her, but he found the condition that he must renounce his Roman Catholic faith unacceptable. Unable to make progress by diplomacy, he turned to force and left France for Scotland in the spring of 1708 in the hope of raising an army. His ship reached the **RIVER FORTH** safely but was forced back to sea by an English fleet and eventually returned to France.

For some years, he fought with the French army, distinguishing himself at the Battle of Oudenarde (1708) and the Battle of Malplaquet (1709), but the terms of the Treaty of Utrecht (which ended the War of the Spanish Succession in 1713) stipulated that he would have to leave France. He retired to Lorraine but set out for Scotland again in 1715, when **JOHN ERSKINE,** Earl of Mar, led the first **JACOBITE REBELLION.** After landing at Peterhead on 22 December, he headed for a coronation ceremony at **SCONE,** but his dreams were to be dashed again. Though Bobbing John Mar had amassed an army of 12,000 men, he was no general. The town of Perth was taken, but **STIRLING** and **EDINBURGH** resisted, and a raid into England petered out at Preston. A battle against the government troops at the **BATTLE OF SHERIFFMUIR** on 13 November was indecisive and the Highlanders who had rallied to the Jacobite cause, lacking decisive leadership and seeing little progress, began to head for home. By early 1716, the rebel army had disintegrated, and, in February, James was forced to flee to France again.

Stuart never returned to the lands he claimed to rule, but he did continue to seek sponsorship for an invasion to restore his Crowns. In 1719, Spain prepared a fleet in support of his cause but, after setting sail from Cadiz, most of the ships were driven back by storms in the Bay of Biscay. The small force which did reach Scotland surrendered at Glenshiel. That was the final throw of the dice. For the remainder of his life, James lived in Rome. On 1 September 1719, he married Maria Clementina Sobieska, the granddaughter of King John III of Poland. She gave him two sons — **CHARLES EDWARD STUART** (Bonnie Prince Charlie) in 1720 and Henry Stuart in 1725 — but the marriage was as disastrous as most of James's other activities and Maria retired to a convent for two years between 1725 and 1727. James himself had health problems and gradually Jacobites began to look to his elder son for leadership. He died on 1 January 1766 and was buried in St Peter's Church in Rome with all the dignity due to a sovereign, but by that time the Jacobite cause was lost.

STUART, JOHN CRICHTON (1793–1848). Stuart, the second Marquess of Bute, deserves much of the credit for turning **CARDIFF,** the capital of Wales, into one of the major British centres of industrial activity during the 19th century. The elder son of John, the first Marquess, and his wife, Elizabeth, he succeeded to the title at the age of only six months following his father's death as a result of a riding accident. He spent his early years in Scotland, being cared for by his mother at her family home in Dumfries, but, after her death in 1797 and that of his grandmother two years later, he moved between the Bute residences in England and the mainland of Europe then, from 1809 until 1814, spent much time travelling on the continent. At 21, he took over control of the estates left to him by his father and his maternal grandfather, the Earl of Dumfries, but an eye disease which troubled him throughout his life made reading and writing difficult so he left many of the day-to-day management tasks to others. However, he had developed a keen interest in land improvement and development and, guided by David Stewart, his Estate Surveyor, began to consider the possibility of building dock facilities at Cardiff in order to facilitate the export of coal from his properties in South Wales. A plan was prepared by engineer James Green in 1828, revised by **THOMAS TELFORD** the following year and approved by Parliament in 1830.

Construction was delayed because the projected costs were such that Bute, one of the richest men in Britain, was faced with investing almost his entire fortune in the scheme. In the end, he decided to accept the risks, and building works began in 1837. The Bute West Dock opened in 1839 but, for the first few years, was plagued by problems. Faulty workmanship necessitated the closure of some sections in 1840 so that repairs could be carried out, the chief contractor (Daniel Storms) went bankrupt and some of the first port officials had to be sacked for embezzlement or inefficiency. However, by 1843, the quays were all operational and, by the end of the century, they had turned Cardiff into one of the world's major ports.

Bute's interests were not confined to the promotion of commerce. Although he was a poor orator, he spoke regularly in the House of Lords, arguing the causes of Roman Catholic emancipation, greater freedom for the Jewish community and the abolition of slavery within British territories abroad. He also advocated the repeal of the corn laws but, more conservatively, championed the causes of the established Church and opposed Parliamentary reforms. Also, he acted as Queen Victoria's High Commissioner to the General Assembly of the **CHURCH OF SCOTLAND** between 1842 and 1846, receiving much praise for his conduct at the time of the **DISRUPTION OF THE CHURCH OF SCOTLAND.**

When he died on 18 March 1848, his passing was hardly mentioned by *The Times*, primarily because his eye ailment had restricted his hunting, shooting and other aristocratic activities so he was little known on the London scene. However, in Wales the press went to town, lauding him for his contribution to the creation of wealth and employment in Cardiff. He was buried at Kirtling (near Cambridge) and his estates passed to his son, also John, who used some of the proceeds to reconstruct Cardiff Castle.

STUART, MARY. (See **MARY, QUEEN OF SCOTS**).

STUARTS. The Stuarts ruled Scotland from 1371 until 1714 and England from 1603 until 1714. Originally, the name was spelled *Stewart* but, during the reign of Mary Queen of Scots, when there was much contact between Scotland and France, the forms *Stuart* and *Steuart* became common because the French alphabet does not contain the letter *w*. The family can be traced to 11th-century Brittany, where it provided stewards to the counts of Dol. It arrived in Scotland about 1136, when Walter, third son of Alan (the fourth steward of Dol), entered the service of King **DAVID II**. Alexander Stewart, Walter's eldest son, inherited the island of Bute (see **JOHN CRICHTON STUART**) through his marriage to Jean (daughter of James, Lord of Bute), and fought against the Vikings at the **BATTLE OF LARGS** (1263). His grandson, also Walter, commanded part of the Scottish army at the **BATTLE OF BANNOCKBURN** (1314), earning the reward of a knighthood on the field from King **ROBERT THE BRUCE.** The following year, Sir Walter married Marjorie, Bruce's daughter, and, in 1371, their only child became **ROBERT II,** the first Stuart monarch. The dynasty was plagued by ill-fortune and prone to grandiose gestures, providing some of the great romances and tragedies of Scottish history. Of the 13 crowned heads who were to follow Robert, six died brutal deaths, and, as a result, seven in succession took the throne as minors, leaving Scotland's nobles to squabble over control of the kingdom. The direct male line ended with **JAMES V,** who was succeeded by **MARY, QUEEN OF SCOTS,** his infant daughter. Her only son, **JAMES VI,** united Scotland and England under one sovereign in 1603 (see **UNION OF THE CROWNS**). The line ended in 1714, when Queen Anne died childless, and was replaced by the Hanoverians, who survived the challenges of the exiled **JAMES STUART** (The Old Pretender) and **CHARLES EDWARD STUART** (Bonnie Prince Charlie). The legitimate royal line of Stuarts ended in 1807 with the death of Henry, James's younger son, who left no heirs. (See **ROBERT III; JAMES I–IV.**)

SUNNINGDALE AGREEMENT, 1973–74. This agreement between the British, Irish and Northern Ireland (executive-designate) governments created a Council of Ireland to discuss matters of mutual concern in **ULSTER.** The concord had been negotiated on the United Kingdom's behalf by Edward Heath's Conservative Party government but it was bitterly opposed by the Loyalist community, who argued that it weakened British sovereignty in the province (Britain had agreed to unification of Ireland, but only if the majority in Ulster concurred with the change: until then, Northern Ireland was to remain part of the United Kingdom). A general strike, called in protest, virtually closed down the Northern Irish economy until 1974 when the Labour Party won the General Election and refused to recognize the agreement. It was superseded, in 1985, by the **ANGLO-IRISH AGREEMENT** and followed, in 1993, by the **ULSTER DECLARATION.** (See **DEVOLUTION; THE TROUBLES**).

SWANSEA. A seaport lying at the mouth of the River Tawe, some 40 miles northwest of **CARDIFF,** Swansea is one of the principal cities in south Wales. The settlement originally developed around a castle, built by Henry de Newburgh during the Norman occupation of Britain in the early 11th century, but its growth stems largely from the 18th century, when copper smelting, the manufacture of earthenware and the export of coal provided the foundation for a growing industrial economy. A 17-mile canal, completed in 1798, linked the harbour to the coal fields and port expansion programmes (which followed the diversion of the river in 1845) enhanced the attractiveness of the site to manufacturers. Steel, copper, tinplate and zinc production all provided employment as, from 1918, did oil refining. Ships arriving at the harbour brought crude oil, grain, metal ores (notably copper, iron and nickel), rubber and timber. Coal (particularly anthracite), coke, refined oil, manufactured goods and tinplate dominated the export trade. Swansea suffered badly from enemy action during the Second World War, especially in February 1941, when most of its commercial core was destroyed by air raids. Also, the decline in demand for heavy industrial goods during the national recession of the 1970s and 1980s caused considerable unemployment. However, the planning authorities have had some success in attracting new, light industry (particularly to the east of the city) and the rebuilt shopping area provides retail facilities for a wide hinterland. Swansea is also a centre for university and technical education, a headquarters of one of the unitary **LOCAL GOVERNMENT** authorities established in 1996 and a bishopric of the **CHURCH IN WALES.** At the time of the 1991 census, it had a population of 174,000.

—T—

TACKSMAN. This term is derived from the Old Scottish word *tack,* meaning lease or tenure of land, or interests in any customs or taxes derived from land. Essentially, the tacksmen were middlemen, leasing land from **CLAN** chiefs and major landholders, subletting to small farmers, and administering estates. They were much involved in the **HIGHLAND CLEARANCES** and often loathed for their self-interest and harsh rent-collecting methods.

TAFF VALE CASE, 1900–1901. A strike against the Taff Vale Railway Company led to a court case in which it was concluded that trade unions could be sued for damages by a company against which they were striking. (Injunctions were used to prevent picketing and union funds were confiscated in the dispute). The case led to increased emphasis on political activity by the labour unions and to the important swelling of membership of the Labour Representation Committee, which, in 1906, became the Labour Party.

TANISTRY. Leaders of Celtic societies (particularly in Scotland and Ireland) were elected by an assembly of all family heads. They had to be adult, possess all their mental faculties and have no physical deformity. Once appointed, they held the position for life. The same assembly appointed a tanist (or heir) — the eldest and most worthy man of the same blood (that could be the new leader's son but might also be a brother, nephew or cousin). The system was abolished in Scotland during the reign of **JAMES I** and replaced by the English practice of primogeniture. Tanistry prevented children from inheriting the role of chief but led to much conflict between families, each of which believed that its representative should be chosen.

TARTAN. Although check patterns which involve repetition of a basic design (or sett) were common in many parts of the world, tartans are now widely regarded as distinctively Scottish. They are produced by weaving coloured threads in stripes which cross at right angles; the strands stretched by the loom are known as the warp and those which pass over and under them as the weft or woof. The earliest pictorial representations of tartan dress date from the 17th century, and by 1747 it had become a sufficiently significant element of clothing in the **SCOTTISH HIGHLANDS** for its use to be proscribed by the Hanoverian government in the wake of the second **JACOBITE REBELLION.** It is not at all certain, however, that, by that time, individual **CLANS** had adopted distinctive tartans: there are several portraits of the period which show individuals wearing a variety of designs. Although the ban on wearing tartan was not lifted until 1782, during the period of proscription its use was permitted to members of regiments of the British Army raised in the Highlands. These regiments began a process of standardization, ensuring that all men were dressed in the same pattern and colours, and their uniforms were later adopted by many private citizens. During the early years of the 19th century, the writings of Sir **WALTER SCOTT** fuelled enormous interest in matters Scottish, and, when King **GEORGE IV** donned the **KILT** for his state visit to **EDINBURGH** in 1822, it was clear that tartan had been accepted by the aristocracy. Queen Victoria's love affair with Scotland (see **BALMORAL CASTLE**) emphasized the fashion and a host of tartans was invented to meet public demand. Many of these were given clan names and, not surprisingly, were adopted by people with the appropriate surname. Frequently, different manufacturers used the same name for very different designs, allowing some individuals a choice of colour schemes. Gradually, the brighter coloured setts became known as dress tartans and the more muted patterns as hunting tartans (many dress tartans are readily identifiable by the large amount of white in the pattern, as with the Dress Stewart, the tartan adopted by the Royal Family). Later, improvements in the manufacture and use of dyes allowed the threadmakers to tone down the bolder colours and the weavers to produce more subdued checks, which became known as ancient tartans. Designs are still being produced and now include an American **ST ANDREW**'s tartan and one for each of the Canadian provinces. They are recorded by the Scottish Tartans Society.

TAY BRIDGE DISASTER. During a storm on the night of 28 December, 1879, the railway bridge connecting **DUNDEE** to Fife, across the River Tay, collapsed under a train. Seventy-five passengers and crew were killed. The two mile long bridge, designed by Thomas Bouch (who received a knighthood for his work), had 85 spans and was 88 feet high. It had been opened only the previous year. The official enquiry into the disaster published the results of its findings in 1880 and placed the blame squarely on Bouch (who had not made sufficient allowance for wind pressure on the structure) and the contractors (who, left unsupervised, had used imperfect metal castings). Bouch died on 30 October the same year, his health undermined by the effects of the accident and its aftermath. A new bridge was built in 1887, only a few yards west of the first, the stumps of which can still be seen.

TELFORD, THOMAS (1757–1834). A civil engineer and architect, who laid foundations for the Industrial Revolution through the construction of roads, bridges and canals, Telford was born in Westerkirk (Dumfries) on 9 August 1757. He attended the village school but learned little more than basic literacy and numeracy before being apprenticed to a stonemason at the age of 14. He worked in Dumfries and **EDINBURGH** until 1782, when he moved to London to assist in the building of Somerset House. From there he went to Portsmouth (1784) and then to Shropshire, where he was appointed Surveyor of Public Works (1787). He became Agent and Engineer with the Ellesmere Canal Company in 1793 and solved the problem of crossing the valleys of the River Ceiriog and the River Dee by constructing two cast-iron aqueducts, feats which brought him much public acclaim. In 1801, he returned to Scotland to undertake a series of government projects, which included the cutting of the route for the Caledonian Canal between Fort William and **INVERNESS.** At the same time, he embarked on road improvements between

Shrewsbury, Chester and Holyhead, incorporating the Menai Straits and River Conway suspension bridges in his plans. As the expansion of the railways threatened the canal companies' freight operations, his skills were increasingly sought by entrepreneurs keen to make water transport more attractive (for example, he designed a tunnel at Harecastle for the Trent and Mersey Canal). He was also responsible for the design of St Katharine Dock on the River Thames in London and for the Gota Canal in Sweden. His contribution to transport was recognized by his colleagues, who made him the first President of the Institute of Civil Engineers (1818). He died in London on 2 September 1834.

TEST ACT. In 1681, the **THREE ESTATES** enacted legislation which required all holders of public office to reject Roman Catholicism, swear to maintain the Protestant faith and recognize the absolute power of the Crown (thereby rejecting those clauses of the **NATIONAL COVENANT** which advocated a Parliament free to take decisions without royal interference). The provisions of the Act split the country and many prominent individuals (including Sir James Dalrymple, President of the Court of Session) opted for exile rather than deny their beliefs. (See **APOLOGETICAL DECLARATION**).

THANE. The functions of the Thane were similar to those of the **SHERIFF**, but the office was hereditary and was particularly common in Scotland.

THOMAS, DYLAN MARLAIS (1914–53). A passionate and often difficult poet, Dylan Thomas was born in **SWANSEA** on 27 October 1914, the only son of David and Florence Thomas. He attended the local grammar school, where his father taught English, but left at the age of 16 to work as a trainee journalist on the *South Wales Evening Post*. Inevitably, his rebellious, flamboyant personality annoyed the guardians of Welsh convention, and, in 1934, he went to London, where he earned money by broadcasting, writing and film making and spent it in fashionable drinking clubs. He was unable to rid himself of his roots, however, and shortly after his marriage to Caitlin Macnamara, in 1937, returned to Laugharne (near Carmarthen). The poetry and stories he wrote at that time reflect his exuberant, restless lifestyle — introspective, surrealistic and obsessed with sexual and religious themes (see, for example, *Twenty-Five Poems*, published in 1936, and *The Map of Love*, which appeared in 1939).

Thomas was medically unfit for national service during the Second World War and spent his time writing film scripts from homes in London, Cardiganshire and Oxfordshire, eventually returning to Laugharne in 1949. The autobiographical short stories, *Portrait of the Artist as a Young Dog* (1940), were published during this itinerant period, recalling his youth in Swansea, and by the time *Deaths and Entrances* went on sale in 1946 he had built up a considerable following, which admired his romantic, rhetorical style, his mysticism and his depiction of relationships with the natural world. *Collected Poems 1934–52* (1952) was another success, partly because Thomas was still something of an antihero as a result of his wild living, hard-drinking lifestyle, partly because his radio broadcasts and popularity with student groups kept him close to his market and partly because his public seemed fascinated by the paradoxes of a man given to hedonism but proclaiming a deepening Christian faith. He was also much appreciated in the United States, where he died, on 9 November 1953, shortly after taking part in a reading of *Under Milk Wood*, the radio play which describes life in a Welsh village and his best known work.

THOMSON, WILLIAM (1824–1907). One of the most remarkable of 19th-century British physicists, Thomson made major contributions to pure as well as to applied science. He was born in **BELFAST** on 26 June 1824 but, at the age of eight, moved with his family to **GLASGOW** following his father's appointment to the post of Professor of Mathematics at the University there. In 1841, he became a student at Cambridge University and, after graduating in 1845, went to work in Paris with Henri Regnault, investigating the thermal properties of steam. In 1846, still only 22, he was appointed Professor of Mathematics and Natural Philosophy at Glasgow University, where he stayed for the next 53 years while his fertile mind led him into explorations of a vast range of scientific nooks and crannies. In 1848, stimulated by a meeting with physicist James Prescott Joule, he developed an absolute scale of temperature, which was based on the principles of thermodynamics and measured in °K (degrees Kelvin). Three years later, he outlined the fundamental relationships between heat loss and energy conservation which became known as the second law of thermodynamics (which states that that it is not possible for heat to be converted to mechanical energy without any flow of heat to a cooler body).

By 1854, Thomson had become interested in submarine telegraphy and had demonstrated, mathematically, that the speed of signalling along a lengthy cable must be inversely proportional to the square of that cable's length. He was consulted on the problems encountered during the laying of the first transatlantic cable in 1857-58 and subsequently carried out a series of experiments designed to improve the efficiency with which messages were transmitted. In the course of these studies, he invented the mirror galvanometer and the siphon recorder, which he patented in 1867 making him a wealthy man. He also redesigned the ship's compass, developed a mechanism which calculated the depth of water by measuring its pressure, invented a tide predictor and a tide guage, perfected tables which helped locate the position of a ship on the high seas and published over 300 scientific papers. His own company, Kelvin and White, manufactured the gadgets he invented.

Thomson's achievements were widely recognized. He was knighted in 1866, elected President of the Royal Society in 1890, raised to the peerage as Baron Kelvin of Largs in 1892, awarded the Order of Merit in 1902 and appointed Chancellor of Glasgow University in 1904. He died at his home near Largs on 17 December 1907 and was buried in Westminster Abbey (London) beside Sir Isaac Newton.

THREE ESTATES. Scotland's Parliament was known as the Three Estates because the ecclesiastical, military and mercantile power bases of the realm were represented through the bishops, the nobles and the freemen of the **BURGH**s. The Estates first appears in the historical records during the reign of King **DAVID II,** wielding considerable power because the monarch was more interested in pleasure than in government. Members of the Parliament, although subject to the King, were responsible for administering justice, shaping foreign policy, controlling the country's expenditure and raising taxes to meet national needs.

TINTERN ABBEY. Tintern, sited on a meander in the deep, wooded valley of the River Wye, five miles north of Chepstow, was founded by Walter de Clare, the Norman Lord of Chepstow, as a site for Cistercian monks in 1131. The present abbey was constructed between 1220 and 1287 (by which time the order was cultivating over 3000 acres of arable land in the lowlands of south Wales and western England) and, by 1536, when Henry VIII broke up the monastic system and redistributed its wealth, was the richest in Wales. The buildings are now owned by the state and open to visitors. William

Wordworth's poem — *Lines Composed a Few Miles above Tintern Abbey* — composed in 1798, describes the "steep woods and cliffs" which make Tintern's location so attractive but makes no reference to the abbey itself.

TOCHER. In Scotland, the tocher was a marriage dowry. It was intended to support the children borne by the woman and was returned to her family if she was barren.

TOWER HOUSES. (See **FORTIFIED HOUSES**).

TREATY OF UNION, 1707. The Act of Settlement, passed by the English Parliament in 1701 and designed to secure the Protestant Hanoverian succession to the throne, precipitated an angry response from the Scots (see **ACT ANENT PEACE AND WAR; ACT OF SECURITY**). England, provoked by the reaction of its northern neighbour, retaliated with legislative measures which threatened the destruction of the Scottish economy unless arrangements were made for full political integration of the two countries (see **ALIEN ACT**). In the early spring of 1705, representatives of both nations met in London and, in April 1706, a draft treaty of union was placed before the Scots Parliament. Under its provisions, Scotland would retain its own legal system (see **LEGAL SYSTEM: SCOTLAND**) and established Church (the **CHURCH OF SCOTLAND**), the royal **BURGH**s would keep the privileges attached to their status and the country would receive nearly £400,000 sterling to liquidate its public debt. In addition, merchants would have the right to trade freely in England and investments in the Company of Scotland Trading to Africa and the Indies (which organized the ill-fated **DARIEN SETTLEMENT**) would be repaid with five per cent interest. But the people would lose their Parliament, and only 45 representatives would watch over their interests in the proposed House of Commons at Westminster, a small coterie swamped by the 513 English MPs. Sixteen **SCOTTISH REPRESENTATIVE PEERS** would be admitted to the House of Lords.

For three months, Scotland agonised over the options. Debates in the **THREE ESTATES** were impassioned, there were riots in **EDINBURGH,** the army was disaffected, **GLASGOW** was taken over by a mob and English troops along the border were augmented. But, on 16 January 1707, the deed was done: the Three Estates ratified the treaty by 110 votes to 67, effectively signing its own death warrant. A **JACOBITE** ballad protested that "We are bought and sold for English gold" by "a parcel of rogues", but that was a sentiment born more of passion than logic. Hardheaded economic realities had prevailed, with legislators opting for the prospect of prosperity through union with a powerful neighbour rather than for poverty with political freedom.

TRIMBLE, WILLIAM DAVID (1944–). Leader of the **ULSTER UNIONIST PARTY** since 1995, Trimble is the son of William and Ivy Trimble. Raised in the relatively liberal atmosphere of County Down, he was educated at Bangor Grammar School and Queen's University **BELFAST,** then qualified as a barrister in 1969. Initially, he embarked on an academic career, lecturing in the law department at Queen's University for 22 years from 1968, but he was increasingly attracted by politics and, at a by-election in 1990, won the seat at Upper Bann, one of the most unionist in **ULSTER.** His election as party leader, following the resignation of **JAMES MOLYNEAUX,** was a surprise to many commentators. Politically the least experienced of the five candidates, Trimble had a hardline Protestant background which apparently appealed to the grassroots loyalists whose votes determined the outcome of the ballot. A former member of the right-wing **VANGUARD UNIONIST PROGRESSIVE PARTY,** he had been a vociferous opponent of the **ANGLO-IRISH AGREEMENT** and uncompromising in his opposition to the inclusion of **SINN FEIN** in peace talks before it unequivocally rejected terrorism. A member of the **ORANGE ORDER,** he has a notoriously short temper, but is an effective media performer with a formidable grasp of detail and an ability to argue his case clearly. Following his election, he undertook a series of meetings with potential allies and opponents in Belfast, Dublin, London and Washington and, early in 1996, suggested that elections should form the core of the Ulster peace process, a proposal which was endorsed by Prime Minister John Major and led some journalists to speculate that Trimble might be mellowing. At that time, Major's Conservative Party government had only a small majority in the House of Commons and relied heavily on the Ulster Unionists for support, so Trimble had a considerable influence on policies related to Northern Ireland. That changed in May of the following year, when a convincing general election victory gave the Labour Party a 179 seat Parliamentary majority. Within weeks the new Prime Minister — **ANTHONY CHARLES LYNTON BLAIR** — had initiated talks with the nationalist organizations, including **SINN FEIN.** Initially, Trimble remained aloof, arguing that he would not participate in discussions unless members of the **IRISH REPUBLICAN ARMY** surrendered their arms. However, under pressure from Ulster business leaders and influenced by polls taken in the province, he eventually agreed to join the negotiations, becoming the first Protestant Unionist leader to sit at the same table as Sinn Fein representatives since Ireland was partitioned in 1922.

TROSSACHS, THE. An area of the **SCOTTISH HIGHLANDS** northwest of **STIRLING,** the Trossachs became a focus for 19th-century travellers following the enormous success of **WALTER SCOTT'**s narrative poem, *Lady of the Lake* (1810), and his novel, *Rob Roy* (1818), both of which used romanticized word pictures of the mountains and **LOCH**s as settings for dramatic action. Queen Victoria, William Wordsworth and Samuel Taylor Coleridge were all captivated by a landscape which is sometimes called 'Scotland in miniature' because it contains, in a small area, the heather-clad hillsides, wooded glens, tumbling burns and trout-stocked lochs which are integral components of tourist stereotypes of the country. Most of the upland is used for sheep rearing, but many of the lower slopes have been reafforested and Loch Katrine acts as a reservoir, providing water for **GLASGOW.** Callander (at the eastern end of the region) is the major settlement, devoted largely to providing facilities for visitors. (See **ROB ROY MACGREGOR**).

TROUBLES, THE. Although originally used with reference to the period 1918–21, when Ireland was plagued by civil war, the term has, more recently, been applied to the modern period of strife in **ULSTER.** It began with the renewed nationalist campaign during the 1960s, when civil rights marches and violent disturbances became increasingly common (a march in **LONDONDERRY** in October 1968, broken up by a police baton charge, is often regarded as the start of this phase of the troubles). In response, the **B-SPECIALS** were called up and, in September 1970, the Provisional **IRISH REPUBLICAN ARMY** (IRA) broke off from its parent body to begin a campaign of bombing. Troops were stationed in the province in increasing numbers and authorized to use rubber bullets in an attempt to retain order and, in February 1971, the first British soldier was killed. In August of that year, internment without jury trial was introduced for some offenders but, even so, the violence escalated. **BLOODY SUNDAY** (30 January 1972) saw British troops kill 13 demonstrators in Londonderry and, in February, the Parachute Regiment base at Aldershot England was bombed, killing seven people.

In March, **DIRECT RULE** from London replaced the Unionist government (see **ULSTER UNIONIST PARTY**). The **SUNNING-DALE AGREEMENT** failed after a general strike in 1974, and, in November of that year, Birmingham pubs were bombed, killing 21. In January 1976, the Special Air Service (SAS) was sent to Ulster as a result of the assassinations of ten Protestants by the IRA but neither it nor a peace movement, which was formed after three children were killed and which received the Nobel prize in 1976, could bring calm. (See **PEACE PEOPLE**). In 1979, Airey Neave, a Conservative Party Member of Parliament, was assassinated near the House of Commons and, in August 1979, Lord Louis Mountbatten (along with three companions) was murdered by a bomb placed on his fishing boat. Hunger strikes in prisons led to ten IRA and **IRISH NATIONAL LIBERATION ARMY** prisoners dying and, in July 1982, 11 bandsmen were killed by an explosion in Regents Park (London). In September 1983, 28 Provisional IRA prisoners escaped from the Maze prison (**BELFAST**), the largest breakout in British history, and, just before Christmas, five people were killed by a bomb outside Harrods' store in London. In October 1984, a further five died following a bomb explosion at the Grand Hotel (Brighton, England) during the Conservative Party Conference and Prime Minister Margaret Thatcher narrowly escaped with her life. In November 1987, 11 died at a Remembrance Sunday Service at Enniskillen, and, in March 1988, three IRA suspects were shot by the SAS in Gibraltar. A bomb killed 11 bandsmen at Deal in September 1989, and, in April 1992, the City of London was rocked by a bomb at the Baltic Exchange. In March 1993, two children died in an attack on shoppers at Warrington (Cheshire, England), and, in April 1993, a massive bomb destroyed the Bishopsgate area in the City of London, with damage costing billions of pounds to repair.

Bombings, assassinations and interreligious sectarian killings by paramilitary groups intensified in October 1993 and led to the **UL-STER DECLARATION**. By that time, almost 3,400 people had died since the Troubles began in 1968 — 1,940 had been killed by Republicans (mainly the IRA), 900 by **ULSTER LOYALISTS,** 361 by the security forces and over 160 by unknown persons or groups. In December, the British Prime Minister, John Major, and the Irish Taoiseach, Albert Reynolds, affirmed the right of both the unionist and the republican communities to free political thought and opened the possibility of changes to the constitution of Ulster, and membership of the Irish Republic, if a majority of the people wished it, thus challenging the gunmen of both sides to forsake violence and work democratically for their ends. At midnight on 31 August 1994, **SINN FEIN** and the IRA announced a ceasefire.

During the months that followed, in Dublin and (more cautiously) in London, the first steps were taken toward a resumption of normal political processes in Northern Ireland and a dialogue with the Nationalist leaders was initiated. However, at 5.30 pm on 9 February 1996, the IRA called off its ceasefire and, at 7.01 the same evening, a bomb was detonated at Canary Wharf, in London Dockland's new office district, killing two people and causing widespread building damage.

On 27 July 1997, following a general election which had brought the Labour Party to power in London, the IRA again announced that it would end attacks on soldiers, police and property but would not give up its arms. Later in the year, the new Prime Minister (**ANTHONY CHARLES LYNTON BLAIR**) met **GERARD ADAMS** (leader of Sinn Fein) and **WILLIAM DAVID TRIMBLE** led the Ulster Unionist Party into talks with the British government and the nationalists (the first time a Protestant political leader from Ulster had entered negotiations with Sinn Fein since Ireland was partitioned in 1922). (See **ALLIANCE PARTY; ANGLO-IRISH AGREEMENT; ANGLO-IRISH TREATY; ANGLO-IRISH WAR; ANTI-PARTITION LEAGUE; APPRENTICE BOYS; HUMPHREY ATKINS; BELFAST; BLOODY FRIDAY; BLOODY SUNDAY; BOGSIDE; BASIL BROOKE; PETER BROOKE; JAMES CHICHESTER-CLARK; PRIVATE LEE CLEGG AFFAIR; COMBINED LOYALIST MILITARY COMMAND; CURRAGH INCIDENT; DEMOCRATIC UNIONIST PARTY; EASTER RISING; BRIAN FAULKNER; FIANNA FAIL; GERRY FITT; HOME RULE; JOHN HUME; DOUGLAS HURD; IRISH FREE STATE; IRISH NORTHERN AID COMMITTEE; IRISH PEOPLE'S LIBERATION ORGANIZATION; THOMAS KING; ROY MASON; BRIAN MAWHINNEY; PATRICK MAYHEW; JAMES MOLYNEUX; TERENCE O'NEILL; IAN PAISLEY; PEACE MOVEMENT; JAMES PRIOR; FRANCIS PYM; MERLYN REES; ROYAL ULSTER CONSTABULARY; SUNNINGDALE AGREEMENT; ULSTER DEFENCE ASSOCIATION; ULSTER DEFENCE REGIMENT; ULSTER FREEDOM FIGHTERS; ULSTER POPULAR UNIONIST PARTY; UNIONIST PARTY OF NORTHERN IRELAND; UNITED ULSTER UNIONIST PARTY; VANGUARD UNIONIST PROGRESSIVE PARTY; WILLIAM WHITELAW**).

MARGARET TUDOR (1489–1541). The eldest daughter of King Henry VII of England, Margaret was born in Westminster on 29 November 1489 and spent her childhood years at the English court before marrying King **JAMES IV** of Scotland on 8 August 1503 as part of a package designed to ensure peace between the neighbouring nations. The three children she bore between 1507 and 1510 all died in infancy and the fourth, born in 1512, succeeded his father (as **JAMES V**) in September 1513 at the age of only 17 months. Appointed Regent and made the boy's sole guardian, the Queen embarked on a series of shifting political alliances which were to mark the remainder of her life. In the early 16th century, Scottish opinion was divided over the relative merits of alliance with England and France. Margaret, not surprisingly in view of her parentage, inclined to the former, and, on 6 August 1514, married a supporter and counsellor, Archibald Douglas, Earl of Angus (see **EARLS AND MARQUESSES OF DOUGLAS**). However, under the terms of James IV's will, her regency lapsed with the wedding, and, the following year, John Stewart, Duke of Albany and leader of the pro-France faction, was invited by Parliament to succeed her. The queen, fearing for her life, fled to England, where she bore Douglas a daughter (Margaret), who was to become the mother of **HENRY DARNLEY**.

Queen Margaret returned to Scotland in 1516, made peace with Stewart but became increasingly estranged from her husband. Her brother, Henry VIII of England, opposed any suggestion of a divorce, and Margaret, alienated from her former supporters, attached herself more closely to the Stewart circle. In 1527, the divorce achieved, she married John Stewart and again became an influential figure in the discussions which shaped Scottish politics. However, an injudicious betrayal of secrets to the English King in 1534 precipitated a rift with her son (now ruling the Scottish kingdom in his own right) and a decline in her power. She died at Methven Castle on 18 October 1541 but bequeathed a considerable genetic legacy to her people because it was through Queen Margaret that the **STEWARTS** were able to claim the throne of England in 1603 and finally unite the two kingdoms under one sovereign, James VI and I.

TWEED, RIVER. The longest river in southeast Scotland, the Tweed flows eastward for 97 miles from its source in the **SOUTHERN UPLANDS** to the North Sea at Berwick-upon-Tweed. For the last 17 miles or so, it forms the boundary between Scotland and England. The upper reaches have been dammed to provide water for **EDINBURGH**, reducing the volume of water downstream but also controlling flooding on the arable and pasture lands in the lower valley. The Tweed has a catchment area of some 1,900 square miles and, with its tributaries, provided water power for the wool textile industry which developed in Galashiels, Melrose and other towns along its course. Its relatively pure waters also serve as spawning grounds for salmon. (See **THE BORDERS**).

TWEEDSMUIR, BARON. (See **JOHN BUCHAN**).

TYRONE REBELLION. There were two revolts which involved the O'Neills, Earls of Tyrone, in conflict with the English in **ULSTER.** They are sometimes referred to as the O'Neill Rebellions.

1559-67. Shane O'Neill, son of Conn Bacach, Earl of Tyrone, disputed the succession, supported by the English, of his illegitimate brother, Matthew, to the Earldom. Murdering his brother in 1558, he attacked the loyalist O'Donnells and the Scottish MacDonnells, plotted with Spain and the supporters of **MARY, QUEEN OF SCOTS,** and attempted to wrest Ulster from the control of Queen Elizabeth I of England. Until his own murder in 1567, he effectively ruled Ulster.

1594-1603. Hugh O'Neill, 2nd Earl of Tyrone, had been educated in England and, when he returned to Ulster in 1580, was given the earldom and a royal commission, in the hope that he would subdue the Irish and persuade them to accept English rule. By 1594, he was plotting with the Papacy and with Spain against England and secured a decisive victory at the **BATTLE OF YELLOW FORD** in 1598. His Spanish support evaporated at the **BATTLE OF KINSALE** in 1601, and he surrendered to the English in March 1603. He was pardoned by King James VI and I and allowed to keep his lands. In 1607, he fled to Rome, where he died in 1616. (See **BATTLE OF THE FORD OF THE BISCUITS; GALLO-GLASSES**).

—U—

ULSTER. Although *Ulster* is now used as a synonym for *Northern Ireland*, the name has a long historical pedigree. During the fifth century, the area was known as Ulaid and was an important base of **ST PATRICK**'s Christian missions. By the eigth century, it was dominated by the O'Neill dynasty but, from about 800, suffered a series of attacks from the Vikings and, during the reign of Henry II (1154–

89) fell under Norman domination. In 1205, King John (Henry's youngest son) created an earldom of Ulster and conferred it on Hugh de Lacy, confirming English authority. The modern Province of Northern Ireland, created by the **ANGLO-IRISH TREATY** of 1921, is slightly smaller than the historic kingdom of Ulster, consisting of the counties of Antrim, Armagh, Derry, Down, Fermanagh and Tyrone.

ULSTER DECLARATION. In December 1993, the British Prime Minister (John Major) and the Irish Taoiseach (Albert Reynolds) agreed to the possibility of constitutional change in Northern Ireland if a majority of the people wished it. They challenged the gunmen of the **IRISH REPUBLICAN ARMY** and the **ULSTER LOYALIST** paramilitary groups to cease terrorism and join democratic discussions on the future of the province. (See **THE TROUBLES**).

ULSTER DEFENCE ASSOCIATION (UDA). The UDA is a hard line **ULSTER LOYALIST** paramilitary organization formed in 1971 from a coalition of vigilante groups which had defended Protestant areas of **BELFAST** during periods of violence inspired by the **IRISH REPUBLICAN ARMY** (IRA) the previous year. A largely working-class movement, it initially supported industrial strikes as a means of achieving political ends and advocated negotiation, rather than violence, as a means of ending **THE TROUBLES.** However, it also became associated with extensive gangsterism and extortion rackets. Then, in 1991, the **ULSTER FREEDOM FIGHTERS** (UFF) — one of its numerous branches — initiated a murder campaign targeting Roman Catholics. The government's response was to ban the organization, but that simply served to reduce the amount of information passed to the security forces and encourage militant young men to attach themselves to the UFF, with a consequent increase in sectarian killings. When the IRA announced a ceasefire in 1994, the UDA responded, but its members held on to their guns, and, with the **ULSTER VOLUNTEER FORCE** (UVF), it remained one of the strongest paramilitary groups in the province.

ULSTER DEFENCE REGIMENT (UDR). The UDR was established in 1970, following the recommendations of a government inquiry into policing in Northern Ireland. That inquiry, chaired by Lord Hunt, criticised the **B-SPECIALS** and proposed their replacement by a part-time military force recruited in the Province. The original intention was that the UDR would have representatives from both religious communities in **ULSTER** and that it would not be heavily armed, but it very quickly became the focus of complaint by nationalist sympathisers, who felt that it was being dominated by members of Protestant paramilitary groups. Ultimately, those allegations were justified by events because several members of the UDR were convicted of sectarian killings and, following an investigation in 1989–90, John Stevens (Deputy Chief Constable of Cambridgeshire) revealed that there was evidence that UDR soldiers had passed imformation on suspected republican terrorists to the loyalist organizations. Under pressure from **ULSTER LOYALISTS,** the government steadily increased the power of the weapons members of the Regiment could carry and it became one of the **IRISH REPUBLICAN ARMY** (IRA)'s principal targets. By the time its nine battalions were merged with the Royal Irish Rangers to form the Royal Irish Regiment in 1992, 197 serving officers and 47 former officers had been murdered.

ULSTER FREEDOM FIGHTERS (UFF). The UFF, which first came to public notice in 1973, is the murder squad operated by the **ULSTER DEFENCE ASSOCIATION** (UDA). An extreme Protestant group, it claims to have killed many Roman Catholics (for example, of the 38 known assassinations by pro-unionist groups in 1992, the UFF was probably responsible for 21, including a 15-year-old boy). Churches, schools and senior politicians have all been targets of the organization's violence.

ULSTER LOYALISTS. This name is given to all citizens of Northern Ireland who want the province to remain part of the United Kingdom but is particularly used to refer to paramilitary groups and political parties. (See **BOGSIDE; BATTLE OF THE BOYNE**).

ULSTER POPULAR UNIONIST PARTY (UPUP). The UPUP was founded in 1980 by Sir James Kilfedder (Member of Parliament for North Down), who believed that Enoch Powell had too much influence on the shaping of **ULSTER UNIONIST PARTY** policy. It won five seats at the 1981 local government elections in Northern Ireland but suffered from criticisms that it was strongly focused on one individual, and, by 1985, many members were turning away to the larger political parties. However, a small core of support remained and managed to maintain representation on two local councils.

ULSTER PROTESTANT LEAGUE (UPL). The UPL was formed in

BELFAST in 1931 in an attempt to safeguard the jobs of Northern Ireland Protestants during the Great Depression. It held many rallies, characterised by inflammatory anti-Catholic speeches, which contributed to the outbreak of violence in the city in 1935.

ULSTER UNIONIST COUNCIL. The bulk of the ULSTER UNIONIST PARTY became known as the Ulster Unionist Council, or the Official Ulster Unionists, when, in 1971, the Democratic Unionist Party broke away from this majority grouping of Unionists in ULSTER.

ULSTER UNIONIST PARTY (UUP). The UUP is the largest political party in Northern Ireland. It has its roots in the Ulster Unionist Council, formed in 1905 and committed to keeping Ireland within the United Kingdom. Following partition of the island in 1920, the UUP provided the Northern Ireland Government at STORMONT and remained in power without a break until DIRECT RULE from London was imposed in 1972. Until the late 1960s, it was a broad church (albeit a Protestant church), reflecting opinion across a wide range of the political spectrum and united largely by opposition to the loosening of ties with Britain. However, the tensions caused by the growing civil rights protests led to the formation of splinter groups, and the traditional alliance with the Conservative Party in Westminster became strained when the Northern Ireland Parliament was suspended. Always uneasy about the UK government's policy of involving the Republic of Ireland in discussions on the future of ULSTER, the UUP forced a series of by-elections when all 15 of its MPs resigned their seats following the signing of the ANGLO-IRISH AGREEMENT in 1985. Fourteen were promptly reelected, a result which the party leadership claimed was a demonstration of support for its reluctance to deal with the south, but the return of a Conservative Government at the 1987 General Election, implying widespread British support for Prime Minister Margaret Thatcher's tactics on the Northern Ireland issue, caused the party hierarchy to rethink its policy. Change was gradual, but, in 1992, the UUP leader, JAMES MOLYNEAUX, accompanied by senior members of the organization, took part in talks with Irish Republic politicians in Dublin and, the following year, criticism of the DOWNING STREET DECLARATION was significantly less strident than that emanating from other unionist camps in Ulster. In 1995, Molyneaux resigned the leadership of the party and was replaced by DAVID TRIMBLE, by reputation a hardliner, but the months following the change brought no significant change of strategy. The Ulster Unionist Party currently holds ten of Northern Ireland's 18 House of Commons seats and won 32.7 per cent of the Ulster vote at the 1997 General Election.

ULSTER VOLUNTEER FORCE (UVF). The UVF is one of the two largest of the Protestant paramilitary organizations in Northern Ireland (see also **ULSTER DEFENCE ASSOCIATION [UDA]**). It was originally formed in 1912–13 when Sir **EDWARD CARSON** and Sir **JAMES CRAIG** established a private army of over 200,000 Protestants determined to prevent the government from granting independence to Ireland as one unit. Armed with German rifles smuggled into the province, its members, drawn from all social classes, were encouraged to enlist in the British Army at the outbreak of the First World War. They formed the 36th (Ulster) Division and died in droves at the Battle of the Somme (1916).

The movement reorganized in 1919, when the war ended, and was heavily involved in the violence which preceded the partition of the island two years later. Ultimately, the UVF units were integrated as a part-time (or B category) force in the **ULSTER SPECIAL CONSTABULARY** (see **B-SPECIALS**), effectively legitimizing the organization.

In 1966, the UVF's name was revived by a small group of hardline **ULSTER LOYALISTS,** led by Augustus 'Gusty' Spence, a shipyard worker who objected to Prime Minister **TERENCE O'NEILL**'s policy of improving the civil rights of the Roman Catholic community. A series of bombings and killings led to Spence's imprisonment for the manslaughter of a Catholic barman and the banning of his organization. However, the violence ultimately led to O'Neill's resignation in 1969 and the proscription fuelled the movement's popularity. More disciplined than the UDA but committed to a programme of violence, it became increasingly attractive to working class males, in particular, over the next two decades. Avowedly antisocialist, it has forged links with mainland right-wing groups such as the National Front. (See **PROGRESSIVE UNIONIST PARTY**).

UNDEB YR ANNIBYNWYR CYMRAEG. (See **UNION OF WELSH INDEPENDENTS**).

UNDERTAKERS. This general term refers to a person who undertakes, or performs, political or government duties in return for crown patronage. In the 16th century it was applied to those who rented Crown lands in Ireland, but during the reigns of James VI and I, Charles I and Charles II it had a broader meaning encompassing people who attempted to influence Parliamentary voting in support of the sovereign. In the 18th century it came to refer to a group of Irish politicians who controlled law and order and carried out executive duties for the crown in return for local control of patronage. They were crucial to secure the province for England at a time when there was no permanent Crown nominee in direct control.

UNION (BRITAIN AND IRELAND) ACT, 1 January 1800. This Act of Parliament, much opposed in Ireland, was an attempt to control the Irish territories after the **IRISH REBELLION** of 1798. By giving the Irish the right to send MPs to Westminster, it was thought that the legislation would generate a form of Catholic emancipation without specific legislation on this point.

UNION OF THE CROWNS (1603). Although, during the Middle Ages, Scotland and England were frequently at war, there were periods of peace, many of them precipitated by marriages between members of the nobility from opposite sides of the border. One such alliance was that, in 1503, between the Scottish King, **JAMES IV,** and **MARGARET TUDOR,** daughter of England's Henry VII. Margaret's fourth child, born in 1512, succeeded to the throne as **JAMES V** when his father died at the **BATTLE OF FLODDEN** the following year. In 1538, James married **MARY OF GUISE,** and, four years later, she gave him a daughter, who became **MARY, QUEEN OF SCOTS,** while still an infant.

In England, Margaret's brother had been crowned King Henry VIII after their father's death in 1509, and had married Catherine of Aragon the same year. By 1526, however, he was thoroughly infatuated with Anne Boleyn and sought papal approval for a divorce on the grounds that Catherine had previously been married to his elder brother, Arthur, who had died in 1502. Pope Clement VII refused to rule on the matter but, in 1533, Thomas Cranmer, Archbishop of Canterbury, annulled the marriage and, the following year, Parliament formally approved his action.

Many influential Roman Catholics were unwilling to accept the authority either of Cranmer or of Parliament. They argued that all the children of Henry's relationship with Anne, and all those born to subsequent relationships, were illegitimate. As a result, when he died in 1547, they maintained that the rightful successor to the throne should be his niece, Mary Queen of Scots, not Elizabeth, the only child of the union with Anne. The friction between the two women plagued politics in both kingdoms and was terminated only by Mary's execution, on Elizabeth's orders, in 1587.

In 1565, Mary had married **HENRY DARNLEY,** and that ill-fated match produced one child, James, born the following year and raised in the Protestant ethos of post Reformation Scotland. James became King on his mother's death but made little protest to Elizabeth about what many of his subjects believed was an unjustified murder. Intent on following Elizabeth to the English throne, he saw no point in annoying her. For 16 years, he dangled at the end of her string, tormented because she refused to name him as her successor, but, on 24 March 1603, she died, childless, and the English Parliament, where James had powerful allies, declared him King. For the first time, Scotland and England were united under a single Monarch. (See **TREATY OF UNION**).

UNION OF PARLIAMENTS. (See **TREATY OF UNION**).

UNION OF WALES AND ENGLAND, 1536, 1543. Two Acts of Parliament finally secured the effective absorption of Wales into England. They removed the **MARCHER LORDS,** imposing English-style county administration and an English legal system based upon the Justices of the Peace, and establishing the English language as the official language of officialdom in the **PRINCIPALITY.**

UNION OF WELSH INDEPENDENTS (UNDEB YR ANNIB-YNWYR CYMRAEG). Formed in 1872, the union is a voluntary association of some 600 Welsh Congregational churches, with 115 ministers. (Congregationalism in Wales dates from 1639, when the first church was opened in Gwent.) Each is Calvinistic in doctrine and maintains independent government of its own activities. Services are conducted in **WELSH.** In 1997, the churches had about 45,000 worshippers (a 50 per cent decline over the preceding 25 years). (See **CHURCH IN WALES; PRESBYTERIAN CHURCH OF WALES**).

UNIONIST PARTY OF NORTHERN IRELAND (UPNI). In 1973, the majority of members of the **ULSTER UNIONIST PARTY** (UUP) rejected the **SUNNINGDALE AGREEMENT,** which proposed that **ULSTER** should be governed by an executive consisting of members of the major political parties in the Province. Brian Faulkner, who had been intimately involved in the negotiations, responded by resigning from the leadership of the UUP and setting up the UPNI. He regarded the new party as a modernising force, prepared to share power with the strongly Roman Catholic **SOCIAL DEMOCRATIC AND LABOUR PARTY,** but it failed to make an impact either at local government polls or at General Elections and was wound up in 1981.

UNITED FREE CHURCH OF SCOTLAND (UF Church). The UF Church was formed on 31st October 1900 through the amalgamation of 1077 congregations from the **FREE CHURCH OF SCOTLAND** and 599 from the **UNITED PRESBYTERIAN CHURCH.** A minority group of Free Church members decided to maintain its independence and, in 1901, sought a ruling by the Scottish courts that it had legal title to all of the properties owned by the mother Church prior to the union. Ultimately, in 1904, its claim was upheld by the House of Lords (the highest court in the United Kingdom) but the UF Church managed to retain all of the buildings which the remnant Free Church could not utilize. Moreover, the experience bound the united congregations in a common cause, helping to overcome many of the differences which might otherwise have troubled the newly-formed institution. It established theological colleges in **ABERDEEN, EDINBURGH** and **GLASGOW** and gained a considerable reputation for scholarship, for missionary activity (particularly in Africa) and for leadership in ecumenical movements. By 1909, links were being established with the **CHURCH OF SCOTLAND.** It was clear that the main obstacle to a reunification between the mother church and the secessionists was the UF Church's insistence on freedom from state control but an Act of Parliament, which disestablished the Church of Scotland in 1921, removed many of the difficulties. In 1929, the formerly warring parties were reconciled and the bulk of the UF Church was taken back into the Church of Scotland fold. However, a minority elected to maintain its independence and continue to worship under the United Free Church banner. It became the first Scottish **PRESBYTERIAN** church to admit women to the ministry and, by 1997, had about 6,700 members in 71 churches but, like many minority religious organizations, faced considerable financial and administrative problems as a result of a steep decline in the number of communicants (over 60 per cent between 1970 and 1997).

UNITED IRISHMEN, SOCIETY OF, 1791. This Irish secret Society was founded in 1791 as a reform association, with both Catholic and

Protestant members. By 1795, inspired by the French Revolution, it had become a republican, anti-English movement, intent on Irish independence. It organized the fateful **IRISH REBELLION** of 1798, but declined as a force after that defeat and especially after the Banishment Act of 1798, which excluded members from Ireland. Many fled to America, Germany and France.

UNITED KINGDOM UNIONIST PARTY (UKUP). The UKUP was formed in 1995 specifically to fight a Parliamentary by-election at the North Down constituency, a Protestant middle-class area on the edge of **BELFAST,** in Northern Ireland. Its candidate — Bob McCartney — won the contest and narrowly retained the seat at the general election two years later. The party opposes all suggestions that the counties of **ULSTER** should be united with the Irish Republic, maintaining that Northern Ireland should remain British because the majority of the province's citizens prefer that allegiance. However, unlike the other unionist groups, it tends to align itself with the Labour Party rather than the Conservative Party on domestic and foreign policy issues.

UNITED PRESBYTERIAN CHURCH (UP Church). In 1847, two groups, which had their roots in 18th century schisms within the **CHURCH OF SCOTLAND,** amalgamated to form the United Presbyterian Church. The United Secession Church brought 400 congregations into the new body, the Presbytery of Relief 118. Over the next 50 years, the UP Church earned a considerable reputation for missionary activity (especially in India and China) and for unbending opposition to state aid for religious organizations (on the grounds that state aid led to state control). In 1863, recognizing that it had much in common with the **FREE CHURCH OF SCOTLAND,** it entered discussions which explored the possibilities of union but these were broken off ten years later, foundering on the rocks of doctrinal difference and internal Free Church politics. However, over the next 25 years, a series of changes on both sides brought the parties back to the negotiating table, and, in 1900, they joined together as the **UNITED FREE CHURCH OF SCOTLAND.** None of the UP congregations dissented.

UNITED SCOTSMEN, SOCIETY OF, 1796. Inspired by the **SOCIETY OF UNITED IRISHMEN,** this was a secret society espousing independence for Scotland, universal suffrage and cooperation with similar revolutionary groups in France and Ireland. With support mainly from the weaving districts of central Scotland, the Society agitated to little effect and faded away after the arrest of its leader, George Mealmaker, in 1798, and its proscription by Parliament in 1799.

UNITED ULSTER UNIONIST COUNCIL. The Council (also known as the Loyalist Coalition) was formed early in 1974 by members of the **OFFICIAL UNIONISTS,** the **DEMOCRATIC UNIONIST PARTY,** and the **VANGUARD UNIONIST PROGRESSIVE PARTY,** all of whom opposed the **NORTHERN IRELAND POWER SHARING EXECUTIVE** and the concept of a **NORTHERN IRELAND ASSEMBLY.** It co-operated with **ULSTER LOYALIST** paramilitary groups and the Ulster Workers' Council to organize a general strike, which brought the province to its economic knees and caused the Executive to disband. In 1975, it won 47 of the 78 seats on the **NORTHERN IRELAND CONSTITUTIONAL CONVENTION,** prepared a report which condemed the **SOCIAL DEMOCRATIC AND LABOUR PARTY** and recommended a Westminster-type administration for **ULSTER,** with a principle of majority rule. The report, although accepted by the Convention, was rejected by minority parties and by the British government. By 1976, the Convention had failed to reach agreement on a new form of administration for Northern Ireland and was disbanded. Shortly afterwards, the Council disintegrated.

UNITED ULSTER UNIONIST PARTY (UUUP). The UUUP was formed in 1977 by a members of the **VANGUARD UNIONIST PROGRESSIVE PARTY** who were opposed to suggestions that the organization would be willing to participate in a government for Northern Ireland which would include representatives of the dominantly Roman Catholic **SOCIAL DEMOCRATIC AND LABOUR PARTY.** However, the more conservative elements of the Protestant community found the policies of the Rev **IAN PAISLEY**'s **DEMOCRATIC UNIONIST PARTY** more appealing and, after failing to win any seats at the elections for the **NORTHERN IRELAND ASSEMBLY** in 1982, the party fell apart.

—V—

VANGUARD UNIONIST PROGRESSIVE PARTY (VUPP). The VUPP was formed in 1973 by former members of the **ULSTER UN-**

IONIST PARTY and became the most right-wing of the loyalist parties committed to keeping Northern Ireland part of the United Kingdom. Linked to the Ulster Vanguard movement, which had emerged the previous year and had held a series of fascist-style rallies across the Province, it was strongly opposed to the imposition of **DIRECT RULE** from London and advocated the introduction of more severe measures against the **IRISH REPUBLICAN ARMY**. In 1977, a group of dissidents, annoyed at the prospect of a coalition with the **SOCIAL DEMOCRATIC AND LABOUR PARTY**, broke away to form the **UNITED ULSTER UNIONIST PARTY** and, the following year, the organization was wound up.

VINEGAR HILL, BATTLE OF, 21 June 1798. Fought during the **IRISH REBELLION** of 1798, this engagement was a struggle between a rebel army of some 16,000 men, led by Father John Murphy, and an English government force, led by Lieutenant-General Gerard Lake and comprising some 10,000 men, mostly Irish yeomanry and militia regiments. The government forces gained a substantial victory on Vinegar Hill, near Enniscorthy, in County Wexford, killing or wounding at least 4,000 of the rebels. Murphy was captured and hanged at Wexford and the episode effectively ended the rebellion.

VOLUNTEERS. (See **IRISH VOLUNTEERS**).

—W—

WALES, STATUTE OF. (See **STATUTE OF RHUDDLAN**).

WALLACE, WILLIAM (*c.* 1270–1305). The second son of Sir Malcolm Wallace of Elderslie and his wife Jean, William Wallace led the resistance to Edward I's attempts to incorporate Scotland within his kingdom. His initial success against the invading forces was at Lanark in May 1297, when he burned the castle and killed the **SHERIFF** installed by the English. On 11 September, however, he struck a more significant blow when, by skillful use of the local topography, he defeated a force led by John de Warenne, Earl of Surrey, in the **BATTLE OF STIRLING BRIDGE.** Surrey was forced to retreat to York and Scotland, for a time, was virtually free of English overlordship. Wallace was knighted and became known as the Guardian of the Kingdom.

The English returned in 1298, with Edward himself leading the army. Wallace retreated, laying waste the countryside as he went and thus depriving the advancing troops of food. On 22 July, he decided to fight at the **BATTLE OF FALKIRK** but Edward's force, although greatly weakened by hunger, put the Scots to flight. The victory brought the English King little immediate gain because, unable to feed his army, he had to retreat south to Carlisle but Wallace's reputation as a military leader lay in ruins. He resigned the Guardianship and appears to have left Scotland for France, though the details of his activities after the battle are unclear. By 1305, he had certainly returned because, on 5 August, he was betrayed and imprisoned in Dumbarton Castle. From there, he was taken to London and, on 23 August, indicted on a charge of treason. Wallace denied the offence on the grounds that he had never sworn allegiance to Edward, but was condemned to death without trial. That same day he was hanged, drawn and quartered. His head was placed on London Bridge as an inspiration to the English and his limbs exhibited at Perth, **STIRLING,** Berwick and Newcastle as an example to the Scots. Edward, however, never managed to quell Scottish resistance to his occupation of the country and Wallace became a folk-hero. Many of the stories of his activities appear to be wholly apocryphal (some stem from a 15th-century romance allegedly composed by the minstrel, Blind Harry) but they appealed to the Scottish temperament. In 1861, as an act of atonement for neglecting his memory, a monument was erected in his name near Stirling. According to a contemporary account, 100,000 people attended the opening ceremony on 24 June.

WATT, JAMES (1736–1819). The inventor of the rotary steam engine, Watt was born in Greenock, on 19 January 1736, to James Watt (a shipowner and merchant) and his wife, Agnes. He was educated at Greenock Academy and worked in his father's business before being sent to London, at the age of 19, to take up an apprenticeship with instrument maker John Morgan. After only a few months he was back in Scotland, worn out by the long hours and the poverty, but, in 1757, he found another job as mathematical instrument maker at **GLASGOW** University. Seven years later, he was asked to repair a model of the Newcomen steam engine, a simple device consisting of a piston which moved up and down within a cylinder. The cylinder was filled with steam, cold water was sprayed in and the steam condensed, forming a partial vacuum underneath the piston. The piston dropped, creating a pump action, then was raised by a lever and the process was repeated. While making the repair to the model, Watt discovered that a high proportion of the steam was being wasted, much of it in reheating the bottom of the cylinder after it had been cooled by the spray. He conducted a series of experiments into the properties of steam, studying the relationships between density, pressure and temperature. On the basis of his results, he reasoned that the engine would be more efficient if the bottom of the cylinder was kept hot and if the steam was condensed in a separate unit. Further experiments demonstrated the practical value of these improvements and, in 1769, he obtained a patent for his design.

With the financial help of industrialist John Roebuck, a full-scale engine was constructed at Kinneil (near Linlithgow), allowing Watt to make further refinements. Roebuck's financial situation deteriorated and he had to withdraw from the association but, in 1775, Watt met Matthew Bolton, who manufactured metal goods at his Soho plant in Birmingham. They formed a partnership, with Bolton supplying finance and plant while Watt supplied creative genius. In essence, it was Watt's conversion of the piston action steam engine into a rotary device which provided the breakthrough and made the machine attractive to industrialists. A patent for the invention was issued in 1781 and covered five different methods of achieving the rotating action. In 1782 and 1784, further patents were acquired as Watt continued to develop his machine, increasing power and efficiency. By the mid-1780s, his invention had virtually replaced the Newcomen engine, primarily because it could do the same work on only one-quarter of the fuel and therefore was much cheaper to run. In 1780, Watt retired from business and gave his share of the partnership to his two sons. He died at Heathfield Hall, his Birmingham home, on 19 August 1819. The watt — a unit of electrical power — was named after him.

WEE FREES. (See **FREE CHURCH OF SCOTLAND**).

WELSH. Modern Welsh is a descendant of British, the language spoken by the Celts, who inhabited the British Isles when the Romans arrived during the first century AD, and differs from English in phonetics, vocabulary and grammatical structure. The acquisition of skills in Latin was necessary for all those who had dealings with the invaders but the Brythonic tongue survived in the more hilly, less subjugated, west of the country and, by the sixth century, a recognizably Welsh language had evolved. Known to those who use it as Cymraeg (anglicized as Cymric and derived from *cymro*, the word for *compatriot*), it is spoken by 508,000 people in the **PRINCIPAL-**

ITY (18.7 per cent of the population aged three and over at the time of the 1991 census). Geographically, its strength varies greatly, with proportionately fewer speakers in south Wales and more in the north and west (only 2.4 per cent of Gwent residents speak the language, for instance, compared with 61.0 per cent in Gwynedd).

The story of Welsh in recent decades has been one of inexorable decline (the proportion of the principality's population speaking the language halved between 1931 and 1991) but, largely because it has become one of the symbols of Welsh nationality and therefore has political implications, attempts have been made to stem the tide. A Welsh language television channel was created in 1981 and now broadcasts over 30 hours of programmes each week. The Government-appointed **WELSH LANGUAGE BOARD (BWRDD YR IAITH GYMRAEG)**, established in 1988, is charged with promoting use of the language and the **WELSH LANGUAGE SOCIETY, PLAID CYMRU** and other organizations act as pressure groups furthering the interests of Welsh speakers. In addition, much of the teaching in schools is now undertaken in Welsh and census returns indicate that the proportion of 10–15 year olds speaking the language is higher than the proportion of speakers in the 30–44 age group. (See **EISTEDDFODD; GAELIC; WILLIAM MORGAN; IOLO MORGANWG; WELSH TRUST; WILLIAM SALESBURY; WILLIAM WILLIAMS**).

WELSH DEVELOPMENT AGENCY. Established by the Labour Government in 1976, the Agency has a remit to further the economic development of Wales by providing jobs, encouraging efficient business practices and enhancing the environment in order to attract employment. Its Board members, appointed by the **SECRETARY OF STATE FOR WALES,** include representatives from the trade unions, industry and commerce. Based in **CARDIFF,** it has an annual budget of some £170 million.

WELSH LANGUAGE ACT (1967). This legislation, passed by the Labour government at a time of growing support for the nationalists (see **PLAID CYMRU**) and the militant stance adopted by the **WELSH LANGUAGE SOCIETY,** gave the Welsh and English languages parity, for most official purposes, within Wales.

WELSH LANGUAGE BOARD (BWRDD YR IAITH GYMRAEG). Originally established as an advisory group by the Conservative Government in 1988, the Board was reconstituted in 1994 as a statutory organization with a remit to promote the use of **WELSH** and ensure that the Welsh and English languages are treated equally by public bodies. Based in **CARDIFF,** it has 14 members appointed by the **SECRETARY OF STATE FOR WALES** and drawn from a wide range of backgrounds, including education, television and the arts.

WELSH LANGUAGE SOCIETY (CYMDEITHAS YR IAITH GYMRAEG). There have been two **WELSH** Language Societies. The first, known in English as the Society for the Utilisation of the Welsh Language, was formed in 1885 at the national **EISTEDD-FOD** in Aberdare, with **WILLIAM ABRAHAM** playing a leading role. In order to make itself acceptable to the authorities, it campaigned for formal recognition of the Welsh language on the grounds that it could be used to give school pupils a knowledge of English. In 1887, the society gave evidence, with some success, to a royal commission which had been set up to conduct an enquiry into elementary education. The recommendations of that commission led to a system of payments to schools which taught Welsh grammar and included lessons on translation from Welsh to English. The moves were limited, and made grudgingly, but were the first steps towards the establishment of a school curriculum taught in the Welsh language to Welsh speakers.

The second society was formed as a result of a radio broadcast by writer Saunders Lewis on 13 February 1962. Calling on Welsh speakers to take a more active part in getting formal recognition for their native tongue, he asked listeners "to make it impossible to conduct local or central government business without the Welsh language". His appeal found a receptive audience, particularly among young people, and a Welsh Language Society was formed during a **PLAID CYMRU** summer school at Pontarddulais later in the year. It immediately adopted high-profile tactics and, during the late 1960s, became increasingly militant, painting out signs written in English and disrupting traffic in its attempts to get Welsh used on such official documents as birth certificates. Although there were many people who objected to the damage and disruption, the movement gained considerable support. Throughout the 1970s, Welsh forms of town names became more common, government documents were printed in both languages and television devoted more time to programmes in Welsh. The society is still active but now adopts a less aggressive stance, having achieved many of its aims. (See **WELSH LANGUAGE BOARD**).

WELSH LAWS. (See **CYFRAITH HYWEL DDA**).

WELSH NOT. During the late 19th- and early 20th-centuries, education authorities made a determined effort to stamp out **WELSH**-speaking among children. The campaign, in part, was an attempt to anglicize Wales but it also reflected a widely-held belief that acquisition of English was essential for young people seeking social and economic advancement. In schools, a child caught speaking Welsh had to place a block of wood with a cord (known as a *not,* the Welsh for *Knot)* round his or her neck. That child listened for any other pupil speaking Welsh and told the teacher, who transferred it to the culprit. The person wearing the not at the end of the school day was punished, usually by caning. In effect, the campaign simply increased bilingualism because many children (particularly in north and west Wales) spoke Welsh when they got home.

WELSH OFFICE. The office is the headquarters of government business in Wales and is headed by the **SECRETARY OF STATE FOR WALES,** supported by a Parliamentary Private Secretary and two Under-Secretaries of State. It is responsible for a wide range of matters affecting the **PRINCIPALITY,** including agriculture and fisheries, economic and regional planning, education, environmental matters, forestry, health and the personal social services, housing, local government, roads, tourism, and town and country planning.

WELSH PARLIAMENTARY COMMITTEE. In 1907, a Welsh Parliamentary Committee was formed so that any Bill, introduced to the House of Commons, which dealt solely with Welsh matters could be formally considered by MPs representing constituencies in Wales. In practice, it is rarely convened (even the Welsh Language Bill, which passed through Parliament in 1993, was debated by a conventional Standing Committee rather than by the Welsh Parliamentary Committee).

WELSH TRUST. In 1674, clergyman Thomas Gouge persuaded wealthy merchants and landowners, most of them from London, to provide funds for a charitable trust which would publish devotional books in **WELSH** and establish English language schools in Wales. His aim — to provide "little garrisons against Popery" — found support amongst Anglicans as well Nonconformists and, within a year, over 2,000 children were learning to read and write in English at 87 schools based in the major towns. By 1678, over 5,000 books had been distributed, most of them religious in nature and promoting Christian codes of conduct. The movement, which was much criticized by those who could see no reason why Welsh children should have to learn English before their souls were saved, was driven largely by the force of Gouge's personality and ground to a halt after his death in 1681.

WESTERN ISLES. These islands, also known as the Outer **HEBRIDES,** lie off the west coast of Scotland between latitudes 55° 35' and 58° 30' North and longitudes 5° 26' and 8° 26' West. They form a crescent-shaped chain and, consisting largely of gneiss, contain some of the oldest rock formations known to science. Under Norse domination from the eigth century, the Western Isles became part of Scotland in 1266 and developed the **CLAN** structure typical of the **SCOTTISH HIGHLANDS.** The introduction of a money economy from the mid-18th century caused much social upheaval and forced many islanders to emigrate to the mainland and abroad, particularly Canada and Australia. **CROFTING** is the traditional way of life, with root and arable crops supplemented by cattle raising, sheep farming and fishing. Harris tweed has a worldwide market but is dependent on changing fashions and is still a cottage industry. Tourism, too, is important though expansion is limited by the islands' isolation from the main population centres of the United Kingdom and Europe. Stornoway, on Lewis, is the main settlement.

WHEATLEY REPORT (1969). The report of the Royal Commission on Local Government in Scotland (usually known as the Wheatley Report after the chairman, Lord Wheatley) recommended far reaching changes to the local government system (see **LOCAL GOVERNMENT: SCOTLAND**). Arguing that the system of over 400 authorities, which had been established since the late 19th century, was confusing and inefficient, the commissioners proposed that the **BURGH** councils, county councils and district councils should be replaced by a two-tier system. Seven regional authorities would take responsibility for major planning initiatives, personal social services (notably education, health and social work), housing provision and some other functions. At a more local level, 37 district authorities would deal with environmental matters (including building control, refuse collection and provision of recreational amenities), housing improvements and assistance to industry. The broad outlines of the plan were accepted by the government (though exceptions were made for the **ORKNEY ISLANDS,** the **SHETLAND ISLANDS** and the

WESTERN ISLES) and were implemented in 1975.

WHISKY. A drink derived from the distillation of fermented barley and malt, whisky has long been associated with Scotland and Ireland (the word is an anglicization of the **GAELIC** *uisge beatha*, meaning *the water of life*). It is first mentioned in Scotland in 1494 but may have been known by the tenth century or even earlier. Scotland quickly became the centre of production after Robert Stein of Kilbagie (near Alloa) turned distilling into a factory industry in 1826, using spring water from peat bog areas to give many distinctive flavours. The bulk of the output is blended (that is, the product of a number of distilleries is mixed) but single malts (whiskies from a single, named, distillery) are more fashionable and command higher prices. Most of the producers operating in Scotland are branches of multinational companies, such as Seagram, which have been closing stills in the face of falling demand. (In the 1976, there were 129 Scottish distilleries; by 1996, the number had fallen to 87). Smaller amounts of the spirit are produced in **ULSTER** and Wales. (See **MALT TAX**).

WHITEBOYS. This term was applied to peasant agrarian protestors in Ireland from about 1762 and is a reference to the white smocks that they wore. More generally, it was used with reference to all land and agricultural objectors who resorted to violent acts until the **IRISH REBELLION** of 1798. Discontent began in Munster, especially in Limerick, but quickly spread and anger was aimed at the enclosures, tithe payments, native Irish leaseholder evictions, high rents and poor prices for produce. The Whiteboys terrorized many areas, burning houses and destroying crops and field boundaries, even attacking a detachment of troops in 1786. Their leader was known as *Captain Danger,* and they were opposed at first only by local volunteers raised by the gentry. They were finally suppressed by military patrols, mass transportation to Botany Bay in Australia, and the ultimate failure of the Rebellion. Similar agitation continued into the early 19th century, with groups using names such as *Whitefeet, Thrashers* and *Rightboys.* (See **GALLOWAY LEVELLERS**).

WHITELAW, WILLIAM STEPHEN IAN (1918–). As the first **SECRETARY OF STATE FOR NORTHERN IRELAND,** Whitelaw exerted considerable influence in Edward Heath's Conservative government between 1970 and 1974. He was born in Nairn on 28 June 1918, the son of William and Helen Whitelaw, but never knew his father, who died of wounds received during the First World War while his son was still an infant. Whitelaw was educated at Winchester School and Cambridge University then, in 1939, received a commission in the Scots Guards. He served with distinction during the Second World War, reaching the rank of major, commanding a tank squadron during the Normandy invasion and receiving the military cross for bravery. At the end of the conflict, he served for a time in Palestine before leaving the service in 1947 to look after the family estates in northwest England.

In 1955, Whitelaw was elected MP for Penrith, a safe Conservative seat which he represented for 28 years. He was made Parliamentary Private Secretary at the Board of Trade (1956), then to Chancellor of the Exchequer Peter Thorneycroft at the Treasury (1957–58), before becoming Assistant Government Whip (1959–61), Lord Commissioner to the Treasury (1961) and Parliamentary Secretary at the Ministry of Labour (1962–64). From 1964 until 1970, while the Conservatives were in opposition, Whitelaw acted as Chief Whip then, following victory in the General Election, returned to government as leader of the House of Commons and Lord President of the Council. Two years later, he moved to the Northern Ireland post, with the responsibility of introducing **DIRECT RULE** to the province.

A genial politician with a reputation for unflappability, Whitelaw enhanced his standing during a two year period in office which found him enduring the wrath of **ULSTER LOYALISTS** (who had lost their Parliament at **STORMONT**) and an increase in terrorist activity by the **IRISH REPUBLICAN ARMY** (IRA). In 1972, he held secret meetings with IRA leaders in an attempt to find a solution to **THE TROUBLES,** but was unable to agree to the nationalists' demands, which included an amnesty for all political prisoners, withdrawal of troops from the province and acceptance of the principle that the future of Northern Ireland should be decided by the people of the whole island, not just those in **ULSTER.** A discussion paper, which he produced later that year, led to government proposals for a **NORTHERN IRELAND POWER SHARING EXECUTIVE.** For seven weeks between 5 October and 21 November 1973, he used his considerable diplomatic skills to engineer an agreement that the **ALLIANCE PARTY,** the **SOCIAL DEMOCRATIC AND LABOUR PARTY** and the **ULSTER UNIONIST PARTY** would all participate but, before the final arrangements were made, he was made Secretary of State for Employment and replaced at the **NORTHERN IRELAND OFFICE** by **FRANCIS PYM.**

Whitelaw's time at the Department of Employment was as difficult as that at Stormont because he was faced with an industrial crisis in the form of a strike by coal miners which led to reductions in electricity supply and, ultimately, to a state of emergency. These events precipitated a General Election in February 1974 and drove the Conservatives from office. In opposition, Whitelaw took on the role of party chairman, attempting to heal the inevitable divisions caused by the election defeat, and, in 1975, stood as a candidate in the election for leadership of the party. He lost to Margaret Thatcher but offered to serve under her and was made deputy leader. Between 1979 and 1983, he was Home Secretary in Thatcher's first administration but was never happy in the job; an opponent of capital punishment, he was often criticized for failing to take suitably rigorous measures to reduce the crime rate and, although dutifully loyal in public, found himself at odds with the Prime Minister's radical agenda for social and economic change. In 1983, he was given a hereditary viscountcy (one of only two awarded since 1964) and made leader of the House of Lords, where he found his negotiating skills tested by a body which opposed many of the legislative proposals accepted by the House of Commons. He suffered a stroke in 1987, retired from politics the following year, and was knighted in 1990. Apart from Parliament and his family, Whitelaw's great passion is **GOLF**; he represented Cambridge University between 1936 and 1939, was a selector for the British Walker Cup team in 1953, and captained the Royal and Ancient **GOLF** Club at **ST ANDREWS** in 1969–70. (See **GERARD ADAMS**).

WIGLEY, DAFYDD (1943–). The leader of **PLAID CYMRU,** the Welsh nationalist party, Wigley was born on 1 April 1943 in Caernarvon, where his father (Elfyn) was county treasurer. He was educated at the local grammar school and at Rydal School in Colwyn Bay before going to Manchester University, where he graduated with a BSc degree in 1964. Initially, he sought to establish a career in business, working with the finance staff of the Ford Motor Company (as the youngest member of the company's executive team) from 1964 until 1967, then with Mars Ltd as chief cost accountant and financial planning manager (1967–71) and with Hoover Ltd as financial controller at its **MERTHYR TYDFIL** plant (1971–74). However, he had contested Merioneth for the nationalists at the 1970 General Election and, in 1974, won the seat at Caernarvon. In the House of Commons, he took particular interest in matters relating to industry, employment and minority groups as well as those dealing specifically with Wales. He also has a particular concern for the mentally and physically handicapped, sponsoring a Disabled Persons

Act in 1981 and serving as the president of the Spastics Society for Wales from 1985 until 1990. Wigley was first elected president of Plaid Cymru in 1981 and held the post for three years, standing down because of the terminal illness of two of his sons. In 1991, he was elected for a second time and has forged a Parliamentary alliance with the **SCOTTISH NATIONAL PARTY,** sharing limited resources and promoting common causes.

WIGTOWN MARTYRS, 11 May 1685. This incident is the subject of some confusion. By 1694 the **COVENANTERS** in Scotland had been reduced to a small but active group known as the **CAMERONIANS** who refused to accept royal authority and who issued the **APOLOGETICAL DECLARATION** in direct defiance of the crown. Two women, 65 year-old Margaret McLauchlan, and 18 year-old Margaret Wilson, were tied to stakes on the beach at Wigtown and guarded until they were drowned by the incoming tide. It is disputed whether this punishment was for refusing to disown the Declaration, or for refusing to forsake their religious beliefs, and it is further in doubt whether they actually did die in this way, but the action certainly worsened the religious tensions north of the border at a critical time in the history of Anglo-Scottish affairs.

WILD GEESE. This term was applied, from about 1720, to Irish mercenaries recruited to foreign, usually Roman Catholic, armies. The **JACOBITE** cause was present in, especially, France and Spain, and large numbers of Irishmen joined the forces of those two Catholic countries. In France, there were so many that separate Irish Brigades were formed and these fought on many occasions for their adopted country up to the beginning of the French Revolution.

WILLIAM I (1143–1214). The grandson of King **DAVID I** (and known as The Lion, probably because he adopted the lion rampant on his coat of arms), William ruled Scotland from 1165 until his death. He extended the feudal system introduced by his grandfather, established additional **BURGH**s and improved the legal network through the appointment of **SHERIFF**s and royal justices. In effect, he also expanded his kingdom by bringing the north of the country under his control despite the strong opposition of the Earls of **ORKNEY.** Relationships with England, however, were less encouraging. Intent on adding Northumberland to his estates, William supported a rebellion against Henry II in 1173 but was captured the following year and had to accept Henry as overlord of his country under the treaty of Falaise. The Treaty was revoked by Richard II in 1189, but, although William retained his dreams, he died without pushing Scotland's boundaries any further to the south.

WILLIAMS, WILLIAM (1717–91). One of the leaders of the 18th century **METHODIST REVIVAL,** Williams was the greatest hymn writer the Welsh nation has produced. He was born at Cefn-coed (near Llandovery) to farmer John Williams and his wife, Dorothy. His father, an elder at the independent Calvinist church at Cefnarthen, intended him to become a doctor and ensured that the boy was given a good education both locally and at the nonconformist Llwynllwyd Academy, where he received a sound grounding in the classics. However, in 1738, Williams heard **HOWEL HARRIS** preaching in Talgarth and, moved by the experience, decided to become a minister. He was ordained a deacon in 1740 and became curate at the upland parishes of Llanwrtyd, Llanfihangel Abergwesyn and Llanddewi Abergwesyn in Breconshire, but his association with Methodism prevented him from advancing to higher posts in the Anglican church. In 1743, he resigned his curacy and worked as an itinerant preacher with **DANIEL ROWLAND,** travelling widely to establish and organize Methodist communities all over Wales (in his old age, Williams calculated that he had travelled over 148,000 miles, spending as much of his adulthood on the back of a horse as he had done at home). In 1749, he married Mary Francis of Llansawel and, using some of her money, bought land near an estate at Pantycelyn, which his mother had inherited. From then, he became widely known as Williams Pantecelyn and, although continuing his work as a preacher, supported his family of five girls and two boys by farming and commerce (he was an efficient businessmen who made a satisfactory income by selling tea).

After Harris and Rowland quarrelled in the early 1750s, Williams became Welsh methodism's creative force, expressing its beliefs in over 90 books and 800 hymns. The first collection (*Aleluia*) had been published in 1744 but *Caniadau y Rhai sydd ar y Môr o Wydr* (*The Songs of Those Who Are on the Sea of Glass*), which appeared in 1762, did much to rejuvenate the revival process. As well as the hymns, Williams wrote several poems and a number of texts in which he attempted to interpret individual experience in a scientific context. He died on 11 January 1791, but many of his hymns, which make much use of Bible imagery and appeal to the emotions rather than the intellect, are still sung. Perhaps the best known is *Guide Me, O Thou Great Jehovah*, originally published as a pamphlet in

1772. The English form, usually sung to the tune *Cwm Rhondda* (*Rhondda Valley*), is a free translation from the **WELSH** by Williams Pantecelyn and Peter Williams (1727–96).

WLADFA GYMREIG, Y (THE WELSH COLONY). (See **PATAGONIA**).

WOOD'S HALFPENCE, 1722. In the early 18th century, Ireland had no official mint to produce coinage, there was a severe shortage of small coins and a great many base coins were still in circulation from earlier reigns. In 1722, the Duchess of Kendal, mistress to King George I, was granted a patent to produce halfpence and farthings (quarter pence) in Ireland, and promptly sold the rights to William Wood, an ironmaster from Wolverhampton, for the immense sum of £10,000. The patent rights caused uproar — the Irish parliament had not been consulted, there was claimed to be an excessive difference between the face value of the coins and their intrinsic metal content and Jonathan Swift railed against the coins in *The Drapier's Letters*, claiming they would destroy the Irish economy. Sir Isaac Newton declared their copper content to be adequate, but most Irish people, including the Archbishop of Dublin, refused to accept the coins minted by Wood. By 1725, Robert Walpole was forced to withdraw the patent, and Wood was granted £24,000 from the Irish pension list in compensation (but under an assumed name to quieten opposition in Ireland).

WORCESTER AFFAIR, 1704. The early 18th century was a period of particularly poor relations between England and Scotland, after the failure of the Scottish **DARIEN SETTLEMENT** (in which English trading interests had played a large part) and the seizure by the English East India Company of the *Annandale*, the last ship to belong to the **COMPANY OF SCOTLAND.** In August 1704, an English vessel, the *Worcester*, was seized in the **RIVER FORTH** in an act of retaliation and, on contrived evidence of piracy, the captain and two crew members were summarily executed by a Scottish Court of Admiralty. This disgraceful episode was condoned by the English Privy Council, which was fearful of Scottish revolt as a result of the Darien experience.

—Y—

YELLOW FORD, BATTLE OF THE, 14 August 1598. This was Hugh O'Neill's greatest victory over the English in Ireland during the **TYRONE REBELLION.** Leading a rebel force of 5,600 men, he ambushed a government army of 4,220 cavalry and infantry near Armagh and killed 2,000 of them (including their commander, Sir Henry Bagenal, who was O'Neill's brother-in-law). The victory fuelled a massive upsurge in support for the Rebellion. (See **BATTLE OF KINSALE; BATTLE OF THE FORD OF THE BISCUITS**).

YORK, TREATY OF (1237). An agreement between King **ALEXANDER II** of Scotland and Henry III of England, the treaty determined that the border between the two countries would run from the mouth of the **RIVER TWEED** in the east, along the Cheviot Hills to the Solway Firth in the west. Alexander renounced his claims to Northumberland, Cumberland and Westmorland, paving the way for the establishment of a national boundary very similar to the present administrative division between Scotland and England.

YOUNG IRELAND. This began as a middle-class, intellectual nationalist movement in Ireland in 1841, led by the poet Thomas Davies. Its views were expressed in its publication, *The Nation,* and it published historical romances and nationalist poems and songs. The movement became more militant after the **IRISH POTATO FAMINE** and, in response to the 1848 revolution in France and encouragement from the Young Italy movement, become known as the 'Physical Force Party'. It attempted its own abortive rising in 1848, which resulted in the transportation of many of its leaders and its demise as a republican force in the island.

YOUNG WALES. This political and cultural nationalist movement was founded in 1886 as Cymru Fydd (Future Wales) by intellectual Welsh Liberals, in emulation of the earlier **YOUNG IRELAND** movement. It campaigned for **HOME RULE** for Wales through the Liberal Party and enjoyed a brief spell of influence in the early 1890s, but poor leadership, general lack of support in Wales for separation and intense internal dissensions led to the demise of the movement by 1900.

BIBLIOGRAPHY

The range of literature dealing with Scotland, Wales and Northern Ireland is wide, so the selection of texts listed below represents the tip of a very large iceberg. In particular, it excludes all material published before 1970, primarily because the texts below cite the earlier material, but also because the recent texts are more readily obtainable by readers who may not have access to British libraries. In addition, journal articles have been omitted, along with nonprint sources of information, such as microfiche collections and compact discs.

Many of the publications listed in the bibliography of Volume 1 of the Dictionary (*Historical Dictionary of the United Kingdom: England and the United Kingdom*), by the same authors and published by Scarecrow Press in 1997, cover the United Kingdom as a whole and contain references to the Celtic nations. In order to expand the coverage in this volume as much as possible, these works are not listed again here. Also, the text of the first volume itself contains many entries dealing with individuals and events relevant to Scotland, Wales and Northern Ireland, such as Prime Ministers born in these parts of Britain, and battles fought between the Scots and the English on English soil.

Specific aspects of the history of the Celtic fringe are covered by the periodicals published by specialist interest groups and include such titles as the *Journal of Welsh Ecclesiastical History, Scottish Studies* and the *Ulster Journal of Archaeology*. In addition, such newspapers as the *Belfast Telegraph*, the *Western Mail* and the *Scotsman* provide contemporary interpretations of events and obituaries of distinguished individuals. Also, the press in the Republic of Ireland regularly covers events in Ulster and provides an alternative view of the United Kingdom media.

In addition an ever-increasing range of sites containing historical information is available on the internet. For example, Edinburgh University's School of Scottish Studies provides access to published articles at www.pearl.arts.ed.ac.uk

Collections of official statistics dealing with United Kingdom (such as *Regional Trends*) often contain sections which list data for Scotland, Wales and Northern Ireland, and the government bodies responsible for these areas — the Scottish Office, the Welsh Office and the Northern Ireland Office — provide regular reports and policy documents which supplement the output from academic sources (for example, the Welsh Office publishes *Welsh Economic Trends* and *Welsh Social Trends* biannually). Most of these are available from Her Majesty's Stationery Office, 49 High Holborn, London WC1V 6HB; Telephone 0171 873 0011. The decennial census returns also provide statistical breakdowns for each area, and are particularly valuable for studies of population distribution and structure.

Scotland is also fortunate in having the *Third Statistical Account*, with one volume for each county and major city. The commentaries which the *Account* contains are variable in quality (many are written by local figures, such as parish ministers), but they include insights which scholars jealous of academic reputations might not have incorporated and they provide an intriguing summary of conditions in the nation during the second half of the 20th century.

For convenience, the entries listed below are grouped according to territory rather than topic. The coverage is not exhaustive, but it will provide the researcher with a solid foundation on which to build investigations.

Volume 1 of this two-volume Historical Dictionary is:

Panton, Kenneth J., and Keith A. Cowlard. *Historical Dictionary of the United Kingdom: Volume 1, England and the United Kingdom.* Lanham, Md.: Scarecrow Press, 1997.

Scotland

Adam, Frank. *The Clans, Septs and Regiments of the Scottish Highlands.* Edinburgh: Johnston and Bacon, 1970.

Adams, Ian. *The Making of Urban Scotland.* London: Croom Helm, 1978.

Aitken, A. J., and Tom McArthur, eds. *Languages of Scotland.* Edinburgh: Chambers, 1979.

Aitken, A. J., Matthew P. McDiarmid, and Derick S. Thompson, eds. *Bards and Makars: Scottish Language and Literature.* Glasgow: University of Glasgow Press, 1977.

Akrigg, G. P. V., ed. *The Letters of King James VI and I.* Berkeley: University of California Press, 1984.

Allan, David. *Virtue, Learning and the Scottish Enlightenment; Ideas of Scholarship in Early Modern History.* Edinburgh: Edinburgh University Press, 1993.

Anderson, Alan Orr. *Early Sources of Scottish History, AD 500 to 1286.* 2 vols. Stamford, England: Paul Watkins, 1990.

Anderson, Marjorie O. *Kings and Kingship in Early Scotland.* Edinburgh: Scottish Academic Press, 1980.

Anderson, R. *Images of Aberdeen.* Derby, England: Areadon Books,

1994.

Anderson, R. D. *Education and Opportunity in Victorian Scotland*. Edinburgh: Edinburgh University Press, 1989.

Anderson, R. G. W. *The Playfair Collection and the Teaching of Chemistry in the University of Edinburgh, 1713–1858*. Edinburgh: Royal Scottish Museum, 1978.

Anderson, R. G. W. and A. D. C. Simpson, eds. *The Early Years of the Edinburgh Medical School*. Edinburgh: Royal Scottish Museum, 1976.

Anderson, W. E. K., ed. *The Journal of Sir Walter Scott*. Oxford: Clarendon Press, 1972.

Antony, R. *Herds and Hinds: Farm Labour in Lowland Scotland, 1900–1939*. East Linton, Scotland; Tuckwell Press 1996.

Armit, Ian, ed. *Beyond the Brochs: Changing Perspectives on the Later Iron Age in Atlantic Scotland*. Edinburgh: Edinburgh University Press, 1991.

——————. *The Archaeology of Skye and the Western Isles*. Edinburgh: Edinburgh University Press, 1996.

——————. *Celtic Scotland*. London: Batsford, 1997.

Ash, Marinell. *The Strange Death of Scottish History*. Edinburgh: Ramsay Head Press, 1980.

Ashmore, P. J. *Neolithic and Bronze Age Scotland*. London: Batsford, 1996.

Ashworth, William, and Mark Pegg. *1946–1982: The Nationalized Industry*. Vol. 5 of *The History of the British Coal Industry*. Oxford: Clarendon Press, 1986.

Aspinwall, Bernard. *Portable Utopia: Glasgow and the United States, 1820–1920*. Aberdeen, Scotland: Aberdeen University Press, 1984.

Bailey, Patrick. *Orkney*. Newton Abbot, England: David and Charles, 1995.

Ball, Martin, ed. *The Celtic Languages*. London: Routledge, 1993.

Ballantyne, John H., and Brian Smith. *Shetland Documents, 1580–1611*. Lerwick, Scotland: Shetland Islands Council and Shetland Times, 1994.

Bannerman, John. *Studies in the History of Dalriada*. Edinburgh: Scottish Academic Press, 1974.

Bardgett, Frank D. *Scotland Reformed: The Reformation in Angus and the Mearns*. Edinburgh: John Donald, 1989.

Barnard, Alfred. *The Whisky Distilleries of the United Kingdom*. Edinburgh: Mainstream, 1987.

Barrow, G. W. S. *The Anglo-Norman Era in Scottish History*. Oxford: Clarendon Press, 1980.

————. *David I of Scotland (1124–1153): The Balance of New and Old.* Reading, England: University of Reading, 1985.

————. *The Kingdom of the Scots: Government, Church and Society from the Eleventh to the Fourteenth Century.* London: Edward Arnold, 1973.

————. *Kingship and Unity: Scotland 1000–1306.* Edinburgh: Edinburgh University Press, 1989.

————. *Robert Bruce and the Community of the Realm of Scotland.* Edinburgh: Edinburgh University Press, 1988.

————. *Scotland and Its Neighbours in the Middle Ages.* London: Hambledon Press, 1992.

————. *The Scottish Tradition: Essays in Honour of Ronald Gordon Cant.* Edinburgh: Scottish Academic Press, 1974.

Barrow, G. W. S., and W. W. Scott, eds. *The Acts of William I, King of Scots, 1165–1214.* Edinburgh: Edinburgh University Press, 1971.

Barthrop, Michael, and G. A. Embleton. *The Jacobite Rebellions, 1689–1745.* London: Osprey, 1982.

Bartram, Peter. *David Steel: His Life and Politics.* London: W. H. Allen, 1981.

Batey, Colleen E., Judith Jesch, and Christopher D. Morris. *The Viking Age in Caithness, Orkney and the North Atlantic: Select Papers from the Eleventh Viking Congress, Thurso and Kirkwall. 22 August–1 September 1989.* Edinburgh: Edinburgh University Press, 1993.

Bawcutt, Priscilla. *Gavin Douglas: A Critical Study.* Edinburgh: Edinburgh University Press, 1976.

Baynes, John. *The Jacobite Rising of 1715.* London: Cassell, 1970.

Beard, Geoffrey. *The Work of Robert Adam.* Edinburgh: John Bartholomew, 1978.

Beaton, Elizabeth. *Scotland's Traditional Houses: Country, Town and Coastal Homes.* Edinburgh: Her Majesty's Stationery Office, 1997.

Bede, Tim. *MacRoots: How to Trace Your Scottish Ancestors.* Loanhead, Scotland: Macdonald, 1982.

Begg, H. M., C. M. Lythe, and R. Sorley. *Expenditure in Scotland 1961–1971.* Edinburgh: Scottish Academic Press, 1975.

Begg, Tom. *Housing Policy in Scotland.* Edinburgh: Donald, 1996.

Bell, Alan, ed. *Lord Cockburn: a Bicentenary Commemoration, 1779–1979.* Edinburgh: Scottish Academic Press, 1979.

————. *Scott Bicentenary Essays.* Edinburgh: Scottish Academic Press, 1973.

Bell, G. T. *A Prospect of Sutherland.* Edinburgh: Birlinn, 1995.

Benn, Caroline. *Keir Hardie.* London: Hutchinson, 1992.

Berresford Ellis, P. *Celt and Saxon: The Struggle for Britain, AD 410–*

937. London: Constable, 1993.

Berry, C. Leo. *The Young Pretender's Mistress: Clementine Walkinshaw (Comtesse d'Albestroff), 1720–1802*. Edinburgh: Skilton, 1977.

Binding, Paul. *Robert Louis Stevenson*. London: Oxford University Press, 1974.

Bingham, Caroline. *James I of England*. London: Weidenfeld and Nicolson, 1981.

—————. *James V: King of Scots, 1512–1542*. London: Collins, 1971.

—————. *James VI of Scotland*. London: Weidenfeld and Nicolson, 1979.

—————. *The Kings and Queens of Scotland*. London: Weidenfeld and Nicolson, 1976.

—————. *Scotland Under Mary Stuart: an Account of Everyday Life*. London: Allen and Unwin, 1971.

—————. *The Stewart Kingdom of Scotland, 1371–1603*. London: Weidenfeld and Nicolson, 1974.

Bingham, Madeleine. *Scotland under Mary Stuart: An Account of Everyday Life*. London: Allen and Unwin, 1971.

Black, George F. *The Surnames of Scotland*. Edinburgh: Birlinn, 1993.

Black, Jeremy. *Culloden and the '45*. Stroud, England: Alan Sutton, 1993.

Blaug, Mark, ed. *David Hume (1711–1776) and James Steuart (1712–1780)*. Aldershot, England: Edgar, 1991.

Boardman, Stephen. *The Early Stewart Kings: Robert II and Robert III*. East Linton, Scotland: Tuckwell Press, 1996.

Bold, Alan. *A Burns Companion*. London: Macmillan, 1991.

—————. *The Letters of Hugh MacDiarmid*. London: Hamish Hamilton, 1984.

—————. *MacDiarmid: Christopher Murray Grieve — A Critical Biography*. London: John Murray, 1988.

Bongie, L. L. *The Love of a Prince: Bonnie Prince Charlie in France 1744–1748*. Vancouver, Canada: University of British Columbia Press, 1986.

Booth, Bradford A., and Ernest Mehew, eds. *The Letters of Robert Louis Stevenson*. 4 vols. New Haven, Conn.: Yale University Press, 1994.

Bowes, Alison, and Duncan Sim, eds. *Demands and Constraints: Ethnic Minorities and Social Services in Scotland*. Edinburgh: Scottish Council For Voluntary Organisations, 1991.

Boyd, K. B., and I. L. Boyd. *The Hebrides: A Natural History*. London: Collins, 1990.

Boyd, Kenneth M. *Scottish Church Attitudes to Sex, Marriage and the Family, 1850–1914*. Edinburgh: John Donald, 1980.

Bradley, J. M. *Ethnic and Religious Identity in Modern Scotland*. Aldershot, England: Avebury, 1996.

Brady, Frank. *James Boswell: The Later Years*. New York: McGraw-Hill, 1984.

Brand, J. *The National Movement in Scotland*. London: Routledge, 1978.

Brander, Michael. *The Emigrant Scots*. London: Constable, 1982.

──────. *The Original Scotch: A History of Scotch Whisky from the Earliest Days*. London: Hutchinson, 1974.

──────. *World Directory of Scottish Associations*. Glasgow: Neil Wilson, 1996.

Bray, Elizabeth. *The Discovery of the Hebrides: Voyages to the Western Isles, 1745-1883*. Edinburgh: Birlinn, 1996.

Breeze, David J. *The Northern Frontiers of Roman Britain*. London: Batsford, 1982.

──────. *Roman Scotland*. London: Batsford, 1996.

──────, ed. *Studies in Scottish Antiquity Presented to Stewart Cruden*. Edinburgh: John Donald, 1984.

Breitenbach, Esther, and Eleanor Gordon, eds. *Out of Bounds: Women in Scottish Society, 1800–1945*. Edinburgh: Edinburgh University Press, 1992.

Brice, Katherine. *The Early Stuarts, 1603–1640*. London: Hodder and Stoughton, 1994.

Brock, William R. *Scotus Americanus: A Survey of the Sources for Links Between Scotland and America in the Eighteenth Century*. Edinburgh: Edinburgh University Press, 1982.

Brooke, Daphne. *Wild Men and Holy Places: St. Ninian, Whithorn and the Medieval Realm of Galloway*. Edinburgh: Canongate Press, 1994.

Brooker, W. D. *A Century of Scottish Mountaineering*. Leicester, England: Scottish Mountaineering Club, 1993.

Brooks, D. *Wild Men and Holy Places: St Ninian, Whithorn and the Medieval Realm of Galloway*. Edinburgh: Canongate Press, 1994.

Brotherstone, Terry, and D. J. Witherington. *Aspects of Aberdeen's History Since 1794*. Glasgow: Cruithne Press, 1996.

Brotherstone, Terry, ed. *Covenant, Charter and Party: Traditions of Revolt and Protest in Modern Scottish History*. Aberdeen, Scotland: Aberdeen University Press, 1989.

Brown, Alice, David McCrone, and Lindsay Paterson. *Politics and Society in Scotland*. Basingstoke, England: Macmillan, 1996.

Brown, Callum G. *The Social History of Religion in Scotland since 1730*. London: Methuen, 1987.

Brown, Jennifer M., ed. *Scottish Society in the Fifteenth Century*. London: Edward Arnold, 1977.

Brown, Gordon, and James Naughtie. *John Smith: Life and Soul of the*

Party. Edinburgh: Mainstream, 1994.

Brown, Keith. *Bloodfeud in Scotland, 1573–1625*. Edinburgh: John Donald, 1986.

—————. *Kingdom or Province?: Scotland and the Regal Union, 1603–1715*. Basingstoke, England: Macmillan, 1992.

Brown, Michael. *James I*. Edinburgh: Canongate Academic, 1994.

Brown, Stewart J. *Thomas Chalmers and the Godly Commonwealth of Scotland*. Oxford: Oxford University Press, 1982.

Brown, Stewart J. and Fry, M. *Scotland in the Age of Disruption*. Edinburgh: Edinburgh University Press, 1993.

Brown, Vivienne. *Adam Smith's Discourse: Canonicity, Commerce and Conscience*. London: Routledge, 1994.

Bruce, Robert V. *Bell: Alexander Graham Bell and the Conquest of Solitude*. London: Gollancz, 1973.

Bryan, Gordon. *Scottish Nationalism and Cultural Identity in the Twentieth Century: An Annotated Bibliography of Secondary Sources*. Westport, Conn.: Greenwood Press, 1984.

Bryden, D. J. *Scottish Scientific Instrument Makers, 1600-1900*. Edinburgh: Royal Scottish Museum, 1972.

Bryden, John, and George Houston. *Agrarian Change in the Scottish Highlands: The Role of the Highlands and Islands Development Board in the Agricultural Economy of the Crofting Counties*. London: Martin Robertson, 1976.

Brydon, Robert. *The Scottish Coronation Journey of King Charles I*. Kirkcaldy, Scotland: Sporting Partnership, 1993.

Buchan, Alasdair. *The Right to Work: The Story of the Upper Clyde Confrontation*. London: Calder and Boyars, 1972.

Buchan, William. *John Buchan: A Memoir*. London: Buchan and Enright, 1982.

Buchanan, Joni. *The Lewis Land Struggle - Na Gaisgich*. Stornoway, Scotland: Acair, 1996.

Buchanan, Meg, ed. *St Kilda: The Continuing Story of the Islands*. Edinburgh: Her Majesty's Stationery Office, 1995.

Buchanan, Patricia Hill. *Margaret Tudor: Queen of Scots*. Edinburgh: Scottish Academic Press, 1985.

Buckle, Henry Thomas. *On Scotland and the Scotch Intellect*, edited by H. J. Hanham. Chicago: University of Chicago Press, 1970.

Buckroyd, J. *Church and State in Scotland, 1660–81*. Edinburgh: John Donald, 1980.

Burns, Peter, and Pat Woods. *Oh, Hampden in the Sun...* Edinburgh: Mainstream, 1997.

Butt, John. *Robert Owen: Prince of Cotton Spinners*. Newton Abbot, England: David and Charles, 1971.

Butt, John, and J. T. Ward, eds. *Scottish Themes: Essays in Honour of Professor S. G. E. Lythe*. Edinburgh: Scottish Academic Press, 1976.

Buxton, B. *Mingulay: An Island and Its People*. Edinburgh: Birlinn, 1995.

Cage, R. A. *The Scottish Poor Law, 1745–1845*. Edinburgh: Scottish Academic Press, 1981.

—————, ed. *The Scots Abroad: Labour, Capital, Enterprise, 1750–1914*. London: Croom Helm, 1985.

Calder, Angus. *Revolving Culture: Notes from the Scottish Republic*. London: I. B. Tauris, 1994.

Calder, Jenni. *RLS: A Life Study*. Glasgow: Richard Drew, 1990.

—————. *Scotland in Trust: The National Trust for Scotland*. Glasgow: Richard Drew, 1990.

—————. *Stevenson and Victorian Scotland*. Edinburgh: Edinburgh University Press, 1981.

Cameron, Alan. *Bank of Scotland, 1695–1995: A Very Singular Institution*. Edinburgh: Mainstream, 1995.

Cameron, D. K. *Willie Gavin, Crofter Man — A Portrait of a Vanished Lifestyle*. Edinburgh: Birlinn, 1995.

Cameron, E. A. *The Land for the People?: The British Government and the Scottish Highlands*. East Linton, Scotland: Tuckwell Press, 1996.

Cameron, N. M. de S. *Dictionary of Scottish Church History and Theology*. Edinburgh: T. and T. Clark, 1993.

Campbell, Alan B. *The Lanarkshire Miners; A Social History of Their Trade Unions, 1775–1874*. Edinburgh: John Donald, 1979.

Campbell, Donald. *Playing for Scotland: A History of the Scottish Stage, 1715–1965*. Edinburgh: Mercat Press, 1996.

Campbell, Ian. *Kailyard*. Edinburgh: Ramsay Head, 1981.

—————, ed. *Nineteenth Century Scottish Fiction: Critical Essays*. Manchester: Carcanet New Press, 1979.

Campbell, J. L. *Canna: The Story of a Hebridean Island*. Edinburgh: Canongate Press, 1994.

Campbell, N., and R. M. S. Smellie. *The Royal Society of Edinburgh (1783–1983): The First Two Hundred Years*. Edinburgh: Royal Society of Edinburgh, 1983.

Campbell, R. H. *Owners and Occupiers: Changes in Rural Society in South-West Scotland before 1914*. Aberdeen, Scotland: Aberdeen University Press, 1991.

—————. *The Rise and Fall of Scottish Industry: 1707–1939*. Edinburgh: John Donald, 1980.

—————. *Scotland since 1707: The Rise of an Industrial Society*. Edinburgh: John Donald, 1985.

Campbell, R. H., and Andrew S. Skinner. *Adam Smith.* London: Croom Helm, 1982.

—————, eds. *The Origins and Nature of the Scottish Enlightenment.* Edinburgh: John Donald, 1982.

Campbell, T. D. *Adam Smith's Science of Morals.* London: Allen and Unwin, 1971.

Cannon, Roderick D. *The Highland Bagpipe and Its Music.* Edinburgh: John Donald, 1995.

Cant, Ronald Gordon. *The University of St Andrews: A Short History.* Edinburgh: Scottish Academic Press, 1970.

Capaldi, Nicholas. *David Hume: The Newtonian Philosopher.* Boston: Twayne, 1975.

Carruthers, A., ed. *The Scottish Home.* Edinburgh: National Museums of Scotland, 1996.

Carswell, David. *Scott and His Circle.* Freeport, N.Y.: Books For Libraries Press, 1971.

Carter, Ian. *Farmlife in Northeast Scotland, 1840–1914: The Poor Man's Country.* Edinburgh: John Donald, 1979.

Carter, J. J., and C. A. McLaren. *Crown and Gown, 1495–1995 — An Illustrated History of the University of Aberdeen.* Aberdeen, Scotland: Scottish Cultural Press, 1995.

Chambliss, J. E. *The Life and Labours of David Livingstone, Covering His Entire Career in Southern and Central Africa.* Westport, Conn.: Negro Universities Press, 1970.

Chapman, Malcolm. *The Gaelic Vision in Scottish Culture.* London: Croom Helm, 1978.

Checkland, Olive. *Philanthropy in Victorian Scotland.* Edinburgh: John Donald, 1980.

Checkland, Olive, and Sydney G. Checkland. *Industry and Ethos: Scotland, 1832–1914.* Edinburgh: Edinburgh University Press, 1989.

Checkland, Olive, and Margaret Lamb, eds. *Health Care as Social History: The Glasgow Case.* Aberdeen, Scotland: Aberdeen University Press, 1982.

Checkland, Sydney G. *Scottish Banking: A History, 1695–1973.* Glasgow: Collins, 1975.

—————. *The Upas Tree: Glasgow, 1875–1981.* Glasgow: Glasgow University Press, 1982.

Cheyne, A. C., ed. *The Practical and the Pious: Essays on Thomas Chalmers (1780–1847).* Edinburgh: St Andrew Press, 1985.

—————. *The Transforming of the Kirk: Victorian Scotland's Religious Revolution.* Edinburgh: St. Andrews Press, 1983.

Chitnis, Annand C. *The Scottish Enlightenment: A Social History.* London: Croom Helm, 1976.

Church of Scotland. *Lifestyle Survey.* Edinburgh: Church of Scotland, 1987.

Church, Roy, Alan Hall and John Kanefsky. *1830–1913, Victorian Pre-Eminence.* Vol. 3 of *The History of the British Coal Industry.* Oxford: Clarendon Press, 1987.

Claeys, Gregory. *Machinery, Money and the Millenium: the New Moral Economy of Owenite Socialism, 1815–60.* Princeton, N.J.: Princeton University Press, 1987.

Clark, Ronald W. *Balmoral: Queen Victoria's Highland Home.* London: Thames and Hudson, 1981.

Close-Brooks, Joanna. *Exploring Scotland's Heritage: The Highlands.* Edinburgh: Her Majesty's Stationery Office, 1995.

Cloyd, E. L. *James Burnett, Lord Monboddo.* Oxford: Clarendon Press, 1972.

Clutton-Brock, T. H., and S. D. Aldon. *Red Deer in the Highlands.* Oxford: BSP Professional Books, 1989.

Clyde, R. *From Rebel to Hero: The Image of the Highlander.* East Linton, Scotland: Tuckwell Press, 1995.

Coley, Linda. *Britons: Forging the Nation, 1707–1837.* London: Pimlico, 1994.

Collinson, Patrick. *The English Captivity of Mary Queen of Scots.* Sheffield, England: University of Sheffield, Department of History, 1987.

Connachan Holmes, J. R. A. *Country Houses of Scotland.* Colonsay, Scotland: House of Lochar, 1995.

Costello, Sean, and Tom Johnstone, ed. *Famous Last Words: Two Centuries of Obituaries from* The Scotsman. Edinburgh: Mercat Press, 1996.

Couldrey, V. *A Celebration of Scottish Landscape: Painters of Scotland.* Nairn, Scotland: Thomas and Lochar, 1993.

Coull, J. R. *The Sea Fisheries of Scotland: A Historical Geography.* Edinburgh: John Donald, 1996.

Coventry, Martin. *The Castles of Scotland: A Comprehensive Reference and Gazetteer to More Than 1700 Castles.* Edinburgh: Goblinshead, 1995.

Cowan, Edward J. *Montrose: For Covenant and King.* London: Weidenfeld and Nicolson, 1977.

Cowan, Henry. *John Knox, the Hero of the Scottish Reformation.* New York: AMS Press, 1970.

Cowan, Ian B. *Regional Aspects of the Scottish Reformation.* London: Historical Association, 1978.

————. *The Scottish Covenanters, 1660–1688.* London: Gollancz,

1976.

————. *The Scottish Reformation: Church and Society in Sixteenth Century Scotland*. London: Weidenfeld and Nicolson, 1982.

Cowan, Ian B., and David E. Easson. *Medieval Religious Houses: Scotland*. London: Longman, 1976.

Cowan, Ian B., P. H. R. Mackay and Alan Macquarrie. *The Knights of St John of Jerusalem in Scotland*. Edinburgh: Scottish Historical Society, 1983.

Cowan, Ian B., and Duncan Shaw, eds. *The Renaissance and Reformation in Scotland: Essays in Honour of Gordon Donaldson*. Edinburgh: Scottish Academic Press, 1983.

Coutts, Ben. *A Scotsman's War*. Edinburgh: Mercat Press, 1996.

Craig, David. *On the Crofters' Trail*. London: Pimlico, 1997.

Craig, Maggie. *Damn Rebel Bitches: The Women of the '45*. Edinburgh: Mainstream, 1997.

Craig, W. S. *History of the Royal College of Physicians of Edinburgh*. Oxford: Blackwell Scientific, 1976.

Craigie, James. *A Bibliography of Scottish Education, 1872–1972*. London: University of London Press, 1972.

————. *A Bibliography of Scottish Education before 1872*. London: University of London Press, 1970.

Craik, Roger. *James Boswell (1740–1795): The Scottish Perspective*. Edinburgh: Her Majesty's Stationery Office, 1994.

Craik, Roger, and John St Clair. *The Advocates' Library: 300 Years of a National Institution*. Edinburgh: Her Majesty's Stationery Office, 1989.

Cramb, A. *Who Owns Scotland Now?* Edinburgh: Mainstream, 1996.

Crathorne, Nancy. *Tennant's Stalk: The Story of the Tennants of the Glen*. London: Macmillan, 1973.

Crawford, Barbara E. *Scandinavian Scotland*. Leicester: Leicester University Press, 1987.

————. *Scandinavian Settlement in Northern Britain*. Leicester, England: Leicester University Press, 1996.

Crawford, Robert, ed. *Robert Burns and Cultural Authority*. Edinburgh: Edinburgh University Press, 1997.

Cruden, Stewart. *The Scottish Castle*. Edinburgh: Spurbooks, 1981.

————. *Scottish Medieval Churches*. Edinburgh: John Donald, 1986.

Cruft, Kitty, and Andrew Fraser, eds. *James Craig, 1744–1795: The Ingenious Architect of the New Town of Edinburgh*. Edinburgh: Mercat Press, 1995.

Cruickshank, Marjorie. *A History of the Training of Teachers in Scot-*

land. London: University of London Press, 1970.

Cruickshanks, E., and J. Black. *The Jacobite Challenge.* Edinburgh: John Donald, 1988.

Crumley, Jim. *The Road and the Miles: A Homage to Dundee.* Edinburgh: Mainstream, 1996.

Cullen, L. M., and T. C. Smout, eds. *Comparative Aspects of Scottish and Irish Economic and Social History, 1600–1900.* Edinburgh: John Donald, 1976.

Cummings, W. A. *The Age of the Picts.* Stroud, England: Alan Sutton, 1995.

Cummings, A. J. G., and T. M. Devine, eds. *Industry, Business and Society in Scotland since 1700: Essays Presented to Professor John Butt.* Edinburgh: John Donald, 1994.

Cuthbert, O. D. *The Life and Letters of an Orkney Naturalist — the Rev George Low, 1747-1866: A Case Study.* Kirkwall, Scotland: Orkney Press, 1995.

Daiches, David. *Charles Edward Stuart: The Life and Times of Bonnie Prince Charlie.* London: Thames and Hudson, 1973.

——————. *Literature and Gentility in Scotland.* Edinburgh: Edinburgh University Press, 1982.

——————, ed. *The New Companion to Scottish Culture.* Edinburgh: Polygon, 1993.

——————. *Robert Burns.* Edinburgh: Spurbooks, 1981.

——————. *Robert Burns and His World.* London: Thames and Hudson, 1971.

——————. *Robert Burns: The Poet.* Edinburgh: Saltire Society, 1994.

——————. *Scotch Whisky: Its Past and Present.* London: Deutsch, 1978.

——————. *Scotland and the Union.* London: John Murray, 1977.

——————. *Sir Walter Scott and His World.* New York: Viking Press, 1971.

Daiches, David, and Jean Jones, ed. *Hotbed of Genius.* Edinburgh: Edinburgh University Press, 1986.

Damer, S. *Glasgow: Going for a Song.* London: Lawrence and Wishart, 1990.

——————. *From Moorepark to Wine Alley: The Rise and Fall of a Glasgow Housing Estate.* Edinburgh: Edinburgh University Press, 1989.

Dand, Charles Hendry. *The Might Affair: How Scotland Lost Her Parliament.* Edinburgh: Oliver and Boyd, 1972.

Dankert, Clyde E. *Adam Smith: Man of Letters and Economist.* Hicksville, N.Y.: Exposition Press, 1974.

Danziger, Marlies K., and Frank Brady, eds. *Boswell: The Great Biographer, 1789–1795*. London: Heinemann, 1989.

Darton, M. *The Dictionary of Place Names in Scotland*. Orpington, England: Dobby, 1994.

Davie, George E. *The Scottish Enlightenment, and Other Essays*. Edinburgh: Polygon, 1991.

Davies, Hunter. *The Teller of Tales: In Search of Robert Louis Stevenson*. London: Sinclair-Stevenson, 1994.

Davies, R. R. *Domination and Conquest: The Experience of Ireland, Scotland and Wales, 1100–1300*. Cambridge: Cambridge University Press, 1990.

Dennison, Walter Traill. *Orkney Folklore and Sea Legends*. Kirkwall, Scotland: Orkney Press, 1995.

Denniston, Robin, and Magnus Linklater, eds. *Anatomy of Scotland*. Edinburgh: Chambers, 1992.

Devine, T. M. *Clanship to Crofters' War: The Social Transformation of the Scottish Highlands*. Manchester: Manchester University Press, 1994.

—————. *Exploring the Scottish Past: Themes in the History of Scottish Society*. East Linton, Scotland: Tuckwell, 1995.

—————, ed. *Farm Servants and Labour in Lowland Scotland, 1770–1914*. Edinburgh: John Donald, 1984.

—————, ed. *Lairds and Improvement in the Scotland of the Enlightenment*. Glasgow: Scottish Historical Conference Trust, 1979.

—————, ed. *Scottish Elites: Proceedings of the Scottish Historical Studies Seminar, University of Strathclyde, 1991–1992*. Edinburgh: John Donald, 1994.

—————, ed. *Scottish Emigration and Scottish Society: Proceedings of the Scottish Historical Studies Seminar, University of Strathclyde, 1990–1991*. Edinburgh: John Donald, 1992.

—————. *A Scottish Firm in Virginia: 1776–1777: W. Cunninghame and Co.*. Edinburgh: Scottish History Society, 1984.

—————. *The Tobacco Lords: A Study of the Tobacco Merchants of Glasgow and Their Trading Activities, 1740–90*. Edinburgh: Edinburgh University Press, 1990.

—————. *The Transformation of Rural Scotland: Social Change and the Agrarian Economy, 1660–1815*. Edinburgh: Edinburgh University Press, 1994.

Devine, T. M., and Rosalind Mitchison. *1760–1830*. Vol. 1 of *People and Society in Scotland:* Edinburgh: John Donald, 1988.

Devine, T. M., and David Dickson, eds. *Ireland and Scotland, 1600–1850: Parallels and Contrasts in Economic and Social Development*.

Edinburgh: John Donald, 1983.

Devine, T. M., and Gordon Jackson, eds. *Glasgow: Beginnings to 1830*. Manchester: Manchester University Press, 1994.

Devine, T. M. and Richard J. Findlay, eds. *Scotland in the 20th Century*. Edinburgh: Edinburgh University Press, 1996.

Devlin, D. D. *The Author of Waverley: A Critical Study of Walter Scott*. London: Macmillan, 1971.

Dick, Michael. *The 4.15 to Cartsdyke: A Tale of Two Shipyards: Scotts' and the Greenock Dockyard*. Durham, England: Pentland Press, 1993.

Dickinson, W. Croft. *Scotland from Earliest Times to 1603*. Oxford: Clarendon Press, 1977.

Dickson, Tony, and James H. Treble. *1914–1990*. Vol. 3 of *People and Society in Scotland*. Edinburgh: John Donald, 1990.

——————, ed. *Scottish Capitalism: Class, State and Nation from before the Union to the Present*. London: Lawrence and Wishart, 1980.

Dilworth, M. *Scottish Universities in the Late Middle Ages*. Edinburgh: Edinburgh University Press, 1995.

Dingwall, Helen M. *Late Seventeenth-Century Edinburgh: A Demographic Study*. Aldershot, England: Scolar Press, 1994.

——————. *Physicians, Surgeons and Apothecaries: Medical Practice in 17th Century Edinburgh*. East Linton, Scotland: Tuckwell Press, 1995.

Dobson, David. *Scottish American Heirs, 1683–1883*. Baltimore: Genealogical Publishing, 1990.

——————. *Scottish Emigration to Colonial America, 1607–1785*. Athens: University of Georgia Press, 1994.

Dodgson, Robert A. *Land and Society in Early Scotland*. Oxford: Clarendon Press, 1981.

Donald, Peter. *An Uncounselled King: Charles I and His Scottish Troubles, 1637–1641*. Cambridge: Cambridge University Press, 1990.

Donaldson, Gordon. *All the Queen's Men: Power and Politics in Mary Stewart's Scotland*. London: Batsford, 1983.

——————. *The Auld Alliance: The Franco-Scottish Connection*. Edinburgh: The Saltire Society, 1985.

——————. *The Faith of the Scots*. London: Batsford, 1990.

——————. *Mary, Queen of Scots*. London: English Universities Press, 1974.

——————. *A Northern Commonwealth: Scotland and Norway*. Edinburgh: Saltire, 1990.

——————. *Scotland, Church and Nation Through Sixteen Centuries*. Edinburgh: Scottish Academic Press, 1972.

——————. *Scotland: James V to James VII.* Edinburgh: Oliver and Boyd, 1974.

——————. *Scotland: The Shaping of a Nation.* Nairn, Scotland: David St John Thomas, 1993.

——————. *Scotland's History: Approaches and Reflections.* Edinburgh: Scottish Academic Press, 1995.

——————, ed. *Scottish Church History.* Edinburgh: Scottish Academic Press, 1985.

——————. *Scottish Historical Documents.* Glasgow: Neil Wilson, 1997.

——————. *Scottish Kings.* New York: Barnes and Noble, 1992.

——————. *The Sources of Scottish History.* Edinburgh: University of Edinburgh, 1978.

Donaldson, Gordon, and Robert S. Morpeth. *Who's Who in Scottish History?* Welsh Academic Press, 1996.

Donaldson, William. *The Jacobite Song: Political Myth and National Identity.* Aberdeen, Scotland: Aberdeen University Press, 1988.

Donnachie, Ian. *Historic New Lanark: The Dale and Owen Industrial Community since 1785.* Edinburgh: Edinburgh University Press, 1993.

——————. *A History of the Brewing Industry in Scotland.* Edinburgh: John Donald, 1979.

Donnachie, Ian, Christopher Harvie and Ian S. Wood. *Forward! Labour Politics in Scotland, 1888–1988.* Edinburgh: Polygon, 1989.

Donnachie, Ian, and George Hewitt. *A Companion to Scottish History: From the Reformation to the Present.* London: Batsford, 1989.

Donnachie, Ian, J. Hume and M. Moss. *Scotland.* (Historical Industrial Scenes Series) Buxton, England: Moorland, 1977.

Donnachie, Ian, and Christopher Whateley, eds. *The Manufacture of Scottish History.* Edinburgh: Polygon, 1992.

Donnison, D., and A. Middleton. *Regenerating the Inner City: Glasgow's Experience.* London: Routledge and Kegan Paul, 1987.

Donovan, Arthur. *Philosophical Chemistry in the Scottish Enlightenment: The Doctrines and Discoveries of William Cullen and Joseph Black.* Edinburgh: Edinburgh University Press, 1975.

Donovan, Arthur, and Joseph Prentiss. *James Hutton's Medical Dissertation.* Philadelphia, Pa.: American Philosophical Society, 1980.

Dorward, David. *Scotland's Place-Names.* Edinburgh: Mercat Press, 1995.

Douglas, Andrew M. *Church and School in Scotland.* Edinburgh: St Andrew Press, 1985.

Douglas, Gordon. *Charles Edward Stuart: The Man, the King, the Leg-*

end. London: Hale, 1975.

——————. *Robert Burns: A Life.* London: Hale, 1976.

Douglas, Hugh. *Bonnie Prince Charlie in Love: The Private Passions of Prince Charles Edward Stuart.* Stroud, England: Alan Sutton, 1995.

Dow, F. *Cromwellian Scotland.* Edinburgh: John Donald, 1979.

Drummond, Andrew L., and James Bulloch. *The Church in Late Victorian Scotland.* Edinburgh: St Andrew Press, 1973.

——————. *The Church in Victorian Scotland, 1843–1874.* Edinburgh: St Andrew Press, 1975.

——————. *The Scottish Church, 1688–1843: The Age of the Moderates.* Edinburgh: St Andrew Press, 1973.

Duff, D, ed. *Queen Victoria's Highland Journals.* Exeter, England: University of Exeter, 1980.

Dunbar, J. Telfer. *History of Highland Dress.* London: Batsford, 1979.

Dunbar, John G. *The Architecture of Scotland.* London: Batsford, 1978.

——————, ed. *The Acts of Robert I, King of Scots, 1306-1329.* Edinburgh: Edinburgh University Press, 1988.

——————. *James I, King of Scots, 1424–1437.* Glasgow: University of Glasgow, 1984.

——————. *Scotland: The Making of the Kingdom.* Edinburgh: Oliver and Boyd, 1975.

——————. *Scotland's Relations with England: A Survey to 1707.* Edinburgh: Saltire Society, 1994.

Dunbar, John G., and Ian Fisher. *Iona: A Guide to the Monuments.* Edinburgh: Her Majesty's Stationery Office, 1995.

Dunlop, Jean. *The British Fisheries Society, 1786–1993.* Edinburgh: John Donald, 1978.

Durie, Alastair J. *The Scottish Linen Industry in the Eighteenth Century.* Edinburgh: John Donald, 1979.

Durkacz, Victor Edward. *The Decline of the Celtic Languages: A Study of Linguistic and Cultural Conflict in Scotland, Wales and Ireland from the Reformation to the Twentieth Century.* Edinburgh: John Donald, 1983.

Durkan, John, and James Kirk. *The University of Glasgow, 1451–1577.* Glasgow: University of Glasgow Press, 1977.

Dwyer, John, and Richard B. Sher, eds. *Sociability and Society in Eighteenth-Century Scotland.* Edinburgh: Mercat Press, 1993.

Dwyer, John, Roger A. Mason and Alexander Murdoch, eds. *New Perspectives on the Policies and Culture of Early Modern Scotland.* Edinburgh: John Donald, 1982.

Edwards, Kevin J., and Ian B. M. Ralston, eds. *Scotland: Environment and Archaeology, 8000 BC–AD 1000.* London: John Wiley and

Sons, 1997.

Edwards, Owen Dudley. *Burke and Hare*. Edinburgh: Mercat Press, 1993.

Edwards, Owen Dudley, and George Shepperson, eds. *Scotland, Europe and the American Revolution*. Edinburgh: University of Edinburgh, 1976.

Ellis, P. Berresford, and Seumas Mac A'Ghobhainn. *The Scottish Insurrection of 1820*. London: Gollancz, 1970.

Erickson, Carolly. *Bonnie Prince Charlie: A Biography*. New York: Morrow, 1989.

Everitt, C. W. F. *James Clerk Maxwell: Physicist and Natural Philosopher*. New York: Scribner's, 1975.

Ewan, E. *Townlife in Fourteenth-Century Scotland*. Edinburgh: Edinburgh University Press, 1990.

Farmer, Lindsay. *Criminal Law, Tradition and Legal Order: Crime and the Genius of Scots Law, 1747 to the Present*. Cambridge: Cambridge University Press, 1996.

Fawcett, Arthur. *The Cambuslang Revival: The Scottish Evangelical Revival of the Eighteenth Century*. London: Banner of Truth Trust, 1971.

Fawcett, Richard. *The Architectural History of Scotland: From the Accession of the Stewarts to the Reformation, 1371–1560*. Edinburgh: Edinburgh University Press, 1994.

——————. *Scottish Abbeys and Priories*. London: Batsford, 1994.

——————. *Scottish Cathedrals*. London: Batsford, 1997.

Feacham, Richard. *Guide to Prehistoric Scotland*. London: Batsford, 1977.

Fedosov, D. *The Caledonian Connection: Scotland-Russia Links — Middle Ages to Early Twentieth Century*. Aberdeen, Scotland: Centre for Scottish Studies, 1996.

Fenton, Alexander. *Scottish Country Life*. Edinburgh: John Donald, 1976.

——————. *The Shape of the Past: Essays in Scottish Ethology*. Edinburgh: John Donald, 1986.

Fenton, Alexander, and Bruce Walker. *The Rural Architecture of Scotland*. Edinburgh: John Donald, 1981.

Fenwick, Hubert. *The Auld Alliance*. Kineton, England: Roundwood Press, 1971.

——————. *Scotland's Historic Buildings*. London: Hale, 1974.

Ferguson, D. M. *Shipwrecks of North East Scotland*. Aberdeen, Scotland: Aberdeen University Press, 1991.

Ferguson, J. De Lancey, ed. *The Letters of Robert Burns*, 2 vols. Oxford: Clarendon Press, 1985.

Ferguson, John P. S. *Scottish Family Histories*. Edinburgh: National Library of Scotland, 1986.

Ferguson, William. *Scotland: 1689 to the Present*. Edinburgh: Mercat Press, 1992.

—————. *Scotland's Relations with England: A Survey to 1707*. Edinburgh: John Donald, 1977.

Finlay, Richard J. *Independent and Free: Scottish Politics and the Origins of the Scottish National Party, 1918–1945*. Edinburgh: John Donald, 1984.

Finlayson, Iain. *The Moth and the Candle: A Life of James Boswell*. London: Constable, 1984.

—————. *The Scots*. London: Constable, 1987.

Finnie, M. *Shetland: An Illustrated Architectural Guide*. Edinburgh: Royal Incorporation of Architects in Scotland, 1990.

Fisher, Andrew. *William Wallace*. Edinburgh: John Donald, 1986.

Fisher, I. *Iona: A Guide to the Monuments*. Edinburgh: Her Majesty's Stationery Office, 1995.

Fisher, Joe. *The Glasgow Encyclopedia*. Edinburgh: Mainstream, 1994.

Fisher, Richard B. *Joseph Lister, 1827–1912*. London: Macdonald and Jane's, 1977.

Fiske, Roger. *Scotland in Music: A European Enthusiasm*. Cambridge: Cambridge University Press, 1983.

Fissell, Mark Charles. *The Bishops' Wars: Charles I's Campaigns against Scotland, 1638–1640*. Cambridge: Cambridge University Press, 1994.

Fitzhugh, Robert Tyson. *Robert Burns, the Man and the Poet: A Round Unvarnished Account*. London: W. H. Allen, 1971.

Flinn, Michael, ed. *Scottish Population History from the 17th Century to the 1930s*. Cambridge: Cambridge University Press, 1977.

Flinn, Michael W., and David Stoker. *1700–1830, the Industrial Revolution*. Vol 2 of *The History of the British Coal Industry*. — Oxford: Clarendon Press, 1984.

Fojut, Noel, and Denys Pringle. *The Ancient Monuments of Shetland*. Edinburgh: Her Majesty's Stationery Office, 1993.

Fojut, Noel, Denys Pringle and Bruce Walker. *The Ancient Monuments of the Western Isles*. Edinburgh: Her Majesty's Stationery Office, 1994.

Forbes, Duncan. *Hume's Philosophical Politics*. Cambridge: Cambridge University Press, 1975.

Forrester, Duncan B., and Douglas M. Murray. *Studies in the History of Worship in Scotland*. Edinburgh: T. and T. Clark, 1984.

Forster, Margaret. *The Rash Adventurer: The Rise and Fall of Charles Edward Stuart*. London: Secker and Warburg, 1973.

Forster, Walter Roland. *The Church before the Covenants: The Church of Scotland, 1596–1638*. Edinburgh: Scottish Academic Press, 1975.

Foster, John, and Charles Woolfson. *Politics of the UCS Work-in: Class Alliances and the Right to Work*. London: Lawrence and Wishart, 1986.

Foster, Sally M. *Picts, Gaels and Scots*. London: Batsford/Historic Scotland, 1996.

Fowler, Richard Hindle. *Robert Burns*. London: Routledge, 1988.

Fraser, Antonia. *King James VI of Scotland, I of England*. London: Weidenfeld and Nicolson, 1974.

—————. *Mary Queen of Scots*. London: Mandarin, 1989.

Fraser, David. *Land and Society in Neolithic Orkney*. 2 vols. Oxford: British Archaeological Reports, 1983.

Fraser, George MacDonald. *The Steel Bonnets: The Story of the Anglo-Scottish Border Reivers*. London: HarperCollins, 1995.

Fraser, Hamish, and R. J. Morris. *1830–1914*. Vol 2 of *People and Society in Scotland*. Edinburgh: John Donald, 1990.

Friel, J. P., and W. G. Watson, eds. *Pictish Studies: Settlement, Burial and Art in Dark Age Northern Britain*. Oxford: British Archaeological Reports, 1984.

Fry, M. *Patronage and Principle: A Political History of Modern Scotland*. Aberdeen: Aberdeen University Press, 1987.

—————. *The Dundas Despotism*. Edinburgh: Edinburgh University Press, 1992.

Furgol, Edward M. *A Regimental History of the Covenanting Armies, 1639–1651*. Edinburgh: John Donald, 1990.

Fyfe, Cameron. *The Layman's Guide to Scotland's Law*. Edinburgh: Mainstream, 1995.

Galbraith, Russell. *Without Quarter: A Life of Tom Johnstone*. Edinburgh: Mainstream, 1996

Galloway, Bruce. *The Union of England and Scotland, 1603–1608*. Edinburgh: John Donald, 1986.

Geddes, John, ed. *Great Scots: A Condensed Biographical Dictionary of 1450 Notable Scots*. Ilfracombe, England: Stockwell, 1974.

Geddes, Olive. *The Laird's Kitchen: Three Hundred Years of Food in Scotland*. Edinburgh: Her Majesty's Stationery Office, 1994.

—————. *A Swing through Time: Golf in Scotland, 1457–1743*. Edinburgh: Her Majesty's Stationery Office, 1992.

Geipel, John. *The Viking Legacy: The Scandinavian Influence on the English and Gaelic Languages*. Newton Abbot, England: David and Charles, 1971.

General Register Office of Scotland. *1991 Census: Key Statistics for Localities in Scotland*. Edinburgh: Her Majesty's Stationery Office,

1995.

Gerber, Pat. *Stone of Destiny*. Edinburgh: Canongate, 1997.

Gibb, Andrew. *Glasgow: The Making of a City*. London: Croom Helm, 1983.

Gibbon Williams, Andrew. *Craigie: The Art of Craigie Aitchison*. Edinburgh: Canongate, 1996.

Gibson, John S. *Lochiel of the '45: The Jacobite Chief and the Prince*. Edinburgh: Edinburgh University Press, 1994.

――――. *Playing the Scottish Card: The Franco-Jacobite Invasion of 1708*. Edinburgh: Edinburgh University Press, 1988.

Gifford, Douglas, and Dorothy Macmillan. *A History of Scottish Women's Writing*. Edinburgh: Edinburgh University Press, 1997.

Gifford, John. *Highlands and Islands*. (Buildings of Scotland Series). London: Penguin Books, 1992.

Gilbert, I. *The Symbolism of the Pictish Stones in Scotland: A Study of Origins*. Edinburgh: Speedwell Books, 1995.

Gilbert, John M. *Hunting and Hunting Reserves in Medieval Scotland*. Edinburgh: John Donald, 1979.

Gilbertson, D. D., J. P. Gratten and M. Kent. *The Outer Hebrides of Scotland: Studies of the Last 14,000 Years*. Sheffield, England: Sheffield Academic Press, 1996.

Glendinning, Mile, Ranald MacInnes and Aonghus MacKechnie. *A History of Scottish Architecture from the Renaissance to the Present Day*. Edinburgh: Edinburgh University Press, 1996.

Glendinning, M., and S. Muthesius. *Tower Block: Modern Public Housing in England, Scotland, Wales and Northern Ireland*. New Haven, Conn.: Yale University Press, 1994.

Glover, Janet R. *The Story of Scotland*. London: Faber, 1977.

Gold, John R., and Margaret M. Gold. *Imagining Scotland: Tradition and Promotion in Scottish Tourism since 1750*. Aldershot, England: Scolar Press, 1995.

Goodman, Anthony, and Anthony Tuck, eds. *War and Border Societies in the Middle Ages*. London: Routledge, 1992.

Goodman, Jean. *Debrett's Royal Scotland*. Exeter: Webb and Bower, 1983.

Gordon, Archie. *A Wild Flight of Gordons*. London: Weidenfeld and Nicolson, 1985.

Gordon, George, ed. *Perspectives of the Scottish City*. Aberdeen, Scotland: Aberdeen University Press, 1985.

Gordon, George, and Brian Dicks, eds. *Scottish Urban History*. Aberdeen, Scotland: Aberdeen University Press, 1983.

Gordon, J. E., and D. G. Sutherland. *The Quaternary of Scotland*. London: Chapman and Hall, 1993.

Goring, Rosemary, ed. *Chambers Scottish Biographical Dictionary.* Edinburgh: Chambers, 1992.

Gourlay, R. *Sutherland: An Archaeological Guide.* Edinburgh: Birlinn, 1996.

Gow, Ian, and Alistair Rowan. *Scottish Country Houses, 1600–1914.* Edinburgh: Edinburgh University Press, 1995.

Graham-Campbell, D. *Perth: The Fair City.* Edinburgh: John Donald, 1994.

Grant, Alexander. *Independence and Nationhood: Scotland 1306–1469.* London: Edward Arnold, 1984.

Grant, Alexander, and Keith J. Stringer. *Medieval Scotland — Crown, Lordship and Community: Essays Presented to G. W. S. Barrow.* Edinburgh: Edinburgh University Press, 1993.

Grant, I. F. *The Lordship of the Isles.* Edinburgh: Mercat Press, 1982.

Gray, Malcolm. *The Fishing Industries of Scotland, 1790–1914: A Study in Regional Adaptation.* Oxford: Oxford University Press, 1978.

Gray, Robert Q. *The Labour Aristocracy in Victorian Edinburgh.* Oxford: Clarendon, 1976.

Green, Martin. *A Biography of John Buchan and His Sister Anna: the Personal Background of Their Literary Work.* Lampeter, Wales: Mellen Press, 1990.

Greig, J. Y. T. *David Hume.* New York: Garland, 1983.

Grigor, Iain Fraser. *Mightier than a Lord: The Highland Crofters' Struggle for the Land.* Stornoway, Scotland: Acair, 1979.

Grimble, Ian. *Clans and Chiefs.* London: Blond and Briggs, 1980.

——————. *Highland Man.* Inverness, Scotland: Highlands and Islands Development Board, 1980.

——————. *Scottish Clans and Tartans.* London: Hamlyn, 1982.

——————. *The Sea Wolf: The Life of Admiral Cochrane.* London: Blond and Briggs, 1978.

Gulvin, Clifford. *The Tweedmakers: A History of the Scottish Fancy Woollen Industry, 1690–1914.* Newton Abbot, England: David and Charles, 1973.

Haakonssen, Knud. *The Science of a Legislator: The Natural Jurisprudence of David Hume and Adam Smith.* Cambridge: Cambridge University Press, 1981.

Halliday, James. *Scotland: A Concise History, BC to 1990.* Edinburgh: Gordon Wright, 1990.

Halliday, Robert S. *The Disappearing Scottish Colliery: A Personal View of Some Aspects of Scotland's Coal Industry since Nationalisation.* Edinburgh: Scottish Academic Press, 1990.

Hamilton, David. *The Healers: A History of Medicine in Scotland.* Edinburgh: Canongate Press, 1981.

Hamilton, Duke of. *Maria R: Mary Queen of Scots — The Crucial Years.* Edinburgh: Mainstream, 1991.

Hamilton-Edwards, Gerald. *In Search of Scottish Ancestry.* Chichester, England: Phillimore, 1983.

Hann, D. *Government and North Sea Oil.* London: Macmillan, 1986.

Hanson, W. S., and E. A. Slater, eds. *Scottish Archaeology; New Perceptions.* Aberdeen, Scotland: Aberdeen University Press, 1991.

Hardie, William. *Scottish Painting, 1837 to the Present.* London: Studio Vista, 1994.

Harding, D. W., ed. *Later Prehistoric Settlement in South-East Scotland.* Edinburgh: University of Edinburgh, 1982.

Hardy, Forsyth. *Scotland in Film.* Edinburgh: Edinburgh University Press, 1990.

Hargrave, Andrew. *Silicon Glen; Reality or Illusion? A Global View of High Technology in Scotland.* Edinburgh: Mainstream, 1985.

Hargreaves, John D. *Aberdeenshire to Africa: Northeast Scots and British Overseas Expansion.* Aberdeen, Scotland: Aberdeen University Press, 1982.

Harris, A., M. G. Lloyd, and D. Newlands. *The Impact of Oil on the Aberdeen Economy.* Aldershot, England: Gower, 1988.

Hart, Francis Russell. *Lockhart as a Romantic Biographer.* Edinburgh: Edinburgh University Press, 1971.

——————. *The Scottish Novel: A Critical Survey.* London: John Murray, 1978.

Harvie, Christopher. *Cultural Weapons: Scotland and Survival in a New Europe.* Edinburgh: Polygon, 1992.

——————. *Fool's Gold: The Story of North Sea Oil.* Edinburgh: Canongate Press, 1995.

——————. *No Gods and Precious Few Heroes: Scotland since 1914.* Edinburgh: Edinburgh University Press, 1993.

——————. *Scotland and Nationalism: Scottish Society and Politics, 1707–1994.* London: Routledge, 1994.

Haswell-Smith, Hamish. *The Scottish Islands: A Comprehensive Guide to Every Scottish Island.* Edinburgh: Canongate Press, 1996.

Hatcher, John. *Before 1700: Towards the Age of Coal.* Vol. 1 of *The History of the British Coal Industry.* Oxford: Clarendon Press, 1993.

Haws, Charles H. *Scottish Parish Clergy at the Reformation, 1540–1574.* Edinburgh: Scottish Record Office, 1972.

Haythornthwaite, J. A. *Scotland in the Nineteenth Century: An Analytical Bibliography of Material Relating to Scotland in Parliamentary*

Papers, 1800–1900. Aldershot, England: Scolar Press, 1993.

Hecht, Hans. *Robert Burns: The Man and His Work.* Ayr, Scotland: Alloway Publishing, 1981.

Hechter, Michael. *Internal Colonialism: The Celtic Fringe in British National Development, 1536–1966.* London: Routledge and Kegan Paul, 1975.

Hellman, George Stanley. *The True Stevenson: A Study in Clarification.* New York: Haskell House, 1972.

Henderson, Diana. *The Scottish Regiments.* London: HarperCollins, 1996.

Henry, Francoise. *The Book of Kells.* London: Thames and Hudson, 1974.

Henry, Peter, Jim MacDonald and Halina Moss, eds. *Scotland and the Slavs: Selected Papers from the Glasgow-90 East West Forum.* Nottingham: Astra, 1993.

Herron, Frank. *Labour Market in Crisis: Redundancy at Upper Clyde Shipbuilders.* London: Macmillan, 1975.

Hewison, W. S. *The Diary of Patrick Fea of Stove, Orkney, 1766-96.* East Linton, Scotland: Tuckwell Press, 1996.

Hewitson, Jim. *Tam Blake & Co.: The Scots in America, 1540-1940.* Edinburgh: Canongate Press, 1995.

Hill, C. W. *Edwardian Scotland.* Edinburgh: Scottish Academic Press, 1977.

Hirst, Francis W. *Adam Smith.* Folcroft, Pa.: Folcroft Library Editions, 1977.

Hogg, James. *Memoirs of the Author's Life and Familiar Anecdotes of Sir Walter Scott,* edited by Douglas Mack. Edinburgh: Scottish Academic Press, 1972.

Hollander, Samuel. *The Economics of Adam Smith.* Toronto, Canada: University of Toronto Press, 1973.

Hollis, Patricia. *Jennie Lee: A Life.* Oxford: Oxford University Press, 1997.

Holloway, James, and Lindsay Errington. *The Discovery of Scotland: The Appreciation of Scottish Scenery through Two Centuries of Painting.* Edinburgh: National Gallery of Scotland, 1978.

Holmes, Timothy, ed. *David Livingstone: Letters and Documents, 1841–1872.* London: James Currey, 1990.

Hont, Istvan, and Michael Ignatieff, eds. *Wealth and Virtue: The Shaping of Political Economy in the Scottish Enlightenment.* Cambridge: Cambridge University Press, 1983.

Hood, Neil. *Multinationals in Retreat: The Scottish Experience.* Edinburgh: Edinburgh University Press, 1982.

Hook, Andrew. *Scotland and America: A Study of Cultural Relations, 1750–1835.* Glasgow: Blackie, 1975.

Hook, Michael, and Walter Ross. *The Forty-Five: The Last Jacobite Rebellion*. Edinburgh: Her Majesty's Stationery Office, 1995.

Hope, V., ed. *Philosophers of the Scottish Enlightenment*. Edinburgh: Edinburgh University Press, 1984.

Hopkins, Paul. *Glencoe and the End of the Highland War*. Edinburgh: John Donald, 1986.

Houston, R. A., and I. D. Whyte, eds. *Scottish Society, 1500–1800*. Cambridge: Cambridge University Press, 1989.

Howarth, Thomas. *Charles Rennie MacKintosh and the Modern Movement*. London: Routledge, 1977.

Hudson, Benjamin T. *The Kings of Celtic Scotland*. London: Greenwood Press, 1994.

Hudson, William Henry. *Sir Walter Scott*. Folcroft, Pa.: Folcroft Library Editions, 1972.

Hughes, Kathleen. *Celtic Britain in the Early Middle Ages: Studies in Welsh and Scottish Sources*. Woodbridge, England: Boydell, 1980.

Hume, John R., *The Industrial Archaeology of Glasgow*. Glasgow: Blackie, 1974.

Hume, John R. and Michael S. Moss. *Beardmore: The History of a Scottish Industrial Giant*. London: Heinemann Educational, 1979.

—————. *Clyde Shipbuilding from Old Photographs*. London: Batsford, 1975.

Humes, Walter M., and Hamish M. Paterson, eds. *Scottish Culture and Scottish Education, 1880–1980*. Edinburgh: John Donald, 1983.

Hunter, James. *The Claim of Crofting: The Scottish Highlands and Islands, 1930–1990*. Edinburgh: Mainstream, 1991.

—————. *A Dance Called America: The Scottish Highlands, the United States and Canada*. Edinburgh: Mainstream, 1994.

—————. *Glencoe and the Indians*. Edinburgh: Mainstream, 1997.

—————. *The Making of the Crofter Community*. Edinburgh: John Donald, 1976.

—————. *On the Other Side of Sorrow: Nature and People in the Scottish Highlands*. Edinburgh: Mainstream, 1995.

Hunter, S. Leslie. *The Scottish Educational System*. Oxford: Pergamon, 1972.

Hustwick, Ian. *Moray Firth Ships and Trade during the Nineteenth Century*. Aberdeen, Scotland: Scottish Cultural Press, 1994.

Hutchinson, I. G. C. *A Political History of Scotland, 1832-1924: Parties, Elections and Issues*. Edinburgh: John Donald, 1986.

Huxley, Elspeth. *Livingstone and His African Journeys*. London: Weidenfeld and Nicolson, 1974.

Ingham, Keith P. D., and James Love. *Understanding the Scottish*

Economy. Oxford: Robertson, 1983.

Inverness Field Club. *The Dark Ages in the Highlands: Ancient Peoples, Local History, Archaeology.* Inverness, Scotland: Inverness Field Club, 1972.

Irwin, David, and Francina Irwin. *Scottish Painters at Home and Abroad, 1700–1900.* London: Faber and Faber, 1975.

Jack, R. D. S. *The Italian Influence on Scottish Literature.* Edinburgh: Edinburgh University Press, 1972.

Jackson, A. *The Symbol Stones of Scotland.* Kirkwall, Scotland: Orkney Press, 1984.

Jackson, G., and S. G. E. Lythe. *The Port of Montrose: A History of Its Harbour, Trade and Shipping.* Dundee, Scotland: Hutton Press, 1993.

Jackson, K. *The Problem of the Picts.* Edinburgh University Press, 1980.

Jackson, Michael. *Whisky.* London: Dorling Kindersley, 1987.

James, Alwyn. *Scottish Roots: A Step-by-Step Guide for Ancestor Hunters in Scotland and Overseas.* Edinburgh: Saltire Society, 1995.

Jarrett, T. *St Andrews Golf Links: The First 600 Years.* Edinburgh: Mainstream, 1995.

Jarvie, Grant. *Highland Games: The Making of the Myth.* Edinburgh: Edinburgh University Press, 1991.

Jarvie, Grant, and Graham Walker, eds. *Scottish Sport in the Making of a Nation.* Leicester: Leicester University Press, 1994.

Jarvis, Rupert C. *Collected Papers on the Jacobite Risings,* 2 vols. Manchester: Manchester University Press, 1971 (Vol. 1) and 1972 (Vol. 2).

Jeal, Tim. *Livingstone.* New York: Putnam, 1973.

Jedrej, C., and M. Nuttall. *White Settlers: The Impact of Rural Repopulation in Scotland.* Luxembourg: Harwood Academic, 1996.

Jeffret, R., and I. Watson. *Images of Glasgow: A Pictorial History of Clydeside's People and Places.* Derby, England: Beedon Books, 1995.

Jenner, M. *Scotland through the Ages.* London: Michael Joseph, 1987.

Johnson, David. *Music and Society in Lowland Scotland in the Eighteenth Century.* London: Oxford University Press, 1972.

Johnson, Edgar. *Sir Walter Scott: The Great Unknown.* London: Hamish Hamilton, 1970.

Johnston, J. B. *Placenames of Scotland.* Edinburgh: SR Publications, 1970.

Johnston, T. L., N. K. Buxton and D. Mair. *Structure and Growth of the Scottish Economy.* London: Collins, 1971.

Johnston, W. T. *Scottish Historians and Histories of Scotland.* London: Officina, 1992.

Jones, Charles. *A Language Suppressed: The Pronunctiation of the Scots Language in the 18th Century.* Edinburgh: John Donald, 1996.

Jones, Charles, ed. *Edinburgh History of the Scots Language.* Edinburgh: Edinburgh University Press, 1997.

Jones, H. R., ed. *Crime and the Urban Environment: The Scottish Experience.* Aldershot, England: Gower Press, 1993.

Jones, Peter, ed. *Philosophy and Science in the Scottish Enlightenment: Essays.* Edinburgh: John Donald, 1988.

Kay, M. *The Dundee Book: An Anthology of Living in the City.* Edinburgh: Mainstream, 1995.

Kearney, Hugh. *The British Isles: A History of Four Nations.* Cambridge: Cambridge University Press, 1989.

Keating, Michael. *Remaking Urban Scotland: Strategies for Local Economic Development.* Edinburgh: Edinburgh University Press, 1986.

Keating, Michael, and David Bleiman. *Labour and Scottish Nationalism.* London: Macmillan, 1979.

Keating, M. and A Middleton. *Remaking Urban Scotland: Strrategies for Local Economic Development.* Edinburgh: Edinburgh University Press, 1986.

Keay, John, and Julia Keay, eds. *Collins Encyclopaedia of Scotland.* London: HarperCollins, 1994.

Kellas, James G. *Modern Scotland.* London: Allen and Unwin, 1980.

———. *The Scottish Political System.* Cambridge: Cambridge University Press, 1989.

Kelsall, Helen, and Keith Kelsall. *Scottish Lifestyle 300 Years Ago: New Light on Edinburgh and Border Families.* Aberdeen, Scotland: Scottish Cultural Press, 1993.

Kemp, Arnold. *The Hollow Drum: Scotland since the War.* Edinburgh: Mainstream, 1993.

Kemp, Hilary. *The Jacobite Rebellion.* London: Almark, 1975.

Kenyon, J. P. *The Stuarts.* London: Severn House, 1977.

Keppie, Lawrence. *Scotland's Roman Remains: An Introduction and Handbook.* Edinburgh: John Donald, 1986.

Kerr, W. G. *Scottish Capital on the American Credit Frontier.* Austin: Texas State Historical Association, 1976.

Kidd, Colin. *Subverting Scotland's Past: Scottish Whig Historians and the Creation of an Anglo-British Identity, 1688–1830.* Cambridge: Cambridge University Press, 1993.

Knox, Roger T. *How Scotland Voted: An Analysis of Scottish Local Government Elections, 1984–1988, by Constituency and by District.* Milton Keynes, England: Open University Press, 1989.

Knox, William, ed. *Scottish Labour Leaders 1918–1939: A Biographi-*

cal Dictionary. Edinburgh: Mainstream, 1984.

Kratzmann, Gregory. *Anglo-Scottish Literary Relations, 1430–1550*. Cambridge: Cambridge University Press, 1980.

Kybett, Susan Maclean. *Bonnie Prince Charlie: A Biography*. London: Unwin Hyman, 1988.

Laing, Lloyd. *The Archaeology of Late Celtic Britain and Ireland, c. 400–1200 AD*. London: Methuen, 1975.

Laing, L., and J. Laing. *The Picts and the Scots*. Stroud, England: Alan Sutton, 1993.

Lamont, Stewart, ed. *St Andrew's Rock: The State of the Church of Scotland*. London: Bellew, 1992.

Larner, Christina, Christopher Hyde Lee and Hugh V. McLachlan. *A Source Book of Scottish Witchcraft*. Glasgow: University of Glasgow, 1977.

Larner, Gerald, and Celia Larner. *The Glasgow Style*. Edinburgh: P. Harris, 1979.

Lea, K. J. *A Geography of Scotland*. Newton Abbot, England: David and Charles, 1977.

Lee, Clive. *Scotland and the UK: The Economics of the Union*. Manchester: Manchester University Press, 1994.

Lee, Maurice. *Government by Pen: Scotland under James VI and I*. Urbana: University of Illinois Press, 1980.

——————. *Great Britain's Solomon: James VI and I in His Three Kingdoms*. Urbana: University of Illinois Press, 1990.

——————. *The Road to Revolution: Scotland under Charles I, 1625–37*. Urbana: University of Illinois Press, 1985.

Lellenberg, Jon L., ed. *The Quest for Sir Arthur Conan Doyle: Thirteen Biographers in Search of a Life*. Carbondale: Southern Illinois University Press, 1987.

Leneman, L., ed. *Perspectives in Scottish Social History: Essays in Honour of Rosalind Mitchison*. Aberdeen, Scotland: Aberdeen University Press, 1988.

Lenman, Bruce P. *An Economic History of Modern Scotland, 1660–1976*. London: Batsford, 1977.

——————. *Integration and Enlightenment: Scotland, 1746–1832*. Edinburgh: Edinburgh University Press, 1992.

——————. *The Jacobite Cause*. Glasgow: Drew, 1986.

——————. *Jacobite Clans of the Great Glen, 1650–1784*. Aberdeen, Scotland: Scottish Cultural Press, 1995.

——————. *Jacobite Risings in Britain, 1689–1745*. Aberdeen, Scotland: Scottish Cultural Press, 1995.

Lenman, Bruce P., and John S. Gibson. *The Jacobite Threat*. Edinburgh:

Scottish Academic Press, 1990.

Levack, B. P. *The Formation of the British State: England, Scotland and the Union, 1603–1707.* Oxford: Clarendon Press, 1987.

Levitt, Ian. *Poverty and Welfare in Scotland, 1890–1948.* Edinburgh: Edinburgh University Press, 1988.

Levitt, Ian, and Christopher Smout. *The State of the Scottish Working Class in 1843.* Edinburgh: Scottish Academic Press, 1979.

Lewis, T. M., and I. H. McNicoll. *North Sea Oil and Scotland's Economic Prospects.* London: Croom Helm, 1978.

Lindgren, J. Ralph. *The Social Philosophy of Adam Smith.* The Hague, Netherlands: Martinus Nijhoff, 1973.

Lindsay, Ian G., and Mary Cosh. *Inveraray and the Dukes of Argyll.* Edinburgh: Edinburgh University Press, 1973.

Lindsay, Jean. *The Scottish Poor Law: Its Operation in the North-East.* Ilfracombe, England: Stockwell, 1975.

Lindsay, Maurice. *The Burns Encyclopedia.* London: Hale, 1995.

——————. *The Castles of Scotland.* London: Constable, 1994.

——————. *History of Scottish Literature.* London: Hale, 1992.

Linklater, Eric. *The Royal House of Scotland.* London: Macmillan, 1970.

Linklater, Magnus. *Massacre: The Story of Glencoe.* London: Collins, 1982.

Livesay, H. C. *Andrew Carnegie and the Rise of Big Business.* Boston: Little, Brown, 1975.

Livingstone of Bachuil, Alastair, Christian W. H. Aikman and Betty Stuart Hart, eds. *Muster Roll of Prince Charles Edward Stuart's Army, 1745–46.* Aberdeen, Scotland: Aberdeen University Press, 1984.

Livingstone, Sheila. *Scottish Customs.* Edinburgh: Birlinn, 1995.

Lockhart, Douglas G. *The Construction and Planning of New Urban Settlements in Scotland in the Eighteenth Century.* Wiesbaden, Germany: Harrassowitz, 1991.

Lockhart, J. G. *The Life of Robert Burns.* New York: AMS Press, 1974.

——————. *The Life of Sir Walter Scott.* New York: AMS Press, 1983.

Lockhart, Sir Robert Bruce. *Scotch: The Whisky of Scotland in Fact and Story.* London: Putnam, 1981.

Logue, Kenneth J. *Popular Disturbances in Scotland, 1780–1815.* Edinburgh: John Donald, 1979.

Low, Donald A. *The Songs of Robert Burns.* London: Routledge, 1993.

Loyn, Henry. *The Vikings in Britain.* Oxford: Blackwell, 1994.

Lyall, Francis. *Of Presbyters and Kings: Church and State in the Law of Scotland.* Aberdeen, Scotland: Aberdeen University Press, 1980.

Lynch, Michael. *Scotland: A New History.* London: Pimlico, 1992.

—————, ed. *Mary Stewart: Queen in Three Kingdoms.* Oxford: Blackwell, 1988.

Lynch, Michael, Michael Spearman and Geoffrey Stell, eds. *The Scottish Medieval Town.* Edinburgh: John Donald, 1988.

Lythe, Charlotte, and Madhavi Majmudar. *The Renaissance of the Scottish Economy?* London: Allen and Unwin, 1982.

Lythe, S. G. E., and J. Butt. *An Economic History of Scotland, 1100–1939.* Glasgow: Blackie, 1975.

Maan, B. *The New Scots: The Story of Asians in Scotland.* Edinburgh: John Donald, 1992.

MacArthur, Mairi. *Columba's Isle: Iona From Prehistory to the Present Day.* Edinburgh: Edinburgh University Press, 1995.

—————. *Iona.* Granton-on-Spey, Scotland: Colin Baxter, 1997.

McArthur, Colin, ed. *Scotch Reels: Scotland in Cinema and Television.* London: BFI Publishing, 1982.

McArthur, Tom, and Peter Waddell. *The Secret Life of John Logie Baird.* London: Hutchinson, 1986.

McConnell, D. *The Strome Ferry Railway Riot of 1883.* Dornoch, Scotland: Dornoch Press, 1993.

McCoy, F. N. *Robert Baillie and the Second Scots Reformation.* Berkeley: University of California Press, 1974.

McCrone, David. *Understanding Scotland: The Sociology of a Stateless Nation.* London: Routledge, 1992.

McCrone, David, Stephen Kemdrick and Pat Shaw, eds. *The Making of Scotland.* Edinburgh: Edinburgh University Press, 1989.

McCrone, David, Angela Morris and Richard Kiely. *Scotland the Brand: The Making of Scottish Heritage.* Edinburgh: Edinburgh University Press, 1995.

MacDonald, A. A., Michael Lynch and Ian B. Cowan, eds. *The Renaissance in Scotland: Studies in Literature, Religion, History and Culture Offered to John Durkan.* Leiden, Netherlands: E. J. Brill, 1994.

MacDonald, I. *Voices from War: Personal Recollections of War in Our Century by Scottish Men and Women.* Edinburgh: Mercat Press, 1995.

MacDonald, I. R. *Glasgow's Gaelic Churches: Highland Religion in an Urban Setting, 1690-1995.* Edinburgh: Knox Press, 1996.

MacDonald, Malcolm. *Edinburgh.* Cambridge: Pevensey Press, 1985.

MacDonald, Roderick, and Huw Thomas. *Nationality and Planning in Scotland and Wales.* Cardiff: University of Wales Press, 1997.

McDonald, R. A. *The Kingdom of the Isles — Scotland's Western Seaboards, c. 1100-c. 1336.* East Linton, Scotland: Tuckwell Press, 1996.

MacDougall, Ian. *Voices from the Hunger Marches.* 2 vols. Edinburgh: Polygon, 1990 (Vol 1) and 1991 (Vol 2).

MacDougall, Ian, ed. *Essays in Scottish Labour History: a Tribute to W. H. Marwick.* Edinburgh: John Donald, 1978.

—————. *Militant Miners: Recollections of John McArthur, Buckhaven, and Letters, 1924–26, of David Proudfoot, Methil, to G. Allen Hutt.* Edinburgh: Polygon, 1981.

MacDougall, Norman. *James III: A Political Study.* Edinburgh: John Donald, 1982.

—————. *James IV.* Edinburgh: John Donald, 1989.

MacDougall, Norman, ed. *Church, Politics and Society: Scotland 1408–1929.* Edinburgh: John Donald, 1983.

—————. *Scotland and War: AD 79–1918.* Edinburgh: John Donald, 1991.

McFarland, E. W. *Ireland and Scotland in the Age of Revolution; Planting the Green Bough.* Edinburgh: Edinburgh University Press, 1994.

McGill, Jack. *Crisis on the Clyde: The Story of Upper Clyde Shipbuilders.* London: Davis-Poynter, 1973.

McGladdery, Christine. *James II.* Edinburgh: John Donald, 1990.

McGurk, Caroline. *Robert Burns and The Sentimental Era.* East Linton, Scotland: Tuckwell Press, 1997.

McIan, R. R. *The Clans of the Scottish Highlands: The Costumes of the Clans.* London: Pan, 1980.

Macinnes, Allan I. *Charles I and the Making of the Covenanting Movement, 1625–1641.* Edinburgh: John Donald, 1991.

—————. *Clanship, Commerce and The House of Stuart, 1603-1788.* East Linton, Scotland: Tuckwell Press, 1996.

McIntyre, Ian. *Dirt and Deity: A Life of Robert Burns.* London: HarperCollins, 1995.

MacIvor, Iain. *Dumbarton Castle.* Edinburgh: Historic Scotland, 1993.

—————. *Edinburgh Castle.* London: Batsford, 1993.

—————. *Fort George.* Edinburgh: Scottish Development Department, 1988.

Mackay, Donald. *Scotland's Rural Land Use Agencies.* Aberdeen, Scotland: Scottish Cultural Press, 1995.

MacKay, Donald I. *Scotland: The Framework for Change.* Edinburgh: Harris, 1979.

Mackay, James. *Allan Pinkerton: The Eye Who Never Slept.* Edinburgh: Mainstream, 1996.

—————. *Little Boss: A Life of Andrew Carnegie.* Edinburgh: Mainstream, 1997.

Mackay, James A. *Burnsiana.* Ayr, Scotland: Alloway Publishing, 1988.

—————, ed. *The Complete Letters of Robert Burns.* Ayr, Scotland: Alloway Press, 1987.

—————. *RB: A Biography of Robert Burns.* Edinburgh: Mainstream, 1992.

—————. *Robert the Bruce, King of Scots.* London: Hale, 1974.

—————. *William Wallace: Brave Heart.* Edinburgh: Mainstream, 1995.

Mackay, Sheila. *Behind the Facade: Four Centuries of Scottish Interiors.* Edinburgh: Her Majesty's Stationery Office, 1995.

—————. *The Forth Bridge: A Picture History.* Edinburgh: Her Majesty's Stationery Office, 1993.

McKean, C., D. Walker and F. A. Walker. *Central Glasgow: An Illustrated Architectural Guide.* Edinburgh: Royal Incorporation of Architects in Scotland, 1993.

Mackenzie, Agnes Mure. *Robert Bruce, King of Scots.* Freeport, NY: Books For Libraries Press, 1970.

Mackenzie, Alexander. *History of the Highland Clearances.* Edinburgh: Mercat Press, 1994.

MacKenzie, John. *David Livingstone and the Victorian Encounter with Africa.* London: National Portrait Gallery, 1996.

Mackenzie, R. Shelton. *Sir Walter Scott: The Story of His Life.* Folcroft, Pa.: Folcroft Library Editions, 1977.

Mackie, J. D. *A History of Scotland.* London: Allen Lane, 1978.

McKinlay, Alan, and R. J. Morris eds. *The ILP on Clydeside, 1893–1932: From Foundation to Disintegration.* Manchester: Manchester University Press, 1991.

MacKinnon, K. M. *Language, Education and Social Processes in a Gaelic Community.* London: Routledge and Kegan Paul, 1977.

Mackintosh, John P. *John P. Mackintosh on Scotland.* London: Hyman, 1982.

MacLaren, A. Allan. *Religion and Social Class: The Disruption Years in Aberdeen.* London: Routledge, 1974.

MacLaren, A. Allan, ed. *Social Class in Scotland: Past and Present.* Edinburgh: John Donald, 1976.

McLaren, Moray. *Bonnie Prince Charlie.* London: Hart-Davis, 1972.

Maclean, Charles. *St Kilda: Island on the Edge of the World.* Edinburgh: Canongate Press, 1996.

Maclean, Fitzroy. *Bonnie Prince Charlie.* New York: Atheneum, 1989.

—————. *A History of the Highland Clans.* London: Adelphi, 1996.

—————. *Scotland: A Concise History.* London: Thames and Hudson, 1993.

MacLean, G. ed. *Culture and Society in the Stuart Restoration.* Cambridge: Cambridge University Press, 1995.

McLean, Iain. *Keir Hardie*. London: Allen Lane, 1975.

Maclean, Lorraine, ed. *The Hub of the Highlands: The Book of Inverness and District*. Inverness, Scotland: Inverness Field Club, 1975.

—————. *The Middle Ages in The Highlands*. Inverness, Scotland: Inverness Field Club, 1981.

Macleod, John. *Scottish Theology in Relation to Church History Since the Reformation*. Edinburgh: Banner of Truth Trust, 1974.

Macleod, J. *Highlanders: A History of the Gael*. London: Hodder and Stoughton, 1996.

McLynn, F. J. *Charles Edward Stuart: A Tragedy in Many Acts*. London: Routledge, 1988.

—————. *France and the Jacobite Rising of 1745*. Edinburgh: Edinburgh University Press, 1981.

—————. *The Jacobite Army in England, 1745: The Final Campaign*. Edinburgh: John Donald, 1983.

—————. *The Jacobites*. London: Routledge, 1985.

—————. *Robert Louis Stevenson: A Biography*. London: Hutchinson, 1985.

McMaster, Graham. *Scott and Society*. Cambridge: Cambridge University Press, 1981.

Macmillan, Duncan. *Scottish Art in the 20th Century*. Edinburgh: Mainstream, 1994.

McNaghten, Angus. *Burns' Mrs Riddell: A Biography*. Peterhead, Scotland: Volturna Press, 1975.

McNamee, Colm. *The Wars of the Bruces: Scotland, England and Ireland, 1306-1328*. East Linton, Scotland: Tuckwell Press, 1997.

McNeil, P. G. B., and H. L. McQueen. *An Atlas of Scottish History to 1707*. Edinburgh: Scottish Cultural Press, 1997.

MacNeill, Duncan H. *The Historical Scottish Constitution*. Edinburgh: Albyn Press, 1971.

McNeill, Peter, and Ranald Nicholson, eds. *An Historical Atlas of Scotland, c. 400–c. 1600*. St Andrews, Scotland: Atlas Committee of the Conference of Scottish Medievalists, 1975.

MacPhail, I. M. M. *The Crofters War*. Stornoway, Scotland: Acair, 1989.

—————. *Dumbarton Castle*. Edinburgh: John Donald, 1979.

Macquarrie, Alan. *The Saints of Scotland: Essays in Scottish Church History, AD 450-1093*. Edinburgh: John Donald, 1997.

—————. *Scotland and the Crusades: 1095–1560*. Edinburgh: John Donald, 1985.

Macqueen, Hector L. *Common Law and Feudal Society in Early Medieval Scotland*. Edinburgh: Edinburgh University Press, 1993.

McRoberts, David, ed. *Modern Scottish Catholicism, 1878–1978.* Glasgow: J. Burns, 1979.

McSmith, Andy. *John Smith: A Life, 1938–1994.* London: Mandarin, 1993.

MacSween, Ann, and Mick Sharp. *Prehistoric Scotland.* London: Batsford, 1989.

McWilliam, Colin. *Scottish Townscape.* London: Collins, 1975.

Mair, Craig. *A Star for Seamen: The Stevenson Family of Engineers.* London: John Murray, 1978.

Mair, Douglas, ed. *The Scottish Contribution to Modern Economic Thought.* Aberdeen, Scotland: Aberdeen University Press, 1990.

Makey, Walter. *The Church of the Covenant, 1637–1651: Revolution and Social Change in Scotland.* Edinburgh: John Donald, 1979.

Marr, Andrew. *The Battle for Scotland.* London: Penguin, 1992.

Marsden, John. *The Illustrated Life of St Columba.* Edinburgh: Floris Books, 1995.

Marshall, Gordon. *Presbyterians and Profits: Calvinism and the Development of Capitalism in Scotland, 1560–1707.* Oxford: Clarendon Press, 1980.

Marshall, Rosalind K. *Bonnie Prince Charlie.* Edinburgh: Her Majesty's Stationery Office, 1988.

—————. *Dynasty: The Royal House of Stuart.* Edinburgh: National Galleries and National Museums of Scotland, 1990.

—————. *Mary of Guise.* London: Collins, 1977.

—————. *Queen of Scots.* Edinburgh: Her Majesty's Stationery Office, 1986.

—————. *Virgins and Viragos: A History of Women in Scotland from 1880–1980.* London: Collins, 1983.

—————. *Women in Scotland, 1660–1780.* Edinburgh: National Galleries of Scotland, 1979.

Marshall, William. S. *The Billy Boys: A Concise History of Orangeism in Scotland.* Edinburgh: Mercat Press, 1996.

Martine, Roderick. *Royal Scotland.* Edinburgh: Harris, 1983.

—————. *Scottish Clan and Family Names: Their Arms, Origins and Tartans.* Edinburgh: Bartholomew, 1987.

Mason, Roger A. *John Knox on Rebellion.* Cambridge: Cambridge University Press, 1993.

Mason, Roger A, ed. *Scots and Britons: Scottish Political Thought and the Union of 1603.* Cambridge: Cambridge University Press, 1994.

—————. *Scotland and England, 1286–1815.* Edinburgh: John Donald, 1987.

Mason, Roger A., and Norman Macdougall, eds. *People and Power in*

Scotland: Essays in Honour of T. C. Smout. Edinburgh: John Donald, 1992.

Massie, Alan. *Edinburgh.* London: Sinclair-Stevenson, 1994.

Maxwell, Gordon S. *The Romans in Scotland.* Edinburgh: Mercat Press, 1989.

Maxwell, Stephen, ed. *Scotland, Multinationals and the Third World.* Edinburgh: Mainstream, 1992.

Mays, Deborah. *The Architecture of Scottish Cities.* East Linton, Scotland: Tuckwell Press, 1997.

Meek, D. E. *Tuath is Tighearna (Tenants and Landlords).* Edinburgh: Scottish Academic Press, 1996.

Mellars, Paul, ed. *Excavations on Oronsay: Prehistoric Human Ecology on a Small Island.* Edinburgh: Edinburgh University Press, 1987.

Meller, H. *Patrick Geddes: Social Evolutionist and City Planner.* London: Routledge, 1990.

Menzies, Gordon, ed. *The Scottish Nation.* London: British Broadcasting Corporation, 1972.

──────. *Who Are the Scots?* London: British Broadcasting Corporation, 1971.

Metcalf, D. M., ed. *Coinage in Medieval Scotland, 1100–1600.* Oxford: British Archaeological Reports, 1977.

Michie, R. C. *Money, Mania and Markets: Investment, Company Formation and the Stock Exchange in Nineteenth Century Scotland.* Edinburgh: John Donald, 1981.

Middlemiss, N. L. *Clydeside. Vol. 2 of British Shipbuilding Yards.* Gateshead, England: Shield Publications, 1994.

Midwinter, Arthur. *Local Government in Scotland: Reform or Decline?* London: Macmillan, 1996.

Midwinter, Arthur, Michael Keating and James Mitchell. *Politics and Public Policy in Scotland.* London: Macmillan, 1991.

Miller, John. *James II: A Study in Kingship.* London: Methuen, 1991.

Miller, Karl. *Cockburn's Millenium.* London: Duckworth, 1975.

Miller, P. *James [The Old Pretender].* London: Allen and Unwin, 1971.

Millgate, Jane. *Walter Scott: The Making of the Novelist.* Edinburgh: Edinburgh University Press, 1984.

Millman, R. N. *The Making of the Scottish Landscape.* London: Batsford, 1975.

Minowitz, Peter. *Profits, Priests and Princes: Adam Smith's Emancipation of Economics from Politics and Religion.* Stanford Calif.: Stanford University Press, 1993.

Minto, C. S. *Victorian and Edwardian Edinburgh from Old Photographs.* London: Batsford, 1970.

Mitchell, James. *Conservatives and the Union: A Study of Conservative Party Attitudes to Scotland.* Edinburgh: Edinburgh University Press, 1990.

Mitchison, Rosalind. *All the Sweets of Being: The Life of James Boswell.* Edinburgh: Mainstream, 1995.

——————. *A History of Scotland.* London: Methuen, 1990.

——————. *Life in Scotland.* London: Batsford, 1978.

——————. *Lordship to Patronage: Scotland, 1603–1745.* Edinburgh: Edinburgh University Press, 1990.

Moffat, Alistair. *Remembering Charles Rennie Mackintosh: An Illustrated Biography.* Lanark, Scotland: Colin Baxter Photography, 1989.

Moncreiffe of that Ilk, Sir Iain. *The Highland Clans: The Dynastic Origins, Chiefs and Backgrounds of the Clans and Some Other Families Connected with Highland History.* London: Barrie and Jenkins, 1982.

Moody, David. *Scottish Family History.* London: Batsford, 1988.

Moore, John N. *The Maps of Glasgow: A History and Cartography to 1865.* Glasgow: Glasgow University Library, 1996.

Morgan, Kenneth O. *Keir Hardie: Radical and Socialist.* London: Weidenfeld and Nicolson, 1975.

Morice, G. P. *David Hume: Bicentenary Papers.* Edinburgh: Edinburgh University Press, 1977.

Morrill, John, ed. *The Scottish National Covenant in its British Context, 1638–1651.* Edinburgh: Edinburgh University Press, 1990.

Morris, R. J., and W. H. Fraser, eds. *People and Society in Scotland, 1830-1914.* Edinburgh: John Donald, 1990.

Moss, Michael S. *The Making of Scotch Whisky: A History of the Scotch Whisky Distilling Industry.* Edinburgh: James and James, 1981.

Moss, Michael S., and John R. Hume. *Workshop of the British Empire: Engineering and Shipbuilding in the West of Scotland.* London: Heinemann, 1977.

Mossner, Ernest Campbell. *The Life of David Hume.* Oxford: Clarendon Press, 1980.

Mossner, Ernest Campbell, and Ian Simpson Ross, eds. *The Correspondence of Adam Smith.* Oxford: Clarendon Press, 1977.

Mowat, Ian R. M. *Easter Ross, 1750–1850: The Double Frontier.* Edinburgh: John Donald, 1981.

Mowat, Sue. *The Port of Leith: Its History and Its People.* Edinburgh: John Donald, 1995.

Muir, Edwin. *John Knox: Portrait of a Calvinist.* Freeport, NY: Books for Libraries Press, 1971.

Mullay, Sandy. *The Edinburgh Enyclopedia.* Edinburgh: Mainstream,

1996.

Munn, Charles W. *The Scottish Provincial Banking Companies, 1747–1864.* Edinburgh: John Donald, 1981.

Murdoch, Alexander. *The People Above: Politics and Administration in Mid-Eighteenth Century Scotland.* Edinburgh: John Donald, 1980.

Murray, Norman. *The Scottish Hand Loom Weavers, 1790–1850: A Social History.* Edinburgh: John Donald, 1978.

Murray, W. H. *Rob Roy MacGregor: His Life and Times.* Edinburgh: Canongate Press, 1995.

Neat, Timothy. *The Summer Walkers: Travelling People and Pearl Fishers in the Highlands of Scotland.* Edinburgh: Canongate, 1996.

Nicholson, Ranald. *Scotland: The Later Middle Ages.* Edinburgh: Oliver and Boyd, 1974.

Nicolaisen, W. H. *Scottish Placenames: Their Study and Significance.* London: Batsford, 1976.

Nimmo, Ian. *Edinburgh: The New Town.* Edinburgh: John Donald, 1991.

Niven, D. *The Development of Housing in Scotland.* London: Croom Helm, 1979.

Norton, David Fate. *The Cambridge Companion to Hume.* Cambridge: Cambridge University Press, 1994.

Norton, D. F., and M. J. Norton. *The David Hume Library.* Edinburgh: Edinburgh Bibliographical Society in association with the National Library of Scotland, 1996.

Noxon, James. *Hume's Philosophical Development: A Study of His Methods.* Oxford: Clarendon Press, 1973.

O'Connor, Anne, and D. V. Clarke, eds. *From the Stone Age to the 'Forty Five: Studies Presented to R. B. K. Stevenson.* Edinburgh: John Donald, 1983.

Oram, Richard. *Angus and The Mearns: A Historical Guide.* Edinburgh: Birlinn, 1996.

—————. *Moray and Badenoch: A Historical Guide.* Edinburgh: Birlinn, 1996.

—————. *Scotland's Kings and Queens.* Edinburgh: Her Majesty's Stationery Office, 1997.

—————. *Scottish Prehistory.* Edinburgh, Birlinn, 1997.

Orel, Harold, Henry L. Snyder and Marilyn Stokstad, eds. *The Scottish World: History and Culture of Scotland.* London: Thames and Hudson, 1981.

Orr, Willie. *Deer Forests, Landlords and Crofters: The Western Highlands in Victorian and Edwardian Times.* Edinburgh: John Donald, 1982.

Ovenden, Richard. *John Thomson (1837-1921): Phtographer.* Edinburgh:

Her Majesty's Stationery Office, 1997.

Owens, Joe, ed. *Miners 1984–1994: A Decade of Endurance*. Edinburgh: Polygon, 1994.

Pagan, Anne. *God's Scotland? The Story of Scottish Christian Religion*. Edinburgh: Mainstream, 1988.

Pálsson, Hermann, and Paul Edwards. *Orkneying Saga: The History of the Earls of Orkney*. London: Hogarth Press, 1978.

Parman, Susan. *Scottish Crofters: A Historical Ethnography of a Celtic Village*. Fort Worth, Texas: Holt, Rinehart and Winston, 1990.

Parry, Graham. *The Golden Age Restor'd: The Culture of the Stuart Court, 1603–1642*. Manchester: Manchester University Press, 1981.

Parry, M. L., and T. R. Slater, eds. *The Making of the Scottish Countryside*. London: Croom Helm, 1980.

Parsler, Ron, ed. *Capitalism, Class and Politics in Scotland*. Farnborough, England: Gower, 1980.

Parsler, Ron, and D. Shapiro, eds. *The Social Impact of Oil on Scotland*. Gower: 1980.

Paterson, Len. *The Light in the Glens: the Rise and Fall in the Puffer Trade*. Colonsay, Scotland: House of Lochar, 1996.

Paterson, Lindsay. *The Autonomy of Modern Scotland*. Edinburgh: Edinburgh University Press, 1994.

Paterson, Raymond Campbell. *For the Lion: A History of the Scottish Wars of Independence, 1296–1357*. Edinburgh: Donald, 1996.

————. *My Wound is Deep: A History of the Later Anglo-Scots Wars*. Edinburgh: John Donald, 1997.

Patrick, John. *Scotland: The Age of Achievement*. London: John Murray, 1976.

Payne, Peter L. *Colvilles and the Scottish Steel Industry*. Oxford: Clarendon Press, 1979.

————. *The Early Scottish Limited Companies, 1856–1895: an Historical and Analytical Survey*. Edinburgh: Scottish Academic Press, 1980.

Pearce, Susan M., ed. *The Early Church in Western Britain and Ireland: Studies Presented to C. A. Ralegh Radford*. Oxford: British Archaeological Reports, 1982.

Pearson, Hesketh. *Johnson and Boswell: The Story of Their Lives*. London: Cassell, 1987.

Peebles, High B. *Warshipbuilding on the Clyde: Naval Orders and the Property of the Clyde Shipbuilding Industry, 1880–1939*. Edinburgh: John Donald, 1987.

Penelhum, Terence. *Hume*. London: Macmillan, 1975.

Perceval-Maxwell, M. *The Scottish Migration to Ulster in the Reign of*

James I. London: Routledge and Kegan Paul, 1990.

Petzch, Helmut. *Architecture in Scotland*. London: Longman, 1971.

Phillipson, N. T. *The Scottish Whigs and the Reform of the Court of Session, 1785-1830*. Edinburgh: Stair Society, 1990.

Phillipson, N. T., and Rosalind Mitchison, eds. *Scotland in the Age of Improvement: Essays in Scottish History in the Eighteenth Century*. Edinburgh: Edinburgh University Press, 1996.

Pittock, Murray. *The Invention of Scotland: The Stuart Myth and the Scottish Identity, 1638 to the Present*. London: Routledge, 1991.

—————. *The Myth of the Jacobite Clans*. Edinburgh: Edinburgh University Press, 1995.

—————. *Poetry and Jacobite Politics in Eighteenth-Century Britain and Ireland*. Cambridge: Cambridge University Press, 1994.

Plowden, Alison. *Elizabeth Tudor and Mary Stewart — Two Queens in One Isle*. Totowa, N. J.: Barnes and Noble, 1984.

Pollard, T., and A. Morrison. *The Early Prehistory of Scotland*. Edinburgh: Edinburgh University Press, 1996.

Pollock, Lawrence, and Ian McAllister. *A Bibliography of United Kingdom Politics: Scotland, Wales and Northern Ireland*. Glasgow: University of Strathclyde, Centre for the Study of Public Policy, 1980.

Pope-Hennessy, James. *Robert Louis Stevenson*. London: Cape, 1974.

Pottinger, Morris. *Parish Life on The Pentland Firth*. Thurso, Scotland: White Maa Books, 1997.

Pottle, Frederick Albert. *James Boswell: The Earlier Years*. New York: McGraw-Hill, 1985.

Prebble, John. *The Highland Clearances*. London: Secker and Warburg, 1971.

—————. *The King's Jaunt: George IV in Scotland, August 1822*. London: Collins, 1988.

—————. *The Lion in the North: a Personal View of Scotland's History*. London: Penguin, 1981.

—————. *Mutiny: Highland Regiments in Revolt, 1743–1804*. Harmondsworth, England: Penguin, 1977.

Price, Glanville. *The Languages of Britain*. London: Edward Arnold, 1984.

Purser, John. *Scotland's Music: A History of the Traditional and Classical Music of Scotland from Early Times to the Present Day*. Edinburgh: Mainstream, 1992.

Rae, John. *The Life of Adam Smith*. Bristol: Thoemmes, 1990.

Ralph, Robert. *William McGillivray: A Hebridean Naturalist's journal, 1817-1818*. Stornoway, Scotland: Acair, 1995.

Ransford, Oliver. *David Livingstone: The Dark Interior*. London: John

Murray, 1978.

Reeks, Lindsay S. *Scottish Coalmining Ancestors.* Baltimore: Galway Press, 1986.

Reese, Peter. *Wallace: A Biography.* Edinburgh: Canongate Press, 1996.

Reid, David, ed. *The Party-Coloured Mind: Prose Relating to the Conflict of Church and State in Seventeenth Century Scotland.* Edinburgh: Scottish Academic Press, 1982.

Reid, Fred. *Keir Hardie: The Making of a Socialist.* London: Croom Helm, 1978.

Reid, J. M. *Scotland's Progress: The Survival of a Nation.* London: Eyre and Spottiswoode, 1971.

Reid, Norman H., ed. *Scotland in the Reign of Alexander III.* Edinburgh: John Donald, 1990.

Reid, W. Stanford, ed. *The Scottish Tradition in Canada.* Toronto: McClelland and Stewart, 1976.

Rendall, Jane. *The Origins of the Scottish Enlightenment.* London: Macmillan, 1978.

Renfrew, Colin, ed. *The Prehistory of Orkney, BC 4000–1000 AD.* Edinburgh: Edinburgh University Press, 1993.

Rentoul, John. *Tony Blair.* London: Little Brown, 1995.

Rice, C. Duncan. *The Scots Abolitionists, 1833–1861.* Baton Rouge: Louisiana State University Press, 1981.

Richards, Eric. *A History of the Highland Clearances. 2 vols.* London: Croom Helm, 1982 (Vol. 1) and 1985 (Vol. 2).

—————. *The Leviathan of Wealth: The Sutherland Fortune in the Industrial Revolution.* London: Routledge, 1973.

Richards, John, and Margaret Richards. *Timber Frame Houses in the Scottish Countryside.* Edinburgh: Her Majesty's Stationery Office, 1994.

Riddell, John F. *Clyde Navigation: A History of the Development and Deepening of the River Clyde.* Edinburgh: John Donald, 1979.

Riley, Patrick William Joseph. *King William and the Scottish Politicians.* Edinburgh: John Donald, 1979.

—————. *The Union of England and Scotland: A Study of Anglo-Scottish Politics in the Eighteenth Century.* Manchester: Manchester University Press, 1978.

Riesen, R. A. *Criticism and Faith in Late Victorian Scotland: A. B. Davidson, William Robertson Smith and George Adam Smith.* Lanham, Md.: University Press of America, 1985.

Ritchie, Anna. *Govan and Its Early Medieval Sculpture.* Stroud, England: Alan Sutton, 1994.

—————. *Iona.* London: B. T. Batsford, 1997.

—————. *Orkney.* Edinburgh: Her Majesty's Stationery Office, 1997.

—————. *Picts: an Introduction to the Life of The Picts and to the Carved Stones in the Care of The Secretary of State for Scotland.* Edinburgh: Her Majesty's Stationery Office, 1989.

—————. *Prehistoric Orkney.* London: Batsford, 1995.

—————. *Scotland BC.* Edinburgh: Her Majesty's Stationery Office, 1988.

—————. *Viking Scotland.* London: Batsford, 1993.

Ritchie, Anna, and David J. Breeze. *Invaders of Scotland: An Introduction to the Archaeology of the Romans, Scots, Angles and Vikings.* Edinburgh: Her Majesty's Stationery Office, 1991.

Ritchie, Graham, ed. *The Archaeology of Argyll.* Edinburgh: Edinburgh University Press, 1997.

Ritchie, Graham, and Mary Harman. *Exploring Scotland's Heritage: Argyll and the Western Isles.* Edinburgh: Her Majesty's Stationery Office, 1995.

Ritchie, Graham, and Anna Ritchie. *The Ancient Monuments of Orkney.* Edinburgh: Her Majesty's Stationery Office, 1995.

—————. *Scotland: Archaeology and Early History.* London: Thames and Hudson, 1991.

Roberts, John L. *Lost Kingdoms: Celtic Scotland and The Middle Ages.* Edinburgh: Edinburgh University Press, 1997.

Robbins, Keith. *Nineteenth Century Britain: Integration and Diversity.* Oxford: Clarendon Press, 1988.

Robertson, Anne S. *The Antonine Wall: A Handbook to the Surviving Remains.* Glasgow: Glasgow Archaeological Society, 1990.

Robertson, C. J. A. *The Origins of the Scottish Railway System, 1722–1844.* Edinburgh: John Donald, 1983.

Robertson, John. *The Scottish Enlightenment and the Militia Issue.* Edinburgh: John Donald, 1985.

—————, ed. *A Union for Empire: Political Thought and the British Union of 1707.* Cambridge: Cambridge University Press, 1995.

Robertson, S., and L. Wilson. *Scotland's War.* Edinburgh: Mainstream, 1995.

Robinson, Eric, and Douglas McKie, eds. *Partners in Science: Letters of James Watt and Joseph Black.* London: Constable, 1970.

Robinson, W. Stitt. *James Glen: From Scottish Provost to Royal Governor of South Carolina.* Westport, Conn.: Greenwood Press, 1996.

Ross, Ian Simpson. *Lord Kames and the Scotland of His Day.* Oxford: Clarendon Press, 1972.

Ross, Stewart. *The Stewart Dynasty.* Nairn, Scotland: Thomas and Lochar, 1993.

Roxburgh, James M. *The School Board of Glasgow, 1873–1919.* London: University of London Press, 1971.

Royal Commission on the Ancient and Historical Monuments of Scotland. *Argyll: An Inventory of the Monuments. 7 vols.* Edinburgh: Her Majesty's Stationery Office, 1971 (Vol. 1), 1975 (Vol. 2), 1980 (Vol. 3), 1982 (Vol. 4), 1984 (Vol. 5), 1988 (Vol. 6), 1992 (Vol. 7).

——————. *Dundee on Record: Images of the Past.* Edinburgh: Her Majesty's Stationery Office, 1992.

——————. *North-East Perth: An Archaeological Landscape.* Edinburgh: Her Majesty's Stationery Office, 1990.

——————. *South-East Perth: An Archaeological Landscape.* Edinburgh: Her Majesty's Stationery Office, 1994.

Royal Scottish Geographical Society. *The Early Maps of Scotland to 1850.* Edinburgh: Royal Scottish Geographical Society, 1973 (Vol. 1) and 1983 (Vol. 2).

Rubenstein, Jill. *Sir Walter Scott: A Reference Guide.* Boston, Mass.: G. K. Hall, 1978.

Ruge, Friedrich. *Scapa Flow 1919.* Shepperton, England: Ian Allan, 1973.

Rykwert, Joseph. *The Brothers Adam: The Men and the Style.* London: Collins, 1985.

The 1745 Association. *A Jacobite Anthology: To Commemmorate the 250th Anniversary of the Rising of 1745.* Aberdeen, Scotland: Scottish Cultural Press, 1995.

Sadler, John. *Scottish Battles: from Mons Graupius (AD 84) to Culloden (1746).* Edinburgh: Canongate Press, 1996.

Sage, Donald. *Memorabilia Domestica: Or, Parish Life in the North of Scotland.* Edinburgh: Albyn Press, 1975.

Salter, M. *The Castles of Grampian and Angus.* Malvern, England: Folly Publications, 1995.

Sanderson, Elizabeth C. *Women and Work in Eighteenth-Century Edinburgh.* London: Macmillan, 1995.

Sanderson, Margaret H. B. *Ayrshire and the Reformation: People and Change, 1490-1600.* East Linton, Scotland: Tuckwell Press, 1997.

——————. *Cardinal of Scotland: David Beaton, c. 1494–1546.* Edinburgh: John Donald, 1986.

——————. *Robert Adam and Scotland: Portrait of an Architect.* Edinburgh: Her Majesty's Stationery Office, 1992.

——————. *Scottish Rural Society in the Sixteenth Century.* Edinburgh: John Donald, 1982.

Savage, Robert C. Woosnam, ed. *Charles Edward Stuart and the Jacobites.* Edinburgh: Her Majesty's Stationery Office, 1995.

Saville, Richard. *Bank of Scotland — A History.* Edinburgh: Edinburgh

University Press, 1996.

Scarlett, James Desmond. *The Tartans of the Scottish Clans.* Glasgow: Collins, 1975.

Schrank, G. *An Orkney Estate: Improvements at Graemeshall.* East Linton, Scotland: Tuckwell Press, 1996.

Scott, Ian. *The Life and Times of Falkirk.* Edinburgh: John Donald, 1994.

Scott, Paul H., ed. *Scotland: A Concise Cultural History.* Edinburgh: Mainstream, 1993.

————. *Scotland: An Unwon Cause.* Edinburgh: Canongate Books, 1997.

Scott, Ronald McNair. *Robert the Bruce, King of Scots.* London: Hutchinson, 1982.

Scott, Tom. *Tales of Sir William Wallace.* Edinburgh: Gordon Wright, 1981.

————. *The Scottish Clans and Their Tartan: History of Each Clan and Full List of Septs.* London: Cassell, 1985.

Scottish National Portrait Gallery. *The Art of Jewellery in Scotland.* Edinburgh: Her Majesty's Stationery Office, 1991.

Scottish Office. *Scottish Rural Life: A Socio-economic Profile of Rural Scotland.* Edinburgh: Her Majesty's Stationery Office, 1992.

Scottish Record Office. *Tracing Scottish Local History.* Edinburgh: Her Majesty's Stationery Office, 1994.

Selby, John. *Over the Sea to Skye: The Forty-five.* London: Hamilton, 1973.

Shapiro, Michael J. *Reading 'Adam Smith': Desire, History and Value.* Newbury Park, Calif.: Sage, 1993.

Sharlin, Harold Issadore. *Lord Kelvin: The Dynamic Victorian.* University Park, Pa.: Pennsylvania State University Press, 1979.

Sharp, James J. *The Flower of Scotland: A History of Scottish Monarchy.* Perth, Scotland: Melven Press, 1981.

Shaw, John Stuart. *The Management of Scottish Society, 1707–1764: Power, Nobles, Lawyers, Edinburgh Agents and English Influences.* Edinburgh: John Donald, 1983.

Sher, Richard B. *Church and University in the Scottish Enlightenment: The Moderati Literati of Edinburgh.* Edinburgh: Edinburgh University Press, 1985.

Sher, Richard B., and Jeffrey R. Smitten. *Scotland and America in the Age of Enlightenment.* Edinburgh: Edinburgh University Press, 1990.

Shortland, M., ed. *Hugh Miller and the Controversies of Victorian Science.* Oxford: Clarendon Press, 1996.

Shuldhalm-Shaw, Patrick, Emily B. Lyle and Peter A. Hall, eds. *The Greig-Duncan Folk Song Collection, 6 vols.* Aberdeen, Scotland: Aberdeen University Press, 1981 (Vol. 1), 1983 (Vol. 2), 1987 (Vol. 3), 1990 (Vol. 4) and 1995 (Vols. 5 and 6).

Shyllon, Folarin. *James Ramsay: The Unknown Abolitionist.* Edinburgh: Canongate, 1977.

Simpson, Grant G. *Scottish Handwriting: An Introduction to the Reading of Documents.* Edinburgh: Bratton Publishing, 1973.

—————. *Scotland and the Low Countries.* East Linton, Scotland: Tuckwell Press, 1996.

—————. *The Scottish Soldier Abroad, 1247–1967.* Edinburgh: John Donald, 1992.

Simpson, Kenneth, ed. *Burns Now.* Edinburgh: Canongate Academic, 1994.

Simpson, Peter. *The Independent Highland Companies: 1603–1760.* Edinburgh: John Donald, 1996.

Sinclair, Cecil. *Tracing Scottish Local History.* Edinburgh: Her Majesty's Stationery Office, 1994.

—————. *Tracing Your Scottish Ancestors: A Guide to Ancestor Research in the Scottish Record Office.* Edinburgh: Her Majesty's Stationery Office, 1990.

Sinclair-Stevenson, Christopher. *Inglorious Rebellion: The Jacobite Risings of 1708, 1715 and 1719.* London: Hamilton, 1971.

Skinner, Andrew S., and Thomas Wilson, eds. *Essays on Adam Smith.* Oxford: Clarendon Press, 1975.

Slaven, Anthony. *The Development of the West of Scotland, 1750–1960.* London: Routledge, 1975.

Slessor, Malcolm. *The Politics of Environment: Including a Guide to Scottish Thought and Action.* London: Allen and Unwin, 1972.

Small, A., ed. *The Picts: A New Look at Old Problems.* Dundee, Scotland: Dundee University Press, 1987.

Small, Alan, Charles Thomas and David M. Wilson. *St Ninian's Isle and Its Treasure.* London: Oxford University Press, 1973.

Smellie, Alexander. *Men of the Covenant: The Story of the Scottish Church in the Years of the Persecution.* Edinburgh: Banner of Truth Trust, 1975.

Smith, Alan G. R., ed. *The Reign of James VI and I.* London: Macmillan, 1973.

Smith, Donald. *Celtic Travellers: Scotland in the Age of the Saints.* Edinburgh: Her Majesty's Stationery Office, 1997.

Smith, H. D. *Shetland Life and Trade, 1550–1914.* Edinburgh: John Donald, 1984.

Smith, Janet Adam. *Buchan: A Biography.* Oxford: Oxford University Press, 1985.

Smith, John. *Cheesemaking in Scotland: A History.* Clydebank, Scotland: Scottish Dairy Association, 1995.

Smith, Maurice. *Paper Lions: The Scottish Press and National Identity.* Edinburgh: Polygon, 1994.

Smout, T. C. *A Century of the Scottish People, 1830–1950.* London: Collins, 1986.

—————. *A History of the Scottish People, 1560–1830.* London: Collins, 1970.

—————, ed. *Scotland and Europe, 1200–1850.* Edinburgh: John Donald, 1986.

Smout, T. C., and Sydney Wood. *Scottish Voices, 1745–1960.* London: Fontana, 1991.

Smyth, Alfred P. *Scandinavian Kings in the British Isles, 850–880.* Oxford: Oxford University Press, 1977.

—————. *Warlords and Holy Men: Scotland AD 80–1000.* London: Edward Arnold, 1984.

Somerset Fry, Peter, and Fiona Somerset Fry. *The History of Scotland.* London: Routledge, 1985.

Somerville, Robert. *Scotia Pontifica: Papal Letters to Scotland before the Pontificate of Innocent III.* Oxford: Clarendon Press, 1982.

Sopel, Jon. *Tony Blair: The Moderniser.* London: Michael Joseph, 1995.

Spaven, Malcolm. *Fortress Scotland: A Guide to the Military Presence.* London: Pluto Press, 1983.

Speck, W. A. *The Butcher: The Duke of Cumberland and the Suppression of the 45.* Oxford: Blackwell, 1981.

Sprott, Gavin. *Robert Burns: Pride and the Passion — The Life, Times and Legacy.* Edinburgh: Her Majesty's Stationery Office, 1997.

Squair, Olive M. *Scotland in Europe: A Study in Race Relations.* Inverness, Scotland: Graphis, 1977.

Stanley, Sir Henry Morton. *How I Found Livingstone.* New York: Arno, 1970.

Steel, David. *Against Goliath: David Steel's Story.* London: Weidenfeld and Nicolson, 1984.

Steel, Tom. *The Life and Death of St Kilda.* London: HarperCollins, 1994.

—————. *Scotland's Story.* London: HarperCollins, 1994.

Steer, K. A., and J. W. M. Bannerman. *Late Medieval Monumental Sculpture in the West Highlands.* Edinburgh: Royal Commission on the Ancient and Historical Monuments of Scotland, 1977.

Steven, Maisie. *Parish Life in Eighteenth Century Scotland: A Review of the Old Statistical Account.* Aberdeen, Scotland: Scottish Cultural Press, 1995.

Stevenson, David. *Alasdair MacColla and the Highland Problem in the*

Seventeenth Century. Edinburgh: John Donald, 1980.

——. *Highland Warrior: Alasdair MacColla and the Civil Wars.* Edinburgh: Saltire Society, 1994.

——. (with translations by Peter Graves). *Scotland's Last Royal Wedding: The Marriage of James VI and Anne of Denmark.* Edinburgh: John Donald, 1997.

——. *Revolution and Counter-Revolution in Scotland, 1641–1651.* London: Royal Historical Society, 1977.

——. *Scottish Covenanters and Irish Confederates: Scottish-Irish Relations in the Mid-Seventeenth Century.* Belfast: Ulster Historical Foundation, 1981.

——, ed. *The Government of Scotland under the Covenanters, 1637–1651.* Edinburgh: Scottish History Society, 1982.

——. *The Scottish Revolution, 1637–44: The Triumph of the Covenanters.* Newton Abbot, England: David and Charles, 1973.

Stevenson, David, and Wendy Stevenson. *Scottish Texts and Calendars: An Analytical Guide to Serial Publications.* London: Royal Historical Society, 1987.

Stevenson, Jack. *Exploring Scotland's Heritage: Glasgow, Clydeside and Stirling.* Edinburgh: Her Majesty's Stationery Office, 1995.

Stones, Jeffrey. *Illustrated Maps of Scotland: From Blaeu's Atlas Novus of the 17th Century.* London: Studio Editions, 1991.

——. *The Pont Manuscript Maps of Scotland: Sixteenth Century Origins of a Blaeu Atlas.* Tring, England: Map Collector Publications, 1989.

Stones, E. L. G., ed. *Anglo-Scottish Relations, 1174–1328: Some Selected Documents.* Oxford: Clarendon Press, 1970.

Stones, E. L. G. and Grant G. Simpson. *Edward and the Throne of Scotland, 1290–1296: An Edition of the Record Sources for the Great Cause, 2 vols.* Oxford: Oxford University Press, 1977 (Vol. 1) and 1978 (Vol. 2).

Strang, Charles Alexander. *Borders and Berwick.* Edinburgh: Rutland Press, 1994.

Strawhorn, J., and K. Andrew. *The History of Prestwick.* Edinburgh: John Donald, 1994.

Stringer, K. J. *Earl David of Huntingdon, 1152–1219: A Study in Anglo-Scottish History.* Edinburgh: Edinburgh University Press, 1985.

——, ed. *Essays on the Nobility of Medieval Scotland.* Edinburgh: John Donald, 1985.

Stroud, Barry. *Hume.* London: Routledge, 1977.

Stuart, Margaret. *Scottish Family History: A Guide to Works of Reference on the History and Genealogy of Scottish Families.* Baltimore:

Genealogical Publishing, 1978.

Sunter, Ronald M. *Patronage and Principle: A Political History of Modern Scotland.* Aberdeen, Scotland: Aberdeen University Press, 1987.

Supple, Barry. *1913–1946: The Political Economy of Decline.* Vol. 4 of *The History of the British Coal Industry:* Oxford: Clarendon Press, 1987.

Sutherland, Elizabeth. *In Search of the Picts: A Celtic Dark Age Nation.* London: Constable, 1994.

—————. *The Pictish Guide: A Guide to the Pictish Stones.* Edinburgh: Birlinn, 1997.

Szechi, Daniel. *The Jacobites: Britain and Europe, 1688–1788.* Manchester: Manchester University Press, 1994.

Tabraham, Chris. *Scottish Castles.* London: Batsford, 1997.

Tabraham, Chris, and Doreen Grove. *Fortress Scotland and the Jacobites.* London: Batsford/Historic Scotland, 1995.

Tait, A. A. *The Landscape Garden in Scotland.* Edinburgh: Edinburgh University Press, 1980.

Tamaki, Norio. *The Life Cycle of the Union Bank of Scotland, 1830–1954.* Aberdeen: Aberdeen University Press, 1983.

Taylor, William. *The Military Roads in Scotland.* Newton Abbot, England: David and Charles, 1976.

Tennant, Charles. *The Radical Laird: A Biography of George Kinloch, 1775–1833.* Kineton, England: Roundwood Press, 1970.

Thomas, Charles. *The Early Christian Archaeology of North Britain.* London: Oxford University Press, 1971.

Thomas, Donald. *Cochrane: Britannia's Last Sea-King.* London: Deutsch, 1978.

Thomas, L. M., ed. *Settlement in Scotland: 1000 BC–AD 1000.* Edinburgh: Scottish Archaeological Forum, 1980.

Thompson, Laurence. *The Enthusiasts: A Biography of John and Katherine Bruce Glasier.* London: Gollancz, 1971.

Thompson, William P. L. *History of Orkney.* Edinburgh: Mercat Press, 1987.

Thomson, Derek, ed. *The Companion to Gaelic Scotland.* Oxford: Blackwell, 1983.

Thomson, W. P. L. *History of Orkney.* Edinburgh: Mercat Press, 1987.

—————. *Lord Henry Sinclair's 1492 Rental of Orkney.* Kirkwall, Scotland: Orkney Press, 1996.

Tiltman, Ronald Frank. *Baird of Television.* New York: Arno Press, 1974.

Tomasson, Katherine, and Francis Buist. *Battles of the '45.* London: Batsford, 1978.

Tranter, Nigel. *The Fortified House in Scotland, 5 Vols.* Edinburgh:

Mercat Press, 1986.

——————. *Rob Roy MacGregor.* Edinburgh: Canongate Press, 1995.

——————. *The Story of Scotland.* Glasgow: Neil Wilson, 1993.

Trevor, Muriel. *The Shadow of a Crown: The Life Story of James II of England and VII of Scotland.* London: Constable, 1988.

Turnbull, Michael T. R. B. *Scotland: The Facts.* Edinburgh: Chambers, 1991.

Turner, Frederick. *John Muir: From Scotland to the Sierra.* Edinburgh: Canongate Press, 1997.

Turnock, David. *The Historical Geography of Scotland since 1707.* Cambridge: Cambridge University Press, 1982.

——————. *The Making of the Scottish Rural Landscape.* Aldershot, England: Scolar Press, 1995.

——————. *The New Scotland.* Newton Abbot, England: David and Charles, 1979.

Tweedsmuir, John Buchan, Baron. *Always a Countryman.* London: Hale, 1971.

Tweyman, Stanley, ed. *David Hume: Critical Assessments.* London: Routledge, 1994.

Van der Vat, Dan. *The Grand Scuttle: The Sinking of the German Fleet at Scapa Flow.* Edinburgh: Birlinn, 1997.

Wagenknecht, Edward. *Sir Walter Scott.* New York: Continuum, 1991.

Walker, Fred. M. *Song of the Clyde: A History of Clyde Shipbuilding.* Cambridge: Stephens, 1984.

Walker, Graham, and Tom Gallagher. *Sermons and Battle Hymns: Protestant Popular Culture in Modern Scotland.* Edinburgh: Edinburgh University Press, 1990.

Walker, William. *Juteopolis: Dundee and Its Textile Workers, 1885–1923.* Edinburgh: Scottish Academic Press, 1979.

Wall, Joseph Frazier. *Andrew Carnegie.* New York: Oxford University Press, 1970.

Watson, Don. *Caledonia Australis: Scottish Highlanders on the Frontier of Australia.* Sydney, Australia: Collins, 1984.

Watson, Godfrey. *Bothwell and the Witches.* London: Hale, 1975.

Watson, W. J. *A History of the Celtic Placenames of Scotland.* Edinburgh: Birlinn, 1993.

Watt, D. E. R. *A Biographical Dictionary of Scottish Graduates to AD 1410.* Oxford: Clarendon Press, 1977.

Waugh, D. J. *Shetland's Northern Links: Language and Religion.* Edinburgh: Scottish Society for Northern Studies, 1996.

Waxman, Wayne. *Hume's Theory of Consciousness.* Cambridge: Cambridge University Press, 1994.

Way of Plean, George, and Romilly Squire. *Scottish Clan and Family Encyclopaedia*. Glasgow: HarperCollins, 1994.

Webster, Bruce, ed. *The Acts of David II: King of Scots 1329–1371*. Edinburgh: Edinburgh University Press, 1982.

——————. *Scotland from the Eleventh Century to 1603*. London: Sources of History, 1975.

——————. *Scotland in the Middle Ages: The Making of an Identity*. Basingstoke, England: Macmillan, 1994.

West, E. G. *Adam Smith: The Man and His Works*. Indianapolis, Ind.: Liberty Press, 1976.

Westwood, Peter J. *The Deltiology of Robert Burns*. Dumfries, Scotland: Creedon, 1994.

Whateley, Christopher A., ed. *John Galt, 1779–1979*. Edinburgh: Ramsay Head Press, 1979.

Whetstone, Ann E. *Scottish County Government in the Eighteenth and Nineteenth Centuries*. Edinburgh: John Donald, 1981.

Whitehead, G. Kenneth. *Half a Century of Scottish Deerstalking*. Shrewsbury, England: Swan Hill Press, 1996.

Whittington, G., and I. D. Whyte, eds. *An Historical Geography of Scotland*. London: Academic Press, 1983.

Who's Who in Scotland? Irvine: Carrick Media. (Published annually).

Whyte, Donald. *A Dictionary of Scottish Emigrants to Canada before Confederation*. Toronto, Canada: Ontario Genealogical Society, 1986.

Whyte, Ian D. *Agriculture and Society in Seventeenth Century Scotland*. Edinburgh: John Donald, 1979.

——————. *Scotland before the Industrial Revolution: An Economic and Social History, c. 1500–c. 1750*. London: Longman, 1995.

Whyte, Ian D., and Kathleen Whyte. *The Changing Scottish Landscape, 1500–1800*. London: Routledge, 1991.

Wickham-Jones, C. R. *Scotland's First Settlers*. London: Batsford, 1994.

Wigan, Michael. *The Scottish Highland Estate: Preserving and Environment*. Shrewsbury, England: Swan Hill Press, 1991.

Wight, Daniel. *Workers Not Wasters — Masculine Respectability, Consumption and Unemployment in Central Scotland: A Community Study*. Edinburgh: Edinburgh University Press, 1993.

Wightman, A. *Who owns Scotland?* Edinburgh: Canongate, 1996.

Williamson, Arthur H. *Scottish National Consciousness in the Age of James VI: The Apocalypse, the Union and the Shaping of Scotland's Public Culture*. Edinburgh: John Donald, 1979.

Williamson, E., A. Riches and M. Higgs. *Glasgow*. London: Penguin, 1990.

Willis, Douglas. *The Story of Crofting in Scotland.* Edinburgh: John Donald, 1991.

Wills, Jonathan. *A Place in the Sun: Shetland and Oil — Myths and Realities.* Edinburgh: Mainstream, 1991.

Wills, V., ed. *Reports on the Annexed Estates, 1755–1769.* Edinburgh: Her Majesty's Stationery Office, 1973.

Willsher, Betty, and Doreen Hunter. *Stones: A Guide to Some Remarkable Eighteenth Century Gravestones.* Edinburgh: Canongate Press, 1978.

Wilson, A. N. *The Laird of Abbotsford: A View of Sir Walter Scott.* Oxford: Oxford University Press, 1980.

Wilson, Alexander. *The Chartist Movement in Scotland.* Manchester: Manchester University Press, 1970.

Wilson, Gordon M. *Alexander McDonald, Leader of the Miners.* Aberdeen, Scotland: Aberdeen University Press, 1982.

Wilson, Ross. *Scotch: The Formative Years.* London: Constable, 1970.

Winch, Donald. *Adam Smith's Politics: An Essay in Historiographic Revision.* Cambridge: Cambridge University Press, 1978.

Winter, Denis. *Haig's Command: A Reassessment.* London: Viking, 1991.

Withers, Charles W. J. *Gaelic in Scotland, 1698–1981: The Geographical History of a Language.* Edinburgh: Donald, 1984.

—————. *Gaelic Scotland: the Transformation of a Culture Region.* London: Routledge, 1988.

Womack, P. *Improvement and Romance: Constructing the Myth of the Highlands.* London: Macmillan, 1989.

Wood, Ian S., ed. *Scotland and Ulster.* Edinburgh: Mercat Press, 1994.

Wood, N. *Scottish Placenames.* Edinburgh: Chambers, 1989.

Wood, Stephen. *The Auld Alliance: Scotland and France — The Military Connection.* Edinburgh: Mainstream, 1989.

—————. *In the Finest Tradition: The Royal Scots Dragoon Guards (Carabiniers and Greys) — Its History and Treasures.* Edinburgh: Mainstream, 1988.

Woosnam-Savage, Robert, ed. *1745: Charles Edward Stuart and the Jacobites.* Edinburgh: Her Majesty's Stationery Office, 1995.

Wormald, Jenny. *Court, Kirk and Community: Scotland, 1470–1625.* Edinburgh: Edinburgh University Press, 1991.

—————. *Lords and Men in Scotland: Bonds of Manrent, 1442–1603.* Edinburgh: John Donald, 1985.

—————. *Mary Queen of Scots: A Study in Failure.* London: George Philip, 1988.

Worsdall, Frank Gilmour. *The Glasgow Tenement: A Way of Life.* Glasgow: Drew, 1989.

Wright, S. Fowler. *The Life of Sir Walter Scott*. New York: Haskell House, 1971.

Yarwood, Doreen. *Robert Adam*. London: Dent, 1970.

Yeoman, Peter. *Medieval Scotland*. London: Batsford, 1995.

Young, Douglas. *Scotland*. London: Cassell, 1971.

Young, Eric. *The Law of Planning in Scotland*. Glasgow: William Hodge, 1978.

——————. *Scottish Planning Appeals: Decisions on Law and Procedure*. Edinburgh: William Green, 1991.

Young, James Douglas. *The Rousing of the Scottish Working Class*. London: Croom Helm, 1979.

Young, John R. *The Scottish Parliament, 1639–1661: A Political and Constitutional Analysis*. Edinburgh: John Donald, 1996.

Young, Margaret D. *The Parliaments of Scotland: Burgh and Shire Commissions. 2 Vols.* Edinburgh: Scottish Academic Press, 1992 (Vol. 1) and 1993 (Vol. 2).

Youngson, A. J. *After the Forty-Five: The Economic Impact on the Scottish Highlands*. Edinburgh: Edinburgh University Press, 1973.

——————. *The Making of Classical Edinburgh*. Edinburgh: Edinburgh University Press, 1988.

——————. *The Prince and the Pretender: A Study in the Writing of History*. London: Croom Helm, 1985.

Zweig, Stefan. *The Queen of Scots*. London: Cassell, 1987.

Wales

Aaron, Jane, Teresa Rees, Sandra Betts and Moira Vincentelli, eds. *Our Sisters' Land: The Changing Identities of Women in Wales*. Cardiff: University of Wales Press, 1997.

Adams, Sam, and Gwilym Rees Hughes, eds. *Triskel One: Essays on Welsh and Anglo-Welsh Literature*. Swansea, Wales: Christopher Davies, 1971.

Ainsworth, William Harrison. *Beau Nash, or, Bath in the Eighteenth Century*. Bath, England: Chivers, 1977.

Aitchison, John, and Harold Carter. *A Geography of the Welsh Language, 1961–1991*. Cardiff: University of Wales Press, 1994.

——————. *The Welsh Language, 1961–1981: An Interpretative Atlas*. Cardiff: University of Wales Press, 1985.

Alban, J. R. *Swansea 1184–1984*. Swansea, Wales: Swansea City Council/*South Wales Evening Post*, 1984.

——————. *The Three Nights Blitz: Select Contemporary Reports Re-*

lating to Swansea's Air Raids of February, 1941. Swansea, Wales: City of Swansea, 1994.

Allchin, A. M. *Praise above All: Discovering the Welsh Tradition.* Cardiff: University of Wales Press, 1995.

Allday, Helen D. *Insurrection in Wales: the Rebellion of the Welsh Led by Owen Glyn Dwr (Glendower) against the English Crown in 1400.* Lavenham, England: Terence Dalton, 1981.

Andrews, J. A., ed. *Welsh Studies in Public Law.* Cardiff: University of Wales Press, 1970.

Archer, Michael Scott. *The Welsh Post Towns before 1840.* London: Phillimore, 1970.

Arthur, Nigel. *Swansea at War.* Urmston, England: Archive Publications, 1988.

Ashworth, William, and Mark Pegg. *The Nationalized Industry. Vol. 5 of The History of the British Coal Industry: 1946–1982.* Oxford: Clarendon Press, 1986.

Atkinson, Michael, and Colin Baber. *The Growth and Decline of the South Wales Iron Industry, 1760–1880.* Cardiff: University of Wales Press, 1987.

Baber, Colin, and L. J. Williams, eds. *Modern South Wales: Essays in Economic History.* Cardiff: University of Wales Press, 1986.

Baker, Colin. *Aspects of Bilingualism in Wales.* Clevedon, England: Multilingual Matters, 1985.

Baker, Philip, and Robert Higham. *Hen Domen, Montgomery: A Timber Castle on the English-Welsh Border.* London: Royal Archaeological Institute, 1982.

Balchin, W. G. V., ed. *Swansea and Its Region.* Swansea, Wales: University College of Swansea, 1971.

Ball, Martin, ed. *The Celtic Languages.* London: Routledge, 1993.

Barber, Chris. *Mysterious Wales.* Newton Abbot, England: David and Charles, 1982.

Barnes, Tudor, and Nigel Yates, eds. *Carmarthenshire Studies.* Carmarthen, Wales: Carmarthenshire County Council, 1974.

Bartlett, Robert. *Gerald of Wales, 1146–1223.* Oxford: Clarendon Press, 1982.

Bartrum, P. C. *Welsh Genealogies, A.D. 1400–1500 18 vols.* Aberystwyth: National Library of Wales, 1983.

Bassett, T. M. *The Welsh Baptists.* Swansea, Wales: Ilston House, 1977.

Batstone, Cyril. *Rhondda Remembered.* Barry, Wales: Stewart Williams, 1983.

Beddoe, Deirdre. *Welsh Convict Women: A Study of Women Transported from Wales to Australia, 1787–1852.* Barry, Wales: Stewart

Williams, 1979.

Benjamin, E. Alwyn. *Penarth, 1841–1871: A Glimpse of the Past.* Cowbridge, Wales: D. Brown, 1980.

Benny, Dave. *Males and Cinema: The First Hundred Years.* Cardiff: University of Wales Press, 1996.

Betts, Clive. *The Political Conundrum: Wales and Its Politics in the Century's Last Decade.* Llandysul, Wales: Gomer Press, 1993.

Bevins, Richard E. *A Mineralogy of Wales.* Cardiff: National Museum of Wales, 1994.

Boon, G. C. *Cardiganshire Silver and the Aberystwyth Mint in Peace and War.* Cardiff: National Museum of Wales, 1981.

Boon, G. C., and J. M. Lewis, eds. *Welsh Antiquity.* Cardiff: Welsh Folk Museum, 1976.

Borrow, George. *Wild Wales: Its People, Language Scenery.* Llandysul, Wales: Gomer Press, 1995.

Bowen, D. Q. *The Llanelli Landscape: The Geology and Geomorphology of the Country around Llanelli.* Llanelli, Wales: Llanelli Borough Council, 1980.

Bowen, E. G. *Saints, Seaways and Settlements in the Celtic Lands.* Cardiff: University of Wales Press, 1977.

Brinnin, John Malcolm. *Dylan Thomas in America.* N. Y.: Paragon House, 1989.

Bromwich, Rachel, A. O. H. Jarman, and Brynley F. Roberts, eds. *The Arthur of the Welsh: The Arturian Ledgend in Medieval Welsh Literature.* Cardiff: University of Wales Press, 1991.

Brown, John H. *The Valley of the Shadow: An Account of Britain's Worst Mining Disaster — The Senghenydd Explosion.* Port Talbot, Wales: Alun Books, 1981.

Brown, Roger Lee. *The Tribulations of a Mountain Parish: Glyncorrwg, Queen Anne's Bounty and the Ecclesiastical Commission.* Cardiff: Tair Eglwys Press, 1988.

Burnham, Helen. *A Guide to Ancient and Historic Wales: Clwyd and Powys.* Cardiff: Her Majesty's Stationery Office, 1995.

Butler, L. A. S. *Denbigh Castle, Town Walls and Friary, Clwyd.* London: Her Majesty's Stationery Office, 1976.

Butt, Philip. *The Welsh Question: Nationalism in Welsh Politics, 1945–1970.* Cardiff: University of Wales Press, 1975.

Campbell, John. *Nye Bevan and the Mirage of British Socialism.* London: Weidenfeld and Nicolson, 1987.

Carr, A. D. *Medieval Anglesey.* Llangefni, Wales: Anglesey Antiquarian, 1982.

——————. *Medieval Wales.* Basingstoke, England: Macmillan, 1995.

——————. *Owen of Wales: The End of the House of Gwynedd.* Cardiff: University of Wales Press, 1991.

Carradice, Phil. *The Book of Pembroke Dock: The Story of a Town Created to Build Ships.* Buckingham: Barracuda Books, 1991.

——————. *The Last Invasion: The Story of the French Landing in Wales.* Griffithstown, Wales: Village Publishing, 1992.

Carter, Harold, ed. *National Atlas of Wales.* Cardiff: University of Wales Press, 1980.

Carter, Harold, and W. K. Davies, eds. *Urban Essays: Studies in the Geography of Wales.* London: Longman, 1970.

Carter, Harold and Sandra Wheatley. *Merthyr Tydfil in 1851: A Study of the Spatial Structure of a Welsh Industrial Town.* Cardiff: University of Wales Press, 1982.

Chadwick, Nora K. *The British Heroic Age: The Welsh and the Men of the North.* Cardiff: University of Wales Press, 1976.

Chapman, John. *A Guide to the Parliamentary Enclosures in Wales.* Cardiff: University of Wales Press, 1992.

Chappell, Edgar L. *History of the Port of Cardiff.* Cardiff: Merton Priory Press, 1994.

Charles, B. G. *George Owen of Henllys: A Welsh Elizabethan.* Aberystwyth: National Library of Wales Press, 1973.

Charles-Edwards, T. M. *The Welsh Laws.* Cardiff: University of Wales Press, 1989.

Charles-Edwards, T., Morfydd E. Owen and D. B. Walters. *Lawyers and Laymen.* Cardiff: University of Wales Press, 1986.

Church, Roy, Alan Hall and John Kanefsky. *1830–1913, Victorian Pre-Eminence. Vol. 3 of The History of the British Coal Industry.* Oxford: Clarendon Press, 1986.

Claeys, Gregory. *Machinery, Money and the Millenium: The New Moral Economy of Owenite Socialism, 1815–60.* Princeton N. J.: Princeton University Press, 1987.

Clancy, Joseph P. *The Earliest Welsh Poetry.* London: Macmillan, 1970.

Clews, Roy. *To Dream of Freedom.* Talybont, Wales: Y Lolfa, 1980.

Cloke, Paul, Mark Goodwin and Paul Milbourne. *Rural Wales: Community and Marginalization.* Cardiff: University of Wales Press, 1997.

Cole, David, ed. *The New Wales.* Cardiff: University of Wales Press, 1990.

Colyer, Richard J. *Roads and Trackways of Wales.* Ashbourne, England: Moorland, 1984.

——————. *The Welsh Cattle Drovers: Agriculture and the Welsh Cattle Trade before and during the Nineteenth Century.* Cardiff: University of Wales Press, 1976.

Cowley, F. G. *The Monastic Order in South Wales, 1066–1349*. Cardiff: University of Wales Press, 1977.

Crawshay, Richard. *The Letterbook of Richard Crawshay: 1788–1797*, edited by Chris Evans. Cardiff: South Wales Record Society, 1990.

Cule, John. *Wales and Medicine: A Source-List for Printed Books and Papers Showing the History of Medicine in Relation to Wales and Welshmen*. Aberystwyth: National Library of Wales, 1980.

Curtis, Tony, ed. *Wales, the Imagined Nation: Studies in Cultural and National Identity*. Bridgend: Poetry Wales Press, 1986.

Daunton, M. J. *Coal Metropolis: Cardiff, 1870–1914*. Leicester: Leicester University Press, 1977.

Davies, Charlotte Hull. *Welsh Nationalism in the Twentieth Century: The Ethnic Option and the Modern State*. New York: Praeger, 1989.

Davies, D. Hywel. *The Welsh Nationalist Party, 1925–1945: A Call to Nationhood*. Cardiff: University of Wales Press, 1983.

Davies, David James Llewelfryn, and J. A. Andrews, eds. *Welsh Studies in Public Law*. Cardiff: University of Wales Press, 1970.

Davies, E. T. *Religion and Society in the Nineteenth Century*. Llandybie, Wales: Christopher Davies, 1981.

Davies, Elwyn. *Mild Majesty: A Welsh Childhood, 1912 to 1924*. Llandysul, Wales: Gomer Press, 1987.

Davies, G. *Overseas Investment in Wales: The Welcome Invasion*. Llandybie, Wales: Christopher Davies, 1976.

Davies, James A., ed. *Heart of Wales: An Anthology*. Bridgend, Wales: Seren Books, 1993.

Davies, John. *Broadcasting and the BBC in Wales*. Cardiff: University of Wales Press, 1994.

——————. *Cardiff and the Marquesses of Bute*. Cardiff: University of Wales Press, 1980.

——————. *A History of Wales*. London: Penguin, 1994.

Davies, Oliver. *Celtic Christianity in Early Medieval Wales: The Origins of the Welsh Spiritual Tradition*. Cardiff: University of Wales Press, 1996.

Davies, R. R. *The Age of Conquest: Wales, 1063–1415*. Oxford: Oxford University Press, 1991.

——————. *Conquest, Coexistence and Change: Wales, 1063–1415*. Oxford: Clarendon Press, 1987.

——————. *Domination and Conquest: The Experience of Ireland, Scotland and Wales, 1100–1300*. Cambridge: Cambridge University Press, 1990.

——————. *Lordship and Society in the March of Wales, 1282–1400*. Oxford: Clarendon Press, 1978.

Davies, Robert Rees, R. A. Griffiths et al, eds. *Welsh Society and Nationhood: Historical Essays Presented to Glanmor Williams.* Cardiff: University of Wales Press, 1984.

Davies, Russell. *Secret Sins: Sex, Violence and Society in Carmarthenshire, 1870-1920.* Cardiff: University of Wales Press, 1996.

Davies, Walter Haydn. *The Right Place — The Right Time: Memories of Boyhood Days in a Welsh Mining Community.* Swansea, Wales: Christopher Davies, 1975.

Davies, Wendy. *An Early Welsh Microcosm: Studies in the Llandaff Charters.* London: Royal Historical Society, 1978.

—————. *The Llandaff Charters.* Aberystwyth: National Library of Wales, 1979.

—————. *Patterns of Power in Early Wales.* Oxford: Clarendon Press, 1990.

—————. *Wales in the Early Middle Ages.* London: Pinter, 1989.

Davies, W. R., ed. *The United Nations at Fifty: The Welsh Contribution.* Cardiff: University of Wales Press, 1995.

Davies, Wynford. *The Curriculum and Organization of the County Intermediate Schools, 1880-1926.* Cardiff: University of Wales Press, 1989.

Doble, G. H. (edited by D. Simon Evans). *Lives of the Welsh Saints.* Cardiff: University of Wales Press, 1993.

Dodd, Arthur H. *The Industrial Revolution in North Wales.* Cardiff: University of Wales Press, 1971.

—————. *A Short History of Wales: Welsh Life and Customs from Prehistoric Times to the Present Day.* London: Batsford, 1977.

—————. *Studies in Stuart Wales.* Cardiff: University of Wales Press, 1971.

Doel, Melanie, and Martin Dunkerton. *Is It Still Raining in Aberfan: A Pit and Its People.* Almeley, England: Logaston Press, 1991.

Drower, George. *Kinnock.* South Woodham Ferrers, England: The Publishing Corporation, 1994.

Dumville, D. N., and Brooke, C. N. L., eds. *The Church and the Welsh Border in the Central Middle Ages.* Woodbridge, England: Boydell, 1986.

Durkacz, Victor Edward. *The Decline of the Celtic Languages: A Study of Linguistic and Cultural Conflict in Scotland, Wales and Ireland from the Reformation to the Twentieth Century.* Edinburgh: John Donald, 1983.

Eames, Aled. *Ships and Seamen of Anglesey, 1558–1918: Studies in Maritime and National History.* Llangefni, Wales: Anglesey Antiquarian

Society, 1973.

Eaton, George. *A History of Neath from Earliest Times.* Swansea, Wales: Christopher Davies, 1987.

Egan, David. *Coal Society: A History of the South Wales Mining Valleys, 1840–1980.* Llandysul: Gomer Press, 1987.

—————. *People, Protest and Politics: Case Studies in Nineteenth Century Wales.* Llandysul, Wales: Gomer Press, 1987.

Ellis, Alice Thomas. *Wales: An Anthology.* London: Collins, 1989.

Ellis, E. L. *University College of Wales, Aberystwyth, 1872–1972.* Cardiff: University of Wales Press, 1972.

Ellis, Osian. *The Story of the Harp in Wales.* Cardiff: University of Wales Press, 1991.

Evans, Catherine, and Steve Dodsworth. *Below the Bridge: A Photo-Historical Survey of Cardiff's Docklands to 1983.* Cardiff: National Museum of Wales, 1984.

Evans, Chris. *'The Labyrinth of Flames': Work and Social Conflict in Early Industrial Merthyr Tydfil.* Cardiff: University of Wales Press, 1993.

Evans, David Gareth. *A History of Wales, 1815–1906.* Cardiff: University of Wales Press, 1989.

Evans, Eifion. *Daniel Rowland and the Great Evangelical Awakening in Wales.* Edinburgh: Banner of Truth Trust, 1985.

—————. *Howel Harris, Evangelist, 1714–1773.* Cardiff: University of Wales Press, 1974.

—————. *Two Welsh Revivalists: Humphrey Jones, Dafydd Morgan and the 1859 Revival in Wales.* Bridgend: Evangelical Library of Wales, 1985.

Evans, Estyn. *The Personality of Wales.* Cardiff: BBC Wales, 1973.

Evans, Evan David. *A History of Wales, 1660–1815.* Cardiff: University of Wales Press, 1976.

Evans, Gwynfor. *Land of My Fathers: 2000 Years of Welsh History.* Swansea, Wales: John Penry Press, 1974.

—————. *Welsh Nation Builders.* Llandysul, Wales: Gomer Press, 1988.

Evans, Leslie Wynne. *Education in Industrial Wales 1700–1900: A Study of the Works Schools System in Wales during the Industrial Revolution.* Cardiff: Avalon, 1971.

Evans, W. Gareth. *Education and Female Emancipation: The Welsh Experience, 1847-1914.* Cardiff: University of Wales Press, 1990.

Ferris, Paul. *Dylan Thomas.* New York: Dial Press, 1977.

Fishlock, Trevor. *Wales and the Welsh.* London: Cassell, 1972.

Flinn, M. W., and David Stoker. *1700–1830: The Industrial Revolution.*

Vol. 2 of The History of the British Coal Industry. Oxford: Clarendon Press, 1984.

Foot, Michael. *Aneurin Bevan, 1945–1960.* London: Paladin, 1975.

Ford, Patrick K., ed. *Mabinogi and Other Medieval Welsh Tales.* Berkeley: University of California Press, 1977.

Foulkes, David, J. Barry Jones and R. A. Wilford, eds. *The Welsh Veto: The Wales Act 1978 and the Referendum.* Cardiff: University of Wales Press, 1983.

Francis, David J. *The Border Vale of Glamorgan.* Barry, Wales: Stewart Williams, 1976.

Francis, Hywel, and David Smith. *The Fed: A History of the South Wales Miners in the Twentieth Century.* London: Lawrence and Wishart, 1980.

Fraser, David. *The Adventurers.* Cardiff: University of Wales Press, 1976.

Gantz, Jeffrey, ed. *The Mabinogion.* Harmondsworth, England: Penguin, 1976.

Garlick, Raymond. *An Introduction to Anglo-Welsh Literature.* Cardiff: University of Wales Press, 1972.

Gater, Dilys. *The Battles of Wales.* Llanrwst, Wales: Gwasg Carreg Gwalch, 1991.

Gaunt, Peter. *A Nation under Siege: the Civil War in Wales, 1642–48.* Cardiff: Her Majesty's Stationery Office, 1991.

Geen, A. G. *Decision Making and Secondary Education: A Case Study.* Cardiff: University of Wales Press, 1986.

George, Kenneth D., and Lynn Mainwaring, eds. *The Welsh Economy.* Cardiff: University of Wales Press, 1988.

Gerald of Wales. *The Journey through Wales and the Description of Wales,* translated by Lewis Thorpe. Harmondsworth, England: Penguin, 1978.

Gillham, Mary, John Perkins and Clive Thomas. *A Guide to the Taf Valley from Quakers Ford to Aberfan.* Vol. 1 of *The Historic Taf Valleys.* Merthyr Tydfil, Wales: Merthyr Tydfil and District Naturalists Society, 1979.

Ginswick, J., ed. *The Mining and Manufacturing Districts of South Wales and North Wales.* Vol. 3 of *Labour and the Poor in England and Wales, 1849–51).* London: Cass, 1983.

Glastonbury, B. *Homeless near a Thousand Homes: A Study of Families without Homes in South Wales and the West of England.* London: Allen and Unwin, 1971.

Glendinning, M., and S. Muthesius. *Tower Block: Modern Public Housing in England, Scotland, Wales and Northern Ireland.* New Haven, Conn.: Yale University Press, 1994.

Glenn, Charles. *The Lords of Cardiff Castle*. Swansea, Wales: Christopher Davies, 1976.

Glover, Brian. *Prince of Ales: The History of Brewing in Wales*. Stroud, England: Alan Sutton, 1993.

Grant, G. *Social Atlas of Gwynedd*. Caernarvon, Wales: Gwynedd County Council, 1979.

Grant, Raymond M. J. *On the Parish: An Illustrated Source Book on the Care of the Poor under the Old Poor Law Based on Documents from the County of Glamorgan*. Cardiff: Glamorgan Archive Service, 1988.

——————. *The Parliamentary History of Glamorgan, 1542–1976*. Swansea, Wales: Christopher Davies, 1978.

Gregory, Donald. *Wales before 1066: A Guide*. Llanrwst, Wales: Gwasg Carreg Gwalch, 1989.

——————. *Wales before 1536: A Guide*. Capel Garmon, Wales: Gwasg Carreg Gwalch, 1993.

Gresham, Colin A. *Eifionydd: A Study in Landownership from the Medieval Period to the Present Day*. Cardiff: University of Wales Press, 1973.

Griffiths, Ralph A., ed. *Boroughs of Medieval Wales*. Cardiff: University of Wales Press, 1978.

——————. *The City of Swansea: Challenges and Change*. Gloucester, England: Alan Sutton, 1990.

——————. *Sir Rhys ap Thomas and His Family: A Study in the Wars of the Roses and Early Tudor Politics*. Cardiff: University of Wales Press, 1993.

——————. *Conquerors and Conquered in Medieval Wales*. Stroud, England: Alan Sutton, 1994.

——————. *The Principality of Wales in the Later Middle Ages* 2 Vols. Cardiff: University of Wales Press, 1972.

Griffiths, Robert. *S. O. Davies — A Socialist Faith*. Llandysul, Wales: Gomer Press, 1983.

Gross, Joseph. *A Brief History of Merthyr Tydfil*. Newport, Wales: Starling Press, 1980.

Gruffydd, R. G. *'In That Gentile Country...': The Beginnings of Puritan Nonconformity in Wales*. Bridgend, Wales: Evangelical Library of Wales, 1975.

——————. *The Translating of the Bible into the Welsh Tongue*. London: British Broadcasting Corporation, 1988.

Gwyndaf, Robin. *Welsh Folk Tales*. Cardiff: National Museum of Wales, 1995.

Hannan, Patrick, ed. *Wales on the Wireless: A Broadcasting Anthology*.

Llandysul, Wales: Gomer Press, 1988.

Harper, Peter S., and Eric Sunderland, eds. *Genetic and Population Studies in Wales*. Cardiff: University of Wales Press, 1986.

Harris, C. C. *Redundancy and Recession in South Wales*. Oxford: Blackwell, 1987.

Harris, Robert. *The Making of Neil Kinnock*. London: Faber, 1984.

Haslam, Richard. *Powys (Montgomeryshire, Radnorshire, Breconshire)*. Buildings of Wales Series, Harmondsworth, England: Penguin. 1979.

Hatcher, John. *Before 1700: Towards the Age of Coal. Vol. 1 of The History of the British Coal Industry*. Oxford: Clarendon Press, 1993.

Hearne, Derrick. *The ABC of the Welsh Revolution*. Talybont, Wales: Y Lolfa, 1982.

——————. *The Rise of the Welsh Republic*. Talybont, Wales: Y Lolfa, 1982.

Hechter, Michael. *Internal Colonialism: The Celtic Fringe in British National Development, 1536–1966*. London: Routledge and Kegan Paul, 1975.

Henken, Elissa R. *National Redeemer: Owain Glyndwr in Welsh Tradition*. Cardiff: University of Wales Press, 1996.

Herbert, Trevor, and Gareth Elwyn Jones, eds. *Edward I and Wales*. Cardiff: University of Wales Press, 1988.

——————. *People and Protest: Wales, 1815–1880*. Cardiff: University of Wales Press, 1988.

——————. *Post-War Wales*. Cardiff: University of Wales Press, 1988.

——————. *The Remaking of Wales in the Eighteenth Century*. Cardiff: University of Wales Press, 1988.

——————. *Tudor Wales*. Cardiff: University of Wales Press, 1988.

——————. *Wales, 1880–1914*. Cardiff: University of Wales Press, 1988.

——————. *Wales between the Wars*. Cardiff: University of Wales Press, 1988.

Hignell, Andrew. *A 'Favorit' Game: Cricket in South Wales Before 1914*. Cardiff: University of Wales Press, 1992.

Hilling, John B. *Cardiff and the Valleys*. London: Lund Humphries, 1973.

——————. *The Historic Architecture of Wales*. Cardiff: University of Wales Press, 1977.

——————. *Llandaf: Past and Present*. Barry, Wales:Stewart Williams, 1978.

Hillman, Judy, and Peter Clarke. *Geoffrey Howe: A Quiet Revolutionary*. London: Weidenfeld and Nicolson, 1988.

Hopkins, Anthony, ed. *Medieval Neath: Ministers' Accounts, 1262–1316*. Pontypool, Wales: Nidum Publications, 1988.

Hopkins, K., ed. *Rhondda: Past and Future.* Porth, Wales: Rhondda Borough Council, 1974.

Houlder, Christopher. *Wales, An Archaeological Guide: The Prehistoric, Roman and Early Medieval Field Monuments.* London: Faber and Faber, 1978.

Howell, Brian E. *Early Modern Pembrokeshire, 1536–1815. Vol 3 of Pembrokeshire County History.* Haverfordwest, Wales: Pembrokeshire Historical Society, 1987.

Howell, David W. *Land and People in Nineteenth Century Wales.* London: Routledge and Kegan Paul, 1978.

——————. *Patriarchs and Parasites: The Gentry of South-West Wales in the Eighteenth Century.* Cardiff: University of Wales Press, 1986.

Howell, Raymond. *A History of Gwent.* Llandysul, Wales: Gomer Press, 1988.

Hubbard, Edward. *Clwyd (Denbighshire and Flintshire).* Buildings of Wales Series. Harmondsworth, England: Penguin. 1986.

Hughes, Anne. *The Diary of a Farmer's Wife, 1796–1797.* London: Allen Lane, 1980.

Hughes, Glyn Tegai. *Williams Pantycelyn.* Cardiff: University of Wales Press, 1983.

Hughes, Kathleen. *Celtic Britain in the Early Middle Ages: Studies in Welsh and Scottish Sources.* Woodbridge, England: Boydell, 1980.

Hughes, Oliver Wynne. *Every Day Was Summer: Childhood Memories of Edwardian Days in a Small Welsh Town.* Llandysul, Wales: Gomer Press, 1989.

Hughes, Wendy. *The Story of Gower.* Capel Garmon, Wales: Gwasg Carreg Gwalch, 1992.

Hume, Ian, and W. T. R. Pryce, eds. *The Welsh and Their Country: Selected Readings in the Social Sciences.* Llandysul, Wales: Gomer Press, 1986.

Humphreys, Emyr. *The Taliesin Tradition.* Bridgend, Wales: Seren, 1990.

Humphrys, G. *Industrial South Wales.* Newton Abbot, England: David and Charles, 1972.

Hyde, H. A., and S. G. Harrison. *Welsh Timber Trees: Native and Introduced.* Cardiff: National Museum of Wales, 1977.

Jack, R. Ian. *Medieval Wales — The Sources of History: Studies in the Uses of Historical Evidence.* London: Sources of History and Hodder and Stoughton, 1972.

James, Arnold, and John E. Thomas. *Union to Reform: A History of the Parliamentary Representation of Wales, 1536 to 1832.* Llandysul, Wales: Gomer Press, 1986.

——————. *Wales at Westminster.* Llandysul, Wales: Gomer Press,

1981.

James, Brian L., and David J. Francis. *Cowbridge and Llanblethian: Past and Present*. Barry, Wales: Stewart Williams, 1979.

James, David W. *St Davids and Dewisland: A Social History*. Cardiff: University of Wales Press, 1981.

James, Lawrence. *The Golden Warrior: The Life and Legend of Lawrence of Arabia*. London: Abacus, 1995.

James, Terrence. *Carmarthen: An Archaeological and Topographical Survey*. Carmarthen, Wales: Carmarthenshire Antiquarian Society, 1980.

Jarman, Alfred Owen Hughes, and Gwilym Rees Hughes, eds. *A Guide to Welsh Literature*. 2 vols. Swansea, Wales: Christopher Davies, 1976 (Vol. 1) and 1979 (Vol. 2).

Jarman, Eldra, and A. O. H. Jarman. *The Welsh Gypsies: Children of Abram Wood*. Cardiff: University of Wales Press, 1991.

Jarvis, Branwen. *Goronwy Owen*. Cardiff: University of Wales Press, 1986.

Jenkins, Dafydd, and Morfydd E. Owen, eds. *The Welsh Law of Women*. Cardiff: University of Wales Press, 1980.

Jenkins, David. *The Agricultural Community in South-West Wales at the Turn of the Century*. Cardiff: University of Wales Press, 1971.

Jenkins, Geraint H. *The Foundations of Modern Wales: Wales 1642–1780*. Oxford: Clarendon Press, 1987.

———. *Literature, Religion and Society in Wales: 1660–1730*. Cardiff: University of Wales Press, 1978.

———. *Protestant Dissenters in Wales, 1639–1689*. Cardiff: University of Wales Press, 1992.

———. *The University of Wales: An Illustrated History*. Cardiff: University of Wales Press, 1993.

Jenkins, Geraint H., and J. Beverley Smith, eds. *Politics and Society in Wales, 1840–1922*. Cardiff: University of Wales Press, 1988.

Jenkins, Gwyn. *Wales*. London: Batsford, 1975.

Jenkins, J. Geraint. *Getting Yesterday Right: Interpreting the Heritage of Wales*. Cardiff: University of Wales Press, 1992.

———. *Life and Tradition in Rural Wales*. Stroud, England: Alan Sutton, 1991.

———. *Maritime Heritage: The Ships and Seamen of Southern Ceredigon*. Llandysul, Wales: Gomer Press, 1982.

Jenkins, Nigel. *Gwalia in Khasia*. Llandysul, Wales: Gomer Press, 1995.

Jenkins, Philip. *A History of Modern Wales, 1536–1990*. London: Longman, 1992.

———. *The Making of a Ruling Class: The Glamorgan Gentry*,

1640–1790. Cambridge: Cambridge University Press, 1983.

John, Angela V. *Our Mother's Land: Chapters in Welsh Women's History, 1830-1939.* Cardiff: University of Wales Press, 1991.

John, Arthur H., and Glanmor Williams, eds. *Industrial Glamorgan from 1700 to 1970. Vol. 5 of Glamorgan County History.* Cardiff: Glamorgan County History Trust, 1980.

John, Brian. *Honey Harfat: A Haverfordwest Miscellany. Haverfordwest Town and Country, 1479–1979.* Newport, Wales: Greencroft Books, 1979.

————. *Pembrokeshire.* Newton Abbot, England: David and Charles, 1976.

Jones, Aled. *Press, Politics and Society: A History of Journalism in Wales.* Cardiff: University of Wales Press, 1993.

Jones, Anthony. *Welsh Chapels.* Stroud, England: Alan Sutton, 1996.

Jones, Brynmor. *A Bibliography of Anglo-Welsh Literature, 1900–1965.* Swansea, Wales: Library Association (Wales and Monmouthshire Branch), 1970.

Jones, David J. V. *Before Rebecca: Popular Protests in Wales, 1793–1835.* London: Allen Lane, 1973.

————. *The Last Rising: The Newport Insurrection of 1839.* Oxford: Clarendon Press, 1985.

————. *Rebecca's Children: A Study of Rural Society, Crime and Protest.* Oxford: Clarendon Press, 1989.

————. *Crime in Nineteenth Century Wales.* Cardiff: University of Wales Press, 1992.

————. *Crime and Policing in the Twentieth Century: The South Wales Experience.* Cardiff: University of Wales Press, 1976.

Jones, E. D. *Victorian and Edwardian Wales from Old Photographs.* London: Batsford, 1972.

Jones, Emyr Wyn. *Bosworth Field and Its Preliminaries: A Welsh Retrospect.* Liverpool: Modern Welsh Publications, 1984.

Jones, Francis. *Historic Carmarthenshire Homes and Their Families.* Carmarthen, Wales: Carmarthenshire Antiquarian Society, 1987.

Jones, Gareth. *The Gentry and the Elizabethan State.* Swansea, Wales: Christopher Davies, 1977.

Jones, Gareth Elwyn. *Controls and Conflicts in Welsh Secondary Education, 1889–1944.* Cardiff: University of Wales Press, 1982.

————. *Modern Wales: A Concise History.* Cambridge: Cambridge University Press, 1994.

————. *Which Nation's School?: Direction and Devolution in Welsh Education in the Twentieth Century.* Cardiff: University of Wales Press, 1997.

Jones, Gwyn, ed. *The Oxford Book of Welsh Verse in English.* Oxford: Oxford University Press, 1977.

Jones, Haydn. *Accounting, Costing and Cost Estimation: Welsh Industry, 1700–1830.* Cardiff: University of Wales Press, 1985.

Jones, Ieuan Gwynedd, ed. *Aberystwyth, 1277–1977: Eight Lectures to Celebrate the Seventh Centenary of the Borough.* Llandysul, Wales: Gomer Press, 1977.

——————. *Communities: Essays in the Social History of Victorian Wales.* Llandysul, Wales: Gomer Press, 1987.

——————. *Explorations and Expeditions: Essays in the Social History of Victorian Wales.* Llandysul, Wales: Gomer Press, 1981.

——————. *Health, Wealth and Politics in Victorian Wales.* Swansea, Wales: University College Swansea, 1979.

——————. *Mid-Victorian Wales: The Observers and the Observed.* Cardiff: University of Wales Press, 1992.

Jones, Ieuan Gwynedd, and David Williams, eds. *The Religious Census of 1851: the Calendar of Returns Relating to Wales.* 2 vols. Cardiff: University of Wales Press, 1976 (Vol. 1) and 1981 (Vol. 2).

Jones, J. Barry, and R. A. Wilford. *Parliament and Territoriality: The Committee on Welsh Affairs, 1979-1983.* Cardiff: University of Wales Press, 1986.

Jones, J. Graham. *The History of Wales: A Pocket Guide.* Cardiff: University of Wales Press, 1990.

Jones, J. Gwynfor., ed. *Class, Community and Culture in Tudor Wales.* Cardiff: University of Wales Press, 1989.

——————. *Concepts of Order and Gentility in Wales, 1540–1640.* Llandysul, Wales: Gomer Press, 1992.

——————. *Early Modern Wales* c. *1525–1640.* Basingstoke, England: Macmillan, 1994.

——————. *Wales and the Tudor State: Government, Religious Change and the Social Order, 1534–1603.* Cardiff: University of Wales Press, 1989.

Jones, Noragh. *Living in Rural Wales.* Llandysul, Wales: Gomer Press, 1993.

Jones, Peter Ellis. *Bangor, 1883-1988: A Study in Municipal Government.* Cardiff: University of Wales Press.

Jones, R. Merfyn. *The North Wales Quarrymen, 1874–1922.* Cardiff: University of Wales Press, 1981.

Jones, R. Merfyn, and D. Ben Rees. *Liverpool Welsh and Their Religion.* Liverpool: Cyhoeddiadau Modern Cymreig, 1984.

Jones, R. Tudur. *Vavasor Powell.* Swansea, Wales: Gwasg John Penry, 1971.

Jones, Robert Brinley, ed. *Anatomy of Wales.* Peterston-Super-Ely: Gwerin Publications, 1972.

Jones, Robert Brinley. *The Old British Tongue: The Vernacular in Wales, 1540–1640.* Cardiff: Avalon Books, 1970.

Jones, T. Gwynn. *Welsh Folklore and Folk-Custom.* Cambridge: Brewer, 1979.

Jones, Thomas. *Rhymney Memories.* Aberystwyth: National Library of Wales, 1990.

Jones, Whitney R. D. *David Williams: The Anvil and the Hammer.* Cardiff: University of Wales Press, 1986.

Jones, Wyn. *Thomas Edward Ellis (1859-1899).* Cardiff: University of Wales Press, 1986.

Kearney, Hugh. *The British Isles: A History of Four Nations.* Cambridge: Cambridge University Press, 1989.

Kenyon, John R., and Richard Avent. *Castles in Wales and the Marches: Essays in Honour of D. J. Cathcart King.* Cardiff: University of Wales Press, 1987.

Kightly, Charles. *A Mirror of Medieval Wales: Gerald of Wales and His Journey of 1188.* Cardiff: Welsh Historic Monuments, 1988.

Kissack, Keith. *Monmouth: The Making of a Country Town.* London: Phillimore, 1975.

Lambert, W. R. *Drink and Sobriety in Victorian Wales, c. 1820–c. 1895.* Cardiff: University of Wales Press, 1983.

Laugharne, Peter J., ed. *Aneurin Bevan: A Parliamentary Odyssey — Speeches at Westminster.* Liverpool: Manuties Press, 196.

Leapman, Michael. *Kinnock.* London: Unwin Hyman, 1987.

Lee, Jennie. *My Life with Nye.* London: Cape, 1980.

Leng, P. J. *The Welsh Dockers.* Ormskirk, England: Heskeths, 1981.

Lewis, Dillwyn. *The History of Llantrisant.* Risca, Wales: Starling Press, 1975.

Lewis, W. J. *Born on a Perilous Rock: Aberystwyth Past and Present.* Aberystwyth, Wales: Cambrian News, 1980.

Lieven, Michael. *Senghennydd: The Universal Pit Village, 1890–1930.* Llandysul, Wales: Gomer, 1994.

Lindsay, Jean. *The Great Strike: A History of the Penrhyn Quarry Dispute of 1900–1903.* Newton Abbot, England: David and Charles, 1987.

———. *A History of the North Wales Slate Industry.* Newton Abbot, England: David and Charles, 1974.

Linnard, William. *Welsh Woods and Forests: History and Utilization.* Cardiff: National Museum of Wales, 1982.

Littlewood, Kevin. *From Reform to Charter: Merthyr Tydfil, 1832–1838.*

Merthyr Tydfil, Wales: Merthyr Tydfil Heritage Trust, 1990.

Lloyd, Humphrey. *The Quaker Lloyds in the Industrial Revolution.* London: Hutchinson, 1975.

Lloyd, J. E. *A History of Wales.* 2 vols. Carmarthen, Wales: Golden Grove Press, 1988.

Lovett, Richard, ed. *Wales 100 Years Ago: The Beauty of Old Wales Illustrated.* London: Bracken Books, 1985.

Lowe, J. B. *Welsh Country Workers' Housing, 1775–1875.* Cardiff: National Museum of Wales, 1985.

——————. *Welsh Industrial Workers' Housing, 1775–1875.* Cardiff: National Museum of Wales, 1977.

Ludlum, Stuart D., ed. *Exploring the Wild Welsh Coast 100 Years Ago.* London: Thames and Hudson, 1985.

Lynch, Frances. *A Guide to Ancient and Historic Wales: Gwynedd.* Cardiff: Her Majesty's Stationery Office, 1995.

MacDonald, Roderick, and Huw Thomas. *Nationality and Planning in Scotland and Wales.* Cardiff: University of Wales Press, 1997.

Madgwick, P. J., Non Griffiths and Valerie Walker. *The Politics of Rural Wales: A Study of Cardiganshire.* London: Hutchinson, 1973.

Malkin, Benjamin Heath. *The Scenery, Antiquities and Biography of South Wales from Material Collected during Two Excursions in the Year 1803.* London: SR Publishers, 1970.

May, John, comp. *Reference Wales.* Cardiff: University of Wales Press, 1994.

——————. *The Yearbook of Welsh Dates.* Cardiff: Castle Publications, 1989.

Michael, D. P. M. *The Mapping of Monmouthshire.* Bristol: Regional Publications, 1985.

Miles, Dillwyn. *The Royal National Eisteddfod of Wales.* Swansea, Wales: Christopher Davies, 1977.

Miles, John. *Gerald of Wales: Giraldus Cambriensis.* Llandysul, Wales: Gomer Press, 1974.

——————. *Princes and People of Wales.* Risca, Wales: Starling Press, 1977.

Millward, Roy and Adrian Robinson. *Landscapes of North Wales.* Newton Abbot, England: David and Charles, 1978.

Molloy, Pat. *And They Blessed Rebecca: An Account of the Welsh Toll-Gate Riots, 1839–1844.* Llandysul, Wales: Gomer Press, 1983.

Moore, D., ed. *Wales in the Eighteenth Century.* Swansea, Wales: Christopher Davies, 1976.

Moore, Patricia, ed. *Glamorgan Sheriffs.* Cardiff: University of Wales Press, 1995.

Morgan, Alun. *Porthcawl: Its History and Development.* Cowbridge, Wales: D. Brown, 1973.

—————. *Porthcawl, Newton and Nottage: A Concise Illustrated History.* Cowbridge: D. Brown, 1987.

—————. *The South Wales Valleys in History: A Guide to the Literature.* Aberfan, Wales: Ty Toronto, 1974.

Morgan, Dennis. *The Cardiff Story: A History of the City from Its Earliest Times to the Present.* Cowbridge, Wales: D. Brown and Sons, 1991.

Morgan, Derec Llwyd. *Williams Pantycelyn.* Caernarvon, Wales: Gwasg Pantycelyn, 1983.

Morgan, Jane. *Conflict and Order: The Police and Labour Disputes in England and Wales, 1900–1939.* Oxford: Clarendon Press, 1987.

Morgan, Kenneth O. *Modern Wales: Politics, Places and People.* Cardiff: University of Wales Press, 1995.

—————. *Rebirth of a Nation: Wales, 1880–1980.* Oxford: Clarendon Press, 1981.

—————. *Wales in British Politics, 1868–1922.* Cardiff: University of Wales Press, 1980.

Morgan, Prys. *The Eighteenth Century Renaissance.* Swansea, Wales: Christopher Davies, 1981.

—————. *Iolo Morganwg.* Cardiff: University of Wales Press, 1975.

Morgan, Prys, ed. *Glamorgan Society, 1780–1980. Vol. 6 of Glamorgan County History.* Cardiff: Glamorgan County History Trust, 1988.

Morgan, Prys, and David Thomas, eds. *Wales: The Shaping of a Nation.* Newton Abbot, England: David and Charles, 1984.

Morgan, Rhodri. *Cardiff: Half-and-Half a Capital.* Llandysul, Wales: Gomer Press, 1994.

Morgan, T. J., and Prys Morgan. *Welsh Surnames.* Cardiff: University of Wales Press, 1985.

Morgan, W. J., ed. *The Welsh Dilemma.* Llandybie, Wales: Christopher Davies, 1973.

Morris, Jan. *The Matter of Wales: Epic Views of a Small Country.* Harmondsworth, England: Penguin, 1986.

Morris, John, ed. *Nennius: British History and the Welsh Annals.* London: Phillimore, 1980.

Musson, Chris. *Wales from the Air: Patterns of Past and Present.* Aberystwyth: Royal Commission on the Ancient and Historical Documents in Wales, 1994.

Nash, Gerallt D. *Timber-Framed Buildings in Wales.* Cardiff: National Museum of Wales, 1995.

Nashold, James, and George Tremlett. *The Death of Dylan Thomas.* Edinburgh: Mainstream, 1997.

Newman, John. *Glamorgan (Mid Glamorgan, South Glamorgan and West Glamorgan)*. Buildings of Wales Series, London: Penguin, 1995.

Nicholas, Thomas. *The History and Antiquities of Glamorganshire and Its Families*. Barry, Wales: Stewart Williams, 1970.

Noble, Frank, ed. *Offa's Dyke Reviewed*. Oxford: British Archaeological Reports, 1983.

Osmond, John. *Creative Conflict: The Politics of Welsh Devolution*. Llandysul, Wales: Gomer Press, 1977.

──────────. *The National Question Again: Welsh Political Identity in the 1980s*. Llandysul, Wales: Gomer Press, 1985.

──────────. *Police Conspiracy*. Talybont, Wales: Y Lolfa, 1984.

Owen, D. Huw. *Settlement and Society in Wales*. Cardiff: University of Wales Press, 1989.

Owen, G. D. *Wales in the Reign of James I*. London: Royal Historical Society and The Boydell Press, 1988.

Owen, Trefor M. *Welsh Folk Customs*. Llandysul, Wales: Gomer Press, 1987.

Owen, T. R., ed. *The Upper Palaeozoic and Post Palaeozoic Rocks of Wales*. Cardiff: University of Wales Press, 1974.

Paget, Mary, ed. *Man of the Valleys: The Recollections of a South Wales Miner*. Gloucester: Alan Sutton, 1985.

Palmer, Alan. *Princes of Wales*. London: Weidenfeld and Nicolson, 1979.

Palmer, Marilyn. *The Richest of All Wales: The Welsh Potosi or Esgair Hir and Esgair Fraith Lead and Copper Mines of Cardiganshire*. Sheffield, England: Northern Mine Research Society, 1983.

Parry, Cyril. *The Radical Tradition in Welsh Politics: A Study of Liberal and Labour Politics in Gwynedd, 1900–1920*. Hull, England: University of Hull, 1970.

Parry-Jones, Daniel. *Welsh Country Upbringing*. Upton-Upon-Severn, England: Ffynnon Press, 1976.

Pearce, David J., ed. *Bridgend 900: A Brief Chronology of the Bridgend District from the Coming of the Normans, 1093–1993*. Bridgend, Wales: D. Brown and Sons.

Pearce, Susan M., ed. *The Early Church in Western Britain and Ireland: Studies Presented to C. A. Ralegh Radford*. Oxford: British Archaeological Reports, 1982.

Peate, Iowerth C. *Tradition and Folk Life: A Welsh View*. London: Faber and Faber, 1972.

Perkins, John, Jack Evans and Mary Gillham. *In the Brecon Beacons National Park*. Vol. 2 of *The Historic Taf Valleys*. Merthyr Tydfil, Wales: Merthyr Tydfil and District Naturalists Club, 1982.

Perkins, John, Clive Thomas and Jack Evans. *From the Taf Confluence at Cefn-Coed-y-Cymmer to Aberfan.* Vol. 3 of *The Historic Taf Valleys.* Merthyr Tydfil, Wales: Merthyr Tydfil and District Naturalists Club, 1986.

Philip, Alan Butt. *The Welsh Question: Nationalism in Welsh Politics, 1945–70.* Cardiff: University of Wales Press, 1975.

Phillips, J. R. S. *The Justices of the Peace in Wales and Monmouthshire, 1541–1689.* Cardiff: University of Wales Press, 1975.

Phillips, Roger. *Tredegar: The History of an Agricultural Estate, 1300–1956.* Upton-upon-Severn, England: Self Publishing Association, 1990.

Pierce, T. Jones. *Medieval Welsh Society: Selected Essays.* Cardiff: University of Wales Press, 1972.

Pollock, Lawrence and Ian McAllister. *A Bibliography of United Kingdom Politics: Scotland, Wales and Northern Ireland.* Glasgow: Centre for the Study of Public Policy (University of Strathclyde), 1980.

Pounds, N. J. G., ed. *The Cardiff Area: Proceedings of the 139th Summer Meeting of the Royal Archaeological Institute.* London: Royal Archaeological Institute, 1993.

Pretty, David A. *The Rural Revolt that Failed: Farmworkers' Trade Unions in Wales, 1889–1950.* Cardiff: University of Wales Press, 1989.

Price, Emyr. *Lord Cledwyn of Penrhos.* Caernarvon, Wales: Cyhoeddiadau Mei, 1990.

Price, Glanville. *The Languages of Britain.* London: Edward Arnold, 1984.

Price, Mary. *A Modern Geography of Wales.* Swansea, Wales: Christopher Davies, 1974.

Pride, Emrys. *Rhondda My Valley Brave.* Risca, Wales: Starling Press, 1975.

Protheroe-Jones, Robert. *Welsh Steel.* Cardiff: National Museum of Wales, 1995.

Pugh, T. B., ed. *The Middle Ages.* Vol. 3 of *Glamorgan County History.* Cardiff: University of Wales Press, 1971.

Ramage, Helen. *Portraits of an Island: Eighteenth Century Anglesey.* Llangefni, Wales: Anglesey Antiquarian Society, 1987.

Redknap, Mark. *The Christian Celts: Treasures of Late Celtic Wales.* Cardiff: National Museum of Wales, 1995.

Rees, D. Ben. *Chapels in the Valley: A Study in the Sociology of Welsh Conformity.* Upton-Upon-Severn, England: Ffynnon, 1975.

——————. *Wales: The Cultural Heritage.* Ormskirk, England: G. W. and A. Hesketh, 1981.

Rees, D. Morgan. *The Industrial Archaeology of Wales.* Newton Abbot,

England: David and Charles, 1975.

Rees, Gareth, and Teresa Rees, eds. *Poverty and Social Inequality in Wales*. London: Croom Helm, 1980.

Rees, Sian. *A Guide to Ancient and Historic Wales: Dyfed*. Cardiff: Her Majesty's Stationery Office, 1992.

Rees, William. *An Historical Atlas of Wales from Early to Modern Times*. London: Faber and Faber, 1972.

Reeves, A. C. *The Marcher Lords*. Llandybie, Wales: Christopher Davies, 1983.

Richards, Brinley. *History of the Llynfi Valley*. Cowbridge, Wales: D. Brown, 1982.

Richards, H. P. *David Williams (1738–1816): Author, Philosopher, Educationist, Politician and Founder of the Royal Literary Fund*. Cowbridge, Wales: D. Brown, 1980.

—————. *A History of Caerphilly*. Cowbridge, Wales: D. Brown, 1975.

Richter, Michael. *Giraldus Cambriensis: The Growth of the Welsh Nation*. Aberystwyth, Wales: National Library of Wales, 1976.

Riden, Philip. *Cowbridge Trades and Tradesmen, 1660–1750*. Cardiff: University College, Cardiff, 1981.

Robbins, Keith. *Nineteenth Century Britain: Integration and Diversity*. Oxford: Clarendon Press, 1988.

Roberts, C. W. *A Legacy from Victorian Enterprise*. Gloucester: Alan Sutton, 1983.

Roberts, John W. *Medieval Welsh Monasteries*. Cardiff: University of Wales Press, 1987.

Roberts, R. O., ed. *Farming in Caernarvonshire around 1800*. Caernarvon, Wales: Caernarvonshire County Record Office, 1973.

Roberts, Tony. *Castles and Ancient Monuments of West Wales*. Fishguard, Wales: Abercastle Publications, 1989.

Robinson, David M. *Cowbridge: The Archaeology and Topography of a Small Market Town in the Vale of Glamorgan*. Swansea, Wales: Glamorgan-Gwent Archaeological Trust, 1980.

Rodenberg, Julius. *Aspects of Britain: Wales*. London: Her Majesty's Stationery Office, 1993.

—————. *An Autumn in Wales (1856): Country and People, Tales and Songs*. Cambridge: D. Brown, 1985.

Ross, J. E., ed. *Radical Adventurer: The Diaries of Robert Morris, 1772–1774*. Bath, England: Adams and Dart, 1971.

Rowan, Eric, ed. *Art in Wales, 2000BC–AD1850: An Illustrated History*. Cardiff: University of Wales Press, 1978.

—————. *Art in Wales, 1850–1980: an Illustrated History*. Cardiff:

University of Wales Press, 1985.

Rowlands, John. *Holyhead: People, Prosperity and Poverty.* Caernarvon, Wales: Gwynnedd Library Service.

Savory, Hubert N., ed. *Early Glamorgan: Pre-History and Early History. Vol. 2 of Glamorgan County History.* Cardiff: Glamorgan County History Trust, 1984.

Senior, Michael. *Anglesey: The Island's Story.* Llanrwst, Wales: Gwasg Carreg Gwalch, 1987.

Sinclair, Andrew. *Dylan Thomas: Poet of His People.* London: Michael Joseph, 1975.

Skidmore, Ian. *Owain Glyndwr: Prince of Wales.* Swansea, Wales: Christopher Davies, 1978.

Smith, Dai. *Aneurin Bevan and the World of South Wales.* Cardiff: University of Wales Press, 1993.

—————. *Wales! Wales?* London: Allen and Unwin, 1984.

Smith, David, ed. *A People and a Proletariat: Essays in the History of Wales, 1780–1980.* London: Pluto Press, 1980.

Smith, David, and Gareth Williams. *Fields of Praise: The Official History of the Welsh Rugby Union.* Cardiff: University of Wales Press, 1980.

Smith, J. Beverley, ed. *Medieval Welsh Society.* Cardiff: University of Wales Press, 1972.

Smith, Peter. *Houses of the Welsh Countryside.* London: Her Majesty's Stationery Office, 1988.

Soden, R. W. *A Guide to Welsh Parish Churches.* Llandysul, Wales: Gomer Press, 1984.

Soulsby, Ian N. *Cardiff: a Pictorial History.* Chichester, England: Phillimore, 1989.

—————. *The Towns of Medieval Wales: A Study of Their History, Archaeology and Early Topography.* Chichester, England: Phillimore, 1983.

Spurgeon, C. J. *The Castle and Borough of Aberystwyth.* Aberystwyth, Wales: Ceredigion District Council, 1975.

Stead, P. P. *Coleg Harlech, the First Fifty Years.* Cardiff: University of Wales Press, 1977.

Stephens, Meic, ed. *The Arts in Wales, 1950–1975.* Cardiff: Welsh Arts Council, 1979.

—————. *The Oxford Companion to the Literature of Wales.* Oxford: Oxford University Press, 1986.

—————. *A Reader's Guide to Wales.* London: National Book League, 1973.

—————. *The Welsh Language Today.* Llandysul, Wales: Gomer

Press, 1979.

Stephenson, David. *The Governance of Gwynedd*. Cardiff: University of Wales Press, 1984.

—————. *The Last Prince of Wales*. Buckingham: Barracuda Books, 1983.

Supple, Barry. *1913–1946, the Political Economy of Decline. Vol. 4 of The History of the British Coal Industry*. Oxford: Clarendon Press, 1987.

Sylvester, Dorothy. *A History of Gwynedd (Anglesey, Caernarvonshire, Merioneth)*. Chichester, England: Phillimore, 1983.

Symons, M. V. *Coal Mining in the Llanelli Area:16th Century to 1829*. Llanelli, Wales: Llanelli Borough Council, 1979.

Taylor, Arnold J. *Caernarfon Castle*. Cardiff: Welsh Historic Monuments, 1986.

—————. *Conway Castle and Town Walls*. Cardiff: Welsh Historic Monuments, 1986.

—————. *Four Great Castles: Caernarfon, Conwy, Harlech, Beaumaris: An Essay*. Newtown, Wales: Gwasg Gregynog, 1983.

—————. *The King's Works in Wales, 1227–1330*. London: Her Majesty's Stationery Office, 1974.

Taylor, J. A., ed. *Culture and Environment in Prehistoric Wales: Selected Essays*. Oxford: British Archaeological Reports, 1980.

Thomas, Alan R. *The Linguistic Geography of Wales: A Contribution to Welsh Dialectology*. Cardiff: University of Wales Press, 1976.

Thomas, D. Aneurin, ed. *The Welsh Elizabethan Catholic Martyrs: The Trial Documents of Saint Richard Gwyn and of the Venerable William Davies*. Cardiff: University of Wales Press, 1971.

Thomas, David, ed. *Wales: A New Study*. Newton Abbot, England: David and Charles, 1977.

Thomas, Hilary W., ed. *The Diaries of John Bird of Cardiff, Clerk to the First Marquess of Bute, 1790–1803*. Cardiff: South Wales Record Society and Glamorgan Archive Service, 1987.

Thomas, Hugh. *A History of Wales, 1485–1660*. Cardiff: University of Wales Press, 1972.

Thomas, I. *William Morgan and His Bible*. Cardiff: University of Wales Press, 1988.

Thomas, Mair Elvet. *The Welsh Spirit of Gwent*. Cardiff: University of Wales Press, 1988.

Thomas, Ned. *The Welsh Extremist: A Culture in Crisis*. London: Gollancz, 1971.

Thomas, Peter D. G. *Politics in Eighteenth Century Wales*. Cardiff: University of Wales Press, 1997.

Thomas, W. S. K. *The History of Swansea: From Rover Settlement to the Restoration*. Llandysul, Wales: Gomer Press, 1990.

——————. *Stuart Wales*. Llandysul, Wales: Gomer Press, 1988.

Thorne, Roy. *Penarth: a History*. Risca, Wales: Starling Press, 1975.

Thorpe, Lewis. *Gerald of Wales: The Journey through Wales and the Description of Wales*. Harmondsworth, England: Penguin, 1978.

Toulson, Shirley. *Walking Round Wales: The Giraldus Journey*. London: Michael Joseph, 1988.

Trenberth, Sian. *Cymry Enwog Heddiw: Welsh Greats of Today*. Stroud, England: Alan Sutton, 1993.

Twamley, Bill. *Cardiff and Me Sixty Years Ago: Growing Up during the Twenties and Thirties*. Newport, Wales: Starling Press, 1984.

Vaughan-Thomas, Wynford. *The Princes of Wales*. Kingswood, England: Kaye and Ward, 1982.

——————. *The Splendour Falls: The Story of the Castles of Wales*. Cardiff: HTV Cymru, 1973.

——————. *Wales: A History*. London: Michael Joseph, 1985.

Verrill-Rhys, Leigh, and Deirdre Beddoe, eds. *Parachutes and Petticoats: Welsh Women Writing on the Second World War*. Dinas Powys, Wales: Honno, 1992.

Walker, David, ed. *A History of the Church in Wales*. Penarth, Wales: Church in Wales Publications, 1976.

——————. *Medieval Wales*. Cambridge: Cambridge University Press, 1990.

——————. *The Norman Conquerors*. Swansea, Wales: Christopher Davies, 1977.

Walker, Mandy. *From Dowlais to Tremorfa: The Story of a Cardiff Steelmaking Company*. Cardiff: Tremorfa Books, 1993.

Wallace, Ryland. *'Organise! Organise! Organise!': A Study of Reform Agitations in Wales, 1840–1886*. Cardiff: University of Wales Press, 1991.

Warner, Philip. *Famous Welsh Battles: Where Battles Were Fought, Why They Were Fought, How They Were Won and Lost*. London: Fontana, 1977.

Wenger, G. Clare. *Mid-Wales: Deprivation or Development — A Study of Patterns of Employment in Selected Communities*. Cardiff: University of Wales Press, 1980.

Whittle, Elisabeth. *A Guide to Ancient and Historic Wales: Glamorgan and Gwent*. Cardiff: Her Majesty's Stationery Office, 1992.

——————. *Historic Gardens of Wales: An Introduction to Parks and Gardens in the History of Wales*. Cardiff: Her Majesty's Stationery Office, 1992.

Wilding, P. *Poverty: The Facts in Wales*. London: Child Poverty Action Group, 1977.

Wiliam, Eurwyn. *Farm Buildings of North-East Wales, 1550–1900*. Cardiff: National Museum of Wales, 1982.

————. *The Historical Farm Buildings of Wales*. Edinburgh: John Donald, 1986.

Wilks, Ivor. *South Wales and the Rising of 1839: Class Struggle as Armed Struggle*. London: Croom Helm, 1984.

Williams, A. H., ed. *John Wesley in Wales, 1739–1790: Entries from His Journal and Diary Relating to Wales*. Cardiff: University of Wales Press, 1971.

Williams, Chris. *Democratic Rhondda: Politics and Society, 1885-1951*. Cardiff: University of Wales Press, 1996.

Williams, David. *A History of Modern Wales*. London: John Murray, 1977.

Williams, David H. *The Welsh Cistercians*. 2 vols. Caldey Island, Wales: Cyhoeddiadiadau Sistersiaidd, 1984.

Williams, E. A. *The Day before Yesterday: Anglesey in the Nineteenth Century*. Beaumaris, Wales: G. Wynne-Griffiths, 1988.

Williams, Glanmor, ed. *Early Modern Glamorgan from the Act of Union to the Industrial Revolution*. Vol. 4 of Glamorgan County History. Cardiff: Glamorgan County History Trust, 1974.

————. *Owain Glyndwr: Prince of Wales*. Cardiff: University of Wales Press, 1993.

————. *Recovery, Reorientation and Reformation: Wales c. 1415–1642*. Oxford: Clarendon Press, 1987.

————. *The Reformation in Wales*. Bangor, Wales: Headstart History, 1991.

————. *Religion, Language and Nationality in Wales: Historical Essays*. Cardiff: University of Wales Press, 1979.

————. *Renewal and Reformation: Wales c. 1415–1642*. Oxford: Oxford University Press, 1993.

————, ed. *Swansea: An Illustrated History*. Swansea, Wales: Christopher Davies, 1990.

————. *Wales and the Act of Union*. Bangor, Wales: Headstart History, 1992.

————. *The Welsh and Their Religion: Historical Essays*. Cardiff: University of Wales Press, 1991.

————. *The Welsh Church from Conquest to Reformation*. Cardiff: University of Wales Press, 1976.

Williams, Glyn, ed. *Crisis of Economy and Ideology: Essays on Welsh Society, 1840–1980*. Bangor, Wales: British Sociological Association, 1983.

————. *The Desert and the Dream: A Study of Welsh Colonization in Chubut, 1865–1915*. Cardiff: University of Wales Press, 1975.

————, ed. *Social and Cultural Change in Contemporary Wales*. London: Routledge and Kegan Paul, 1978.

————. *The Welsh in Patagonia: The State and the Ethnic Community*. Cardiff: University of Wales Press, 1991.

Williams, Gwyn. *An Introduction to Welsh Literature*. Cardiff: University of Wales Press, 1992.

————. *The Land Remembers: A View of Wales*. London: Faber and Faber, 1977.

Williams, Gwyn A. *Madoc: The Making of a Myth*. Oxford: Oxford University Press, 1987.

————. *The Merthyr Rising*. Cardiff: University of Wales Press, 1988.

————. *The Search for Beulah Land: The Welsh and the Atlantic Revolution*. London: Croom Helm, 1980.

————. *The Welsh in Their History*. London: Croom Helm, 1982.

————. *When Was Wales? A History of the Welsh*. London: Black Raven Press, 1985.

Williams, Gwyn A. *The Merthyr Rising*. Cardiff: University of Wales Press, 1995.

Williams, J. Gwyn. *The University Movement in Wales*. Cardiff: University of Wales Press, 1993.

Williams, Herbert. *Battles in Wales*. Cardiff: John Jones, 1975.

Williams, Jac L., and Gwilym Rees Hughes, eds. *The History of Education in Wales*. Swansea, Wales: Christopher Davies, 1978.

Williams, John. *Digest of Welsh Historical Statistics*. 2 vols. Cardiff: Welsh Office, 1985.

Williams, Moelwyn. *The Making of the South Wales Landscape*. London: Hodder and Stoughton, 1975.

Williams, Rhodri, ed. *Prison Letters of John Jenkins*. Talybont, Wales: Y Lolfa, 1981.

Williams, Roger, and David Jones. *The Bitter Harvest: The Tragic History of Coalmining in Gwent*. Cwmbran, Wales: Village Publishing, 1988.

————. *The Cruel Inheritance: Life and Death in the Coalfields of Glamorgan*. Pontypool, Wales: Village Publishing, 1990.

Williams-Jones, Keith, ed. *The Merioneth Lay Subsidy Roll, 1292–3*. Cardiff: University of Wales Press, 1976.

Winterbottom, Derek. *The Vale of Clwyd: A Short History*. Denbigh, Wales: Gee and Son, 1982.

Northern Ireland

Adams, Gerry. *Before the Dawn*. London: Heinemann, 1996.

——————. *Cage Eleven*. Dingle, Irish Republic: Brandon, 1990.

——————. *Falls Memories*. Dingle, Irish Republic: Brandon, 1983.

——————. *A Pathway to Peace*. Cork, Irish Republic: Mercier Press, 1988.

Adams, James, Robin Morgan and Anthony Bambridge. *Ambush: The War between the SAS and the IRA*. London: Pan, 1988.

Adelman, Paul. *Great Britain and the Irish Question, 1800–1922*. London: Edward Arnold, 1996.

Akenson, Donald Harman. *Education and Enmity: The Control of Schooling in Northern Ireland, 1920–1950*. Newton Abbot, England: David and Charles, 1973.

Andrews, J. H. *Plantation Acres: An Historical Study of the Irish Land Surveyor and His Maps*. Belfast: Ulster Historical Foundation, 1985.

Aretxaga, Begona. *Shattering Silence: Women, Nationalism and Political Subjectivity in Northern Ireland*. Princeton, N. J.: Princeton University Press, 1997.

Armstrong, David, and Hilary Saunders. *A Road Too Wide: The Price of Reconciliation in Northern Ireland*. Basingstoke, England: Marshalls, 1985.

Arthur, Max. *Northern Ireland: Soldiers Talking*. London: Sidgwick and Jackson, 1987.

Arthur, Paul. *Government and Politics of Northern Ireland*. London: Longman, 1984.

——————. *The People's Democracy, 1968–1973*. Belfast: Blackstaff Press, 1974.

Arthur, Paul, and Keith Jeffrey. *Northern Ireland since 1968*. Oxford: Blackwell, 1996.

Aughey, Arthur. *Under Siege: Ulster Unionism and the Anglo-Irish Agreement*. Belfast: Blackstaff Press, 1989.

Aughey, Arthur, and Duncan Morrow, eds. *Northern Ireland Politics*. Harlow, England: Longman, 1995.

Baker, J. *The McMahon Family Murders and the Belfast Troubles, 1920–22*. Belfast: Glenravel Local History Project, 1993.

Bardon, Jonathan. *Belfast: An Illustrated History*. Belfast: Blackstaff Press, 1982.

——————. *A History of Ulster*. Belfast: Blackstaff, 1992.

Barritt, Denis P. *Northern Ireland — A Problem to Every Solution*. London: Quaker Peace and Service, 1982.

Barritt, Denis P., and Charles F. Carter. *The Northern Ireland Problem:*

A Study in Group Relations. London: Oxford University Press, 1972.

Barry, T. B. *The Archaeology of Medieval Ireland*. London: Methuen, 1987.

Bartlett, Thomas, and D. W. Hayton, eds. *Penal Era and Golden Age: Essays in Irish History, 1690–1800*. Belfast: Ulster Historical Foundation, 1979.

Barton, Brian. *Blitz: Northern Ireland and the Second World War*. Chester Springs, Pa.: Dufour Editions, 1989.

—————. *Brookeborough: The Making of a Prime Minister*. Belfast: Queen's University of Belfast, 1988.

Barton, Brian, and Patrick J. Roche, eds. *The Northern Ireland Question: Perspectives and Policies*. Aldershot, England: Avebury, 1994.

Barzilay, David. *The British Army in Ulster*. 4 vols. Belfast: Century, 1973 (Vol. 1), 1975 (Vol. 2), 1978 (Vol. 3) and 1981 (Vol. 4).

Belfrage, Sally. *The Crack: A Belfast Year*. London: Deutsch, 1987.

Bell, Desmond. *Acts of Union: Youth Culture and Sectarianism in Northern Ireland*. Basingstoke, England: Macmillan, 1990.

Bell, Geoffrey. *The Protestants of Ulster*. London: Pluto Press, 1976.

Bell, John Bowyer. *The Secret Army: The IRA, 1916–1979*. Dublin: Academy Press, 1979.

Bell, Robert. *The Book of Ulster Surnames*. Belfast: Blackstaff Press, 1988.

—————, ed. *Troubled Times: Fortnight Magazine and the Troubles in Northern Ireland, 1970–91*. Belfast: Blackstaff Press, 1991.

Benn, George. *A History of the Town of Belfast*. Ballynahinch, Northern Ireland: Davidson, 1979.

Beresford, David. *Ten Men Dead: The Story of the 1981 Irish Hunger Strike*. London: Grafton, 1987.

Bew, Paul. *Conflict and Conciliation in Ireland, 1890–1910*. Oxford: Clarendon Press, 1987.

Bew, Paul, Peter Gibbon and Henry Patterson. *Northern Ireland, 1921–1994: Political Forces and Social Classes*. London: Serif, 1995.

Bew, Paul, and Gordon Gillespie. *Northern Ireland: a Chronology of the Troubles, 1968–1993*. Dublin: Gill and Macmillan, 1993.

—————. *The Northern Ireland Peace Process, 1995-1996: A Chronology*. Washington, D. C.: Serif, 1996.

Bew, Paul, and Henry Patterson. *The British State and the Ulster Crisis: From Wilson to Thatcher*. London: Verso, 1985.

Birrell, Derek, and Alan Murie. *Policy and Government in Northern Ireland: Lessons of Devolution*. Dublin: Gill and Macmillan, 1980.

Bishop, Patrick, and Eamonn Mallie. *The Provisional IRA*. London: Heinemann, 1987.

Black, Eileen, ed. *Kings in Conflict: Ireland in the 1690s*. Belfast: Ulster Museum, 1990.

Blaney, Roger. *Belfast: 100 Years of Public Health, 1888–1988*. Belfast: Belfast City Council, 1988.

Bleakley, David. *Faulkner: Conflict and Consent in Irish Politics*. London: Mowbrays, 1974.

Boal, Frederick W., and J. N. H. Douglas, eds. *Integration and Division: Geographical Perspectives on the Northern Ireland Problem*. London: Academic Press, 1982.

Boulton, David. *The UVF, 1966–1973: An Anatomy of Loyalist Rebellion*. Dublin: Torc Books, 1973.

Bourke, Cormac. *Patrick: The Archaeology of a Saint*. Belfast: Her Majesty's Stationery Office, 1993.

Bowen, D. *The Protestant Crusade in Ireland, 1800–1870*. Dublin: Gill and Macmillan, 1978.

Bowman, John. *De Valera and the Ulster Question, 1917–1973*. Oxford: Oxford University Press, 1982.

Boyce, D. G. *The Irish Question and British Politics, 1868–1986*. Basingstoke, England: Macmillan, 1988.

——————. *Nationalism in Northern Ireland*. London: Croom Helm, 1982.

Boyce, D. G., ed. *The Revolution in Ireland, 1879–1923*. London: Macmillan, 1988.

Boyd, Andrew. *Brian Faulkner and the Crisis of Ulster Unionism*. Tralee, Irish Republic: Anvil Books, 1972.

——————. *Holy War in Belfast*. Belfast: Pretani, 1987.

Boyle, Kevin, and Tom Hadden. *Northern Ireland: The Choice*. Harmondsworth, England: Penguin, 1994.

Boyle, Kevin, Tom Hadden and Paddy Hillyard. *Law and State: The Case of Northern Ireland*. London: Martin Robertson, 1975.

——————. *Ten Years on in Northern Ireland: The Legal Control of Political Violence*. London: Cobden Trust, 1980.

Bradford, Norah. *A Sword Bathed in Heaven: The Life, Faith and Cruel Death of the Rev. Robert Bradford, B.Th., M.P*. Basingstoke, England: Pickering, 1984.

Brady, Ciaran, Mary O'Dowd, and Brian Walker, eds. *Ulster: An Illustrated History*. London: Batsford, 1989.

Breen, Richard, ed. *Social Attitudes in Northern Ireland: The Fifth Report*. Belfast: Appletree Press, 1996.

Breen, Richard, Paula Devine and Gilliam Robinson, eds. *Social Attitudes in Northern Ireland: The Fourth Report, 1994–1995*. Belfast: Appletree Press, 1995.

Brett, Charles E. *Housing a Divided Community*. Dublin: Institute of Public Administration, 1986.

Brewer, John D., and Kathleen Magee. *Inside the RUC: Policing in a Divided Society*. Oxford: Clarendon Press, 1990.

British Broadcasting Corporation. *Ulster Castles and Defensive Buildings*. London: British Broadcasting Corporation, 1977.

Brooke, Peter. *Ulster Presbyterianism*. Dublin: Gill and Macmillan, 1987.

Bruce, Steve. *God Save Ulster! The Religion and Politics of Paisleyism*. Oxford: Clarendon Press, 1986.

—————. *The Edge of the Union*. Oxford: Oxford University Press, 1994.

—————. *The Red Hand: Protestant Paramilitaries in Northern Ireland*. Oxford: Oxford University Press, 1986.

Buchanan, R. H., and B. M. Walker, eds. *Province, City and People: Belfast and Its Region*. Antrim, Northern Ireland: Greystone, 1987.

Buckland, Patrick. *The Factory of Grievances: Devolved Government in Northern Ireland, 1921–1939*. Dublin: Gill and Macmillan, 1979.

—————. *A History of Northern Ireland*. Dublin: Gill and Macmillan, 1981.

—————. *Ulster Unionism and the Origins of Northern Ireland, 1886–1922. Vol 2 of Irish Unionism:* London: Macmillan, 1973.

—————. *James Craig, Lord Craigavon*. Dublin: Gill and Macmillan, 1980.

Budge, Ian, and Cornelius O'Leary. *Belfast: Approach to Crisis — A Study of Belfast Politics, 1613–1970*. London: Macmillan, 1973.

Burton, Frank. *The Politics of Legitimacy: Struggles in a Belfast Community*. London: Routledge, 1978.

Byrne, Francis John. *Irish Kings and High-Kings*. London: Batsford, 1973.

Byrne, Sean. *Growing Up in a Divided Society: The Influence of Conflict on Belfast School Children*. Cranbury, N. J.: Fairleigh Dickinson University Press, 1997.

Cairns, Ed. *Caught in Crossfire: Children and the Northern Ireland Conflict*. Belfast: Appletree, 1987.

Callaghan, James. *A House Divided: The Dilemma of Northern Ireland*. London: Collins, 1973.

Campbell, Flann. *The Dissenting Voice: Protestant Democracy in Ulster from Plantation to Partition*. Belfast: Blackstaff Press, 1991.

Canavan, Tony. *Frontier Town: An Illustrated History of Newry*. Belfast: Blackstaff Press, 1989.

Carr, A. *The Belfast Labour Movement, 1885–93*. Belfast: Athol Books, 1974.

Catterall, Peter, and Sean McDougall, eds. *The Northern Ireland Question in British Politics*. London: Macmillan, 1996.

Chambers, George. *Faces of Change: The Belfast and Northern Ireland Chambers of Commerce and Industry, 1783–1983*. Belfast: Northern Ireland Chamber of Commerce and Industry, 1984.

Chubb, Basil. *The Government and Politics of Northern Ireland*. London: Longman, 1992.

Clark, Wallace. *Linen on the Green: An Irish Mill Village, 1730–1982*. Belfast: Universities Press, 1983.

—————. *Rathlin: Its Island Story*. Limavady, Northern Ireland: North-West Books, 1988.

Clarke, Liam. *Broadening the Battlefield: The H-Blocks and the Rise of Sinn Fein*. Dublin: Gill and Macmillan, 1987.

Clarkson, L. A., and E. M. Crawford. *Ways to Wealth: The Cust Family of Eighteenth-Century Armagh*. Belfast: Ulster Society, 1985.

Clifford, Brendan. *Government without Opposition*. Belfast: Athol Books, 1986.

—————. *Parliamentary Sovereignty and Northern Ireland*. Belfast: Athol Books, 1985.

Compton, Paul A. *Northern Ireland: A Census Atlas*. Dublin: Gill and Macmillan, 1978.

—————, ed. *The Contemporary Population of Northern Ireland and Population-Related Issues*. Belfast: Institute of Irish Studies (Queen's University), 1981.

Conroy, John. *Belfast Diary: War as a Way of Life*. Boston, Mass.: Beacon Press, 1995.

Coogan, Timothy Pat. *On the Blanket: The Inside Story of the IRA Prisoners' 'Dirty' Protest*. Boulder, Co.: Rinehart, Roberts, 1997.

—————. *The IRA*. London: HarperCollins, 1993.

—————. *The Troubles: Ireland's Ordeal, 1966–1995, and the Search for Peace*. London: Hutchinson, 1995.

Corlett, John. *Aviation in Ulster*. Belfast: Blackstaff Press, 1981.

Cormack, Robert J., and Robert D. Osborne, eds. *Discrimination and Public Policy in Northern Ireland*. Oxford: Clarendon Press, 1991.

Cronin, Sean. *Washington's Irish Policy, 1916–1986*. Dublin: Amvil, 1987.

Cullen, L. M. *An Economic History of Ireland since 1660*. London: Batsford, 1972.

Curl, James Steven. *The Londonderry Plantation, 1609–1914: The History, Architecture and Planning of the Estates of the City of London and Its Livery Companies in Ulster*. Chichester, England: Phillimore, 1986.

Curran, Frank. *Derry — Countdown to Disaster.* Dublin: Gill and Macmillan, 1986.

Dane, Mervyn. *The Fermanagh B-Specials.* Enniskillen, Northern Ireland: W. Trimble, 1970.

Darby, John. *Conflict in Northern Ireland: The Development of a Polarised Community.* Dublin: Gill and Macmillan, 1976.

——————. *Intimidation and the Control of Conflict in Northern Ireland.* Dublin: Gill and Macmillan, 1986.

——————, ed. *Northern Ireland: The Background to the Conflict.* Belfast: Appletree Press, 1983.

Darby, John, and A. Williamson, eds. *Violence and the Social Services in Northern Ireland.* London: Heinemann, 1978.

Day, Angelique, and Patrick McWilliams. *The Ordnance Survey Memoirs of Ireland.* Vols. 1–22 and 27–32. Belfast: Queen's University, 1990 (Vols. 1–6), 1991 (Vols. 7–11), 1992 (Vols. 12–17), 1993 (Vols. 18–22), 1994 (Vol. 27) and 1995 (Vols. 28–32).

Day, Angelique, Patrick McWilliams and Noirin Dobson. *The Ordnance Survey Memoirs of Ireland.* Vols. 23–26. Belfast, Queen's University, 1993 (Vol. 23) and 1994 (Vols. 24–26).

Department of the Environment for Northern Ireland. *Historic Monuments of Northern Ireland.* Belfast: Her Majesty's Stationery Office, 1983.

Deutsch, Richard R. *Northern Ireland, 1921–1974: A Select Bibliography.* New York: Garland, 1975.

Deutsch, Richard R., and Vivien Magowan. *Northern Ireland, 1968–73: A Chronology of Events.* 3 vols. Belfast: Blackstaff Press, 1973 (Vol. 1), 1974 (Vol. 2) and 1975 (Vol. 3).

Devlin, Paddy. *Straight Left: An Autobiography.* Belfast: Blackstaff Press, 1994.

——————. *Yes, We Have No Bananas: Outdoor Relief in Belfast, 1920–39.* Belfast: Blackstaff Press, 1981.

Dewar, Michael. *The British Army in Northern Ireland.* London: Arms and Armour Press, 1985.

Dillon, Martin. *The Dirty War.* London: Hutchinson, 1990.

——————. *The Shankhill Butchers: A Case Study of Mass Murder.* London: Hutchinson, 1989.

Dillon, Martin, and Denis Lehane. *Political Murder in Northern Ireland.* London: Penguin, 1973.

Downey, James. *Them and Us: Britain, Ireland and the Northern Question, 1969–82.* Dublin: Ward River Press, 1983.

Dunlop, Eull (ed). *Mid-Antrim: Articles on the History of Ballymore and District.* 2 vols. Ballymena, Northern Ireland: Mid-Antrim Historical Group, 1981 (Vol. 1) and 1983 (Vol. 2).

Dunn, Seamus. *Facets of the Conflict in Northern Ireland.* New York: St Martins Press, 1995.

Edwards, Owen Dudley. *The Sins of Our Fathers: Roots of Conflict in Northern Ireland.* Dublin: Gill and Macmillan, 1970.

Elliott, Marianne. *Partners in Revolution: The United Irishmen and France.* New Haven, Conn.: Yale University Press, 1982.

Elliott, Sydney. *Northern Ireland Parliamentary Election Results, 1921–1972.* Chichester, England: Political Reference Publications, 1973.

Ellis, Peter Berresford. *The Boyne Water: The Battle of the Boyne, 1690.* London: Hamish Hamilton, 1976.

Evans, E. Estyn. *Mourne Country: Landscape and Life in South Down.* Dundalk, Irish Republic: Dundalgan Press, 1978.

Evason, Eileen. *On the Edge: A Study of Poverty and Long-Term Unemployment in Northern Ireland.* London: Child Poverty Action Group, 1985.

Evelegh, R. *Peace-Keeping in a Democratic Society: The Lessons of Northern Ireland.* London: Hurst and Company, 1978.

Fairweather, Eileen, Roisin McDonough and Melanie McFadyean. *Only the Rivers Run Free: Northern Ireland — The Women's War.* London: Pluto, 1984.

Faligot, Roger. *Britain's Military Strategy in Ireland: The Kitson Experiment.* Dingle, Irish Republic: Brandon, 1983.

Farrell, Michael. *Arming the Protestants: The Formation of the Ulster Special Constabulary and the Royal Ulster Constabulary, 1920–27.* London: Pluto Press, 1983.

—————. *Northern Ireland: The Orange State.* London: Pluto Press, 1976.

—————. *The Poor Law and the Workhouse in Belfast, 1838–1948.* Belfast: Public Record Office of Northern Ireland, 1978.

Faul, Denis, and Raymond Murray. *British Army and Special Branch RUC Brutalities.* Cavan, Irish Republic: A. Bey, 1972.

Faulkner, Brian. *Memoirs of a Statesman.* London: Weidenfeld and Nicolson, 1978.

Fields, Rona M. *Northern Ireland: Society under Siege.* New Brunswick, N. J.: Transaction, 1980.

—————. *A Society on the Run: A Psychology of Northern Ireland.* Harmondsworth, England: Penguin, 1973.

Fisk, Robert. *The Point of No Return: The Strike Which Broke the British in Ulster.* London: Deutsch, 1975.

—————. *In Time of War: Ireland, Ulster and the Price of Neutrality, 1939–45.* London: Deutsch, 1983.

Fitzgibbon, Constantine. *Red Hand: The Ulster Colony.* New York:

Warner, 1973.

Fitzpatrick, Rory. *God's Frontiersmen: The Scots-Irish Epic.* London: Weidenfeld and Nicolson, 1989.

Flackes, W. D., and Sydney Elliott. *Northern Ireland: A Political Directory, 1968–1993.* Belfast: Blackstaff Press, 1994.

Foot, Paul. *Who Framed Colin Wallace?* London: Macmillan, 1989.

Foster, Roy F. *Modern Ireland, 1600–1972.* London: Allen Lane, 1988.

Gaffikin, Frank, and Mike Morrissey. *Northern Ireland: The Thatcher Years.* London: Zed, 1990.

Gailey, Alan. *Rural Houses of the North of Ireland.* Edinburgh: John Donald, 1984.

Gallagher, Eric, and Stanley Worrall. *Christians in Ulster, 1968–80.* Oxford: Oxford University Press, 1982.

Gibbon, P. *The Origins of Ulster Unionism: The Formation of Popular Protestant Politics and Ideology in Nineteenth-Century Ireland.* Manchester: Manchester University Press, 1975.

Gillespie, Raymond. *Colonial Ulster: The Settlement of East Ulster, 1600–1641.* Cork, Irish Republic: Press for the Irish Committee of Historical Sciences, 1985.

Gillespie, Raymond, and Harold O'Sullivan, eds. *The Borderlands: Essays on the History of the Ulster-Leinster Border.* Belfast: Queen's University of Belfast, 1989.

Glassie, Henry. *Passing the Time: Folklore and History of an Ulster Community.* Dublin: O'Brien Press, 1982.

Glendinning, M., and S. Muthesius. *Tower Block: Modern Public Housing in England, Scotland, Wales and Northern Ireland.* New Haven, Conn.: Yale University Press, 1994.

Goldring, Maurice. *Belfast: From Loyalty to Rebellion.* London: Lawrence and Wishart, 1991.

Gordon, David. *The O'Neill Years: Unionist Politics, 1963–1969.* Belfast: Athol Books, 1989.

Grant, Alexander, and Keith J. Stringer, eds. *Uniting The Kingdom: the Making of British History.* London: Routledge, 1995.

Gray, John. *City in Revolt: James Larkin and the Belfast Dock Strike of 1907.* Belfast: Blackstaff Press, 1985.

Gray, Tony. *The Orange Order.* London: Bodley Head, 1972.

Greaves, Desmond. *The Irish Crisis.* London: Lawrence and Wishart, 1972.

Green, Arthur J. *Devolution and Public Finance: Stormont from 1921 to 1972.* Glasgow: University of Strathclyde, 1979.

Greer, Alan. *Rural Politics in Northern Ireland: Policy Networks and Agricultural Development Since Partition.* Aldershot, England:

Avebury Press, 1996.

Gribbon, Sybil. *Edwardian Belfast: A Social Profile.* Belfast: Appletree, 1982.

Guelke, Adrian. *Northern Ireland: The International Perspective.* Dublin: Gill and Macmillan, 1988.

Hadden, Tom, and Kevin Boyle. *The Anglo-Irish Agreement.* London: Sweet and Maxwell, 1989.

Hadfield, Brigid, ed. *Northern Ireland: Politics and the Constitution.* Buckingham: Open University Press, 1992.

Hamill, Desmond. *Pig in the Middle: The Army in Northern Ireland, 1969–1984.* London: Methuen, 1985.

Hammond, David, ed. *Songs of Belfast.* Dublin: Gilbert and Dalton, 1978.
—————. *Steelchest, Nail in the Boot and the Barking Dog: The Belfast Shipyard.* Belfast: Flying Fox Films, 1986.

Hamond, Fred. *Antrim Coast and Glens: Industrial Heritage.* Belfast: Her Majesty's Stationery Office, 1991.

Harbinson, John F. *The Ulster Unionist Party, 1882–1973: Its Development and Organization.* Belfast: Blackstaff Press, 1973.

Harbison, Jeremy, and Joan Harbison, eds. *A Society under Stress: Children and Young People in Northern Ireland.* Shepton Mallett, England: Open Books, 1980.

Harkness, David. *Ireland in the Twentieth Century: Divided Island.* Basingstoke, England: Macmillan, 1996.
—————. *Northern Ireland since 1920.* Dublin: Helicon Press, 1983.

Harris, Richard, Clifford Jefferson and John Spencer. *The Northern Ireland Economy: A Comparative Study in the Economic Development of a Peripheral Region.* London: Longman, 1990.

Harris, Rosemary. *Prejudice and Tolerance in Ulster: A Study of Neighbours and 'Strangers' in a Border Community.* Manchester: Manchester University Press, 1972.

Healy, T. M. *The Great Fraud of Ulster.* Dublin: Anvil, 1971.

Hechter, Michael. *Internal Colonialism: The Celtic Fringe in British National Development, 1536–1966.* London: Routledge and Kegan Paul, 1975.

Henry, Francoise. *The Book of Kells.* London: Thames and Hudson, 1974.

Hepburn, A. C. *The Conflict of Nationality in Modern Ireland.* London: Edward Arnold, 1980.

Heskin, Ken. *Northern Ireland: A Psychological Analysis.* Dublin: Gill and Macmillan, 1980.

Hezlet, Arthur. *The 'B' Specials: A History of the Ulster Special Constabulary.* London: Tom Stacey, 1972.

Hickey, John. *Religion and the Northern Ireland Problem.* Dublin: Gill and Macmillan, 1984.

Hidden, A. E., and C. J. Latimer. *Science and Technology: Belfast and Its Region*. Belfast: Queen's University of Belfast, 1987.

Holliday, Laura, ed. *Children of 'The Troubles': Our Lives in the Crossfire of Northern Ireland*. New York: Pocket Books, 1997.

Holmes, Finlay. *Henry Cooke*. Belfast: Christian Journals, 1981.

Holroyd, Fred, and Nick Burbridge. *War without Honour*. Hull, England: Medium, 1989.

Home, Leo. *Being Unemployed in Northern Ireland: An Ethnographic Study*. Cambridge: Cambridge University Press, 1990.

Hoppen, K. Theodore. *Ireland since 1800: Conflict and Conformity*. Harlow:Longman, 1989.

Hull, Roger H. *The Irish Triangle: Conflict in Northern Ireland*. Princeton, N. J.: Princeton University Press, 1976.

Jackson, Alvin. *The Ulster Party: Irish Unionists in the House of Commons, 1884–1911*. Oxford: Clarendon Press, 1989.

Jackson, John, and Sean Doran. *Judge Without Jury: Diplock Trials in the Adversary System*. Oxford: Clarendon Press, 1996.

Jalland, Patricia. *The Liberals and Ireland: The Ulster Question in British Politics to 1914*. Brighton, England: Harvester Press, 1980.

Jeffery, Keith, ed. *The Divided Province: The Troubles in Northern Ireland, 1969–1985*. London: Orbis, 1985.

Jennings, Tony, ed. *Justice Under Fire: The Abuse of Civil Liberties in Northern Ireland*. London: Zwan, 1988.

Jones, Thomas. *Ireland 1918–1925. Vol. 3 of Whitehall Diary* edited by Keith Middlemass. London: Oxford University Press, 1971.

Kearney, Hugh. *The British Isles: A History of Four Nations*. Cambridge: Cambridge University Press, 1989.

Kee, Robert. *The Green Flag: The Turbulent History of the Irish National Movement*. New York: Delacorte Press, 1972.

Kelley, Kevin J. *The Longest War: Northern Ireland and the IRA*. London: Zed Press, 1988.

Kelly, Henry. *How Stormont Fell*. Dublin: Gill and Macmillan, 1972.

Kennedy, Dennis. *The Widening Gulf: Northern Attitudes to the Independent Irish State, 1919–49*. Belfast: Blackstaff Press, 1988.

Kennedy, Liam. *Two Ulsters: A Case for Repartition*. Belfast: Queen's University, 1986.

Kennedy, Liam, and Philip Ollerenshaw, eds. *An Economic History of Ulster, 1820–1940*. Manchester: Manchester University Press, 1985.

Kennedy-Pipe, Caroline. *The Origins of the Troubles in Northern Ireland since 1968*. Harlow, England: Longman, 1996.

Kenney, James F. *The Sources for the Early History of Ireland: Ecclesi-*

astical — An Introduction and Guide. Dublin: Irish University Press, 1979.

Kenny, Anthony. *The Road to Hillsborough: The Shaping of the Anglo-Irish Agreement.* Oxford: Pergamon Press, 1986.

Keogh, Dermot, and Michael H. Haltzon, eds. *Northern Ireland and the Politics of Reconciliation.* Cambridge: Cambridge University Press, 1994.

Killen, John. *John Bull's Famous Circus: Ulster History through the Postcard, 1905–1985.* Dublin: O'Brien Press, 1985.

Kingsmore, Rona K. *Ulster-Scots Speech: A Sociolinguistic Study.* Tuscaloosa, Ala.: University of Alabama Press, 1995.

Knight, James, and Nicholas Baxter-Moore. *Northern Ireland: The Elections of the Twenties.* London: Arthur McDougall Fund, 1972.

Lacy, Brian. *Siege City: The Story of Derry and Londonderry.* Belfast: Blackstaff Press, 1990.

Laffan, Michael. *The Partition of Ireland, 1911–1925.* Dublin: Dublin Historical Association, 1983.

Laing, Lloyd. *The Archaeology of Late Celtic Britain and Ireland, c. 400–1200 AD.* London: Methuen, 1975.

Lambkin, B. K. *Opposite Religions Still?: Interpreting Northern Ireland After the Conflict.* Aldershot, England: Avebury Press, 1996.

Longford, Frank Pakenham, Earl of, and Anne McHardy. *Ulster.* London: Weidenfeld and Nicolson, 1981.

Loughlin, James. *Gladstone, Home Rule and the Ulster Question.* Dublin: Gill and Macmillan, 1986.

—————. *The Ulster Question since 1945.* Basingstoke, England: Macmillan, 1994.

Lubenow, W. C. *Parliamentary Politics and the Home Rule Crisis: The British House of Commons in 1886.* Oxford: Clarendon Press, 1988.

McAllister, I. *The Northern Ireland Social Democratic and Labour Party: Political Opposition in a Divided Society.* London: Macmillan, 1977.

Macaulay, Ambrose. *Patrick Dorrian, Bishop of Down and Connor, 1865–85.* Dublin: Irish Academic Press, 1987.

McCann, Eamonn. *Bloody Sunday in Derry: What Really Happened.* Dingle, Irish Republic: Brandon, 1992.

—————. *War and an Irish Ghetto.* London: Pluto, 1980.

McCaughan, Michael, and John Appleby, eds. *The Irish Sea: Aspects of Maritime History.* Belfast: Queen's University of Belfast, 1989.

McClean, Raymon. *The Road to Bloody Sunday.* Dublin: Ward River Press, 1983.

McCloskey, John. *Statistical Report of Ballinascreen, Kilcronaghan, Desertmartin, Banagher, Dungiven and Boveva in the County of Lon-*

donderry, edited by D. O'Kane. Ballinascreen, Northern Ireland: Ballinascreen Historical Society, 1983.

MacCurtain, Margaret. *Tudor and Stuart Ireland.* Dublin: Gill and Macmillan, 1972.

McCutcheon, W. A. *The Industrial Archaeology of Northern Ireland.* Belfast: Her Majesty's Stationery Office, 1980.

McDonnell, Pat. *They Wrought among the Tow: Flax and Linen in County Tyrone, 1750–1900.* Belfast: Ulster Historical Foundation, 1990.

McGarry, John, and Brendon O'Leary. *Explaining Northern Ireland: Broken Images.* Malden, Mass.: Blackwell Press, 1995.

—————, (eds). *The Future of Northern Ireland.* Oxford: Clarendon Press, 1990.

McGuffin, John. *The Guinea Pigs.* Harmondsworth, England: Penguin, 1974.

—————. *Internment.* Tralee, Irish Republic: Anvil, 1973.

McKittrick, David. *Despatches from Belfast.* Belfast: Blackstaff Press, 1989.

McMinn, J. R. B. *Against the Tide: A Calendar of the Papers of Rev. J. B. Armour, Irish Presbyterian Minister and Home Ruler.* Belfast: Proni, 1985.

McNeill, T. E. *Anglo-Norman Ulster: The History and Archaeology of an Irish Barony, 1177–1400.* Edinburgh: John Donald, 1980.

—————. *Carrickfergus Castle, County Antrim.* Belfast: Her Majesty's Stationery Office, 1981.

MacNiocaill, Gearoid. *Ireland before the Vikings.* Dublin: Gill and Macmillan, 1972.

Macrory, Patrick. *The Siege of Derry.* London: Hodder and Stoughton, 1980.

Magee, J. *Northern Ireland: Crisis and Conflict.* London: Routledge and Kegan Paul, 1974.

Maguire, Maria. *To Take Arms: A Year in the Provisional IRA.* London: Macmillan, 1973.

Maguire, W. A. *Belfast.* Keele, England: Ryburn Publishing, 1993.

—————. *The Downshire Estates in Ireland, 1801–1845: The Management of Irish Landed Estates in the Early Nineteenth Century.* Oxford: Clarendon Press, 1972.

Mallory, J. P. *Navan Fort: The Ancient Capital of Ulster.* Belfast: Ulster Archaeological Society, 1985.

Mallory, J. P., and T. E. McNeil. *The Archaeology of Ulster: From Colonisation to Plantation.* Belfast: Queen's University of Belfast, 1991.

Maltby, Arthur. *The Government of Northern Ireland, 1922–72: A Catalogue and Breviate of Parliamentary Papers.* Dublin: Irish University Press, 1974.

Mansergh, P. N. S. *The Irish Question, 1840–1921*. London: Allen and Unwin, 1975.

Marrinan, Patrick. *Paisley: Man of Wrath*. Tralee, Irish Republic: Anvil, 1973.

Miller, David W. *Queen's Rebels: Ulster Loyalism in Historical Perspective*. Dublin: Gill and Macmillan, 1978.

——————, ed. *Peep O'Day Boys and Defenders: Selected Documents on the Disturbances in County Armagh, 1784–1796*. Belfast: Public Record Office of Northern Ireland, 1990.

Mitchell, Brian. *On the Banks of the Foyle: Historic Photographs of Victorian and Edwardian Derry*. Belfast: Friar's Bush, 1989.

Moffatt, Chris, ed. *Education Together for a Change: Integrated Education and Community Relations in Northern Ireland*. Belfast: Fortnight Educational Trust, 1993.

Moloney, Ed, and Andy Pollak. *Paisley*. Swords, Irish Republic: Poolbeg, 1986.

Moody, T. W. *Davitt and the Irish Revolution, 1846–82*. Oxford: Clarendon Press, 1981.

——————. *The Ulster Question, 1603–1973*. Dublin: Mercier Press, 1978.

Morrison, John. *The Ulster Cover-Up*. Lurgan, Northern Ireland: Ulster Society, 1993.

Morton, G. *Elizabethan Ireland*. London: Longman, 1971.

Moss, Michael S., and John R. Hume. *Shipbuilders to the World: 125 Years of Harland and Wolff, Belfast, 1861–1986*. Belfast: Blackstaff, 1986.

Moxon-Browne, Edward. *Nation, Class and Creed in Northern Ireland*. Aldershot, England: Gower, 1983.

Mullin, T. H. *Ulster's Historic City: Derry, Londonderry*. Coleraine, Northern Ireland: Coleraine Bookshop, 1986.

Munck, Ronnie, and Bill Rolston. *Belfast in the Thirties: An Oral History*. Belfast: Blackstaff Press, 1987.

Murphy, Desmond. *Derry, Donegal and Modern Ulster, 1790–1921*. Londonderry, Northern Ireland: Aileach Press, 1981.

Murray, Dominic. *Worlds Apart: Segregated Schools in Northern Ireland*. Belfast: Appletree Press, 1985.

Murray, Raymond. *The SAS in Ireland*. Cork, Irish Republic: Mercier Press, 1990.

Nelson, Sarah. *Ulster's Uncertain Defenders: Protestant Political, Paramilitary and Community Groups and the Northern Ireland Conflict*. Belfast: Appletree Press, 1984.

O'Brien, Brendan. *The Long War: The IRA and Sinn Fein, 1985 to Today.* Dublin: O'Brien Press, 1993.

O'Brien, Conor Cruise. *States of Ireland.* London: Hutchinson, 1972.

O'Clery, Conor. *Daring Diplomacy: Clinton's Secret Search for Peace in Northern Ireland.* Boulder, Co.: Rinehart, Roberts, 1997.

O'Corrain, Donncha. *Ireland before the Normans.* Dublin: Gill and Macmillan, 1972.

O'Day, Alan. *Political Violence in Northern Ireland: Conflict and Conflict Resolution.* New York: Praeger, 1997.

──────, ed. *Dimensions of Irish Terrorism.* New York: G. K. Hall, 1994.

O'Day, Alan, and Yonah Alexander, eds. *Ireland's Terrorist Trauma: Interdisciplinary Perspectives.* New York: Harvester Wheatsheaf, 1989.

O'Doherty, Shane. *The Volunteer: A Former IRA Man's True Story.* London: Fount, 1993.

O'Dowd, Liam, Bill Rolston and Mike Tomlinson. *Northern Ireland: Between Civil Rights and Civil War.* London: CSE Books, 1980.

O'Halley, Padraig. *The Uncivil Wars: Ireland Today.* Belfast: Blackstaff Press, 1983.

O'Halloran, Clare. *Partition and the Limits of Irish Nationalism.* Dublin: Gill and Macmillan, 1987.

O'Leary, Cornelius, Sydney Elliot and R. A. Wilford. *The Northern Ireland Assembly, 1982–1986: A Constitutional Experiment.* London: Hurst, 1988.

Oliver, John Andrew. *Working at Stormont: Memoirs.* Dublin: Institute of Public Administration, 1978.

O'Malley, Padraig. *Biting at the Grave: The Irish Hunger Strikes and the Politics of Despair.* Boston, Mass.: Beacon Press, 1991.

──────. *Northern Ireland: Questions of Nuance.* Belfast: Blackstaff Press, 1990.

──────. *The Uncivil Wars: Ireland Today.* Belfast: Blackstaff Press, 1983.

O'Neill, Terence. *The Autobiography of Terence O'Neill: Prime Minister of Northern Ireland, 1963–69.* London: Hart-Davis, 1972.

Orr, Philip. *The Road to the Somme: Men of the Ulster Division Tell Their Story.* Belfast: Blackstaff Press, 1987.

O'Snodaigh, Padraig. *Hidden Ulster: The Other Hidden Ireland.* Dublin: Clodhanna Teo, 1973.

Osborne, R. D., and R. J. Cormack, eds. *Religion, Education and Employment.* Belfast: Appletree Press, 1983.

Osborne, R. D., R. J. Cormack and R. L. Miller, eds. *Education Policy in Northern Ireland.* Belfast: Policy Research Institute (Queen's University and University of Ulster), 1987.

Paor, Liam de. *Divided Ulster.* London: Penguin, 1970.

Patterson, Henry. *Class Conflict and Sectarianism: The Protestant Working Class and the Belfast Labour Movement, 1868–1920.* Belfast: Blackstaff Press, 1980.

Pearce, Susan M., ed. *The Early Church in Western Britain and Ireland: Studies Presented to C. A. Ralegh Radford.* Oxford: British Archaeological Reports, 1982.

Perceval-Maxwell, M. *The Scottish Migration to Ulster in the Reign of James I.* London: Routledge and Kegan Paul, 1990.

Pollak, Andy, ed. *A Citizens' Inquiry: The Opsahl Report on Northern Ireland.* Dublin: Lilliput Press, 1993.

Pollock, Lawrence, and Ian McAllister. *A Bibliography of United Kingdom Politics: Scotland, Wales and Northern Ireland.* Glasgow: Centre for the Study of Public Policy (University of Strathclyde), 1980.

Probert, Belinda. *Beyond Orange and Green: The Political Economy of the Northern Ireland Crisis.* London: Zed Press, 1978.

Prior, Lindsay. *The Social Organization of Death: Medical Discourse and Social Practices in Belfast.* New York: St Martins Press, 1989.

Purdie, Bob. *Politics in the Streets: The Origins of the Civil Rights Movement in Northern Ireland.* Belfast: Blackstaff Press, 1990.

Rees, Merlyn. *Northern Ireland: A Personal Perspective.* London: Methuen, 1985.

Robbins, Keith. *Nineteenth Century Britain: Integration and Diversity.* Oxford: Clarendon Press, 1988.

Robinson, Gillian. *Cross-Community Marriage in Northern Ireland.* Belfast: Queen's University of Belfast, 1992.

Robinson, Philip S. *The Plantation of Ulster: British Settlement in an Irish Landscape, 1600–1670.* Dublin: Gill and Macmillan, 1984.

Roche, Patrick J., and Brian Barton, eds. *The Northern Ireland Question: Myth and Reality.* Aldershot, England: Avebury, 1991.

Roebuck, Peter, ed. *Plantation to Partition: Essays in Ulster History in Honour of J. L. McCracken.* Belfast: Blackstaff Press, 1981.

Rolston, Bill, and Mike Tomlinson. *Unemployment in West Belfast: The Obair Report.* Belfast: Beyond the Pale, 1988.

Rose, Richard. *Governing without Consensus: An Irish Perspective.* Boston Beacon Press, 1971.

—————. *Northern Ireland: A Time of Choice.* London: Macmillan, 1976.

Rowthorn, Bob, and Naomi Wayne. *Northern Ireland: The Political Economy of Conflict.* Cambridge: Polity Press, 1988.

Ruane, Joseph, and Jennifer Todd. *The Dynamics of Conflict in Northern Ireland: Power, Conflict and Emancipation.* Cambridge: Cambridge University Press, 1996.

Ryder, Chris. *The RUC: A Force Under Fire.* London: Methuen, 1989.

——————. *The Ulster Defence Regiment: An Instrument of Peace.* London: Methuen, 1991.

Shannon, Elizabeth. *I Am of Ireland: Women of the North Speak Out.* Amherst, Mass.: University of Massachusetts Press, 1997.

Sharrock, David, and Mark Devenport. *Man of War, Man of Peace?: The Unauthorised Biography of Gerry Adams.* Basingstoke, England: Macmillan, 1997.

Shea, Patrick. *Voices and the Sound of Drums: an Irish Autobiography.* Belfast: Blackstaff Press, 1988.

Sluka, Jeffrey A. *Hearts and Minds, Water and Fish: Support for the IRA and INLA in a Northern Ireland Ghetto.* Greenwich, Conn.: JAI Press, 1989.

Smith, David J., and Gerald Chambers. *Inequality in Northern Ireland.* Oxford: Clarendon Press, 1991.

Smyth, Clifford. *Ian Paisley: Voice of Protestant Ulster.* Edinburgh: Scottish Academic Press, 1987.

Spencer, John, Richard Harris and Clifford Jefferson, eds. *The Northern Ireland Economy.* London: Longman, 1990.

Stetler, Russell. *The Battle of Bogside: The Politics of Violence in Northern Ireland.* London: Sheed and Ward, 1970.

Stevenson, David. *Scottish Covenanters and Irish Confederates: Scottish-Irish Relations in the Mid-Seventeenth Century.* Belfast: Ulster Historical Foundation, 1981.

Stevenson, Johnathan. *'We Wrecked the Place': Contemplating an End to the Northern Ireland Troubles.* New York: Free Press, 1996.

Stewart, A. T. Q. *The Narrow Ground: Aspects of Ulster, 1609–1969.* London: Faber and Faber, 1977.

Stringer, Peter, and Gillian Robinson, eds. *Social Attitudes in Northern Ireland, 1990–91.* Belfast: Blackstaff Press, 1991.

——————. *Social Attitudes in Northern Ireland: The Second Report, 1991–1992.* Belfast: Blackstaff Press, 1992.

——————. *Social Attitudes in Northern Ireland: The Third Report, 1992–1993.* Belfast: Blackstaff Press, 1993.

Sugden, John and Alan Bairner. *Sport, Sectarianism and Society in a Divided Ireland.* Leicester: Leicester University Press, 1993.

Sweetman, Rosita. *On Our Knees: Ireland 1972.* London: Pan, 1972.

Teague, Paul, ed. *Beyond the Rhetoric: Politics, the Economy and Social Policy in Northern Ireland.* London: Lawrence and Wishart,

1987.

Toibin, Colm. *Walking along the Border*. London: Queen Anne Press, 1988.

Toolis, Kevin. *Rebel Hearts: Journeys Within the IRA's Soul*. New York: St Martins Press, 1996.

Townshend, Charles. *The British Campaign in Ireland, 1919–1921*. Oxford: Oxford University Press, 1975.

Utley, T. E. *The Lessons of Ulster*. London: Dent, 1975.

Van Voris, W. H. *Violence in Ulster: An Oral Documentary*. Amherst, Mass.: University of Massachusetts Press, 1975.

Walker, Brian M. *Sentry Hill: An Ulster Farm and Family*. Belfast: Blackstaff Press, 1981.

—————. *Ulster Politics: The Formative Years, 1868–1886*. Belfast: Ulster Historical Foundation, 1989.

Walker, Graham S. *The Politics of Frustration: Harry Midgley and the Failure of Labour in Northern Ireland*. Manchester: Manchester University Press, 1985.

Wallace, Martin. *Northern Ireland: 50 Years of Self-Government*. Newton Abbot, England: David and Charles, 1971.

Walsh, Pat. *From Civil Rights to National War: Northern Ireland Catholic Politics, 1964–1974*. Belfast: Athol Books, 1989.

Ward, Alan J., ed. *Northern Ireland: Living with the Crisis*. London: Aldwych Press, 1988.

Watt, David, ed. *The Constitution of Northern Ireland*. London: Heinemann, 1981.

Weritzner, John. *Policing Under Fire: Ethnic Conflict and Police-Community Relations in Northern Ireland*. New York: State University of New York Press, 1995.

White, Barry. *John Hume: Statesman of the Troubles*. Belfast: Blackstaff Press, 1984.

Whyte, John H. *Interpreting Northern Ireland*. Oxford: Clarendon Press, 1990.

Wichert, Sabine. *Northern Ireland since 1945*. Harlow, England: Longman, 1994.

Wiener, Ron. *The Rape and Plunder of the Shankhill*. Belfast: Farset Co-operative Press, 1980.

Wilson Gordon (with Alf McCreary). *Marie: A Story from Enniskillen*. London: Collins, 1990.

Wilson, Tom. *Ulster: Conflict and Consent*. Oxford: Basil Blackwell, 1989.

Wood, Ian S., ed. *Scotland and Ulster*. Edinburgh: Mercat Press, 1994.

Woodman, P. C. *Excavations at Mount Sandel, 1973–77, County Lon-*

donderry. Belfast: Her Majesty's Stationery Office, 1985.

Wright, Frank. *Northern Ireland: A Comparative Analysis.* Dublin: Gill and Macmillan, 1987.

——————. *Two Lands on One Soul.* Dublin: Gill and Macmillan, 1996.

APPENDIX

ENTRIES IN VOLUME 1

ENGLAND AND THE UNITED KINGDOM

Abdication Crisis
Aberdeen, Earl of
Abhorrers
Abjuration, Oath of
Abjuration of the Realm
Abortion
Aboukir Bay, Battle of
Abyssinian Campaign
Abyssinian War
Accession, Treaty of
Acre, Battles of
Act of Parliament
Act of Settlement, 1652
Act of Settlement, 1662
Act of Settlement, 1701
Act of Succession
Act of Supremacy, 1534
Act of Supremacy, 1559
Act of Uniformity
Act of Union
Addington, Henry
Addled Parliament
Admiralty
Aethelbald
Aethelbert I
Aethelfrith
Aethelred I
Aethelred II
Aethelstan
Aethelwulf
Afghan Wars
Africa, Scramble for
African Company
Agincourt, Battle of
Agricultural Revolution

Air Transport
Albert, Prince
Albuera, Battle of
Aldermaston Marches
Alfred the Great
Alliance, the
Alma, Battle of
American Revolution
American Revolutionary War
American War of Independence
Andrew, Prince
Angevins
Angles
Anglo-American War
Anglo-French Treaty
Anglo-German Agreement
Anglo-German Naval Agreement
Anglo-Japanese Alliance
Anglo-Polish Alliance
Anglo-Russian Entente
Anglo-Saxon Chronicle
Anglo-Saxons
Anglo-Soviet-Iranian Treaty
Anjou, House of
Anne
Anne, Princess
Anne of Cleves
Anne of Denmark
Anti-Corn Law League
Appeasement
Arcadia Conference
Archbishop of Canterbury
Arcos Raid
Arkwright, Richard
Armistice Day

Charles II
Charles, Prince
Chartism
Chatham, Earl of
Chevy Chase, Ballad or Battle of
Chief Secretary to the Treasury
Chiltern Hundreds
Chivalry, Orders of
Church of England
Churchill, John
Churchill, Winston Leonard
  Spencer
Cinque Ports
Citizen's Charter
City
City of London
Civil List, the
Civil War (first)
Civil War (second)
Clarendon Code
Clarke, Kenneth Harry
Clean Air Act
Clive, Robert
Clive of Plassey, Baron
Cnut
Coal
Cod Wars
Colombo Plan
Combination Acts
Command Paper
Common Land
Common Law
Common Market
Commonwealth, the
Commonwealth of Nations
Communist Party
Comprehensive Schools
Concorde
Confederation of British Industry
  (CBI)
Conscription
Conservative Party

Consolidated Fund
Consolidation Bill
Constituency
Constitution, British
Constitutional Monarchy
Continental System
Conventicle Act
Convention Parliament, 1660
Convention Parliament, 1689
Cook, James
Cooper, Anthony Ashley
  (1621-83)
Cooper, Anthony Ashley
  (1801-85)
Co-operative Movement
Copyhold
Corn Laws
Coronation
Corporation of London
Cotswold Hills
Cotton Industry
Council Housing
Country Party
County
Coupon Election
Court of Appeal
Court Party
Cranmer, Thomas
Crecy, Battle of
Cricket
Crimean War
Cripps, Richard Stafford
Cromwell, Oliver
Cromwell, Thomas
Cropredy Bridge, Battle of
Cross Bencher
Crown
Crown Colony
Crown Courts
Crown Dependency
Crown Lands
Crusades

Gas
Gascoyne-Cecil, Robert Arthur
  Talbot
Gaunt, John of
General Election
General Strike
General Synod
Gentry
George I
George II
George III
George IV
George V
George VI
George, St
George Cross
Georgian
Ghent, Treaty of
Gladstone, William Ewart
Glorious Revolution
Goderich, Viscount
Gold Standard
Golden Jubilee
Good Parliament
Gordon, Charles George
Gordon Riots
Government
Governor General
Grammar Schools
Grand Alliance, 1689
Grand Alliance, 1701
Grand Alliance (coal)
Grand Remonstrance
Great Britain
Great Depression
Great Depression: Agriculture
Greater London Council (GLC)
Great Exhibition
Great Fire of London
Great Plague
Great Seal
Green Party

Greenham Common
Greenwich Meridian
Grenville, George
Grenville, Baron William
Grenville, William Syndham
Grey, Charles
Grey, Earl
Grey, Jane
Guild
Guildford Four
Gulf War
Gunpowder Plot
Gwyn, Nell
Habeas Corpus
Hadrian's Wall
Hailsham, Viscount
Hamilton-Gordon, George
Hanoverians
Hansard
Hanseatic League
Hardicanute
Harold I
Harold II
Hastings, Battle of
Hastings, Warren
Hattersley, Roy Sydney George
Healey, Denis Winston
Hearth Tax
Heath, Edward Richard George
Heenan, John Carmel
Henry I
Henry II
Henry III
Henry IV
Henry V
Henry VI
Henry VII
Henry VIII
Hexham, Battle of
High Commission
High Court of Justice
Hillforts

Monarch, the
Monetarism
Monmouth Rebellion
Montfort, Simon de
Montgomery, Bernard Law
More, Thomas
Morrison, Herbert Stanley
Mosley, Oswald
Mount Badon, Battle of
Mountbatten, Louis Francis
   Albert Victor Nicholas
Munich Agreement
Munich Air Tragedy
Municipal Corporations Act
Muscovy Company
Nanking, Treaty of
Napoleonic Wars
Naseby, Battle of
Nassau Agreement
National Anthem
National Debt
National Economic Development
   Council (NEDDY)
National Front
National Health Service (NHS)
National Lottery
National Parks
National Service
National Trust
Nationalization
Navarino, Battle of
Navigation Acts
Nelson, Horatio
Neolithic
New Model Army
New Towns
Newark, Battle of
Newburn Ford, Battle of
Newbury, Battles of
Newcastle, Duke of
Newcastle-Upon-Tyne
Newton, Isaac

Nightingale, Florence
Nile, Battle of the
Nineteen Propositions
Nonconformists
Normans
North, Frederick
North, Lord
Northampton, Battle of
North Briton
Northeast Passage
North-South Divide
Northwest Passage
Northern Ireland
Northern Rebellion
Nuclear Deterrent
Nuclear Energy
Obscene Publications Act
Offa
Official Secrets Act
Oil
Oil Crisis
Ombudsman
Omdurman, Battle of
Open Field System
Opium Wars
Opposition, the
Ordinances
Ordination of Women
Ordnance, Board of
Ordnance Survey (OS)
Osborne Judgement
Otterburn, Battle of
Oudenarde, Battle of
Outlaw
Owen, David Anthony Llewellyn
Oxford
Oxford and Asquith, Earl of
Oxford Parliament, 1258
Oxford Parliament, 1641
Pacifico, David
Palaeolithic
Palmerston, Viscount

Pankhurst, Emmeline
Paris, Treaty of
Parish
Parliament
Parliament Act
Parliamentarians
Parliamentary Private Secretary
Parliamentary Privilege
Parliamentary Reform
Parliamentary Secretary
Parliamentary Under-Secretary of State
Parr, Catherine
Passchendaele, Battle of
Pax Britannica
Paymaster General
Peasants' Revolt
Peel, Robert
Peerage
Pelham, Henry
Penal Laws
Peninsular War
Pennines, the
Penny Post
Penruddock's Rising
Perceval, Spencer
Percy, Henry
Persian War
Peterloo Massacre
Petition of Right
Petitioners
Philip, Prince
Phillips, Mark Antony Peter
Phoney War
Pilgrimage of Grace
Pilgrim Fathers
Pitt the Elder, William
Pitt the Younger, William
Place Acts
Placemen
Planning, Town and Country
Plantagenets

Plantations of Ireland
Plassey, Battle of
Plug Riots
Pocket Boroughs
Poitiers, Battle of
Police
Poll Tax
Pollution Control
Polytechnics
Poor Law
Popish Plot
Poplarism
Portland, Duke of
Postmaster General
Post Office
Potsdam Conference
Potteries, the
Powell, John Enoch
Prehistoric Britain
Prescott, John Leslie
President of the Board of Trade
Preston, Battle of
Pride's Purge
Prime Minister
Prince of Wales
Princess Diana
Princess of Wales
Princess Royal
Printing
Prisons
Private Bill
Private Member's Bill
Privatization
Privy Council
Privy Seal
Profumo Scandal
Protectorate
Protectorate, the
Provisions of Oxford
Provisions of Westminster
Public House
Public Record Office (PRO)

Seven Years War
Severn, River
Sex Discrimination Act
Sexual Offences Act
Seymour, Jane
Shackleton, Ernest Henry
Shadow Minister
Shaftesbury, Earl of (1621–83)
Shaftesbury, Earl of (1801–85)
Shelburne, Earl of
Sheriff
Ship Money
Shipbuilding
Shire
Short Parliament
Shrewsbury, Battle of
Sidmouth, Viscount
Sinking Fund
Sir
Six Acts
Slave Trade
Snowdon, Lord
Social and Liberal Democratic
 Party (SLDP)
Social Democratic Party (SDP)
Solicitor General
Somme, Battle of the
South African War
South Sea Bubble
Spa Fields Riot
Spanish Armada
Spanish Civil War
Spanish Succession, War of the
Speaker, the
Special Air Service (SAS)
Special Operations Executive
 (SOE)
Spencer, Diana Frances
Splendid Isolation
Spurs, Battle of the
Stamford Bridge, Battle of
Stamp Acts

Standing Army
Stanley, Edward George Geoffrey
 Smith
Star Chamber
State Lottery
Statute of Merton
Steel
Stephen
Stephenson, George
Sterling
Stewart, Robert
Stewarts
Stock Exchange
Stoke, Battle of
Stone Age
Stonehenge
Street Offences Act
Stuart, John
Stuarts
Sudanese Wars
Suez Crisis
Suffragettes
Supreme Court of Judicature
Supreme Governor
Swing Riots
Synod of Whitby
Tamworth Manifesto
Temperance Movement
Temple, Henry John
Test Acts
Tewkesbury, Battle of
Thames, River
Thatcher, Margaret Hilda
Thatcherism
Thirty Years War
Thorpe, John Jeremy
Three-Day Week
Throckmorton Plot
Times, The
Tinchebrai, Battle of
Titanic, The
Tithe

William the Conqueror
William Rufus
Wilson, James Harold
Window Tax
Windsor
Windsor Castle
Winter of Discontent
Witan
Witchcraft
Wolfe, James
Wolfenden Report
Wolsey, Thomas
Wool Industry

Woolsack
Worcester, Battle of
Wyatt's Rebellion
Wycliffe, John
Yalta Conference
Yangtse Agreement
Yeomen
York
Yorkists
Ypres, Battles of
Zimmermann Telegram
Zinoviev Letter
Zulu War

ABOUT THE AUTHORS

KENNETH J. PANTON is Associate Professor of Geography, and Assistant Director of British Studies Programs, at the University of Southern Mississippi. A journalist before entering the academic world, he was educated at the University of Edinburgh (where he won the Vans Dunlop Scholarship) and at King's College, London where he gained his Ph.D. At posts in British and North American Universities, he has pioneered international education programs and published analyses of patterns of religion and language.

KEITH A. COWLARD retired from the post of Head of the Department of Geography at London Guildhall University in 1997. He was born in the historic town of Canterbury and educated at the University of Leeds, where he took his bachelor's degree and his doctorate. He has published widely in geography, history and planning focusing on the identification of social class areas in 19th century cities and on the economic transformation of London's Docklands. Throuhout his career, he maintained a strong commitment to international education.